Handbook of Research on Artificial Intelligence in Government Practices and Processes

Jose Ramon Saura
Rey Juan Carlos University, Spain

Felipe Debasa
Rey Juan Carlos University, Spain

A volume in the Advances in Electronic Government, Digital Divide, and Regional Development (AEGDDRD) Book Series

Published in the United States of America by
IGI Global
Information Science Reference (an imprint of IGI Global)
701 E. Chocolate Avenue
Hershey PA, USA 17033
Tel: 717-533-8845
Fax: 717-533-8661
E-mail: cust@igi-global.com
Web site: http://www.igi-global.com

Library of Congress Cataloging-in-Publication Data

Names: Saura, José Ramón, 1992- editor. | Debasa, Felipe, 1974- editor.
Title: Handbook of research on artificial intelligence in government practices and
  processes / José Ramón Saura, and Felipe Debasa, editor.
Description: Hershey, PA : Information Science Reference, [2022] | Includes
  bibliographical references and index. | Summary: "This book identifies
  the main uses that governments make of artificial intelligence and
  outlines define citizens' concerns about their privacy, covering topics
  that are essential to understanding how governments should use
  artificial intelligence in their practices and processes"-- Provided by
  publisher.
Identifiers: LCCN 2021048729 (print) | LCCN 2021048730 (ebook) | ISBN
  9781799896098 (Hardcover) | ISBN 9781799896111 (eBook)
Subjects: LCSH: Artificial intelligence. | Artificial
  intelligence--Government policy.
Classification: LCC Q335 .A665 2022 (print) | LCC Q335 (ebook) | DDC
  006.301--dc23/eng/20211109
LC record available at https://lccn.loc.gov/2021048729
LC ebook record available at https://lccn.loc.gov/2021048730

This book is published in the IGI Global book series Advances in Electronic Government, Digital Divide, and Regional Development (AEGDDRD) (ISSN: 2326-9103; eISSN: 2326-9111)

British Cataloguing in Publication Data
A Cataloguing in Publication record for this book is available from the British Library.

For electronic access to this publication, please contact: eresources@igi-global.com.

Advances in Electronic Government, Digital Divide, and Regional Development (AEGDDRD) Book Series

Zaigham Mahmood
University of Derby, UK & North West University, South
Africa

ISSN:2326-9103
EISSN:2326-9111

MISSION

The successful use of digital technologies (including social media and mobile technologies) to provide public services and foster economic development has become an objective for governments around the world. The development towards electronic government (or e-government) not only affects the efficiency and effectiveness of public services, but also has the potential to transform the nature of government interactions with its citizens. Current research and practice on the adoption of electronic/digital government and the implementation in organizations around the world aims to emphasize the extensiveness of this growing field.

The **Advances in Electronic Government, Digital Divide & Regional Development (AEGDDRD)** book series aims to publish authored, edited and case books encompassing the current and innovative research and practice discussing all aspects of electronic government development, implementation and adoption as well the effective use of the emerging technologies (including social media and mobile technologies) for a more effective electronic governance (or e-governance).

COVERAGE

- Urban Development, Urban Economy
- Case Studies and Practical Approaches to E-Government and E-Governance
- E-Citizenship, Inclusive Government, Connected Government
- Social Media, Web 2.0, and Mobile Technologies in E-Government
- E-Governance and Use of Technology for Effective Government
- Knowledge Divide, Digital Divide
- Issues and Challenges in E-Government Adoption
- Citizens Participation and Adoption of E-Government Provision
- Online Government, E-Government, M-Government
- Current Research and Emerging Trends in E-Government Development

IGI Global is currently accepting manuscripts for publication within this series. To submit a proposal for a volume in this series, please contact our Acquisition Editors at Acquisitions@igi-global.com or visit: http://www.igi-global.com/publish/.

Titles in this Series

For a list of additional titles in this series, please visit: www.igi-global.com/book-series

701 East Chocolate Avenue, Hershey, PA 17033, USA
Tel: 717-533-8845 x100 • Fax: 717-533-8661
E-Mail: cust@igi-global.com • www.igi-global.com

List of Contributors

Table of Contents

Section 3
Case Studies on Artificial Intelligence Government Practices

Section 4
AI and Its Applications in Education

Detailed Table of Contents

Section 1
From Artificial Intelligence to Good Governance: Theory, Framework, and Policy

This section introduces the main uses of artificial intelligence (AI) in the processes and practices applied by governments. Section 1 analyzes different frameworks and policies that reflect the development of AI in public administrations from a theoretical perspective.

This chapter explores the global context of the deformation of political reality in relation to artificial intelligence (AI). The chapter discusses the need to understand the importance of geopolitics for good governance. Likewise, the chapter examines, from a historical perspective, the planetary governance structures that have been characterized through the following three fundamental pillars: (1) the exercise of power over a specific territory, (2) the inequality between the central executive and administered regional structures, and finally, (3) the implementation of a political project through various forms of influence from the political, economic, institutional, social, ideological, and technological perspectives. The chapter concludes with an analysis of the future of AI in public governance practices and processes.

The greatest revolution in technology to date is artificial intelligence (AI). With rapid technological advances, government agencies, business, and academia are looking for guidance and standards around artificial intelligence. Several of the AI applications can be viewed as algorithms that make decisions, raising the question of when society will attempt to delegate decision making processes to computers. A crucial practical application should be in mind while creating a theoretical taxonomy about decisions and their context, in terms of norms, laws, and policies. Using artificial intelligence (AI), this study proposes a policy framework for the country by analysing FATE (fairness, accountability, transparency, and explainability). This study examines three core areas, namely public policy, artificial intelligence (AI), and decision making. As a means to better understand public policy, a description of how decision-making processes are based on the concept of artificial intelligence is presented.

Chapter 3

John G. McNutt, University of Delaware, USA
Lauri Goldkind, Fordham University, USA

Artificial intelligence technology offers a wealth of opportunities for government to serve its constituencies and address its mission. Technology providers paint a picture of unlimited possibilities and the fulfillment of dreamlike visions. The reality is often different with failed projects or efforts with negative consequences for social justice and human rights. This situation often leads to angry resistance from multiple groups. What accounts for these different fates? This chapter examines how these efforts develop within a community systems approach and how this accounts for positive and negative outcomes.

Chapter 4

Jorge Chauca García, University of Malaga, Spain

Social behavior is central to the rise of artificial intelligence (AI). This chapter studies the global internet network as a repository of data that companies and governments use as a valuable commercial and geopolitical tool. But in the face of this optimistic vision of global information management, society must ensure freedom and privacy in the community. The denunciation of abuses and the need to set ethical and political limits to the use of AI in relation to social behavior and its contexts is today a priority task, nor do we want to fall into a dystopian society. The border between freedom and AI is marked by ethics.

Chapter 5

Felipe Debasa, Rey Juan Carlos University, Spain

In 2016 the term 4th Industrial Revolution was coined to define a new era in history based on commercial and industrial activity connected through the internet. Connections to the network and the internet of things facilitate that activity and processes can be stored, generating large volumes of data. Algorithms can analyze and process this data to create new added value. Algorithms already control many basic sectors of the economy and society. Although with some initial rejection, the users have assumed as normal that the algorithms set the prices of supply and demand in the provision of goods and services or that they make investment proposals in financial markets. This new way of acting has created the circular economy, but also a new economic model based on very high amounts of data that comes under the name surveillance capitalism. An economic model based on virtuality, with data as raw materials and driven by algorithms, generates new challenges also in security.

Section 2
Artificial Intelligence Regulation and Control Initiatives

Various initiatives regulate the use of AI in the public sector globally. Section 2 analyzes current norms and laws, as well as the initiatives to control the development and application of AI in the society.

Cities reflect the social, political, and technological evolution of humanity. The implementation of new technologies in urban areas facilitate these changes. For that reason, decision-making processes in urban management have changed significantly in recent decades. At present, artificial intelligence and the supporting data infrastructures represent a new urban paradigm where city governance must attend to proper urban development while considering its citizens' opinions. However, AI requires continuous data collection to feed the algorithms. Collecting this data may raise privacy issues that vulnerate citizens' rights and personal data. Even if Europe and its member states possess highly protective privacy laws, this is still a significant concern for many citizens in urban decision-making processes. This chapter collects the European legal framework regarding AI data infrastructures and the European Green Deal to measure their potential impact on urban transformation. Also, the relationship between fundamental urban principles and the city-governance are analysed.

Starting from a brief reference to the concept and typology of political democracy systems, the authors present in this chapter some of the most important challenges that the use of new information and communication technologies entails in both spheres of political decisions (from power or choosing power). It is logical to question and open a debate regarding the democratic validity of its use, since fake news, misinformation, bubble filters undoubtedly influence the propaganda of political parties and affect the message and its effectiveness. On the other hand, the new technological communication paradigm applied to the democratic electoral system, technically possible, also raises interesting considerations regarding its eventual institutionalization and its legitimacy in comparison with the classical model of participation.

The European Union has begun its legal development on artificial intelligence and is presented as one of the least advanced legal fields by the European institutions. Since the communication of the Commission on Artificial Intelligence for Europe was developed, different works have been addressed, such as the coordination plan on artificial intelligence of December 2018 and the White Paper on Artificial Intelligence, guiding excellence and trust to European citizens and businesses. The challenge facing Europe and Spain is not to be left behind, lagging the great powers that are making a very notable investment effort, seeking to develop this technology that is already impacting our societies. The work presents the major milestones of European action and outlines the ambitious future that awaits the European Union and Spain in the coming years, but is still unclear if there is not a decisive action implemented by all the powers concern.

Chapter 9

In this digital computer-based ecosystem, governments use mechanisms of data extraction which are barely identified by citizens. Therefore, among the data extracted from institutional e-platforms, computer-based transactions play an important role in this process. This research study aims to shed light on the data mining techniques used by governments and public institutions, identify which are the most commonly used, and expose the privacy risks they may pose to citizens. The chapter is made through a systematic literature review with two main keywords: "big data" and "government." This study intends to answer the following research questions: What are the key techniques used by governments to extract data? May these tools pose risks to citizens?

Section 3
Case Studies on Artificial Intelligence Government Practices

Section 3 presents case studies applied to AI strategies used by governments in the last decade. The chapter discusses strategies developed by governments in different scenarios, challenges, and opportunities using case studies of several industries.

Chapter 10

The use of artificial intelligence (AI) by governments represents a radical transformation of governance, which has the potential for a lean government to provide personalised services that are efficient and cost-effective. This represents the next frontier of digital-era governance (DEG), which is an extension of the traditional bureaucratic model representing digital manifestations of instrumental rationality. However, the use of AI also introduces new risks and ethical challenges (such as biased data, fairness, transparency, the surveillance state, and citizen behavioural control) that need to be addressed by governments. This chapter critiques DEG enabled by AI. The authors argue for adopting a public values perspective for managing AI ethical dilemmas. Through a cross-case analysis of 30 government AI implementations, four primary AI use cases are outlined. Furthermore, a conceptual model is developed that identifies relationships between AI ethical principles and public values as drivers of AI adoption by citizens. Finally, six propositions are outlined for future research.

Chapter 11

In this chapter, the authors analyse the Chinese social credit system and its impact and implementation on Western democratic systems to address the challenges posed by terrorist threats and social tensions. The case around which this chapter is structured is the Chinese social credit, projected in a short period of time to other countries. This analysis focuses on the motivations that lead China to develop and implement this system and the type of policies pursued around social credit. The authors also analyse the tools on which it is based and the debate that the implementation of a system of population control of these dimensions brings about.

Chapter 12
    Niranjan Devkota, Research Management Cell, Quest International College, Lalitpur, Nepal
    Rabin Paudel, Quest International College, Lalitpur, Nepal
    Seeprata Parajuli, Research Management Cell, Quest International College, Lalitpur, Nepal
    Udaya Raj Paudel, Quest International College, Lalitpur, Nepal
    Udbodh Bhandari, Quest International College, Lalitpur, Nepal

Recent advances in technology in the fields of artificial intelligence (AI) and machine learning (ML) are significantly changing business environment. In the high-tech competitive edge, it has the immense use of computerized knowledge analytics, particularly for information management and the industrial sector. This study aims to analyze adoption of artificial intelligence among Nepalese industries, how industries are ready to adopt AI, challenges being faced and ways for improvement. Findings of the study revealed that on average 20.77% industries are ready in terms of technological sufficiency, 29.91% industries are ready in terms of management efficiency, and 39.23% industries are ready in terms of value creation potential in the firm for the adoption of AI intelligence. Further, 56% industries stated that small market size and lack of skilled manpower are the major challenges for AI adoption. Therefore, this study concludes that as stated by 44% industries, if they get adequate and relevant support from government, it would be easier for them to adopt AI.

Chapter 13
    José Emilio Pérez-Martínez, Rey Juan Carlos University, Spain

This chapter deals with one of the hottest issues in recent years: the application of artificial intelligence to surveillance systems and the movements against this type of surveillance in Spain. The authors show how, in the face of the advance of facial recognition technologies in more and more aspects of our lives in Spain and around the world, movements of response and rejection to this new model of society are being organised. The cases of UNIR and Mercadona are analysed in this text as representative of the state of these debates in the Spanish public sphere.

Chapter 14
    Emilio Sanchez de Rojas Díaz, EAE Businnes School, Rey Juan Carlos University, Spain
    Elena Bulmer, EAE Businnes School, Rey Juan Carlos University, Spain
    Carlos R. Quijano Junquera, Rey Juan Carlos University, Spain

The aim of this chapter is to address the use of artificial intelligence in managing GSC, restructuring it, and providing it with enough flexibility to meet the challenges and risks that the current situation—

characterized by uncertainty—could threaten including integrity and correct operation. To do this, the authors propose to address issues such as what is a supply chain, what are risks and how risks can affect the management of the supply chain, particularly in the face of the COVID-19 outbreak. Optimizing supply chains and integrating all processes, from suppliers to customers, through warehouses, is a typical target for artificial intelligence (AI). It will be of critical importance to migrate towards 'Agile' strategies, suitable for the uncertain times we live in, incorporating a timely risk analysis and allowing routine decisions to be taken within the framework of AI.

Chapter 15

Felipe Debasa, Rey Juan Carlos University, Spain
Yuliia Andriichenko, Taras Shevchenko National University, Ukraine
Nataliia Popova, Taras Shevchenko National University of Kyiv, Ukraine

Ukraine is a European state situated in the middle of the spheres of power and influence of the European Union and Russia. After the fall of the Soviet Union communist regime, Ukraine maintained a significant number of Russian citizens who now promote the country in international politics. In front of them, a larger number of Ukraine citizens show their preferences to join to the European Union. Thus, the country is being polarized due to some political forces exploit these contradictions for authorities' defamation and to their own benefits. This chapter presents an analysis of a wide selection of Yuliia Tymoshenko's speeches using computer tools that allow the analysis of a large volume of data.

Section 4
AI and Its Applications in Education

Section 4 introduces the use of AI in the education sector and reviews different processes that governments should apply to appropriately and safely use AI in the educational sector. This chapter also explores the main uses and practices of AI in the education sector.

Chapter 16

Ana María Lacárcel, Universidad de Murcia, Spain

Due to the undeniable increase in the impact that artificial intelligence systems have on numerous aspects of society, the teaching-learning process is increasingly influenced by these, producing the need to know the participating agents and applicable approaches for their implementation. Therefore, the main purpose of this chapter is to obtain an overview of the elements and challenges involved in the application of artificial intelligent devices in education. In this sense, the information presented below characterizes some of these systems through the way in which they personalize learning based on the peculiarities of the students and makes specific reference to the operation of some of them, such as the intelligent tutor system and exploratory learning environments.

Chapter 17

José Ramón Saura, Rey Juan Carlos University, Spain

Universities have adapted their teaching systems to integrate new educational techniques focused on technology and education as fundamental pillars of their development. This chapter proposes the analysis of the fields that encompass the use of artificial intelligence in universities using teaching innovation strategies. The chapter identifies the skills and examples that teachers should understand in order to use artificial intelligence to improve their teaching methods. With this objective, seven interviews have been carried out with university professors in which they explain the use of artificial intelligence and the need to acquire technical knowledge relative to teaching innovation. The results of the research present the main uses and the knowledge needed for university teachers to be able to carry out teaching innovation tasks using artificial intelligence. Finally, implications for university-industry and university teachers are discussed.

For some years now, we have been living through times of the rapid interaction of technologies in society, and this has been an authentic revolution. Many speak of this moment as a fourth industrial revolution that is going to significantly change the way we see the world and interact with other people. Among these technologies, without a doubt, one of the most outstanding has been artificial intelligence (AI), which is so present in the daily lives of people looking for patterns that are used in numerous fields of action. In education, the advance of AI has been very significant, and all governments are seeking to make policies that involve AI in education in order to improve the academic results of students. It is for this reason that we must analyze how this improves implementation and improvement to the education of the 21st century.

This exploratory and pedagogical chapter has proposed new ways of using artificial intelligence in education. The uses of artificial intelligence have been linked to the education sector in order to improve the active listening actions and decision-making of governments. The results identify and discuss seven educational uses of artificial intelligence. From the government's point of view, three uses of artificial intelligence to improve the educational sector have been identified. By using the present study insights and the prospects for governments initiatives proposed, the authors have covered a scope of the uses of artificial intelligence and outlined the role that governments should maintain for efficient development and optimization strategy in education.

Preface

In recent years, the use of artificial intelligence (AI) by governments has become one of the challenges that public administrations should urgently address. AI is a technology that has a significant impact on the decisions and actions taken by public administrations in the medium and long term (Chen, 2009).

Accordingly, in the coming years, the influence of AI will pose innumerable challenges to governments due to its potential development in public administrations (Chen & Wen, 2021). For instance, part of the work currently performed by public employees may be carried out by devices that automatically work with AI (Al-Mushayt, 2019; Saura et al., 2022). Furthermore, owing to the prediction capacity of AI, better decisions could be made, and policies focused on improving communication with country citizens and residents could be developed. Likewise, AI can also promote agreements with the private sector based on efficiency insights that AI provides to organizations (Bansal et al., 2022).

However, despite its advantages, AI can also cause imbalances in governmental work structures and organizational models—and this can occur not only in terms of effectiveness of the performed tasks, but also in relation to the legal response that the decisions made with the use of AI may have. Together with innovation, AI shows that there are many cases where the global leadership of institutions can be marked in relation to technology, its adaptability, and its development applied to traditional management and structure models (Ashok et al., 2022).

The clear development of AI is transforming many aspects in the daily life of society. In the public sector, with regard to national priorities, citizen security defense or prevention strategies could be valuable strategies for governments (Mehta & Shukla, 2022). At the same time, governments must be able to adapt each of their actions and redefine the different ways in which policies are designed to protect privacy of both workers and citizens (Pandit et al., 2022).

At this point, a fundamental principle for the successful development of an AI tools and applications that citizens and other societies can trust is international collaborations (Valle-Cruz et al., 2018). Accordingly, although the use of AI is being progressively implemented in public institutions, a legal and regulatory framework should still be developed to ensure that practices focused on data collection and treatment are adequate (Zhang et al., 2021). To date, most of the public institutions that have proposed the development and inclusion of AI in their programs have focused their development on the issues directly linked to the daily activities of public agencies (Boyd & Wilson, 2017).

Furthermore, governments extensively use AI to identify specific projects for the development of public products and services in the near future. In addition, there are several initiatives for collaboration between different sectors and industries where collaborations between the public and private sectors are the main drivers for the creation of innovation (Chatterjee & Sreenivasulu, 2019). In addition, there are also initiatives where projects and actions focused on the prediction of citizen's behaviors, in both medium and long term, allow governments to anticipate the demand and requirements of the society (Alqudah & Muradkhanli, 2021). Overall, several projects focused on the development of automation and routines in processes to boost efficiency in public administrations have recently been developed (Saura et al., 2021).

In general, using AI in the domain of public administrations can boost decision making and improve the evaluation of alternatives and processes occurring in the states of emergency (like COVID-19 pandemic) (Saura et al. 2022a)

However, there remains the need to ensure ethical uses to preserve citizens' privacy. Similarly, AI capacity to develop behavioral prediction strategies should also be always ensured (Sharma et al., 2021). Furthermore, promoting the development of tools and platforms focused on the use of AI for the benefit of public administrations must be a priority in today's data-centric era.

APPLICATION OF ARTIFICIAL INTELLIGENCE IN GOVERNMENT PRACTICES AND PROCESSES

In the present-day global culture where the development of new technologies has become one of the main tools for innovation, boosting the economy, proposing new regulations, and making decisions made with the help of AI have become essential for public actors and public institutions (Nijkamp et al., 2001).

Governments need to update their practices and processes with the appropriate use of new technologies and their subsequent adoption by the society (Saura et al., 2021a). Accordingly, governments must use AI as a way to identify the demands of society, anticipate user behavior based on data analysis, develop intelligent applications, or offer new insights that would facilitate the development of policies, thereby contributing to the creation of an increasingly efficient and sustainable society (de Sousa et al., 2019).

In this context, AI has become one of the fundamental pillars for the actions, practices, and processes that governments must develop, based on user behavior data in both connected and digital environments (Cath et al., 2018). Yet, it should also be noted that prediction, automation, and mass use features that AI provides to governments can jeopardize users' privacy and free decision making.

Today, governments can use algorithms working with AI to interfere with citizens' decision-making capacity, launch new prediction and monitoring systems of citizen behavior, or implement new alert models to increase national security (Zheng et al., 2018). Overall, concerns about personal privacy and security problems remain among the main topics that should be developed in this field of research (Djeffal, 2020).

Similarly, democracy in relation to users' decision making, political communications, or massive data extraction using AI is the fundamental source for the development of research in the present volume. Each nation state develops operations in its specific cultural and economic context and, although AI can be adapted to different norms and cultures, governments should be able to contextualize their use of AI using country-specific perspectives and values (Saura et al., 2021b).

Accordingly public services should propose the development of actions that will generate interactions between the private and public sectors, with the aim to cause an impact on services that depend on public administration (Suh et al., 2020). Beyond proposing new regulations focused on the use of AI, governments should inform their citizens about the capacity and influence of the use of AI in public services (Esteve et al., 2020). Therefore, each of the different scenarios where AI can be applied should be fully understood by citizens (Sun & Medaglia, 2019).

To this end, new educational communication protocols should be proposed, with a particular focus on making citizens understand the definition of AI and how governments can legally propose uses that work with the collection and analysis of massive data while respecting users' privacy (Wang et al., 2021). Confronting the new challenges of the new connected society, confidence in the AI technology should become an important part of governmental communication strategies (Saura et al., 2021d).

This edited volume is a useful source of information for a number of actors, including politicians, who can analyze case studies of other governments in relation to AI, data analysts, who can identify the main techniques for data collection and analysis developed by governments in relation to AI, and journalists, who are in charge of sharing information in a way understandable to citizens (Antebi & Dolinko, 2020).

This volume is also important for public figures, executives, data researchers, communication specialists, and academics who explore the use of AI in any industry, such as education or production processes, digital democracy initiatives, geopolitics, as well as in political communications or supply chains that drive the processes developed by governments (Ribeiro-Navarrete et al., 2021).

Covering most of current applications of AI by governments, the present volume provides a comprehensive overview of this research and offer meaningful theoretical and practical applications and implications. In what follows, we present a brief outline of the structure of this volume.

ORGANIZATION OF THIS BOOK

The first contribution, Chapter 1, explores the global context of the deformation of political reality in relation to AI. The chapter discusses the need to understand the importance of geopolitics. This chapter also examines, from a historical perspective, the planetary governance structures that have been characterized through the following three fundamental pillars: (1) the exercise of power over a specific territory, (2) the inequality between the central executive and administered regional structures and, finally, (3) the implementation of a political project through various forms of influence from the political, economic, institutional, social, ideological, and technological perspectives.

Furthermore, Chapter 2 analyzes the revolution in technology in relation to AI. This chapter discusses how, with rapid technological advances, government agencies, business, and academia are looking for guidance and standards around AI. The authors also analyze different applications that should be considered while creating a theoretical taxonomy about decisions and their context in terms of norms, laws, and policies. Based on the results of this analysis, the chapter proposes a policy framework for the country by analyzing FATE (Fairness, Accountability, Transparency and Explainability) and examining three core areas—namely public policy, artificial intelligence (AI), and decision making.

For its part, Chapter 3 focuses on a wealth of opportunities that AI offers for the government to serve its constituencies and address its mission. The authors analyze the unlimited possibilities and the fulfillment of dreamlike visions when using AI. Highlighting that the reality is often different and involves failed projects or efforts with negative consequences for social justice and human rights in relation to AI, the authors examine and discuss how these efforts develop within a community systems approach, and how this accounts for positive and negative outcomes.

Next, Chapter 4 is devoted to the analysis of social behavior as a central axis to the rise of AI. This chapter studies the global Internet network as a repository of data that companies, and governments use as a valuable commercial and geopolitical tool. However, in the face of this optimistic vision of global information management, the authors indicate that the society should ensure freedom and privacy in the community. The chapter concludes with a discussion of the denunciation of abuses and the need to set ethical and political limits to the use of AI in relation to social behavior and its contexts as priority tasks.

In the next contribution, the authors of Chapter 5 discuss the development of algorithms to control many basic sectors of the economy and society. The authors argue that, despite some initial rejection, the users have assumed as normal that the algorithms set the prices of supply and demand in the provision of goods and services or that they make investment proposals in financial markets. The chapter analyzes how this new way of acting has created not only the so-called circular economy, but also Surveillance Capitalism, a new economic model based on virtuality and very high amounts of data; using data as raw material and driven by algorithms, the latter model generates new challenges in security.

Similarly, Chapter 6 highlights the role of cities in the technological environment. The authors argue that cities reflect social, political, and technological evolution of the humanity. In this ecosystem, the decision-making processes in urban management have significantly changed in recent decades due to AI. AI and the supporting data infrastructures represent a new urban paradigm where city governance must attend to appropriate urban development while considering its citizens' opinions. However, this chapter discusses whether these data may raise privacy issues that violate citizens' rights and personal data. In addition, using the European legal framework regarding AI data infrastructures and the European Green Deal, the authors measure a potential impact of AI on urban transformation and the relationship between fundamental urban principles and the good city-governance.

In Chapter 7, the authors present some of the important challenges associated with the use of new information and communication technologies in both spheres of political decisions. Considering that fake news, misinformation, and bubble filters can influence propaganda of political parties and affect associated messages, it is logical to start a debate on the democratic validity of the use of AI. On the other hand, the authors also discuss whether the new technological communication paradigm applied to the democratic electoral system also raises interesting considerations regarding its eventual institution-alization and its legitimacy in comparison with the classical model of participation.

Furthermore Chapter 8 is concerned with the challenge of the European Union for the development of AI. The author argues that, since the development of communication of the Commission on AI for Europe, different works have been addressed, such as the coordination plan on AI of December 2018 and the White Paper on AI, guiding excellence and trust to European citizens and businesses. Chapter 8 also outlines major milestones of European action and outlines the ambitious future that awaits the European Union and Spain in the upcoming years.

Likewise, Chapter 9 identifies different mechanisms that governments use for data extraction, iden-tifying the importance of institutional e-platforms and computer-based transactions. This chapter aims to shed light on the data-mining techniques used by governments and public institutions, as well as identifies which techniques are the most used and expose the privacy risks they may pose to citizens. The chapter is based on a systematic literature review with two main keywords: *Big Data* and *govern-ment*. The chapter intends to answer the following research questions: What are the key techniques used by governments to extract data? May these tools pose risks to citizens?

Next, in Chapter 10, the authors present the next frontiers of digital-era governance (DEG), which is an extension of the traditional bureaucratic model representing digital manifestations of instrumen-tal rationality. However, the use of AI also introduces new risks and ethical challenges that need to be addressed by governments. Through a cross-case analysis of 30 government AI implementations and 4 primary AI use cases, the authors argue for the adoption of public values perspective to manage AI ethical dilemmas. Furthermore, a conceptual model is developed that identifies relationships between AI ethical principles and public values as drivers of AI adoption by citizens.

Furthermore, Chapter 11 analyzes the Chinese social credit system and its impact and implementation on Western democratic systems. The overarching goal of this contribution is to address the challenges posed by terrorist threats and social tensions. The case around which this chapter is structured is the Chinese social credit, projected in a short period of time to other countries. This analysis focuses on the motivations that have led China to develop and implement this system and the type of policies pursued around social credit. The authors also analyze the tools on which it is based and the debate initiated by the implementation of a system of population control of these dimensions.

In Chapter 12, the authors discuss recent advances in technology in the fields of AI and machine learning. The chapter aims to analyze adoption of AI among Nepalese industries to understand industries' readiness to adopt AI, challenges being faced, as well as ways for improvement. The chapter findings reveal that, with regard to the adoption of AI intelligence, on average 20.77% industries are ready in terms of technological sufficiency, 29.91% industries are ready in terms of management efficiency, and 39.23% industries are ready in terms of value creation potential in the firm. Furthermore, in 56% of industries, the small market size and the lack of skilled manpower remain major challenges for AI adoption. The chapter concludes that, as stated by 44% industries, adequate and relevant support from government would facilitate industries' adoption of AI.

Likewise, Chapter 13 deals with one of the hottest issues in recent years: the application of AI to surveillance systems and the movements against this type of surveillance in Spain. To this end, the authors analyze the advances of technologies such as facial recognition. The chapter focuses on UNIR and Mercadona cases, which are analyzed as representative cases in the Spanish public sphere.

Furthermore, Chapter 14 addresses the use of AI in managing and restructuring supply chains with sufficient flexibility to meet the challenges and risks coming from the current uncertain situation that could threaten its integrity and correct operation. The authors address the issues such as what a supply chain is, what risks are, and how these risks can affect the management of the supply chain, particularly in the face of the COVID-19 outbreak. Optimizing supply chains and integrating all processes, from suppliers to customers, through warehouses, is a typical target for AI. Accordingly, it is of critical importance to migrate towards 'agile' strategies, i.e. strategies that are suitable for the current uncertain times and incorporate a timely risk analysis, thus allowing routine decisions to be taken within the framework of AI.

Chapter 15 focuses on Ukraine, a European state situated at the intersection of power and influence of the European Union and Russia. After the collapse of the Soviet Union communist regime, Ukraine maintained a significant portion of Russian citizens who now promote the country in international politics. Against them, a larger number of Ukraine citizens show their preferences to join to the European Union. Accordingly, the country is being polarized due to some political forces that exploit these contradictions for authorities' defamation and to their own benefit. This article presents an analysis of a wide selection of Yuliia Tymoshenko's speeches using computer tools that work with machine learning that allow the analysis of a large volume of data.

In Chapter 16, the authors analyze the impact that AI systems on numerous aspects of the society. More specifically, the chapter reviews challenges involved in the application of AI-based devices in education. Accordingly, the authors characterize some of relevant systems, with a particular focus on intelligent tutor systems and exploratory learning environments.

Next, Chapter 17 discusses new educational techniques focused on technology and education as fundamental pillars of the development of teaching systems at universities. The chapter proposes the analysis of the fields that encompass the use of AI in universities using teaching innovation strategies. The chapter identifies the skills and examples that teachers should understand in order to use AI to improve their teaching methods. The data analyzed in this chapter include seven interviews on the use of AI with university professors who discussed the need to acquire technical knowledge relative to teaching innovation. The results reported in this chapter reveal the main uses and knowledge needed for university teachers to be able to carry out teaching innovation tasks using AI.

Chapter 18 discusses the changes brought by the Fourth Industrial Revolution to the world and the way that people interact with each other. The author analyzes AI and its role in modifying people's daily lives by looking at the patterns used in numerous fields of action. In education, advances of AI have been particularly significant, and all governments are now seeking to implement policies that involve AI in order to improve students' academic results. It is for this reason that we should carefully analyze how AI implementation would improve the education of the XXI century.

Finally, Chapter 19 is an exploratory and pedagogical chapter that proposes new ways of using AI in education. In this chapter, the uses of AI are linked to the education sector in order to improve the active listening actions and decision-making of governments. The results reveal seven educational uses of AI. From the governmental point of view, the authors identify three uses of AI that improve the educational sector. Chapter 19 provides meaningful insights and outlines new prospects to analyze governments initiatives associated with AI.

REFERENCES

Al-Mushayt, O. S. (2019). Automating E-government services with artificial intelligence. *IEEE Access: Practical Innovations, Open Solutions, 7*, 146821–146829. doi:10.1109/ACCESS.2019.2946204

Alqudah, M. A., & Muradkhanli, L. (2021). Artificial Intelligence in Electric Government; Ethical Challenges and Governance in Jordan. *Electronic Research Journal of Social Sciences and Humanities, 3*, 65–74.

Antebi, L., & Dolinko, I. (2020). Artificial intelligence and policy: A review at the outset of 2020. *Strategic Assessment, 23*(1), 94–100.

Ashok, M., Madan, R., Joha, A., & Sivarajah, U. (2022). Ethical framework for Artificial Intelligence and Digital technologies. *International Journal of Information Management, 62*, 102433. doi:10.1016/j.ijinfomgt.2021.102433

Bansal, M., Sirpal, V., & Choudhary, M. K. (2022). Advancing e-Government using Internet of Things. In *Mobile Computing and Sustainable Informatics* (pp. 123–137). Springer. doi:10.1007/978-981-16-1866-6_8

Boyd, M., & Wilson, N. (2017). Rapid developments in artificial intelligence: how might the New Zealand government respond? *Policy Quarterly, 13*(4).

Cath, C., Wachter, S., Mittelstadt, B., Taddeo, M., & Floridi, L. (2018). Artificial intelligence and the 'good society': The US, EU, and UK approach. *Science and Engineering Ethics, 24*(2), 505–528. PMID:28353045

Chatterjee, S., & Sreenivasulu, N. S. (2019). Personal data sharing and legal issues of human rights in the era of artificial intelligence: Moderating effect of government regulation. *International Journal of Electronic Government Research, 15*(3), 21–36. doi:10.4018/IJEGR.2019070102

Chen, H. (2009). AI, e-government, and politics 2.0. *IEEE Intelligent Systems, 24*(5), 64–86. doi:10.1109/MIS.2009.91

Chen, Y. N. K., & Wen, C. H. R. (2021). Impacts of Attitudes Toward Government and Corporations on Public Trust in Artificial Intelligence. *Communication Studies, 72*(1), 115–131. doi:10.1080/10510974.2020.1807380

de Sousa, W. G., de Melo, E. R. P., Bermejo, P. H. D. S., Farias, R. A. S., & Gomes, A. O. (2019). How and where is artificial intelligence in the public sector going? A literature review and research agenda. *Government Information Quarterly, 36*(4), 101392. doi:10.1016/j.giq.2019.07.004

Djeffal, C. (2020). Artificial Intelligence and Public Governance: Normative Guidelines for Artificial Intelligence in Government and Public Administration. In *Regulating Artificial Intelligence* (pp. 277–293). Springer. doi:10.1007/978-3-030-32361-5_12

Esteve, M., Campion, A., Gascó, M., & Mikhaylov, S. (2020). The Challenges of Organizational Factors in Collaborative Artificial Intelligence Projects. *Social Science Computer Review*.

Mehta, N., & Shukla, S. (2022). Pandemic Analytics: How Countries are Leveraging Big Data Analytics and Artificial Intelligence to Fight COVID-19? *SN Computer Science, 3*(1), 1–20. doi:10.100742979-021-00923-y PMID:34778841

Nijkamp, P., Poot, J., & Vindigni, G. (2001). Spatial dynamics and government policy: An artificial intelligence approach to comparing complex systems. In *Knowledge, Complexity and Innovation Systems* (pp. 369–401). Springer. doi:10.1007/978-3-662-04546-6_18

Pandit, P., Krishnamurthy, K. N., & Bakshi, B. (2022). Artificial Intelligence (AI) and Big Data Analytics for the COVID-19 Pandemic. In *Assessing COVID-19 and Other Pandemics and Epidemics using Computational Modelling and Data Analysis* (pp. 1–17). Springer. doi:10.1007/978-3-030-79753-9_1

Ribeiro-Navarrete, S., Saura, J. R., & Palacios-Marqués, D. (2021). Towards a new era of mass data collection: Assessing pandemic surveillance technologies to preserve user privacy. *Technological Forecasting and Social Change, 167*, 120681. doi:10.1016/j.techfore.2021.120681 PMID:33840865

Saura, J. R., Palacios-Marqués, D., & Ribeiro-Soriano, D. (2022a). Exploring the boundaries of Open Innovation: Evidence from social media mining. *Technovation*, 102447. Advance online publication. doi:10.1016/j.technovation.2021.102447

Saura, J. R., Ribeiro-Soriano, D., & Palacios-Marqués, D. (2021). Using data mining techniques to explore security issues in smart living environments in Twitter. *Computer Communications, 179*, 285–295. doi:10.1016/j.comcom.2021.08.021

Saura, J. R., Ribeiro-Soriano, D., & Palacios-Marqués, D. (2021b, July 15). Setting privacy "by default" in social IoT: Theorizing the challenges and directions in Big Data Research. *Big Data Research, 25*, 100245. doi:10.1016/j.bdr.2021.100245

Saura, J. R., Palacios-Marqués, D., & Ribeiro-Soriano, D. (2021a). How SMEs use data sciences in their online marketing performance: A systematic literature review of the state-of-the-art. *Journal of Small Business Management*, 1–36. doi:10.1080/00472778.2021.1955127

Saura, J. R., Ribeiro-Soriano, D., & Iturricha-Fernández, A. (2022). Exploring the challenges of remote work on Twitter users' sentiments: From digital technology development to a post-pandemic era. *Journal of Business Research, 142*(March), 242–254. doi:10.1016/j.jbusres.2021.12.052

Saura, J. R., Ribeiro-Soriano, D., & Palacios-Marques, D. (2021c). Evaluating security and privacy issues of social networks based information systems in Industry 4.0. *Enterprise Information Systems*, 1–17. doi:10.1080/17517575.2021.1913765

Sharma, M., Luthra, S., Joshi, S., & Kumar, A. (2021). Implementing challenges of artificial intelligence: Evidence from public manufacturing sector of an emerging economy. *Government Information Quarterly*, 101624. doi:10.1016/j.giq.2021.101624

Suh, J., Yoo, S., Park, J., Cho, S. Y., Cho, M. C., Son, H., & Jeong, H. (2020). Development and validation of an explainable artificial intelligence-based decision-supporting tool for prostate biopsy. *BJU International, 126*(6), 694–703. doi:10.1111/bju.15122 PMID:32455477

Sun, T. Q., & Medaglia, R. (2019). Mapping the challenges of Artificial Intelligence in the public sector: Evidence from public healthcare. *Government Information Quarterly, 36*(2), 368–383. doi:10.1016/j.giq.2018.09.008

Valle-Cruz, D., & Sandoval-Almazan, R. (2018, May). Towards an understanding of artificial intelligence in government. In *Proceedings of the 19th Annual International Conference on Digital Government Research: Governance in the Data Age* (pp. 1-2). 10.1145/3209281.3209397

Wang, C., Teo, T. S., & Janssen, M. (2021). Public and private value creation using artificial intelligence: An empirical study of AI voice robot users in Chinese public sector. *International Journal of Information Management, 61*, 102401. doi:10.1016/j.ijinfomgt.2021.102401

Zhang, W., Zuo, N., He, W., Li, S., & Yu, L. (2021). Factors influencing the use of artificial intelligence in government: Evidence from China. *Technology in Society, 66*, 101675. doi:10.1016/j.techsoc.2021.101675

Zheng, Y., Yu, H., Cui, L., Miao, C., Leung, C., & Yang, Q. (2018, April). SmartHS: An AI platform for improving government service provision. *Thirty-Second AAAI Conference on Artificial Intelligence*.

Section 1
From Artificial Intelligence to Good Governance: Theory, Framework, and Policy

This section introduces the main uses of artificial intelligence (AI) in the processes and practices applied by governments. Section 1 analyzes different frameworks and policies that reflect the development of AI in public administrations from a theoretical perspective.

Chapter 1
Geopolitics, Governance, and AI

Jose Manuel Azcona Pastor
Rey Juan Carlos University, Spain

Fernando Gil González
Rey Juan Carlos University, Spain

ABSTRACT

This chapter explores the global context of the deformation of political reality in relation to artificial intelligence (AI). The chapter discusses the need to understand the importance of geopolitics for good governance. Likewise, the chapter examines, from a historical perspective, the planetary governance structures that have been characterized through the following three fundamental pillars: (1) the exercise of power over a specific territory, (2) the inequality between the central executive and administered regional structures, and finally, (3) the implementation of a political project through various forms of influence from the political, economic, institutional, social, ideological, and technological perspectives. The chapter concludes with an analysis of the future of AI in public governance practices and processes.

INTRODUCTION: ARTIFICIAL INTELLIGENCE AND THE TRANSMISSION OF KNOWLEDGE

Geopolitics is geared towards cooperation through exchange, transactions, negotiation etc. Concerning the public sphere, there is interest and the common will of nation-states, coexistence rules, or even political institutions, which all constitute organizational elements of international politics (Miailhe et al., 2020: 56-64). As a matter of fact, the global system comprises a set of strategies implemented by different subjects and countries. In this case, the role of global leadership and the formulation of agenda all emphasize social work strategies. On the other hand, geopolitics in the public sphere is an instrument of power, governance, control, and domination that avoids subjugation by another institutional element (Mesa, 2014: 107). In another vein, the concept of post-truth (Morales, 2018: 29) allows us to understand the global context embodied in the deformation of political reality. Even so, it is necessary to know and integrate some of the geopolitical realities, despite being governed by hypocrisy, which is usually ruthless and treacherous in nature (Baños, 2017: 12). On the other hand, it must be added that, historically,

DOI: 10.4018/978-1-7998-9609-8.ch001

planetary governance structures have been characterized by three fundamental pillars. First, the exercise of power over a specific territory. Secondly, the inequality between the central executive and administered regional structures and finally, the implementation of a political project through various forms of influence from the political, economic, institutional, social, ideological, and technological points of view.

Artificial Intelligence is mainly focused on the centralization of power in the hands of a few political, economic, military, and social agents (Bárcena et al., 2018: 33-34). In fact, digital empires would benefit from economies of scale, and in this manner, accelerate their concentration of power. They would become the major instruments governing international affairs, and thus return to a bloc logic. Such networks and digital instruments would spread on a continental scale, especially in the cases of the United States and China, while other political and supranational actors, such as Europe, would adopt more conservative strategies. In addition, surveillance is associated with the use of cameras, delving deeper into public places as occurs regarding numerous megacities such as London, New York, New Delhi, Shanghai or Rio de Janeiro (Bauman and Lyon, 2013: 9). As a matter of fact, surveillance, from the point of view of control, exists in the form of passports, biometric scanners, etc. Likewise, there is security control as regards online purchases or political participation on the internet. Other methods of social monitoring for artificial intelligence in geopolitics comprise the tax identification document, the use of codes or passwords to access a building, purchase of products online and, lastly internet searches (Lyon, 2005: 66). Against this backdrop, to understand the geopolitics of the 21st century, it is vital to consider the following question: What is the significance of new technologies in this new world and their link with politics in today's world? In the first place, the idea of phenomenological magnitude, understood as a coercive strategy in the abuse of power must be highlighted. Next, the idea of expansion in data processing (Saura and Palacios, 2021b) to explain surveillance or to analyze elements of control in geopolitics and Artificial Intelligence must be delved into. In fact, between the twentieth and twenty-first centuries, we would have to rethink the issue; to what extent do they allow us to know and have a critical view of surveillance today? The answer is liquid control, which is an instrument to guide us, as well as serve to pinpoint changes in security and surveillance. However, surveillance is blurred as regards consumption in society today. On the other hand, there are bits, which comprise the personal data extracted (Janssen, 2020) for an end or a purpose without a fixed objective, as a result of the pressure stemming from the demands of security, publicity, or propaganda. Furthermore, it would be necessary to analyze the concept of postmodernity from the time of the Marxist theories. Subsequently, to understand the concept, it is essential to carry out an in-depth analysis regarding some experts such as G. Deleuze, who discusses the idea of the society of control, which grows vertically in the same way a climbing plant does (Deleuze, 1992: 3). However, current surveillance is incentivized by staples, that is, everything that is established as liquid ends up dissolving at some point in history. On the other hand, some experts consider the concept of surveillance to consist of a panoptical system (Rhodes, 1998: 308), understood as a model of compressed information that is used in *iPhones* or *iPads*. Nevertheless, there are other electronic technologies such as firewalls or windows, integrated into software architecture. Other forms of control in geopolitics are oriented to the use of the *Smartphone* or *PNR*. In short, the need arises to understand safety as regards business by using digital techniques to analyze geopolitics in a current historical context. In this respect, it is possible to explain that politics consists of bringing together public and private interests at the local, regional, state, supranational or even international level. It is important to understand that political control is evident in the field of institutions, in administration or, even, in police states. For that reason, there is a set of networks, which is a product of social fragmentation, since modernity is liquid and must be free. Therefore, we must expunge, *in illo tempore*, social networks, especially for uncontrolled surveillance and, in this way, use them with a more orderly and updated purpose to avoid citizen problems such as the Occupy movement (Chomsky, 2012).

Adiaforization exists in personal data as occurs with DNA or with passwords (Flanagan, 2010: 93). On numerous occasions, there is a need to delve into personal data or, even, to obtain knowledge of the fragmented data that is duplicated which leads to greater credibility than what could be contributed by a person. In actual fact, software designers insist on the idea of a liquid modernity consisting of the use of search criteria, according to the historical-technological context or, even, in the methods of social control as seen in the Orwellian example of *Big Brother*, which is an instrumental organ that dominates the ideologies of citizens. We also have Smartphone tracking with barcodes, chips, *QR* codes... However, the chips locate where the products are by means of the sale. In short, in everyday life, as citizens, we are controlled by the movements and speed of electrical signals. Regarding the secrecy level, we must delve into national security or, on the contrary, into commercial competition. In short, in the panoptical world of liquid modernity, such personal information exists because a proportion of the data is kept in the private and public spheres (Bauman, 2000: 11). Drones are sophisticated visualization devices that are almost as imperceptible as other government alliances. It is worth noting their use in clashes, to make armed conflict invisible for the country or nation-state that initiates or undertakes it (Parker, 2010: 23).

Drones are programmed to fly by themselves to initiate espionage or, failing that, geopolitical surveillance. This causes concern about the existence of an ever-increasing tsunami of data (Whitlock, 2011). Indeed, in geopolitics, we must try to bolster anonymity. We cannot willingly sacrifice our right as citizens to privacy, for a reasonable price, like a flock of sheep. Secondly, there is access to the internet through web pages with the collective intelligence of two billion users who use their e-mail, messages, photos, or exchange data.

As a matter of fact, we surrender our personal autonomy in the manner of a civil contract. Thus, there is public consumption using gadgets which are easier to handle, but the fact of the matter is that there is a major use of drones or network operators attempting to influence reality. However, the internet does not rob us of our identity; it rather reflects our identity because as consumers, we leave our data at the mercy of data merchants, without any control whatsoever, and we barely worry about our privacy. In short, we must pay attention to what the Internet and social networks reveal concerning social relations since the violation of privacy should matter to us. That is, privacy has become a place of confinement and the owner of a private space sentenced, condemned and abandoned to his fate that wants to be understood by social media consumers by sharing secrets (Saura, 2021). This is all due to the ego of citizens who provide a massive amount of information, at a ridiculous price, to talk show hosts and television or radio collaborators. Failing that, it could result in living death or social exclusion since one does not belong to the select information club. The sociological field (Marx and Muschert, 2008) is mainly related to digitization and social networks since there are two universes: online and offline, and as to the worlds, there is the virtual world which is very fast and the real world, with a slower pace, alluding *stricto sensu* to the fable of the hare and the tortoise. In actual fact, human relationships advance according to the law of minimum effort since the digital and virtual path allows one to connect with others with barely any interaction with the people in the different social groups. Nevertheless, for technology, the real world is anachronistic and almost claustrophobic because it avoids socialization practices in real life. On the other hand, it is necessary to highlight the panopticons, which consitute the fundamental element of technological development, during the 20th and 21st centuries. This mechanism is based on the encryption of text messages, WhatsApp, e-mails etc., while, in the case of drones -mechanical dragonflies-, information intelligence after September 11, 2001 or military technology, are more effective to prosecute crimes classified as murders, in the different national or international criminal codes. In the field of security in each country, the horrors or torture in Syria must be explained and analyzed. This is proven by the terrorist groups of Islamic nationalism. Likewise, to understand security, diseases, the risks of nightlife, parents protecting children or even the existence of risks and vulnerabilities must be mitigated. It is fundamental to have elements of surveillance and tracking techniques while allowing individuals in the public sphere to exercise their own disputable executive, legislative and judicial power through indi- vidualization, resources, and social skills. In short, the fall of the Twin Towers, unleashed an unbridled obsession with digital surveillance and it was essential to do this with the help of technology. On the other hand, there is an increased fear of shrouding decisions in a halo of secrets while, in the case of the Internet, surveillance is hidden. In sum, the sophistication of data storage technology makes it possible to obtain a reasoned response in the shortest possible time (Tester, 2004: 147).

Civilization is currently at a crossroads due to the use of outdated energy sources such as oil or fossil fuels; this must be radically changed if we do not want to destroy the planet or want to evolve accord- ingly as a modernized society. In addition, there are serious problems such as climate change or even the beginning of a post-carbonic society (Ayres, 2010: 11). In 1990, the third industrial revolution began, and from the Third Millennium, the use of digital policies was encouraged. In short, it is essential to understand that the third industrial revolution must set the foundations of the collaborative era between social, political, and economic agents, otherwise society will drift in an uncertain direction. In industry or in business markets it is possible to collaborate using new tools such as the internet or renewable energies to strengthen the future of society through scientific-technological results. However, regarding the revolution of technologies and communication, there are platforms such as Apple and AOL (Rifkin, 2011:191-193) targeting this purpose.

As a matter of fact, thanks to digitization, CO_2 emulsions have decreased on our planet. There are elements or ways of change, after digitization, concerning aspects of communication, organization or even management etc. Thus, in the 21st century, the fundamental pillars of the third industrial revolution are: the transition of renewable or green energy; transformation in the building stock, the deployment of technology leading to the increase of Artificial Intelligence or hydrogen storage that began to develop in the early years of the Third millennium. So, do we need to manage the energy needs of a complex global economy based on soft energies? It is important to delve into the idea of the existence of electronic motor vehicles in the supply network. However, the creation of the energy regime of buildings was fundamental, from the first years of the new millennium, to promote the sustainability of the planet. Secondly, we have the technological platforms of the European Union, among which there are public and private research initiatives, concerning new areas such as promotion of transportation, electricity or even technology (GWEC, 2009: 10). In sum, the third industrial revolution is the fundamental element to consolidate the practices of international and national politics through the new political mentality among the new generations that are connected to social networks and the Internet. Hence inter-nautical links are inclined to divide the world, thus consolidating a marked turn in international geopolitics. Political performance, in relation to real creation, exists in economic transformation and change in political values or even changes in globalization as regards the continent, as a means of communication of the third industrial revolution and a vision or action plan of the Union European. Consequently, after the beginnings of the third industrial revolution, globalization is declining and it is vital to reunify the continents, promote the cooperation of financial aid or even the rise of solar sources as elements of energy transformation. In short, the intercontinental era must adapt slowly at the level of international relations, geopolitics and politics of the biosphere (Rifkin, 2010: 584) and this can only be done with the help of technology and

Artificial Intelligence as regards universities and the development of teaching technology applications or, even, serve to promote renewable energies using Nano-technology or biotechnology.

BIG DATA CONVERGENCE: MACHINE LEARNING

Artificial Intelligence is being driven by convergence and industrial maturity of techno-scientific trends. In fact, big data consists of the processing of huge amounts of data as well as machine learning (the ability of computers to know and understand the field of commerce) and the rise of data in the cloud. However, for more than half a century, Artificial Intelligence, as a field of study, has made it possible to understand the acceleration of the increase in computing power, while the recent availability of massive warehouses and flows of digital data has enabled the deployment of very powerful solutions based on machine learning. Although one may be tempted to think that Artificial Intelligence is a neutral tool, it is not in a vacuum devoid of social interests (Miaihe, 2018: 105). Big data, computing power and knowledge mechanical systems are actually a part of a complex socio-technical system in which human beings have played and will continue to play a prominent role in the globalized world. Therefore, it is not really about Artificial Intelligence but rather about collective intelligence, which increasingly involves global, interdependent and open communities of actors with their own power dynamics, while engineering teams construct large sets of data produced by consumers, sellers, workers, users, citizens, etc. In sum, there are macro-data design algorithms that interpret some results and determine the organization of our societies through the use of smart phones and objects, which are increasingly interconnected with billions of people using Artificial Intelligence daily, and which contribute to the training and development of their cognitive and sociability skills. Specific business models, at the industrial level, are the basis of the convergence between big data, computing power and machine learning. What distinguishes giants, such as the United States, is their inventiveness and contribution to the development of research and technology. First, we distinguish the groups that initially propose the sale of products and services of telematic windows and applications which recommend services for online sale. As to the others, it is a matter of exploiting the data of users to sell them diverse commercial services, as occurs with the Facebook or Google companies (Hernández, 2018: 8). On the other hand, the economic model of these corporations is also based on the close collaboration of their highly varied activities which are coherently linked. For example, instant messaging service and payments such as the case of some platforms and applications that have been billed large sums of money in China. This interferes with the functionalities of various Applications. However, some big data experts have denounced the excesses of the major platforms. In cases where their products have undoubtedly benefited users around the world, these companies also participate in zero-sum contests to get our attention, which they need to monetize their products and services. Some businesses are constantly forced to outperform their competitors because the different platforms depend on the latest advances in neuroscience to deploy increasingly persuasive and addictive techniques, aimed at keeping users glued to their computers. By doing this, they influence our perception of reality, our decisions, or behaviors. The massification of data and processing capacities are necessary for machine learning but, the rise to power of Artificial Intelligence almost inevitably questions a market dynamic that is monopolistic within a specific economic area and oligopolistic at a global level (Rodríguez, 2018: 16). In this way, we are witnesses to a centralization of digital power in the hands of these computer empires. The development of Artificial Intelligence, with the sources in hand, corresponds to the dynamics of economies of scale and scope, as well as the effects of direct and indirect networks, such as digital platforms that are in a position to collect and structure consumer data, and attract and fund talents capable of mastering the most advanced functions of Artificial Intelligence. These systems also give these talents access to processing power and user bases large enough to further develop their Artificial Intelligence capabilities.

In short, the machine learning algorithms used in certain applications are also transferable to others within the framework of a discipline called learning by transfer, which further favors strategic digital game actors. In fact, Alpha Zero, a source program developed by Google, is based on the Alpha Go model, which is structured through the dynamics of learning the transfer process. To some extent, the present dominance of the world market arises naturally from the components required for the development of Intelligence Artificial within the framework of the digital economy. However, this logic will inevitably be modified by the continuous process of convergence between hardware and software, which pushes operators to provide different solutions.

THE QUESTION OF SOVEREIGNTY OF GOVERNMENTS

National and international actors are increasingly aware of the strategic, economic and military risks related to Artificial intelligence practices. They also anticipate their impact on elections, as evidenced by the interference in the 2016 and 2020 United States presidential elections or in the referendum on Brexit. Thus, Canada, China, South Korea, Denmark, the Commission European, Finland, Mexico, Japan, Italy, India, the Baltic and Scandinavian countries, United Arab Emirates, Taiwan, United Kingdom and Singapore which, in the last year and a half, have presented strategies to enhance the use and development of Intelligence Artificial. These strategies address education, research, and learning in a variety of ways. Development, digital infrastructures, public services and social ethics. Not all countries can aspire to leadership in this area. Rather, it is about identifying and building up the comparative advantages and meeting the specific needs of the nation. Some states focus on scientific research, others on cultivating talent and education (Bruffee: 1999: 66), others on the adoption of Artificial Intelligence in administration or ethics and inclusion. The actors characterized by their aspiration to global leadership include not only the United States and China, but also the European Union. However, countries like Canada, France, and the UK also have an ambitious strategy and they are making significant investments and progress in Artificial Intelligence. Other countries are specializing in specific aspects, following a successful niche market strategy. India, for example, aims to become a place for the encouragement and promotion of Artificial Intelligence, specializing in specific applications for developing countries. On the other hand, Poland is exploring and developing aspects related with cybersecurity and military uses, while the government of the United Arab Emirates launched its digitized strategy in the fall of 2017, creating, in this way, the world's first artificial intelligence ministry.

THE SINO-AMERICAN DUOPOLY THE UNITED STATES AND CHINA

The United States and China, currently constitute a kind of Artificial Intelligence duopoly based on the critical dimensions of their markets and their *laissez-faire* policies with respect to the protection of personal data. Their competence is particularly evident in a trade war that began with the imposition by the administration of the president of the United States, Donald Trump, by applying a 25% tariff on

Chinese products, which included products derived from Artificial Intelligence, with an approximate value of thirty-four billion dollars. China then retaliated by imposing 25% tax barriers on five hundred and forty American products. Shortly after, in August 2017, Washington launched an investigation against China (Chesney, 2019: 147), accusing it of unfair administrative, financial, and commercial practices concerning matters of intellectual property, particularly in the technological sphere. On the other hand, the Chinese boom began in March 2016, when the South Korean company Go, Lee Sewol, suffered major defeat by DeepMind's Artificial Intelligence program, Alpha Go (Corella, 2017). In July 2017, the Chinese capital published an especially ambitious national strategy aimed at reaching an estimated market of 15.7 trillion dollars by 2030. It still intends to become the privileged center for Artificial Intelligence innovation, nine years from now. In accordance with this policy, which is closely targeted at the highest levels of the state, the Chinese tech ecosystem will pursue an offensive investment strategy and reinforcement of Artificial Intelligence capabilities. On the other hand, for instance, one of the solvent companies like Alibaba contributed fifteen billion dollars to research and development (R&D), a figure which is comparable to that of the American giants such as Amazon, which invested 16.1 billion dollars in R&D in 2017. Following this, Artificial Intelligence advanced quickly while the Chinese teams, for example, won the ImageNet visual recognition competition in 2016 and 2017. On the other hand, China has also integrated digital and Artificial Intelligence in its geopolitical strategy. However, since 2016, its Digital Belt and Road initiative for the construction of infrastructures to connect Asia, Africa and Europe has included a digital component in the said program. The latest development regarding the program was the creation of a new international center of excellence for the digital silk routes, in the case of Thailand, from the winter of 2018.

BLOC GEOPOLITICS? THE DIGITAL SITUATION OF THE EUROPEAN UNION

The European Union has fallen behind China and the United States in technological and industrial terms. In 2013, a report issued by the French Senate expressed concern upon observing the Old Continent become a kind of digital colony. The situation has not improved in recent years. The European approach appears to consist of leveraging its multi-million consumer market to lay the foundations of an ethical industrial model of Artificial Intelligence, while renegotiating de facto strategic partnership with the United States. Thus, in April 2018, -when the European Commission published its Artificial Intelligence program-, the Swedish Minister of Digital Development stated that it was not expected for China to do so in the same way as Europe. Indeed, with a functioning democracy and legal system, Europe must consider Artificial Intelligence to be fundamental for the future. Competing with China, or competing with the United States is of course important, but if we do not create the necessary legal and ethical framework, as a continent, we are doomed to failure (Lu veto; 2008: 5). Europe lags behind in private investment in Intelligence Artificial, which amounted to approximately 2.4 to 3.2 billion euros in 2016, and 5-7 billion in 2020, as compared to three times as many millions on the Asian continent and up to five times as much in the United States, although, despite the size of the convergence of the so-called big data, it is driven by computer and machine learning. Constantly forced to outperform their competitors, the different platforms depend on the latest advances in neuroscience to deploy increasingly more persuasive and addictive techniques to keep users glued to their screens. By so doing, they influence our perception of reality, our choices and behaviors in a powerful and hitherto completely unregulated form of soft power. In fact, the development of Artificial Intelligence and its use throughout the world is therefore a type of domination that, by non-coercive means, influences the behavior of actors or even defines their very interests. In this sense, one can speak of a political project on the part of digital empires, intertwined with the mere pursuit of profit. (Attina, 2001: 190). Along with the critical masses of data and processing capabilities necessary for Machine Learning, the rise to power of Artificial Intelligence almost inevitably sets in motion a market dynamic that is monopolistic within a given and oligopolistic economic area at the global level. We are thus witnessing a centralization of digital power in the hands of these digital empires. The development of sophisticated technology corresponds to the dynamics of the economies of scale and scope, as well as the effects of direct and indirect networks: large digital platforms can collect and structure more data on consumers, and attract and fund the rare talents capable of mastering the most advanced functions of Artificial Intelligence. In fact, these platforms can also provide these talents with the necessary access to processing power and user bases which are sufficiently large enough to further develop their Artificial Intelligence capabilities. The machine learning algorithms used in certain applications are also transferable and have benefitted political blocs even more. Specifically, Alpha Go learned with video games, playing against itself, without human experts and thanks to strict training it managed to beat the best computers at chess. However, to a certain extent, the current dominance of the world market emerges from the components required for the development of Artificial Intelligence in the digital economy. In sum, this logic will naturally be accentuated by the continuing process of convergence between hardware and software, which is pushing operators to resort to developing their own solutions and critical components since, the centralization of digital power around a few actors is what characterizes a new kind of digital empire. As previously stated, the European Union has remained far behind China and the United States from the commercial, technological, and / or digital perspectives. In fact, for less than a decade, there has been great concern concerning the possibility of the European continent being digitally controlled by the US or China and Russia within a few years (Koerner, 2020: 1). Indeed, the European approach appears to consist of tapping into its market of 500 million consumers to lay the foundations of an ethical industrial model of Artificial Intelligence, while renegotiating a de facto strategic partnership with the United States. Despite the size of its market, which has yet to be digitally integrated, with its acknowledged scientific excellence and its entrepreneurial and creative vigor, there are few European models. Therefore, its growth is slowed by the lack of a digital industrial and capitalist surface of the old continent. It is difficult, under these conditions, to avoid the purchase of European digital data by American and Chinese giants, as was the case of the British company DeepMind, a pioneer in the field of Artificial Intelligence, which was bought by Google in 2014 for half a billion dollars, or in the case of the purchase of Cuka, one of the key German robotics corporations, by the Chinese home appliance giant Midea in 2016, which paid about four billion dollars for the German subsidiary. As the co-founder of Darty pointed out in a recent opinion article, the artificial intelligence revolution is perceived in technophobic Europe, to a greater degree than in China or the United States because of a foreign wave that threatens its socio-economic model, and from which it must be protected. Therefore, driven by dominant industrial players, who have not succeeded in carrying out their own digital transformation, Europeans seek to regulate and reduce the Artificial Intelligence revolution instead of gearing it towards certain purposes. Furthermore, there is a universalist ambition, which is more conservative than progressive. The result is the search for a European model of Artificial Intelligence that links the assertion of sovereignty and the pursuit of power with respect for human dignity. Nevertheless, balancing these three objectives will not be easy, because by regulating from a position of extreme weakness and industrial dependence in relation to the Americans or the Chinese, Europe is likely to block its own rise to global domination. This is the risk that the General Data

Protection Regulation is likely to pose for Europe's ambitions of power. Subsequently, the European Commission announced an increase of 1,500 million euros regarding its investments in research and innovation in Artificial Intelligence for 2018-2020, within the framework of the Horizon 2020 program. Artificial Intelligence makes it possible to influence voters in democratic countries, authoritarian states or, it can also reinforce population control. As such, the major platforms must integrate these ethical and political concerns into their strategy. In short, Artificial Intelligence, like any technological revolution, offers considerable opportunities, but it also presents a host of economic, social, and political risks that exponentially overlap with these (Bale, 2019: 47).

EPILOGUE: WHERE ARE WE HEADED?

Finally, several questions need to be raised, among which the following may be highlighted: how should we act and survive in the jungle of geopolitics? Is Artificial Intelligence essential to understand the public sphere? To resolve these questions, it would be necessary to know the intentions and capabilities of the new digital member in international geopolitics. Artificial intelligence has become an element of significant competitive power. This is the reality which the member states of the European Union must face. On the other hand, Intelligence Artificial is poised to influence the global balance of power and the relationship between fifteen states, as well as, geopolitics, in general. In our field, the European Union, must take this challenge seriously and commit to the changes that are underway in the world. For this reason, it is time for Europe to invest more time, effort and money to ensure that the European continent benefit from the international challenges that Artificial Intelligence is introducing, while at the same time mitigating the downsides of the said development. For Artificial Intelligence to be adopted in any of these three sets of functions, it must demonstrate comparable or greater efficacy than that of humans at a comparable cost. Thus, in the situation where legislators trust in the ability of human analysts to put an agreement concerning the control of strategically important weapons into effect, they are unlikely to transfer the said processes to a completely new and untested system. In any case, implementation will not simply be a case of handing over the keys or flipping a switch. It seems there will not be Artificial Intelligence agents who are willing to take on human roles. Rather, Artificial Intelligence will increasingly be paired with human analysts to take part in activities and projects. In this way, human-machine agents offer the greatest promise in the foreseeable future and represent the maximum opportunity for a gradual transition that is far removed from exclusive human supervision as regards these tasks.

Theoretically, the pairings allow the combination of the best qualities of human and machine intelligence: the machine can process huge amounts of data quickly while the human can detect and correct where necessary, as well as understand, frame and respond to the results in ways that interact with existing policy mechanisms. Some efforts have already been made to begin to design an ethical or legal framework for autonomous systems. More recently, in May 2018, a Non-Governmental Organization, signed a new declaration on the protection of rights, equality and non-discrimination in the systems of machine learning. On the other hand, within the framework of international law of human rights and emphasizing the responsibilities of human rights actors in the public and private sectors, as outlined in the Toronto Declaration, which aims to ensure that new machine learning technologies, and Artificial Intelligence and related data systems more broadly, incorporate principles of respect for inclusion and non-discrimination. Nonetheless, reaction time, in the human context, might not be adequate for their coupling or need for greater autonomy. Even if a fundamental change in autonomy-driven warfare is not an immediate prospect, the consequences in terms of changes in norms and standards of how policy makers view and respond to threats are likely to be radical. In fact, certain weapons were anticipated to define the legality of the development and use of autonomous weapons. These steps are welcome, but they are at the initial stages. However, this study does not attempt to cover the full scope or breadth of the implications of Artificial Intelligence technologies for politics but to point out that there are important areas, including public health or law, in which Artificial Intelligence systems can be transformative in ways that directly impact the processes of the international system in the next twenty years. In short, it is necessary to focus on the application of Artificial Intelligence from military, economic and citizen security perspectives, in the field of privacy (Saura and Palacios, 2021), to avoid the fall of the European Union at the hands of the major digital empires.

CONCLUSION

The study is original because it delves into the mechanisms of robotics, as the ultimate goal of Artificial Intelligence, as explained by a group of experts. However, -despite the post-canonical statements-, Artificial Intelligence does not manage an improvement, due to the sequence of determined patterns, in the lives of human beings but, rather, what reflects - and is explained in this chapter - It is that the brilliant minds of the field that have fostered this field of study have oriented it mainly to the economic field and, therefore, is not considered human feelings, in terms of robotics and artificial intelligence. On the other hand, the European Union must be competitive by developing a set of techniques, as well as new ways of working, in the aforementioned matter, to avoid being eaten up by the Chinese and United States markets. In short, to understand that Artificial Intelligence, as it is working, is a tool to unite the hybrid feelings between human beings and machines in order to have a certain sensitivity in technological advances.

REFERENCES

Ayres, R. U. (2010). *Ayres, Crossing in the Energy Divide: Moving from Fossil Fuel, Dependence to a Clean-Energy Future*. Wharton Publishing.

Bale, N. (2019, March). Artificial Intelligence: Risk Assessment and Considerations for the Future. *International Journal of Computers and Applications*, *181*(43), 47–49. doi:10.5120/ijca2019918529

Baños, P. (2017). Así se domina el mundo. Ariel.

Bárcena, A. (2016). The new digital revolution from the consumer Internet to the industrial Internet. ECLAC y United Nations.

Bauman, Z. (2000). *Liquid Modernity*. Polity.

Bruffee, K. A. (1999). *Collaborative Learning: Higher Education, Interdependence and the Authority of Knowledge*. Baltimore University Press.

Carton, S. (2016). Why the rise of Donald Trump should make us doubt the Hype about. *Artificial Intelligence*, 1–3.

Chomsky, N. (2012). Ocupar Wall Street. Ediciones Urano.

Corbella, J. (2017). Inteligencia Artificial Arpa Jo. *Diario La Vanguardia*. https://www.lavanguardia.com/ciencia/20171019/432171399410/inteligencia-artificial-alphago-zero-juego-go-deepmind.html

Deleuze G. (1992, Winter). Postscripts of the societies of control. *October*, 59.

Flanagan, K. (2010). *Bauman's Implicit Theology*. Palgrave.

Global Wind 2008 Report (Bélgica). (2009). *Big data o como los datos masivos están cambiando el mundo", Ciudad de México*. Dirección General de Divulgación de la Ciencia, UNAM, n° 241, pp. 8-13.

Janssen, M., Brous, P., Estevez, E., Barbosa, L. S., & Janowski, T. (2020). Data governance: Organizing data for trustworthy Artificial Intelligence. *Government Information Quarterly*, *37*(3), 101493. doi:10.1016/j.giq.2020.101493

Koerner, K. (2020). How will the EU become an AI superstar? In *Digital Economic and structural change*. Deutsche Bank.

Lu, L., & Etzkowitz, H. (n.d.). Strategic challenges for creating knowledge-based innovation in China: Transforming triple helix university-government-industry relations. Journal of Technology Management in China, 3(1), 5–11.

Lyon, D. (2005). The border is everywhere IDcards, surveillance and the others. In *Global Surveillance and Policing, Collumption* (pp. 66–82). Willan.

Mesa Escobar, E. (2014). Esfera público: entre lo público y la política en la construcción de la opinión política. *Revista Departamento de Ciencia Política*, *5*, 105-117.

Miailhe, N., Hodes, C. R., Buse, C., Lannquist, & Jeanmaire, C. (2020). Geopolítica de la inteligencia artificial. *Política Exterior*, *34*(193), 56-69.

Mialhe, N. (2018). The geopolitics of artificial intelligence: The return of empires? *Politique Etrangere*, *3*, 107–118.

Morales Campos, E. (2018). *La posverdad y las noticias falsas: el uso ético de la información*. Instituto de Investigaciones Bibliotecológicas y de la Información de la UNAM.

Parker, K. (n.d., Dec. 5). Can the City on a Hill Survive? *Washington Post*, p. 23.

Rhodes, L. (1998). Panoptical intimacies. *Public Culture*, *10*(2), 308.

Ribeiro-Navarrete, S., Saura, J. R., & Palacios-Marqués, D. (2021). Towards a new era of mass data collection: Assessing pandemic surveillance technologies to preserve user privacy. *Technological Forecasting and Social Change*, *167*, 120681. doi:10.1016/j.techfore.2021.120681 PMID:33840865

Rodríguez Manzano, A. (n.d.). *El uso de los datos masivos para salvar vidas*. Dirección General de Divulgación de la Ciencia, UNAM, n° 241, pp. 16-19.

Saura, J. R., Ribeiro-Soriano, D., & Palacios-Marqués, D. (2021). Using data mining techniques to explore security issues in smart living environments in Twitter. *Computer Communications*, *179*, 285–295. doi:10.1016/j.comcom.2021.08.021

Saura, J. R., Ribeiro-Soriano, D., & Palacios-Marqués, D. (2021b, July). Setting privacy "by default" in social IoT: Theorizing the challenges and directions in Big Data Research. *Big Data Research*, *25*, 15. doi:10.1016/j.bdr.2021.100245

Tester, K. (2004). *The Social Thought of Zgymunt Bauman*. Palgrave. doi:10.1057/9780230505681

VVAA. (2018). Transitions from war to peace. Presents and futures of Iran. Politique Étrangère, 3, 216.

Whitlock, C. (2011, Apr. 29). Gorgon Stare surveillance system gazes over Afghan war zone. *The Washington Post*.

Chapter 2
A Policy Framework Towards the Use of Artificial Intelligence by Public Institutions:
Reference to FATE Analysis

Priyadarsini Patnaik
Birla Global University, India

ABSTRACT

The greatest revolution in technology to date is artificial intelligence (AI). With rapid technological advances, government agencies, business, and academia are looking for guidance and standards around artificial intelligence. Several of the AI applications can be viewed as algorithms that make decisions, raising the question of when society will attempt to delegate decision making processes to computers. A crucial practical application should be in mind while creating a theoretical taxonomy about decisions and their context, in terms of norms, laws, and policies. Using artificial intelligence (AI), this study proposes a policy framework for the country by analysing FATE (fairness, accountability, transparency, and explainability). This study examines three core areas, namely public policy, artificial intelligence (AI), and decision making. As a means to better understand public policy, a description of how decision-making processes are based on the concept of artificial intelligence is presented.

INTRODUCTION

In today's technological age, artificial intelligence (AI) has become a major revolution that will disrupt every aspect of modern life (Chen, 2018). Various industries have already adopted AI to some extent. Similarly, the adoption of Artificial Intelligence (AI) technologies by government is being based on 'success stories' generated by the private sector (in areas such as health, taxation, and education). AI assists in this extremely complex process while offering advantages of automation apply, such as low human dependency, reliability, and efficiency. Artificial intelligence is helping companies sort through data and identify patterns that could empower them to make better decisions, revealing previously hidden

DOI: 10.4018/978-1-7998-9609-8.ch002

information, (Pencheva, I.,et.al 2020) Data-driven decision-making is at the heart of this advancement by helping public entities make better access of data. By the help of AI, better decisions and governance with this latest generation of techniques can be achieved. Some states have already seen the potential of AI to help guide their decisions. With more access to data sources, applications supported by artificial intelligence will become more common in government . Again, Artificial intelligence tools reduce judgmental errors, which can be seen in public policy applications that use AI which reduces uncertainty associated with human limitations, thereby improving performance.

A number of countries across sectors, numerous government bodies, public organizations are leveraging data, artificial intelligence, and algorithms in their decision-making processes. Also, government is using big data analysis system for swift policy decisions, by considering artificial intelligence (AI) for making quick decisions, (de Sousa, W. G et.al.2019) To facilitate this, it has started working on implementing policy decisions defined by AI and begun basic research to facilitate this. Also, the combination of big data and machine learning algorithms could enable public sector organisations to improve their operations and provide better service delivery models. According to a 2017 report by Deloitte Insights, AI could free up government workers' time by up to 30% within five to seven years, (articles/3832_AI-augmented-government/DUP_AI-augmented-government.pdf) It's also expected to make routine tasks more efficient. AI has the potential to save the government a huge amount of money. It could also help avoid waste and fraud. So, AI is being used by many government customers to improve processes and cut costs. Most national strategies support the use of AI in the public sector, which is aimed at improving the quality of public services and increasing efficiency. Since, governments have access to a wealth of data, a number of types of information are accessible to the government, including data generated by organisations, programs and external agencies, as well as data generated by the Internet of Things (IoT). Government portal services are increasingly improved through the use of artificial intelligence-guided chatbots as tools for improving artificial intelligence, (Wang, Y et.al. 2020) .

Moreover, while a number of techniques have been developed to aid in research in the field of AI, understanding how AI will impact workers, organizations, the economy and government still unexamined (Faraj et.al.2018; Brynjolfsson & Mitchell, 2017). After technology has been adopted and diffused, it takes years for the production processes, the performance of organizations, legal issues, and social issues to transform, (Brynjolfsson & Mitchell, 2017). Furthermore, the privacy of personal information is a critical issue raised by AI, (Butterworth, 2018; Čerka et al., 2017), as a result public sector activities could be affected (positively or negatively) by these factors. These considerations lead to recognize a large gap in knowledge regarding AI's application in the public sector; although initiatives exist in several governmental sectors, it is still necessary to systematize information about AI's motivations, processes, outcomes, and results (Liu & Kim, 2018; Fernandes et al., 2018 Kouziokas, 2017; Pan, 2016; Ayoub & Payne, 2016). Since, the use of AI in government has been identified as a promising area of application this study demonstrated how different public administrations in the public domain are exploring the possibility of using AI to improve their policies and operations. Hence, the potential of AI in the public sector needs to be tapped, and extensive research is still required to truly harness the technologies and to address important issues/needs, (Androutsopoulou, A., et.al.2019) However, public sector organizations face challenges in adopting and implementing artificial intelligence as well as implementing these technologies in government(Kankanhalli, A et.al 2019), hence a comprehensive framework is recommended .

OBJECTIVE OF THIS STUDY

Artificial intelligence and big data will profoundly transform governments all over the world. Therefore, it is essential that public managers and policymakers have access to a useful analysis on adapting those services more effectively. In this study, the challenges posed by the adoption of Artificial Intelligence in public sector of India were analysed. This article provided a summary of key themes in the field of artificial intelligence, such as the benefits and challenges of AI throughout the policy process, as well as its implications for the public sector and proposed policy solutions and examined the challenges of incorporating these technologies into public sector operations whereas the research was designed to review various AI frameworks for government sector and proposed a framework that addressed the challenges identified.

BACKGROUND

AI in Government Sector

As AI adoption grows, providing advanced data analytics opportunities, many sectors, including smart government, benefit from its increased use, (Kankanhalli, A .et.al.2019) Smart government is envisioned being an adaptive advancement of egovernment, as a result to quick digital change in technology to innovative the ways government can engage citizens, be more accountable, and work more seamlessly (Gil-Garcia et.al.2016). The primary purpose of government is to enhance the effectiveness of governance and the wellbeing of citizens (Chatterjee et al. 2018). The use of intelligent (AI) technologies is therefore closely linked to the development of government. Besides transport, medicine, general public protection, and security, other areas can also benefit from it. Over the past few decades, databases with large numbers of records are becoming increasingly available and a new generation of artificial intelligence methods is built on data instead of algorithms (Tecuci, 2012). Thus AI continuously processes and interprets data at faster rates to perform both routine and non-routine tasks (Brynjolfsson & Mitchell, 2017; Frey & Osborne, 2017; Newell & Marabelli, 2015).

How Can AI Support Government?

Machine learning and artificial intelligence have been widely used in various industries for years whereas machine intelligence can be used to improve making decisions and solving problems with quality (Buzzle et.al.2017). Due to the efficiency gains that private firms can achieve through the use of AI, governments have started adopting these technologies for various tasks such as public safety, education, and health, (Capgemini, 2017). According to a report by Harvard, government agencies should consider AI applications in areas such as resource allocation, data compilation, and repetitive tasks (Mehr, 2017). There are a number of benefits of using AI in the public sector. The majority of them are related to cost cutting, improved productivity, and reducing public servants' workload, generation of new employment opportunities, and resolving resource problems while improvising citizens' satisfaction (Williamson, B.et.al.2018 ; Capgemini, 2017; William et al., 2017; White House, 2016; Ebbers.et.al.2016). One of the most notable examples is the reduction of the administrative burden of public agencies.

An array of programs is already supported by AI globally. It requires an exceptional amount of analytical ability to know what skills will be required to support a particular program in advance and to be able to anticipate that need in advance. Automation of these processes by machines can greatly amplify the effect of AI. If humans are liberated to be used elsewhere in the organisation, then they can really be used to support the AI-led processes instead of only answering business questions with numbers.

Artificial Intelligence in Governance

Social Welfare

Detecting bogus benefits claims: Billions of dollars are lost by governments each year due to bogus claims. For example, during the coronavirus pandemic, it is estimated that £1.5 billion was lost in bogus Universal Credit claims in the United Kingdom. AI-powered forgery systems will help governments track down large scale corruption and welfare programme corruption. It can also check social media profiles

Healthcare

Artificial intelligence (AI) can be used to avoid disease spread. Using graph analytics to discover linkages with a recognized viral carrier, like in the instance of China during COVID-19. Although triaging patients has long been practised in hospital emergency departments, it has become vital after the advent of the coronavirus. AI-powered technologies can evaluate patient records to anticipate risk scores, allowing doctors to prioritise their patients.

Surveillance

AI surveillance is the practice of using machine learning and deep learning algorithms to analyse photos, videos, and data captured by Surveillance cameras. Though AI-powered surveillance allows governments to identify individuals from surveillance footage using techniques such as face recognition, the ethical aspect of AI-powered surveillance is still debatable.

Military

Autonomous Drones

UAVs (Unmanned Combat Aircraft Vehicles) or autonomous military drones are military weapons that have varying levels of autonomy and can carry missiles or other similar combat payloads under real-time human control.

Self-Driving Shuttles

Shuttles that operate autonomously can transport people along predetermined paths at speeds of less than 50km per hour, whether on industrial campuses, city centres, or suburban neighbourhoods. There is an expectation that self-driving shuttle trials will accelerate rapidly because compared to the automotive segment, the shuttle segment has fewer regulations and greater consumer confidence.

Education

Machine learning techniques can assist in providing tailored education. AI can assess a student's development and identify contradictions between the areas being taught and the areas yet to be grasped. Also, several newsrooms are already using Natural Language Generation (NLG) for developing automated content.

Fire Prediction

To better anticipate wildfires, ML and DL algorithms track the dryness of woods.

Public Relations

Governments can use chatbots to do a range of things, such as:

- Schedule meetings
- Answer FAQs
- Direct inquiries to the proper department within administration
- Fill out a form
- Assisting with document searches
- Assisting with recruitment (e.g., United States Army)

Law Enforcement

Developers of AI-based technologies are currently investigating the use of facial recognition, discourse acknowledgment, and robo-cops for various applications .India is still developing its mechanical capabilities in order to fully adopt AI solutions with a purpose to enforce the law.

Speech and Facial Recognition

Speech recognition allows a person's spoken words to be transformed into text by identifying their sounds through a microphone .

Defense in Safeguard

Knowledge, observation and surveillance, robot officers, digital protection, hazard landscape investigation, and smart weaponry frameworks are all examples of AI applications. Out of the aspects observed, the only one where the use of independent frameworks is being considered is security. However, many of these initiatives are still in their early phases.

Application of AI in India

This section aims to explore the territory of AI in Indian governance by distinguishing its uses and patterns. India's legislature has begun to employ artificial intelligence to assist in the dissemination of taxpayer-funded organisations to the general public.

US-India AI Initiative

Founded in March 2021, the Indo-US Science and Technology Forum (IUSSTF) promotes AI innovation through sharing ideas, experiences, and finding new research opportunities and bilateral collaboration between the US and India.

Applied AI Research Centre in Telangana

As part of a collaboration with Intel India, International Institute of Information Technology, Hyderabad (IIIT-H) and Public Health Foundation of India (PHFI), the Telangana government launched INAI (Intel AI) in October 2020.(i.e. applied AI research centre) to conduct various research on Artificial Intelligence.

MCA Portal

The Ministry of Corporate Affairs (MCA) has released version 3.0 of its portal, MCA 21, which uses predictive analytics, artificial intelligence, and machine learning to make regulatory filings easier for businesses. The goal of the redesign is to make conducting business easier and to improve compliance monitoring.

AI Portal

The Government of India unveiled a specialized artificial intelligence (AI) platform, India AI, in June 2020, built collaboratively by MeitY and NASSCOM. India AI is expected to be a central centre for AI-related projects in India.

National Research Foundation

Under National Education Policy (NEP) 2020, National Research Foundation aims to research in Artificial Intelligence (AI) to promote linkages between R&D, academia, and industry while also strengthening the system of governance of research-related organisations."

Promoting AI in Schools

AI is most commonly used in dynamic, understudy administrations, understudy progress checking, and personalised learning. Despite the fact that India has a diverse range of dialects, it does not appear that many of the arrangements made in this country are focused on language. AI has all the makings of being the most commonly used system in the setup. In accordance with the National Education Policy

2020, National Council of Educational Research and Training (NCERT) attempts to introduce a basic AI course to secondary school students.

AI, Governments, and Decision Making

All of the benefits of automation, such as dependability, efficiency, and elimination of human involvement, apply to the usage of AI in businesses." "Furthermore, in terms of decision-making, whereas a systems analyst in a specific industry can make fast and effective decisions based on the experiences, AI can help others with much less experience do the same. This study has examined best practises around government usage and governance of AI with the purpose of assisting policymakers and practitioners all around world in making smart decisions on AI strategy, governance, ethics, governance, and risk.

- According to recent news, the Japanese government is investigating the use of artificial intelligence (AI) for quick policy decision-making as it meets with Palantir Inc to examine the company's large data analysis technology. To that end, it has begun fundamental research and planning to adopt AI-based policy decisions for national concerns like as defence, national security, and trade management, as well as to restrict the transmission of the new coronavirus. This latest action is in line with Japanese Prime Minister Yoshihide Suga's objectives, who has requested that the government expedite preparations for his centrepiece new digital agency, which will advance Japan's digitalization. A lot of public institutions in several countries across industries are now employing data, AI, and algorithms for decision-making mechanisms, similar to the Japanese government.
- In the United Kingdom, for example, one in every three councils is utilising computer algorithms to assist in making judgments about benefit claimants and other welfare issues. .
- India, on the other hand, has not lagged behind. In partnership with the Indian Space Research Organisation, the state governments of Delhi and Uttar Pradesh are now employing AI-based applications to find criminal "hotspots" that will aid in decision-making processes. The state of Andhra Pradesh is also using AI in education to supervise youngsters and dedicate student-focused attention to detecting and preventing school dropouts and academic failure.
- In Africa, the WildTrack programme uses artificial intelligence to match crowd-sourced photos of animal footprints in the wild to a database of recognised footprints. This is a vital tool for animal conservation because of the spatial footprint that animals might leave.
- Supporting workforce planning is a common requirement of advanced analytics for Australian government organisations.

AI Policy and Ethics in Public Sector

Government entities, industries, and academics are looking for direction and practice guidelines around AI and ethics as they try to keep up with quickly expanding technology. Many AI applications can be classified as algorithmic decision making, which begs another question of whether public sector should try to transfer decision-making mechanisms to computer programmes as a society. Though, AI is already being used by governments and private actors to make judgments still there is a distinction between deciding which buildings to check based on a computer-generated risk assessment and deciding a criminal penalty. Having a pressing practical application in mind to build a theoretical taxonomy of decisions and their settings, asking how their distinctions and similarities should be reflected in a society's norms, laws, and regulations concerning automation. According to Varakantham, An, Low, and Zhang (2017), intelligent cities may be used to build a whole nation, with AI playing a key role in improving citizen quality of life. As advocated by Centre for Ethics and Data Innovation, this indicates the breadth of this technology's usefulness, necessitating the establishment of norms (Grant, Eltoukhy, & Asfour, 2014). As a result, AI policies and ethical consequences pervade all layers of the programme. This situation demonstrates the importance of seriously considering the potential good and negative repercussions of AI deployment in publicly owned sectors. According to Halaweh (2018), the argument regarding AI's use should take place in the realm of laws and policies, with the goal of avoiding errors, prejudices, misinterpretations, as well as other issues. It is critical to highlight that AI be utilised as intended; otherwise, if sufficient supervision and regulations are not in place, undesired human behaviours such as bias and discrimination might be mimicked by the computer. Mikhaylov et al. (2018) highlighted this concern by stating that dealing with the potential of developing unfairness complications and eliminating discrimination in legal pronouncements is a major challenge in AI application in government sector. However, it is possible that the enterprise that built the algorithm is based in another country, in which case the citizen's hypothetical legal action could be conducted in a painful international legal lawsuit. Furthermore, it is believed that AI-related policies in public segment should address methodological challenges. Klijn and Teisman (2010) emphasised the need of cyber security since there's always the possibility that data may be corrupted to fulfil personal agendas and objectives.

Legal Considerations

The structure of bureaucratic as well as administrative challenges is diverse, much as the potential usage of AI across sub-parts. A generic AI approach doesn't work; instead, each subdivision must examine logical prompts unique to itself, as well as the innovation's specific applications. As a result, moral and legitimate concerns must be classified into broad categories, use of such each issue differs from segment to segment. . For example, fair treatment in foresight policing may indicate towards concerns about sensible doubt,' There is, however, an absence of commitment to the rules of International Humanitarian Law (IHL) that apply during conflicts between armed groups in independent weaponry frameworks. One of the most important aspects of the administration segment is responsibility. When a government body exercises its 'open capacity,' it is reliant on the full range of fundamental rights, as well as legitimate rights include the right to data. As a result, the edge of responsibility, involvement, supervision, and obligation brought about by particular on-screen characters using AI in the assembly or social security space may be lower than that of the safe fair and equal treatment or straightforwardness requirements that the administration must face.

CHALLENGES OF AI EXECUTION FOR SMART GOVERNANCE

While Governments and administrations in India have tremendous potential for utilizing AI, the nation's monetary, mechanical, and administrative realities present unique challenges that must be recognised and addressed when constricting strategy and implementing innovation.

Data Privacy

Data governance is a process that ensures that the data used for the intended purpose is appropriate and transparent. The most crucial issue is data, specifically data safety and confidentiality. For modelling decision-making that counts on AI, understanding the prevailing barriers is essential. Furthermore, it risks causing a dearth of public data sources. In today's AI world, personal data is commonly used to collect insights, so government agencies may be concerned about releasing too much personal data without risking a data breach. In order to build trust with stakeholders - including the government and the public - the methodology behind AI processes must be clearly communicated. AI technology has been used to embed transparency in the process of creating intelligence, which is a popular new application of AI technology in recent years. Public involvement will make the intelligence process more effective, be bought in, and become owned by the public and other stakeholders. With more access to data sources, applications supported by artificial intelligence will become more common in government, including the use of sensors on smartphones. Artificial intelligence will be integrated into a number of government processes, making citizen interactions with government agencies that impact their lives much smoother.

The Internet is required for data collecting and processing in Internet - of - things AI applications. As a result, these IoT applications, like regular web applications, are subject to cyber security risks (Ahmadi et al. 2018; de Bruijn & Janssen 2017). Personal privacy and trust may be jeopardised as a result of this discrepancy in data gathering and use. The problem of determining who owns data and what benefits are obtained through a chain of IoT applications is similarly related to the data privacy issue (Bailey & Coleman 2018). Individuals, organisations, and government agencies own the sensing devices or the facilities that deploy the sensors, however, their expertise in evaluating this raw data may be limited and provide public value. As a result, other companies are allowed to complete over these tasks. These businesses may be able to help asset owners or other parties by maintaining and analysing data. Authorities, for example, collect the data and then provide traffic advice for drivers using cameras embedded in vehicles.

AI has an unlimited amount of processing power, which allows it to store data (Winter and Davidson, 2019). Data storage costs have been reduced as a result and many industries have uncovered the value of valuable data that has been trapped in big volumes of data (Calo et al., 2016). When making decisions, there are many factors to consider when identifying patterns related to important outcomes in the data. Data can be a valuable asset, but it can also generate noise - irrelevant information that is useless in decision-making. In today's AI world, where personal data is commonly used to collect insights, government agencies may be concerned about releasing too much personal data without risking a data breach. In order to build trust with stakeholders - including the government and the public - the methodology behind AI processes must be clearly communicated. Public involvement will make the intelligence process more effective, be bought in, and become owned by the public and other stakeholders.

Improved Limit and Improved Comprehension of Developing Advances

There is a need to create limits within the legislative for convincing execution of AI-driven solutions across divisions. This would also necessitate greater reactivity, comprehension, and familiarity with data advancements, which the persons in charge of putting the plan into action - such as educators, police officers, or government officials - may lack, (Philomina, M. J.et.al.2016) Given that the advancement of AI-driven arrangements in administration is largely sought after through partnerships with the private sector, much of this limit construction may need to come from the private sector. It is, nonetheless, a challenge to ensure that vital lines of communication between the architect working in this sector and the administration body accepts the innovations.

Trust

Across divisions, a recognised problem stems from the significant potential susceptibility of any system that has been content to use traditional instruments rather than algorithmic models, particularly astute models. At the local level, law enforcement officers, police and the use of techniques that do not involve using artificial intelligence has been thoroughly trained to gain hands-on experience with them. To be realistic, their expertise and preparation typically do not entail the use of ICTs, (Sane R., 2017) Despite their enthusiasm for the key benefits of developing independent and unique solutions, the functionalities of the security authorities do not trust the frameworks being developed by CAIR, (Goudarzi, S. et.al.2018)

At the same time, there's a concern about the potential social vulnerability posed by the various instruments that are being utilized for the development of AI. This issue is not restricted to the police officers and instructors working in the grassroots level. The various divisions of the police force are aware of the potential social vulnerability posed by the various frameworks and instruments utilized for various purposes. As a result, they are not utilizing AI or any other computerized instruments. Across the divisions, the potential social vulnerability posed by the utilization of instruments and algorithmic models is a concern. In most cases, police officers and instructors have gotten ready to utilize procedures that are not based on the same approach or procedures.

Risk of a Systemic Bias

Across the globe, artificial intelligence is being used in public sector applications. As a means of advancing public policy objectives as well as assisting citizens in interacting with government, also, in government, artificial intelligence (AI) has a variety of potential applications. However, there are potential risks associated with using AI in government, such as biases emerging, a lack of transparency in making decisions using AI, and the responsibility attached to any decisions made by AI. In government, AI should be used in a way that protects privacy, is compatible with legacy systems, and formulated to support evolving workloads. So this study tries to provide a summary of key themes in the field of artificial intelligence, such as the benefits and challenges of AI throughout the policy process .In addition to aligning with the book's objective it also ensures readers' needs are met at the same time. Additionally, a domain expert in a particular field could make better decisions in terms of decision-making. Several of the AI applications can be viewed as algorithms that make decisions, raising the question of when society will attempt to delegate decision making processes to computers.

While AI-based judgments might improve accuracy, the adoption of technologies that perpetuate societal bias is a major worry. This necessitates more transparency into algorithmic or machine learning decision-making processes, as well as means to understand and audit how an AI agent makes judgments or assigns classifications. Finally, bias (injustice) in AI applications, such as intellectually stimulating systems, has detrimental repercussions. . For example, there could be systemic racism in the Artificial intelligence system due to a biased training techniques, (Angwin et.al.2016). This algorithm assigns a risk score to those detained by the police in order to forecast recidivism.. This implies that law enforcement authorities are unable to observe their underlying judgement and learning mechanisms. As a result, ensuring openness in AI and machine learning systems has become critical (Hofman, Sharma, & Watts, 2017)

Literature GAP

Although AI is already being used in many government departments, its adoption is still relatively slow and small as compared to private sector . Since, many challenges involved in implementing AI in government, many public institutions are still not ready to adopt it. According to a survey conducted by Gartner revealed that about 26 percent of government CIOs are actively experimenting with AI and 36 percent are planning to deploy AI (Gartner report, October 2021) but employees are hesitant to adopt it. Despite the small efforts to use AI in states and communities, the desire to try it has become increasingly useful. Also, the technology stack in government is very outdated. It's not being upgraded at the same rate as in the private sector. There are a lot of people who don't have the necessary expertise to implement AI in the public sector. This is a huge reason why the technology is still so slow to spread. The public is not convinced that AI is the right tool for government. This is why the public should be more transparent when it comes to adopting AI. Even though concern is understanding and auditing how an artificial intelligence algorithm makes decisions, and how to increase transparency by keeping algorithms and decision-making processes transparent (Schiff, D. S., et.al.2021) To maintain transparency there is no well-defined standard . But researchers have been researching on FATE (Fairness, Accountability, Transparency and Explainability). Despite the widespread attention that has been focused on the issues of FATE, little is discussed within research communities,(Mayfield et al., 2019; Holmes et al., 2018; Porayska-Pomsta & Rajendran, 2019; Holstein & Doroudi, 2019). However, the challenges to FATE of AI have been addressed in the past through studies that focused on the domain-specific requirements,(Green & Hu, 2018; Holstein et al., 2019; Mayfield et al., 2019). So, in an effort to stay relevant and find guidance on AI and ethical practices, government agencies, industry, and academia are searching for guidance. This is why it is critically important that academic communities investigate what ethical and fairness look like in technology-based public institution .Further, there is no explicit discussion of ethical issues related to AI technology previously. Hence, this study proposed a FATE framework and discussed how it impacts usefulness, trustworthiness and convenience which further supports in AI adoption.

RESEARCH METHODOLOGY

To conduct this study, focus group discussions and other sources were used, such as company websites, journals and periodicals, various reports on AI published by the Indian Government, literature studies, and policies on AI implemented in different locations in India. An outline of recommendations is available after the studies. As a result, the AI policy will be able to be framed by the authorities.

Proposed FATE Model

Despite the fact that AI covers policy and ethical consequences, the research examined are largely concerned with providing solutions to practical problems. It was discovered that the technique to be employed in the execution of the solutions offered is determined by the type of difficulty in each circumstance. The procedures, on the other hand, supply the resources required in the development of solutions, which include algorithms and techniques for processing data and providing answers. Fairness, Transparency, accountability, explainability are four more systems based on artificial intelligence for handling these difficulties according to this study . FATE keeps bringing up important points to think about when designing and developing algorithmic applications (Diakopoulos & Koliska, 2016; Shin et al., 2020). These concerns are important in order to understand AIs and their outcomes; however they are divisive and understudied (Dörr & Hollnbuchner, 2017). FATE difficulties are commonly mentioned in the present conversation on AI trust without even a clear understanding of how these concerns connect to trust (Shin et al., 2020). Because fundamentally biased algorithm might pose serious hazards in AI implementation, hence a discussion on how to build systems that seem to be fair, transparent, and accurate is urgently needed (Lee, 2018).

Figure 1. FATE model

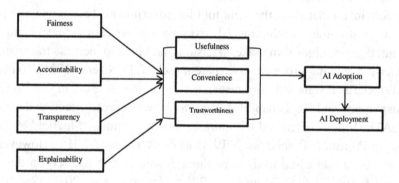

This proposed model consists of four constructs fairness, accountability, transparency and explainability which give rise to usefulness and convenience. Usefulness and convenience collectively increases the trustworthiness to adopt and deploy AI. Any organization or individuals are much more likely to use reliable systems if they are acquainted with how data is being collected, analysed, and provided (Rai, 2020). Users of algorithms can comprehend the system's reasoning (Renijith et al., 2020). In order to build user confidence, algorithm providers endeavour to verify accuracy and authenticity of results. Transparency, fairness, and accuracy all work together to enhance trustworthiness in algorithms (Shin et al., 2020). People are more likely to experience better trustworthiness when honest, fair, and accurate services are provided. High degrees of transparency in algorithm can provide people a sense of trust, which can lead to increased happiness and usage.

Fairness

Although algorithmic fairness has indeed been lauded alongside the rise of AI, there is no universally accepted definition of fairness (Shin & Park, 2019). It's crucial to think as to what fairness implies in the perspective of a user case. The formation or transmission of unfair prejudice is a crucial outcome to avoid while creating Artificial intelligence systems (Diakopoulos, 2016). In contrast to popular belief, the reality of AI functioning does not always operate fairly. A mechanism can yield biased results for particular individuals and organisations if it is not designed with impartiality in mind at every step. Establishing ethical frameworks, emphasizing current legal norms, where appropriate and essential binding norms can be introduced to develop a trustworthy, fair, and accountable strategy for deploying AI. A focus on persons who may be harmed should also be addressed. The implementation of public services, including strategy and planning, demands a constantly evolving understanding of what end users want, whether those are frontline workers or citizens.. End-user groups that are significant to government agencies should be identified.

Accountability

Whilst algorithmic accountability has yet to be conceived or operationally defined and the relevance of algorithmic accountability policies has been debated alongside practical measures. Because discriminatory and black-boxed algorithm can evolve into hazardous hazards, the AI industry as a whole should be ready to address pertinent questions regarding accountability. The vulnerabilities make it critical to create algorithm fair, accountable, transparent, and interpretable, and furthermore reliable and commonly understood, (Donghee Shin 2020) .Establishing accountability is a fundamental that is tested whenever the "characteristics and entitlements that the embedded norms generate are hidden within dark boxes." From a variety of perspectives, the many applications of computations in administrations could lead to what Frank Pasquale refers to as a "Discovery Society," in which hazy ('dark boxed') computations characterise the orientation of day-to-day presence, (Pasquale, F. 2015). However, because of the figurative 'black box' that transforms contribution into observable yields, determining functional responsibility and assessment requirements remains a major challenge. Ex post facto assessment of the algorithmic evaluation's effect is a common way to end an evaluation. This may not be an adequate indication of the calculation's accuracy. Furthermore, if AI governance is used, there must be on-going forms of communication so that the individuals affected by the technology is made constantly aware of how the technology is being used to make decisions that may influence their day-to-day existence. The argument over AI responsibility revolves around who is responsible for the consequences of AI services (Shin & Park, 2019). According to Diakopoulos (2016), algorithm developers must be made responsible for the outcomes of the AI. Although there are differing perspectives on who is to blame for AI, the adverse outcomes of undesired and unforeseen outcomes are significant. Biometric identification by AI has discriminated against certain ethnicities and genders. Many experts have started questioning the method of attributing blame for damages caused by algorithmic reportage that produces unequal and discriminating results (Shin & Park, 2019).

Transparency

AI can be easily interpreted whenever there is transparency, and algorithms can be explained in terms of how specific results are obtained. There is a growing demand for transparency and comprehensibility in order to make algorithms understandable to individuals (Cramer et al., 2008). What signifies transparency is the most debated topics (Sloan & Warner, 2017). In this context, Shin and Park (2019) suggest the term algorithms transparency, which they describe as the necessity that consumers comprehend how well an AI system makes a choice or makes a forecast. Transparency, according to Diakopoulos and Koliska (2016), means that algorithmic inputs, which must be accessible. Algorithmic visibility, explainability, and interpretability are all words that are linked to algorithmic transparency, (Meijer, 2014). Transparency is a process to determine if relevant information is being used, (Courtois & Timmermans, 2018). Moreover if people can understand how the mechanism works (Shin et al., 2020)

Artificial intelligence faces a number of challenges, including: transparency. Intelligence process and outcomes lack confidence without it. Additionally, it could result in the disappearance of public data sources. This problem is exacerbated in India because the legal executive has yet to voice a position opposing the rules, requiring the designated authority to pay close attention to the situation. Before using computations in the condemnation method, the Indian legal system must adhere to the various calls, (Ahmad T., 2014) to establish a uniform condemnation method to achieve that the dynamical contributions to the calculation is as consistent as possible. Transparency is a topic worth considering in each of the above sub-sectors, (NITI Aayog Report) However, depending on which sub-part is being discussed, the impact of a lack of clarity may differ. A prediction policing computation lacks transparency, which can be considered a violation because it legitimately affects an individual's liberties and freedoms, whereas absence of transparency in a computation constructing a learning path for Right to Information claims.

Explainability

Explainability refers to the ability to communicate the use, purpose, and outcomes of an algorithm in simple terms. It might be useful in situations when "technical transparency" doesn't often deliver the appropriate level of clarity. The regulations related agencies must have adequate visibility into data processing activities in order to accurately supervise the government's decision-making based on data analytics. It's important to recognize between "technical transparency" and "explainability" in this context. One of the most difficult aspects of AI is figuring out what occurs during the training of deep network. Because of accountability and transparency, explainability may become a more significant concept in the public sector. In this way, what is anticipated of an explainable AI is that its behaviours are understandable by humans. Explainability is associated with two concepts: interpretability and transparency. These concepts' are vital in AI content, especially when the system is human-cantered. Despite the existence of research in the academic literature, there is still no definite consensus on explainability (Sokol,K.,Flach,P. 2020). However, if AI is to be used by people, it must be specified with specific criteria in order to be understandable. Legislation relating to data protection may have a number of effects which may require models to be understandable in the context of offering a description for a choice that is taken automatically. These explanations allow algorithms to be scrutinised to see if the decisions they have made were reasonable and unbiased (Hacker. P.et.al.2020). Overall, while explainable algorithms still has a bit of a way to go, the introduction of explainability constraints would almost give these models a boost. Explainability, in algorithms, is analogous to the notion of transparency in that which relates to the strategies in AI applications that should be understandable by humans (Ehsan & Riedl, 2019). Explainability refers to the degree to which an instance's obtained features are linked to its prediction model in a way that humans can comprehend (Rai, 2020). Algorithmic AI systems give recommendations or make suggestions based on a black boxed method that most people really don't understand (Renijith et al., 2020). There seems to be no definitive explanation of how the AI created particular outputs in most existing AI systems. This lack of specifics could be due to the fact that most end users are unable to comprehend or grasp highly specialised programming skills.

Usability of the Proposed Model

The electronic relationship between government, citizens and AI builds a revolutionary internet system, which completely fulfils what's needed of heterogeneous (when it comes to both format and content) information and understanding resources, along with particular handling methodologies and resources. The working platform allows the smooth integration of solutions and guarantees their particular interoperability from the perspective of technology and graphical user interface to establish an informational structure for acquiring and describing the various perspectives of stakeholders. The proposed solution is general and does not impose any limitations on the technologies used in the back-end. It improves and enables significant relationship between government and the public. This solution makes it simple to access interconnected services and simplifies a variety of related requirements. Its interoperable set of web applications can be organised appropriately to suit the underlying objectives of acquiring, relevant data. This strategy employs a two-tier design that easily connects the following service categories listed below:

- Data management services – It helps in providing, processing, preserving, sharing, and archiving big data from a variety of sources and formats. To properly address the underlying metadata and ontology concerns, data analysis services are substantially enhanced. In fact, this layer's (data layer) services handle the life span of the many streaming data that will be used to construct and maintain the system's base of knowledge..

- Knowledge processing services - Analysing and interpreting high-performance data is example of knowledge processing services that take advantage of the most popular huge data processing techniques. Advanced text mining algorithms like information extraction, argumentative mining will aid in the extraction of significant contextual information from unprocessed administrative texts, and also web forums and blogs. Recommendations for data mining can analyse the aforesaid sources of data in such a way that essential information components and patterns in the data are discovered, and they are effectively associated with real citizen needs and government interventions. Such linkages could, for example, disclose how individuals view previous government judgments or evaluate public' relevance feedback to guide future government actions. The suggested technique uses a variety of tried-and-true techniques and algorithms, such as Deep Neural network, K-means. This layer's (knowledge layer) services offer a complex inference engine that improves the connection between both the citizens and government.

DISCUSSION

This paper dwells on the challenges that public administration faces when trying to implement AI technologies. In response to a review of multiple AI frameworks pertaining to smart governance, the authors developed a research framework that incorporates AI to assist in organizing the literature and identifying areas where understanding is lacking. Considering the framework proposed and literature gaps, this study developed an initial research agenda for AI for smart governance. Research agendas for future directions are described here in four areas i.e., performing domain-specific studies, taking a closer look at implementation after adoption studies and evaluating these systems, and by supplementing the methodologies and theoretical frameworks currently available.

Artificial Intelligence (AI) could perhaps improve a few unnecessary auxiliary components in the release of governmental capacities. The arrangement of this innovation across sub-parts, according to the findings, is yet on the horizon. This contextual analysis identified few sub-parts such as: law implementation, instruction, security, privacy, trust are the major factors of AI applications in public sectors . Also, too much reliance on AI frameworks, protection, risk task, inclination and distinction in procedure and straight forwardness and fair treatment are among them.

Implementation and evaluation studies go beyond adoption studies to address specifically issues that adversely affect the deployment of AI systems, and expand the set of research methodologies and theoretical foundations presently available. How to establish transparent interface, fair mechanisms, and integrate explainability in the interface would really be essential problems to address in AI deployment. The importance of using a FATE by proposed methodology while designing AI systems and applications was presented in this study where building trust and attaining synergy among major stakeholders for effective AI deployment in reality was discussed. According to the findings, AI and emerging algorithms must go beyond operational transparency and technological accuracy to meet actual human needs and requirements. As a result, for user-centred AI architecture, comprehending algorithmic experiences would be critical for anticipating users' future interests. The algorithm perception model elucidates how information is exchanged and with whom or what they communicate, as well as the ramifications of integrating FATE with accessibility aspects and behavioural patterns. AI's ultimate purpose is to do user-centred algorithms operations. The proposed model in this research identified the major challenges in AI deployment and how to overcome those. Further established a fair relationship between FATE and trustworthiness to provide a beginning step toward accomplishing the long-term objectives.

Theoretical Implication

The researcher draws on the deeper studies of various social and scientific fields to address the needs for transparency, fairness, explainability and accountability in machine learning and artificial intelligence. In this study, a model of algorithmic qualities describing transparency, accountability, fairness, and explainability was developed. A favorable perception of AI was developed largely as a result of FATE's qualities. The study focused on how features of the FATE Model affected the adoption of AI in public domain. It analysed how these features influenced users' convenience, trustworthiness, usefulness which further helps in AI implementation, deployment and adoption. The characteristics that attribute to algorithmic features has played a crucial role in deciding on the best option for them. It can help users make informed decisions about their algorithms. This study tried to contribute to the literature on FATE and algorithms in the context of artificial intelligence. It highlighted the importance of establishing the antecedents of user trust and the role of fairness, transparency and ethics in generating trust in an AI system. This work contributed to the explorations of how to approach and develop AI-based systems that support users while avoiding algorithmic discrimination and unfair situations.

The model shows that FATE is a heuristic tool to evaluate trust in an algorithm. It is typically used by users with limited expertise to evaluate algorithms. Individuals who use algorithmic trust often develop their own processes related to FATE. A user's perceived usefulness or convenience is not automatic rather it is dependent on how they react to the information that FATE provides. A relationship between FATE and the user's perception about algorithm services can be described as heuristic. Perceptions of algorithmic FATE are also influenced by the algorithms' actual performance.

As AI becomes more prevalent, FATE will become more important. The significance of this factor is evidenced by the finding of the relationship between FATE and AI adoption. This study established the relationships between FATE and usefulness, convenience, trustworthiness in order to explore the design of AI adoption. Due to the increasing importance of FATE in AI, it is commonly considered that the relationship between humans and machines is a critical factor in the development of AI. The relationship between trustworthiness and FATE has been acknowledged . This study investigated the link between FATE, AI adoption and deployment .This research work studied the qualities of algorithms under the FATE framework which can be used to develop user-centered algorithms that are designed to work seamlessly with AI. They can be useful for developers of AI and other algorithmic services. As AI continues to transform how technology can be interacted, the need for fair algorithms and transparent interaction will become more critical.

Further, this study supported the FATE model in terms of addressing the issues of transparency and explainability in AI. Trust between users and AI is key to cultivating a more transparent environment. This can help users feel more secure and confident in their data collection process. As AIs become more sophisticated, they will be able to provide more precise and accurate results that are tailored to individual user needs and interests. The study revealed that the development of AI systems and applications should start with a FATE-by-design approach. This approach can help build consensus among various stakeholder groups and achieve collaboration across various platforms. This study provided insights into how AI can be utilized in various fields of research. This study shows how this knowledge can be used to improve processes related to public sector AI utilization. By developed FATE framework, government practitioners can build a robust knowledge base for their AI implementation. This should include all the relevant documents and data that the AI is expected to handle.

There are two notions that are important to the content of AI: interpretability and transparency (Sokol,K. & Flach,P.2020). These notions help explain how decisions are made and why they were made, Hacker et al. (2020) .Towards the accountability to work effectively and to ensure that decision-making processes are improved with AI systems, governments should make it clear how they operate. When a public sector uses AI-based systems for interaction with users, a clear, accessible notification is necessary for users. In order for AI to be used appropriately in the public sector, it must be transparent hence AI algorithms should be transparent in the public sector.

Practical Implication

Artificial Intelligence (AI) in public services can help improve the efficiency of public organizations by helping them provide better services.AI could help citizens answer their frequently asked questions and provide them with information on various topics such as welfare payments, immigration decisions, and infrastructure planning. With the advent of technology, many administrative tasks have been automated. The rise of artificial intelligence in public sectors has been widely discussed in this study and it was found that AI solutions in public services help improve the efficiency and quality of services provided by public servants. The point where technology can allow agencies to get rid of many of their administrative tasks has come. Also, AI-powered cognitive applications are helping government run more smoothly. It is transforming the way public-sector employees get their work done. It's already replacing some jobs and making new professions happen. It helps government run better, ranging from reducing paperwork to identifying criminal suspects through facial recognition. These AI powered technology can help to identify fraudulent transactions and predict future criminal acts.

The key to AI implementation is learning how to find patterns and anomalies in large amounts of data. Developers of AI must ensure that their data protection is guaranteed which ensures that they can handle all the data that they collect and use it for their outputs. This could affect people's trust in the system's processing of their data and further can affect their privacy and prevent them from being exploited. Since the data is an important part of AI technology, it should be used by developers and researchers with limitation. The protection of personal data is often subject to contractual obligations, commercial confidentiality, and statistical confidentiality. This framework should provide effective methods and techniques that can safeguard the sensitive data.

Managerial Implication

AI technology has been used to embed transparency in the process of creating intelligence, which is a popular new application of AI technology in recent years .The use of AI in government has been identified as a promising area of application. This study also shows that different public administrations in the public domain are exploring the possibility of using AI to improve their policies and operations. The combination of big data and machine learning algorithms could enable public sector organisations to improve their operations and provide better service delivery models. This study has provided policymakers and government authorities with much to think about when developing comprehensive AI policy. In today's AI world, where personal data is commonly used to collect insights, government agencies may be concerned about releasing too much personal data without risking a data breach. In order to build trust with stakeholders - including the government and the public - the methodology behind AI processes must be clearly communicated. Public involvement will make the intelligence process more effective, be bought in, and become owned by the public and other stakeholders.

LIMITATIONS AND FUTURE SCOPE OF RESEARCH

The focus group discussions, literature reviews, and consultations with different stakeholders with experience from different developed countries in AI policy discussions have been used to outline some key initiatives to incorporate into the AI policy framework in India for making it more impactful and comprehensive. However, India has yet to formulate a comprehensive AI policy. As a result, the suggested key points real-time scenarios were not possible to verify. It tends to be foresighted to predict how the recommended suggestions will be carried out in the future. However, the study was confined to AI in the government sector, rather than a specific area of expertise of government function. As a result, it is suggested that the employment of AI in specific areas or roles should be examined further in future research.

Furthermore, India is a big country with a diverse cultural and socioeconomic landscape and has an impact on policy execution. The subject of ethnicity, personal conviction, and culture has not been thoroughly examined in this study. This is something that future studies should concentrate on.

Machine learning and AI are becoming mainstream in many fields of society. However, their ethical and social implications are still very complex. Ethical and social questions arise when it comes to using AI for humans. To make it work seamlessly and avoid exposing users to discrimination and to make sure that the systems that we rely on are ethical and fair, future study can develop computational methods that are both ethical and innovative.

CONCLUDING REMARKS

The goal of this research was to examine how a comprehensive AI strategy may be framed in all aspects. In order to accomplish this, the study took a methodical approach, examining the role of AI in various government industries and proposed a policy framework for AI. Following that, the policy framework for AI in India has been thoroughly discussed. In addition, by resolving the anticipated hurdles, this study examined the prospects of AI adoption in India's public sectors. Through a review of relevant literature, this study contributed to the existing knowledge regarding artificial intelligence (AI) in the government sector. Overall, this study has succeeded in showing the various areas of government where AI applications are being developed, as well as the benefits that are being realised. Finally, certain inputs that could be incorporated in the formulation of a comprehensive AI strategy for India were suggested, followed by a comprehensive conclusion.

For each function, the present state of study was described, along with numerous types of AI applications. A framework for this research for public-sector AI solutions was offered too. Surprisingly, rules and ethical concerns of AI use pervade all layers of this technology's deployment. In this regard, it is suggested that a previous discussion with society concerning the employment of AI in government sector should be held. Though, some countries have already established institutions to regulate any future initiatives in this area, concerns have been raised about coding and data falsification, as well as the absorption of poor human behaviour into the computer. In addition, the research identified a number of AI solutions that add value to public institutions. The outcomes of these initiatives can be improved by collaborating with other government entities. In this study, various benefits of AI implementation were described in an organized manner to allow practitioners and researchers to utilize information provided by the current study's findings to generate future studies and strategies.

AI is evolving with different digital transformation methodologies and strategies.. Governments and the public sector, on the other hand, can use AI to do more, satisfy workforce and citizens, and make unimaginable advancements. The use of AI for a range of programs is already widespread across the globe. The topic of this article is still in its embryonic stages and more research is needed to ensure that the theory offers real value to practitioners. In the paper, the author analysed the current literature critically, identifying its strengths and limitations, and proposed future research to fill knowledge gaps to enhance understanding of the topic. Research findings will provide policymakers with the necessary information to formulate appropriate strategies for the current adoption and acceptance of AI in government sector. By incorporating AI into every element of their operation, the government and the public sector benefit hugely. The Gartner Group in October 2021, reports that governments are increasing investment in artificial intelligence, but their employees are still hesitant. Hence, senior executives must show how technology helps government workers get their work done in order to address early apprehension. However, privacy and security, compatibility with existing systems, and growing workflows must all be considered when using AI in government. Public Sector may ensure their success by meticulously preparing each stage with the assistance of technology and deployment professionals.

REFERENCES

Ahmad, T. (2014, April). *Sentencing Guidelines: India*. Retrieved from https://www.loc.gov/law/help/sentencing-guidelines/india.php

Ahmadi, H., Arji, G., Shahmoradi, L., Safdari, R., Nilashi, M., & Alizadeh, M. (2018). The application of internet of things in healthcare: A systematic literature review and classification. *Universal Access in the Information Society*, 1–33.

Ananny, M., & Crawford, K. (2018). Seeing without knowing: Limitations of the transparency ideal and its application. *New Media & Society*, *20*(3), 973–989. doi:10.1177/1461444816676645

Androutsopoulou, A., Karacapilidis, N., Loukis, E., & Charalabidis, Y. (2019). Transforming the communication between citizens and government through AI-guided chatbots. *Government Information Quarterly*, *36*(2), 358–367. doi:10.1016/j.giq.2018.10.001

Angwin, J., Larson, J., Mattu, S., & Kirchner, L. (2016). *Machine Bias*. Retrieved Feb 23, 2019, https://www.propublica.org/article/machine-bias-risk-assessments-incriminal-sentencingñ.

Ayoub, K., & Payne, K. (2016). Strategy in the age of artificial intelligence. *Journal of Strategic Studies*, *39*(5–6), 793–819. .1088838 doi:10.1080/01402390.2015

Bailey, J., & Coleman, Y. (2018). *Urban IoT and AI: How can cities successfully leverage this synergy?* Retrieved Feb 23, 2019, from https://aibusiness.com/future-cities-iotaio/ñ

Brynjolfsson, E., & Mitchell, T. (2017). What can machine learning do? Workforce implications. *Science*, *358*(6370), 1530–1534. .aap8062 doi:10.1126/science

Butterworth, M. (2018). The ICO and artificial intelligence: The role of fairness in the GDPR framework. *Computer Law & Security Review*, *34*(2), 257–268. doi:10.1016/j.clsr.2018.01.004

Buzzle. (n.d.). *Unbelievably Brilliant Applications of Artificial Intelligence*. Retrieved January 8, 2018, from https://www.buzzle.com/articles/applications-of-artificialintelligence.html

Calo, R., Froomkin, M., & Kerr, I. (2016). *Robot Law*. Edward Elgar Publishing. doi:10.4337/9781783476732

Capgemini. (2017). *Unleashing the potential of Artificial Intelligence in the Public Sector*. Retrieved from https://www.capgemini.com/consulting/wp-content/uploads/sites/30/2017/10/ai-in-public-sector.pdf

Čerka, P., Grigienė, J., & Sirbikytė, G. (2017). Is it possible to grant legal personality to artificial intelligence software systems? *Computer Law & Security Review*, *33*(5), 685–699. doi:10.1016/j.clsr.2017.03.022

Chatterjee, S. (2020). AI strategy of India: Policy framework, adoption challenges and actions for government. *Transforming Government: People, Process and Policy*, *14*(5), 757–775. doi:10.1108/TG-05-2019-0031

Chatterjee, S., Kar, A. K., & Gupta, M. P. (2018). Success of IoT in smart cities of India: An empirical analysis. *Government Information Quarterly*, *35*(3), 349–361. doi:10.1016/j.giq.2018.05.002

Chen, N. (2018). *Are robots replacing routine jobs?* [Thesis]. Harvard University.

Courtois, C., & Timmermans, E. (2018). Cracking the tinder code. *Journal of Computer-Mediated Communication*, *23*(1), 1–16. doi:10.1093/jcmc/zmx001

Cramer, H., Evers, V., Ramlal, S., van Someren, M., Rutledge, L., Stash, N., Aroyo, L., & Wielinga, J. (2008). The effects of transparency on trust in and acceptance of a content-based art recommender. *User Modeling and User-Adapted Interaction, 18*(5), 455–496. doi:10.100711257-008-9051-3

De Bruijn, H., & Janssen, M. (2017). Building cybersecurity awareness: The need for evidence-based framing strategies. *Government Information Quarterly, 34*(1), 1–7. doi:10.1016/j.giq.2017.02.007

de Sousa, W. G., de Melo, E. R. P., Bermejo, P. H. D. S., Farias, R. A. S., & Gomes, A. O. (2019). How and where is artificial intelligence in the public sector going? A literature review and research agenda. *Government Information Quarterly, 36*(4), 101392. doi:10.1016/j.giq.2019.07.004

Diakopoulos, N. (2016). Accountability in algorithmic decision making. *Communications of the ACM, 59*(2), 58–62. doi:10.1145/2844110

Diakopoulos, N., & Koliska, M. (2016). Algorithmic transparency in the news media. *Digital Journalism, 5*(7), 809–828. .2016.1208053 doi:10.1080/21670811

Discussion Paper on National Strategy for Artificial Intelligence | NITI Aayog | National Institution for Transforming India. (n.d.). Retrieved from https://niti.gov.in/content/nationalstrategy- ai-discussionpaper

Ebbers, W., Jansen, M., Pieterson, W., & van de Wijngaert, L. (2016). Facts and feelings: The role of rational and irrational factors in citizens' channel choices. *Government Information Quarterly, 33*(3), 506–515. doi:10.1016/j.giq.2016.06.001

Ehsan, U., & Riedl, M. (2019). *On design and evaluation of human-centered explainable AI systems.* ACM

Faraj, S., Pachidi, S., & Sayegh, K. (2018). Working and organizing in the age of the learning algorithm. *Information and Organization, 28*(1), 62–70. 1016/j.infoandorg.2018.02.005

Fernandes, E., Holanda, M., Victorino, M., Borges, V., Carvalho, R., & van Erven, G. (2018). Educational data mining: Predictive analysis of academic performance of public school students in the capital of Brazil. *Journal of Business Research, 94*, 335–343. doi:10.1016/j.jbusres.2018.02.012

Frey, C. B., & Osborne, M. A. (2017). The future of employment: How susceptible are jobs to computerisation? *Technological Forecasting and Social Change, 114*, 254–280. doi:10.1016/j.techfore.2016.08.019

Gil-Garcia, J. R., Zhang, J., & Puron-Cid, G. (2016). Conceptualizing smartness in government: An integrative and multi-dimensional view. *Government Information Quarterly, 33*(3), 524–534. doi:10.1016/j.giq.2016.03.002

Goudarzi, S., Khaniejo, N., & the Centre for Internet and Society. (2018, March 18). *AI and Governance.* Retrieved from https://cis-india.org/internet-governance/files/ai-in-governance

Grant, J., Eltoukhy, M., & Asfour, S. (2014). Short-term electrical peak demand forecasting in a large government building using artificial neural networks. *Energies, 7*(4), 1935–1953. doi:10.3390/en7041935

Green, B., & Hu, L. (2018). The Myth in the Methodology: Towards a Recontextualization of Fairness in Machine Learning. *Proceedings of the International Conference on Machine Learning: The Debates Workshop.*

Hacker, P., Krestel, R., Grundmann, S., & Naumann, F. (2020, December). Explainable AI under Contract and Tort Law: Legal Incentives and Technical Challenges. *Artificial Intelligence and Law*, *28*(4), 16. doi:10.100710506-020-09260-6

Halaweh, M. (2018). Viewpoint: Artificial intelligence government (Gov. 3.0): The UAE leading model. *Journal of Artificial Intelligence Research*, *62*, 269–272. doi:10.1613/jair.1.11210

Hofman, J. M., Sharma, A., & Watts, D. J. (2017). Prediction and explanation in social systems. *Science*, *355*(6324), 486–488. doi:10.1126cience.aal3856 PMID:28154051

Holmes, W., Bektik, D., Whitelock, D., & Woolf, B. P. (2018). Ethics in AIED: Who Cares?. In *International Conference on Artificial Intelligence in Education (AIED 2018)* (pp. 551–553). 10.1007/978-3-319-93846-2

Holmes, W., Bialik, M., & Fadel, C. (2019). *Artificial Intelligence in Education. Promises and Implications for Teaching and Learning*. Center for Curriculum Redesign.

Holstein, K., & Doroudi, S. (2019). Fairness and Equity in Learning Analytics Systems (FairLAK). *Companion Proceedings of the Ninth International Learning Analytics & Knowledge Conference (LAK 2019)*.

Holstein, K., Wortman Vaughan, J., Daumé, H. III, Dudík, M., & Wallach, H. (2019). Improving Fairness in Machine Learning Systems: What do Industry Practitioners Need? In *Proceedings of the ACM CHI Conference on Human Factors in Computing Systems (CHI'19)*. ACM. doi:10.1145/3290605.3300830

Kankanhalli, A., Charalabidis, Y., & Mellouli, S. (2019). *IoT and AI for smart government: A research agenda*. Academic Press.

Klijn, E., & Teisman, G. R. (2010). Institutional and strategic barriers to public – Private partnership: An analysis of Dutch cases. *Public Money & Management*, 37–41. doi:10.1111/1467-9302.00361

Kouziokas, G. N. (2017). The application of artificial intelligence in public administration for forecasting high crime risk transportation areas in urban environment. *Transportation Research Procedia*, *24*, 467–473. .05.08310.1016/j.trpro.2017.05.083

Lee, M. (2018). Understanding perception of algorithmic decisions. *Big Data & Society*, *5*(1), 1–16. doi:10.1177/2053951718756684

Liu, S. M., & Kim, Y. (2018). Special issue on internet plus government: New opportunities to solve public problems? *Government Information Quarterly*, *35*(February), 88–97. doi:10.1016/j.giq.2018.01.004

Mayfield, E., Madaio, M., Prabhumoye, S., Gerritsen, D., McLaughlin, B., Dixon-Román, E., & Black, A. W. (2019). Equity Beyond Bias in Language Technologies for Education. In *Proceedings of the Fourteenth Workshop on Innovative Use of NLP for Building Educational Applications* (pp. 444-460). 10.18653/v1/W19-4446

Mehr, H., Ash, H., & Fellow, D. (2017). *Artificial intelligence for citizen services and government*. Ash Center for Democratic Governance and Innovation: Harvard Kennedy School. Retrieved from https://ash.harvard.edu/files/ash/files/ artificial_intelligence_for_citizen_services.pdf

Meijer, A. (2014). Transparency. In M. Bovens, R. E. Goodin, & T. Schillemans (Eds.), *Oxford handbook of public accountability* (pp. 661–672). Oxford University Press. doi:10.1093/oxfordhb/9780199641253.013.0043

Mikhaylov, S. J., Esteve, M., & Campion, A. (2018). Artificial intelligence for the public sector: Opportunities and challenges of cross-sector collaboration. *Philosophical Transactions - Royal Society. Mathematical, Physical, and Engineering Sciences, 376*(2128), 20170357. Advance online publication. doi:10.1098/rsta.2017.0357 PMID:30082303

Newell, S., & Marabelli, M. (2015). Strategic opportunities (and challenges) of algorithmic decision-making: A call for action on the long-term societal effects of "datification." *Journal of Strategic Information Systems, 24*(1), 3–14. 1016/j.jsis.2015.02.001

Pan, Y. (2016). Heading toward artificial intelligence 2.0. *Engineering, 2*(4), 409–413. doi:10.1016/J.ENG.2016.04.018

Pasquale, F. (2015). *The black box society: The secret algorithms that control money and information.* Harvard University Press. doi:10.4159/harvard.9780674736061

Pencheva, I., Esteve, M., & Mikhaylov, S. J. (2020). Big Data and AI–A transformational shift for government: So, what next for research? *Public Policy and Administration, 35*(1), 24–44. doi:10.1177/0952076718780537

Philomina, M. J., & Amutha, S. (2016). Information and communication technology awareness among teacher educators. *International Journal of Information and Education Technology (IJIET), 6*(8), 603–606. doi:10.7763/IJIET.2016.V6.759

Porayska-Pomsta, K., & Rajendran, G. (2019). Accountability in Human and Artificial Intelligence Decision-Making as the Basis for Diversity and Educational Inclusion. In *Artificial Intelligence and Inclusive Education* (pp. 39–59). Springer. doi:10.1007/978-981-13-8161-4_3

Rai, A. (2020). Explainable AI. *Journal of the Academy of Marketing Science, 48*(1), 137–141. doi:10.100711747-019-00710-5

Renijith, S., Sreekumar, A., & Jathavedan, M. (2020). An extensive study on the evolution of context-aware personalized travel recommender systems. *Information Processing & Management, 57*(1), 102078. doi:10.1016/j.ipm.2019.102078

Sane, R. (2017, April 11). *Budgeting for the police.* Retrieved from https://www.livemint.com/

Schiff, D. S., Schiff, K. J., & Pierson, P. (2021). Assessing public value failure in government adoption of artificial intelligence. *Public Administration*, padm.12742. doi:10.1111/padm.12742

Shin, D. (2010). The effects of trust, security and privacy in social networking. *Interacting with Computers, 22*(5), 428–438. doi:10.1016/j.intcom.2010.05.001

Shin, D. (2019). Toward fair, accountable, and transparent algorithms. *Javnost. The Public, 26*(3), 274–290. doi:10.1080/13183222.2019.1589249

Shin, D. (2020). User Perceptions of Algorithmic Decisions in the Personalized AI System:Perceptual Evaluation of Fairness, Accountability, Transparency, and Explainability. *Journal of Broadcasting & Electronic Media, 64*(4), 541–565. Advance online publication. doi:10.1080/08838151.2020.1843357

Shin, D., & Park, Y. (2019). Role of fairness, accountability, and transparency in algorithmic affordance. *Computers in Human Behavior, 98*, 277–284. doi:10.1016/j.chb.2019.04.019

Shin, D., Zhong, B., & Biocca, F. (2020). Beyond user experience. *International Journal of Information Management, 52*, 1–11. fomgt.2019.102061 doi:10.1016/j.ijin

Sloan, R., & Warner, R. (2017, May/June). When is an algorithm transparent? *IEEE Security and Privacy*. Advance online publication. doi:10.2139srn.3051588

Sokol, K., & Flach, P. (2020). Explainability Fact Sheets: A Framework for Systematic Assessment of Explainable Approaches. In *Fairness, Accountability, and Transparency (FAT* '20), January 27–30, 2020, Barcelona, Spain*. ACM. Available: https://arxiv.org/abs/1912.05100

Varakantham, P., An, B., Low, B., & Zhang, J. (2017). Artificial intelligence research in Singapore: Assisting the development of a smart nation. *AI Magazine, 38*(3), 102–105. doi:10.1609/aimag.v38i3.2749

Wang, Y., Zhang, N., & Zhao, X. (2020). Understanding the determinants in the different government AI adoption stages: Evidence of local government chatbots in China. *Social Science Computer Review*. doi:10.1177/0894439320980132

White House. (2016). *Artificial Intelligence, Automation, and the Economy*. Retrieved from https://www.whitehouse.gov/sites/whitehouse.gov/files/images/ EMBARGOEDAIEconomyReport.pdf

William, E., Schatsky, D., & Viechnicki, P. (2017). *AI-augmented government using cognitive technologies to redesign public sector work*. Deloitte University Press. Retrieved from https://www2.deloitte.com/content/dam/insights/us/articles/3832_AI-augmentedgovernment/DUP_AI-augmented-government.pdf

Williamson, B., Pykett, J., & Nemorin, S. (2018). Biosocial spaces and neurocomputational governance: Brain-based and brain-targeted technologies in education. *Discourse (Berkeley, Calif.), 39*(2), 258–275. doi:10.1080/01596306.2018.1394421

Winter, J. S., & Davidson, E. (2019). Governance of artificial intelligence and personal health information, digital policy. *Regulation & Governance, 21*(3). Advance online publication. doi:10.1108/DPRG-08-2018-0048

KEY TERMS AND DEFINITIONS

AI Deployment: Deployment is the method by which you integrate a machine learning model into an existing production environment to make practical business decisions based on data. It is one of the last stages in the machine learning life cycle and can be one of the most cumbersome.

Artificial Intelligence: AI is the development of computer systems that are able to perform tasks that would require human intelligence.

Data Privacy: It refers to the information privacy and protection of data and concern with the proper handling of sensitive data.

FATE: Fairness, accountability, transparency and explainability.

Governance: Governance is all the processes of interaction be they through the laws, norms, power or language of an organized society over a social system.

Government: Government, the political system by which a country or community is administered and regulated.

Policy Framework: A policy framework is document that sets out a set of procedures or goals, which might be used in negotiation or decision-making to guide a more detailed set of policies, or to guide ongoing maintenance of an organization's policies.

Chapter 3
Intersectoral Collaboration and Social Justice Concerns in Artificial Intelligence Implementation at the Community Level

John G. McNutt

iD https://orcid.org/0000-0002-5172-9163

University of Delaware, USA

Lauri Goldkind

Fordham University, USA

ABSTRACT

Artificial intelligence technology offers a wealth of opportunities for government to serve its constituencies and address its mission. Technology providers paint a picture of unlimited possibilities and the fulfillment of dreamlike visions. The reality is often different with failed projects or efforts with negative consequences for social justice and human rights. This situation often leads to angry resistance from multiple groups. What accounts for these different fates? This chapter examines how these efforts develop within a community systems approach and how this accounts for positive and negative outcomes.

INTRODUCTION

Artificial intelligence technologies offer a wealth of opportunities for government to serve constituencies and realize its mission. Private technology providers paint a picture of unlimited possibilities and the fulfillment of dreamlike visions. The reality is often different with failed projects or efforts with negative consequences causing the damaging of the community's human rights and the exacerbation of existing inequalities. These efforts can also interact with other AI projects in the commercial and civic

DOI: 10.4018/978-1-7998-9609-8.ch003

spaces. This state of affairs often leads to angry resistance from multiple groups. What accounts for these different outcomes? Understanding the nature of local communities is an important part.

This chapter explores AI implementations in the public sector offering ideas about successful and unsuccessful community engagement. It proposes a model for considering engagement decisions using a participatory decision-making model, suggesting key decision points for the government to consider when making choices about implementation. The chapter examines how these efforts might develop within a community with a community information ecosystem and how this accounts for positive and negative outcomes (Goldkind & McNutt, 2019). It also suggests that efforts that blend various key stakeholders including civic technologists, advocacy groups, community members and civil servants may lead to more successful outcomes.

LITERATURE REVIEW

The Promise and Peril of Artificial Intelligence in Government and Communities

Artificial Intelligence is an important force in the future of society (West & Allen, 2018; West 2018; Engin & Treleaven, 2019; Goldkind, 2020; Ribeiro-Navarrete, Saura & Palacios-Marqués, 2021; Saura, Ribeiro-Soriano & Palacios-Marqués, 2021; Janssen, Brous, Estevez, Barbosa & Janowski, 2020; Saura, Ribeiro-Soriano & Palacios-Marqués, 2021). It holds the promise of a more effective and responsive government, more accurate decision making and greater health and wellbeing for citizens and a more productive economy. It can have transformative effects on a community or society. At the same time, there are equally alarming possibilities, especially in the areas of privacy and surveillance, the labor market and personal freedom. Artificial intelligence represents another major step in the transition toward a digital world.

Darrell West argues that "Today, AI generally is thought to refer to "machines that respond to stimulation consistent with traditional responses from humans, given the human capacity for contemplation, judgment, and intention (West and Allen, 2018)". While this is certainly more modest than some projections, it potentially represents significant potential improvements in many areas of life.

There are many benefits and potential applications of Artificial Intelligence in government. AI has shown potential benefits across public health, climate change, public administration and decision-making, disaster prevention and response, improving government-citizen interaction, personalization of services, interoperability, analyzing large amounts of data, detecting abnormalities and patterns (Valle-Cruz, et al, 2019). Chatbots and smart systems can facilitate customer services for benefits and permits. AI systems can assist in resource allocation and can identify areas of new or potential need. AI can speed permits and licenses for businesses and homeowners. The technology of Artificial Intelligence can protect us from terrorists, criminals and other malefactors. AI can also protect us from diseases and support more effective treatments. The possibilities are almost endless.

It needs to be noted that Artificial Intelligence technology is commonly combined with other families of technology including robotics, data science-related technologies, the Internet of Things, cloud-based research, automation and so forth. The boundaries between these technologies are often thin. This also means that, in many cases, multiple technologies combine to form an approach to a problem or issue.

Autonomous vehicles, for example, use technology from Artificial Intelligence but also employ sensor technology (IOT), robotics and a host of other methods.

There is also a dark side to Artificial Intelligence (Sloane, 2019). While resistance to Artificial intelligence is sometimes irrational, there are very real reasons to be concerned (West, 2018). Even when the technology is properly planned and implemented there are negative direct or primary effects and externalities.

The most direct threat to well being is in employment and labor market dynamics. It is clear that technology in general and Artificial Intelligence, in particular, has the potential to affect the labor market. Projections are that AI will not only eliminate jobs but that the employment risk will not be confined to low-skilled positions (West & Allen, 2018; 2020; West, 2018). There is a long history of technology reducing the need for workers, but the coming wave is considered to be severe. While local governments can take modest action to alleviate this disruption but cannot completely prevent the disruption. This will have implications for poverty, inequality, unemployment and underemployment and economic justice.

More to the point of government use of AI, Artificial intelligence can perpetuate bias and discrimination and even spawn new types of oppression (Mitchell, Potash, Barocas, D'Amour & Lum, 2021; Eubanks, 2019; Inclezan & Pradanos, 2017). The algorithms that control artificial intelligence are postulated on certain assumptions. These expectations might perpetuate existing inequalities in the social order. The status that people have in society is the result of certain forces that often reflect previous oppression (See Buolamwini, 2016). When those relationships are enshrined in mathematical models, they deliver decisions that reflect the original oppression. These decisions continue to reinforce the oppression. These issues have been particularly harmful in the criminal justice and child welfare systems (Završnik, 2019; Keddell, 2019).

The technology that makes Artificial Intelligence possible depends on large amounts of accurate and current data. Like human decisions, better data (and hence a smaller zone of uncertainty) leads to better Artificial Intelligence decisions. Conversely, bad data or obsolete data leads to problematic decisions. It also stands to reason that biased data will lead to biased results.

In addition to bias, the limitations of the technology need to be carefully considered. Facial recognition technology is a case in point (Najibi, 2020). It is not only not completely accurate, but it also has a much harder time identifying persons of color reliably (Jones,2020). Given that this, and other types of surveillance technology, operate on technology that may have intrinsic biases, the connection to security and law enforcement can be concerning.

Technology, like artificial intelligence, holds risks that the legal system has not yet completely considered. This means that legal and policy protections are not fully implemented. Many of these items are legislation or regulations that have not been passed or created as well as legal decisions that still can be overturned by higher courts.

Artificial Intelligence technologies can be part of efforts at better and more efficient government services and potentially fairer decision-making. It has the potential to enhance evidence-based and data-informed policymaking. However, automated decision-making systems can perpetuate racism, sexism and other forms of bias (Benjamin, 2019). The benefits are wonderful but the perils are real.

Local Communities and Artificial Intelligence: When we talk about smart cities and intelligent communities, it is important to recognize that these entities are actually placed based in human communities with community-level social institutions, of which government is only one. The assumption that these other components lack the ability to determine events is shortsighted at best and foolhardy at worst.

Technology for government is often obtained the way that other goods and services are secured—through a procurement system. This is a standard system that engages in processes like competitive bidding, proposal evaluation and contract negotiation. Typically, the vendor and the governmental entity are involved.

A fuller understanding of communities and their unique characteristics is often lost in discussions where vendors deal with the bureaucracy only (Halegoua, 2020). Many technology proposals are standard solutions with minimal adaptation to local conditions. The procurement system is designed to achieve a cost-effective and reliable solution, not to gauge community acceptability.

All parties are shocked when they encounter pointed resistance (see Halegoua, 2020) to a new technology tool, but that can happen. In 2020 there was a massive outcry in the United Kingdom over the use of an algorithm to provide a substitute score for a public exam made impossible by the COVID 19 pandemic.

This is part of a larger discussion of governmental failure to procure technology and hire technologists (McGuinness & Schank, 2021) but what is salient here is the ability of government activities via Artificial Intelligence to impact human lives. Understanding communities is critical to predicting how they will respond. If one equates community with local government or the part of local government that does procurement, there is the possibility of serious miscalculation. This can lead to poor utilization, passive resistance or even active confrontation. It is critical to consider all of the major players in a community.

What is a Community? The term community has many conceptions and approaches. To be specific, in this chapter we are discussing local geographic communities as opposed to communities of practice or online communities. Warren's (1978) classic definition is still relevant today "…that combination of social units and systems that perform the major social functions relevant to the meeting of people's needs ". In Warren's approach communities are systems that discharge several social functions: Production-Distribution-Consumption, Socialization, Social Control, Social Participation and Mutual Support. These are addressed by community institutions (such as the government, the economy and the family) and ultimately by organizations, groups and individuals. Each of these participants might have different positions on artificial intelligence matters and many have active interests in the world of artificial intelligence.

While some consider relating to local government (or more correctly the local government bureaucracy) working with the community, that is rarely correct. Local government is one player in a multiplayer field. Lack of involvement with the entire community means that expectations can be different across stakeholder groups and where resistance may arise. The process of technology adoption and institutionalization is often a long and complex one (Rogers, 2003).

Purchasing and installing a facial recognition system or a predictive policing effort is not the same as acquiring other types of technology. There are far more serious consequences for the community if the program either doesn't work or has substantial side effects.

CONCEPTUAL MODEL

Major Participants in Public Artificial Intelligence at the Community Level: In general, the local political economy of a community can be divided into three sectors: (1) the commercial sector; (2) the governmental sector and (3) the nonprofit and voluntary action sector (See Figure One).

Figure 1. Major sectors in the community

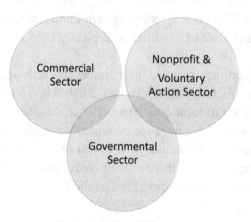

At one time, the three sectors were clearly demarcated and exceptions to the classification were rare. That situation has changed and there is a great deal of cross-sectoral interaction. The blurring of sector boundaries (Bills, 1993) has been pronounced in the past five decades and the process not only continues but intensifies. Adding to the complexity of the situation, the rise of self-organized citizen groups has created another new complication in the formally well-ordered typology. Government and nonprofit owned businesses, the rise of B-Corporations, contracting for government services (Smith & Lipsky, 1993) and a host of other developments have made the boundaries unclear.

THE GOVERNMENTAL SECTOR

The government sector needs to be understood in light of the division between the political system and the bureaucracy. The political system is the ultimate decision-maker for the government sector at the community level and frequently consists of executive, legislative and judicial branches. Government, at the local level, interacts with the government at higher (national, regional or even international) levels. While there are certain limits, this component of government represents the power and authority of the public sector.

The political system is highly sensitive to politically powerful groups in the community and elsewhere. The business community is usually one of these groups, but there are always others (see Walker, 2014). This can result in decisions that are often problematic for those in other sectors of the community.

Another issue is support for the government. Trust in government is challenging in many areas and this makes governing more difficult (Pérez-Morote, Pontones-Rosa & Núñez-Chicharro, 2020). Demonstrations and other political tools can create situations where decisions have to be carefully considered, but lack of citizen support can also be problematic. This is especially true if a certain amount of coproduction is needed. A related issue, polarization has created issues for many local governments and promises to continue and even intensify. Finally, the influx of misinformation adds to the seriousness of these forces. What this means is that in some quarters even benign interventions are often seen as threatening. This has been particularly troubling in the COVID-19 pandemic as mistrust in government (combined with mistrust in science) has led to resistance to vaccines and other public health techniques.

The bureaucracy, on the other hand, consists of public employees. Their authority and funding come from the fruits of the political system. They provide law enforcement, Public Works (roads and bridges), code and regulation enforcement, tax collection, education and a host of other functions. Many of the functions of the bureaucracy are prime candidates for partial or complete automation with Artificial Intelligence. Ideally, the civil servants who make up the bureaucracy are insulated from politics, but this is not always the case. In recent years, the size of the government bureaucracy has declined as a result of devolution.

This is often the part of the community that acquires or procures artificial intelligence applications, although approval from the political system is occasionally necessary. Government adoption of technology has often lagged behind the other sectors (McBride, et al, 2020; McGuinness & Schank, 2021). A skilled workforce is often difficult to hire within the strictures of civil service and procurement regulations often create additional barriers to acquiring technology resources (McGuinness & Schank, 2021).

Governments collect a wide variety of data as part of their activities. This data can be the basis for Artificial Intelligence efforts. There are often limits to this data and older data collection systems are often at risk from method deterioration. Survey response rates, for example, have been declining for quite some time (Stedman, et al, 2019). This creates issues for governmental organizations that depend on this data. Data collected by organizations in other sectors is often critical to supporting government decision-making.

Government has much to gain from artificial intelligence, but the path is far from clear. Other sectors will have a role here and how this set of relationships is negotiated will influence success.

THE COMMERCIAL OR BUSINESS SECTOR

The commercial sector, in most communities, consists of a variety of organizations of different sizes and structures. These include manufacturing, retail, service and financial enterprises as well as a variety of professional and skilled labor firms. The commercial sector frequently represents a considerable sector of the community's economic base and defines a substantial component of the local labor market.

The Commercial Sector has considerable influence on the political life of many communities (Walker, 2014; Walker & Rea, 2014). Local Interest Groups, such as affiliates of the Chamber of Commerce and the National Association of Manufacturers, trade and labor organizations and business-oriented nonprofits (such as the Jaycees) represent business interests.

While it varies from organization to organization, the commercial sector makes substantial use of technology and overall has made substantial investments in newer technology breakthroughs, such as analytics, big data, machine learning, high-performance computing and artificial intelligence. At least part of the commercial sector enjoys expertise in many areas of Artificial Intelligence that is far more sophisticated than that processed by many local governments. Corporate volunteers, through efforts like Code for America (David, McNutt & Justice, 2015) and Data4Good (Howson, Beyer, Idoine & Jones, 2018) can help local governments build more sophisticated applications than is possible with native expertise.

Commercial organizations collect data both as an operational necessity and as a strategic asset. Data is an essential part of many of the technology tools and gives these organizations potentially powerful insights into markets, customers, and the organization's environment. This data is often sold to third parties for marketing and other uses.

Data philanthropy efforts are of fairly recent vintage and involve using corporate data to solve community problems (McKeever, Greene, MacDonald & Tatian, 2018). Examples include using data from the rating site Yelp to guide health department inspections or using data from the ride-sharing platform Uber to help plan transportation programming. These are sometimes provided directly to the government and sometimes provided through structures referred to as data collaboratives (Verhulst & Young, 2019).

Given the commercial sector's political and economic power, it is difficult to see how its wishes can be ignored. The sector can be a considerable ally to artificial intelligence efforts but commercial interests must be engaged for synergy to occur. Commercial organizations have a stake in the wellbeing of local communities and the health of local governments. Cooperative efforts between the sectors can benefit both parties.

THE NONPROFIT AND VOLUNTARY ACTION SECTOR

The nonprofit sector is a highly complex group of organizations that range from very small voluntary associations to large hospitals and universities. Churches, political parties, social action groups, fraternal organizations, trade associations, labor unions, human services providers and advocacy organizations are typically nonprofits.

Defining the nonprofit sector is difficult and often controversial. Some take the view that all nonprofits are incorporated organizations that enjoy some type of government status. In the United States and many nations throughout the world, that group accounts for only part of the sector (Smith, 2000). Many nonprofits are unincorporated voluntary associations. Also referred to as grassroots associations, the organizations are created for the interests of their members. Social movement organizations and social advocacy groups can be one or the other.

The barrier between government and the nonprofit sector has been weakened over the past six decades. Purchase of service contracting has transferred many formally governmental functions to the nonprofit sector (Smith & Lipsky, 1993; Goldkind & McNutt, 2019). Nonprofit organizations are substantial players in politics. Political parties, political action committees and advocacy and interest groups are all nonprofits.

Nonprofit technology, at the sector level, has always lagged behind the commercial sector (McNutt, Guo, Goldkind & An, 2018). On balance, some nonprofits have highly sophisticated technology and others have created highly advanced technology-related efforts. Universities and hospitals are often nonprofit organizations and many of these rival commercial organizations in their use of technology.

The line between the nonprofit sector and the commercial sector has always been less than that with government and there are many crossover establishments. The idea of social enterprise and the creation of corporations that include elements of both (such as B-Corporations) is a move toward erasing the lines.

Civic and Voluntary Action is an important aspect of the nonprofit sector. For years this meant advocacy groups and formally organized systems. In the past two decades, there has been a shift toward self-organizing, solo advocacy, civic hacking, crowdsourcing and coproduction. This means that citizens can create their own organizations or efforts and use them to address community issues. This can mean protesting the actions of other organizations, modifying other organizations from within, and/or creating new efforts that address community issues. This isn't altogether new but the rise of cooperative technology (such as Web 2.0 based technologies) has promoted a wide variety of efforts that would have been nearly impossible without these tools. This has led some to refer to this development as a *cooperative society* (Jemielniak & Przegalinska, 2020).

Virtual nonprofits are going to play an interesting role in the future of the sector. Freed from some of the constraints of the bricks-and-mortar nonprofit sector, they have the potential to reinvent the sector in various ways (McNutt, Brainard, Zeng & Kovacic, 2016).

The nonprofit and voluntary action sector has much to add to AI efforts at the local level. A strong partnership can add much to the implementation potential of a new system.

Communities are essential to the well-being of society. They are instrumental in meeting the needs of most people. While it is easy to consider the components in isolation from each other, communities are interdependent systems. Action taken in one area of the community is frequently felt in others.

<u>What Resistance Looks Like: Opposition to Artificial Intelligence Tools:</u> Resistance from the community or its constituent parts can make AI technology implementation difficult to impossible. Community action is a well understood and well documented phenomenon (McNutt, 2018). At one point it can be noncompliance or passive resistance. Political pressure comes in many forms including lobbying, organized demonstrations, traditional and social media campaigns, petitions, lawsuits and electoral campaigns. Table 1 looks at the options available to opponents.

Table 1. Techniques for opposition to Artificial Intelligence efforts by local government

Passive Techniques	Traditional Techniques	Conflict Strategies
Noncompliance Providing incorrect or partially correct information	Lawsuits Political Pressure Electoral Strategies Community Organization Administrative Lobbying Social Media Campaigns Data Based Organizing Media Strategies	Demonstrations Civil Disobedience

What seemed like a straightforward decision can easily transition into a program and career-ending mess. For instance, in Los Angeles county in the United States, community advocates and community leaders have organized a group called, Stop LAPD (Los Angeles Police Department) Spying Coalition focused on removing AI-enhanced surveillance tools from poor communities (Laynor, 2021).

On balance, a successful and well supported effort can bring major benefits and smooth implementation. Supporters can smooth over opposition and provide the resources needed.

Communities have an information ecology that includes a wide range of information from a variety of sources (Goldkind & McNutt, 2019). Sharing the data that different stakeholders have can create a database on community functioning that is worthy of the tools that artificial intelligence brings to the table.

Communities can make Artificial Intelligence activities successful and well supported or unworkable and chaotic. Technologists who aim for the "City on a Hill" should consider community involvement critical.

METHODOLOGY

Communities Considered

Communities and their major components must be involved in major decisions that involve Artificial Intelligence. While it is impractical to involve every constituent in every technology decision, public administrators need a set of guidelines to plan and structure this involvement. The approach taken here proposes three possible strategies based on the degree of potential controversy in the decision.

ANALYSIS AND DISCUSSION

Strategies for Acquiring Artificial Intelligence

If we understand that involving communities is important in making technology decisions, then a strategy for said involvement is needed. Extensive community involvement is clearly not needed in all AI decisions, but in other situations, considerable input and involvement are needed.

Three levels of community involvement in acquiring AI technology is proposed here: (1) a standard procurement model where community involvement is kept at a minimum, (2) A Limited Community Involvement approach that brings in representatives of relevant units and (3) an Extensive Community Involvement Effort that solicits broad community involvement. Each of these approaches is described below.

Figure 2. Strategies of Artificial Intelligence acquisition

Standard Procurement Approach

This is the approach that is most familiar to government workers are represents a rational approach to purchasing goods and services. There are well established approaches to making this process work. As long as the impact of the AI technology is both internal and has a limited impact on the community, this is an adequate approach. AI tools that support a worker's individual efforts (such as a decision support system for a health care worker or an engineer) are one example of things that can be placed in this category. Many processes are so internal to government that their impact outside is negligible.

While community input isn't essential in this case, expertise from the community might be very useful to government procurement professionals. These relationships can often be invaluable to decision-makers. This speaks to the need to create these networks at the local level.

Limited Community Involvement Approach

This strategy involves engaging a limited set of community stakeholders around an issue. An AI-based system for assessing business taxes might require significant input from business and professional service groups, but larger population groups might be indifferent.

A community task force might be one approach to this or a survey of potential stakeholders. Care should be taken to involve all of the relevant stakeholders. At the very least, community education about the new technology is essential. A technology champion (a well-respected person who is willing to advocate for the technology) is helpful in making the implementation process work and this person can be identified within a community task force. In addition, the task force might surface some information that the implementers were unaware of and are critical to implementation.

It is easy to rationalize avoiding this step but the costs of doing so can be considerable. Making technology work is not the same as making it work in the community.

Extensive Community Involvement Approach

AI offers many wonderful gifts but some come with huge potential consequences. These need to be carefully considered by a larger cross-section of the community and these stakeholders must be meaningfully involved.

AI tools such as predictive policing, facial recognition, algorithmic decision making in child protective services (Eubanks, 2018) or school achievement tracking fall into this category. They promise to make life and death decisions easier but this type of application needs serious consideration. The results of the functioning of these tools is often controversial and their impact can be substantial.

This approach requires broad representation from across the community and true community problem solving. Living or Innovation labs might be a useful approach for AI implementations of this type (van Veenstra & Kotterink, 2017). Community hearings should be considered and carefully organized.

Technology, at this level, should be adopted on a trial basis. Careful monitoring of both the outcomes and externalities is important and it may be considered good practice to create an oversight group to judge the progress of the project.

MANAGERIAL IMPLICATIONS AND PRACTICAL/SOCIAL IMPLICATIONS

Making Decisions About Artificial Intelligence

Technology is both a gift and a curse, magic and a nightmare. Like any other government asset, it needs to be carefully managed. Government, as a protector of the public interest, must be especially careful and must involve stakeholders to the extent possible.

Some technology is low risk. A word processor, spreadsheet or simple database has little potential for mischief. AI that guides the users of these items is probably low risk as well. Other technology affects many people and its use has major impacts on their lives. The former is probably the bulk of government technology procurement.

At the same time, some technology is not considered benign. Technology that makes major decisions about a person's life and future is definitely taken seriously. Facial recognition technology that can add your name to a terrorism watch list is one example, but evidence shows that its ability to operate successfully on nonwhite subjects is deeply troubling (Cave & Dihal, 2020). Algorithms that can determine government benefits, identify suspects for police, determine areas that need additional law enforcement presence, identify parents who pose a risk to their children are taken very seriously by those who are the targets of such decisions. Using these tools will be controversial and will require political capital and skill to put into place. Table 2 provides a rough characterization of Artificial Intelligence related tools considered by their degree of Controversy.

Table 2. Artificial Intelligence tools by degree of controversy

Low Controversy	Medium Controversy	High Controversy
• AI Supported Office Applications • Internal Fraud Control Artificial Intelligence • Employee Tracking	• AI Fraud Prediction • License Plate readers and other IoT Sensors coupled with AI • AI backed benefit eligibility. • Algorithms for School Choice	• Predictive Policing • Facial Recognition • Child Protection Case identification Algorithms

Many of these Artificial Intelligence tools are particularly threatening to populations that are already vulnerable. The poor, minority communities, immigrants and others are often identified by Artificial intelligence applications as needing attention. These are groups that often fear the attention of public agencies. Robert Kennedy (1964) once said that "The poor man looks upon the law as an enemy, not as a friend. For him, the law is always taking something away. Even completely well intentioned actions can be distrusted and resisted by organizations that represent the poor and the downtrodden.

Governments don't always understand this perspective. It is also very possible that those who develop the software may not appreciate either the fear that exists or some aspects of the local situation that is critical. Software applications are typically developed outside the community and are based on assumptions that may not hold in specific areas.

Making a Decision with Community Input: While the community should be a consideration in every decision, it might be practical to create a metric for the degree of involvement. Table 3 presents a decision matrix for community-oriented decisions about Artificial Intelligence tools.

Table 3. Community involvement and Artificial Intelligence

	Low Community Impact	High Community Impact
Low Potential Controversy	Standard Procurement	Limited Community Involvement Effort
High Potential Controversy	Limited Community Involvement Effort	Extensive Community Involvement Effort

For lower impact/low controversy AI decisions, standard procurement methodologies should be adequate. In those situations with low community impact or low controversy, a limited community involvement effort should be adequate, but care needs to be exercised in important cases. Finally, in those cases where there is very high impact and very high controversy, a more substantial community involvement approach is needed.

It should be noted that if the acquisition of technology proves to be riskier than originally thought, it stands to reason that a more protective system should be substituted. The prudent practice involves being prepared for this eventuality.

This means changing what are standard ways of addressing procurement decisions where Artificial Intelligence is concerned. It is clear that this will not be a simple matter. A network of laws and regulations surround current practice and a set of tools and techniques have grown up to implement the mainstream model. Still, the changes are worth making, especially in this case.

CONCLUSION AND LIMITATIONS

Artificial intelligence promises much to the future of government. In order to realize those gifts, local governments need to reach out to their communities and involve them in the technology acquisition decisions and the decisions about how the technology is implemented. Many local governments would tell you that they already understand what their communities want and need. Some do but others clearly don't. Civic unrest and civic apathy signal that something is amiss. Trust in government is another indicator of lack of fit between government and community.

Communities are complex and their nature changes over time. They have important constituencies. Ignoring or black boxing these subgroups means risking resistance and worse. On balance, involving multiple groups means not only more support but more resources. Businesses and nonprofits, as well as citizen groups, have access to human and material resources that government might lack.

While this type of involvement strategy is useful for making procurement decisions, there is a better way. Community-led technology movements such as Civic Technology (Suri, 2013; David, McNutt & Justice, 2018; David, Justice & McNutt, 2015; McNutt, Justice, Melitski, Ahn, Siddiqui, Carter & Kline, 2016) promise a more comprehensive and long term approach. Civic technology builds strong partnerships with other parts of the community and involves volunteers in addressing community issues including those related to government technology. There are other models of community technology that offer additional possibilities (Winschiers-Theophilus, Zaman & Stanley, 2019; Alperstein, 2021).

While involving communities in technology decision-making is a worthy goal, the creation of technology-based community partnerships is a much better outcome. This type of approach promises better implementation, superior technology choices and better resource availability. The idea of government technology as part of a robust community network is an exciting development.

This analysis is limited by our place in time and the need to map out a general approach that might work for many local governments. As technology and practice evolve, we can expect that changes and refinements will be necessary.

Artificial Intelligence brings the promise of considerable new capacity to communities throughout the world. Local governments must take advantage of these new tools while avoiding the perils. The time when governments could work in separation from or even opposition to their communities is over.

REFERENCES

Ahn, M. J., & Chen, Y. C. (2020, June). Artificial intelligence in government: potentials, challenges, and the future. In *The 21st Annual International Conference on Digital Government Research* (pp. 243-252). 10.1145/3396956.3398260

Alperstein, N. (2021). Exploring Issues of Social Justice and Data Activism: The Personal Cost of Network Connections in the Digital Age. In Performing Media Activism in the Digital Age (pp. 143-177). Palgrave Macmillan.

Androutsopoulou, A., Karacapilidis, N., Loukis, E., & Charalabidis, Y. (2019). Transforming the communication between citizens and government through AI-guided chatbots. *Government Information Quarterly*, *36*(2), 358–367. doi:10.1016/j.giq.2018.10.001

Arevian, A. C., O'Hora, J., Jones, F., Mango, J., Jones, L., Williams, P. G., ... Wells, K. B. (2018). Participatory technology development to enhance community resilience. *Ethnicity & Disease*, *28*(Suppl 2), 493–502. doi:10.18865/ed.28.S2.493 PMID:30202203

Belfield, H. (2020, February). Activism by the AI community: Analysing recent achievements and future prospects. In *Proceedings of the AAAI/ACM Conference on AI, Ethics, and Society* (pp. 15-21). 10.1145/3375627.3375814

Benjamin, R. (2019). Assessing risk, automating racism. *Science*, *366*(6464), 421–422. doi:10.1126cience.aaz3873 PMID:31649182

Billis, D. (1993). Sector blurring and nonprofit centers: The case of the United Kingdom. *Nonprofit and Voluntary Sector Quarterly*, *22*(3), 241–257. doi:10.1177/0899764093223006

Buolamwini, J. (2016). *The algorithmic justice league*. Medium. https://medium. com/mit-media-lab/the-algorithmic-justice-league-3cc4131c5148

Cave, S., & Dihal, K. (2020). The whiteness of AI. *Philosophy & Technology*, *33*(4), 685–703. doi:10.100713347-020-00415-6

Ceccaroni, L., Bibby, J., Roger, E., Flemons, P., Michael, K., Fagan, L., & Oliver, J. L. (2019). Opportunities and risks for citizen science in the age of artificial intelligence. *Citizen Science: Theory and Practice*, *4*(1), 29. doi:10.5334/cstp.241

David, N., Justice, J. B., & McNutt, J. G. (2015). Smart Cities are Transparent Cities: The Role of Fiscal Transparency in Smart City Governance. In P. R. B. Manuel (Ed.), *Transforming City Governments for successful Smart Cities. Empirical Experiences*. Springer. doi:10.1007/978-3-319-03167-5_5

David, N., Justice, J. B., & McNutt, J. G. (2018). Smart Cities, Transparency, Civic Technology and Reinventing Government. In Smart Technologies for Smart Governments. Transparency, Efficiency and Organizational Issues. Berlin: Springer.

Engin, Z., & Treleaven, P. (2019). Algorithmic government: Automating public services and supporting civil servants in using data science technologies. *The Computer Journal*, *62*(3), 448–460. doi:10.1093/comjnl/bxy082

Eubanks, V. (2018). *Automating inequality: How high-tech tools profile, police, and punish the poor.* St. Martin's Press.

Feldstein, S. (2019). The road to digital unfreedom: How artificial intelligence is reshaping repression. *Journal of Democracy, 30*(1), 40–52. doi:10.1353/jod.2019.0003

Goldkind, L. (2021). Social Work and Artificial Intelligence: Into the Matrix. *Social Work, 66*(4), 372–374. Advance online publication. doi:10.1093wwab028 PMID:34279661

Goldkind, L., & McNutt, J. G. (2019). We could be unicorns: Human services leaders Moving from Managing Programs to Managing Information Ecosystems. *Human Service Organizations, Management, Leadership & Governance, 43*(4), 269–277. doi:10.1080/23303131.2019.1669758

Goldkind, L., Wolf, L., & Freddolino, P. P. (Eds.). (2018). *Digital social work: Tools for practice with individuals, organizations, and communities.* Oxford University Press.

Halegoua, G. (2020). *Smart cities.* MIT Press. doi:10.7551/mitpress/11426.001.0001

Harris, M. (2012). Nonprofits and business: Toward a subfield of nonprofit studies. *Nonprofit and Voluntary Sector Quarterly, 41*(5), 892–902. doi:10.1177/0899764012443735

Hou, Y., & Lampe, C. (2017, June). Sustainable hacking: characteristics of the design and adoption of civic hacking projects. In *Proceedings of the 8th International Conference on Communities and Technologies* (pp. 125-134). ACM. 10.1145/3083671.3083706

Howson, C., Beyer, M. A., Idoine, C. J., & Jones, L. C. (2018). *How to Use Data for Good to Impact Society.* Gartner. https://www.gartner.com/doc/3880666/use-data-good-impact-society

Inclezan, D., & Pradanos, L. I. (2017). A critical view on smart cities and AI. *Journal of Artificial Intelligence Research, 60*, 681–686. doi:10.1613/jair.5660

Janssen, M., Brous, P., Estevez, E., Barbosa, L. S., & Janowski, T. (2020). Data governance: Organizing data for trustworthy Artificial Intelligence. *Government Information Quarterly, 37*(3), 101493. doi:10.1016/j.giq.2020.101493

Jemielniak, D., & Przegalinska, A. (2020). *Collaborative society.* MIT Press. doi:10.7551/mitpress/11587.001.0001

Jones, C. (2020). Law Enforcement Use of Facial Recognition: Bias, Disparate Impacts on People of Color, and the Need for Federal Legislation. *NCJL & Tech., 22*, 777.

Kassens-Noor, E., & Hintze, A. (2020). Cities of the future? The potential impact of artificial intelligence. *AI, 1*(2), 192-197.

Keddell, E. (2019). Algorithmic justice in child protection: Statistical fairness, social justice and the implications for practice. *Social Sciences, 8*(10), 281. doi:10.3390ocsci8100281

Kennedy, R. F. (1963). *Robert F. Kennedy's address to University of Chicago Law School students on Law Day, May 1, 1964.* https://mag.uchicago.edu/law-policy-society/lawyers-responsibility-redefined

Krafft, P. M., Young, M., Katell, M., Lee, J. E., Narayan, S., Epstein, M., ... Barghouti, B. (2021, March). An Action-Oriented AI Policy Toolkit for Technology Audits by Community Advocates and Activists. In *Proceedings of the 2021 ACM Conference on Fairness, Accountability, and Transparency* (pp. 772-781). 10.1145/3442188.3445938

Laynor, G. (2021). Artificial Whiteness: Politics and Ideology in Artificial Intelligence by Yarden Katz. *Information & Culture*, *56*(3), 356–357.

McBride, K., van Noordt, C., Misuraca, G., & Hammerschmid, G. (2021). Towards a Systematic Understanding on the Challenges of Procuring Artificial Intelligence in the Public Sector. doi:10.31235/osf.io/un649osf.io/un649

McGuinness, T. D., & Schank, H. (2021). *Power to the Public: The Promise of Public Interest Technology*. Princeton University Press. doi:10.2307/j.ctv18b5dbz

McKeever, B., Greene, S., MacDonald, G., Tatian, P., & Jones, D. (2018). *Data philanthropy: Unlocking the power of private data for public good*. Urban Institute.

McNutt, J. G. (Ed.). (2018). Technology, Activism and Social Justice in a Digital Age. Oxford University Press.

McNutt, J. G., Brainard, L., Zeng, Y., & Kovacic, P. (2016). Information and Technology In and For Associations and Volunteering. In Palgrave Handbook of Volunteering and Nonprofit Associations. Palgrave Macmillan.

McNutt, J. G., & Goldkind, L. (2020). Civic Technology and Data for Good: Evolutionary Developments or Disruptive Change in E-Participation? In Digital Government and Achieving E-Public Participation: Emerging Research and Opportunities (pp. 124-142). IGI Global.

McNutt, J. G., Guo, C., Goldkind, L., & An, S. (2018). Technology in Nonprofit organizations and voluntary action. *Voluntaristics Review*, *3*(1), 1–63. doi:10.1163/24054933-12340020

McNutt, J. G., Justice, J. B., Melitski, M. J., Ahn, M. J., Siddiqui, S., Carter, D. T., & Kline, A. D. (2016). The diffusion of civic technology and open government in the United States. *Information Polity*, *21*(2), 153–170. doi:10.3233/IP-160385

Medaglia, R., Gil-Garcia, J. R., & Pardo, T. A. (2021). Artificial Intelligence in Government: Taking Stock and Moving Forward. *Social Science Computer Review*. doi:10.1177/08944393211034087

Mehr, H. (2017). Artificial intelligence for citizen services and government. *Ash Cent. Democr. Gov. Innov. Harvard Kennedy Sch*, (August), 1–12.

Mitchell, S., Potash, E., Barocas, S., D'Amour, A., & Lum, K. (2021). Algorithmic fairness: Choices, assumptions, and definitions. *Annual Review of Statistics and Its Application*, *8*(1), 141–163. doi:10.1146/annurev-statistics-042720-125902

Musikanski, L., Rakova, B., Bradbury, J., Phillips, R., & Manson, M. (2020). Artificial intelligence and community well-being: A proposal for an emerging area of research. *International Journal of Community Well-Being*, *3*(1), 39–55. doi:10.100742413-019-00054-6

Najibi, A. (2020). *Racial discrimination in face recognition technology*. Harvard University. https://sitn.hms.harvard.edu/flash/2020/racial-discrimination-in-face-recognition-technology/

Noble, S. U. (2018). *Algorithms of oppression*. New York University Press. doi:10.2307/j.ctt1pwt9w5

Pérez-Morote, R., Pontones-Rosa, C., & Núñez-Chicharro, M. (2020). The effects of e-government evaluation, trust and the digital divide in the levels of e-government use in European countries. *Technological Forecasting and Social Change*, *154*, 119973.

Quaintance, Z. (2021, December 5). What Can Local Government Do to Avoid Inequitable Tech? *Governing*. https://www.governing.com/community/what-can-local-government-do-to-avoid-inequitable-tech

Rakova, B., Yang, J., Cramer, H., & Chowdhury, R. (2021). Where responsible AI meets reality: Practitioner perspectives on enablers for shifting organizational practices. *Proceedings of the ACM on Human-Computer Interaction, 5*(CSCW1), 1-23. 10.1145/3449081

Ribeiro-Navarrete, S., Saura, J. R., & Palacios-Marqués, D. (2021). Towards a new era of mass data collection: Assessing pandemic surveillance technologies to preserve user privacy. *Technological Forecasting and Social Change*, *167*, 120681. doi:10.1016/j.techfore.2021.120681 PMID:33840865

Robinson, P., & Johnson, P. A. (2021). Pandemic-Driven Technology Adoption: Public Decision Makers Need to Tread Cautiously. *International Journal of E-Planning Research*, *10*(2), 59–65. doi:10.4018/IJEPR.20210401.oa5

Rogers, E. M. (2003). *Diffusion of Innovations* (5th ed.). Free Press.

Saura, J. R., Ribeiro-Soriano, D., & Palacios-Marqués, D. (2021, July 15). Setting privacy "by default" in social IoT: Theorizing the challenges and directions in Big Data Research. *Big Data Research*, *25*, 100245. doi:10.1016/j.bdr.2021.100245

Saura, J. R., Ribeiro-Soriano, D., & Palacios-Marqués, D. (2021). Using data mining techniques to explore security issues in smart living environments in Twitter. *Computer Communications*, *179*, 285–295. Advance online publication. doi:10.1016/j.comcom.2021.08.021

Sloane, M. (2019). Inequality is the name of the game: thoughts on the emerging field of technology, ethics and social justice. In *Weizenbaum Conference* (p. 9). DEU.

Smith, D. H. (2000). Grassroots associations. *Sage (Atlanta, Ga.)*.

Smith, S. R., & Lipsky, M. (1993). *Nonprofits for hire*. Harvard University Press. doi:10.4159/9780674043817

Stedman, R. C., Connelly, N. A., Heberlein, T. A., Decker, D. J., & Allred, S. B. (2019). The end of the (research) world as we know it? Understanding and coping with declining response rates to mail surveys. *Society & Natural Resources*, *32*(10), 1139–1154. doi:10.1080/08941920.2019.1587127

Thinyane, M., Goldkind, L., & Lam, H. I. (2018). Data collaboration and participation for sustainable development goals—A case for engaging community-based organizations. *Journal of Human Rights and Social Work*, *3*(1), 44–51. doi:10.100741134-018-0047-6

Valle-Cruz, D., Alejandro Ruvalcaba-Gomez, E., Sandoval-Almazan, R., & Ignacio Criado, J. (2019, June). A review of artificial intelligence in government and its potential from a public policy perspective. In *Proceedings of the 20th Annual International Conference on Digital Government Research* (pp. 91-99). Academic Press.

van Veenstra, A. F., & Kotterink, B. (2017, September). Data-driven policy making: The policy lab approach. In *International Conference on Electronic Participation* (pp. 100-111). Springer.

Verhulst, S. G., & Young, A. (2019). The potential and practice of data collaboratives for migration. In *Guide to Mobile Data Analytics in Refugee Scenarios* (pp. 465–476). Springer.

Walker, E. T. (2014). *Grassroots for hire: Public affairs consultants in American democracy.* Cambridge University Press.

Walker, E. T., & Rea, C. M. (2014). The political mobilization of firms and industries. *Annual Review of Sociology, 40,* 281–304.

Warren, R. L. (1978). The Community in America. Rand McNally.

West, D. M. (2018). *The future of work: Robots, AI, and automation.* Brookings Institution Press.

West, D. M., & Allen, J. R. (2018). *How artificial intelligence is transforming the world.* Report. Brookings Institution.

West, D. M., & Allen, J. R. (2020). *Turning Point: Policymaking in the Era of Artificial Intelligence.* Brookings Institution Press.

Winschiers-Theophilus, H., Zaman, T., & Stanley, C. (2019). A classification of cultural engagements in community technology design: Introducing a transcultural approach. *AI & Society, 34*(3), 419–435.

Wirtz, B. W., Weyerer, J. C., & Sturm, B. J. (2020). The dark sides of artificial intelligence: An integrated AI governance framework for public administration. *International Journal of Public Administration, 43*(9), 818–829.

Završnik, A. (2019). Algorithmic justice: Algorithms and big data in criminal justice settings. *European Journal of Criminology.*

Chapter 4
Social Behaviour and Artificial Intelligence:
The Myth of Sisyphus in Question

Jorge Chauca García
University of Malaga, Spain

ABSTRACT

Social behavior is central to the rise of artificial intelligence (AI). This chapter studies the global internet network as a repository of data that companies and governments use as a valuable commercial and geopolitical tool. But in the face of this optimistic vision of global information management, society must ensure freedom and privacy in the community. The denunciation of abuses and the need to set ethical and political limits to the use of AI in relation to social behavior and its contexts is today a priority task, nor do we want to fall into a dystopian society. The border between freedom and AI is marked by ethics.

INTRODUCTION

Social behaviour begins with language, but its channels continue to multiply throughout the development of our species. The rise of artificial intelligence (AI) is making more complex a panorama that itself it is already. The global Internet network is a colossal data repository that companies and governments use as a valuable tool, but in the face of this optimistic vision of global management, the canon of society has appeared since its inception: to ensure freedom in community. Privacy is a guiding element of the political structure and the exponential growth of information channels could put it at risk. It is not about recovering a past of denial of technological progress or predicting a dystopian future, but it is about denouncing abuses and setting ethical and political limits to the use of AI in relation to social behaviour and its contexts (Saura, Ribeiro-Soriano y Palacios-Marqués, 2021a).

These limits are given spontaneously and unpredictably by us, apart from any regulation. Human behaviour in stressful situations is capable of outsmarting AI in its predictions, we have very recent and clarifying cases in this regard that puts into question the successes of automation. Algorithms are nourished by our activity and social networks, are they capable of predicting what may interest us or

DOI: 10.4018/978-1-7998-9609-8.ch004

rather what we frequent or make us frequent? Social behaviour in times of crisis dislocates AI and its patterns, no matter how much the human footprint is digitized and ready to be evaluated as a consumer, user or in the political game, for example. The ability of AI does not penetrate human emotion, but it does penetrate the faculty of manipulation. From the smart phone onwards, computing transforms information and can even exceed human capacity in certain competitions. But is man condemned to repetition or does he act in a more unpredictable way?

The original challenge is to study the fine line that separates dependence from independence, repetition from freedom. The added value of the study is, precisely, to approach AI from a purely ethical and social reflection perspective.

THE BORDER BETWEEN FREEDOM AND AI

Human freedom is one of the universals inherited from the Enlightenment. High modernity has bequeathed to late modernity that we live a host of political, social or communication experiences that today are questioned by the extraordinary rise of the means of knowledge control. If Hobbes sacrificed freedom for security (2008), while Locke set himself up as the antecedent of liberalism (2010), today both are in danger. It is no longer a controversy or cultural struggle between freedom and security, if we want between individual and community, but between truth and lies, reflection or perpetuation, autonomy or manipulation by selection and repetition.

AI is a technological resource whose depository mind is human, we mean that it reproduces what it received. The data entered is done by human hands based on registered social behaviours. But these behaviours, in turn, reproduce, transmit and bias behaviours. Knowledge about society and its consumption habits or information margin is biased by itself, by everything quantitative that it is possible to collect, study and process. Is it possible, perhaps, the social transformation or that of knowledge from these premises, or is it an eternal loop that feeds itself without apparent end?

The term "Artificial Intelligence" (AI) is applied when a machine mimics the cognitive functions that humans associate with other human minds, such as learning or solving problems (Russell & Norvig, 2009). The human being makes decisions based on the information that he collects from the outside through the senses. The brain from the birth of the person is processing that information, shaping the personality of the individual, accumulating memory information and all this serves in the decision-making process. In contrast, AI tries to imitate that human behaviour, and systems such as neural networks and machine learning systems have been developed so that the machine itself makes those decisions. AI works using large amounts of data with fast, iterative processing and intelligent algorithms, allowing software to automatically learn from patterns or characteristics in the data.

Russell & Norvig propose how four approaches have been followed based, on the one hand, on the mental process and reasoning, and on the other, on behaviour.

Systems that think like humans. An effort to make computers think, like machines with minds, in the strict sense (Haugeland, 1985). The automation of activities that we link with human thought processes, such as the aforementioned key decision-making or problem solving and learning processes (Bellman, 1978).

Systems that act like humans. The development of machines with the capacity to perform functions that when performed by people require intelligence (Kurzweil, 1990). Or following Rich & Knight, the study of how to get computers to perform tasks that humans do better, for the moment (1991).

Systems that think rationally. The study of mental faculties through the use of computational models (Charniak & McDermott, 1985). According to Winston, studying the calculations that make it possible to perceive, reason and act (1992).

Systems that act rationally. Computational Intelligence is the study of the design of intelligent agents (Poole, Mackworth & Goebel, 1998). AI would thus be related to intelligent behaviours in artefacts (Nilsson, 1998).

Machine learning is one of the main approaches to AI. It is an aspect of computing in which computers or machines have the ability to learn without being programmed to do so. It uses algorithms to learn from patterns in the data. There are three types of machine learning, and the functions that we want them to carry out will depend on whether we use some algorithms or others:

Reinforced learning, in which a machine learns certain patterns through repetitions of trial and error to obtain a reward. In a game, for example, an algorithm would try different paths until it found the one that gave it the prize. It is thus useful for performing automated tasks. In this case, algorithms such as Dynamic programming or Q-learning are used.

Supervised learning. In these cases, the machine is offered a set of data that serves as the basis for the system to find a specific solution. But, in addition, the algorithms are also taught the result that we intend to obtain so that, through analysis, they are able to find a relationship. Some of the algorithms we use for this type of learning are decision trees or Naive Bayes classifications.

Unsupervised learning. In unsupervised learning, we do not provide the system with output data to find a relationship between variables, but only input data to find patterns of similarity between elements. This is more complicated to process by the algorithm, since having less data requires a more complex development to be able to analyse conceptual structures. There are unsupervised algorithms of different categories, such as cluster and association algorithms.

Most of the latest generation browsers include machine learning methods - usually Bayesian - to classify email and eliminate junk or spam messages. Our personal information is also processed and analysed by tools that will suggest patterns and filter the information for us (Hernández Orallo, Ramírez Quintana y Ferri Ramírez, 2004). Once again, social media and its security are key (Saura, Riberiro-Soriano y Palacios-Marqués, 2021b). But it is essential to influence individual freedom against the repetitive filter of technology. Here lies the originality, in the ethical and humanistic perspective.

There is even a manual on Computer Ethics (Berleur & Brunnstein, 2001). A path on which it would be pertinent to continue working, since AI brings new problems, namely: human beings could lose their jobs due to automation - which takes us back to the industrial or agricultural Luddism of the 18th and 19th centuries; You could also have excessive or insufficient leisure time for personal and social fulfilment or lose the sense of being unique, that is, of singularity. On the other hand, the successful use of AI systems could lead to loss of responsibility or, being fatalistic, it could spell the end of the human race or at least lead to the loss of some of its so jealously won private rights.

It is in this last context that the relationship between the proper handling of data, the correct decision-making of intelligent machines and the relationship with the freedom of decision of the human being and its social context is framed. Weizenbaum also pointed out that voice recognition technology could lead to extensive wiretapping, and hence loss of civil liberties (1976). He did not envision a world threatened by terrorists that would shift the balance of control that people are willing to accept, but would rightly acknowledge that AI has the potential to produce surveillance in large numbers. The US government's Echelon classified system consists of a network of listening posts, antenna fields, and radar stations. It is backed by computers that use language translation, voice recognition and keywords that seek to automatically screen all traffic from phone calls, emails or faxes, among others. Some people acknowledge that computerization leads to loss of privacy. Thus, Sun Microsystems CEO Scott McNealy meditated on our inevitable zero privacy. There are those who disagree with the previous statement. For example, Judge Louis Brandeis in 1890 claimed privacy as an inalienable right.

But government practices limit or favor social control according to the media, popular or political response that is faced. The recent pandemic has shown it (Ribeiro-Navarrete, Saura y Palacios-Marqués, 2021).

MEN AND MACHINES: FROM CONFLICT TO INTERDEPENDENCE IN NETWORKS

The machine, object of destruction by the Luddites during the readjustment to the industrialization process, was and continues to be the centre of controversy, although its presence is already unquestionable in the cutting-edge and globalized technology of the present 21st century. However, it is worth remembering the Neo-Luddite current, faced with the impacts of technology in aspects such as the environment, while its predecessors did so for social reasons of another nature as the main force of their actions (Noble, 2000 and Sale, 1995).

Just a few decades ago, the destruction of machines could be resumed at least in futuristic fiction. In this sense, Isaac Asimov concluded one of his most accurate books with a prediction: "The Machine is driving our future not only or simply as a direct answer to our direct questions, but as a general answer to the situation in the world and to human psychology as a whole" (2007: 371). Indeed, social behaviour and attitude towards knowledge are beyond our control, at least from the data collected by AI. In any case, little is out of its reach today, and at this point public ethics, data privacy, and personal freedom and security come into play. At the end of the aforementioned text by Asimov, the lament for a painful continuity like that of Sisyphus is expressed in a very graphic way. Humanity was always "at the mercy of economic and sociological forces that it did not understand, the vagaries of the weather and the hazards of war" (2007: 372). Now the ubiquitous machines dominate it. The prejudice against the machines of the protagonist of the book mutates, at least partially, thanks to the knowledge, previous phase of the recognition: could machines and humans coexist beneficially? There are attempts in this regard (Oliver, 2020).

This repetition, which fell as a punishment on the Sisyphus of Hellenic mythology, comes to represent a hard, perennial and absurd work. Pushing a stone up the side of a mountain that rolled down again and again before reaching the top. The scene was replicated, despite the cunning of its protagonist, who had been "the most cunning of men" (Homer, 1962: 6 [VI, 153]). But, despite the cyclical mythological didactics, the changes or novelties –in this case of the technique– that thread the innovation are of a complex nature that goes beyond mere intention. Human existence is not repetition, but a process in transformation, whose limit is to see "identity threatened" (Etzioni, 1995: 380).

The current interdependence incorporates the idea of networks within a border thinking (Mignolo, 2013: 390). The local and the global play as much as freedom and security or ethics and technology, AI in this case. Indirect domination "plays a great role in the international sphere" (Baños, 2017: 166), already surpassed Foucault's dialectic between dominated and domineering, although it can be admitted that power relations are intrinsic to other types of relationships (2012: 118), such as those established by data analysis and AI at a global level and their conditioning and conditioned role of social behaviour. More current, although under review, we find Carl Schmitt's political perspective between friend-foe.

Fortunately, the universe is not just a panoply of schemes processed by machines, since to make such a mistake would be to sin in a technological reductionism on reality far from metaphysics or the consciousness of existence. AI has philosophical implications that have already been masterfully highlighted by José Luis González Quirós. From him we collect a synthesis on the point that concerns us. The very name of AI as a discipline is the work of John McCarthy in the fifties of the 20th century and as a consequence of previous military research, that is, in an international context marked by the Second World War and the subsequent Cold War or third wave of globalization –all marked by technological systems–.

Technological advances and the possibility for machines to store memory according to given instructions are in the pioneering works of Türing and Von Neumann. The development of computing is at the base of AI. But these machines have not reached human capacity, even if many point in that direction in the short term. AI has a dubious cognitive capacity in the sense pointed out by Judea Pearl on understanding, because "as long as machines do not learn to deal with the cause-effect scheme [...] as long as they function as mere approximations to probability curves, their intelligence will be extremely insufficient". Neither machines that think, nor mere calculations –in which aspect they do surpass man–, rather it seems that they have exceeded the limits "imposed by a simple routine of following the rules" (González Quirós, 2019: 132-134). In addition, human behaviour is the object of analysis from different theories that deal with the formation of attitudes, which comes to mean its complexity, far from reductionism. An unresolved issue. The behaviour of a person depends on biological, cultural, moral and perception factors of the current affairs to which it responds. From its multiple combinations we obtain infinite attitudes and behaviours (Cobo, 2003: 128-129). Perhaps more than those achievable by AI calculations, regardless of the ethics and free will that characterize our species from the beginning. *Homo sapiens* thrived on their capacity for accommodation and curiosity.

Technology plays a prominent social role due to its widespread use in all possible scenarios. Its etymology is Greek (Medina, 1995), and it accompanies us from our individual birth and as a species. But it also raises a series of problems, among which the axiological question the values of its use in relation to freedom, justice or ethics (Aguilar Gordón, 2011: 148). The technology developed by AI is omnipresent, yes, a considerable effort of domination, "but human intelligence can suffice for much more" (Camus, 1995: 150). Optimism.

AI, as we saw, is an efficient processor of knowledge, but not of behaviours. subject to freedom and human ethics. However, it tries and there is no shortage of people beyond fiction who believe that it will achieve this goal. A knowledge base that accumulates reasoning related to how the user faces the problem (Alonso Martínez, 1992: 2). But a machine that can simulate human intelligence collides head-on with its consciousness. It is true that it can develop methods and algorithms that allow the intelligent behaviour of computers, and that the rise of techniques and applications of AI is extraordinary, but I think it is very difficult to resolve that it can apply the Kantian ethics that flows from so many pages that yes it would be possible to memorize.

The machine is fed with data (the information of the senses in humans), processes that information and generates an output data (decision making). We have reached this point, thanks to the great data processing capacity of the current digital machines. Today's large computers can process large amounts of information so that we can feed the self-learning algorithm with a large volume of data. The more data, the better or more reliable the result will be, but the question arises when the origin of the data that feeds the algorithm is questioned.

Music or video platforms collect hundreds of data daily about the tastes of their users. Mobile telephony joined this dynamic. And not only in relation to the favourite genres, but also to the quantitative aspects of audition or viewing. And even preferences per day and a series of variables to extract all kinds of data. With this colossal amount of data, an AI project can guess the relationship with the content of consumption and, thus, proceed to recommend some options or others. The recommendation comes directly from recorded social behaviour, but perhaps the machine just amplifies our behaviour, to the extent that it magnifies our repeated decisions and feeds them back. Automatic algorithms could sometimes produce a breakthrough in misinformation in the way that unethical behaviour is magnified. We can also interpret the foregoing as a mere simplification of our behaviour, insofar as it reaches an equilibrium in which the information from which it is fed, and which serves to suggest behaviours., generates a behaviour similar to the initial one. In this sense, it could be said that there is no advance in knowledge since there could be a balance between the starting information and the induced behaviour.

The existence of dis-informative content on YouTube has been verified, as well as the incidence of the YouTube algorithm in the information recommendation processes. The responsibility for the circulation of this type of content is not only YouTube and its producers, since traditional media channels act as a gateway to dis-informative content (Sued, 2020). As a renowned philosopher asserted: "It is thus that in the world of the end of metaphysics it becomes impossible to speak of the truth" (Vattimo, 2010: 129).

The exercise of full digital citizenship must include critical understanding and audiovisual literacy in the face of potentially dis-informative content. An *echo chamber* is the metaphorical description of a situation in which information, ideas or beliefs are amplified by transmission and repetition in a closed system where different or competing visions are censored, prohibited or are minority represented. The term refers by analogy to the acoustic echo chamber where sounds reverberate. (Jamieson & Capella, 2008). Some algorithms censor and others misinform.

The expression "Search Engine Manipulation Effect" (SEME), was used in August 2015 by two American academics who demonstrated that the vote of 20% or more undecided could be chosen based on the results offered by Google (Epstein & Robertson, 2015). In this sense, Cathy O'Neil warned about the blind trust placed in algorithms to obtain objective results (2016). The architecture of the Internet has a tremendous influence on what is done and what is seen, the algorithms influence which content is spread more on Facebook and other social networks, which appears privileged in Google searches. However, the user is not forewarned or trained to understand how the data is collected and classified. The opacity of the algorithms introduces a democratic dysfunction in society.

The use of these new technologies can lead to a dehumanization of the processes. Making the majority of decision-making dependent on machines. The phenomenon is also contemplated from a recurring utopian perspective, thinking that everything or almost everything can be solved by means of AI. It is essential to open a deep debate on the ethical consequences of new technologies and how they shape or affect behaviour and not the other way around. If we change the motivations for our civic and moral behaviour, it is likely that we will also change the very nature of such behaviour (Morozov, 2013).

EPILOGUE TO AN OPEN DEBATE

There is no doubt that AI has a number of unquestionable advantages. The possibilities of error are minimized and we can obtain greater precision, when doing computations and comparing large amounts of data. It can perform complex and dangerous tasks for humans, such as space exploration or mining.

These machines can be helpful in overcoming the limitations that humans have. They facilitate our daily life, knowing and predicting needs, tastes and interests. For example, digital assistant applications and smartphone predictions that are already widely used today. But they also bring disadvantages from an opposite perspective, like any new technology or new industrial or technological stage, they are not without drawbacks. New systems are expensive and require time to implement. Investment in artificial intelligence is very high when dealing with complex systems. A multitude of professional profiles will have to be reconverted to coexist with AI, within the framework of greater versatility. Jobs where routine or repetitive tasks are performed will progressively disappear, with the subsequent problem of rising unemployment.

Also, AI does not integrate creativity among its advantages. Machines do not think, they work under given parameters, so the creative capacity remains absent. For the same reason, the jobs that provide the greatest creative load will be the last or the most difficult to replace in this landscape of changes and adaptations. Along with the lesser or greater creativity, work related to emotions or emotional treatment can be added, virtues so human that they cannot be triumphantly replaced by intelligent machines (Lee, 2018).

British scientist Stephen Hawking warned about the risks of not controlling AI. In an article published in *The Independent*, he assured that "the success in the creation of AI would be the greatest event in human history. Unfortunately, it could also be the last, unless we learn how to avoid risks" (2014).

Framed in SDG4 (Sustainable Development Goal 4 of the 2030 Agenda, which seeks an inclusive, equitable, permanent and quality education), UNESCO (United Nations Educational, Scientific and Cultural Organization) recognizes that, uncontrolled, the development of AI can deepen the existing divisions and inequalities in the world, and that no one should be left behind against their will, whether in enjoying the benefits of AI or in protecting against its negative consequences, and calls for ensuring ethical, transparent and auditable use of education data and algorithms. (Beijing Consensus, 2019).

The Select Committee on Artificial Intelligence of the House of Lords (UK Parliament, 2018: 1.056-1.057) was appointed on 29 June 2017 to consider the economic, ethical and social implications of advances in artificial intelligence, and to make recommendations. Its objective was to answer the following questions regarding: the pace of technological change, impact on society, public perception, industry, ethics, the role of the Government, learning from others.

With regards to Ethics, the ethical implications of the development and use of artificial intelligence and how can any negative implications be resolved was asked. Amongst all the recommendations made by the people and institutions that participated, it was mentioned about the existing guidance BS 8611:2016 "Guide to the ethical design and application of robots and robotic systems" was written by a BSI committee of experts that included scientists, academics, ethicists, philosophers and users. It provides guidance on potential hazards and protective measures, including ethical hazards arising from the growing number of robots and autonomous systems being used in everyday life. There were concerns about the rights of individuals, including privacy rights, that should be strengthened and upheld in the GDPR and UK-equivalent data protection laws. And also concerns about the great amount of data used that could pose a risk of misuse or misinformation. AI is actually not sufficiently intelligent right now, and this could lead to discriminatory actions.

Consumers and citizens will not permit a lack of transparency in those areas that are most personal to them, for example, decisions around education, housing, mortgage financing or employment. The key here is how organisations can enable their systems such that there is explainable AI. While the technology may not necessarily fully enable this today, organisations must anticipate that consumers want sufficient explanations and that organisations will be accountable for their use of the AI. By fairness, we should like to ensure that algorithms will not discriminate against any particular subgroup of the population. If we train a machine learning system to emulate past biased human decisions (for example in making hiring decisions), we are implicitly training the system to replicate previous human bias. In addition, developers may simply overlook the potential for difficulties, as evidenced in Google's early image recognition

Geopolitics is geared towards cooperation through exchange, transactions, negotiation etc. Concerning the public sphere, there is interest and the common will of nation-states, coexistence rules, or even political institutions, which all constitute organizational elements of international politics (Miailhe, Hodes, Çetin, Lannquist & Jeanmaire, 2020: 56-69). As a matter of fact, the global system comprises a set of strategies implemented by different subjects and countries.

In geopolitics, certainly, there is a redistribution between countries not in view of their size and strength, but rather introduces their speed and consummate technological degree as one more but determining variable. Complex globalization is dominated by great connectivity as a sign of the present time (Aznar Fernández-Montesinos, 2019: 106). AI could be a fourth industrial revolution with all its unimaginable derivatives, since "technology has been considered a key factor in the definition of a civilization" (Aznar Fernández-Montesinos, 2019: 5). But we must never forget to establish guiding principles of ethics in AI, "the object of a multiplicity of proposals" (Ortega Klein, 2020: 2), disparity and ambiguity that show how embryonic the subject is.

Liquid modernity refers to a lost opportunity, whose promising alternative can slip through your hands due to its fluid nature. We are witnessing "a redistribution and reassignment of the dissolution powers of modernity" (Bauman, 2004: 12).

We finish as we begin. The Orwellian dystopia of extreme control of society calls into question our freedom (Orwell, 2012), but now security is also called into question. In addition, if social behaviour sets the standard for AI, we can fall into what another dystopian writer announced: "the most dangerous enemies of truth and freedom, the solid and unshakable cattle of the majority" (Bradbury, 2012: 124). An approach from ethics on behavior and social networks on the extraordinary boom is necessary (Saura, Palacios-Marqués e Iturricha-Fernández, 2021).

Trust has always been a more than powerful link in all areas of history and relationships between men. An AI with a future, who will have it, must organize data reliably (Janssen, Brous, Estévez, Barbosa y Janowski, 2020). Trust and personal and social ethics are part of the elementary principles of human nature, although their combinations are changing, this truth must be preserved, as suggested by Mary Shelley (1994: 21). The literature conforms to this rule. But the uncertainty about the future is also shared.

The theoretical contribution affects the study of AI from the humanistic perspective, but away from global considerations and closer to the individual and their rights, where its scientific value and originality reside. This dimension must be applied to data analysis and the complex world of social networks, since the human being often puts improvisation, whim or any other passion before the repetitive and predictable.

REFERENCES

Aguilar Gordón, F. (2011). Reflexiones filosóficas sobre la tecnología y sus nuevos escenarios. *Sophia. Colección de Filosofía de la Educación, 11*, 123–172.

Alonso Martínez, M. (1992). *Conocimiento y Bases de Datos: una propuesta de integración inteligente* [Unpublished doctoral dissertation]. Universidad de Cantabria, Santander, España.

Asimov, I. (2007). *Yo, robot*. Edhasa.

Aznar Fernández-Montesinos, F. (2019). Inteligencia artificial y geopolítica. *Claves de Razón Práctica*, *267*, 106–114.

Aznar Fernández-Montesinos, F. (2019). *La inteligencia artificial como factor geopolítico*. Documento de análisis IEEE 18/2019. https://www.ieee.es/Galerias/fichero/docs_analisis/2019/DIEEEA18_2019FEDAZN_IAgeopolitica.pdf

Baños, P. (2017). Así se domina el mundo. *Ariel*.

Bauman, Z. (2004). *Modernidad líquida*. FCE.

Beijing Consensus on artificial intelligence and education. Outcome document of the International Conference on Artificial Intelligence and Education "Planning education in the AI era: Lead the leap". (2019). http://www.moe.gov.cn/jyb_xwfb/gzdt_gzdt/s5987/201908/W020190828311234688933.pdf

Bellman, R. E. (1978). *An introduction to Artificial Intelligence: Can Computers Think?* Boyd & Fraser Publishing Company.

Berleur, J., & Brunnstein, K. (Eds.). (2001). *Ethics of Computing: Codes, Spaces for Discussion and Law*. Chapman and Hall.

Bradbury, R. (2012). *Fahrenheit 451*. Penguin Random House Grupo Editorial.

Camus, A. (1995). *El mito de Sísifo*. Alianza Editorial.

Charniak, E., & McDermott, D. (1985). *Introduction to Artificial Intelligence*. Addison-Wesley.

Cobo, C. E. (2003). El comportamiento humano. *Cuadernos Americanos*, *29*, 114–130.

Epstein, R., & Robertson, R. E. (2015). The search engine manipulation effect (SEME) and its possible impact on the outcomes of elections. *Proceedings of the National Academy of Sciences of the United States of America*, *112*(33), 512–521. doi:10.1073/pnas.1419828112 PMID:26243876

Etzioni, A. & E. (1995). *Los cambios sociales. Fuentes, tipos y consecuencias*. FCE.

Foucault, M. (2012). *Un diálogo sobre el poder y otras conversaciones*. Alianza Editorial.

González Quirós, J. L. (2019). La inteligencia artificial y la realidad restringida: Las estrecheces metafísicas de la tecnología. *Naturaleza y Libertad*, *12*(12), 127–158. doi:10.24310/NATyLIB.2019.v0i12.6271

Haugeland, J. (Ed.). (1985). *Artificial Intelligence: The Very Idea*. MIT Press.

Hawking, S. (2014, Dec. 4). AI could be the end of Humanity. *The Independent*. https://www.independent.co.uk/news/science/stephen-hawking-ai-could-be-end-humanity-9898320.html

Hernández Guerrero, J. A. (2016, July 11). Solucionismo. *Diario de Cádiz*. https://www.diariodecadiz.es/opinion/articulos/Solucionismo_0_1043595790.html

Hernández Orallo, J., Ramírez Quintana, M. J., & Ferri Ramírez, C. (2004). *Introducción a la minería de datos*. Pearson Educación.

Hobbes, T. (2008). *Leviatán o la materia, forma y poder de un Estado eclesiástico y civil*. Alianza Editorial.

Jamieson, K. H., & Cappella, J. N. (2008). *Echo Chamber: Rush Limbaugh and the Conservative Media Establishment*. Oxford University Press.

Janssen, M., Brous, P., Estévez, E., Barbosa, L. S., & Janowski, T. (2020). Gobernanza de datos: Organización de datos para una inteligencia artificial confiable. *Government Information Quarterly, 37*(3), 101493. doi:10.1016/j.giq.2020.101493

Kurzweil, R. (1990). *The Age of Intelligent Machines*. MIT Press.

Lee, K.-F. (2018). *How AI can save our humanity*. https://www.youtube.com/watch?v=ajGgd9Ld-Wc

Locke, J. (2010). *Segundo Tratado sobre el Gobierno Civil*. Alianza Editorial.

Medina, M. (1995). Tecnología y filosofía: Más allá de los prejuicios epistemológicos y humanistas. *Isegoría, 12*(12), 180–196. doi:10.3989/isegoria.1995.i12.249

Miailhe, N., Hodes, C., Çetin, R. B., Lannquist, Y., & Jeanmaire, C. (2020). Geopolítica de la Inteligencia Artificial. *Política Exterior, 34*(93), 56–69.

Mignolo, W. D. (2013). *Historias locales / diseños globales. Colonialidad, conocimientos subalternos y pensamiento fronterizo*. Akal.

Morozov, E. (2013). *To Save Everything, Click Here: The Folly of Technological Solutionism*. Public Affairs.

Nilsson, N. J. (1998). *Artificial Intelligence: A New Synthesis*. Morgan Kaufmann.

Noble, D. F. (2000). *Una visión diferente del progreso. En defensa del luddismo*. Alikornio.

O'Neil, C. (2016). *Weapons of Math Destruction: How Big Data Increases Inequality and Threatens Democracy*. Crown Publishers.

Oliver, N. (2020). *Inteligencia artificial, naturalmente. Un manual de convivencia entre humanos y máquinas para que la tecnología nos beneficie a todos*. Ministerio de Asuntos Económicos y Transformación Digital.

Ortega Klein, A. (2020). *Geopolítica de la ética en Inteligencia Artificial*. Documento de trabajo 1/2020 Real Instituto Elcano. https://www.realinstitutoelcano.org/wps/wcm/connect/acc09d1e-3138-4436-b77b-ec5926ea0983/DT1-2020-Ortega-Geopolitica-de-la-etica-en-Inteligencia-Artificial.pdf?MOD=AJPERES&CACHEID=acc09d1e-3138-4436-b77b-ec5926ea098

Orwell, G. (2012). *1984*. Penguin Random House Grupo Editorial.

Poole, D., Mackworth, A. K., & Goebel, R. (1998). *Computational Intelligence: A logical approach*. Oxford University Press.

Ribeiro-Navarrete, S., Saura, J. R., & Palacios-Marqués, D. (2021). Towards a new era of mass data collection: Assessing pandemic surveillance technologies to preserve user privacy. *Technological Forecasting and Social Change, 167*, 120681. https://doir.org/10.1016/j.techfore.2021.120681

Rich, E., & Knight, K. (1991). *Artificial Intelligence*. MacGraw-Hill.

Russell, S. J., & Norvig, P. (2009). *Artificial intelligence. A modern approach*. Prentice Hall.

Sale, K. (1995). *Rebels Against the Future. The Luddites and Their War on the Industrial Revolution: Lesson for the Computer Age*. Addison-Wesley Publishing Company.

Saura, J. R., Palacios-Marqués, D., & Iturricha-Fernández, A. (2021). Ethical Design in Social Media: Assessing the main performance measurements of user online behavior modification. *Journal of Business Research, 129*(May), 271–281. https://doi.org./10.1016/j.jbusres.2021.03.001

Saura, J. R., Ribeiro-Soriano, D., & Palacios-Marqués, D. (2021, July 15). Setting privacy "by default" in social IoT: Theorizing the challenges and directions in Big Data Research. *Big Data Research, 25*, 100245. doi:10.1016/j.bdr.2021.100245

Saura, J. R., Ribeiro-Soriano, D., & Palacios-Marqués, D. (2021). Using data mining techniques to explore security issues in smart living environments in Twitter. *Computer Communications, 179*, 285–295. doi:10.1016/j.comcom.2021.08.021

Shelley, M. (1994). *Frankenstein o el moderno Prometeo*. Valdemar.

Sued, G. (2020). El algoritmo de YouTube y la desinformación sobre vacunas durante la pandemia de COVID-19. *Chasqui. Revista Latinoamericana de Comunicación, 145*(145), 163–180. doi:10.16921/chasqui.v1i145.4335

UK Parliament. (2018). *Select Committee on Artificial Intelligence, Collated Written Evidence Volume*. https://www.parliament.uk/globalassets/documents/lords-committees/artificial-intelligence/ai-written-evidence-volume.pdf

Vattimo, G. (2010). *Adiós a la verdad*. Gedisa.

Weizenbaum, J. (1976). *Computer Power amd Human Reason. From judgment to calculation*. W. H. Freeman & Co Ltd.

Winston, P. H. (1992). *Artificial Intelligence*. Addison-Wesley.

Chapter 5
Algorithms, Social Rejection, and Public Administrations in the Current World

Felipe Debasa

Rey Juan Carlos University, Spain

ABSTRACT

In 2016 the term 4th Industrial Revolution was coined to define a new era in history based on commercial and industrial activity connected through the internet. Connections to the network and the internet of things facilitate that activity and processes can be stored, generating large volumes of data. Algorithms can analyze and process this data to create new added value. Algorithms already control many basic sectors of the economy and society. Although with some initial rejection, the users have assumed as normal that the algorithms set the prices of supply and demand in the provision of goods and services or that they make investment proposals in financial markets. This new way of acting has created the circular economy, but also a new economic model based on very high amounts of data that comes under the name surveillance capitalism. An economic model based on virtuality, with data as raw materials and driven by algorithms, generates new challenges also in security.

INTRODUCTION

Automaton, Clocks, Computers, and Apps

To understand what technology stands for, it is important to define technology as a set of skills, knowledge, and instruments. This statement is needed to be emphasized since the current perception about technology is everything that includes microchips and that moves with electricity. The first computers were mechanical machines that appeared thousands of years ago designed exclusively for mathematical and arithmetic operations. These have evolved over the centuries, differing in three aspects, all of them mechanical automatons, clocks, and punch cards (Pikhart, 2020).

DOI: 10.4018/978-1-7998-9609-8.ch005

Firstly, the automaton is considered the predecessors of today's robots (Wimsatt, 1939). Examples of mechanical automaton were found in the 13th century, specifically in the Islamic world. Although afterwards, they were widespread in Europe during the Scientific Revolution. They were not considered watches, but they were works of art for the rich with no utility. They used to play instruments, and some of them were programmable through roller systems. Programming an automaton was simple being able to change music. As the precision of the mechanisms improved, a higher quality was achieved in the automatons, both in the movements and the things they could do. Some were programmable by means of a system of rollers very similar to the ears of corn. For those who played musical instruments, the melodies could be changed. The bases of these mechanisms were the same as those of watchmaking, so some famous automata manufacturers were also watchmakers. Automatons were human or animal shaped objects, animated by mechanical mechanisms, programmed by means of logical systems of combinations, which, according to the interlocutor, act as if they were living beings. The goal of the artisan was to ensure there were no difference between the living being and the automaton.

Figure 1. Poster about an exhibition of automata in the United States probably in year 1826. It indicates that people will be able to see various automatas. One who plays chess, another who plays the trumpet and others who dance.
Source: Library of the Congress, USA.

Currently, the theory of automata is a branch of the theory of computation whose final exponent will be the Turing machine. Therefore, the final path of automata is to overcome the human mind. This exercise is achieved by the supercomputer manufactured by IBM in 1996 to play chess, Deep Blue (Campbell et al., 2002). The supercomputer must be considered by history, the beginning of the era of AI (Debasa and Sánchez, 2021).

Secondly, mechanical watches. They were also typical of the time of the scientific and industrial revolution, unlike the automaton, these do have specific utilities. Watches were used to measure the time and cycles such as the month, the day of the year, the season and even the moon phase and calculate astral positions. The clocks are programmable due to the continuous mismatches with the time since the measurement of time was not very accurate. Additionally, one of the main attractions of these objects, being able to manipulate them. In addition to their own functions, many of them included small automatisms such as pendulums or animated objects. The so-called *"memento mori"* was very popular at the end of the 16th century, which included skulls to opened and close the eyes, or slogans that moved slogans in front of the mouth.

Figure 2. Unknown soldier posing with his pocket watch as a status symbol (1861 and 1865)
Source: Library of the Congress, USA.

Finally, the last case of mechanical computing were punch cards. They were used in the 7th century to introduce melodies into music boxes. During the Industrial Revolution punch cards went to the looms to introduce patterns on it (Wallén, 2008). The purpose was anyone with little knowledge could incorporate very complex patterns into the designs of the fabrics. The next step comes in the 19th century with analytical machines. By means of the punched cards, a mechanical communication was established between the programmer and the device in which very simple programming commands could be included. Thus, it is considered the first programmable algorithms in history appear. One of the functions for which punch card machines began to be used was to establish censuses. One of the first steps taken by the newly established National Socialists in power in Germany was to carry out a census to identify ethnic groups such as Jews or Gypsies. This census was carried out thanks to the collaboration between IBM and the National Socialism government with the close collaboration of the CEO of IBM, Thomas J. Watson. Controversy exists over whether punch cards made the Holocaust possible (Medina, 2008; Black, 2012).

Figure 3. Young underage woman working on a punch card machine. Year 1917.
Source: Library of the Congress, USA

What it is considered as the first digital electronic computer was designed during World War II by the German Konrad Zuse in 1941. Its invention was significant due to the computer was able to execute external programs different from the object for which the computer had been created. It was an improvement on a previous programmable system, but it did not admit external programs. Therefore, only had one utility, the one for which it had been designed. Zuse's invention allowed what it is known today as computer programs to work. Historiography has not given Zuse his rightful role as the inventor of the modern computer, going unnoticed in many cases. Electronic computers were originally great devices that occupied closets and even entire rooms. They were only available to public institutions, companies, and universities.

Figure 4. In the image ENIAC, acronym for Electronic Numerical Integrator and Computer. This computer developed years after Zuse's, and mistakenly considered the first in history.
Source: Library of the Congress, USA.

The most important step for the generalization of computers will be the appearance of microcomputers in the seventies, which gives way to home computers in the eighties. At this time, two distinct types of technologies will be developed. Personal computers and video game consoles. Both use programs not to function, but to perform very different activities. These programs are the direct antecedents of current apps. Although the connections of the equipment by means of networks already existed, these were very infrequent. The Internet was not yet implemented at the user level and all the computer equipment worked autonomously, that is, without any type of connection between them, much less with servers.

In the nineties, a very rudimentary incipient mobile telephony became generalized with equipment that only served to talk on the phone (Farley, 2005). Telephone networks would gradually incorporate services such as incoming call identification or text messages. At this time mobile phone calls were still very expensive, then users began to devise a touch system to communicate. By identifying the receiving telephone, the sending telephone number, by means of so-called hang up and call, the receiver saw the number of rings received. For example, a single tap could mean – *"I'm fine"* – a double tap – *"I'm bored"* – and a triple tap – *"call me urgent"*. Faced with these situations, the telephone companies considered charging for the establishment of calls, a situation that never occurred. A similar situation is the one that occurred a century and a half earlier with postal shipments. Situation that led to the invention of the postage stamp in 1840.

The great leap in mobile telephony occurs with the entry of the 3rd generation of Universal Mobile Telecommunications Systems, 3G - UMTS. Telephone equipment becomes small computers with a specific graphic operating system. In these devices, thanks to 3G communication networks, programs can be downloaded and installed to carry out actions very different from those of mobile telephony. Then, it can be confirmed, this great leap opens the door to a new economic model based on the confluence of technologies and the hyperconnectivity of things.

At that time, it was unknown that this new economic model that was about to begin was going to be achieve an exponential growth based on machine learning (ML) or big data (Saura et al., 2021). The applications created by then, aimed to offer services in a personalized way, improved the user experience and optimized the service on the rapid computer learning of the data generated. This is how current apps are born including mobile apps, or simply apps.

Generally speaking, it is not recognized the long history applications have. However, as it has discussed previously, apps are not as new as it is thought. Applications have grown exponentially with big data, but also with the confluence of technologies connected to the Internet. At the beginning of the 21st century, mobile phones underwent a great transformation. Complementary devices such as GPS position sensors, high-definition photographic optics, gyroscope, ambisonic microphones and speakers, facial recognition or fingerprints, and recently lidar scanners were integrated into the housing. The inclusion of all these sensors in the housing of a mobile phone, accompanied by specific software, has turned them into smart devices that can be used for countless other things, in addition to calling by phone (Reid, 2018).

The possibilities offered by these devices are exploited by software developers who create programs that have nothing to do with the initial purpose of the telephone or a computer, which aim to facilitate access to user services. Apps have so much improved the user experience on the basis of existing services, provoking a total break about the way of how the market is being understanding. The apps are intended to facilitate access to user services (Gan, 2018).

Application users have the feeling that their comfort space is increased regardless of the place where they request the service, which leads to the apps revolutionizing traditional sectors such as the taxi or the reservation of tables in restaurants. This phenomenon was called in its beginnings as the collaborative economy (Alfonso Sánchez, 2017).

Table 1. Differentiating elements of the app-based economy

Topics
Digital technology
Immediacy
Customization
User control
Transparency
Reputation
Information
Simplicity
Accessibility
Creation of communities
Babel Tower
Uncertainty
Payment
Eliminate intermediation
Direct contact with the producer
Supervision

Source: Author's own elaboration

Table 2. Differentiating elements of the app-based economy

Topic	Description
Digital technology	Apps need sensors to work. These can be integrated into the smartphone or obtain data from other types of sensors located remotely (Ribeiro-Navarrete et al., 2021)
Immediacy	The service contracted through the app is immediate and without waiting. If there is waiting time, the user always has control over the waiting time, being aware of it, thus reducing the stress levels caused by uncertainty.
Customization	Most of the services offered by the applications are based on the user's geolocation in real time, so the service is customized based on the user's location.
User control	The user has a lot of information in real time that allows him to always evaluate the situation of the provision of the service. This information can be shared in many cases with third parties. As in the case of immediacy, it involves reducing the levels of stress caused by uncertainty. The user is always in control of the situation.
Transparency	The service provider and the user have very little room for deception, cheating or mischief. Transparency in the service is practically total.
Reputation	The continuous evaluation of the way of acting of the service provider and the user, constitutes what is called reputation. It is a system in which everyone evaluates everyone. Although technologically possible, in some places reputation measurement systems are blocked due to legal issues. Reputation is the key to accessing new services and opens new business possibilities establishing in itself a new and important discipline (Saura et al., 2021a).
Information	It is very useful in case of further checks or complaints. It is also the database that will be used to offer a better later user experience. In the case of misuse of this data, the door is opened to trade with third parties and the establishment of behavior patterns without the user knowing (Saura et al., 2021b)
Simplicity	Since the fundamentals of programming and web design began, simplicity was established as a fundamental criterion. This same precept reaches the design of the apps that must be simple and intuitive, then they are accessible to all people.
Accessibility	Apps must be accessible to disabled or vulnerable groups.
Creation of communities	The user experience of an app offers a degree of satisfaction that can be shared. This satisfaction allows relationships to be established between users that allow a community to be formed. On the other hand, some services intermediation apps allow service providers and users to carry out transactions directly without the need for intermediaries, thus reinforcing the feeling of community of consumers and users, or producers. The establishment of this type of relationship is what motivated the name of collaborative economy to provide services through apps.
Babel Tower	Many apps fight against the Tower of Babel complex that prevents communication. By means of automatic translation engines it is possible to read in your language what is written in other languages. The translation engines of Chinese applications that are more developed than Western ones are significant.
Uncertainty	The availability of information in real time and the possibility of making decisions about various alternatives built on the predictive basis of the data reduces uncertainty. In addition, another reason that eliminates the stress of the user knowing that in case of failure of the initial option, the system offers exits (Saura et al., 2021c).
Payment	Apps offer numerous facilities to pay for services. Specially if we are in another country with another currency. It also facilitates that the price of the services can be shared automatically in the case of a service performed by several users (Yang et al., 2019).
Eliminate intermediation	One of the bases of this new economic model is the elimination of intermediaries, leaving only the people who cause the added value in the value chain.
Direct contact with the producer	Getting in touch with the producer is one of the greatest assets. The added value is greater when the producer moves away in distance, culture, or language. Thanks to the applications, distant communities that produce in a traditional way can survive.
Supervision	There are mainly two application markets depending on the operating system. Apple and Android. The managers of the application markets carry out a first check to avoid deception in the apps. Once available in the markets, apps must fight for their reputation like other users and producers.

Source: Author's own elaboration

Firstly, this phenomenon caused numerous social rejections on the part of the traditional sectors that were losing market share due to the new technological competition. In many places, social protests appeared calling for apps to be banned, asking governments to leave things as they were, without evolving. The criticism appeared by workers in the traditional sectors who did not understand how customers lost overnight to newly created and inexperienced companies. In addition, in practically all cases, apps only deal with intermediation, so they are companies that provide services without owning the final product. Thus, the paradox arose that the world's largest taxi company did not have a single car and a single driver on the payroll and that the largest company providing room services did not have a single hotel. The lesson learned from that moment was that disruption in the sectors appeared thanks to technology and always external to the sector, never as an evolution of it. In 2016, movements against the sharing economy and apps appeared (Slee, 2017). This phenomenon was known disparagingly as the uberization of the economy, in clear analogy with the app, UBER (Fleming, 2017).

Apps burst onto the market with great anger from the service provider and great joy from the consumer. In the middle of the situation is the political decision-maker who has had to decide how to regulate the new models of goods and services (Collier et al., 2018). The attacks against the new scenario led to the fact that little by little the name of collaborative economy was falling into disuse and that of the circular economy was being used. The concept of circular economy appears in 1989 which presents a new economic model compared to making, using and disposing of (Pearce and Turner). The current definition is not very clear, and the app user considers that his Smartphone and everything related to it, are part of this economic model (Tena and Khalilova, 2016; Kirchherr et al., 2017).

The concept of circular economy evolves to that of collaborative economy, a model in which services are considered to be exchange goods. The model was born with the intention of promoting responsible consumption with the last beneficiary of the planet. One of the main characteristics of this model is that the use of a certain asset prevails over possession with the consequent reduction of materials and optimization of resources (Polanco-Diges and Debasa, 2020).

The initial rejection of private sectors in the use of apps seems to have been overcome. However, this transformation in management models has not yet reached the public sector with force. This chapter analyzes the reasons why Artificial Intelligence (AI) processes are not developing in the public sector. The objective is to clarify the reason why AI generates rejection public administrations processes. In this study, it is presented the fundamentals of Artificial Intelligence (AI) processes, Data, Algorithms and Machine Learning (ML). Firstly, it is clarified the difference between digitizing and automating processes. Following by the identification of those elements for which public administrations find it difficult to use artificial intelligence processes. Finally, this research concludes determining the main causes for which social rejection occurs in the application of AI processes in public administration. The methodology used in this research is mixed. The exploratory results are obtained from specialized bibliography and semi-structured interviews.

DATA AND ALGORITHMS: THE NEW ECONOMIC MODEL

The apps technological basis consists of developing software that, permanently connected to the internet, integrates the multiple sensors of the Smartphone, using algorithms and collecting data. Over time, applications receive and store a greater volume of data that is processed through machine learning (Curry, 2016). Predictive models allow the service to be offered before the user requests it, thereby optimizing costs and resources. There is a perception in society that the data obtained by these applications is the oil of the 21ˢᵗ century and therefore, it must be safeguarded. Users are beginning to be aware of the need to take care of their data and many political institutions are regulating the access, treatment and safeguarding of data. The European Union has one of the most reserved and rigorous models in this regard (Finck, 2018; Hoofnagle et al., 2019).

Apps collect data allowing empirical studies to be carried out in a new discipline, named as application engineering (Geiger et al., 2018). Using the apps involves generating a lot of data, and since almost all of them work online, the data is collected in real time. The data is necessary to provide the service, but once it is used, it is never destroyed, and it is stored indefinitely pending future use (Saura et al., 2021d). National regulations sometimes mandate that data be stored on servers located within national territories or in friendly countries. Legislation is also being developed to regulate the storage of data and protect the rights of users and consumers. Data is the engine of algorithms and algorithms allow machine learning to develop (Moschovakis, 2001). This process is the foundation of AI. That is why data is so important, without it, it would be very difficult to start processes and automations with AI.

The general properties of ML and AI add value to the company (Kietzmann and Pitt, 2019). The algorithms can evaluate markets, looking for opportunities, identifying threats, and predicting the degree of user satisfaction. The algorithms will be able to develop a full degree of autonomy and independence. In this case, civil rights petitions for algorithms are already being raised (Saura et al., 2021e). This approach assumes de facto the possibility that algorithms and robots would have rights.

It has also been found applications to sell used objects, do manual work at home like a barter economy, sell surplus materials or remnants of stock that would have otherwise been thrown away, etc ... By allowing user communities to create their own rules in some cases, they create their means of payment, being able to even exchange goods and services through time coupons. This new economic activity is possible thanks to technology and IoT, being characteristic elements of the IV Industrial Revolution. It is important to highlight without algorithms it cannot be developed (Debasa, 2021).

The app market offers great legal challenges. By accepting the conditions of each app that users install on their Smartphone, it requires to accept legal clauses drafted. However, these legal clauses differ completely from the country the user is from (Western, Eastern, Latin, Anglo-Saxon lawyers, etc...). Every time users click on the app icon, they are entering an island legal independent of the nation or state in which they reside. Although the Smartphone has geolocation devices and the geographical place from which the Internet is accessed is also identifiable, it is not difficult to circumvent these types of controls with a VPN, making the Smartphone escape the controls and censorship of the countries (Saura et al., 2021f).

All these approaches are building a new economic model based on virtuality, in which data allows the construction of new applications with high added value. This new economic model is derogatory defined in 2015 by Shoshana Zuboff, as *Surveillance capitalism*. The author states that the economy allows the commercialization of citizens' personal data for the sole purpose that companies obtain economic benefits. Surveillance capitalism watches over human nature in order to offer the products that the system or AI think the individual needs. For the author it is a new totalitarian order. The greatest fear of technology on the part of neo-Luddites is the possible loss of free will on the part of people. In this sense, it is confirmed this is one of the main causes of the origin of the rejection of technological and digital processes, especially those that involve the implementation of AI processes. Some authors already speak of the dictatorship and the control of algorithms (Fioriglio, 2015). This type of approach is called Neoludism or anarchoprimitivism, and contrasts with the techno-optimism of other sectors or cultural groups such as transhumanists (Vydra and Klievink, 2019).

But why do not these principles are applying to public administrations? The public structures are solid, robust and with a great tradition. They have some advantages, but also some disadvantages. Among the advantages are the institutional strength in the face of revolutionary or anarchic attacks, the solidity in the face of political blackmail, and the capacity to respond to the problems of citizens. These same strengths are the obstacles they present in the face of the challenges of rapid social transformation. The solidity, the robustness and the tradition prevent the necessary resilience of a rapid transformation. In addition, it must be added that the citizen perceives the changes as something negative, so that the political decision-maker does not have one of his priorities, either, to transform the administration.

The Covid-19 epidemic which devastated the world on March 8, 2021, locked up almost the entire world population to confine themselves to their homes (Ribeiro-Navarrete et al., 2021). This forced to accelerate the digital transformation to be able to continue with the work activity. Companies and institutions adopted processes and mechanisms for digitizing processes and teleworking. Online work tools and digital certificates became essential to be able to carry out practically any activity. This fortuitous event transformed ways of life and social customs (Ferreira et al., 2021). The migratory process from the countryside to the city has been slowed down, producing an interest in reverse migration. From cities to the countryside and from populated places to more depopulated ones. The pandemic forced the implementation of digitization and teleworking in public and private institutions, but in public services this adaptation to the new pandemic situation did not imply also adopting process automation or the implementation of AI technology.

The anti-vaccine movement is growing strongly in Europe and the United States with the application of the Covid-19 vaccine. Similarly, the covid passport implemented by the European Union is seen by many users as an element of social control. In some countries this passport is being appealed in national courts precisely because it is an element of control of movements of governments before citizens. This finding shows that the situation generated by Covid-19 and the necessary control measures have increased social rejection of the application of technology by public governments. Citizens and users perceive this type of measure, an increase in control and a loss of freedom.

Finally, affirming that technology, apps and the hyperconnection of things are creating a new economic model based on data, the challenges of this model will no longer be the traditional ones. To this end, Estonia was one of the first countries to grant its army powers to protect national security also in cyberspace and on the Internet, understanding that problems should no longer come through physical space (Herzog, 2011).

MODERNIZE PUBLIC ADMINISTRATIONS, HISTORICAL APPROACH

Political and institutional modernization has been one of the tasks of political statement throughout history. The American Revolution from which the United States of America obtained independence in the 18th century forced the creation of a new legal, political, and constitutional order. The same happens with the French Revolution in Europe, which forces to reconstruct the institutional map when passing from the old regime to the new regime. For the changes that the modernization of public administrations had to carry out, it was necessary to train the population so that they could understand these new concepts. Otherwise, it would be talking about enlightened absolutism and not contemporary societies.

It is a representative example to point out what happens today when people do not acquire digital and technological skills and therefore giving rise to digital divide.

Frederick, the Great or Frederick II of Prussia transformed the public administration based on the following points. Freedom of expression in the press and literature, reduce cases of judicial torture and the death penalty, legal equality of citizens, protection of local businesses and industries, generalized tax cuts to encourage domestic consumption. To prepare the social climate between high officials and the nobility and avoid social rejection of his transformations in the political administration, he used a space for socialization that had been created in London in 1717, Freemasonry. Frederick II was initiated into a Framason knight in 1738 at a Brunswick lodge. Later he becomes the Venerable Master of the King's Lodge and from that position he influences nobles and high officials to enter Freemasonry (Alvarado-Planas, 2021). Frederick the Great promulgates some fracmasonic constitutions at the end of the 17th century, the origin of the current Supreme Council of the 33rd Degree of the Ancient and Accepted Scottish Rite. Freemasonry is a philosophical school aiming to help understand the meaning of life and to be a free citizen with rights. Thus, in the first Masonic degree's people learn to be good person and in the later, good citizens. In these Masonic degrees, the masters who were reaching higher levels had to know and debate on topics such as the nation, tributes, duties and rights of man, freedom of assembly, the institution of the jury or social equality. Each degree in which one is promoted in Freemasonry, is a subject that the teacher must work on. Therefore, it confirms that the high degrees of Freemasonry were a political instrument to fight against ignorance and social rejection in the face of political and institutional reforms in many European and American countries. Hence, it is important to emphasized that the transformations of the administrations have always been complex processes. Moreover, it is necessary to flag out that in this study in any case it is talking about modernization processes that lasted many years or centuries.

The IV Industrial Revolution has erupted drastically, and companies have had to digitalize very quickly. This has been a key matter, either they are digitized or disappear. Covid-19 has left an important trail of wrecks of companies that have not been able to overcome the crisis, while it has been found some other companies overcoming resiliently this situation and even though they have improved. However, there is a perception in society that public services and institutions are not being digitized at the speed of change.

In this study is also analyzed in depth the semi-structured interviews carried out to identify the main causes why the administration has difficulty in modernizing, updating, digitizing, and incorporating an automation of processes.

In table 3, it can be deduced that public administrations are built on very solid and old foundations, being, therefore, immobile. Western countries built based on Roman Law have hyper-regulation. This is a problem that is aggravated in places with provincial-type parliaments or assemblies that can legislate. Implementing technological processes in these places is technically complex and difficult. At the risk of this situation, there are political positions that have among their proposals not to allow the digitization of processes, saying that this goes against the essence of democracy. This type of approach is inserted in the political agendas and then it will be very difficult to fight against them, since they are proud to become political ideas. In the past, transformations took place over years and even centuries. However, now time is limited and if public administrations do not reinvent themselves including digitization and automation, they will cease to be competitive. In this sense, it is quite interesting to cite the case of Estonia.

Table 3. Thematic description table

Topics	Description
Size, bureaucracy, duplication of processes, decentralization.	Old structures, large and complex structures, solid structures.
Resilience	Public administration grows and it is difficult to spoil it.
Public workers	Rejection of the civil service to changes, to modify their living and working conditions, and this implies implementing technology.
Unions	Excessive union power in the civil service that slows down changes. Excessive union power in the civil service that does not want to lose power.
Status	The implementation of technology is perceived by the public worker as a loss of power.
Private initiative	Political attacks on public-private collaboration.
Creativity	The processes of public administrations do not take into account creativity or design. Serve as a lot of institutional apps have very low ratings

Source: Author's own elaboration

Estonia was a communist country that was part of the Union of Soviet Socialist Republics. In 1989 the Berlin wall fell, called in the USSR, the anti-fascist protection wall. The USSR disintegrates in late 1991 and many of its former countries look to the West instead of the East. Estonia inherits from the USSR a complex public system with a lot of bureaucracy. They decided that the best way to transform their institutions was to digitize services to create a new transparent and online system. To this end, the Tiigrihüpe (Tiger Leap) program was developed in 1996 (Runnel et al., 2009). Through a roadmap for digital transformation, a series of measures were imposed such as: Internet access and installation of computer labs in all schools. Collaboration between the public and private sectors and the digital literacy of the population. In 2007 the defense of the Internet network entered the common military doctrine. New versions of the Tiigrihüpe program will arrive in 2012 such as ProgeTiger and IT Academy (Hsu et al., 2019).

The Estonian government has calculated that the savings from using a digital and automated administration is 2% of GDP (Cerdeira, 2020). The final step in this entire digitization process that began with Estonia's new life after the end of the USSR is the automation of processes and the implementation of AI algorithms. The important to highlight that Estonia has a national Artificial Intelligence strategy, named KrattAI, and has ample experience in fighting against social rejection of change thanks to previous experiences in digitization (Dreyling et al., 2021). The name refers to a creature from Estonian mythology who made a pact with its master and took care of tough and difficult tasks. An analogy with the word Robot that also refers to complex and hard work. In Estonia, they currently have about 50 public processes automated by AI and this number is increasing ("New e-Estonia factsheet: National AI 'Kratt' Strategy," 2020). One use of AI applied to the legislature in Estonia is the Hans tool, which deals with the automatic transcription of parliament sessions ("HANS, AI support tool for Estonian Parliament," 2019). The tedious job that stenographers traditionally did.

CURRENT WORLD AND REJECTION OF TECHNOLOGY

Human societies are reluctant to change and evolution. Throughout history, processes of years, centuries and generations were necessary so that the technologies that were appearing, managed to settle. In various parts of the world, it has been found communities that, due to cultural or religious ideas, at a certain moment decided not to use more technology and have been anchored in a past moment in history. The biggest challenge of the Current world is that changes are happening at breakneck speed, and it is very difficult to assimilate them. People reject what they do not understand and avoid what they do not know. The fortuitous event of the appearance of Covid-19 forced the implementation of numerous measures of a global nature and in a very short space of time.

For some, the vaccines against Covid-19 were seen as hopeful points to regain normalcy, but for others represent the essence of state control and the loss of individual freedom. Many companies have used the Covid challenge to reinvent themselves and move forward, while public administrations have slowed down. This study affirms that private companies had to transcend Covid-19 to survive, in a clear Darwinian exercise, while public administrations have no predator in sight that would force them to transform more quickly. The only impulse that a public administration can have to automate processes is the determined will of the political decision-maker. And for this, an action plan is required with a series of measures that act in a coordinated way and in the medium term.

Subsequently, it is analyzed the interviews in depth to extract the main causes of perception of social rejection towards algorithms and AI.

From the interviews carried out it has been obtained the following results:

1. Causes of general rejection (see table 4)
2. Main causes of rejection of the implementation of AI in the processes of public administrations (see table 5)
3. The brakes of automation processes (see table 6)

Table 4. Main causes of general rejection

Causes of General Rejection
Artificial intelligence can escape human control
Artificial intelligence can have sexist and racist biases
Artificial intelligence can escape supervision
Artificial intelligence is not transparent
The intellectual property of the algorithm is unclear
The liability of the algorithm is unclear

Source: Author's own elaboration

ANALYSIS OF EXPLORATORY RESULTS

On the basis of the interviews carried out, it is identified the themes mainly repeated in the interview. Then, it has been considered the most relevant. They are as follows shown in table 7.

Table 5. Main causes of rejection of the implementation of Artificial Intelligence in the processes of public administrations

Causes of Rejection Implementing AI in Public Administration
Automation prevents contact between the official and the citizen
Automation forsakes the citizen
Automation removes the ability to interpret law
Automation makes resource difficult
Process automation destroys traditional employment
Automation can do injustices
The concept of public administration must be linked to that of public officials and not to that of artificial intelligence

Source: Author's own elaboration

Table 6. From the interviews carried out it is obtained the following results in relation to the brakes on the automation of processes

Brakes on the Automation of Processes
The digital divide
Aging population
Non-digitally trained population
The excessive size of the administration
The great power of unions over public employees
The creation of a discourse contrary to digital advancement
Digital rejection
Digital rejection of Apps against human attention
Perception of added value when being cared for by a human
The value of being served by a human and not a bot

Source: Author's own elaboration

Table 7. Main topics repeated in the interview

Topics	Similar Words
Social rejection	Difficult access to technology, especially for ageing population.
Public services	Public administration, public employees, digital divide, taxes.
Public administrative sector	Power, immobility.
Algorithm	Process automation, AI
Private sector	Business, entrepreneurship, logistics
Artificial intelligence	Company, entrepreneurship, medicine, education, security, cybersecurity, value added
IV Industrial Revolution	New era, new economic model, globalization

Source: Author's own elaboration

After having identified the most representative recurring topics from the interviews, all of them are defined in the following table (see table 8).

Table 8. Topics' definition

Topics	Description
Social rejection	It is about the dissatisfaction of a society with a certain issue. Social rejection is measurable and is one of the causes that influence political decision-making. Historically, social rejection has been shaped with propaganda or populist actions, depending on the case. Currently, for a measure not to have social rejection, it requires an action plan that includes a great pedagogy.
Public services	In this study, the public services are understood as the set of services that must be provided by public administrations in each country. The administrations should optimize the services so that their provision is more affordable to the taxpayer, taking into account that they are paid with fees and taxes.
Public sector	All that economic activity that is neither private nor originated by the private sector. It depends directly or indirectly on the states.
Algorithm	Element that makes up artificial intelligence.
Private sector	What is not public. The autonomous initiative of the person or company that starts with capital.
Artificial intelligence	It replaces human action in repetitive performances or those that require minimal decision-making. As artificial intelligence has more data and greater computing power, it will become stronger.
IV Industrial Revolution	The new age. The one we are currently experiencing since 2016.

Source: Author's own elaboration

The interviews carried out show that the situation generated by Covid-19 has not favored the implementation of AI processes in Public Administrations. Although the impact of the pandemic on society has been very high, the public sector does not have the urgent need for resilience that the private sector does. Although some experts consider that Artificial Intelligence would have helped to better fight against the pandemic, especially in logistics and distribution sectors. Most of the society perceives that these processes are implemented only with the intention of establishing greater control. In the event that the public administration decides to implement these processes, combined action plans are urgently needed to combat digital illiteracy and the technological divide, and to train people in skills related to the new disciplines. Ignorance of what an algorithm is widespread.

CONCLUSION

This study confirms the great confusion that exists between the concepts of process digitization and AI. The Covid-19 pandemic accelerated the implementation of process digitization in private companies and public administrations. Digitization has not been accompanied by automation, especially in public administrations. The automation of processes has a high economic cost in the implementation, but later it allows to escalate the cost and make the processes cheaper. Likewise, a qualified workforce is required to manage the programs.

Social rejection of the application of AI processes in the private sectors was very high in the beginning, but with the passage of time the opposition movements were reduced. It is significant that social rejection appears in the sectors of competition for the provision of the service and never by the user, contrary to what happens in the public sector. A greater increase in active policy investments to fight the digital and technological divide coincides with a greater reduction in the level of social rejection. It has also observed that, although the level of social rejection decreases with greater training in technological skills, the residual is more active and is perceived as more violent.

Social rejection behaves differently when it is analyzed public administration scenarios. It mainly originates from two reasons, the digital divide and the political battle. In the case of the digital divide, the behavior is very similar to the social rejection that occurs in the private sectors. But the political battle is very different. Society perceives that the automation of processes through AI in the public sector can escape the control of people to these processes. In this case, a hypothetical dictatorship of algorithms arises. By escaping the algorithms to the control and supervision of the people, the algorithms could act with the same biases that occur in society, that is, discrimination and discretion. One of the institutional solutions proposed so far so that these hypothetical scenarios do not occur, it is that the results of the processes carried out by artificial intelligence have a final human supervision.

Democratic systems with legal systems based on Roman law have very difficult to implement the automation of processes because everything that is not expressly regulated is basically prohibited. Thus, regulating AI in these systems is currently difficult due to the technological divide, and because digital skills are not widespread. In Anglo-Saxon democracies, what is not strictly prohibited is basically allowed, so the implementation of AI in these countries is somewhat easier. However, autocratic systems find it easier to implement these processes, so it is very likely that in a few years there will be a great dysfunction between modern and technological administrations in some parts of the world and others more stagnant in traditional ways of acting.

Finally, there is the cultural question. While in Judeo-Christian and Greco-Latin people's robots are perceived by society as evil and dangerous, in Asian countries digital automatisms are perceived as a great help to people and therefore positive. Yet another approach that will help to bring about a great difference between the European and Asian management models in the coming years. For European administrations to be able to implement AI processes, three main aspects will be required. Fight against the digital divide, optimal social climate, and great political consensus. For this to be carried out without social rejection, it will probably require listening processes through economic and social agents, universities, and political parties.

This chapter serves to prepare public administrations for the need to adapt to the IV Industrial Revolution. In the same way, it recommends an active fight against the digital divide necessary to prepare the social climate necessary for the modernization of the public administrations necessary to face the new situation in history. If this is not done, the difference between the eastern and western management models will be very great in a few years and the countries that have not prepared their administrations will not be competitive to offer opportunities in the new period. This scenario precedes that of a great social and economic crisis and the opening of a direct door to technological poverty that will appear in the next decade. Training in technological skills, especially in algorithms and artificial intelligence will not be an exclusive sector for computer scientists. On the contrary, theoretical and practical implications that are approached from other sectors such as economics, law or history will be necessary. It is an initial study that addresses global aspects of the Western world. In the future, stages could be made focused on the different levels of public administration, on specific geographic areas or on specific procedures or processes within an administration.

REFERENCES

Alfonso Sánchez, R. (2017). Economía colaborativa: Un nuevo mercado para la economía social. *C.I.R.I.E.C. España, 231*(88), 231. doi:10.7203/CIRIEC-E.88.9255

Barnhizer, D. (2016). The future of work: Apps, artificial intelligence, automation and androids. *Artificial Intelligence, Automation and Androids (January 15, 2016)*. Cleveland-Marshall Legal Studies Paper, (289).

Black, E. (2012). *IBM and the Holocaust: the strategic alliance between Nazi Germany and America's most powerful corporation*. Dialog Press.

Campbell, M., Hoane, A. Jr, & Hsu, F. (2002). Deep Blue. *Artificial Intelligence, 134*(1-2), 57–83. doi:10.1016/S0004-3702(01)00129-1

Cerdeira, L. (2020, September 20). *Lo que podemos aprender de Estonia, el país más digitalizado del mundo*. Retrieved December 12, 2021, from Forbes España website: https://forbes.es/empresas/76138/lo-que-podemos-aprender-de-estonia-el-pais-mas-digitalizado-del-mundo/

Collier, R. B., Dubal, V. B., & Carter, C. L. (2018). Disrupting Regulation, Regulating Disruption: The Politics of Uber in the United States. *Perspectives on Politics, 16*(4), 919–937. doi:10.1017/S1537592718001093

Curry, E. (2016). The Big Data Value Chain: Definitions, Concepts, and Theoretical Approaches. *New Horizons for a Data-Driven Economy*, 29–37. doi:10.1007/978-3-319-21569-3_3

Debasa, F. (2018, October 23). *Nuevos retos sociales en la IV Revolución Industrial*. Retrieved December 12, 2021, from Telos Fundación Telefónica website: https://telos.fundaciontelefonica.com/telos-109-regulacion-felipe-debasa-nuevos-retos-sociales-en-la-iv-revolucion-industrial/

Debasa, F. (2021). Digitalisation, pandemics and current world (2019-2021). *UNIO–EU Law Journal, 7*(1), 18–32. doi:10.21814/unio.7.1.3575

Debasa, F., & Sánchez, T. A. (2021). El discurso político de la presidencia Trump antes del covid. *Historia Actual Online*, (56), 21–34.

Dreyling, R., Jackson, E., Tammet, T., Labanava, A., & Pappel, I. (2021). Social, Legal, and Technical Considerations for Machine Learning and Artificial Intelligence Systems in Government. *Proceedings of the 23rd International Conference on Enterprise Information Systems*. 10.5220/0010452907010708

Farley, T (2005). Mobile telephone history. *Telektronikk, 101*(3-4), 22.

Ferreira, L. N., Pereira, L. N., da Fé Brás, M., & Ilchuk, K. (2021). Quality of life under the COVID-19 quarantine. *Quality of Life Research: An International Journal of Quality of Life Aspects of Treatment, Care and Rehabilitation, 30*(5), 1389–1405. Advance online publication. doi:10.100711136-020-02724-x PMID:33389523

Finck, M. (2018). Blockchains and Data Protection in the European Union. *European Data Protection Law Review, 4*(1), 17–35. doi:10.21552/edpl/2018/1/6

Fioriglio, G. (2015, October 28). Freedom, Authority and Knowledge on Line: The Dictatorship of the Algorithm. Retrieved December 12, 2021, from https://ssrn.com/abstract=2728842

Fleming, P (2017). The human capital hoax: Work, debt and insecurity in the era of Uberization. *Organization Studies*, *38*(5), 691-709.

Gan, S. K.-E. (2018). The history and future of scientific phone apps and mobile devices. *Scientific Phone Apps and Mobile Devices*, *4*(1), 2. Advance online publication. doi:10.118641070-018-0022-8

Geiger, F.-X., Malavolta, I., Pascarella, L., Palomba, F., Di Nucci, D., & Bacchelli, A. (2018, May 1). *A Graph-Based Dataset of Commit History of Real-World Android apps*. Retrieved December 12, 2021, from IEEE Xplore website: https://ieeexplore.ieee.org/document/8595172

HANS. (2019, December 18). *AI support tool for Estonian Parliament*. Retrieved December 12, 2021, from e-Estonia website: https://e-estonia.com/hans-ai-support-tool-for-estonian-parliament/

Herzog, S. (2011). Revisiting the Estonian Cyber Attacks: Digital Threats and Multinational Responses. *Journal of Strategic Security*, *4*(2), 49–60. doi:10.5038/1944-0472.4.2.3

Hoofnagle, C. J., van der Sloot, B., & Borgesius, F. Z. (2019). The European Union general data protection regulation: What it is and what it means. *Information & Communications Technology Law*, *28*(1), 65–98. doi:10.1080/13600834.2019.1573501

Hsu, Y.-C., Irie, N. R., & Ching, Y.-H. (2019). Computational Thinking Educational Policy Initiatives (CTEPI) Across the Globe. *TechTrends*, *63*(3), 260–270. doi:10.100711528-019-00384-4

Javier Alvarado Planas. (2021). Monarcas masones y otros príncipes de la Acacia. Madrid Dykinson, S.L.

Kietzmann, J., & Pitt, L. F. (2019). Artificial intelligence and machine learning: What managers need to know. *Business Horizons*. Advance online publication. doi:10.1016/j.bushor.2019.11.005

Kirchherr, J., Reike, D., & Hekkert, M. (2017). Conceptualizing the Circular Economy: An Analysis of 114 Definitions. SSRN *Electronic Journal*. doi:10.2139/ssrn.3037579

Medina, E. (2008). Big Blue in the bottomless pit: The early years of IBM Chile. *IEEE Annals of the History of Computing*, *30*(4), 26–41. doi:10.1109/MAHC.2008.62

Moschovakis, Y. N. (2001). What Is an Algorithm? *Mathematics Unlimited — 2001 and Beyond*, 919–936. doi:10.1007/978-3-642-56478-9_46

New e-Estonia factsheet: National AI "Kratt" Strategy. (2020, June 26). Retrieved December 12, 2021, from e-Estonia website: https://e-estonia.com/new-e-estonia-factsheet-national-ai-kratt-strategy/

Pikhart, M. (2020). Intelligent information processing for language education: The use of artificial intelligence in language learning apps. *Procedia Computer Science*, *176*, 1412–1419. doi:10.1016/j.procs.2020.09.151 PMID:33042299

Polanco-Diges, L., & Debasa, F. (2020). The use of digital marketing strategies in the sharing economy: A literature review. *Journal of Spatial and Organizational Dynamics*, *8*(3), 217–229.

Reid, A. J. (2018). *The smartphone paradox: our ruinous dependency in the Device Age.* Palgrave Macmillan. doi:10.1007/978-3-319-94319-0

Ribeiro-Navarrete, S., Saura, J. R., & Palacios-Marqués, D. (2021). Towards a new era of mass data collection: Assessing pandemic surveillance technologies to preserve user privacy. *Technological Forecasting and Social Change, 167,* 120681. doi:10.1016/j.techfore.2021.120681 PMID:33840865

Runnel, P., Pruulmann-Vengerfeldt, P., & Reinsalu, K. (2009). The Estonian Tiger Leap from Post-Communism to the Information Society: From Policy to Practice. *Journal of Baltic Studies, 40*(1), 29–51. doi:10.1080/01629770902722245

Saura, J. R., Palacios-Marqués, D., & Iturricha-Fernández, A. (2021). Ethical Design in Social Media: Assessing the main performance measurements of user online behavior modification. *Journal of Business Research, 129*(May), 271–281. doi:10.1016/j.jbusres.2021.03.001

Saura, J. R., Palacios-Marqués, D., & Ribeiro-Soriano, D. (2021b). How SMEs use data sciences in their online marketing performance: A systematic literature review of the state-of-the-art. *Journal of Small Business Management.* Advance online publication. doi:10.1080/00472778.2021.1955127

Saura, J. R., Ribeiro-Soriano, D., & Palacios-Marqués, D. (2021a). Setting B2B Digital Marketing in Artificial Intelligence-based CRMs: A review and directions for future research. *Industrial Marketing Management, 98*(October), 161–178. doi:10.1016/j.indmarman.2021.08.006

Saura, J. R., Ribeiro-Soriano, D., & Palacios-Marqués, D. (2021c). Using data mining techniques to explore security issues in smart living environments in Twitter. *Computer Communications, 179,* 285–295. Advance online publication. doi:10.1016/j.comcom.2021.08.021

Saura, J. R., Ribeiro-Soriano, D., & Palacios-Marques, D. (2021d). Evaluating security and privacy issues of social networks based information systems in Industry 4.0. *Enterprise Information Systems,* 1–17. Advance online publication. doi:10.1080/17517575.2021.1913765

Saura, J. R., Ribeiro-Soriano, D., & Palacios-Marqués, D. (2021e, July 15). Setting privacy "by default" in social IoT: Theorizing the challenges and directions in Big Data Research. *Big Data Research, 25,* 100245. doi:10.1016/j.bdr.2021.100245

Saura, J. R., Ribeiro-Soriano, D., & Palacios-Marqués, D. (2021f). From user-generated data to data-driven innovation: A research agenda to understand user privacy in digital markets. *International Journal of Information Management, 60*(October), 102331. doi:10.1016/j.ijinfomgt.2021.102331

Slee, T. (2017). *What's yours is mine against the sharing economy.* Or Books. doi:10.2307/j.ctv62hf03

Tena, E. C., & Khalilova, A. (2016). Economía circular. *Economía Industrial,* (401), 11–20. https://dialnet.unirioja.es/servlet/articulo?codigo=5771932

Vydra, S., & Klievink, B. (2019). Techno-optimism and policy-pessimism in the public sector big data debate. *Government Information Quarterly, 101383*(4), 101383. Advance online publication. doi:10.1016/j.giq.2019.05.010

Wallén, J. (2008). *The history of the industrial robot.* Linköping University Electronic Press.

Watson, H. A., Tribe, R. M., & Shennan, A. H. (2019). The role of medical smartphone apps in clinical decision-support: A literature review. *Artificial Intelligence in Medicine*, *100*, 101707. doi:10.1016/j.artmed.2019.101707 PMID:31607347

Wimsatt, W. K. (1939). *Poe and the chess automaton.* Academic Press.

Yang, W., Li, J., Zhang, Y., & Gu, D. (2019). Security analysis of third-party in-app payment in mobile applications. *Journal of Information Security and Applications*, *48*, 102358. doi:10.1016/j.jisa.2019.102358

APPENDIX 1

Table 9. Identification of the profiles interviewed

Object of the Research	Job Description and Profile	Location
Full professor Law with experience in technology and regulation of technology markets	Full professor Law	Portugal
Identify a Spanish politician with government responsibilities	Mayor	Spain
Sindicalist	Sindicalist	Argentina
Entrepreneur in the tech sector	Entrepreneur	Italy
Entrepreneur in the import/export sector	International Trade	France

APPENDIX 2

Base Question Forms That Have Been Used for Semi-structured Interviews

Question 1: Are private companies digitized at the same speed as public administrations?

Question 2: Do you think that the same is perceived by digitization and automation, or that, on the contrary, the difference is well understood.

Question 3: Is user satisfaction with services offered by algorithms different than with services offered by people?

Question 4: Do you think that the social rejection of technology occurs in a transversal way or by specific sectors?

Question 5: Do you think that the administration should desist from implementing Artificial Intelligence processes?

Section 2
Artificial Intelligence Regulation and Control Initiatives

Various initiatives regulate the use of AI in the public sector globally. Section 2 analyzes current norms and laws, as well as the initiatives to control the development and application of AI in the society.

Chapter 6
Artificial Intelligence in European Urban Governance

Miguel Angel Ajuriaguerra Escudero

https://orcid.org/0000-0001-8618-4194
Rey Juan Carlos University, Spain

Majlinda Abdiu
Universidad de Tirana, Albania

ABSTRACT

Cities reflect the social, political, and technological evolution of humanity. The implementation of new technologies in urban areas facilitate these changes. For that reason, decision-making processes in urban management have changed significantly in recent decades. At present, artificial intelligence and the supporting data infrastructures represent a new urban paradigm where city governance must attend to proper urban development while considering its citizens' opinions. However, AI requires continuous data collection to feed the algorithms. Collecting this data may raise privacy issues that vulnerate citizens' rights and personal data. Even if Europe and its member states possess highly protective privacy laws, this is still a significant concern for many citizens in urban decision-making processes. This chapter collects the European legal framework regarding AI data infrastructures and the European Green Deal to measure their potential impact on urban transformation. Also, the relationship between fundamental urban principles and the city-governance are analysed.

INTRODUCTION

Cities have traditionally been the social meeting point and, in turn, have represented the focus of culture and commerce of many civilisations through the centuries.

In Europe, the urban structure and its buildings have evolved following the theoretical perceptions of geometry, mathematics, philosophy, and politics originally from the Hellenic culture and developed under the wisdom of Plato or Aristotle. In this way, as urban civilisations have overtaken each other, technological advances have allowed notable improvements thanks to the development of infrastructures.

DOI: 10.4018/978-1-7998-9609-8.ch006

That improved the quality of life of its citizens, intertwined territories regardless of distance until now, where the new urban revolution will not take place entirely in a physical environment (Mitchell, 1999).

History shows multiple examples of the bound between urban growth and infrastructures. For instance, the Industrial Revolution meant a rapid development of infrastructures. Water supply, electricity, sanitation, and other infrastructures enabled the cities to transform and grow remarkably. This prosperity attracted many families who migrated from rural regions to the city looking for better living conditions. Later on, at the end of the 19th century, automobiles and their associated infrastructures made the cities grow into suburbs far away from the centre. As cities sprawled the urban planning changed to favour the automobile.

Nowadays, urban transformation is based on telecommunications infrastructures and specifically on the data infrastructures necessary for the correct functioning of AI. This disruptive technology significantly impacts current and future urban developments (Allam & Dhunny, 2019).

Telecommunications have already transformed cities, their daily life, their business, and how people interact with their public space through the Internet and Information and Communication Technologies (Humphreys, 2010). In this way, information infrastructures have become standard elements of the urban framework, including wiring, telecommunication facilities, mobile devices, antennas, storage centres, servers, and other components. All are fundamental elements for a contemporary society where every citizen can manage any activity anywhere and any time in the world. The Covid-19 pandemic, its derived lockdown, and the proliferation of remote work have proven the criticality of these infrastructures (Jallow, Renukappa, & Suresh, 2020).

The urban fabrics of many Western and Asian cities have taken advantage of these infrastructures to favour data interconnection. They have begun strengthening their telecommunications and data infrastructures to develop different AI projects in urban management. These projects will allow decentralising the city's services while increasing the flexibility when answering the citizens' demands. Therefore, architects, developers, and urban managers must understand the urban needs and the necessary infrastructure to deal with them. They are creating more flexible spaces to accommodate the increasingly upcoming future daily life, creating interconnected urban utopias in what seems to be the tremendous urban revolution of the millennium (Yigitcanlar et al. 2020).

However, this utopic future suffers from a significant drawback. Urban governance requires continuous data collection to answer future challenges and threats. This issue is problematic, especially for AI retractors who claim that losing control over personal data will lead to a dystopic future (Ribeiro-Navarrete, Saura, Palacios-Marqués, 2021).

In Europe, citizens are not alien to this transformation or its consequences. The reality of an interconnected world supported by increasingly AI seems irreversible. For this reason, the governing bodies of the European Union have contemplated a legislative framework concerning the development of the European AI Strategy, and it also has specific financing for its development in all the European cities and regions. This funding and the legislative framework respond to citizens' demand for privacy who want to maintain control over their data and ensure their privacy within an infrastructure that cannot function without data.

This chapter exposes the core perspective of the European policies regarding Artificial Intelligence, its associated legal framework, and some significant concerns like data privacy and biased solutions. In contrast with these obstacles, the chapter later presents the main areas where Artificial Intelligence has positively impacted urban governance and several examples of successful AI-driven initiatives in

Europe. Finally, the chapter concludes by discussing the possibilities of these technologies to reshape the urban fabric into a new physical-digital reality.

BACKGROUND

The European Framework for Artificial Intelligence

The European Union aims to lead and become a global example regarding the ethical application of AI. This chapter analyses the current legal framework under development to achieve this goal and ponders its future impact on IA-based urban solutions (Reis, J., Santo, P., & Melão, N. (2020).

The European Artificial Intelligence political structure stands on a collaborative space among the Member States. This collaboration involves a series of communal tasks for AI development and implementation and the regular exchange of information and practices between the Member States to identify trends and facilitate the future achievement of a common European legal framework concerning AI.

This European strategy is essential for the homogeneous development of a safe AI environment in all Member States, mainly considering that the technological development of each state is different, and the implementation of an overall regulatory framework requires a homogeneous environment that allows the all-inclusive development. Therefore, in December 2018, the Commission presented a Coordinated Plan for the Member States. This plan consists of 70 actions that allow more efficient cooperation in crucial areas as relevant as:

- Research
- Investment
- Market uptake
- Skills and talent
- Data and international collaboration

These actions are encompassed to maximise the investment of European funds, with particular reference to research, innovation, and usability of the AI in all Member States. Furthermore, the Action 1st of the White Paper in AI, in which it specifies:

Action 1: The Commission, taking into account the results of the public consultation on the White Paper, will propose to the Member States a revision of the Coordinated Plan to be adopted by end 2020. (European Commission, 2018, p.5)

This aspect is essential to understand the distribution of funds and each Member State's investments. The Commission aims to attract an investment of more than €20 billion per year throughout the decade, encouraging that such investment should be public and private (European Commission, 2018, p.3). To this end, the European Union will make available resources from the Digital Europe Program. Also, to achieve this ambitious goal, the European Structural and Investment Funds will be made available to help the specific needs for the less developed regions, such as rural areas, of each Member State (DiGiacinto, F., 2018).

In order to achieve success in the implementation of a homogeneous AI framework among the Member States, the Commission will facilitate the creation of monitoring centres through the objectives of the European strategy, aligning the AI strategy with other objectives such as the fight against climate change or the environmental degradation. The Action 25 of the White Paper on AI states that:

The Commission will facilitate the creation of excellence and testing centres that can combine European, national and private investments, possibly including a new legal instrument. The Commission has proposed an ambitious and dedicated amount to support world reference testing centres in Europe under the Digital Europe Programme and complemented where appropriate by research and innovation actions of Horizon Europe as part of the Multiannual Financial Framework for 2021 to 2027. (European Commission, 2020, p.5)

This framework for homogeneous AI development and implementation among all the Member States will lead Europe's positioning in the international context to unprecedented success, especially for all European citizens involved in AI regardless of their country of residence. Thus, the European Union will achieve world leadership in the ethical use of AI. In addition, the European partnership within the OECD will help boost the ethical principles of AI worldwide (OECD, 2021).

Thus, the main issues of the European AI strategy lay in the public trust and the efficient development of its regulatory framework. Under this scope, data processing is a fundamental aspect for the success of its strategy and implementation and to prospect the AI ethical leadership in the world.

As AI can only work with a vast amount of data, the key to winning trust towards this technology rest on adequate data collection and treatment policies (Salah et al., 2019). Western public opinion, especially the European one, is susceptible to this subject and is very reticent and feels unprotected about their privacy. At the same time, from a business point of view, it is also essential to highlight the legal uncertainty produced by exploiting business data for AI implementation. Remarkably, given the asymmetries that can occur between citizens willing to transfer data and those who are not. Currently, in the EU, the data use does not have a standard and homogeneous legal framework. Even counting the Commission's efforts to solve this situation, these asymmetries can produce severe biases in the AI implementation and decision-making algorithms. This is one of the most worrying aspects of the European AI implementation strategy. For this reason, a homogeneous and mandatory legal framework for all Member States supposes the application of the fundamental rules and rights that would facilitate the citizen trust and the correct management of their data for any use, including the AI.

The European Union and its AI strategy want to strengthen the popular confidence in this technology through a legal framework designed to protect the fundamental rights of its citizens. The Commission wants to achieve this by a firm policy for data protection and non-discrimination use. This aspect has been reiterative for the European Parliament and the European Council, which had called all Member States for a common legal framework to favour the proper AI function throughout the EU. There is an agreement for AI use, albeit only for military purposes. For that reason, the Commission has proposed a regulatory framework that represents the key to establishing the homogeneous legal framework necessary for IA in all Member States. Minimising the risk of ambiguous standards and uses through the EU.

To prevent AI from altering the founding values of the European Union and violating its citizens' fundamental privacy freedom, the Council of Europe has developed a study to ensure European citizens' fundamental rights when AI is broadly in use. Especially regarding the development of algorithms that avoid the data need risk. Particularly the data that can be considered personal from a legal framework.

The European Commission expresses its concern in this regard and emphasises the following statement from the 81st conference of the Proceedings of Machine Learning Research (Bualamwini & Gebru, 2018):

Certain AI algorithms, when exploited for predicting criminal recidivism, can display gender and racial bias, demonstrating different recidivism prediction probability for women vs men or for nationals vs foreigners. Source: Tolan S., Miron M., Gomez E. and Castillo C. "Why Machine Learning May Lead to Unfairness: Evidence from Risk Assessment for Juvenile Justice in Catalonia", Best Paper Award, International Conference on AI and Law, 2019. (European Commission, 2020, p.11)

According to the 81st conference of the Proceedings of Machine Learning Research, specific AI programs for facial analysis display gender and racial bias. On the other hand, they showed low errors in determining the gender of lighter-skinned men but high errors in determining gender for darker-skinned women. This is a susceptible aspect of data processing and management. Therefore, before the broad implementation, it must be delimited and clarified for ethical, technological development, and use. Mainly since the responsibility for decision-making goes from a human origin to a technological one. This ethical point of view is mandatory for avoiding the treatment of the wrongful data by the AI algorithm itself. For this reason, the definition of AI is fundamental for any development and its implementation in the European legal framework, mainly since it must satisfy both the present and future technology needs of this technology to ensure the ethical and legal treatment of European citizens' data.

Another evidence to highlight the European Commission's responsibility in unravelling different aspects of the AI that may lead to unethical biases is the evolving definition of AI itself. The Coordinated Plan on Artificial Intelligence published in 2018 provides the following definition of IA:

Artificial Intelligence refers to systems that display intelligent behaviour by analysing their environment and taking action — with some degree of autonomy — to achieve specific goals. We are using AI on a daily basis, for example, to block email spam or speak with digital assistants. Growth in computing power, availability of data and progress in algorithms have turned AI into one of the most important technologies of the 21st century. (European Commission, 2018, p.1)

However, after consulting with High-Level Expert Group outside the European Agencies, the Commission refined this definition almost a year later as follows:

Artificial intelligence (AI) systems are software (and possibly also hardware) systems designed by humans that, given a complex goal, act in the physical or digital dimension by perceiving their environment through data acquisition, interpreting the collected structured or unstructured data, reasoning on the knowledge, or processing the information, derived from this data and deciding the best action(s) to take to achieve the given goal. AI systems can either use symbolic rules or learn a numeric model, and they can also adapt their behaviour by analysing how the environment is affected by their previous actions. As a scientific discipline, AI includes several approaches and techniques, such as machine learning (of which deep learning and reinforcement learning are specific examples), machine reasoning (which includes planning, scheduling, knowledge representation and reasoning, search, and optimisation), and robotics (which includes control, perception, sensors, and actuators, as well as the integration of all other techniques into cyber-physical systems). (High-Level Expert Group (HLEG), 2018, p. 1)

This renewed definition emphasises the role the data plays when perceiving reality, interpreting it, and deciding the best course of action. This definition aspect requires special attention from the Commission or the Member States and those involved in the AI development, implementation, and use. For that reason, the origin of the data must also attend to its specific use. It is crucial to highlight that most data derives from citizens living in the more minor European administrative scales, such as municipalities and township associations where most of the European population is concentrated (Giffinger et al., 2007).

In addition to the general European legal framework, it is also essential to focus on the data infrastructure that supports AI, especially according to the data traffic increase. For this data infrastructure, all the different levels of administrations must intervene, mainly the local administrations, if they want to use AI services for correct urban management and planning. Thus, the legal framework and the data infrastructure must meet the following requirements:

- Training data
- Data and record-keeping
- Information to be provided
- Robustness and accuracy
- Human oversight

Of all of them, the training data is the most relevant requirement for achieving the European AI strategy. Furthermore, this is necessary to position the EU in the global leadership of data rights. His can be achieved mainly by promoting the use of ethical AI. Without data, there is no AI.

On the other hand, since 2021, the EU has a clear roadmap for digitalisation, alienated to transform Europe in the next ten years. For that reason, it is essential to align the risks and opportunities that AI has in Europe. Thus, the Commission has established several funding programs, such as Digital Europe and Horizon Europe. In this way, the EU intends to invest 1 billion euros a year in AI to increase this investment up to 20 billion euros per year. This objective is feasible by involving both the private sector and the available economic capacity of each Member State for this purpose.

Also, it is crucial to consider that in response to the Covid-19 crisis, the EU has established aid funds to mitigate the crisis effects among the Member States. These funds, known as Recovery and Resilience Facility (RRF), are considered the opportunity to make the first move regarding the adoption of AI in the common European framework. At least 20% of the available budget should fund necessary measures concerning the digital transition. This will reflect the political efforts made during the 2018-2021 period, especially after the presentation in 2018 of the European Strategy on AI. For that, in 2020, the Commission prepared an official document about the responsibility and security of AI. This document was about the Internet of Things (IoT) and robotics. Since the consultation ended in June 2020, this analysis has highly impacted citizens, Member States, and stakeholders. This has been essential to carry out the legal and practical approach for the future AI policies of implementation in Europe.

Together, these future policies with the different results obtained from the open participation in the AI workshops have raised some relevant issues. The European legal and practical framework for the use of AI must address these concerns. Briefly, these risks are:

- AI systems need to respect a set of specifically designed requirements for adequate traceability by the user of all his information, including the data obtention, processing, and management.

- For a total European legal integration within the various existing AI frameworks, the AI systems must verify their conformity with the legality before being placed on the market or put into service. For that, Member States must guarantee the legal coherence and meet the needs for permitting the data used for the economic operators.
- Establish the limitation for the AI uses. Especially for those that contravene the fundamental values and rights of the European Union citizens.
- Limit the remote biometric identification systems of European citizens. This is one of the most significant and AI-worrying aspects for European citizens and its legal perspective because its citizens will be subjected to data registration in real-time. This could be considered by law as an act of human supervision; for this reason, and following the European legal framework, biometric identification would be prohibited in public spaces unless some exceptional cases are authorised by law.

The Data Used in Europe

Data is the critical element to drive and implement the European strategy for Artificial Intelligence. Also, the urban environment is the area where most of the data will be generated and managed. The European strategy focuses on the European cities as a fundamental part of data production and AI implementation, particularly since digital technologies have entirely transformed the European society and economy. This digital trend is consolidating in both Europe and the world, and currently, data is at the centre of this socio-economic transformation. At the same time, the European Commission has established a new strategy complementary to the AI agenda. This new strategy is concerning data and is known as the European Strategy for Data. This strategy also adds to data and AI's contribution to achieving the European Green Deal.

From the Commission's perspective, citizen data empowerment is the cornerstone of the European leadership on ethical AI. As mentioned before, to meet this leadership goal, the EU is establishing a new legal framework that favours the union principles and responds to the present and future needs regarding the fundamental European rights for data protection and cyber-security. The European policies promote the ethical collection and usage of citizens' data to promote the productivity and competitiveness of the whole European economy while dissolving eventual socio-economical differences among the different Member States. In the same way, the aim is to ensure that this data and AI strategy serve to improve the health of Europeans, improve and protect their environment, and promote the use and transparency of all public services.

Regardless of the legal framework exposed before, it is vital to highlight the growing volume of data and the technological changes that are currently taking place. The data volume is growing from 33 zettabytes in 2018 to an expectation of 175 zettabytes by 2025 (International Data Corporation, 2020). Europe's leadership in AI encompasses the ethical use of data and the needed infrastructure for absorbing the data flow. These infrastructures contemplate the expected data collection, processing, and storage requirements for the next five years. This perspective will transform the current data infrastructure, with an expected 80% increment of the data flow between the various specialised decentralised centres (Quinn, M., & Strauss, 2017).

To achieve the European leadership on the AI and data strategies, the Commission wants to promote economic growth based on overcoming a pattern recognition by predictive techniques that will lead to better decisions, management, and government decisions. Considering that growth depends on available data to fuel AI, these respond and collaborate to the future development of new start-ups and medium-sized companies (SMEs) across the Member States along the whole data value chain. This business aspect was also collected in 2018 by a study of Deloitte, which estimates that the use of non-personal data can represent a business of 1.5 trillion euros by 2027 (Deloitte, 2018).

The improvement of data infrastructures is a critical challenge for the European AI leadership, enabling better social and economic resources management. Primarily when the core of the AI and data efforts aim to confront the current risks about climate change and environmental preservation, in concordance with the objectives of the European Green Deal policies. Thus, the Commission established a plan for a Common European Green Deal Data Space. This plan focused on transforming Europe by 2050, becoming the first climate-neutral continent in the world. The Green Deal strategy incorporates the Common European Green Deal Data Space to promote using data to prioritise actions in such fundamental aspects as climate change, biodiversity, the decrease in pollution, and the growth of the circular economy, both at territorial and at urban scopes. This aspect responds to the initiative "GreenData4all". Moreover, a future Directive will provide open access for all Urban Environmental Information. This initiative is making the necessary transition to a carbon-neutral economy easier for authorities, a severe demand from most European citizens and companies.

Along these lines, different strategies can be implemented with the European Green Deal to put the 0-pollution policy into context through data mining. These strategies will provide better territorial and urban management through IA while ensuring the quality of the air, water, emissions, chemicals, and dangerous substances in the European regions.

From 2014 to the present, the Commission has regulated the following aspects:

- General Data Protection Regulation (GDPR)
- Regulation on the free flow of non-personal data (FFD)
- The Cybersecurity Act (CSA)
- The Open Data Directive

The Commission has engaged European digital diplomacy to include 13 other countries under these policies to expand the EU values. This inclusion will provide their citizens with an adequate level of protection for their data. Thus, the EU is creating an attractive policy that by 2030 will allow the Member States to obtain, process, store and share data, generating a single data market. These aspects anticipate the future urban infrastructures that will favour the data market and reduce the environmental footprint through more efficient resource management.

However, the most significant risk for the European leadership in AI and data lies in the existing fragmentation between the Member States. Also, it is essential to consider the internal economic and social problems that each state faces concerning the differences between regions and cities. For this reason, the Commission promulgates the provision of open data for the general good. Where specifically it is exposed in the Common European Data Spaces:

Data is created by society and can serve to combat emergencies, such as floods and wildfires, to ensure that people can live longer and healthier lives, to improve public services, and to tackle environmental degradation and climate change, and, where necessary and proportionate, to ensure a more efficient fight against crime. Data generated by the public sector as well as the value created should be available for the common good by ensuring, including through preferential access, that these data are used by researchers, other public institutions, SMEs, or start-ups. Data from the private sector can also make a significant contribution as public goods. The use of aggregated and anonymised social media data can, for example, be an effective way of complementing the reports of general practitioners in case of an epidemic. (European Commission, 2020, pp. 6-7)

From an urban management perspective, it is essential to highlight that data mining represents an economic opportunity for the development of SMEs or start-ups. Companies primarily focus on obtaining, processing, storing, and sharing data to develop new software for urban planning, mobility, infrastructures, or any other aspect that can benefit the European leadership and help the local administration in their urban and territorial management. To this end, the Commission has held a series of workshops to reinforce data governance through the concept of Common European Data Spaces.

AI IN EUROPEAN URBAN MANAGEMENT

Main Opportunities for IA Solutions in Urban Management

The European legal framework, as said before, must have a homogeneous fundamental basis for the correct AI development and implementation throughout the Member States of the European Union to favour its global leadership and innovation strategy for an ethical AI. However, to promote the successful implementation of the European AI strategy, the origin of the data that will feed these algorithms must be addressed from an urban perspective, mainly because in Europe, most of the population concentrates in urban areas.

From the urban planning perspective, AI systems are essential for the real-time management of the endowments and services produced in cities (Ji et al., 2021). Many AI applications are still unknown by both urban managers and decision-makers. So, it is also necessary to instruct them on the advantages AI offers to simplify urban management tasks and decision-making. Mainly, concerning:

- traffic management;
- health coordination between health centres;
- emergency management and coordination between first responders,
- infrastructures and urban facilities management;
- environmental and pollution management and predictive maintenance;
- distributed and flexible e-Government regarding the management of licenses, permits, and other administrative matters.

Of all of them, currently, traffic management is the most extended use of AI in the European territory. Nevertheless, these approaches did not contemplate autonomous vehicles during the algorithmic training, which is an unacceptable risk for the European AI strategy and should be addressed as soon as possible by the Commission. It is evident that soon traffic management will work through the mixture of navigation systems, including the hybrid model between drivers and autonomous vehicles (Schwarting et al., 2018).

This aspect is complex according to the current and future urban scenarios for traffic management. In a mixture of users, the driving participation of all vehicles in real-time will lead to the production of massive data that, if managed, will facilitate the traffic, avoiding both jams and accidents thanks to algorithm management. For that reason, the data infrastructure is a crucial element due to the mixture of autonomous and driver users. Furthermore, in an autonomous vehicle traffic management scenario, the car's data must be considered public to provide the necessary data flow to make the AI work appropriately in this context. Nowadays, the public data considered are the destination, scheduled stops, speed and consumption, among others, which may turn insufficient with the inclusion of autonomous vehicles. On the other hand, the AI will help the urban environmental aspects for the physical infrastructures such as the state of the roads, signage, relationship with other vehicles and pedestrians, weather, and emergencies.

The Commission is working on promoting the involvement of AI concerning transportation and mobility, mainly because it is one of the most polluting sectors in the EU. The different administrations are doing much work to digitise all transport systems and logistics hubs to obtain the necessary data to manage the European mobility systems. The "Smart and Sustainable Transport Strategy" applied throughout the European transportation infrastructure encompasses this effort. This strategy to the automakers, which currently generate 25 gigabytes of data per hour, is expected to reach terabytes in the autonomous vehicle case.

Urban pollution is a severe issue that the Commission considered because of its expected growth in the upcoming years. Even if the introduction of electrified transportation will help mitigate the growth of the pollution rate, it is expected to increase 30% by 2025 and 50% by 2050. The AI can manage and reduce the polluting effects in transportation, including freights and passengers. For this reason, the European strategy addressed above for AI, governance, and data is embracing the urban principles included in the European Green Deal in compliance with the United Nations Sustainable Development Goals, significantly mitigating the worst health effects in urban areas for the presence of the pollutants. However, according to European legislation, access to vehicle data is regulated through the Vehicle Approval Legislation. The European Green Deal strategy will consider this regulation, especially for most cities' efforts to decrease air pollution in the main urban areas (Cariolet et al., 2018).

Another aspect to consider regarding the use of AI in European urban management is the data applicability for financial purposes. This aspect also represents a new urban leadership challenge, as the Global Cities phenomenon was before. Nowadays, data represent the key for leadership and competitiveness in different economic dimensions such as logistics, finance, and politics. All those dimensions represent different aspects of the cities and are measurable for the different city rankings. For this reason, the common European Financial Data Space can represent the leadership opportunity for the financial sector in shaping the emerging European Data City.

The European data financial leadership opportunity requires the European legislation requiring all financial institutions to disclose essential data regarding products, transactions, operations, and financial results (Arner et al., 2016). This legal framework represents an opportunity for the urban leadership of European financial cities. For this reason, shortly, the Commission will lay the foundations for the fledgling Digital Finance Strategy. In this way, in April 2020, Eurocities, the network of the leading European cities, developed a response to the Digital Strategy White Paper on AI and the European Data Strategy of the European Commission. Eurocities defends that all programs regarding AI are fundamental for the change in the local governments and urban management. In other words, the future of AI is in the cities, and its future depends on it.

In addition, the digital changes that are taking place and the future use of AI in urban and territorial management are necessary for the competitiveness of European cities. Suppose all scales of government consider to face the current significant risks for humanity, such as climate change, social and migratory crises, or rising sea levels. In that case, all they need is the broad implementation of AI to transform the governance of the city and its society. Especially if we look at the social and urban transformation that Covid-19 has experienced. This crisis has highlighted the urgency of consolidating a digital transformation of European citizenship, transportation, and city management to guarantee social and economic resilience against unexpected future crises.

The role of AI is crucial to assume the management of the urban aspects highlighted before. Regarding the current Covid-19 crisis management in Europe, AI can be a valuable tool for predicting and managing public health emergencies. For that reason, it is essential to try to implement this technology as soon as possible. It mainly highlighted the guarantees provided by the European legal framework regarding the use of personal data for AI in management and health coordination. As previously stated, since in the EU human rights are protected as part of the fundamental European values, the use of AI for urban management should not be an issue. Therefore, it is possible to achieve a successful AI solution for urban management respecting the fundamental European rights and ethics.

From an urban perspective, AI can transform European cities into a more sustainable and inclusive space for all citizens. In particular, using AI, Europe can reach enormous environmental success. For that reason, the Commission has promoted several programs to help local authorities to comply with the Green Deal and other strategies. For example, to reach environmental success, AI and its machine learning through data feeding can help manage many kinds of situations through the IoT, especially when the IoT users cede their data for better personal and community experience. So, AI can predict many urban issues such as level of pollution, behaviour and usability patterns of citizens and tourists, traffic, and parking management concerning the availability of parking space (public and private), and so on. This data flow can highly improve the citizens' lives. Also, it can help the local government adopt policies and investments according to the citizens' actual needs.

Europe should consider all its strategies and try to promote a unique and integrated one related to the broad AI adoption through the Member States (Trauner, 2009), especially if Europe wants to lead the ethical use of AI in the world (Smuha, 2021). In comparison, many Asian cities are increasing their use (Regmi, 2020). Furthermore, the challenges related to its use also increase, highlighting the disruption in security, privacy, and the job market.

This last one is related to response to the immediate change produced in the job market worldwide. Soon, many jobs will become obsolete as a cause of AI implementation. This issue will mainly affect the urban areas as they concentrate the primary labour force. For the European urban leadership in AI implementation, it is essential to consider all the possible scenarios. Mainly if the urban population decrease for the job crisis (Hughes, 2014). For that, the local governments should consider these disruptive technologies for urban planning to grasp the opportunity to develop the Data City. This new paradigm would counter the traditional job loss by creating a high demand for technological experts. Simultaneously, this transformation will help position Europe at the lead of the new digital labour market.

The European Governance Experience in Cities With AI Interests

The reality of AI implementation in European cities is far from other cases, such as in Asian cities. However, implementing technological solutions without a proper conceptualisation and framing may lead to an undesired scenario. For example, the Korean case has led to a ubiquitous hyperconnected technologic-centric implementation with a noticeable vertical approach but without a much needed horizontal perspective (Dimmer, 2021). In the European case, the Commission's efforts to develop AI technologies in the urban spectrum are solid strategies with a perfectly defined goal to integrate all the State Members.

The Commission has set founded several projects under the Horizon 2020, Horizon Europe and other R&D programmes to boost the IA capabilities in urban governance. All these urban projects are related to data management and AI technologies. For instance, the URBANITE project, founded under the H2020 program, aims to facilitate the decision-making process in urban mobility and transformation policies. This project has demonstrated the capabilities of AI in urban governance through several pilots in the following cities: Amsterdam, Bilbao, Helsinki, and Messina. The project demonstrates the advantages of data management, AI, and governance applied to urban solutions. The project's success relied on a continuous flow of information, data, consultation and, partnership with all local agents.

Of all the case studies contemplated by URBANITE, it is essential to mention the case study of Amsterdam, mainly because the digitisation process of this city is considered an example for others. The city has taken part in several other AI and mobility-related projects. For instance, during the three-year-long project Mobility Urban Values – MUV, the City of Amsterdam engaged its citizens towards sustainable mobility choices in their neighbourhood using gamified experiences. In 2020, the most representative results of the program execution were made public.

Another evidence of the city's involvement in AI-driven sustainable mobility is its participation in the Smart CitySDK project. This project aimed to define services that help developers and users access the open data necessary for developing AI technologies, especially in urban fields as Participation, Mobility, and Tourism. Although the City of Amsterdam led the mobility pilot study, other cities like Helsinki, Manchester, Barcelona, Rome, Istanbul, and Lamia have implemented the official API of the project.

These projects demonstrate that a structured IA implementation can lead to beneficial urban management solutions and show the possibilities to expand beyond their initial urban scenario as they can adapt to new deployment as long as the required infrastructures exist. In this sense, they follow the lead of the European IA deployment strategy.

Regarding other European AI experiences, the followings are an example of some relevant initiatives of the last decade in different fields beyond urban mobility:

- VioGén 5.0. is the latest version of the "Integral Follow-up of Gender Violence Cases System" (in Spanish: Sistema VioGén). It was released in March 2019. The system has been in place since the 26th of July of 2007. It was initially launched by the State Security Secretary of the Spanish Ministry of Home Affairs, according to the Organic Spanish Law 1/2004.
- Public Stack for charging infrastructure. This study is a publication commissioned to Waag in collaboration with the Netherlands Enterprise Agency (RVO) and Topsector Energie. This work is in line with the Club van Wageningen guiding principles. This project is related to implementing an energy transition model for arranging physical and digital charging infrastructure for electric vehicles (EV). Also, it is considered the promotion of highly qualified technicians to create a network of changemakers in the Netherlands to work for this proposal.
- Assessment List for Trustworthy. This study was a project developed by a high-level expert group on AI to 'translate the Ethics Guidelines [EC's] into an accessible and dynamic (self-assessment) checklist. The checklist was promoted by both developers and deployers of AI who want to implement the essential European requirements in practice.

These cities and projects represent the beginning of the future urban development and planning established for the European cities. The European cities and their transformation represent the Commission's leadership by applying AI in the most harmonious way possible across all Member States.

MAIN FINDINGS AND RECOMMENDATIONS

After analysing the AI masterplans, data management, and use promoted by the European Commission some Member States and the European cities, the legal framework exposed has a clear message between the leadership and AI implementation on the European soil.

The legal documents and communication clarify that the main goal promoted by the Commission is to achieve global leadership in urban strategies and policies. For that reason, it is necessary to strengthen the European data infrastructures as soon as possible, especially regarding data use, flow, and interoperability. This aspect is fundamental for the management of cities due to the broad data infrastructure needed to collect, manage, analyse, and store for proper AI functioning.

For that reason, an adequate new data infrastructure and some new pilot programs related to AI can help to spread the strategies to other European cities. Thus, the urban areas will be able to promote and incentivise AI implementation through new management projects that will facilitate both the leadership of urban AI technologies and also the compliance of the European Green Deal for more sustainable cities. In order to achieve this goal, the European policies must address the following vital aspects:

- Invest in high-impact European projects regarding data infrastructure and management. Including in these projects: good practices, tools, and standards for the homogenous governance mechanisms in all Member States.
- Establish a common European data space for the use and development of strategic and public interest sectors as the Commission establishes concerning the common European data spaces.

These two aspects are fundamental for developing and implementing AI tools for urban management and governance. Moreover, it can also develop new dimensions: planning for urban uses and resources, management, maintenance, electronic offices, and e-governance, among others.

In this way, the EU hopes to broadly use disruptive AI technologies in urban planning and territorial management. Not just to be a global example of leadership and ethical use of the AI, but also to transform the European cities in a more sustainable way for achieving a better urban quality of life, following the European Green Deal Strategy.

CONCLUSION

The general outlines of our electronic future are clear. However, the details and opportunities of this vast data infrastructure and its relationship with AI are not specified because the European governance of cities and territories has not still reached a consensus concerning the legal framework of all the Member States of the Union.

Nowadays, AI implementation in cities has different speeds depending on the results obtained from European programs and technological business careers. At the same time, the European Commission is making numerous efforts regarding AI strategy and its proper data infrastructure. In addition, social acceptance occurs unevenly among the citizens' participation in European projects between social and political debates.

However, these social and political debates are fundamental to finding new objective and straightforward uses of AI in the urban space. Europe wants to lead this urban transformation technology from an ethical perspective and, it is precisely for this reason that European governance can achieve AI leadership through social acceptance. This consensus is the real opportunity to link the fundamental criteria of individual and citizen privacy in a world of new 24/7 interconnection infrastructures.

The beginning of this chapter introduced how the urban historical evolution is linked with the introduction of new infrastructures as electricity supply, water, roads, and others. Most of these "innovations" were unpopular before their implementation, even when these infrastructures represented a significant urban development and improved the lives of its citizens. In the same way, nowadays, new technological advances and innovative solutions are not safe from their retractors.

Today telecommunications already represent the backbone of urban infrastructures. The telecommunications network itself is the one that supports the correct operation and maintenance of the rest of the urban infrastructures and facilities. In addition, telecommunications support a large part of the social and commercial relations that occur in the West. Furthermore, the effect on distance has been spectacular, minimising interdependence relationships between isolated regions and populations. Thus, in recent decades urban transformation has begun through data infrastructures and, therefore, AI. In addition, cities and the services have begun to plan and manage through a data infrastructure that supports the European AI engine, especially if we want the city physical spaces to serve as elements or smart sensors that facilitate new forms of intelligent interaction and management.

Programs like the European Green Deal support and promote the data infrastructure for AI. The legal framework is promoted among the Member States to give continuity to AI programs in European cities. So, this new infrastructure collaborates on the urban and architectural scale through the transmission networks to facilitate navigation and the usability of urban services beyond traffic. On the other hand, the environment and urban health can improve highly through AI solutions, mainly because the European Green Deal is also a tool to fight and prepare against climate change.

The use of AI on an urban scale represents the new opportunity to solve all the problems that manifest in our cities today. It is a compelling element in which the European Commission wants to lead its ethical use while respecting the privacy of its citizens' data. Moreover, the lack of privacy related to digital phobia is one of the aspects that the European Commission and its legislative framework protect the most.

In addition, the task concerning law and its application among all European states remains unclear. It is essential to value that AI's infrastructure can favour the quality and management of the urban spaces and its citizens and the economic growth. An advantage where business can also be extended without physical need, eliminating the distance from many social interactions. Also, the AI economic boost will embrace the interactions of the circular economy, as the Commission has already pointed out.

Finally, the development of AI and its infrastructures implies an evolution in urban planning and architecture. Each building and street will represent a point in the data infrastructure, and it stands out in the privacy framework of European governance. This urban change will start the social interaction with more robots. The comfort of where we live and the state of the streets concerning their environmental quality, cleanliness, or traffic management will be managed and controlled. Concerning urban planning, this transformation will also take place in all urban facilities serving as sensors for the future electronic neighbourhoods that will make society connected 24 hours a day without the need to travel and generate new social and commercial relationships.

In this way, once the urban transformation of AI completes, it will give way to a metaverse where the virtual society will complement the physical. An aspect that is currently manifesting itself opening to new discussions and regulatory frameworks in which governance, once again, will be essential for its success.

REFERENCES

Allam, Z., & Dhunny, Z. A. (2019). On big data, artificial intelligence and smart cities. *Cities (London, England), 89*, 80–91. doi:10.1016/j.cities.2019.01.032

Arner, D. W., Barberis, J., & Buckey, R. P. (2016). FinTech, RegTech, and the reconceptualisation of financial regulation. *Nw. J. Int'l L. & Bus., 37*(3), 370–413.

Buolamwini, J., & Gebru, T. (2018). Proceedings of the 1st Conference on Fairness, Accountability and Transparency. *Proceedings of Machine Learning Research, 81*, 77–91.

Cariolet, J. M., Colombert, M., Vuillet, M., & Diab, Y. (2018). Assessing the resilience of urban areas to traffic-related air pollution: Application in Greater Paris. *The Science of the Total Environment, 615*, 588–596. doi:10.1016/j.scitotenv.2017.09.334 PMID:28988095

Council of Europe. (2017). *Study on the human rights dimensions of automated data processing techniques (in particular algorithms) and possible regulatory implications.* Council of Europe, Committee of experts on Internet MSI-NET.

Deloitte. (2018). *Realising the economic potential of machine-generated, non-personal data in the EU Report for Vodafone Group.* Deloitte.

DiGiacinto, F. (2018). "European Structural And Investment Funds" 2014-2020 For The Efficiency Of Public Administration. *Curentul Juridic, 73*(2), 26–37.

Dimmer, C. (2021). Smart Cities in Asia: Governing Development in the Era of HyperConnectivity. Cities. *Pacific Affairs, 94*(2), 401–403.

European Commision. (2020). *European Strategy for Data. Communication from the Commission to the European Parliament, the Council, the European Economic and Social Committee and the Committee of the Regions: A European strategy for data* (Publication No. COM (2020) 66). Directorate-General for Communications Networks, Content and Technology.

European Commission. (2018). *Artificial Intelligence for Europe* (Publication No. COM (2018) 237). Directorate-General for Communications Networks, Content and Technology.

European Commission. (2018). *Coordinate Plan on Artificial Intelligence* (Publication No. COM (2018) 795 Final). Directorate-General for Communications Networks, Content and Technology.

European Commission. (2018). *Communication from the Commission to the European Parliament, the European Council, the Council, the European Economic and Social Committee and the Committee of the Regions. Coordinated Plan on Artificial Intelligence* (Publication No. COM (2018) 795 final). Directorate-General for Communications Networks, Content and Technology.

European Commission. (2020). *White Paper On Artificial Intelligence - A European approach to excellence and trust* (Publication No. COM (2020) 65 final). Directorate-General for Communications Networks, Content and Technology.

European Commission. (2020). *European Commission Report on the Safety and Liability Aspects of AI the Internet of Things (IoT) and robotics* (Publication No. COM (2020) 64). Directorate-General for Communications Networks, Content and Technology.

European Commission. (2021). *Communication from the Commission to the European Parliament, the Council, the European Economic and Social Committee and the Committee of the Regions. Fostering a European approach to Artificial Intelligence* (Publication No. COM/2021/205 final). Directorate-General for Communications Networks, Content and Technology.

Giffinger, R., Fertner, C., Kramar, H., & Meijers, E. (2007). *City-ranking of European medium-sized cities*. Cent. Reg. Sci.

Hughes, J. (2014). A strategic opening for a basic income guarantee in the global crisis being created by AI, robots, desktop manufacturing and biomedicine. *Journal of Ethics and Emerging Technologies*, *24*(1), 45–61.

Humphreys, L. (2010). Mobile social networks and urban public space. *New Media & Society*, *12*(5), 763–778. doi:10.1177/1461444809349578

International Data Corporation (IDC). (2020). *IDC's Global DataSphere Forecast Shows Continued Steady Growth in the Creation and Consumption of Data*. IDC.

Jallow, H., Renukappa, S., & Suresh, S. (2020). *The impact of COVID-19 outbreak on United Kingdom infrastructure sector*. Smart and Sustainable Built Environment.

Ji, T., Chen, J. H., Wei, H. H., & Su, Y. C. (2021). Towards people-centric smart city development: Investigating the citizens' preferences and perceptions about smart-city services in Taiwan. *Sustainable Cities and Society*, *67*(102691), 1–14. doi:10.1016/j.scs.2020.102691

Mitchell, W. J. (1999). e-topia: Urban Life, Jim# But Not As We Know It. MIT Press.

Quinn, M., & Strauss, E. (Eds.). (2017). *The Routledge Companion to Accounting Information Systems*. Routledge. doi:10.4324/9781315647210

Regmi, M. B. (2020). Measuring sustainability of urban mobility: A pilot study of Asian cities. *Case Studies on Transport Policy, 8*(4), 1224-1232.

Reis, J., Santo, P., & Melão, N. (2020). Impact of artificial intelligence research on politics of the European Union member states: The case study of Portugal. *Sustainability, 12*(17), 1-25.

Ribeiro-Navarrete, S., Saura, J. R., & Palacios-Marqués, D. (2021). Towards a new era of mass data collection: Assessing pandemic surveillance technologies to preserve user privacy. *Technological Forecasting and Social Change, 167*, 120681. doi:10.1016/j.techfore.2021.120681 PMID:33840865

Salah, K., Rehman, M. H. U., Nizamuddin, N., & Al-Fuqaha, A. (2019). Blockchain for AI: Review and open research challenges. *IEEE Access: Practical Innovations, Open Solutions, 7*, 10127–10149. doi:10.1109/ACCESS.2018.2890507

Schwarting, W., Alonso-Mora, J., & Rus, D. (2018). Planning and decision-making for autonomous vehicles. *Annual Review of Control, Robotics, and Autonomous Systems, 1*(1), 187–210. doi:10.1146/annurev-control-060117-105157

Smuha, N. A. (2021). From a 'race to AI' to a 'race to AI regulation': Regulatory competition for artificial intelligence. *Law, Innovation and Technology, 13*(1), 57–84. doi:10.1080/17579961.2021.1898300

Trauner, F. (2009). From membership conditionality to policy conditionality: EU external governance in South Eastern Europe. *Journal of European Public Policy, 16*(5), 774–790. doi:10.1080/13501760902983564

Yigitcanlar, T., Desouza, K. C., Butler, L., & Roozkhosh, F. (2020). Contributions and risks of artificial intelligence (AI) in building smarter cities: Insights from a systematic review of the literature. *Energies, 13*(6), 1473. doi:10.3390/en13061473

Chapter 7
Digital Democracy:
Political Communications in the Era of New Information and Communication Technologies

Luis Vicente Doncel Fernández
Rey Juan Carlos University, Spain

ABSTRACT

Starting from a brief reference to the concept and typology of political democracy systems, the authors present in this chapter some of the most important challenges that the use of new information and communication technologies entails in both spheres of political decisions (from power or choosing power). It is logical to question and open a debate regarding the democratic validity of its use, since fake news, misinformation, bubble filters undoubtedly influence the propaganda of political parties and affect the message and its effectiveness. On the other hand, the new technological communication paradigm applied to the democratic electoral system, technically possible, also raises interesting considerations regarding its eventual institutionalization and its legitimacy in comparison with the classical model of participation.

EXORDIUM: ABOUT THE CONCEPT OF DEMOCRACY

At the beginning, a brief enunciative incursion on different democratic systems seems necessary, in order to offer an overview of them and thus be able to later place the influence of the new information and communication technologies, well understood that most of the essay is it will refer to the generically most widespread system: representative democracy. But, perhaps, the media themselves tend to modify the system to some extent, an idea that we take, for the moment, as a mere working hypothesis.

When we refer to 'democracy' we refer to a system of political organization in which power resides in the entire citizenry. Decisions acquire legitimacy precisely when they are made by the majority, either directly or indirectly - through representatives elected by the people. We are going to refer, first of all, to pure democracy (or direct democracy), where political power is developed in assembly interaction.

DOI: 10.4018/978-1-7998-9609-8.ch007

Classical Greece is a recurring example of such a system and to some extent we could also include the cantonal mechanism practiced in some areas of Switzerland. Obviously, this system becomes little applicable when the volume of people to participate is excessively large, then direct interaction is replaced by consultative mechanisms, such as plebiscites or binding referendums (Fraguas, 1985).

Sometimes various procedures are used that lead to a semi-direct democracy, with a representative government and reserving certain decisions to some kind of direct democracy. As we will see later, this being one of the nuclei of our reflection, the extension of the Internet makes possible, at least in theory, a possible direct democratic application: digital democracy, technically already possible. It is true that, although it is used to weigh certain tendencies of the voters, it can be said that, currently, it is not used mainly for decisions of wide scope nor, of course, for the direct election of parliamentary representatives.

The most widespread formula in democratic nations, at least in the West, is the so-called liberal democracy. Here the representatives elected by the citizens They are subject to the laws, they must limit their political action and they can never circumvent certain individual or collective rights established in the constitution. In this system, typical of the rule of law, elections for representatives are combined with a plural political offer, respecting a series of fundamental rights of the people and attending to the classic division of powers of the modern rule of law, increasing with political globalization. and its effects, as explained by Azcona (2019):

Social cohesion, rational urban planning and respect for the environment are the vectors for future economic development. The above, within the main idea according to which representative and multi-party democracy has supreme value and the massive middle classes are the ones that make up the structure of progress and stability of developed societies. Globalization has created a flat world.

Representative democracy is usually considered, regardless of its specific types (parliamentary monarchy, parliamentary republic, federal republic), the most effective form when it comes to politically organizing demographically very large nations. It goes hand in hand with the so-called representative government that was installed since the 18th century after the American and French revolutions. The idea of representation demands the expression of the will, germinating a concept of the rule of law "*that links and weaves together the three premises of modern democracy: human rights, the supremacy of the law (and the constitution) and the separation of powers.*" (Olivan and Fernando, 2021). Political interaction in this model implies that voters decide who will be their political representatives, but it is true that sometimes this issue is given - or wants to be given - less importance; the representatives must be responsible and accountable for their political decisions to those who have placed in them the power that, it should not be forgotten, resides in the people. This assumption, undoubtedly, sometimes allows its questioning, as Olivan and Fernando (2017) illustrated:

The truth is that one of the great failures of democratic models has been precisely their inability to manage their aesthetics, that is, their inability to do feel that, beyond proclamations, power is and is exercised by the people. It is not enough for power, in its origin, even in its exercise, to declare itself democratic. Democratic plenitude also entails the visualization of power as a direct expression of the popular masses.

The question is, recalling Thomas's theorem, that what is understood as real is real in its consequences, so if this lack of visibility with respect to the true core of power, perception that may or may not be just a matter of Lack of political communication (or aesthetic-political marketing) is absorbed by citizens, or by them, will have real consequences in political life. It is necessary to study whether the new information and communication technologies will solve or increase this perception.

The new technologies that have emerged since the second half of the 20th century have given rise to a new stage, which goes beyond the classic change in technical innovations in production, illuminating a qualitative change in communication processes, since they generate and process information, occupying the core of the new technological paradigm and influencing not only the economic but also the socio-political. Thus, after this brief conceptual reminder, we come to the exposition of the fundamental nucleus of the essay at hand. It is a question, in fact, of exposing and analyzing whether modern forms communication technologies can - will - change these political representative systems. In the next section we will focus on seeing to what extent this is possible, to what extent communication technologies can be used in political decisions, to elect representatives or to make direct decisions. Likewise, from the perspective of the aforementioned representatives, they can be used to ascertain the popular will and promptly report on the political decisions they make and their effectiveness. In any case, its use may affect political institutions such as universal suffrage, representative assemblies, government control or the plurality of political groups.

As not everything is positive in the use of new information and communication technologies, or at least that is what we think, we must also review some debates regarding their possible negativity: the widespread false news - with the possibility of a more rapid disinformation- and bubble filters raise some questions regarding the goodness of the technological means applied in political communication. In part we find ourselves with the old controversy about the control of technologies and whether or not they are responsible for the negative effects - because no one seems to doubt the positive ones - that they entail, or it is the humans who apply them who must - we must. - bear the responsibility of its unfavorable incidence.

Finally, we will include, as a conclusion, a reflection about what has been studied where, inevitably, the personal position and considerations regarding the writing of the author of this essay are revealed more, which is obvious, they only depend on a specific perspective and do not have conceptually no value beyond the doctrinal circumstance of the contributor.

NEW TECHNOLOGICAL PARADIGM AND POLITICAL COMMUNICATION

Paraphrasing H.G. Wells, we will say that fifty years ago no one could have thought that, in the third decade of the 21st century, we would live in the era of digital communications. And yet it has happened. Web 2.0 (blogs, wikis, social-digital networks, podcasts, cloud, etc.) are surpassing in use and audience even the once powerful television, which succeeded radio broadcasting, like the press, which in turn He had done it with assemblies or gatherings as a leading communicative space. Let's reflect a little more on the so-called social networks, now digital. Social networks have existed since the beginning of social life, of the common life of human beings. As the sociologist and computer scientist Barajas Martínez (2019):

Since the term 'social network' is used both in the field of sociology and in the field of technology and, since they are not the same, some are social structures formed by people and the others are technological tools that they serve as support to the former. [...] We will call the former, the social networks defined in sociology, real social networks and the tools, digital social networks, alluding to the fact that, after all, they are computer prográms.

Digital social networks - Facebook, Linkedin, Twitter, Instagram or WhatsApp - sometimes serve to connect users, at least virtually. Or to inform yourself, biased, as for example in Google or wikis. The aforementioned author analyzes the characteristics and social importance of the most used digital networks, which we briefly synthesize to see their relationship with politics later. For example, Facebook moves into the relationship type 'friendship'. Information (messages, photos, videos, etc.) is shared with so-called digital or virtual friends. And you can value the contributions of 'friends', build groups or pages similar to traditional web pages, but almost always with an informal and playful nature, with friend search functions. Not everything is so idyllic: *"Before creating an account on Facebook, two things must be taken into account. First, that the privacy of the content you post on the network cannot be ensured and, secondly, that your content will be analyzed for commercial or political purposes."* And the algorithms that Facebook uses are used to show us political propaganda based on our behavior on the network, according to the profile that they have attributed to us and, of course, it contributes to the use of big data in electoral campaigns. Linkedin offers contacts between professionals, as well as serving for job search or, from the point of view of companies, to spread their business or glimpse possible candidates in a selection process.

It also enables the creation of groups and social networks in which matters of interest to the members of the group are discussed, which also offers information - explicit or implicit - on the political positions issued or the contacts that one maintains, with all the consequences and political applications that this may entail.

According to the research of James Fowler, an American expert in social network research, the social influence throughout the network moves to the third degree of separation. So I don't think it's a coincidence that Linkedin used this value. Twitter is distinguished by the short length of the messages and allows linking them with the `threads´. Here the relationship is defined as 'follow' and "we are all sovereign to decide who we follow. Which gives rise to a whole relationship policy in order to get the maximum number of followers.

Another characteristic is the hashtags or tags, which make it possible to propose discussion topics that, if they are followed mostly by other users who disseminate them in their messages, ends up being included in the network statistics, and may become a current topic (or trending topics).

These characteristics make the Twitter network, more than a social network, to be a network for the dissemination of ideas, in fact, Wikipedia defines it as 'microblogging'. If to all this we add the mechanism of retweeting, by which a follower can re-tweet a message to his own followers, this sense of diffusion multiplies until it reaches what has come to be called diffusion or viral marketing.

Therefore, it can be said that political events are constantly circulating in this network and that they tend to provoke attitudes for or against in a short period of time.

Instagram applies to the design and display of visual content rather than textual content. Share with Twitter the type of relationship 'follow a' and the content classification (hashtags). It is associated with mobile devices - it was born with smart phones and tablets in the 2010s - although there is a more static web version.

At the beginning, Instagram had a lot of popularity among young audiences and the contents that were shared were special moments from their daily life or images about their personal lifestyle. But soon, without losing this segment, it was expanded to people who share their professional, recreational or artistic activities as a way of creating a personal brand and, finally, companies that do not disdain the opportunity to penetrate their target markets have landed.

And here, of course, political parties and other ideological organizations have also set their sights on influencing opinions and behaviors from there. We could, without a doubt, add others to these digital networks. We will only mention, to finish the example, WhatsApp, an application for creating and organizing chats that was started for mobile phones, but which is now also compatible with the web, and that spreads texts, photos or videos, both family members and professionals, or it disseminates political ideas, being probably the most widely used instant messaging application (it currently has more than two billion users worldwide).

It is doubtful that all of these "cyber social" networks truly enhance real sociability. Although this does not occupy the center of our argument if it has to do with the ability to reach, for example, political agreements. Author such as Rendueles (2013) believes that:

In reality, 2.0 tools have not solved the problem of the fragility of the social bond in modernity or the fragmentation of the postmodern personality, rather they have made it more opaque through the dissemination of computerized social prostheses. [...] Communication technologies have generated a diminished social reality, not an increased one. For the first time, mass culture is more than a metaphor. The Internet has not improved our sociability in a post-community environment, it has simply lowered our expectations regarding social bonding. Nor has it increased our collective intelligence, it simply prompts us to lower the bar for what we consider to be an intelligent comment (one hundred and forty characters is actually a modest threshold).

Rendueles alludes to Kierkegaard's position on the expansion of the press and magazines in the first half of the 19th century.

While most thinkers of the time celebrated the expansion of the press and magazines as a way of democratization, Kierkegaard believed that it was detrimental to political life. Newspapers were on the fringes of power structures, but they made it easy for their readers to hold very vivid opinions on almost any topic of public interest. On the other hand, they did not develop to the same degree the impulse to act accordingly. On the contrary, the saturation of conflicting opinions and information led to indefinitely postpone any important decision. Ultimately, the press destroyed genuine political activity, which for Kierkegaard had to do with intense commitments and risky decisions.

If we compare with the current explosion of information, it is surely legal to conclude that the diagnosis has worsened; Although the mobilizing potential of digital networks exists, it is not easy to accept that it is collective - and reflected - decisions that lead to certain actions. *"The Internet generates an illusion of intersubjectivity that, however, does not compromise us with norms, people and values."* Rendueles' critical judgment deserves, at the very least, a pause in celebrating the positivity of digital communication, at least in the political arena if we want to speak of true democracy. *"Democracy cannot be fragmented into individual decision packages because it has to do with the commitments that constitute us as individuals with some kind of coherence, with a past and some remote expectation of the future. And that is an anthropological reality incompatible with cyberfetishism and sociophobia.*" Really, according to the quoted author, we allow ourselves to doubt: is the digital boom useful for real social life - life together and mutual care - or is it just a piece of props?

"*The truth is that free access to the Internet not only does not immediately lead to political criticism and citizen intervention but, in any case, mitigates them. [...] Empirical evidence consistently suggests that the Internet limits cooperation and political criticism, it does not encourage them.*" And Rendueles adds: "*Actually, the idea that technology can help strengthen and expand the bonds between people is quite exotic.*" To be rigorous, we must say that the truly relevant information that comes to us through new technologies is still fairly controlled and, furthermore, it does not necessarily facilitate sociability or political commitment.

The considered main specialist in the study of the interaction between new technologies and human beings, Turkle (2017) analyzed in an ambitious investigation the challenges that the new digital world poses to us as citizens. "*Although the Internet provides incomparable tools to receive information and mobilize to take action when faced with a problem that worries us, it tempts us to withdraw to what I would call reality online.*" The researcher compares, referring to the contributions of Malcolm Gladwell, online activism, with weak ties, with that supported by stronger ties, such as that carried out during the movement in favor of civil rights in the United States. "*If you want to stand up to political authority, Gladwell says, if you want to take that kind of risk, you need more trusting ties, based on a deeper story.*" We also agree with Rendueles (2013) when the researcher questions, in a hypothetical question with an obvious negative answer, the strength of technological ties: "*Is a conversation in a chat a social bond such as a family relationship or with an affinity group*". Weak ties are those that arise from relationships with acquaintances, or friends of friends - typical in social networks (Saura et al., 2022); While strong ties exist with those whom we really know, we have personal, emotional contacts in some sense and, above all, in whom we trust.

REPERCUSSIONS ON DECISIONS FROM POLITICAL POWER

In this section the question that concerns us is to think about the influence that the aforementioned new communication technologies (and others that we do not make explicit due to space issues) have on political decisions taken from power. We distinguish two vectors in interaction: how public opinion captured in the aforementioned communication forms influences decisions, as the prediction of voting intention is now easier, and how the management of new communication tools shapes public opinion itself. According to Castells (2009), the communication / power connection, with the increasingly high relationship between information technologies and the exercise of power, their access and dissemination, mark a new social - and, therefore, political - difference in favor of those who can impose new symbolic universes, leaving on the sidelines or as mere spectators those who do not control the transmission mechanisms. And this despite the fact that communication through the Internet makes those that previously were exclusively receivers in potential emitters, constituting what Castells calls 'self-communication of the masses'.

As Echeverría (1999) states:

The new information and telecommunication technologies are having a profound social impact on the entire planet, especially in the most developed countries. The rapid growth of the Internet telematics network represents an important step towards the construction of a global, electronic and digital city, which a few years ago I proposed to name Telepolis.

It is true that now any individual, at least those in the most technologically advanced countries, can launch their messages to crowds, but the probability that this will occur and have a substantial impact is much lower than if the sender is a source, government, business, or a large social movement.

The control of the agenda setting, it is well known, largely marks the interest of the audiences in a given period of time. And this happens even though the internet is an open, global network that works in real time and uninterruptedly and is multidirectional. Furthermore, as Castells (1996) indicates:

The inclusion of the majority of cultural expressions within the integrated communication system, based on digitized electronic production and distribution and the exchange of signals, has important consequences for social forms and processes. On the other hand, it considerably weakens the symbolic power of the traditional transmitters external to the system, which they transmit through the social customs codified by history: religion, morality, authority, traditional values, political ideology. It is not that they disappear, but they weaken unless they are recoded in the new system.

And in this new system, the rules of the game and control are not, at least currently, fully balanced, although Castells is optimistic about the future:

The information technology revolution will accentuate its transformative potential. The 21st century will be marked by the completion of the global information superhighway, which will decentralize and spread the power of information, fulfill the promise of multimedia, and increase the pleasure of interactive communication. Electronic communication networks will constitute the backbone of our lives.

That future is not here yet... we will cross that river when we get to it. Now the scene is not so idyllic, although communication is the key element of contemporary developed societies (Castells, 2006).

Relating new technologies and democracy, which concerns us in this essay, and entering a little more in the debate about the plural use of new communication technologies, V. Romano (2004) reminds us that: "*There have always been those who believe that social organization can transform itself by managing existing resources in a more rational way, simply by letting 'progress' run its course.*" There is no doubt that computer networks facilitate communication and have an impact on political life.

The democratic potential of new technologies is attributed to this circumstance. As tools they are undoubtedly powerful. They allow international communication easily, quickly and cheaply. But, for organizational purposes, technology is neutral, as it is used by both the authorities and those who resist it.

For us, the key issue is not that both parts of the binomial use the new communication technologies but the imbalance that still exists today in their use and, of course, the unequal impact that they entail. Romano himself admits that: "*Given the communication possibilities of the Internet, a better-informed citizenry would have more power. And this is where the weak point of the argument that equates information with power lies.*"

Do citizens have sufficient information, for example, on matters such as pollution, safety, health ...? It is a rhetorical question, of course. And if there is not enough information, there can be no rational decisions. Abounding more: "*But the fundamental inequality of power does not reside in informational inequality: those who govern and command do not do so because they know more, often they even know less. Its power lies in the ability to give or deny support to business projects and political groups. Private institutions and their "quasi-public"* associates have the management structures and financial power, the State has the legal institutions and the coercive force, if necessary.

VARIOUS FORMS OF THE TECHNOLOGICAL / POLITICAL LIE

The lie in politics is not a novelty brought by the new communication technologies Courtine (2019) reflected on this in her introduction to Jonathan Swift's classic pamphlet (The Art of Political Lying), making it clear that its effects are present "*in all political reflection from Plato's Republic to the Prince of Machiavelli: Should we hide the truth? the people for their own good, deceive them to safeguard them?*". Here he refers to the lie as a falsehood with a good end, for the benefit of the people; although this is not always the case, obviously, but sometimes to simply make him submissive and, of course, professional politicians are not the only ones to lie. "*Everyone lies: the ministers deceive the people to rule them, and the latter, to get rid of them, circulate slanderous gossip and false rumors.*"

In order to carry out this noble purpose of deceiving to a successful conclusion "*it is necessary to be able to count, first of all, with a mass of credulous people willing to repeat, spread, spread everywhere the false news that others have invented. (Courtine, 2019)*". The truth is that, currently, this diffusion is carried out more quickly, and we could say that in geometric progression, with the new existing media, even more at the disposal of those who hold power, especially in electoral processes, you can see entire shipments of lies. The aforementioned author says that: "*Today the lie is electronic, instantaneous, global. [...] The distinction between truth and lies is becoming more and more complex. Information or intoxication? Nobody can tell them apart anymore. Perhaps we are approaching that ideal state in which political discourse will finally get rid of that ghost of truth, which sometimes still haunts it like atavistic remorse.*" Perhaps a law that punishes politicians who lie, who do not comply with what is stated in their campaigns, would partly avoid so much falsehood, but it is difficult, because the laws are promoted by the politicians themselves, therefore: *lasciate ogni speranza.*

One of the classic forms of this misinformation has been rumors (the rumor is information without contrast, propagated as a truth and that can finally be verified or forgotten), easy to produce since each person usually changes something the news when repeating it. Given its importance, we will expand a little more on the rumors. The study of rumor is ancient. As early as 1726 rumors were defined as: "*false or fabricated reports that are maliciously spread by malicious people, without confirmation, with malicious intent or perhaps for pleasure or pleasure. (1985)*"

It is evident that: "*with the appearance of the internet they have become ubiquitous. In fact, today we are surrounded by them (Sunstein, 2010).*" *It goes to the point that the internet allows people to live in information bubbles or resonance chambers made for them, so that different rumors take hold in different communities.*" Without going into a broad compilation of rumor conceptualizations, we believe it is convenient for a better understanding of this section to collect some relevant definitions.

For Allport et al. (1973) and Postman, initiators of the scientific study of the rumor: "*It is a specific proposition to believe, which is passed from person to person, usually orally, with no reliable evidence to prove it.*" For Sills (1974) who is in charge of the explanation of the rumor in the International Encyclopedia of Social Sciences, the rumors are: "*Descriptions, forecasts or explanations of events that are formed, to a large extent, in informal encounters, and that although not have been confirmed by authorized sources are, however, taken seriously into account by a considerable part of a community interested in it."*

As stated in Pinazo and Molpeceres (2006), Edgar Morin, author of one of the best-known studies on rumors (The Orleans rumor), understands by pure rumor: *"A topical information that circulates in a social group outside of the social communication media and very poorly founded."* According to Kapferer (1989), president of the Foundation for the Study of Information on Rumors: *"We will call rumors the appearance and circulation in the social community of information that has not been publicly confirmed by official sources, or that they have denied."* With these few but authoritative definitions we can appreciate the basic notes of the rumor: unproven propositions, which are transmitted personally and informally without a clear intended recipient and which are disseminated due to the interest of the recipients - later issuers - in said information. In addition, precisely because of the informal chain that is established, the distortion of the initial news is inevitable.

Just to illustrate this question, and without the intention of being exhaustive, we mention the three types of rumors originally proposed by Robert H. Knapp and collected by Pinazo and Molpeceres (2006): *"the rumors that expressed wishes and desires, those that expressed fears and anxieties and the rumors aggressive."* As the referenced authors point out: *"The scheme developed by Knapp to classify rumors was a significant step to facilitate the study of rumor. His scheme has been reduced in current research to a dichotomous focus: a) analyze the spread of rumors of wishes, and b) analyze the spread of rumors of fear."*

Following Runciman (1999) the problem of diluting a rumor is complex. It can be affirmed that, on many occasions, the attempt to dismantle it turns against and the rumor acquires more firmness. Bismarck is credited with the ironic - or not so ironic - phrase: "Do not believe anything until it has been officially disproved." That idea is old, as the old Latin adage reflects: *Plus augmentatur rumors, quando negantur.* When trying to correct the information contained in a rumor, the aforementioned effect is almost always produced, for various reasons:

First, the correction can annoy them and put them on the defensive, if this happens, it can produce dissonance and, for this reason, that strengthen what they believed before. Second, to an unreasonable person the very existence of the correction will tend to confirm the truth of the previous belief. Why bother to correct a claim unless there is some truth to it? Perhaps those who seek to · correct · are insisting too much; insistence confirms the truth of what is denied. Third, correction will focus people's attention on the issue under discussion, and their focus on it may strengthen support for the opinion they already have.

In certain situations, however, contradicting the rumor may not be so negative. *"Now we can identify the circumstances in which the corrections are not so counterproductive. If those who hear the false rumor have no compelling reason to accept it, if their prior knowledge is weak or non-existent, and if they trust those who offer the correction, the corrections will eliminate the false rumors."*

Runciman (1999) offers us here some basic keys to mitigate the effects of a rumor and neutralize it: interest, knowledge and trust in the source. The situation in which the rumor is born is also decisive in its spread: *"When conditions are bad, rumors, both true and false, tend to spread like wildfire. It has been observed that rumors are easy in situations characterized by social tension."* Referring to rumors in general, as indicated in Pinazo and Molpeceres (2006), Mark L. Knapp proposed five tips to prevent their proliferation:

-Firstly, it is advisable that people maintain absolute confidence in the official media (…), so that they do not be tempted to look for information in other sources. - Secondly, it is necessary that the people maintain total faith in their leaders, that they give their trust to the Government (…) Therefore, no means should be spared to avoid mistrust and suspicions, a true breeding ground for rumors. . - When a very important event takes place, disseminate as much information as possible as soon as possible. Rumors are born from questions that people ask spontaneously and for which no answer has been pronounced. These questions respond to the need to understand the event in case some aspect is not seen clearly. –Disseminating information does not guarantee that it necessarily has a receiver. All foci of ignorance must be removed. –Since leisure awakens an avidity for the most insignificant noises capable of disturbing the monotony, it is necessary to keep the population protected from idleness through work or the organization of their free time.

Trust, sufficient communication, knowledge, and activity are the keys that are extracted from this long appointment regarding the fight against rumors and that are repeated in the cases that occur in companies and institutions. Sometimes a rumor can be stopped by breaking the chain of transmission, of contagion, as proposed by Ramon-Cortés (2007): *"Get a potential transmitter to agree not to spread a rumor and to break the chain."* But it is not easy to discover these transmission belts once they are put into operation, not even in digital transmission. In reality, the loss of confidence is very difficult to restore, and personal contact is essential.

I want to say that I have dedicated myself to giving information with all kinds of details about little things that seemed irrelevant to me, but that generated some rumor; (…) I have dedicated myself to explaining to a series of people one by one and personally. (…) And I have noticed that I have regained the lost confidence of some members of the team." "Deep down, good prior personal communication is what even prevents the birth of rumors. [...] Anticipating every possible rumor by providing real and accurate information was the way to avoid `infections´ (Ramon-Cortés, 2007).

The communication policy is essential, a good internal communication system avoids or at least attenuates the rumor. *"My strategy of `breaking the chains´ is clear: I try to offer as much information as possible to avoid that, if missing, it is replaced by rumors."* (Ramon-Cortés, 2007). This action can immunize against rumors, because it is more than likely that they arise, as we saw above, when information about a matter of interest is missing. And it is aggravated by mistrust, which also has to do not only with the credibility of the source, but also with the personal contact of the manager or command with his subordinates or the leader with his followers. Ramon-Cortés exposes a series of actions, skills and attitudes that anyone with others in their charge must consider in order, as far as possible, to immunize themselves against rumors.

We summarize them below:

1 / Know people well. 2 / Know interpersonal relationships. Instead of carrying out large-scale actions involving the entire organization, selective actions must be taken with the key people who can stop the process. 3 / Fight against reservoirs. 4 / Be transparent. 5 / Be clear. 6 / Be quick. 7 / Have courage. 8 / Be upright. (Ramon-Cortés, 2007).

However, as this author points out, these principles do not always and in any case prevent the emergence of a rumor and if it starts, we can take some actions so that at least it does not spread massively: "

1 / Be faster than rumors. Once the presence of rumors in the organization is detected, it is necessary to act urgently. Offer accurate, clear and sufficient information, anticipating the next mutation. You have to objectify the information with real data and counteract the power of rumors with even more powerful messages. 2 / Breaking the chains of contagion. Act on those people who can break the chains of transmission of a certain rumor. Instead of carrying out large-scale actions involving the entire organization, selectively engage with the key people who can stop the process. 3 / Fight against reservoirs. Systematically eliminate sources of rumors: criticism, speculation about the decisions made, misinterpretations ... Do not participate in the transmission of non-verified information. And detect and act with those people who, in each organization, are great reservoirs of rumors, analyzing the reasons that explain the reason for their actions. Only then can they be deactivated. (Ramon-Cortés and Ferran, 2007)

For the least appearance of rumors, we reiterate, personal interaction is decisive and must be based on trust. *"The problem of the extinction of the rumor is above all a question of people: the act of believing depends on who is speaking. If there is no reliable issuer, the fight against rumors is doomed to failure."* (Ramon-Cortés and Ferran, 2007)

And Kapferer (1989) insists on this in his reference to the very birth of the rumor.

Since rumors are often born from mistrust of official versions, the key to prevention is also the credibility of the sources. This trivial recommendation raises, as we have seen, important practical problems. For someone to have credibility, it is not enough to affirm it; it is necessary to have proof of it; that is, to be known as a person who always tells the truth as it is. This precept has a very difficult application in times of crisis, precisely because it often seems preferable not to divulge the information, or to disguise it.

Surely here lies the difficulty: finding credible people because they never manipulate the information. And it is worse, most likely, to tell part of the truth than to say nothing, because the most dangerous liars are those who include a true part of their information that is essentially false.

Falsehood in political communications, rumors and hoaxes (the Royal Spanish Academy defines hoax as false news propagated with some strategic purpose), almost certainly have existed, as we said, since the beginning of social life and, therefore, Hence, since the beginning of democracy. What happens is that now the transmission of disinformation is faster and easier. And this, necessarily, has consequences in the decisions and in the formation of the political conscience of the citizenship. The paradox is that we have more information available, but it is not easy to detect whether this information is true or false. We will briefly review the characteristics of some of these tools and their circulation on digital networks. The so-called fake news - false news -, such as hoaxes, rumors, smoke curtains and probe balloons, have had a considerable increase since the generalization of the Internet, so that they are increasingly present in the information.

According to the Collins dictionary (2017) the word fake was originally used as part of the jargon spoken among criminals who wanted to hide their activities, it began as a verb, and it referred to producing a falsified version of something, such as money or documents. Fake (false) began to be associated with news (news) in comedy shows, but it was in 2005 when the term began to be used as false news disseminated with malicious intentions (Ribeiro-Navarrete et al., 2021; Saura et al., 2021).

Although the main platforms on which these phenomena spread are social networks, the classic mass media also reproduce them, given the immediacy that the transmission of news requires and its lack of contrast on many occasions. Fake news is a big problem and, on many occasions, they even question the acceptance of news that is true (Saura et al., 2021a). It is difficult to assess the certainty of a news item. New technologies allow the spread of false news to increase and for these, as stated in the newspaper La Tribuna (2018), to take possession of space on social networks. Its power is so great that, for example, according to a study carried out by the Association of Internet Users (2018), 70% of Spaniards did not know how to distinguish between true and false news. Knowing the reality allows recipients to find out about the world, but the constant and vast flow of information and false news limit credibility, generating disinformation. Wardle (2017) who calls misinformation "information disorder", explains that it occurs when we refer to news that is not verified, when we share false information to do harm, as well as to bad information that is constructed to harm in a way. conscious through information. Disinformation, strictly speaking, must be understood as a phenomenon that encompasses more than fake news, and welcomes any false information system, which is not entirely accurate and includes a voluntary component of harm to others (Saura et al., 2022a).

Many false news that are spread by the network are mixed with real information, with the aim of confusing the reader, so that the false part is treated as real. The spread of hoaxes on the Internet is becoming an increasingly serious problem. It is true that on certain occasions false information is published due to lack of time, due to the haste to inform the former, due to lack of time to contrast or even due to lack of good sense; This has happened timelessly, but new technologies, especially digital social networks, have made it even easier to spread (Saura et al., 2021b).

On certain occasions, so-called probe balloons are launched to assess the effect that a measurement could have on the affected population and, depending on the reaction that occurs, implant it later or not. The well-known smoke screens can also be used, spreading information to distract from a matter on which the issuer is not interested in paying public attention. The Internet has been an essential vehicle in the growth of various forms of false news, since the anonymity of the network makes its publication less compromised, as well as very fast since millions of people can have instant access to them.

The use of the Internet has made the filters for the publication of content disappear, as it did in traditional media when expert professionals determined whether the information was truthful and relevant to the public; Now any content can be disseminated without any verification for the reader, and if a news reaches you through Facebook or WhatsApp, for example, you can understand it as true and share it automatically (Saura et al., 2021c; Saura et al., 2021d).

Regarding the channels for accessing political information, it must be said that they have been intensely diversified since the beginning of the 21st century, changing a system until then dominated by traditional media: radio, television and the press. This change has not been homogeneous populationally speaking; According to various surveys, clear differences are observed between the different age groups, not only with respect to the use to obtain information, but even in their consumption. These differences are very visible in the age groups under 44 years of age, who mostly consume internet spaces, leaving more aside traditional media, even more so in the age group between 18 and 33 years old and differing from the rest of the sections also by the spaces from Internet used for information, predominantly the use of certain social networks such as Twitter, Instagram and YouTube, different from the age group between 33 and 43, which use more specialized pages and social networks such as Facebook and WhatsApp. From the 44-year-old age group on, the use of the internet to find out about day-to-day politics begins to decline notably in favor of traditional media, although the trend leads to these differences between the different sections being reduced.

When commenting on the possible disinformation in political news, we must mention, at least, the ways in which it reaches society thanks to various techniques that are not appreciable a priori when a political party uses them, most of them related to language and public speaking. In the end, what is hidden behind this is a manipulation of information, orienting it in a position in which it benefits a specific political group or lobby, negatively affecting the adversary.

We will cite, without the intention of being exhaustive, those that we understand to be the most used:

- Demonizations: they consist in qualifying the adversary as an "evil" figure, positioning himself on the opposite side of "the good". This is one of the most used techniques in politics today. We can observe it on a daily basis, when the most populist parties located in extremes pigeonhole their rivals, placing them in a part of the political spectrum (fascism, communism, neoliberalism) or awarding them political measures that do not correspond to their program.
- Deterrent Adjectives: with which we can see how language in politics is a very powerful weapon. The use of dissuasive and negative words is part of common political discourse. They are intended to exclude any type of reply, leaving the argument unanswerable in a way. Some examples of this are adjectives like: shameless, illegitimate, indisputable, disloyal, that we have read or heard more than one once in political communications. They are used to finish off a speech in some way, making it more difficult to refute, as the rival has to justify the other's fallacies; Within the framework of disinformation, they are very important, since they accompany speeches that, although full of lies, are difficult to refute.
- Logans: phrases that are easy to memorize, hooky and that can be recorded in the collective mind. However, they easily hide false messages, difficult to forget due to their social penetrability.
- Scapegoats: it is about charging an adversary with the blame for an event, without delving into the solutions or the real origin of the problem. We can observe it in the question of the current house price, crisis, social conflicts, by blaming the adversary for it and also manipulating the information: the party that uses this technique is positioned as the only one that can solve the problem.
- Spread of Misinformation: Fake news directly or indirectly influences our decision-making as free citizens that we are, and in the case of politics this influence is usually direct, destined to condition and guide our vote towards a political party.

Likewise, virtual social networks are perfect spaces for the proliferation of echo chambers: digital bubbles have become real cases of cultivation and dissemination of false news that are very present in the political scene. They exist for psychosociological principles: to trust 'people who think like me and believe in the things that I believe'. Selective exposure, perception and memory work here, with a confirmation bias enhanced in social networks thanks to the model of fleeting information, based on headlines, which encourages real misinformation and does not deepen.

The problem arises with the quality of the information transmitted or sought, since it is often selected by the networks themselves. Google, in an example that can be extended to other similar media, creates a personalization of the news and the information that the subject is interested in seeing, according to the cookies accepted on the pages they have previously entered. An algorithm constantly tries to crystallize the interests of the user in order to build a profile so that, when entering its page, the contents are appropriate since they have been previously announced. Cookies are files that are downloaded to a computer or a device used (smartphone, tablet, connected television) when accessing certain web pages or applications. Cookies make it possible to collect statistical information, facilitate certain technical functionalities and store and retrieve information about the browsing habits or preferences of a user or her team.

By accepting it, Google understands that those pages that have been accessed are of interest to the person and, therefore, the products or even news from a newspaper of a specific ideology visited will appear first in a similar search. In this way, users, when searching in a browser, access only the news or information that interests them according to, for example, their ideology, leaving aside other information, which results in partial access to reality.

We find the so-called bubble filter that, following Pariser (2017), refers to the informational isolation where users would be trapped as a result of these configurations. Access to information and participation on the web is conditioned by the algorithmic design of the platforms used to enter it, and we cannot escape the aforementioned personalization, since all interaction in Google is like that, with the addition that many Users are not even aware of the bias – ideological, political – in the information. In most cases this information is of a political nature and it is not very daring to affirm that political parties are a source of misinformation, with great impact on society, in their attempt to obtain accessions and, ultimately, votes.

When a political party, or a coalition of several of them, comes to the government of a nation, it usually uses new technologies to increase its power, and there are two circumstances that interest us: the greater availability of tools for information / disinformation and the greater significance of what it circulates through digital social networks that increasingly replace traditional media, so the responsibility derived from this greater power should also be greater in terms of the consequences of the aforementioned effects. Thanks to big data, it will be known quite precisely what we are going to vote for, when quantum computing is fully developed, which is already a new technological race, estimating the experts that it may culminate in 2030-2035; a single computer will be able to do in seconds what today's supercomputers can take 10,000 years, including classified information or private emails. It will be easier to access other people's secrets from the analysis of large databases to which, obviously, not everyone will have the same access. The business race seems led by Google, while geopolitics involves a technological dispute between China, the United States and the European Union.

INCIDENCE OF NEW COMMUNICATION TECHNOLOGIES IN POLITICAL PARTICIPATION

The question that prompts us to reflect in this section focuses on the debate regarding whether the new information and communication technologies (ICT) will change the forms of political participation to some extent. In principle, there seems to be agreement that the technologies currently available allow new forms of political participation. Of incidence in political campaigns or in the evaluation of political leaders.

The connection between the government and citizens can change and there is an increase in participation and democratic awareness, although the democratic countries that exist today are not many more than those counted before the irruption in our lives of ICTs. We will focus first on advocacy in political campaigns. It is well known that:

During the 2008 United States presidential elections there was a drastic increase in the use of the internet in all political campaigns, but Obama's in particular benefited from the power of online social networks and social media (person to person). Many have commented on Obama's extraordinary ability to connect with voters, but even more impressive was his ability to connect voters with others. (Christakis et al., 2010)

And for that the use of online networks was decisive, in the hypothesis that we do not vote alone: *"There is numerous evidence that shows that a single individual's decision to vote increases the chances that others will vote as well."*

The extended "civic duty" to vote seems to be contagious if we know that others do. If a politician manages to be better connected and connect hypothetical voters with each other - in a kind of online activism - he can produce a current of vote in his favor. Christakis et al. (2010) explain that *"the idea of voting is so ingrained that, even, between 20 and 30% of respondents lie when they respond in a poll saying that they have voted in a certain election when they have not."* It is possible that they do so because of a possible fear of social sanctions or, perhaps, because they believe that their electoral action may influence others, participation or abstention, depending on our answer. But *"we have the explanation for why we vote: because we are connected and the decision to go to vote is something rational precisely because of these connections."*

The question that we will rethink later is whether this impact of connections with others when going to a vote can be more effective when it occurs on online networks or through direct and personal presence. For the authors mentioned: *"The use of the Internet and mobile telephony in the Obama presidential campaign demonstrates the true power of online social networks."* (Christakis et al., 2010).

That is, it obtained electoral gains from digital social networks, bringing more people to the polls. It also seems true, as the authors themselves put it, that: *"Activists around the world are starting to use the Internet to organize large-scale demonstrations."* From which we can also deduce that technological networks also serve for the preparation of real concentrations of people who, undoubtedly, also influence electoral decisions, so their incidence is - or can be - double.

There is a nuance, and that is that this happens more easily if there is already some kind of previous personal connection.

From a global point of view, the experience of real social networks indicates that virtual networks can be used to improve the existing flows between friends and relatives in the real world, but we still do not know if the Internet will increase the speed or the scope of social contagion in general. (Christakis et al., 2010)

If we apply this to the decision to vote, it seems that virtual networks are going to influence more if we already know the other: family member, friend, colleague, co-religionist ..., which, on the other hand and together with the concept of identification, it leads us to think that virtual social networks are multiplier tools as long as we have some real social link with the senders of messages in them. *"Our social networks are growing in size and speed [...] But it also gives the impression that these networks are not a new invention. We have lived with them for millions of years."* (Christakis et al., 2010)

And, as we said above, they still work. *"Ideas about behavior can spread even in the absence of direct and frequent personal contact. Still, it appears that the spread of these ideas is based on deep social connections, and therefore additional weak virtual ties will have little or no effect."* (Christakis et al., 2010). The more linked we are to others, the less preponderant is our individuality: *"By concentrating on the connections of a network, the relevance of individuals is diminished when it comes to understanding group behavior."* (Christakis et al., 2010).

What we maintain, following experts in group behavior, Durkheim (1982), is that personal contact, face to face, even more so if it is collective, as occurs in massive social celebrations, electoral events, demonstrations, concentrations or popular festivals, generates a psychosocial spirit of identification and encourages the sharing of ideas and behaviors, often putting aside individual rationality for the sake of subjective sensations that lead to making decisions, sometimes not very rational, that would never have been chosen lonely.

And since, in the end and in the end, one is usually alone in front of the computer or the mobile screen, the effect of interpersonal contagion, produced by the effervescence that others generate when they are there in person and there are many, does not occur in these online contacts. Therefore, since there is a "distant" impact (which, by the way, already occurred in the first television debate between Nixon and Kennedy) we understand that it will never be the same as that made possible by the direct mass presence. Oliván (2017, 2021) explains this question:

The great step is not only in the construction of ideological models, not even in the appearance of groups and masses that follow them, but in that this ideological component is capable of turning these groups into true actors. politicians, with an efficiency even higher than that of family clans or religious groups in the past.

The final objective of a political ideology requires action, generally real, which is what sustains or modifies what exists. You can increase political reflection thanks to digital networks, but reflection without action is of little use. *"Only at the moment when the assembled multitude is capable of acting as an organic unit, when its force reaches the perfect sum of all the individual vectors that compose it, only at that moment, we say, does the political unit appear."* (Durkheim, 1982) Is there political unity in a digital forum? How effective is it for real action?

In any case, the doubt about its effectiveness remains open. We cannot forget that, given the public nature of the forum, a square open to all, the Internet continues to be a fundamentally private space. Users only reach political competition if they are customers of one or another service provider company. In short, there is no public Internet, but the political act needs a recognizable space as everyone's.(Durkheim, 1982)

We add the collective communication deficiency that is undoubtedly seen in digital networks compared to traditional ones. Not only because of the difficulty of not seeing everyone at the same time and not hearing them simultaneously, with the lost nuances of non-verbal communication (kinesic, paralinguistic, proxemic, impact of personal appearance) but because the real distance prevents the degree of collective interaction at emotional levels, which does occur with face-to-face social interaction. Part of the group factor is lost. And this, logically has to influence individual decisions, politically speaking. We will return to this idea, with its corresponding adaptation, in the next section when evaluating the possibility of electronic voting.

ABOUT ELECTRONIC VOTING

Technological advances, since punch card systems began to be used in the 1960s, have made it possible for political elections to be made through electronic systems, sometimes in person and selecting the option on a screen installed in the room. of voting and on other occasions, this is what is most interesting in this essay, at a distance, each voter from his computer, outside the electoral counting center.

So that the latter has not become generalized, with the undoubted economic and temporal advantages that it brings, psychosocial factors are influencing more than the purely technical ones. The most advanced technology in this regard collides with the problem of confidence that the vote cast by this system is actually counted, on the one hand because a cyberattack on said process is far from being unfeasible, but fundamentally because the recount is not carried out by people. with their corresponding supervisors and the technological mechanism and its controls remain outside the technical understanding of the majority of current citizens, which undermines social trust in the system and prevents its widespread implementation: among 188 countries, 14.6% uses electronic voting in national elections, 8.4% regionally and 2.2% locally (Institute for Democracy and Electoral Assistance, 2021).

Electronic voting in polling stations or online, as a trial, has been carried out in Germany, Argentina, Australia, Brazil, Belgium, Canada, Estonia, France, Ireland, Italy, Norway, the Netherlands, Romania, Switzerland, the United Kingdom and Venezuela. In the United States of America and France it has been used in the primary elections of political parties. In September 2000, the European Commission launched a project, with tests in Germany, France and Switzerland, to clarify that fully verifiable online elections that guarantee absolute privacy of votes using fixed and mobile internet terminals were possible.

Why has an electronic voting system not been generalized and implemented? The advantages are evident in terms of reducing the time for collecting and counting votes, avoiding travel - with the corresponding financial savings - and facilitating voting for people with a physical disability, whether this is temporary or not. In contrast, we must mention the possibility of a possible failure in the electronic components of the system, which cannot be ruled out.

The problem is not only a lack of confidence in the technological procedure for voting. There are social components that generate even more doubts. For example, the difficulty of securing the identity of a voter who does so remotely. Despite the fact that a digital document assures us that whoever is casting the vote is the one authorized to do so (and that trusting that this cannot be falsified), no one can certify that they do so privately, freely and at their full will, as it happens when the members of a polling station verify that the person who casts the vote is the one who should do so. In the case of "cyber voting" there may be someone close to them who forces the subject to cast a specific vote, not so in face-to-face voting in which, as is mandatory, there are booths with the ballots so that the privacy of the vote is guaranteed.

In addition, the day of the elections physically going to vote is traditionally, and the traditions weigh on social life, something like a "party of democracy", a kind of ceremonial, and as it is part of the democratic culture it is very complicated may that well-established cultural tradition change. Electoral campaigns, with their rallies and debates, are collective acts with a real presence and culminate in a voting day with people in the streets to go to vote, with lines of people in front of the polling stations, being able to recognize and interact with neighbors, relatives or coreligionists who participate in the vote -which can encourage others to do so- and there is, in general, a group environment that collides with the loneliness of the computer voter.

Deutsch and Gerard (1973) in their classic experimental research on the influence of the group on the individual, have long found that: *The normative social influence on the individual criterion will be greater in the individuals that form a group than in a simple aggregation of individuals. that they do not compose a group."* Go to vote in the company of relatives, or meet neighbors when doing so, to be able to chat in person before and after even though the vote itself is always personal and if we want anonymous, the fact that the town and neighborhood are especially busy in that mission of voting and making it visible, undoubtedly encourage them to do so and give the act a sense similar to the original one of meeting in the agora to make political decisions. Voting alone from a digital device is very different. We do not see groups of people, we do not observe the environment. And this social factor surely influences the fact that, despite its real possibility, electronic voting has not become widespread.

CONCLUSION

The new information and communication technologies are changing the world we used to know, globalization is our new state. This change affects all areas and has an impact, as is obvious, also in political life, seeking the support of these new media to extend and perhaps update the classic concept of democracy. The essence of democracy continues to be participation, those who have the 2009, the Constitutional Court of they delegate power to representatives to exercise it on their behalf. The point is that, given that we are still immersed in the aforementioned change, there are no definitive results on the interaction between politics and new communication technologies. But there are various contributions that, apart from describing the state of the matter and trying to answer some basic questions, can lead us to explain and assess their direction.

Regarding the decisions made by political power, we observe that modern technologies facilitate the knowledge that professional politicians have of the electorate, including the meaning of future votes. In addition, they make it possible to use mechanisms to contrast the measures before they are definitively carried out. The now called social networks are actually digital social networks, or virtual ones. Social networks have always existed, social interaction in groups in which people participate directly are the authentic social networks, without more. Political news has always been disseminated through social networks, the difference is that, currently, with digital networks, this process is perhaps more comfortable and simple and, of course, faster and with more scope, but also more susceptible to the use of political lies, false news, hoaxes, rumors, probe balloons or smoke screens. Political lies, which are certainly not born with new technologies, previously required a certain art, a personal exhibition. Now it is easier to lie and spread misinformation.

On the other hand, there is doubt about whether the use of new technologies allows more political participation. Surely in terms of discussion, political debate, they facilitate its proliferation, but real, direct personal interaction is lost, and despite some sophisticated networks, group conjunction also disappears when making decisions, which has great psychosocial importance. Today it is possible to vote electronically, but the system has not become widespread, despite its undoubted advantages in terms of saving time and financial resources and facilitating voting in certain cases of complicated personal presence, because it raises doubts as to true anonymity the fact itself of the vote and because, undoubtedly, its use would break a long tradition of electoral days, with what this could mean. But, in addition, its massive application would make it easier to carry out something that practicing politicians, who ultimately are the ones who could make the decision to legalize an electronic voting system, would surely not fit very well: the possibility that this type Given its ease of issuance, it is not sequenced every four or five years, but in shorter periods, a year or two, being even feasible to withdraw the vote in full legislature to a party if we understand that it has disappointed us and give it to them to another at any time.

In this essay we have not gone beyond exposing a series of questions that we believe are of interest and that can serve for reflection and debate. The new information and communication technologies have already changed political life, but let us not forget that their creators, human beings, can decide - hopefully democratically - how far their future use will go.

REFERENCES

Allport, G. & Postman, L. J. (1973). La psicología básica del rumor. In *Estudios básicos de psicología social*. Tecnos.

Azcona, J. M. (2019). Historia del tiempo presente. La sociedad actual desde 1945. *Editorial Cátedra URJC-Presdeia, Madrid, 2019*, 565.

Barajas Martinez, J. C. (2019). *Andamos Muy enredados II: Redes Sociales Digitales*. Sociología Divertida. Retrieved June 26, 2021, from: http://sociologiadivertida.blogspot.com/2021/01/andamos-muy-enredados-ii-redes-sociales.html

Castells, M. (1996). La era de la información: Economía, sociedad y cultura. Vol. I, La sociedad red. *Alianza Editorial, Madrid, 1996*, 408.

Castells, M. (2006). La era de la información: Economía, sociedad y cultura. Vol. III. Fin de milenio. Alianza Editorial.

Castells, M. (2009). Comunicación y poder. Editorial Siglo XXI.

Christakis, N. A., Fowler, J. H., Diéguez, A., Vidal, L., & Schmid, E. (2010). Conectados: el sorprendente poder de las redes sociales y cómo nos afectan (No. 302.30285 C4Y.). Madrid: Taurus.

Courtine, J.-J. (2019). *Introducción: El cabal mentir", on: Swift, Jonathan, El arte de la mentira política*. Editorial Sequitur.

Deutsch, M., & Gerard, H. B. (1973). Estudio de las influencias sociales normativas e informativas sobre el criterio individual. In H. Proshansky & B. Seidenberg (Eds.), *Estudios básicos de psicología social* (p. 491). Ed. Tecnos.

Durkheim, É. (1982). *Las formas elementales de la vida religiosa* (Vol. 38). Ediciones Akal.

Echeverría, J. (1999). *Los señores del aire: Telépolis y el Tercer Entorno*. Editorial Destino.

Fraguas, M. (1985). *Teoría de la desinformación*. Editorial Alhambra.

Institute for Democracy and Electoral Assistance. (2021). *The Global State of Democracy Report 2021 - Building Resilience in a Pandemic Era*. Retrieved on January 2021 from: https://www.idea.int/gsod-events

Kapferer, J.-N. (1989). *Rumores: el medio de difusión más antiguo del mundo*. Editorial Plaza y Janés.

Oliván, F. (2017). Antropología de las formas políticas de Occidente. Escolar y Mayo Editors.

Oliván, F. (2021). La ideología de los derechos humanos. Tirant Humanidades.

Pariser, E. (2017). *El filtro burbuja: cómo la web decide lo que leemos y pensamos*. Editorial Taurus.

Pinazo, S., & Molpeceres, M. A. (2006). *¿De boca a oreja? La transmisión del rumor en la comunicación. In Psicología social de la comunicación*. Editorial Pirámide.

Ramon-Cortés, F. (2007). Virus. Un relato sobre el peligro de los rumores en las organizaciones. *Editorial RBA Edipresse, Barcelona, 2007, 83*.

Rendueles, C. (2013). *Sociofobia. El cambio político en la era de la utopía digital*. Editorial Capitán Swing Libros.

Ribeiro-Navarrete, S., Saura, J. R., & Palacios-Marqués, D. (2021). Towards a new era of mass data collection: Assessing pandemic surveillance technologies to preserve user privacy. *Technological Forecasting and Social Change, 167*, 120681. doi:10.1016/j.techfore.2021.120681 PMID:33840865

Romano, V. (2004). Ecología de la comunicación. HIRU.

Runciman, W. G. (1999). *El animal social*. Taurus.

Saura, J. R., Palacios-Marqués, D., & Ribeiro-Soriano, D. (2021c). How SMEs use data sciences in their online marketing performance: A systematic literature review of the state-of-the-art. *Journal of Small Business Management*, 1–36. doi:10.1080/00472778.2021.1955127

Saura, J. R., Palacios-Marqués, D., & Ribeiro-Soriano, D. (2022). Exploring the boundaries of Open Innovation: Evidence from social media mining. *Technovation*, 102447. Advance online publication. doi:10.1016/j.technovation.2021.102447

Saura, J. R., Ribeiro-Soriano, D., & Iturricha-Fernández, A. (2022a). Exploring the challenges of remote work on Twitter users' sentiments: From digital technology development to a post-pandemic era. *Journal of Business Research, 142*(March), 242–254. doi:10.1016/j.jbusres.2021.12.052

Saura, J. R., Ribeiro-Soriano, D., & Palacios-Marqués, D. (2021). Using data mining techniques to explore security issues in smart living environments in Twitter. *Computer Communications, 179*, 285–295. doi:10.1016/j.comcom.2021.08.021

Saura, J. R., Ribeiro-Soriano, D., & Palacios-Marqués, D. (2021a, July 15). Setting privacy "by default" in social IoT: Theorizing the challenges and directions in Big Data Research. *Big Data Research, 25*, 100245. doi:10.1016/j.bdr.2021.100245

Saura, J. R., Ribeiro-Soriano, D., & Palacios-Marqués, D. (2021b). Setting B2B Digital Marketing in Artificial Intelligence-based CRMs: A review and directions for future research. *Industrial Marketing Management, 98*(October), 161–178. doi:10.1016/j.indmarman.2021.08.006

Saura, J. R., Ribeiro-Soriano, D., & Palacios-Marques, D. (2021d). Evaluating security and privacy issues of social networks based information systems in Industry 4.0. *Enterprise Information Systems*, 1–17. doi:10.1080/17517575.2021.1913765

Sills, D. L. (1974). *Enciclopedia internacional de las ciencias sociales* (Vol. 1). Aguilar.

Sunstein, C. R. (2010). *Rumorología*. Editorial Debate.

Turkle, S. (2017). En defensa de la conversación. El poder de la conversación en la era digital. Ático de los libros.

Wardle, C. (2017). *Fake news, it's complicated*. DesinfoLab of the European Union. Retrieved on 14 July 2021 from: https://www.disinfo.eu/academic-source/claire-wardle-2017

Chapter 8
The Artificial Intelligence Implementation Challenge in the European Union and Spain

Julio Guinea Bonillo
Rey Juan Carlos University, Spain

ABSTRACT

The European Union has begun its legal development on artificial intelligence and is presented as one of the least advanced legal fields by the European institutions. Since the communication of the Commission on Artificial Intelligence for Europe was developed, different works have been addressed, such as the coordination plan on artificial intelligence of December 2018 and the White Paper on Artificial Intelligence, guiding excellence and trust to European citizens and businesses. The challenge facing Europe and Spain is not to be left behind, lagging the great powers that are making a very notable investment effort, seeking to develop this technology that is already impacting our societies. The work presents the major milestones of European action and outlines the ambitious future that awaits the European Union and Spain in the coming years, but is still unclear if there is not a decisive action implemented by all the powers concern.

INTRODUCTION

The main developments in the regulations on Artificial Intelligence are based on a previous pillar of the EU integration, the accumulated experience in the construction of the digital single market, as a vital element to complete the construction of the analog single market and perfected in its digital aspect. The accelerated technological transformation that the European Union has undergone has meant accelerating the legislative development around the fields of information and communication technology that are changing the way in which we interact, perform our job functions, we communicate, and we propose lines of business, or we undertake trips to third countries.

A process of technological convergence has begun, after the adoption of the Lisbon strategy, which gradually eliminates the existing gaps between telecommunications, broadcasting, and Information Tech-

DOI: 10.4018/978-1-7998-9609-8.ch008

nology. The European Union should start its own process of construction of a solid capacity in Artificial Intelligence and as a matter of fact, the challenge of this paper is to reflect the construction, the main developments, and the future lines of transformation at the EU and Spanish level, that may, until today, have not been addressed. The methodology requires to read the main primary sources of the Artificial Intelligence documents published by the European Commission, obtain the main inputs from the political discussions done by the EU leaders, and compare with the literature that until today has been written in this topic. The originality of this paper shows, in an orderly manner, the progress and evolution of the Artificial Intelligence implemented in the European Union and Spain, based on solid plans but without the proper attention coming from Member states. Therefore, presents the plans to effectively carry out the biggest transformation in Europe with the implementation of solid systems of Artificial Intelligence.

The roots of this process can be observed at the European Council in Seville, on June 21 and 22, 2002, the e-Europe action plans were adopted, foreseeing the necessary digital impulse that the Union should create with the new millennium. The advances stem from the framework programs in research and development, which since 2004 focused on robotic innovation and would be extended in 2010, under the Durao Barroso Commission, which had a notable determination to focus greater efforts on a powerful agenda digital, overcoming insufficient private investment, boosting productivity, and conveying to Member States the need to modernize public services. It was imperative, in the eyes of the European Commission, to start putting Europe on the rails of the new and flourishing global information society, to fully develop its capabilities.

In the multiannual financial framework from 2014 to 2020, a total of 700 million euros were invested, under the co-financing of innovation and development programs, and in which the private sector completed with a level of investments of around 2,100 million euros. An amount that has made it easier for Europe to acquire remarkable importance in the field of robotics advances, but that did not lead to a take-off of Artificial Intelligence since it is not exclusively comparable to robotics. In the Horizon 2020 program, around 1,100 million euros were dedicated to investigate everything related to Artificial Intelligence and that could be used in space technology, health, in transport, or in the analysis and management of the so-called Big data (Hilderbrandt, 2020).

The Horizon 2020 program would be one of the first mechanisms used when implementing the general lines of the European Digital Agenda. From it, full effects were deployed with the election as the new president of the European Commission to the Luxembourgian, Jean Claude Juncker. In presenting his work plan to the European Parliament, on July 15, 2014, he stressed that a new beginning was necessary for Europe, prioritizing the articulation of the Digital Single Market, based on the previous experience assumed under the development of the analogical single market.

His mandate would strengthen one of the most relevant technological areas of the XXI century and facilitated that, after the arrival of the next Commission, chaired for the first time by a woman, under the German, Ursula von der Leyen. With it, a roadmap in favor of people and sustainability would be undertaken, that is, the social agenda and the environmental agenda, and on the other hand digitization and Artificial Intelligence. To this end, a Communication entitled "Shaping Europe's digital future" was adopted, which highlighted by the Commission the main challenges on which the Union should focus.

Three decisive lines of action were identified for the next five years, given the development of new technologies, among which it should be noted: a technology at the service of people, a fair and competitive digital economy, and an open, democratic and sustainable society in the world in a digital context. In these three fields, Artificial Intelligence is intimately embedded in them, given its great empowerment and expansion experienced in recent years.

THE COMMISSION COMMUNICATION: ARTIFICIAL INTELLIGENCE FOR EUROPE

The Communication is part of the procedure the European Commission follows when faced with a new political challenge. It is a general and open policy document, aimed at EU legislators, to inform them of the situation that exists with respect to a certain issue and, generally, includes proposals to solve the problem with legislative lines that could be adopted in a near future.

Like all Communication, it is usually preceded by a public consultation, in which the Commission invites all interested parties, including citizens, companies, associations, local authorities, etc., to contribute their point of view on the issue addressed. The Commission, understanding that the EU legislation on Artificial Intelligence is failing to reach the appropriate levels of development, proposes advances in which community action could be taken. At that point, it is published a consultation document explaining the issue and inviting interested parties to contribute their point of view. Based on the responses received, possibly combined with the technical advice of consultants and technicians on the matter, it produces a Communication addressed to the Council of Ministers and the European Parliament, in which it offers a series of alternative solutions to the problem and possible advances to specify in the regulatory field. The Council and Parliament will respond, including their choice of what to do about it. On that basis, the Commission will act, possibly drafting legislation if deemed necessary.

On this basis, the first moment in which the Community institutions began to rethink the future of Artificial Intelligence for Europe was from April 25, 2018, with the Communication from the Commission to the European Parliament, the European Council, the Council, the European Economic and Social Committee and the Committee of the Regions on Artificial Intelligence for Europe.

Assuming, in the first place, that Artificial Intelligence is called to transform the lives of the next generations, it is an integral part of the daily work of human beings, helping even when performing multiple tasks from autonomous driving, the choice of a restaurant to go to or provide us with a playlist related to our tastes. The European Commission itself formulates a meaning for the term Artificial Intelligence and applies it *"to systems that manifest intelligent behaviour as they are capable of analysing their environment and taking action with a certain degree of autonomy in order to achieve specific objectives. Systems based on Artificial Intelligence can simply consist of a computer program (for example advanced robots, autonomous cars, drones or internet of things applications)"* (European Commission, 2018, p.1). The Communication was made public 15 days later, after the adoption of the International Agreement on April 10, 2018, among 24 Member States of the Union[1] plus Norway, to increase quantitatively and qualitatively investments and the development of Artificial Intelligence and which was later joined by Romania, Greece and Cyprus in May 2018. It was approved by the European Council in June 2018 and Croatia would join in July of the same year.

The experts participating in the reflection on the future of Artificial Intelligence in Europe have agreed that it is a set of systems like computer programs designed by man and that act autonomously in the analogical, as well as digital environment when they perceive around its data that is interpreted by internal algorithms and this reasoning produces the action that leads to a specific objective.

The countries of the Union are beginning to use Artificial Intelligence in sectors as fundamental as diseases and diagnostic tests, they contribute to clarify the results of medical check-ups and it is applied from the tertiary sector to the primary sector in which the wide range of new Technological opportunities facilitate the work of the agricultural sector, planting, sowing, harvesting or feeding livestock, are tasks that can be automated through the use of Artificial Intelligence.

In fact, Europe today has important elements that can project its strength and consolidate its leading role in the Artificial Intelligence environment. To do this, it is simply necessary to be able to coordinate the actions of the Member States and capitalize on 3 fundamental elements: Researchers, laboratories and emerging companies, whose activities are widely developed in this sector and are poles of innovation and growth in the field of robotics.

Secondly, the Union must be ready to take full advantage of the Digital Single Market, which is made up of the entire set of regulations and directives that have eroded the barriers that existed in the digital environment between the different Member States and, thirdly, it is necessary to make good use of the set of data from the private sector, both industry and research and also from the public sector because Artificial Intelligence is based on constant learning that comes from all data obtained from the real world.

Investment in Artificial Intelligence Planned

One of the great aspects that the European Commission highlights the most is the fact that the economic weight that the European Union maintains as opposed to the investment that is made in terms of Artificial Intelligence is clearly insufficient because it has been around 2,400 to 3,200 million euros in 2016, partially limiting Europe's potential vis-à-vis other international players. Among the Western economies, the United States is one of the countries that invests the most and that together with China are the two giants whose dominance is indisputable (Miailhe, 2020). The latter is undertaking a next-generation Artificial Intelligence development plan that wants to turn Beijing into the Asian capital that competes with Silicon Valley as a pole of extraordinary development, with his government financing the creation of a Technology Park worth more than of 1,700 million euros (Cyman, Gromova & Juchnevicius, 2021).

In that sense, Europe's competitors do not skimp on resources. The Union assumes that it must enhance its technological and industrial capacity, decisively promoting the adoption of Artificial Intelligence in all areas of economic activity, both in the public and private sectors. All the Member States must become aware of the depth that this new technological transformation entails, which will have significant socio-economic effects. For this, it must adopt a whole set of rules that raise ethical standards and safeguard legal security throughout the Union.

Until 2017, only 25% of large European companies and 10% of SMEs had introduced into their production chain and raised their digitization standards. Figures that contrast, in turn, with the fact that a third of the workforce in the European Union lacks sufficient skills to work in the digital environment at a basic level. This is one, if not the largest, of the major elements against which the Union is working to reverse the high figures, insisting that the Member States improve the training of their population, only in this way can Europe take the necessary leap and position itself to the vanguard. But member States are not progressing enough. Taking the case of Spain, the country is involved in constant fighs in favour or against nationalistic causes instead of building solid plans for future adaptation of its people.

The path envisaged by the European Union, to advance in the field of Artificial Intelligence, has required an additional effort from the public and private sectors. Both must work together to generate positive synergies and mutually increase their investment to reach 20,000 million euros. In this sense, the Community Executive plays as a fundamental protagonist, since it is the European Commission that would increase 500 million euros a year in investment since 2018, to boost growth, while it would provide its collaboration with the Member States and maintaining an adequate level of coordination, with which the necessary development objectives could be achieved. Coordination has not been proved to be enough serious at all levels between member states.

This differential fact means that the story in the construction and articulation of Artificial Intelligence in Europe takes on a special role in all economic sectors, which seek their involvement, in order to maximize the benefits with the necessary cooperation of the States, which must coordinate with each other, thus being able to transform economies into highly digitized environments and in which Artificial Intelligence could be inserted at all levels of production processes. With a budget of around 2.7 billion euros, the European Commission has supported the strengthening of research and innovation to maintain the necessary muscle in Europe (Saura, Ribeiro-Soriano & Palacios-Marqués, 2021b), but there is a lack of willingness of the member states to act in a more coordinated manner, as in other areas they have shown a lack of compromise to do so, like in the migration crisis or the Covid crisis.

The European Research Council, having a line of funding that is committed to scientific excellence, has adopted grants under the Marie Skłodowska-Curie action program that are committed to research in Artificial Intelligence. An investigation whose results must redound to business and social benefit, accessible to small and medium-sized enterprises (SMEs) from which the European labour fabric is nourished. The Commission has proposed developing an on-demand Artificial Intelligence platform that facilitates the adoption of this cutting-edge technology by economic operators, promoting a network of digital innovation poles specialized in Artificial Intelligence, as developers of said technology.

In addition, one of the issues that can help promote Artificial Intelligence in Europe is plural access to the data collected. The algorithms with which Artificial Intelligence works are nourished by a set of data and the Commission is aware that only through plural and secure access will this new technological transformation be enhanced, provided that the data does not necessarily require special protection. In this sense, the public sector and the private sector must forge a joint alliance so that, respecting the regulations on Personal Data Protection, the reuse of data is allowed that does not entail a risk on privacy (Ribeiro-Navarrete, Saura & Palacios-Marqués, 2021). Europe is committed to a support centre to share data in common and to provide technical and legal assistance, so that this European data bank can be viewed with all the guarantees.

Socio-Economic Transformation of Europe

The European Commission was aware since 2018 that Artificial Intelligence was called to completely transform all human relationships. A new era that was called to arrive with a somewhat abrupt transition. With a view to avoiding mistakes that occurred in the past, with the arrival of new technologies in work processes, this led to the emergence of social protest movements, such as Luddism, which at the beginning of the 19th century with the destruction of machines, which they came to diminish the need for labour. The Luddites marked an era and Europe must try to prevent this new technological revolution from raising the same misgivings.

For this, it is necessary, given the 3 great challenges facing the Union with the appearance of Artificial Intelligence, that society must be trained and begin to adapt to a new environment in which different skills are required. In principle, start with the education and training of citizens since a major transformation can only be accepted if the foundations are previously laid for a social adaptation through the training of people. This will mean transferring competence knowledge in digital matters so that citizens can develop their daily lives with full normality and functionality.

The European Commission has endorsed a digital education action plan to raise the digital skills and competencies of Europeans and train citizens in this vital area, but member states like Spain have failed to present any plan in this very important matter. Inequality is one of the most obvious risks that can negatively impact the economic balances of the Member States if effective measures are not established so that citizens are trained with knowledge and mastery of new technologies in this new environment. Helping in this work requires European and national structural and investment funds, the amount of which amounted to 2.7 billion euros in the multiannual financial framework from 2014 to 2020, providing specific aid to improve digital capabilities, in the same way as the Social Fund European with an amount of 2.300 million euros, but Spain has not dedicated specific resources to teach citizens or create awareness in the new transformation that AI may bring.

The need to establish specific practices, to increase advanced digital skills, from the academy to the business world, should be emphasized, promoting access to the labour market with excellent training rates. Likewise, at lower levels, such as professional training, learning in Artificial Intelligence must be assumed as a central element of their study plans, in the same way that at higher levels of formal education, postgraduate and doctoral degrees they must increase their research and your attention on this area of knowledge.

On the other hand, it is necessary to increase and strengthen social protection since there will be a great variety of less qualified jobs that, given the development of Artificial Intelligence, will undergo changes or will cease to exist and that will mean hundreds of thousands of people who will end up unemployed and who need to know how to reorient or recycle in their training and give them a new possibility of integrating into the circle of the economy. Indeed, if many jobs are to be destroyed, there will also be millions of jobs called to be created in this area, meanwhile training and protection will be prioritized, so that no one can be left behind, reinforcing social protection such as the minimum living wage so that every human being receives an economic amount that allows him to lead a life with dignity.

Promote Ethical and Legal Respect at the European Level

The European Union is based on values clearly defined in the Treaty of the Union, according to article 2 it establishes that:

the Union is based on the values of respect for human dignity, freedom, democracy, equality, the rule of law and respect for human rights, including the rights of persons belonging to minorities. These values are common to the member states in a society characterized by pluralism, non-discrimination, tolerance, justice, solidarity and equality between women and men.

This shows that if the European Union must adopt rules within the framework of Artificial Intelligence, above all the safeguarding of the dignity of every human being, full respect for the areas of individual and collective freedom, protection of democracy, as an elementary system of government, the assumption of equality as an inescapable principle in social and digital life and the promotion of Human Rights (Završnik, 2020). The General Data Protection Regulation and the rules that have been created to guarantee security in the Digital Single Market contribute positively to this as a fundamental aspect (Saura, Ribeiro-Soriano & Palacios-Marqués, 2021).

Artificial Intelligence must follow the same path and aimed at the common good of society as a whole, bet on transparency in its use, avoiding that algorithm impede the normal development of people or that it is used for malicious purposes (Larsson & Heintz, 2020). The main element to bet on Artificial Intelligence is the fact that it will mean an improvement in human life, the ultimate goal is happiness, not with the aim of using it to put society or the rule of law at risk so a discriminatory system is established.

The Union will bet on the elaboration of an ethical code in the matter of Artificial Intelligence, aligning the Charter of Fundamental Rights and increasing the security and responsibility in the use of the new tools that are created. For this, a rigorous commitment is required in favour of the correct, non-fraudulent action, sponsoring controls and supervision by the Member States and mobilizing so that they are the main interested in providing Artificial Intelligence with counterweights that avoid the excesses that could be derived from its massive use.

COORDINATED PLAN ON ARTIFICIAL INTELLIGENCE IN EUROPE: THE SPANISH CASE

The international Agreement signed on April 10, 2018, between 26 Member States of the Union[2] and Norway, sought to commit member states to a coordinated strategy on Artificial Intelligence and approved by the European Council in June 2018. Based on the voluntary and participatory commitment, sovereignly adopted on the so-called digital day of 2018, The European Commission began to draw up a coordination plan that could facilitate the spread of Artificial Intelligence by each and every one of the Europeans (Zuiderveen Borgesius, 2020).

At the same time, the trust of citizens was valued, safeguarding ethical standards and legitimate business aspirations, accelerating the development of this technology. The first starting point required a design by the Member States of national plans, or also called national strategies, which reflected the main lines of execution of the plan together with an adequate budget. According to consulting firm McKinsey (McKinsey, 2017) Europe invested between 6 and 8 less than North America in Artificial Intelligence and 3 times less than Asia.

The key point of coordination had to start with investment, and the European Union had to structure a growth in Artificial Intelligence investments from the end of 2018, moving towards a goal of 20,000 million euros, for the next decade. This was the most important elemental and transferred a financing line to the Horizon 2020 program of 1,500 million euros for the years 2018 to 2020. However, the objective for the next decade was to combine public and private investments, with the public sector corresponding to an effort of 7,000 million euros and 13,000 to private companies. However, investment would be of little use if fragmentation in the digital market continued, since companies could not assume a true economy of scale and, therefore, completing the articulation of the Digital Single Market becomes critical for the firm development of Artificial Intelligence.

The Creation of a Public-Private Pool

The robotics and big data sectors already maintain a close association between public and private entities, mobilizing more than 4,000 million euros in investments and, however, this same model must be replicated for Artificial Intelligence. The European Commission foresees that only through a reinforcement between private entities and the public sector will it be possible to achieve a development in innovation in this field, for which, we reiterate that the Academy must be a fundamental pillar in the European scientific and industrial environment.

The European Union will mobilize resources, not only to support consolidated companies in the sector, but also emerging ones, such as start-up accelerators, and the European Innovation Council will be created, with a view to supporting the most cutting-edge technological efforts and companies that are willing to innovate, regardless of their size and capacity. Along with joint international collaboration, experimentation support programs should be extended because this type of technology requires numerous tests and programs to test the systems. Requiring suitable laboratories and the adoption of a joint European testing platform that is yet to be finalized.

One of the key points emphasized by the coordination plan is to support the attraction of talent by those professionals whose training allows them to deploy all the capacities in this sector. Europe must try to offer flexibility to obtain the bureaucratic procedures in the Schengen area access and companies must understand that only through correct remuneration will they be able to establish these professionals on Community soil.

As long as Europe does not have sufficiently trained human capital to supply workforce to technology companies, it will be obliged to import workers and the blue card, which is regulated under directive 2009/50 / EC, must contemplate these assumptions. However, not only can the Union be responsible for attracting talent, but the following generations must also be trained in this very specific field with the promotion of specific studies in Artificial Intelligence. The States have been responsible for setting in different research support programs all those that focus on strengthening Artificial Intelligence, and Spain has proved no ambitious enough due to the lack of programs in secondary and high level education.

The European Data Space

Artificial Intelligence in Europe may gain strength and be operational if there are adequate systems to collect data, make it available to public and private entities, based on the premises of trust, availability and a correct infrastructure.

The algorithms that feed the autonomous decision-making processes by robots and computers, guided by Artificial Intelligence systems, require many data to be able to operate. The algorithms can act autonomously, identifying patterns in the data that are supplied to them and can find evidence that the human eye would miss.

The European Union, in order to facilitate the correct provision and processing of data, has adopted the General Data Protection Regulation as the main legal vehicle to provide the Digital Single Market with correct and adequate access to these data, respectful of individual rights. of people. However, the European Data Protection Council is the one that must adopt a proactive role when it comes to ensuring that the processing of data in the field of Artificial Intelligence is carried out in a correct way.

On the other hand, the Regulation on the free circulation of non-personal data was adopted in 2018 and it has allowed to begin unblocking all those data that come from industrial or tertiary processes, that are obtained by computers or machines and that circulate to throughout the Union, to optimize the Artificial Intelligence learning process (European Union, 2018).

The adoption of European data spaces in areas such as energy, the manufacturing sector or other types of companies with significant innovative added value will be enormously valuable, since it will allow common access to data from both the public and private sectors and will allow training to Artificial Intelligence, under a framework of interoperability and clearly defined requirements.

The European Union has already put on the table different initiatives with which it is providing data that stem from space programs, with the Copernicus star program, through which a careful observation of the earth is carried out and millions of photographs are being obtained and of securities that can be used by other companies and companies to create a certain product. At the same time, in the health field, databases with anonymized images related to cancerous ailments are being financed, which facilitates the rapid diagnosis by Artificial Intelligence of other patients who may be undergoing development in early stages of cancer and who can alleviate human suffering (Tsang, Kracov, Mulryne, Strom, Perkins, Dickinson,... & Jones, 2017).

The volume of data that will be created in the coming years is of such magnitude that very high-performance computers will be required, called super computers and under the Eurohpc program, the European Union will allocate adequate funding to print a quantum generational leap in the generation of computers capable of processing Big Data and training experts in the management of Artificial Intelligence. For this, it is vital to acquire a strategic autonomy in the field of the creation and design of processors with a not very high level of energy consumption because this whole range of supercomputers will be a reality in a very few years. Europe cannot depend on external suppliers, it should achieve its own production line for both chips, microchips and processors, with a powerful industry dedicated to supplying the necessary components.

A Coordinated Ethic in the Expansion of Artificial Intelligence

The plan coordinated by the European Union once again claims that citizens will only accept the massive use of Artificial Intelligence as long as it obeys the requirements of: predictability, responsibility, verifiability and respect for fundamental rights and ethics (Vakkuri, 2020). As the professor of ethics, Adela Cortina, has emphasized on numerous occasions, this technology must be used to put the human being at the centre of development and progress, with a view to doing good and be designed to strength the society and not to make it worse.

Based on the work of a group of experts, the ethical guidelines for the responsible use of Artificial Intelligence in the European Union were drawn up. A draft was published at the end of 2018 and in March 2019 the final version was already available, allowing those third countries that did not belong to the European Union to understand the vision that the Union had for this new technological field. In this way, if they shared this same purpose, an international alliance could be configured to strengthen the development of Artificial Intelligence, guided by ethical and responsible standards.

It also involves maintaining a line of study on the possible misuse of this technology, to prevent attacks or abuses by companies or governments that seek to weaken the European Union. Cybersecurity necessarily must be present hand in hand with an ethical action because the conflicts that occur in the world and geopolitical tensions are going to impact the digital environment and will sooner or later seek to sabotage Artificial Intelligence networks (Mosteanu, 2020).

However, if in the future it is necessary to deploy some type of technology that requires joint armed action at the European level, in order to defend our values and rights against possible attacks, ethical and, at the same time, acceptable action will only be accepted by a procedure that the order to neutralize any target will have to be given by a human being, and not by an algorithm that decides on the life or death of other people (Barbé & Badell, 2020).

The National Artificial Intelligence Plan of Spain

The European Union requested that in mid-2019 the member states prepare their coordination plans and make them public regarding the extension of Artificial Intelligence, but in the Spanish case the publication was experienced with a long delay. Until November 2020, the National Artificial Intelligence Strategy (ENIA) was not made official from the Moncloa Palace and it has begun to deploy its effects in 2021.

The Spain Digital 2025 Agenda, published in July 2020, already presented in its line of action 9 on Data Economy and Artificial Intelligence, a priority axis of main action, and supported by the Agenda for Change that had been published in February 2019. The purpose was to set itself "*as a frame of reference for the period 2020-2025 that allows guiding the sectoral plans, state and regional strategies in this matter, in line with the policies developed by the EU, and promoting the transformation of the different economic sectors through public-private cooperation*" (Government of Spain, 2020, p.13).

Its objectives are scientific excellence and innovation in Artificial Intelligence; the projection of the Spanish language, the creation of qualified employment; the transformation of the productive fabric; the generation of an environment of trust in relation to Artificial Intelligence; underline in this process the humanistic values in Artificial Intelligence and, lastly, make it more inclusive and sustainable. Objectives that it fully shares with the ambitious community agenda and the United Nations, through its 2030 Agenda.

The Plan presented 6 strategic axes: 1. Promote scientific research, technological development and innovation in AI. 2. Promote the development of digital capabilities, enhance national talent and attract global talent in Artificial Intelligence. 3. Develop data platforms and technological infrastructures that support AI. 4. Integrate AI into value chains to transform the economic fabric. 5. Promote the use of AI in public administration and in national strategic missions. 6. Establish an ethical and regulatory framework that reinforces the protection of individual and collective rights, in order to guarantee inclusion and social well-being.

Each of these axes addresses a series of action measures. The first assumes the need to create the Spanish Network of Excellence in Artificial Intelligence, the Reinforcement of the system of pre-doctoral and post-doctoral research contracts, the flexibility of the scientific trajectory of the research staff in Artificial Intelligence or the creation of new centres national multidisciplinary technological development that contribute to the consolidation of Artificial Intelligence in Spain; program aid for companies in this sector, strengthen the network of Digital Innovation Centres or the creation of the R + D + i Missions program.

In the second axis, the Development of the National Plan of Digital Competences stands out, the promotion of a greater training offer in Vocational and University Training oriented to AI. The launch of the "SpAIn Talent Hub" Program and the launch of a program to assist in the homologation of international qualifications and accreditations to attract international talent by promoting female talent.

The third axis assumes the creation of the Data Office and the Chief Data Officer. The creation of shared spaces for sectorial and industrial data and decentralized and accessible repositories. The promotion of the National Plan for Language Technologies. The reinforcement of Strategic Supercomputing Capabilities (cloud, edge, quantum) and the implementation of the Data for Social Good Project.

The fourth axis stands out for the launch of aid programs for companies for the incorporation of AI in the production processes of the value chains. The programs to promote the transfer of innovation in AI through the Digital Innovation Centres specialized in Artificial Intelligence of an industrial nature. The launch of the NextTech Public-Private Venture Capital Fund to boost digital entrepreneurship and business growth in AI (scale ups). The development of the National Green Algorithms Program.

The fifth axis seeks to incorporate Artificial Intelligence in public administration to improve efficiency and eliminate administrative bottlenecks. Launch an innovation laboratory for new services and applications of AI in Public Administration (GobTechLab). Promote Artificial Intelligence skills in Public Administrations. Adopt the "Artificial Intelligence for Data-Based Public Management" Program. Promote national strategic missions in the field of public administration where Artificial Intelligence can have an impact (focus on health, justice, employment).

The sixth axis will develop a national seal of quality Artificial Intelligence. It will set up observatories to evaluate the social impact of the algorithms. It will develop the Charter of Digital Rights. It will implement a national governance model of ethics in Artificial Intelligence (IA Advisory Council). Dialogue will be promoted in national and international discussion, awareness and participation forums in relation to Artificial Intelligence and with all this it is expected that Spain will be at the forefront of Artificial Intelligence. Depending on the execution of the planned investment programs, the provision of sufficient resources and the avoidance of negligent administration, the roadmap is adequate to adapt Spain to the new context of global competitiveness in terms of Artificial Intelligence. Ethic as a pillar in the implementation of Artificial Intelligence must be safeguard (Saura, Palacios-Marqués, D. & Iturricha-Fernández, 2021a). After all, great words but with emptiness of ambition because the government in the last years has not proved to take seriously Artificial Intelligence as a priority in all lines of public policies.

THE WHITE PAPER ON ARTIFICIAL INTELLIGENCE - A EUROPEAN APPROACH TO EXCELLENCE AND TRUST

The White Paper is the last piece on which the future legislative articulation in the field of Artificial Intelligence will pivot (De Miguel Asensio, 2020). It was published on February 19, 2020, and offers the European approach through which the regulatory ecosystem in terms of Artificial Intelligence should be sustained, to be developed so that its benefits have effects on the whole of citizens, companies and governments.

The main pillars on which it is based are the political framework, which highlights the main commitments that will have the obligation to be adopted at the regional, national and European level, in order to specify the so-called ecosystem of excellence under a solid research base that grants clear benefits to all value chains.

On the other hand, the regulatory framework that the Union should articulate in the field of Artificial Intelligence is highlighted, based on respect for fundamental rights, consumer rights and legal security to articulate the necessary trust, so that citizens and companies, as well as public bodies can carry out their functions with total normality. Lastly, the European data strategy stands out, as an element that will facilitate the Union to transform its economy into a more agile one when it comes to managing data in the digital environment.

The Realization of an Ecosystem Based on Excellence

The Union is willing to bet on a new adaptation that extracts the advantages of Artificial Intelligence, but for this it recognizes that the economy can only carry out the necessary transformation if there is optimal collaboration between the Member States. For this reason, it not only proposes to review the original coordination plan, but also calls for an effort from the research community, which is currently under serious fragmentation in dispersed centres in each of the Member States, to Europeanize its progress.

In this sense, it is imperative to create a web-like platform that allows the interconnection of teams and specialists, who help and materialize the progress of research, innovation and technical development. The Community Executive is willing to bet on the so-called centres of excellence as reception poles for public-private investment, both European and national as well as from the business sector, which will serve as engines and models of this process.

The European Commission is committed to a skills agenda that consolidates the competences of the population and is reinforced with the Action Plan on Digital Education that will contribute to ensuring that no citizen is left behind in this digital transformation. It will mean a notable improvement in the formation of national educational curricula, so that they contemplate greater and better competences in the digital context.

The Digital Europe program will support universities that are concerned with facilitating academic development for the most cutting-edge researchers and that transform the educational community into a global avant-garde powerhouse. It is not only possible to stick to the purely academic aspect, but also to address the needs of small and medium-sized companies, being supported from digital innovation centres and having the necessary access to financing to be able to implement timely innovations in their value chains and bring Artificial Intelligence to your business. The recovery funds after the coronavirus pandemic will specifically contemplate the companies that carry out the execution of this transformation, to give them help and consolidate them.

Singularly, the Community Executive will allow the Member States to maintain a great deal of autonomy in this process, although this does not prevent them from carrying out the appropriate inquiries and controls, to verify that at least one digital innovation centre within each of the States assume a remarkable level of specialization in Artificial Intelligence. This will make it possible to have European reference centres supervised by the States, but more directly controlled by the Commission.

The European Union will bet on a strategic alliance between the private sector and the public sector in matters of Artificial Intelligence, robotics and data, which will facilitate joint research and obtain the greatest benefits from both sectors. Indeed, the benefits will lead to compliance with one of the keys, which is the promotion by community institutions of the full adoption of Artificial Intelligence by the public administration (Criado, 2021), either in the provision of public services, in the configuration of Smart cities (Tantau, 2021), in health care or by rural administrations that are often more neglected under public investment plans.

In fact, there are already a multitude of scattered rules that address the details of security in the digital field, but none specifically on Artificial Intelligence and some Member States have chosen to create their own regulatory packages (Barfield & Pagallo, 2021). This puts legal coherence in the Union at risk and, therefore, the European Commission proposes the articulation of a specific European regulatory framework in this area, exclusively focused on Artificial Intelligence. An approach is required that considers the risk of these new systems and that interested parties are aware of the applicable law in each specific case.

The new regulatory package, which will mean constitutionalizing the rules over Artificial Intelligence in Europe (De Gregorio, 2021), should focus: the training data and data records by Artificial Intelligence, the information to be provided by the systems, its strength and accuracy; the human supervision that will exist at all times and the specific requirements in the case of certain applications. At the end of the day, the recipients of these regulations will be all citizens, but those who develop and implement this technology, potential users of it, will be particularly affected. Therefore, regardless of whether, or not, they are established in the European Union, they should be subject to these requirements, to avoid the holes through which it would lose complete effectiveness. The need to promptly implement a sophisticated evaluation system is assumed, to previously test Artificial Intelligence that poses a high risk, before putting it into use, with an absolute obligation on the part of all economic subjects to carry them out before letting it be put into operation (De Hoyos Sancho, 2020).

Under the new multiannual financial framework from 2021 to 2027 has been approved with the Next Generation European Union funds, Europe intends to improve its centres of excellence dedicated to Artificial Intelligence research, as well as its governance model (Peña, 2021), to continue with research programs and delve into areas as sensitive as energy, data efficiency, unsupervised machine learning, invest in additional testing facilities and experimentation in Artificial Intelligence with a view to developing the future technologies that are transferred to the health, industrial, transport, manufacturing or agri-food sector. Especially, thinking about the commitment to turn Europe into a low-carbon continent, neutral in CO2 emissions by the year 2050. The European Commission will bet on all those technologies that energetically give Artificial Intelligence greater sustainability and suppose an ecological improvement in the value chain (Hamon, Junklewitz & Sanchez, 2020). However, States must take European rules and plans into real policies and actions and still persist a gap between both, at least in the Spanish case.

CONCLUSION

Artificial Intelligence in the European Union is in full development and investments in this sector have been economically reinforcing. However, it is important to note that its regulatory extension is not very extensive and requires further efforts from member states who have the main responsibility to impact in the life of the citizens through their actions. In fact, as of the 2020 White Paper, the European Commission highlights the need for a governance framework in the field of Artificial Intelligence, which requires concrete measures aligned with the European data strategy, which convert the Union in a global digital nerve centre.

In matters of Artificial Intelligence, everything is yet to be written, consultations will be made with companies, civil society, and academic circles so that they can raise the most appropriate proposals, considering the security and civil liability framework that the Commission has provided. Therefore, the next few years will be decisive to understand the course that Europe is taking in the context of Artificial Intelligence and Spain must dedicate stronger efforts to create awareness of the great impact that has to come. Particularly in education, there are not enough resources dedicate to teach the present and future generations in the domain of Artificial Intelligence. The country still lives in old nineteenth debates arguing in terms of nationalism instead of adopting measures that transforms for better the life of millions of citizens.

Therefore, the originality of this paper has proved in an orderly manner the progress and evolution of the Artificial Intelligence implemented in the European Union, but the lack of capacity and instruments adopted by Spain, without solid plans and proper attention from public institutions at the national, regional and local level, to adapt their society to the new changes that Artificial Intelligence will bring to the country. So, in the case of Spain, the country is going very slow in implementing education reforms and support to the people in the adaptation to the new reality. Ambitious plans without means will mean inefficiency in the medium and long term

REFERENCES

Barbé, E., & Badell, D. (2020). The European Union and lethal autonomous weapons systems: United in diversity? In *European Union Contested* (pp. 133–152). Springer. doi:10.1007/978-3-030-33238-9_8

Barfield, W., & Pagallo, U. (2020). *Advanced Introduction to Law and Artificial Intelligence*. Edward Elgar Publishing. doi:10.4337/9781789905137

Criado, J. I. (2021). Inteligencia Artificial (y Administración Pública). *EUNOMÍA. Revista en Cultura de la Legalidad*, (20), 348–372. doi:10.20318/eunomia.2021.6097

Cyman, D., Gromova, E., & Juchnevicius, E. (2021). Regulation of artificial intelligence in BRICS and the European Union. *BRICS Law Journal*, 8(1), 86–115. doi:10.21684/2412-2343-2021-8-1-86-115

De Gregorio, G. (2021). The rise of digital constitutionalism in the European Union. *International Journal of Constitutional Law*, 19(1), 41–70. doi:10.1093/icon/moab001

De Miguel Asensio, P. A. (2020). Libro Blanco sobre inteligencia artificial: Evolución del marco normativo y aplicación efectiva. *La Ley Unión Europea*, (79), 1–5.

European Commission (2018). Communication to the European Parliament, the European Council, the Council, the European Economic and Social Committee and the Committee of the Regions "Artificial Intelligence for Europe". 237 final.

European Union (2018) Regulation of the European Parliament and of the Council on a framework for the free circulation of non-personal data in the European Union, number 1807.

Government of Spain (2020). National Artificial Intelligence Strategy.

Hamon, R., Junklewitz, H., & Sanchez, I. (2020). *Robustness and explainability of artificial intelligence*. Publications Office of the European Union.

Hildebrandt, M. (2020). The Artificial Intelligence of European Union Law. *German Law Journal*, 21(1), 74–79. doi:10.1017/glj.2019.99

Larsson, S., & Heintz, F. (2020). Transparency in artificial intelligence. *Internet Policy Review*, 9(2), 1–16. doi:10.14763/2020.2.1469

McKinsey. (2017). *Ten imperatives for Europe in the era of Artificial Intelligence and automation*. Author.

Miailhe, N., Hodes, C., Çetin, R. B., Lannquist, Y., & Jeanmaire, C. (2020). Geopolítica de la inteligencia artificial. *Política Exterior, 34*(193), 56-69.

Mosteanu, N. R. (2020). Artificial Intelligence and Cyber Security–A Shield against Cyberattack as a Risk Business Management Tool–Case of European Countries. *Quality - Access to Success*, 21(175).

Peña, J. C. H. (2021). Gobernanza de la inteligencia artificial en la Unión Europea. La construcción de un marco ético-jurídico aún inacabado. *Revista General de Derecho Administrativo*, (56), 13.

Ribeiro-Navarrete, S., Saura, J. R., & Palacios-Marqués, D. (2021). Towards a new era of mass data collection: Assessing pandemic surveillance technologies to preserve user privacy. *Technological Forecasting and Social Change, 167*, 120681. doi:10.1016/j.techfore.2021.120681 PMID:33840865

Sancho, M. D. H. (2020). El libro blanco sobre inteligencia artificial de la Comisión Europea: Reflexiones desde las garantías esenciales del proceso penal como "sector de riesgo". *Revista Española de Derecho Europeo*, (76), 9–44.

Saura, J. R., Palacios-Marqués, D., & Iturricha-Fernández, A. (2021a). Ethical Design in Social Media: Assessing the main performance measurements of user online behavior modification. *Journal of Business Research*, *129*(May), 271–281. doi:10.1016/j.jbusres.2021.03.001

Saura, J. R., Ribeiro-Soriano, D., & Palacios-Marqués, D. (2021). Using data mining techniques to explore security issues in smart living environments in Twitter. *Computer Communications*, *179*, 285–295. Advance online publication. doi:10.1016/j.comcom.2021.08.021

Saura, J. R., Ribeiro-Soriano, D., & Palacios-Marqués, D. (2021b). From user-generated data to data-driven innovation: A research agenda to understand user privacy in digital markets. *International Journal of Information Management*, *60*(October), 102331. doi:10.1016/j.ijinfomgt.2021.102331

Tantau, A., & Şanta, A. M. I. (2021). New Energy Policy Directions in the European Union Developing the Concept of Smart Cities. *Smart Cities*, *4*(1), 241–252. doi:10.3390martcities4010015

Tsang, L., Kracov, D. A., Mulryne, J., Strom, L., Perkins, N., Dickinson, R., ... Jones, B. (2017). The impact of artificial intelligence on medical innovation in the European Union and United States. *Intellectual Property & Technology Law Journal*, *29*(8), 3–11.

Vakkuri, V., Kemell, K. K., Kultanen, J., & Abrahamsson, P. (2020). The current state of industrial practice in artificial intelligence ethics. *IEEE Software*, *37*(4), 50–57. doi:10.1109/MS.2020.2985621

Završnik, A. (2020, March). Criminal justice, artificial intelligence systems, and human rights. In *ERA Forum* (Vol. 20, No. 4, pp. 567-583). Springer Berlin Heidelberg. 10.100712027-020-00602-0

Zuiderveen Borgesius, F. J. (2020). Strengthening legal protection against discrimination by algorithms and artificial intelligence. *International Journal of Human Rights*, *24*(10), 1572–1593. doi:10.1080/13 642987.2020.1743976

KEY TERMS AND DEFINITIONS

Artificial Intelligence: Scientific discipline that deals with creating computer programs that perform operations comparable to those performed by the human mind, such as learning or logical reasoning.

Ethics: Set of moral norms that govern the conduct of the person in any area of life.

European Commission: Executive body of the Union, in charge of ensuring the application of Community law, making recommendations, and adopting decisions under the conditions provided for in the treaties. It is independent of the Member States, although the Commissioners are nationals of the States of the Union, appointed after each election of the European Parliament by the European Council, by qualified majority, in agreement with the President who has previously been appointed by the Plenary of the European Parliament on a proposal from the Council. The mandate of the Commission lasts for 5 years.

European Council: Institution of the European Union established since December 1, 2009, made up of the Heads of State or Government of the Member States, as well as its President and the President of the Commission. Its functions are basically the impulse of the EU and the setting of its political orientations and priorities.

European Parliament: Institution of the European Union of a parliamentary nature that integrates in the institutional system the principle of representative democracy of citizens and political pluralism.

European Union: Voluntary association or federation of sovereign States to which the exercise of normative powers is attributed by means of three fundamental treaties: Treaty on the Functioning of the European Union (TFEU), Treaty on European Union (TEU) and Charter of Fundamental Rights of the European Union.

Next Generation EU: Massive recovery fund of the European Union (EU) of € 750 billion (in constant 2018 prices) agreed on July 21, 2020 by the European Council, after four days of negotiation, to support the member states of the Union hit by the COVID-19 pandemic.

Recovery, Transformation, and Resilience Plan: Is the plan developed by the Spanish Government as a proposal for the management of the Next Generation EU (NGEU) funds in the period 2021-2023, of which 69,500 million euros correspond to non-refundable funds, in addition to have access to another € 67 billion in loans.

ENDNOTES

[1]   Belgium, Bulgaria, Czech Republic, Denmark, Germany, Estonia, Ireland, Spain, France, Italy, Latvia, Lithuania, Luxembourg, Hungary, Marta, Netherlands, Austria, Poland, Portugal, Slovenia, Slovakia, Finland, Sweden and the United Kingdom.

[2]   Belgium, Bulgaria, Czech Republic, Denmark, Germany, Estonia, Ireland, Spain, France, Italy, Latvia, Lithuania, Luxembourg, Hungary, Marta, Netherlands, Austria, Poland, Portugal Slovenia Slovakia, Finland, Sweden and United Kingdom.

Chapter 9
Main Government–Related Data Extraction Techniques:
A Review

Paula González-Padilla
Rey Juan Carlos University, Spain

Ana Fernández López
Rey Juan Carlos University, Spain

Francisco J. S. Lacárcel
University of Alicante, Spain

ABSTRACT

In this digital computer-based ecosystem, governments use mechanisms of data extraction which are barely identified by citizens. Therefore, among the data extracted from institutional e-platforms, computer-based transactions play an important role in this process. This research study aims to shed light on the data mining techniques used by governments and public institutions, identify which are the most commonly used, and expose the privacy risks they may pose to citizens. The chapter is made through a systematic literature review with two main keywords: "big data" and "government." This study intends to answer the following research questions: What are the key techniques used by governments to extract data? May these tools pose risks to citizens?

INTRODUCTION

In recent years, the use of large amounts of data has boosted the digital era in several areas (Al-Sai & Abualigah, 2017), such as corporations and governments, where population has evidenced the mass collection of their data (Zhou et al, 2014). Therefore, big data has turned out to be a key factor and discipline not only in the business field but also in public administrations (Chen & Hsieh, 2014), in order to develop and enhance different initiatives (Wang et al., 2016).

DOI: 10.4018/978-1-7998-9609-8.ch009

It should be noted that data can become a brand-new opportunity for governments as this asset can offer citizen-centric services (Chen & Hsieh, 2014), reduce waste (LaBrie et al., 2018), fight terrorism (Calo, 2016) and corruption (Von Haldenwang, 2004), or even implement protocols for health or social crisis such as COVID-19 pandemic (Saura et al., 2021). However, some authors argue that government data-centric projects do not benefit society even though they have a citizen-centric aim (Gómez, 2015; Huffine, 2015; Lu et al., 2012).

Likewise, governments based on the use of big data techniques, also known as e-governments (Esteves & Joseph, 2008), promote collaboration, productivity, efficiency, and transparency (Von Haldenwang, 2004; McNeal; Zhang & Chen, 2010; Morabito, 2015). In this way, the use of data in the public sector is changing the paradigm into a digital and innovative era where organizational structures are more flexible, thus facilitating processes to users as well as reducing costs (Ebrahim & Iran, 2005).

Of note, we have witnessed how the era of Big Data has boosted the volume, complexity and growth of data generated, where governments collect data from users because of their public functions, in which citizens have to share their information. Nevertheless, public administrations do not value at all citizens' data (Privacilla, 2001) and how it can be used to predict and forecast events or even how people will behave (Saura et al., 2021a).

Data collection, gathering or mining is related to personal information from users. In this context, surveillance capitalism is taking part of a new data-driven era in which the interaction with smart devices in the daily life, generates large amounts of data that are collected and treated by organizations (Zuboff, 2015). Of note, these data extraction techniques are unknown by users because it is normally gathered in hidden ways (Andrejevic, 2014).

Considering that governments have been collecting data for ages (Amankwah-Amoah, 2015), the collection and acquisition techniques developed have improved through all these decades, where the utilization of mobile devices has exponentially grown in recent years. In this way, data collectors are developing how to efficiently gather, extract, interpret and storage these large amounts of data (Zhou et al, 2014).

Of note, in recent years open data governments initiatives have been being developed as they allow to prevent corruption, offer better services to citizens, as well as increase reliability on governments' accountability (Nikiforova & McBride, 2021), nevertheless it may entail data risks if securing rules are not well settled and designed (Bonina & Eaton, 2020).

Related to governments built based on data, smart cities offer a way to manage energy consumption, sustainability, economics' areas, among others, in order to improve every day's people lifes. In this data-driven cities, information and communication technologies, artificial intelligence and machine learning play a key role for its development, as these technologies contribute to manage, collect and treat large amounts of data (Ulla et al., 2020). Therefore, studies related to both IoT and smart cities suggest that security and resilience are critical factors as different devices are interconnected to each other, sharing sensitive information from users (Abdul Ahad et al., 2020).

Additionally, there is a need of developing new strategies, techniques and tools for data extraction since industries such as finance or insurance are exploiting data from their clients to improve their decision-making, and cede and transfer this information to third-parties. Moreover, the different purposes of each sector and organization imply different extraction techniques, affecting how, what, and why data is extracted (Sadowski, 2019).

Therefore, technologies such as location-based services, GPS, external APIS or Bluetooth, among others, are used to track large amounts of data. Therefore, it is said that the Internet and mobile devices are the major source of data extraction (Ribeiro-Navarrete et al., 2021). Besides these techniques, data mining has been widely spread to get insights from the information not only in the business sector but also in the public area (GAO, 2005) while authors point out the privacy risks and concerns entailed. (Wu, 2014).

However, governments have to face challenges such as the need to obtain these techniques, technologies and tools which are offered in the corporate sector with high costs involved (Chen & Hsieh, 2014). In addition, the public sector has to deal with the hassle of the continuous improvements and of these technologies as well as the acquisition of the newest ones in order to stay not only updated but also competitive, which consequently leads to high inherent costs (Günther, Mehrizi, Huysman, & Feldberg, 2017).

Likewise, authors have shown interest in privacy issues that carry collection, process, storage, aggregation and use of personal information, thus sensitive information by governments (Ebrahim & Iran, 2005). In this context, new technologies such as social Internet of Things devices collect data from users who barely know the amount of information they are sharing as privacy "by default" does not strictly protect user information (Saura et al., 2021).

Therefore, there is an urgent need to clarify to citizens that public institutions collect their data when using their websites, which may be one of the most used techniques to gather all this valuable and sensitive information (Gefen et al., 2002; Wu, 2014). The fact is that when contacting and dealing with the public sector, anonymization of data is barely unfeasible or illegal (Mayer-Schonberger & Lazer, 2007a, p. 286).

In this digital computer-based ecosystem, governments use mechanisms of data extraction which are barely identified by citizens. Therefore, among the data extracted from institutional e-platforms, computer-based economic transactions play an important role in this process (Zuboff, 2015). Bearing in mind the importance of data privacy, data governance should thus establish mechanisms to protect this information by minimizing its collection to avoid misusing it (Janssen et al., 2020), safeguarding these data from malware, cybercriminals; or data leaks (Saura et al., 2021)

Considering the statements outlined above, the aim of the present to shed light on the data extraction techniques used by governments. In addition, regarding the importance of the topics outlined above the present study intends to answer the following research questions:

- RQ1. *What are the key techniques used by governments to extract data?*
- RQ2. *May these tools pose risks to citizens?*

Regarding these research questions, identifying what the most commonly used data extraction, collection and treatment techniques are, is an open question.

- To explore data collection technologies used by governments.
- To establish implications for both citizens and public institutions.
- To improve digital initiatives by governments
- To understand how governments extract citizens' data
- To establish a comparison between companies and governments' data extraction techniques
- To identify the main data collection techniques implemented by governments

In this way, seeking to reach the objectives outlined above and extract useful insights, the present study conducts a Systematic Literature Review (SLR) of previous studies based on data extraction techniques, technologies, and methods used by governments.

Of note, the originality of this study lies in a review of relevant scientific literature focused on data extraction techniques by governments, an area which has not been studied in-depth yet. A major contribution is that our results provide meaningful implications for governments and citizens in this field as well as it fills a gap in the literature.

The remainder of this paper is structured as follows. In Section 2, we review the theoretical framework on the concept of data extraction techniques, specifically in the government area. Next, Section 3 presents the methodology. In Section 4, the results are reported followed by a discussion in Section 5. Finally, conclusions are drawn in Section 6.

THEORETICAL FRAMEWORK

Big data techniques used in the public sector and governments have been subject of study on many occasions (Khine & Shun, 2017). Of note, implementing such tools by service providers enables them to understand citizen's behavior, especially when the information is collected from smartphones. In this way, mobile devices have become an undeniable source of data acquisition (Ribeiro-Navarrete et al., 2021), especially in delivering public services. These data can be used to predict and forecast people's intentions with different data techniques and technologies (Pence, 2014).

Regarding Big Data within political science, Clark and Golder (2015) define it as the "technological innovations such as machine learning that have enabled researchers to collect new types of data, such as social network data, or large amounts of traditional data with less expense." It is a way of explaining that this ability now to work with data and optimize results leads to a transformation of the understanding of the political world as it has been known until now.

To capture the value from Big Data, authors Ribeiro-Navarrete et al. (2021) have identified several technologies such as GPS or external ID Network that offered in this case valuable information about COVID-19 among the population for governments. Similarly, Wu (2014) affirms that, when visiting a public institution's website, citizens are tacked in order to collect their personal data. Therefore, exploiting web analytics provides an overview of users' interactions with governments, and let public sector identify needs by analyzing the searched contents to extract value from them (Joseph & Johnson, 2013).

In this Internet context, smartphones are becoming a key factor to extract and build knowledge from users about their habits by considering their clicks, their search history or online transactions, among others. In this way, governments -as well as companies- can predict and forecast public needs or events, so they can act in consequence and offer better public services and accurate solutions by considering performance measurements to increase user engagement (Saura et al., 2021b). Concretely, social networks such as Twitter or Facebook are becoming a new way of obtaining opinions of citizens, thus governments are using them to retrieve data and process it with natural language techniques (Driss et al., 2019).

Considering data as a key asset, researchers such as Saura et al. (2021c) have identified several uses of data sciences in digital marketing used by SMEs. The tools used by SMEs can be also applied by the public sector in order to acquire knowledge from citizens, or to get information from users to better design their online and offline campaigns.

In some other way, the government analyzes data from traffic cameras by using real-time analytics (Aggarwal, 2015), which is considered to be one of the most important technologies in smart cities as it helps to monitor and control traffic jams. Some other significant sources are social media (Chen et al., 2015; Li et al., 2016), Internet of Things, traditional operation systems (Khine & Shun, 2017), or satellites that extract not only data but also images (Lewis and Caplan, 2015). In a nutshell, traditional methods of data collection are being replaced by new technologies. Therefore, in this digital era, big data sources are no longer homogeneous, so this becomes a major challenge for big data technologies hampered by the incomplete data gathered (Chen et al., 2015).

Anshari & Lim (2017) show on their investigation how smartphones enable big data to improve and innovate public services. It is also highlighted the large amount of data created by smartphone users and the need of extracting this useful information from them to establish patterns based on their online activities. Therefore, governments can understand how their countries are behaving by intercepting data from population mobile devices.

According to Hassani et al. (2016) data mining is an important tool used by the public sector to extract insights in order to investigate and prevent crime, but some others such as entity extraction, clustering or support vector machines, among others.

Similarly, Li et al., (2016) conducted research where they highlighted how geospatial data provides meaningful insights from mobile devices. Organizations usually gather this information using mobile mapping, geo-tagged web content, or global navigation satellite system, among others. In this sense, cities that gather real-time data through different sensors are able to forecast, prevent and rapidly respond to disasters or events. Of note, digital platforms such as Twitter are considered to be an asset for real-time data technologies, as the content shared by users can be tracked using Data Sciences (Saura, 2020).

Accordingly, to capture data there is a need of developing specific Big Data techniques that must be mixed up in order to extract insights to solve problems in fields such as economics. Among these tools, some academics such as Chen & Zhang (2014) highlight statistics as a way of collect, compel, and analyze data; data mining as a bunch of methods to define patterns; social network analysis as a technique to identify social behaves; or machine learning as a tool to build knowledge and improve the decision-making, thus the more information governments and corporations have, the better decisions they will take (Abu-Shanab, 2020).

The result of associating concepts such as Big data and government resulted in a new term, smart cities, and a sign of the importance given to the term is that one of the first to use it was IBM, who has had the "smart cities" brand since 2014 (Söderström et al., 2014). What they call smart cities are associated with the promise of concrete benefits (Al Nuami et al., 2015), such as the use of data tools by the government, with higher levels of political transparency, which in turn will generate a better quality of life.

In this context, the rapid development of smart cities serves as an example of how smart networks can store information not only about consumers' energy (Yin et al., 2013) but also from their smart cars, smart house devices or smartphones. Therefore, Chen et al., (2015) highlight that smart cities need to take advantage of improved algorithms to extract insights and support real-time capturing applications. This smart grid, based on computer remote controls, allows interested public entities to monitor large amounts of real-time data in order to improve their decision-making and reduce their costs (Chen et al., 2015). Consequently, several studies affirm that a key element in this digital-government era is the collection of urban big data (Lim et al., 2018).

Regarding how these technologies are implemented, several authors such as Gamage (2016), or Lim et al., (2018) show different smart cities projects in which data is gathered from citizens. This information can be collected from areas such as business, health, natural resources, traffic or taxes, among others. Therefore, smart cities can focus their investments on health services, where data such as diagnosis or treatment data were used to innovate data-based services in this sector. Other techniques are focused on providing an overview for governments from the use of tax processes.

Table 1 "Main sources of data", presented below, shows the main sources of data according to various authors. A total of six authors place social networks as the main source of data, followed by smartphones and smart grids, with a total of four authors respectively. Next, and in a less repetitive way, we find websites, traffic cameras, IoT, traditional operation systems, and satellites. Therefore, it can be stated that social networks, together with smartphones, are, for the most part, the most recurrent data sources.

Table 1. Main sources of data

Authors	Sources							
	Smartphones	Social Networks	Websites	Traffic Cameras	IoT	Smart Grids	Traditional Operation Systems	Satellites
Anshari & Lim (2017)	◉							
Aggarwal (2015)				◉				
Chen et al. (2015)		◉				◉		
Driss et al. (2019)		◉						
Gamage (2016)						◉		
Joseph & Johnson (2013)		◉						
Khine & Shun (2017)							◉	
Lewis and Caplan (2015)								◉
Li et al. (2016)	◉	◉						
Lim et al. (2018)						◉		
Ribeiro-Navarrete et al. (2021)	◉							
Saura et al. (2021b)		◉	◉					
Saura et al. (2021c)	◉	◉	◉					
Wu (2014)			◉					
Yin et al. (2013)					◉	◉		

Source: Self-elaboration

METHODOLOGY

The SLR methodology is chosen for this analysis. An SLR (systematic literature review) is a type of literature review that compiles and critically analyses multiple studies or research papers through a systematic process (Ramírez & García-Peñalvo, 2018). It is a systematic method for identifying, evaluating, and interpreting the work of and interpreting the work of researchers, scholars, and practitioners in a chosen field (Rother, 2007). The goal of an SLR is to provide a comprehensive summary of the available literature relevant to a research question.

In order to carry out this study, a structure similar to that proposed by Saura (2021) was followed, where the key terms of the research were first identified, and then searches were carried out in the databases: Web of Science, Scopus, and Science Direct. We have always worked with research catalogued as scientific articles, in order to obtain more concrete and rigorous results, in addition to filtering and narrowing the searches as much as possible to generate more precise results.

Systematic reviews are studies that gather information previously generated by other authors, they come from articles already published, it is the research on a specific topic, evaluated through a meta-analysis (Ortiz, 2004), which ends with results that are summarized in the conclusions of the study.

For the optimal execution and results of the research, the systematic review must be carried out in a rigorous and objective manner, and strategies that limit errors are usually used (Noble, Scheinost, & Constable, 2019). Some of them are the search for reproducible and explicit selection criteria (Leonelli, 2018), the exhaustive search of all relevant articles on the subject, evaluation of the synthesis and interpretation of the results (Papadopoulos, Versluis, Bauer, Herbst, Von Kistowski, Ali-Eldin, & Iosup, 2019).. In this type of research, quantitative and qualitative points of view are used, and data are collected through primary studies using mathematical and methodological tools to create a combined effect and thus be able to conclude with a synthesis of the evidence that is generated.

One of the strengths of this type of study is that they constitute an efficient research design, have consistency in the generalization of results, are precise in their estimation, and as Ortiz et al. (2004) mention, offer a strict evaluation of the published information. Furthermore, if the aim is to answer the same question through the integration of different studies, the sample size is increased, which in turn increases statistical power (Dickersin & Berlin, 1992).

In this way, the present study follows a literature review as a methodology to classify pertinent studies in the most relevant databases. Therefore, the terms "Government" and "Big Data" have been identified in the literature to determine which studies address the research question. The results are classified and filtered based on previously established selection criteria in order to select the accurate articles, conferences or book chapters. The articles are then carefully studied to determine whether they contain terms relevant to the research. In this way, studies that contain irrelevant specifications are excluded.

Since our object of study are data collection techniques, we focused on publications that include these terms in the following databases, according to the abovementioned search criteria. Specifically, we used the databases Web of sciences (WOS), ScienceDirect, and Scopus. The searches were focusing on titles, abstracts and keywords in order to identify the most relevant contributions in the field. Consequently, a total of 229 related articles were obtained, of which 17 met the established criteria.

Table 2 shows the analysis of different articles extracted from the databases. The following figures 1, 2 and 3 explain the selection process and the reason for selecting the last 17 potential articles.

Table 2. Number of articles found

Database	Number of Results	Number of Relevant Results
Web of Sciences	132	8
Scopus	58	5
Science Direct	39	4
Total	**229**	**17**

Source: Self-elaboration

Figure 1 shows the databases chosen to analyze the research articles. Figure 2 shows the searches performed in the databases, the terms chosen have been Government AND Big Data mainly, when through the searches no results have been found, the following terms have been added; Data Analytics OR Business Intelligence. Finally, Figure 3 shows the main fields in which the searches have been filtered with the terms discussed above.

Figure 1. Terms used in the databases (1)

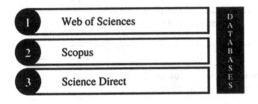

Figure 2. Terms used in the databases (2)

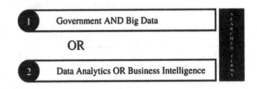

Figure 3. Terms used in the databases (3)

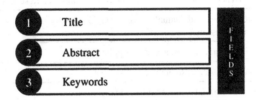

Figure 4. The SLR process

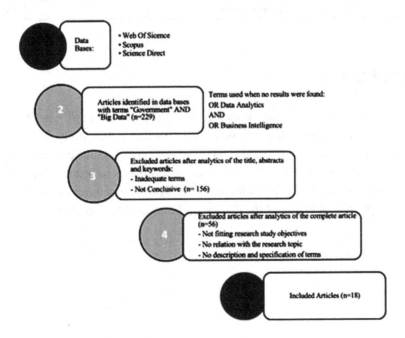

Table 3. Results of the SLR

Authors	Journal	Category
Joseph & Johnson, (2013)	It Professional	Computer Science
Yan (2018)	2018 International Conference on Information Management and Processing (ICIMP)	Computer Science
Anshari et al. (2018)	Proceedings of the 2018 10th International Conference on Machine Learning and Computing	Computer Science
Zainal et al. (2016)	2016 6th international conference on information and communication technology for the Muslim World	Computer Science
Pannu et al. (2016)	2016 IEEE 7th Annual Information Technology, Electronics and Mobile Communication Conference (IEMCON)	Telecommunications
Rozario & Issa, (2020)	Government Information Quarterly	Information Science
Ping (2018)	Proceedings of the 3rd International Conference on Judicial, Administrative and Humanitarian Problems of State Structures and Economic Subjects	Social Sciences
Anthopoulos (2017)	A Tool for Smart Government or an Industrial Trick?	Social Sciences
Jadi & Jie, (2017)	2017 International Conference on Information Society	Computer Science
Gottfried et al. (2021)	Journal of Theoretical and Applied Electronic Commerce Research	Business & Economics
Hagen et al. (2021)	DG. O2021: The 22nd Annual International Conference on Digital Government Research	Computer Science
Abu-Shanab & Harb, (2019)	Electronic Commerce Research and Applications	Business & Economics
Kim et al. (2021)	Public Administration Review	Public Administration
Zhang et al. (2020)	International Journal of Information Management	Information Science
LaBrie et al. (2018)	Technological Forecasting and Social Change	Business & Economics
Archenaa & Anita (2015)	Procedia Computer Science	Computer Science
Rozario et al. (2020)	Government Information Quarterly	Information Science

Source: Self-elaboration

ANALYSIS OF RESULTS

Table 4 "Key terms definition", as its name indicates, is the section where we can see and understand all the more technical and specific terms that, at one point or another in this study, have been discussed and referred to. It is a good place to clarify concepts and to see in a very clear and concrete way everything that involves the resources, techniques and systems used by governments to benefit from and work with data sources. In this way it is intended that the reader understands and links the concepts that are talked about, in order to have a better understanding of the theory, and thus avoid conceptual errors (Cordero, 2019).

Table 4. Key terms definition.

Key Terms	Definition
Amazon Web Services	Amazon Web Services is a collection of public cloud computing services that together form a cloud computing platform, offered over the Internet by Amazon.com. It is used in popular applications such as Dropbox, Foursquare, HootSuite.
Apache Hive	Apache Hive is a data warehousing infrastructure built on top of Hadoop to provide data aggregation, querying, and analytics. Initially developed by Facebook, Apache Hive is now used and developed by other companies such as Netflix and the Financial Industry Regulatory Authority.
API	The application programming interface is a set of subroutines, functions, and procedures that provides a certain library to be used by other software as an abstraction layer.
Artificial Intelligence	The theory and development of computer systems able to perform tasks normally requiring human intelligence, such as visual perception, speech recognition, decision-making, and translation between languages.
Big Data Analytics	Big data, also called massive data, data intelligence, large-scale data or big data, is a term that refers to data sets so large and complex that they require non-traditional data processing software applications to process them properly.
BPM	Is a management discipline composed of methodologies and technologies. Its objective is to improve the performance (efficiency and effectiveness) and optimization of an organization's processes. This is done through the management of processes that must be designed, modeled, organized, documented and optimized on an ongoing basis. It can therefore be described as a process of continuous process improvement.
Big Query	Is a fully managed serverless data warehouse that enables scalable analysis on petabytes of data. It is a platform-as-a-service that supports queries using ANSI SQL. It also has built-in machine learning capabilities.
Cloud Computing	Cloud computing, also known as cloud services, cloud computing, cloud computing, cloud computing or simply "the cloud", is a paradigm that enables computing services to be delivered over a network, usually the Internet.
Cluster	Group of interrelated, geographically concentrated companies and institutions competing in the same business. They generally include: Companies located at various steps of the value chain.
Data Analytics	Data analysis is a process that consists of inspecting, cleaning and transforming data with the objective of highlighting useful information, to suggest conclusions and support decision making.
DBMS	A database management system is a set of programs that allow the storage, modification and extraction of information in a database. Users can access the information using specific query and report generation tools, or by means of applications for this purpose.
Data Mining	Data mining or data exploration is a field of statistics and computer science that refers to the process of attempting to discover patterns in large volumes of data sets using the methods of artificial intelligence, machine learning, statistics and database systems.
Data Science	Is an interdisciplinary field that involves scientific methods, processes and systems to extract knowledge or a better understanding of data in its different forms, whether structured or unstructured, which is a continuation of some fields of data analysis such as statistics, data mining, machine learning, and predictive analytics.
ETL	Extract, Transform and Load is the process that allows organizations to move data from multiple sources, reformat and clean it, and load it into another database, data mart, or data warehouse for analysis, or into another operational system to support a business process.
Framework	Is a standardized set of concepts, practices and criteria for approaching a particular type of problem that serves as a reference for addressing and solving new problems of a similar nature.
Google Trends	Google Trends, also called Google Search Trends, is a Google Labs tool that shows the most popular search terms of the recent past.
GPS	The Global Positioning System, originally Navstar GPS, is a system that allows positioning any object on Earth with an accuracy of up to centimeters, although a few meters is common.
Hadoop	Is a freely licensed software framework for programming distributed applications that handle large volumes of data. It allows applications to work with thousands of networked nodes and petabytes of data.
HTML5	HTML 5 is the fifth major revision of the basic language of the World Wide Web, HTML.
IAAs	Infrastructure as a Service (IaaS) refers to online services that provide high-level APIs used to index low-level infrastructure details such as physical computing resources, location, data partitioning, scaling, security, backup, etc.

continues on following page

Table 4. Continued

Key Terms	Definition
ICTs	Refers to facilities, resources or services necessary for the development of cutting-edge, top-quality research, as well as for the transmission, exchange and preservation of knowledge, technology transfer and the promotion of innovation.
JSON	Is a simple text format for data exchange. It is a subset of the JavaScript object literal notation, although, due to its widespread adoption as an alternative to XML, it is considered a language-independent format.
LSA	Latent semantic analysis is a technique in natural language processing, in particular distributional semantics, for analyzing the relationships between a set of documents and the terms they contain by producing a set of concepts related to the documents and terms.
LDA	In machine learning, is a generative model that allows sets of observations to be explained by unobserved groups that explain why some parts of the data are similar.
LSTM	Short-term memory is an artificial recurrent neural network architecture used in the field of deep learning.
Matching algorithm	Are algorithms used to solve graph matching problems in graph theory. A matching problem arises when a set of edges must be drawn that do not share any vertices. Graph matching problems are very common in daily activities.
Machine Learning	Is the subfield of computer science and a branch of artificial intelligence, which aims to develop techniques that enable computers to learn.
Mobile Computing	Mobile computing is a term used to describe the use of computers without the need to be connected to a network, either by radio, satellite, etc.
Natural Language Processing	Is a field of computer science, artificial intelligence and linguistics that studies the interactions between computers and human language.
Network Analysis	Social network analysis is an interdisciplinary field of study focused on the study of social networks, whose initial motivation is the modeling and study of social phenomena.
Neural Network	Are computational model evolved from various scientific contributions that are recorded in history. It consists of a set of units, called artificial neurons, connected together to transmit signals to each other.
NLP	Is a field of computer science, artificial intelligence and linguistics that studies the interactions between computers and human language.
NNMF	Non-negative matrix factorization, also non-negative matrix approximation, is a group of algorithms in multivariate analysis and linear algebra where a matrix V is factored into two matrices W and H, with the property that all three matrices have no negative elements.
NOSQL	Is a broad class of database management systems that differ from the classical RDBMS model in important respects, the most prominent being that they do not use SQL as their primary query language.
OLAP	Online analytical processing. It is a solution used in the field of the so-called Business Intelligence whose objective is to speed up the querying of large amounts of data.
Opinion Mining	Sentiment analysis refers to the use of natural language processing, text analysis and computational linguistics to identify and extract subjective information from resources.
PLSA	Probabilistic latent semantic indexing is a statistical technique for the analysis of two-mode and co-occurrence data. In effect, one can derive a low-dimensional representation of the observed variables in terms of their affinity to certain hidden variables, just as in latent semantic analysis, from which PLSA evolved.
PVS	Is a software that allows groups to securely conduct votes and elections.
PVSR	Is a visual presentation technique that displays information in fragments and in a sequential manner, providing a relationship between the information displayed and the space/time used that is highly satisfactory.
Really Simple Syndication	Stands for Really Simple Syndication, an XML format for distributing content on the web. It is used to disseminate frequently updated information to users who have subscribed to the content feed.
RFID	Radio frequency identification is a remote data storage and retrieval system that uses devices called RFID tags, cards or transponders. The purpose is to transmit the identity of an object using radio waves.
RNN	Recurrent Neural Network, the structure of an artificial neural network is relatively simple and refers mainly to matrix multiplication.

continues on following page

Table 4. Continued

Key Terms	Definition
Sentiment Analysis	Refers to the use of natural language processing, text analysis and computational linguistics to identify and extract subjective information from resources.
Single Sign On	Single Sign On" or "Unified Sign On" is an authentication procedure that enables a given user to access multiple systems with a single instance of identification.
SQL	Is a domain-specific language used in programming, designed to manage, and retrieve information from relational database management systems.
SVM	Support vector machines or support vector machines are a set of supervised learning algorithms developed by Vladimir Vapnik and his team at AT&T Laboratories. These methods are properly related to classification and regression problems.
TAM	Total Available Market is the total market demand for a product or service.
UTAUT	The unified theory of technology acceptance and use is a model of technology acceptance formulated by Venkatesh et al. in "User acceptance of information technology: Toward a unified view."
VLDBS	Is a database that contains a large amount of data, so much so that it may require specialized architecture, administration, processing and maintenance methodologies.
XML	eXtensible Markup Language, translated as "Extensible Markup Language" or "Extensible Markup Language", is a metalanguage that allows defining markup languages developed by the World Wide Web Consortium used to store data in a readable form.

Source: Self-elaboration

CONCLUSION

The main objective of this research work was to conduct a deeper and clearer study on the different data mining techniques used by governments. The results of this research show that there is an opportunity for improvement in the use of government data. Two clear needs are shown, one about training, and the other about execution by large companies, political institutions and the state, so that strategies can be implemented more efficiently through big data systems that encourage and help predict possible outcomes, and in turn, help improve decision-making processes.

This chapter provides an overview on the current state of the theoretical and empirical literature on Big Data concepts related to government affairs. Today's world, and the speed with which new technologies evolve, means that the paradigm shifts and developments in how to work with the data available to governments are continuous and the opportunities for improvement are consequently also constant. Hence the need for rapid adaptability by agencies to these new ways of obtaining valuable information for their decisions. In this systematic literature review, 50 key terms have been identified and subsequently classified and described.

Furthermore, with respect to the first question posed (What are the main techniques used by governments to extract data?) it can be seen, thanks to the results obtained, that there are a number of them that are most commonly used by governments. It is important to note that some of these techniques, which are defined as such in the study, can be concepts that are also related to indicators or strategies, since they are broad concepts that can be used in different ways depending on the nuance or context in which they are found. Thus we see how the techniques most commonly used by governments are: Artificial Intelligence, Cloud Computing, Data Mining, Data Science, LDA, LSA, Machine Learning, Mobile Computing, NNMF, NLP, Opinion Mining, OLAP, and Sentimental Analysis.

In response to the second question (Can these tools pose risks to citizens?), it can be seen that these are turbulent times for this issue, as there are constant changes in terms of legislation and data use. Users are exposed to certain risks when accepting cookies, or simply by using certain browsers, entering or registering on websites, downloading, using social networks, shopping.... Any action that has to do with the Internet involves leaving data that companies, or in this case, governments, collect and use to their advantage. As the data collected are, essentially, personal data, the issue goes beyond that, since the risks in terms of security and privacy of the user increase, which means that both the user and the company or institution must comply with the law and protect these data as much as possible.

Theoretical Implications

The theoretical implications of the present research are as follows. First, our study summarizes the data extraction techniques used by governments, thus the novelty and originality of our study is that we systematically review these techniques for the very first time. In this way, our results highlight the main benefits and uses of each identified big data tools, so future research may be focused on linking data extraction technologies to government initiatives, programs, and services in order to propose a more effective government organization.

In the 21st century, rapid growth in the development of data-driven technologies used by governments is a recurring topic among researchers. Therefore, our study contributes to a deep understanding of a complex topic, by presenting these techniques in a single article, thus helping academics establish further research.

Likewise, science and technology are advancing rapidly, so consequently this research will be updated as new formulas are developed between Big Data and the use of the same by the states.

In addition, this research reveals several issues to be taken into account in future research, as they are relevant to the development of this new technology and the functions performed by governments.

Practical Implications

Similarly, this study is aimed at all government bodies that want to delve deeper into the subject, improve their results and become more efficient with the resolution of social problems or obtain a greater positive impact with their citizens. Of note, the implementation of a more effective system in these organizations will improve not only the processes involved, such as collection, processing and storage, but also the data quality.

The results of the present study can be used by governments and public institutions to understand which techniques, methods, and tools can be used to collect data. Therefore, the identified technologies summarize the main ways governments gather data from population to improve their strategies, campaigns, and decision-making.

In a data-driven era, these tools let governments reduce their costs, improve their offered services and design better solutions. In this way, our study demonstrates that Big Data techniques are widely used among different organizations to improve their initiatives and structures.

Limitations and Future Research

Several limitations need to be considered when interpreting the results of this review. First, the number of reviewed articles and databases consulted. In this way, the number of articles that meet criteria was reduced due to the lack of research in big data extraction techniques linked to government practices. Second, even though we sought to minimize this issue by including several databases such as Web of sciences (WOS), ScienceDirect, IEEExplore, ACM Digital Library and AIS electronic library, there are more databases available. Additionally, the searches were carried out in English, thus valid articles published in other languages may be left out. Another point to consider and take into account is the fact that technological changes are occurring at such a rapid pace that this study must always be contextualized and placed in time so that it does not lose meaning and coherence.

REFERENCES

Abu-Shanab, E., & Harb, Y. (2019). E-government research insights: Text mining analysis. *Electronic Commerce Research and Applications*, *38*, 100892. doi:10.1016/j.elerap.2019.100892

Abu-Shanab, E. A. (2020). E-government contribution to better performance by public sector. In Open Government: Concepts, Methodologies, Tools, and Applications (pp. 1-17). IGI Global.

Ahad, M. A., Paiva, S., Tripathi, G., & Feroz, N. (2020). Enabling technologies and sustainable smart cities. *Sustainable Cities and Society*, *61*, 102301. doi:10.1016/j.scs.2020.102301

Al Nuaimi, E., Al Neyadi, H., Mohamed, N., & Al-Jaroodi, J. (2015). Applications of big data to smart cities. *Journal of Internet Services and Applications*, *6*(1), 1–15. doi:10.118613174-015-0041-5

Al-Sai, Z. A., & Abualigah, L. M. (2017, May). Big data and E-government: A review. In *2017 8th international conference on information technology (ICIT)* (pp. 580-587). IEEE. 10.1109/ICITECH.2017.8080062

Andrejevic, M. (2014). Big data, big questions| the big data divide. *International Journal of Communication*, *8*, 17.

Anshari, M., Almunawar, M. N., & Lim, S. A. (2018, February). Big data and open government data in public services. In *Proceedings of the 2018 10th International Conference on Machine Learning and Computing* (pp. 140-144). 10.1145/3195106.3195172

Anshari, M., & Lim, S. A. (2017). E-government with big data enabled through smartphone for public services: Possibilities and challenges. *International Journal of Public Administration*, *40*(13), 1143–1158. doi:10.1080/01900692.2016.1242619

Anthopoulos, L. G. (2017). Smart government: A new adjective to government transformation or a trick? *Understanding Smart Cities: A Tool for Smart Government or an Industrial Trick?*, 263-293.

Archenaa, J., & Anita, E. M. (2015). A survey of big data analytics in healthcare and government. *Procedia Computer Science*, *50*, 408–413. doi:10.1016/j.procs.2015.04.021

Archenaa, J., & Anita, E. M. (2015). A survey of big data analytics in healthcare and government. *Procedia Computer Science*, *50*, 408–413. doi:10.1016/j.procs.2015.04.021

Bonina, C., & Eaton, B. (2020). Cultivating open government data platform ecosystems through governance: Lessons from Buenos Aires, Mexico City and Montevideo. *Government Information Quarterly*, *37*(3), 101479. doi:10.1016/j.giq.2020.101479

Chen, C. P., & Zhang, C. Y. (2014). Data-intensive applications, challenges, techniques and technologies: A survey on Big Data. *Information Sciences*, *275*, 314–347. doi:10.1016/j.ins.2014.01.015

Chen, F., Deng, P., Wan, J., Zhang, D., Vasilakos, A. V., & Rong, X. (2015). Data mining for the internet of things: Literature review and challenges. *International Journal of Distributed Sensor Networks*, *11*(8), 431047. doi:10.1155/2015/431047

Chen, H., Chiang, R., & Storey, V. (2012). Business Intelligence and Analytics: From Big Data to Big Impact. *Management Information Systems Quarterly*, *36*(4), 1165–1188. doi:10.2307/41703503

Chen, Y. C., & Hsieh, T. C. (2014). Big data for digital government: Opportunities, challenges, and strategies. *International Journal of Public Administration in the Digital Age*, *1*(1), 1–14. doi:10.4018/ijpada.2014010101

Clark, W. R., & Golder, M. (2015). Big data, causal inference, and formal theory: Contradictory trends in political science?: Introduction. *PS, Political Science & Politics*, *48*(1), 65–70. doi:10.1017/S1049096514001759

Cordero, R. (2019). Qué es un concepto? Theodor W. Adorno y la crítica como método. *Diferencias*, *1*(8).

Dickersin, K., & Berlin, J. A. (1992). Meta-analysis: State-of-the-science. *Epidemiologic Reviews*, *14*(1), 154–176. doi:10.1093/oxfordjournals.epirev.a036084 PMID:1289110

Driss, O. B., Mellouli, S., & Trabelsi, Z. (2019). From citizens to government policy-makers: Social media data analysis. *Government Information Quarterly*, *36*(3), 560–570. doi:10.1016/j.giq.2019.05.002

Ebrahim, Z., & Irani, Z. (2005). E-government adoption: Architecture and barriers. *Business Process Management Journal*, *11*(5), 589–611. doi:10.1108/14637150510619902

Esteves, J., & Joseph, R. C. (2008). A comprehensive framework for the assessment of eGovernment projects. *Government Information Quarterly*, *25*(1), 118–132. doi:10.1016/j.giq.2007.04.009

Gottfried, A., Hartmann, C., & Yates, D. (2021). Mining Open Government Data for Business Intelligence Using Data Visualization: A Two-Industry Case Study. *Journal of Theoretical and Applied Electronic Commerce Research*, *16*(4), 1042–1065. doi:10.3390/jtaer16040059

Günther, W. A., Mehrizi, M. H. R., Huysman, M., & Feldberg, F. (2017). Debating big data: A literature review on realizing value from big data. *The Journal of Strategic Information Systems*, *26*(3), 191–209. doi:10.1016/j.jsis.2017.07.003

Hagen, L., Harrison, T., & Falling, M. (2021, June). Contributions of Data Science to Digital Government Research: Contributions of Data Science to Digital Government Research. In *DG. O2021: The 22nd Annual International Conference on Digital Government Research* (pp. 38-48). Academic Press.

Hassani, H., Huang, X., Silva, E. S., & Ghodsi, M. (2016). A review of data mining applications in crime. *Statistical Analysis and Data Mining: The ASA Data Science Journal*, *9*(3), 139–154. doi:10.1002am.11312

Jadi, Y., & Jie, L. (2017, July). An Implementation Framework of Business Intelligence in e-government systems for developing countries: Case study: Morocco e-government system. In *2017 International Conference on Information Society (i-Society)* (pp. 138-142). IEEE. 10.23919/i-Society.2017.8354689

Janssen, M., Brous, P., Estevez, E., Barbosa, L. S., & Janowski, T. (2020). Data governance: Organizing data for trustworthy Artificial Intelligence. *Government Information Quarterly*, *37*(3), 101493. doi:10.1016/j.giq.2020.101493

Janssen, M., van der Voort, H., & Wahyudi, A. (2017). Factors influencing big data decision-making quality. *Journal of Business Research*, *70*, 338–345. doi:10.1016/j.jbusres.2016.08.007

Joseph, R. C., & Johnson, N. A. (2013). Big data and transformational government. *IT Professional*, *15*(6), 43–48. doi:10.1109/MITP.2013.61

Khine, P. P., & Shun, W. Z. (2017). Big Data for organizations: A review. *Journal of Computer and Communications*, *5*(3), 40–48. doi:10.4236/jcc.2017.53005

Kim, S. (2021). Education and Public Service Motivation: A Longitudinal Study of High School Graduates. *Public Administration Review*, *81*(2), 260–272. doi:10.1111/puar.13262

Kim, S., Andersen, K. N., & Lee, J. (2021). Platform Government in the Era of Smart Technology. *Public Administration Review*, puar.13422. doi:10.1111/puar.13422

LaBrie, R. C., Steinke, G. H., Li, X., & Cazier, J. A. (2018). Big data analytics sentiment: US-China reaction to data collection by business and government. *Technological Forecasting and Social Change*, *130*, 45–55. doi:10.1016/j.techfore.2017.06.029

Leonelli, S. (2018, October). Rethinking reproducibility as a criterion for research quality. In *Including a symposium on Mary Morgan: curiosity, imagination, and surprise*. Emerald Publishing Limited. doi:10.1108/S0743-41542018000036B009

Li, S., Dragicevic, S., Castro, F. A., Sester, M., Winter, S., Coltekin, A., Pettit, C., Jiang, B., Haworth, J., Stein, A., & Cheng, T. (2016). Geospatial big data handling theory and methods: A review and research challenges. *ISPRS Journal of Photogrammetry and Remote Sensing*, *115*, 119–133. doi:10.1016/j.isprsjprs.2015.10.012

Lim, C., Kim, K. J., & Maglio, P. P. (2018). Smart cities with big data: Reference models, challenges, and considerations. *Cities (London, England)*, *82*, 86–99. doi:10.1016/j.cities.2018.04.011

Mergel, I., Rethemeyer, R. K., & Isett, K. (2016). Big data in public affairs. *Public Administration Review*, *76*(6), 928–937. doi:10.1111/puar.12625

Morabito, V. (2015). Big data and analytics for government innovation. In *Big data and analytics* (pp. 23-45). Springer. doi:10.1007/978-3-319-10665-6_2

Nikiforova, A., & McBride, K. (2021). Open government data portal usability: A user-centred usability analysis of 41 open government data portals. *Telematics and Informatics*, *58*, 101539. doi:10.1016/j.tele.2020.101539

Noble, S., Scheinost, D., & Constable, R. T. (2019). A decade of test-retest reliability of functional connectivity: A systematic review and meta-analysis. *NeuroImage, 203*, 116157. doi:10.1016/j.neuroimage.2019.116157 PMID:31494250

Ortiz, Z. (2004). *¿ Qué son las revisiones sistemáticas.* Recuperado de: http://www. scielo. org. co/ scielo. php

Pannu, M., Gill, B., Tebb, W., & Yang, K. (2016, October). The impact of big data on government processes. In *2016 IEEE 7th Annual Information Technology, Electronics and Mobile Communication Conference (IEMCON)* (pp. 1-5). IEEE. 10.1109/IEMCON.2016.7746334

Papadopoulos, A. V., Versluis, L., Bauer, A., Herbst, N., Von Kistowski, J., Ali-Eldin, A., ... Iosup, A. (2019). Methodological principles for reproducible performance evaluation in cloud computing. *IEEE Transactions on Software Engineering.*

Pence, H. E. (2014). What is big data and why is it important? *Journal of Educational Technology Systems, 43*(2), 159–171. doi:10.2190/ET.43.2.d

Ping, J. (2018, August). Opportunities provided by Big Data technology for government management. In *Proceedings of the 3rd International Conference on Judicial, Administrative and Humanitarian Problems of State Structures and Economic Subjects* (Vol. 252, pp. 552-555). 10.2991/jahp-18.2018.113

Ribeiro-Navarrete, S., Saura, J. R., & Palacios-Marqués, D. (2021). Towards a new era of mass data collection: Assessing pandemic surveillance technologies to preserve user privacy. *Technological Forecasting and Social Change, 167*, 120681. doi:10.1016/j.techfore.2021.120681 PMID:33840865

Rozario, A. M., & Issa, H. (2020). Risk-based data analytics in the government sector: A case study for a US county. *Government Information Quarterly, 37*(2), 101457. doi:10.1016/j.giq.2020.101457

Rozario, A. M., & Issa, H. (2020). Risk-based data analytics in the government sector: A case study for a US county. *Government Information Quarterly, 37*(2), 101457. doi:10.1016/j.giq.2020.101457

Sadowski, J. (2019). When data is capital: Datafication, accumulation, and extraction. *Big Data & Society, 6*(1), 2053951718820549. doi:10.1177/2053951718820549

Saura, J. R. (2021). Using data sciences in digital marketing: Framework, methods, and performance metrics. *Journal of Innovation & Knowledge, 6*(2), 92–102. doi:10.1016/j.jik.2020.08.001

Saura, J. R., Palacios-Marqués, D., & Iturricha-Fernández, A. (2021b). Ethical Design in Social Media: Assessing the main performance measurements of user online behavior modification. *Journal of Business Research, 129*(May), 271–281. doi:10.1016/j.jbusres.2021.03.001

Saura, J. R., Palacios-Marqués, D., & Ribeiro-Soriano, D. (2021). Using data mining techniques to explore security issues in smart living environments in Twitter. *Computer Communications, 179*, 285–295. doi:10.1016/j.comcom.2021.08.021

Saura, J. R., Palacios-Marqués, D., & Ribeiro-Soriano, D. (2021c). How SMEs use data sciences in their online marketing performance: A systematic literature review of the state-of-the-art. *Journal of Small Business Management.* Advance online publication. doi:10.1080/00472778.2021.1955127

Saura, J.R., Ribeiro, D., & Palacios-Marqués, E.R. (2021a). From user-generated data to data-driven innovation: A research agenda to understand user privacy in digital markets. *International Journal of Information Management*. .ijinfomgt.2021.102331 doi:10.1016/j

Saura, J. R., Ribeiro-Soriano, D., & Palacios-Marqués, D. (2021). Setting Privacy "by Default" in Social IoT: Theorizing the Challenges and Directions in Big Data Research. *Big Data Research*, *25*, 100245. doi:10.1016/j.bdr.2021.100245

Saura, J. R., Ribeiro-Soriano, D., & Palacios-Marqués, D. (2021d). Setting B2B Digital Marketing in Artificial Intelligence-based CRMs: A review and directions for future research. *Industrial Marketing Management*, *98*(October), 161–178. doi:10.1016/j.indmarman.2021.08.006

Söderström, O., Paasche, T., & Klauser, F. (2014). Smart cities as corporate storytelling. *City*, *18*(3), 307–320. doi:10.1080/13604813.2014.906716

Tsado, Y., Gamage, K. A., Lund, D., & Adebisi, B. (2016, October). Performance analysis of variable Smart Grid traffic over ad hoc Wireless Mesh Networks. In *2016 International Conference on Smart Systems and Technologies* (SST) (pp. 81-86). IEEE. 10.1109/SST.2016.7765637

Ullah, Z., Al-Turjman, F., Mostarda, L., & Gagliardi, R. (2020). Applications of artificial intelligence and machine learning in smart cities. *Computer Communications*, *154*, 313–323. doi:10.1016/j.comcom.2020.02.069

Von Haldenwang, C. (2004). Electronic government (e-government) and development. *European Journal of Development Research*, *16*(2), 417–432. doi:10.1080/0957881042000220886

Wang, H., Xu, Z., Fujita, H., & Liu, S. (2016). Towards felicitous decision making: An overview on challenges and trends of Big Data. *Information Sciences*, *367*, 747–765. doi:10.1016/j.ins.2016.07.007

Wu, Y. (2014). Protecting personal data in E-government: A cross-country study. *Government Information Quarterly*, *31*(1), 150–159. doi:10.1016/j.giq.2013.07.003

Yan, Z. (2018, January). Big data and government governance. In *2018 International Conference on Information Management and Processing (ICIMP)* (pp. 111-114). IEEE. 10.1109/ICIMP1.2018.8325850

Yin, J., Sharma, P., Gorton, I., & Akyoli, B. (2013). Large-Scale Data Challenges in Future Power Grids. *Service Oriented System Engineering (SOSE), 2013 IEEE 7th International Symposium on IEEE*, 324–328.

Zainal, N. Z., Hussin, H., & Nazri, M. N. M. (2016, November). Big data initiatives by governments--issues and challenges: A review. In *2016 6th international conference on information and communication technology for the Muslim World (ICT4M)* (pp. 304-309). IEEE.

Zhang, W., & Chen, Q. (2010, May). From E-government to C-government via Cloud Computing. In *2010 International Conference on E-Business and E-Government* (pp. 679-682). IEEE. 10.1109/ICEE.2010.177

Zhang, W., Wang, M., & Zhu, Y. C. (2020). Does government information release really matter in regulating contagion-evolution of negative emotion during public emergencies? From the perspective of cognitive big data analytics. *International Journal of Information Management*, *50*, 498–514. doi:10.1016/j.ijinfomgt.2019.04.001

Zhou, Z. H., Chawla, N. V., Jin, Y., & Williams, G. J. (2014). Big data opportunities and challenges: Discussions from data analytics perspectives. *IEEE Computational Intelligence Magazine, 9*(4), 62–74. doi:10.1109/MCI.2014.2350953

Zuboff, S. (2015). Big other: Surveillance capitalism and the prospects of an information civilization. *Journal of Information Technology, 30*(1), 75–89. doi:10.1057/jit.2015.5

Section 3
Case Studies on Artificial Intelligence Government Practices

Section 3 presents case studies applied to AI strategies used by governments in the last decade. The chapter discusses strategies developed by governments in different scenarios, challenges, and opportunities using case studies of several industries.

Chapter 10
A Public Values Perspective on the Application of Artificial Intelligence in Government Practices:
A Synthesis of Case Studies

Rohit Madan

Henley Business School, University of Reading, UK

Mona Ashok

https://orcid.org/0000-0002-9827-9104

Henley Business School, University of Reading, UK

ABSTRACT

The use of artificial intelligence (AI) by governments represents a radical transformation of governance, which has the potential for a lean government to provide personalised services that are efficient and cost-effective. This represents the next frontier of digital-era governance (DEG), which is an extension of the traditional bureaucratic model representing digital manifestations of instrumental rationality. However, the use of AI also introduces new risks and ethical challenges (such as biased data, fairness, transparency, the surveillance state, and citizen behavioural control) that need to be addressed by governments. This chapter critiques DEG enabled by AI. The authors argue for adopting a public values perspective for managing AI ethical dilemmas. Through a cross-case analysis of 30 government AI implementations, four primary AI use cases are outlined. Furthermore, a conceptual model is developed that identifies relationships between AI ethical principles and public values as drivers of AI adoption by citizens. Finally, six propositions are outlined for future research.

DOI: 10.4018/978-1-7998-9609-8.ch010

INTRODUCTION

The first wave of technological innovation in governments focussed on digitising back-office operations with the goals of efficiency and cost savings inspired by the New Public Management (NPM) reforms of the 1980s. NPM was driven by the neo-liberal agenda and critique of large bureaucratic structures associated with red tape and cumbersome processes (Bernier et al., 2015; Kamarck, 2004). However, technology took a backseat and was considered simply a tool for achieving managerialism. Succeeding this initial technology implementation which has had mixed results in meeting its innovation goals (Hung et al., 2006), the second wave driven by Artificial Intelligence (AI), however, is transforming the roles and functions of government. Often referred to as the next frontier of digital-era governance (DEG) (Dunleavy et al., 2006), this technologically centred model of governance enabled by AI has the potential for a lean government providing personalised services that are efficient and cost-effective. The use of AI also introduces new risks and ethical challenges such as biased data, fairness, transparency, the surveillance state, and citizen behavioural control (Ashok et al., 2022; Saura et al., 2021A; Ashok, 2018). Maintaining citizen trust and legitimacy of AI-driven governmental services and processes is vital more than ever for sustaining democratic processes (Janssen & van den Hoven, 2015).

The concept of AI, introduced by John McCarthy in 1956, is aimed at developing intelligent machines that can emulate human cognition autonomously (von Krogh, 2018; Washington, 2006). Following an enthusiastic start, progress stalled due to technical limitations; AI was limited to expert systems with specific applications (Haenlein & Kaplan, 2019). At the beginning of the 21st century, with advances in processing speeds and storage, and decreasing computational costs, interest in AI grew exponentially (Haenlein & Kaplan, 2019; von Krogh, 2018). Brynjolfsson and McAfee (2014, p. 7) claim this renewed interest as the "second machine age" where machines are taking over cognitive human tasks.

Dwivedi et al. (2021) discuss the terminological challenges associated with defining AI. The meaning of artificial vs natural is derived from the epistemological assumptions of objectivist or constructivist ideas and scientists and philosophers still do not have a good grasp of what intelligence entails (Ibid.). Following Dwivedi et al. (2021, p. 24) "institutional hybrid" approach, AI for this chapter is defined as emerging technologies that enable machines to "learn, adapt, be creative and solve problems" autonomously (Rosa et al., 2016, p. 6). Scholars (Raisch & Krakowski, 2020; Sousa et al., 2019; von Krogh, 2018) generally agree on the three components of AI: input, often big data; task processing algorithms; and output, either digital or physical.

The primary applications of AI in government are process automation, virtual agents, predictive analytics, resource management, and threat intelligence and security (Ojo et al., 2019; Wirtz et al., 2018). The associated benefits include efficiencies, accelerated processing of cases, workforce redistribution to productive tasks, and enhancing satisfaction and trust in public authorities (Susar & Aquaro, 2019; Wirtz & Müller, 2018). AI represents radical innovation transforming internal organisational structures and introducing new governance models (Ashok et al., 2016). However, the use of AI for making policy decisions is accompanied by ethical dilemmas of fairness, transparency of black-box algorithms, privacy concerns, and respect for human rights (Ashok et al., 2022; Ribeiro-Navarrete et al., 2021; Wirtz et al., 2018). Kuziemski and Misuraca (2020) and Helbing et al. (2019) discuss externalities from the use of AI leading to the detriment of human dignity and well-being such as mass surveillance, profiling, and nudging for incentivising compliance with government direction akin to programming citizens. Mehr et al. (2017) caution AI should not be used solely for its innovation potential but adapted towards a broader social development goal. Citizens expect responsive governments able to meet their personalised needs with the adoption of AI-driven governmental services. The level of trust and legitimacy of government determines expectations of privacy and a fair, equitable, and secure outcome. Erosion of this trust with mismanagement of ethical issues undermines democratic institutions and impacts adoption.

The ethical design of digital technologies is a contemporaneous issue debated in academia and policy (Saura et al., 2021A). The use of AI further intensifies this debate especially in terms of biased data having a detrimental effect on its trustworthiness (Janssen et al., 2020) and consequently marginalising already most at-risk populations. AI has also been discussed from the perspective of maintaining power and control than as an agent for societal advancement (Crawford, 2021). Motivated by these growing concerns, governments and technology companies have published several ethical guidelines for the development of AI solutions. Floridi and Cowls (2019, pp. 6-8) conducted a comparative analysis of leading AI ethical frameworks and developed five AI principles: 'beneficence', 'non-maleficence', 'autonomy', 'justice', and 'explicability'. Jobin et al. (2019)'s analysis of global AI guidelines shows a convergence of these high-level AI principles but divergence on interpretation and application. There is still a large gap in the literature on how to use these macro-level principles during the design and implementation of AI. Ashok et al. (2022) discuss AI ethical impact analysis, balancing AI ethical considerations with societal impact, a critical topic of research and currently a significant gap in literature and policy. In the context of the government's use of AI, these ethical principles need to be front and centre towards balancing societal goals against economic and political objectives.

The literature on the use of AI within governments and its transformation has received far less attention than the role of government as a regulator of these technologies (Kuziemski & Misuraca, 2020; Valle-Cruz et al., 2019). Wirtz et al. (2018)'s literature review of AI in the public sector shows scarce research on AI applications and challenges. The factors affecting AI adoption in governments have not been tested (Valle-Cruz et al., 2019). Scholars (Alsheibani et al., 2018; Jankin et al., 2018; Misuraca et al., 2020) have called for research to understand the adoption of AI-driven government services.

In light of these literature gaps, this chapter explores AI use in governments and argues for an adoption model balancing broader public interests against the ethical risks of AI. The chapter seeks to explore two research questions:

RQ1: How is AI being used in governments?
RQ2: What are the factors that impact citizen adoption of AI-driven governmental services?

The next section critiques public administration paradigms and argues for adopting a Public Values Management (PVM) perspective for exploring the use of AI in governments. This is followed by a review of technology adoption models providing a theoretical basis for exploring citizen adoption of AI-driven governmental services. There is scant empirical evidence on how AI is being implemented in governments (Mikalef et al., 2019). Thus, the authors adopt a cross-case analysis method and through a systematic literature review identify thirty cases. A typology of AI use cases is developed and explicate the balance between AI ethics principles and public values as drivers of adoption by citizens. The resulting conceptual model extends the literature on the current technology adoption models within the context of AI in governments. The model also has practical implications providing a framework for exploring benefits and risks from the use of AI towards achieving citizen adoption.

LITERATURE REVIEW

Public Administration Paradigms

Weber's ideal-type bureaucracy, an embodiment of "techno-scientific" logic separating bureaucrats from political questions of morality and obtaining legitimacy through established laws of the land, assumed a dominant position in the twentieth century as the appropriate organisational design for managing modern and complex capitalist societies (Chris & Susan, 2018, p. 192; Courpasson & Clegg, 2016). Bureaucracy came to be seen as means of maintaining control over the masses and critiqued for elite bureaucrats assuming increasing decision-making power distancing citizens from democratic processes (Chris & Susan, 2018, p. 192). Such neo-liberal ideas garnered mainstream support in the 1970s with stagflation and oil crisis seen as failures of Keynesian policies. The popular discourse moved towards liberating individual entrepreneurial freedoms and limiting the role of the state as an "institutional framework ... [to] guarantee ... integrity of money ... set up military, defence, legal structures ... secure private property rights ... functioning of markets" (Harvey, 2007, p. 2).

Neo-liberalism propagated decentralisation in public administration emboldened by the dominant discourse of market control as the superior form of organising evident from private sector success (Christensen et al., 2007; Hartley et al., 2013). This perception of antiquated hierarchical government structures characterised by inertia and red tape has persisted in practice and scholarship to this date (Perry & Rainey, 1988; Rainey & Bozeman, 2000).

A confluence of neo-liberalism and economic climate led to the set of reforms categorised under NPM beginning in the 1980s with successful political campaigns in the UK, US, and Canada highly critical of governmental bureaucracy (Bernier et al., 2015; Kamarck, 2004). However, following the limited success of NPM and concurrently technology assuming the dominant role of a social actor, two new paradigms are emerging, Public Value Management (PVM) and Digital-era Governance (DEG) (De Vries & Nemec, 2013; Dunleavy et al., 2006; Hood, 1991).

New Public Management (NPM)

NPM became the dominant public administration paradigm in the 1980s seen as a pragmatic synthesis of operating principles borrowed from private sector successes. The three main themes of NPM are "disaggregation" through splitting up of large governmental hierarchies, "competition" adopting marketisation of public services, and "incentivization" through empowering employees and rewarding performance-based management (Dunleavy et al., 2006, p. 470). The American reform movement by Osborne and Gaebler (1992) argued for downsizing public services by focussing on policy development and marketizing service delivery functions while Hood (1991, 1995) in the European context argued for improving the quality of public service delivery by adopting management practices but maintaining the central role of the government. These reforms introduced quasi-markets, managerialism, and performance management metrics (Hartley et al., 2013; Torfing, 2019).

Hood (1991) synthesises NPM critique in four main categories. First, the strong institutional character of the governments resisted cultural change from NPM. Parker (2000)'s examination of Australian public sector organizations supports this view. Notwithstanding a central mandate to adopt NPM, these agencies were resilient and continued to emphasise values of hierarchical and bureaucratic culture. Christensen et al. (2007) argue the inherent multifunctional conflict regarded as a systemic defect in

NPM and resolved through disaggregation and marketisation principles is instead a core organisational trait in public administration that cannot be eliminated. Ashok et al. (2021) show organisational inertia driven by bureaucracy negatively impacts knowledge management practices adoption in UAE public sector despite a national agenda towards innovation and knowledge economy.

Second, public administration scholars (Bryhinets et al., 2020; Dunleavy et al., 2006; Rainey & Bozeman, 2000; Torfing, 2019) concur NPM was politically motivated than based on empirical evidence and has failed to deliver on its promises of reinvention. Dunleavy et al. (2006) argue NPM's performance and disaggregation principles damaged public service ethos and reduced citizens' engagement with government. Skålén (2004, p. 251) empirical research in Sweden contradicts NPM claims of performance-based pay summarising "NPM creates heterogeneous, conflicting and fluid organizational identities, rather than the uniform and stable business identity it is supposed to." NPM led to unintentional consequences of "overbidding" and "free-riding" problems (Hartley et al., 2013, p. 823).

Third, NPM marketisation principles have been critiqued for the implicit assumption of the superiority of market control. Scholars argue pursuit of efficiency initially seen as means towards social goals became ends in themselves (Bannister & Connolly, 2014; Dunleavy et al., 2006; Harvey, 2007). Performance management goals compelled public managers to focus on specific short-term institutional goals while ignoring the broader vision of public service (Bryhinets et al., 2020).

Fourth, Hood (1991, p. 9) argues NPM's claims of "universality" were unfounded with different administrative values having varied implications on the administrative culture. NPM's focus on economic values has been detrimental to the pursuit of external societal goals with public administration becoming internally focused.

The first two critiques on the incongruity and adverse effects of applying market control principles to governments have led to a reversal of NPM changes since early 2000 (Dunleavy et al., 2006). The disaggregated agencies have been consolidated into coherent government-wide processes, however, performance management, marketisation, and incentivisation persist (Ibid.). The first wave of information technology (IT) implementations within the governments was driven by NPM principles of efficiency and cost savings (Cordella & Bonina, 2012). These projects failed to consider the critical importance of technology and its role in transformational change of governments and society at large, the narrative was centred on technology as a tool enabling managerial values (Dunleavy et al., 2006; Ashok, 2018). Ojo et al. (2019) contend NPM even worked against the digital transformation of government through outsourcing and failure of large IT implementations. With the current wave of digital transformation through AI, technology needs to be central and hence, a new paradigm of DEG is emerging.

Following the critiques on the NPM discourse of serving society exclusively through economic goals (Dunleavy et al., 2006) and the proliferation of AI inducing ethical dilemmas, the paradigm of PVM is emerging.

Digital-Era Governance (DEG)

DEG encompasses "complex…changes, which have IT…at their centre, …[and] spread…in many more dimensions simultaneously than was the case with previous IT influences" (Dunleavy et al., 2006, p. 478). The vision of DEG is a lean and smarter state administration driven by big data and advanced analytics (Andrews, 2018). DEG represents a transformation change often described as the second wave of technological development and takes a step further from e-government in locating human-machine interactions at the core of government service delivery; citizens and private agents are governed through co-producing big data and machine interactions (Williamson, 2014).

Dunleavy et al. (2006, p. 480) discuss three primary themes of DEG: "reintegration", "needs-based holism", and "digitalization changes". First, reintegration encompasses consolidating distinct agencies created as a result of the disaggregation agenda of NPM and the establishment of central shared services for the efficient and effective government (Ojo et al., 2019). Second, needs-based holism characterises transformational change between government and citizens through end-to-end reengineering, digital citizen engagement, crowdsourcing of policy ideas, and concepts like agile government (Ibid.). Third, integrating the other two themes is digitalisation change referring to the global trend towards open government and transparency (Ibid.). Paradoxically, quantification of citizen transactions and surveillance without checks leads to a manifestation of Orwell's fictional big brother state (Chris & Susan, 2018; Kuziemski & Misuraca, 2020).

Chris and Susan (2018) argue DEG draws a parallel to Weber's bureaucracy with digital manifestations of efficiency, objectivity, and rationality. Efficiency and cost savings remain the key objectives for the implementation of AI in government (Misuraca et al., 2020). Algorithms have assumed the role of bureaucratic experts representing objectivity by distancing humans from the decision-making process and representing "instrumental rationality in the public sphere" (Dunn & Miller, 2007, p. 353). Similarly, big data represents the ontological assumption of realism capturing the world the way it exists without human subjectivity and engenders legitimacy through data and algorithmic neutrality (Chris & Susan, 2018). With the proliferation of digital technologies, citizens can disseminate information and cultivate their realities weakening the formal rationality and legal dominance of administration, most apparent in fake news, nationalistic campaigns, conspiracy theories, etc. This represents a "control crisis" requiring experts' intervention, where a centralised hierarchy is achieved through a distributed "bureaucracy at distance" (Chris & Susan, 2018, p. 206). Thus, DEG represents an "institutional matrix" consisting of humans, algorithms, data collection devices, and surveillance representing Weber's "techno-scientific" logic through rule-based rationality (Chris & Susan, 2018, p. 207).

Public Value Management (PVM)

The debates on public values grew out of the critique of NPM's claims of being universal in its application. Hood (1991, p. 11) argues governmental strategy is fundamentally dependent on administrative values and discusses three core values as: "…'sigma'…relates to economy and parsimony, 'theta'… relates to honesty and fairness, and 'lambda'…relates to security and resilience." NPM in principle only represents "sigma" values of "cost-cutting, efficiency, and performance management" (Ibid.) and fails to satisfy universality assumptions.

Bannister and Connolly (2014, p. 120) define values as "a mode of behaviour, either a way of doing things or an attribute of a way of doing things, that is held to be right." In the context of technological change in public administration, values ascribe public servants behavioural intention towards goals that "citizens … consider … to be right" (Ibid.). This definition concurs with Schein (1992)'s conceptualisation of values as basic underlying assumptions that drive acceptable norms and are the primary source of motivation and coordination of organizational activity (Daher, 2016; Gregory et al., 2009). Pant and Lachman (1998, p. 197) refer to these as core values that exert "high consensus and high control."

PVM was forwarded by Moore (1995) who popularised the strategic triangle as a pragmatic model for public managers to undertake strategy development. The strategic triangle encompasses public value, legitimacy and support, and the development of operational capabilities (Moore, 1994 1995). The key tenant of PVM is public value creation through government programs and services (Bryhinets et al., 2020; Karkin et al., 2018). As opposed to the NPM tenants of delivering public goods by the most efficient means (Hartley et al., 2016), public values are pluralistic over and above economic values. PVM is derived through democratic processes engendering legitimacy and clearly understanding the public interest and the overall public sphere (Andrews, 2018; Ranerup & Henriksen, 2019). With strategy derived from public values, the operational capacity building turns towards long-term outcomes, public managers shift from results orientation to stakeholder interactions and co-production with citizens (Bryhinets et al., 2020; Karkin et al., 2018; Panagiotopoulos et al., 2019).

In the contemporary e-government literature, PVM is discussed as a new paradigm that can address the challenges of governmental reforms centred on digital technologies (Cordella & Bonina, 2012). Ranerup and Henriksen (2019) contend technology is not only an enabler of value creation but also a mode for engaging citizens. PVM provides an appropriate democratic process for resolving ethical dilemmas with the implementation of AI in the public sector (Andrews, 2018; Panagiotopoulos et al., 2019). PVM orientation helps public managers to ensure the maximisation of aggregate values of all services delivered together (Panagiotopoulos et al., 2019).

Bannister and Connolly (2014, p. 123) adapt Hood (1991)'s taxonomy to analyse the impact of technology on public administration and propose three core values as "duty", "service", and "social". Duty orientation aligns with Hood (1991)'s sigma values adopting a "broader view incorporating non-financial aspects [of public administration]", service orientation falls within lambda values "covering responsibility … to provide good service to customers" and social orientation corresponds to theta values but also incorporate "wider, quasi-political view … [of] social goals" (Ibid.).

Dunn and Miller (2007, p. 353) argue instrumental rationality is embedded in both NPM and Weber's bureaucracy with the main goal of "control of human and material nature on the basis of knowledge." This deduction can be expended to DEG in the form of digital Weberianism where the role of scientific, professional, and technocrat's expertise is being assumed by algorithms (Chris & Susan, 2018). From a critical theory perspective, there is a large gap in the theory and practice of public administration on the "emancipatory" rationality concerned with "critical self-reflection and creation of institutions through moral discourse and ethical reflection" (Dunn & Miller, 2007, p. 354). In addition, ethical dilemmas introduced with the implementation of AI in government further strengthen the need for assuming "emancipatory" rationality in both research and practice. PVM provides an opportunity for such ethical discussions and offers a complementary perspective to DEG in light of AI implementations.

Technology Adoption

Technology adoption models use theories from informatics, sociology, and psychology, and explain potential users' intention to use new digital technology, (Chatterjee & Bhattacharjee, 2020; Williams et al., 2009). Venkatesh et al. (2003) synthesised eight leading technology adoption theories into a UTAUT model that has received wide acceptance and application in research. UTAUT suggests four exogenous constructs as determinants of behavioural intention to adopt a technology, "performance expectancy, effort expectancy, social influence and facilitating conditions" (Venkatesh et al., 2003, p. 447). This model has been used as a theoretical lens to study the adoption of AI such as Chatterjee and Bhattacharjee (2020), Fan et al. (2018), Gao et al. (2015), Wang et al. (2014), Adapa et al. (2017). In many studies, UTAUT has been expanded by adding additional variables such as trust, perceived enjoyment, and personal innovativeness (Chong, 2013). Venkatesh et al. (2012, p. 160) extend UTAUT to UTAUT2 by adding consumer-specific constructs to further incorporate end consumer context. Most recently, Dwivedi et al. (2020, p. 14) performed a meta-analysis of UTAUT usage and further outline a meta-UTAUT model adding attitude as a mediator and several other constructs such as "compatibility, perceived information security, perceived social pressure, perceived innovativeness in IT, resistance to change, perceived enjoyment".

Kim et al. (2007) argue traditional technology adoption models are internally focussed on organisational users with desired outcomes of efficiency. Externally focussed models like UTAUT2 and meta-UTAUT are consumer focussed with profit motive outcomes. Literature on e-government adoption using such models propagates bias towards managerial and economic outcomes driven by NPM tenants (Cordella & Bonina, 2012) and continues to be driving AI implementations. Misuraca et al. (2020) review of 85 AI implementations in the European public sector shows 70% were driven by performance and efficiency goals, with only 30% being focussed on making the government open and none on public values. As well, the expected benefits in 56.5% are internally motivated towards organisational performance and only 27.1% towards social values (Ibid.). Reis et al. (2019) discuss current AI models are heavily skewed towards private sector needs and lack consideration of public values. Furthermore, the discourse on the role of government in directing AI development is divided between the US pursuing a private-sector led agenda and UK and EU propagating a public-private partnership approach (Reis et al., 2019). In either case, there is a concern that lack of public administration scholarship and consideration of public values will once again create conditions whereby the government adopts private sector models with disappointing results similar to NPM-era IT projects.

With the implementation of AI, technological change is growing in complexity. Governments need to build mechanisms able to examine the value judgements behind a decision made by AI (Susar & Aquaro, 2019) and the public value perspective provides one such mechanism. However, there is limited research on exploring the technology adoption from a PVM perspective (Andrews, 2018; Cordella & Bonina, 2012; Karkin et al., 2018; Moore, 2014). Political reform agendas discuss the critical role of technology as a driver of governmental innovation but lack any discussion on the relationship between technology and public values (Bannister & Connolly, 2014). Thus, with ethical dilemmas associated with AI implementation as enumerated by AI principles and the evolving DEG paradigm at the risk of becoming a digital version of Weber's bureaucracy, this chapter aims to develop an AI adoption model that incorporates public values at its core.

CROSS-CASE ANALYSIS

The objective of this chapter was two-fold. First, develop a typology of the use of AI in governments. Second, enumerate the factors that impact citizen adoption of AI-driven governmental services drawing on public administration and technology adoption theories. To achieve these objectives, the authors undertake a case study synthesis approach exploring the phenomenon of AI implementations within governments. Given the scarcity of empirical studies on AI implementations, secondary case studies are used to achieve theoretical saturation on AI use and determinants of adoption. Khan and VanWynsberghe (2008) argue cross-case analysis assist with identifying commonalities and differences in the phenomenon and contributes towards conditional generalisations. Stake (2006, p. 6) discuss themes identified through cross-case analysis that can be used to make assertions about the "quintain", the phenomenon or object being studied. In the current analysis, this is an AI-enabled governmental service or process. As well as cross-case comparisons can support the identification of clusters sharing certain configurations and help build typologies of the phenomenon (Khan & VanWynsberghe, 2008). Denzin (2001) suggest identifying essential elements and components of a phenomenon across multiple cases. These essential elements when clustered within a social context can assist with developing typologies.

Using a sample of 30 representative case studies of AI application in governments (Table 1), qualitative synthesis is conducted to identify AI use cases and determinants of AI adoption.

Table 1. Case studies summary

Case No.	Cases and Summary	Country	AI Use Case	Public Values	AI Principles
1	Annie™ MOORE (Matching and Outcome Optimization for Refugee Empowerment): ML and optimization methods to recommend optimal placements of refugees (OPSI, 2020)	US	Public services delivery	Service Social	Autonomy Beneficence Non-maleficence
2	AuroraAI: personalised AI-driven services for citizens and businesses (Berryhill et al., 2019)	Finland	Public services delivery	Service Social	Beneficence
3	City of Things: development of a smart city (OPSI, 2020)	Belgium	Public services delivery	Social	Beneficence
4	Queensland Land Use Mapping Program (QLUMP): ML and computer vision to automatically map and classify land use features in satellite imagery (OPSI, 2020)	Australia	Public services delivery	Service Social	Explicability
5	MyService: a digital solution enabled by AI/ML to improve veterans' experience when accessing health care (OPSI, 2020)	Australia	Public services delivery	Service	N/A*
6	R2D3: active-waiting robot to at the reception desk of the Department's Home for Disabled Persons (OPSI, 2020)	France	Public services delivery	Service	Beneficence
7	Services Guide: a digital catalogue that centralizes all information regarding public services and Jaque, a virtual clerk based on AI (OPSI, 2020)	Brazil	Public services delivery	Duty Service	Explicability
9	TradeMarker: AI-enabled system for detecting similar trademarks (UNESCAP & Google, 2019)	Israel	Public services delivery	Service	Autonomy
9	UNA: a virtual assistant (OPSI, 2020)	Latvia	Public services delivery	Service	Explicability
10	Aylesbury Vale District Council (AVDC): AI-powered voice control (OPSI, 2020)	UK	Public services delivery	Service	Explicability
11	The Work: a service that recommends jobs without the need to conduct individual searches (OPSI, 2020)	Korea	Public services delivery	Service Social	Explicability

continues on following page

Table 1. Continued

Case No.	Cases and Summary	Country	AI Use Case	Public Values	AI Principles
12	Insights.US: a tool that helps governments and cities obtain insights directly from their stakeholders (OPSI, 2020)	Israel	Public services delivery Regulatory functions	Duty Service	N/A*
13	Converlens: digitally-enabled community engagement in policy and programme design (OPSI, 2020)	Australia	Public services delivery Regulatory functions	Duty Service	Autonomy Explicability
14	Farming the Future: AI in the agricultural sector for sowing advisory and commodity price forecasting (UNESCAP & Google, 2019)	India	Public services delivery Regulatory functions	Service Social	Explicability
15	Better Reykjavik: a crowdsourcing platform for solutions to urban challenges, agenda-setting, participatory budgeting, and policymaking (OPSI, 2020)	Iceland	Regulatory functions	Duty	Beneficence
16	Bomb in a box: use of AI for risk-based reviews of air cargo records (Berryhill et al., 2019)	Canada	Regulatory functions	Service	Explicability
17	CitizenLab: a platform to automatically classify and analyse thousands of contributions collected on citizen participation platforms. (Berryhill et al., 2019)	Belgium	Regulatory functions	Duty	Autonomy Explicability
18	Department for Business, Energy & Industrial Strategy: technological solution to help analyse the cumulative effect of different regulations on business (Forum, 2020)	UK	Regulatory functions	Service	Explicability
19	UK Food Standards Agency: the predictive capability to mitigate against food safety risks (Forum, 2020)	UK	Regulatory functions	Service	Explicability
20	Policing: ML within a policing context for human trafficking mapping; crime 'solvability' estimates; misclassified crime detection; missing person anticipation; geospatial predictive mapping (UNESCAP & Google, 2019)	Unknown	Compliance Regulatory functions	Service	Autonomy Explicability Justice
21	AELOUS: a mid-altitude airborne maritime sensor platform (OPSI, 2020)	Ireland	Compliance	Service	Explicability
22	Fraud detection in social security payments (UNESCAP & Google, 2019)	Australia	Compliance	Justice	Explicability
23	Counterfeit drug detection using Blockchain and AI (OPSI, 2020)	Mongolia	Compliance	Social	Beneficence
24	Serenata de Amor: AI for financial transparency finding misuse of public money by congress members (UNESCAP & Google, 2019)	Brazil	Compliance	Duty Service	Explicability
25	Statement of Interests and Assets system (DIP): monitoring assets and potential conflicts of interest of officials through business intelligence (OPSI, 2020)	Chile	Compliance	Duty Service	N/A*

continues on following page

Table 1. Continued

Case No.	Cases and Summary	Country	AI Use Case	Public Values	AI Principles
26	Slavery from Space: satellite remote sensing data with ML algorithms to detect slavery and monitor antislavery intervention (OPSI, 2020)	UK	Compliance	Social	Beneficence
27	Text analysis: help several government institutions in streamlining and automating their processes, conducting document management audit, removing personal information from nearly 80,000 expired court sentences (OPSI, 2020)	Estonia	Organisational management	Service	N/A*
28	Big Data Analysis for HR efficiency improvement: improve efficiency, develop organisational capacity, improve effectiveness and efficiency, and staff satisfaction. (OPSI, 2020)	Slovenia	Organisational management	Service	Non-maleficence
29	Emergency services forecasting: inform sophisticated machine learning forecasts of hazard probabilities (e.g. flood, cyclone, fire, road crash, rescue, etc.) and evolving exposures (e.g. people, assets) over the coming 10 years (OPSI, 2020)	Australia	Organisational management	Service	Explicability
30	R&D Platform for Investment and Evaluation ("R&D PIE"): provides an evidence-based policy platform to monitor, analyse and manage technologies, talents, and regulatory issues via the PIE model (OPSI, 2020)	Korea	Organisational management	Service	Explicability

* The case descriptions did not outline any specific considerations of risks that can be coded for AI principles.

Methodology

The chapter follows the widely used 'Preferred Reporting Items for Systematic Reviews and Meta-Analyses' (PRISMA) (Moher et al., 2009) methodology to conduct a systematic review and qualitative synthesis of the case studies. The public sector innovation case study archive maintained by OPSI (2020) was used that includes details on 396 cases of public sector innovation (as of March 2021). Using the search terms "artificial intelligence", "big data", and "machine learning", 70 cases were identified for a full-text review. Twenty cases were finally selected for coding after excluding ones that did not involve AI or government context. In addition, through Google Scholar search and following the same exclusion criteria, ten more relevant cases were identified from UNESCAP and Google (2019), Forum (2020), and Berryhill et al. (2019). A range of data was collected for the final 30 cases using desk research to enable triangulation and build the external validity of the findings. These sources included case descriptions published on the case archive databases, government reports, presentations, blogs, news releases, media documents, and website archives.

Qualitative synthesis was conducted using template analysis to identify themes and cluster constituent themes across cases (King, 2004). Data analysis was conducted in three steps as described below. The unit of analysis was the AI-enabled governmental service or an internal process.

In step one, a priori template was developed from the literature that included public values (derived from Bannister and Connolly, 2014) and AI principles (derived from Floridi & Cowls, 2019). In step two, the cases were coded in NVivo identifying the AI use case, objectives, expected outcomes in terms of public values, consideration for AI principle(s), and lessons learned. The resulting themes were organised into constituent and global themes. The final template was developed following a few rounds of reflection and re-organising themes. In step three, results were summarised, and a novel Public Value-based Adoption Model and corresponding propositions were developed.

Results

The case studies are summarised in Table 1. Four themes of AI use are identified. First, compliance involves the use of AI for ensuring citizens, private actors, and governmental agencies abide by the rules and regulations of the land. Second, organisational management involves the use of AI for government administration and internal processes. Third, public service delivery involves the use of AI for delivering public services to a range of stakeholders. Fourth, regulatory functions involve the use of AI for research and policy development. Table 2 shows the definitions and related codes.

Table 2. AI use case definitions and related codes from thematic analysis

AI Use Case	Definition	Codes
Compliance	AI is used for activities related to ensuring citizens, private actors and other governmental agencies adhere to the legislated rules and regulations.	Monitoring and surveillance, fraud detection, counterfeit drug detection, policing, slavery, auditing
Organisational management	AI is used for activities related to the management of internal organisational processes and resources	Streamlining processes, efficiency improvement, budgeting, resource and demand forecasting towards business planning
Public service delivery	AI is used for the delivery of public services to citizens, businesses, and other governmental/NGO bodies.	Refugee resettlement, job recommendations, public engagements, agricultural advisory, land use, administrative claims processing, operations of public service centres, digital catalogue and virtual assistant, trademark registration
Regulatory functions	AI used for activities related to policy development and research	Crowdsourcing, risk-based oversight, predictive regulation, forecasting

Figure 1 shows cases by AI use case. The highest percentage of AI use cases relate to public services delivery at 47% followed by 30% for regulatory functions, 23% for compliance, and 13% for organisational management. Some cases relate to more than one use case and percentages are not exclusive.

Figure 2 shows the cases by country. The sample is global with the largest number of cases from Australia (17%) and the UK (13%).

Table 3 shows the definitions and codes of public values and AI principles identified from the literature and supported by the cases. A map of public values and AI principles by AI use case is shown in Figure 3. The percentages represent the number of cases that mention a particular public value or AI principle by use case; a case may mention more than one public value or AI principal and hence, the percentages are not exclusive.

Figure 1. Cases by AI use case

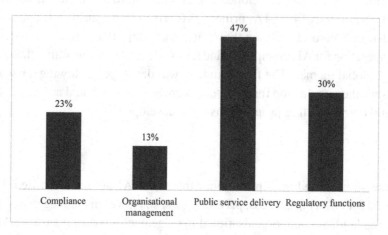

Figure 2. Cases by Country

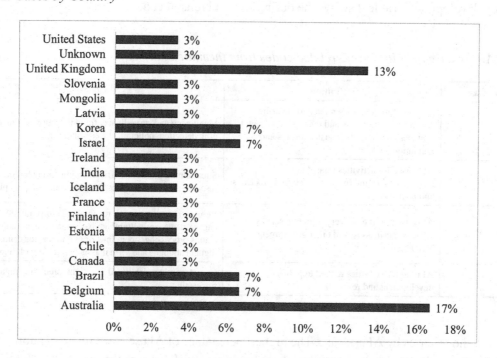

Where black cells represent cited in more than 2/3ʳᵈ cases, grey cells show cited between 1/3ʳᵈ and 2/3ʳᵈ cases, and light grey cells indicate less than 1/3ʳᵈ cases. For cases related to compliance, 71% mention service followed by 29% for duty and social. Service is the only public value for all cases related to organisational management. For cases related to public services delivery, 93% mention service followed by 43% social and 21% duty. For cases related to regulatory functions, 78% mention service followed by 44% duty and 11% social.

Table 3. Public values and AI principles definitions and codes

Constructs	Measures and Definitions	Codes
Public Values (Bannister & Connolly, 2014, pp. Table 2, 123)	Duty orientation: "responsibility to the citizen, politicians, efficient use of public funds, integrity and honesty, democratic will"	Citizen participation, citizen needs, dialogue on the public sphere, inclusive and responsive engagement, government transparency
	Service orientation: "responsiveness, effectiveness, efficiency, transparency"	Streamline processes, resources, and budgets, effectiveness, quality, better planning, efficiency, reducing time, service experience
	Social orientation: "inclusiveness, justice, fairness, equality, respect for citizens, accountability"	Community development, quality of life, access to employment, elimination of counterfeit drugs, environmental concerns, humanitarian efforts, social value
AI Principles (Floridi & Cowls, 2019, pp. 6-8)	Non-maleficence: "do no harm and avoid misuse of privacy and security"	Data privacy, data security, the confidentiality of personal data
	Autonomy: "the power to decide"	Augmenting decision making, free up time for humans to make crucial value judgements
	Explicability: "the knowledge of how AI works and who to hold responsible for its outcomes"	Quality of data, accuracy, explainable AI, trust and awareness, transparency
	Beneficence: "promoting well-being, preserving dignity, and sustaining the planet"	Community development, wellbeing, happiness, quality of life, save lives, inform liberation
	Justice: "the quality of being fair and eliminating discrimination ensuring equal access to the benefits of AI"	Protect vulnerable populations, social biases in machine learning

In terms of AI principles, compliance use cases identify considerations for explicability in 43%, beneficence and justice in 29%, autonomy in 14% cases, and none consider non-maleficence. For organisational management, 50% of cases identify explicability, 25% non-maleficence, and none for autonomy, beneficence, and justice. For public services, 50% identify explicability, 29% beneficence, 21% autonomy, 7% non-maleficence, and none for justice. For regulatory functions, 78% identify explicability, 44% autonomy, 11% beneficence and justice, and none for non-maleficence.

The success criteria and lessons learned were coded into two global themes of external and internal. As the objective of this analysis is citizen adoption, the chapter focuses on the external theme. Three constituent themes were identified under external as shown in Table 4. First, the dominant external theme relates to co-design practices and public-private partnerships. 73% of the cases report a collaborative design process involving citizens and businesses and encouraging public-private collaborations as key to successful adoption. Second, 17% of the cases report communication of benefits vital in successful take-up. Third, 13% report product design as a relevant determinant of higher adoption and discuss simple intuitive design and adaptability of the applications.

DISCUSSION

For the first research question on how AI is being used in government, the cross-case analysis identifies four AI use cases: compliance, regulatory functions, public service delivery, and organisational management. All four use cases support literature regarding the transformational impact of AI, its embedded instrumental rationality, and corresponding ethical dilemmas.

Figure 3. Public values and AI principles by AI use type

AI use type	AI Principles					Public Values		
	Autonomy	Beneficence	Explicability	Justice	Non-maleficence	Duty	Service	Social
Compliance	14%	29%	43%	29%	0%	29%	71%	29%
Organisational management	0%	0%	50%	0%	25%	0%	100%	0%
Public service delivery	21%	29%	50%	0%	7%	21%	93%	43%
Regulatory functions	44%	11%	78%	11%	0%	44%	78%	11%

Key:

cited in over 2/3rd cases

cited in between 1/3rd and 2/3rd cases

cited in less than 1/3rd of cases

Table 4. Externally focussed success criteria and related codes

Global Theme	Constituent Themes	Codes	Percentage of Cases
External	Market the benefits	Communication and promotion of benefits, manage expectations, market the project to citizens, clients understand the benefits	17%
	User interface	Attractive design, lightweight, intuitive to use, make apps interesting to use, human-centred design, design thinking	13%
	Co-design with citizens and stakeholders	Co-design and feedback cycle between all users and stakeholders, consulting process with citizens and businesses, understanding of target users, results of citizen work are used, engagement from different stakeholders, co-creation, bottom- approaches, public-private collaborations, civic volunteers, connecting local knowledge and experience to machine learning, citizen-science platform, social acceptability	73%

Figure 3 shows service is the dominant public value irrespective of AI use case. This concurs with the literature that NPM values of efficiency and cost savings are still driving the majority of AI implementations in government. The use case of public service delivery show social is the second-ranked public value explicating support for external orientation geared towards customer satisfaction and societal reforms. In these cases, AI has been delegated the role of a public agent interacting with citizens and businesses. For fully automated solutions, such as Aylesbury Vale District Council's AI-powered voice control, citizen-government interactions become citizen-AI interactions. The self-learning capabilities of AI risk divergence from its original design towards unexpected influence on citizens' choices. When AI is used for decision augmentation, such as US' Annie™ MOORE on refugee settlement, employees increasingly rely on options suggested by AI which might have a detrimental effect on human learning and knowledge (Berente et al., 2021). AI becomes a salient techno-rational actor learning and influencing public decisions.

The use case of organisational management is internally oriented towards achieving service-oriented values. AI is being used for automating and/or augmenting processes, such as Estonia's text analysis, or directing and evaluating humans, such as Solvenia's HR application. As opposed to expert systems whereby human know-how was embedded as business rules, AI-driven systems incorporate the extreme form of rationality using autonomous learning and correlational knowledge lacking contextual considerations. This is most visibly evident in the regulatory use cases where predictive modelling is used for policy development, such as the UK's predictive solution on the effect of regulations on business. The regulatory functions show duty as the second-ranked public value explicating an internal motive consistent with the ethos of public service to increase transparency and ensure democratic processes for policy development. The use of AI in these use cases have the biggest potential impact on society with policy determining the future of citizens lives and which interventions take precedence. Compliance shows an equal balance of duty and social values explicating the balance between both internal and external goals.

The results also support DEG themes outlined in the literature. The reintegration, needs-based holism, and digitising change themes of DEG (Dunleavy et al., 2006, p. 480) are reflected in Finland's National AI Strategy. This strategy document summarised "developing new operating models to shift from organisation-based activities to systems-wide approaches"; "improve the interoperability of government data, and open up this data to fuel innovation in all sectors"; " public discussion on AI ethics"; and "break down silos within … public services" (Berryhill et al., 2019, pp. 144-148). The specific case of AuroraAI within this national strategy holistically integrates public services from different agencies around three life events: "moving away from study, remaining in the labour market, and family wellbeing after a divorce" (Ibid.). The Services Guide case from Brazil provides another example of DEG themes of reintegration and digitising change by integrating scattered information on public services as an open data digital catalogue and the use of AI as a virtual clerk.

Several cases exemplify the needs-based holism theme of DEG. For example, Belgium's CitizenLab platform uses natural language processing (NLP) and ML to automatically classify thousands of citizen contributions. Similarly, Australia's Converlens assists public servants to manage community engagement using NLP and ML. Australia's use of AI for fraud detection in social security payments, and the use of ML in policing for mapping human trafficking, crime detection, missing person anticipation, and geospatial predictive mapping. The counterfeit drug detection case from Mongolia exemplifies needs-based holism and digitalising change themes. The use of blockchain as an immutable ledger among all stockholders in the supply chain ensures an easy track and trace of counterfeit drugs in real-time.

The four AI use cases explicate the need for a broader public values perspective for exploring AI adoption. Drawing on the consumer choice theory, Kim et al. (2007) developed a Value-based Adoption Model (VAM) that hypothesises perceived value, measured through benefits and sacrifices, as a determinant of adoption intention. VAM has been used extensively to explain the adoption of several AI-based technologies (Hsu & Lin, 2016; Kim et al., 2017; Lau et al., 2019; Yu et al., 2019). Sohn and Kwon (2020) analysis of consumer acceptance of AI-based intelligent products shows VAM performed better than UTAUT in modelling user acceptance. Thus, the authors postulate perceived value of an AI-driven governmental service from a citizen's perspective is measured through public values (a proxy for benefits) and consideration of AI principles (a proxy for sacrifices). The unit of measurement, AI-driven governmental service, is postulated to include uses cases across compliance, regulatory functions, public services delivery, and organisational management in the sense they relate to citizen's perceptions of value generation through consumption of public services, ensuring safety and well-being, or efficient use of public funds. Hence, for the second research question regarding factors influencing citizen adoption of AI-driven governmental services, first two propositions are stated as:

P1: The citizen perception of perceived value associated with AI-driven governmental service is a key
    determinant of adoption intention.
P2: Public values related to service, social, and duty affects the perceived value of AI-driven governmental services.

In terms of AI principles, explicability is dominant regardless of the AI use case. The focus on explicability-related concerns, such as transparency, accuracy, trust, and explainability, align with the dominant service value. A surprising finding is a low percentage for non-maleficence related concerns, especially those relating to data privacy and security. Literature, policy, and media focus extensively on these concerns especially concerning the proliferation of big data (Ribeiro-Navarrete et al., 2021; Saura et al., 2021B). Similarly, justice-related concerns such as discrimination from biased data, equal rights, etc. are also low in the sample. For the public services delivery use type, beneficence considerations are high aligning with social values and reflecting the outward focus. Similarly, for regulatory functions, autonomy considerations are higher reflecting an internal focus on preserving public service jobs and using AI in an augmentation capacity.

This analysis supports the PVM discussion that suggests value orientation that is internally focussed will drive risk mitigation towards accuracy and explainability of data. Hence, this diminishes the considerations for externally focussed societal risks of privacy, discrimination, and justice. The third proposition is stated as:

P3: The citizen perception of risk mitigation related to AI implementation expressed in terms of AI principles affects the perceived value of AI-driven governmental services.

Deducing from the success criterion themes three constructs are identified. First, perceived citizen collaboration is identified as a key determinant of adoption intention. When citizens perceive a strong collaborative process was followed and their needs were considered as evidence of democratic involvement, adoption of such public services will be higher. Second, the "effort expectancy" construct from the UTAUT model (Venkatesh et al., 2003, p. 450) is identified representing the theme of an attractive, intuitive, and adaptive user interface. Third, the "perceived usefulness" construct from the TAM model (Davis, 1989, p. 320) is identified as a measure of the theme around communication of benefits. Hence, three final propositions are stated as:

P4: Perceived collaborative process moderates the relationship between perceived value and adoption intention.
P5: Effort expectancy moderates the relationship between AI principles and perceived value.
P6: Perceived usefulness moderates the relationship between public values and perceived value.

To test these propositions, a Public Values-based Adoption Model is developed as shown in Figure 4.

The definitions of public value and AI principles constructs are derived from literature and case analysis as shown in Table 3. Furthermore, perceived value is defined as the "overall evaluation of the user regarding the benefit and cost of using" an AI-based public service (Kim et al., 2017, p. 1153). Adoption intention is defined as "a desire to use" the new AI-based public service compared to e-government or paper-based alternative (Kim et al., 2017, p. 1153). Effort expectancy is defined as "the degree of ease associated with the use of [AI based public service]" (Venkatesh et al., 2003, p. 450). Perceived usefulness is defined as "the degree to which [citizens] believe an [AI driven public service] would enhance" personal and societal goals (Davis, 1989, p. 320). Perceived collaboration is defined as an overall evaluation of the level of collaboration between the public sector, citizens, and private sector when developing the AI-based public service.

Figure 4. Public Value-based Adoption Model

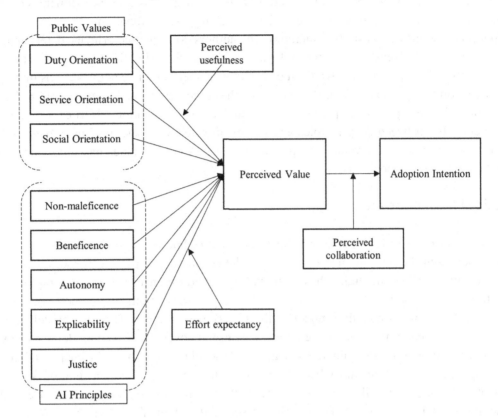

CONCLUSION

In this chapter, the authors aimed to explore the use of AI within governments with a specific focus on the variety of uses and the corresponding citizen adoption. Much of modern government administration has been heavily influenced by the NPM reforms of the 1980s adopting private sector managerial ideas and marketisation of services. With the failures of NPM in bringing forth any meaningful change and the socio-technical transformation of society through AI, DEG is emerging as a new paradigm of governance. However, as much as DEG is hailed as the technological transformation of public administration, the implementation of AI in government introduces several risks.

Following a review of multidisciplinary literature on public administration, AI, and technology adoption, the chapter highlights a critical gap in the use and implementation of AI in government and scant empirical evidence on the determinants of citizen adoption. Furthermore, the majority of technology adoption models focus on internal efficiency and discount the consideration of societal and public values. As a result, AI adoption is being motivated through the efficiency and cost savings ethos (Misuraca et al., 2020) of the NPM-era. Thus, the chapter argues for the adoption of a public values perspective whereby the outcomes of the use of AI are not only related to service values but also incorporate duty and social related values.

In response to these gaps, the authors performed a systematic review of AI implementation cases in government and selected 30 cases for cross-case analysis. Using a range of data sources, the authors conducted a qualitative synthesis and identified four major AI use cases in government: compliance, organisational management, public service delivery, and regulatory functions. Drawing on technology adoption and public administration literature, the authors postulate the primary determinant of AI adoption intention by citizens is the perceived value of the services. Public values are postulated as a proxy for benefits affecting the perceived value. The management of AI principles is postulated as risk mitigation affecting the perceived value. Furthermore, the authors postulate that perceived collaboration moderates the relationship between perceived value and adoption intention, effort expectancy moderates the relationship between AI principles and perceived value, and perceived usefulness moderates the relationship between public values and perceived value. A public values-based adoption model is developed to test these propositions.

Theoretical Implications

This chapter contributes to both public administration and technology adoption literature. Three primary theoretical contributions are highlighted. First, the chapter develops a new typology of AI use in government. This typology highlights the commonalities and differences between AI implementations and their transformational effect on internal processes or government-citizen interactions. Second, the chapter develops a new AI adoption model in the government context. The new model extends the technology adoption literature within the context of AI use in government. The model can be extended to other contexts through future qualitative research and model testing. Third, the chapter addresses the literature gap on using a public values-based perspective to explore the phenomenon of AI use within governments. The authors postulate viewing the benefits of AI in terms of public values, over and above economic measures, is one way of balancing risks associated with the AI principles.

Practical Implications

The practical contribution of this chapter includes both policy and operational implications. First, the typology of AI use cases can be used by policymakers considering regulations on the use of AI within governments. For example, Figure 3 provides a conceptual map of AI principles and public values mapped to each of the AI use cases. Even though limited in terms of generalisability with the small sample size, it provides a starting point on the current state of benefits versus risk considerations in AI implementation projects. A policy intervention towards the desired outcome from AI can then be designed and implemented. Second, citizen adoption is the ultimate measure of the success of AI-driven governmental service. It ensures continued trust and legitimacy in the governmental agency and its actions. The conceptual model with a broader public values perspective will help public managers implementing AI to enumerate and explore the balance between benefits (public values) and risks (AI principles) in terms of achieving a maximised perceived value by the citizens.

Limitations and Future Research

There are two key limitations of this research. First, the data used for the cross-case analysis is limited to secondary published records and documents. The published data might be biased towards highlighting successes and the politically positive view of such implementations. Second, although, the sample of

30 cases achieved theoretical saturation, the findings are limited in terms of inferences of relationships between the constructs and hence its generalisability.

Thus, three future research agendas are suggested. First, collecting primary data through interviews and in-depth case analysis to increase the external validity of the propositions. Second, testing the propositions and the model using mixed-method and quantitative techniques. Third, comparing the proposed Public Values-based Adoption Model results against UTAUT and TAM to determine which model performs better in modelling users' acceptance of AI-driven governmental services.

ACKNOWLEDGMENT

This research received no specific grant from any funding agency in the public, commercial, or not-for-profit sectors.

REFERENCES

Adapa, A., Nah, F. F.-H., Hall, R. H., Siau, K., & Smith, S. N. (2017). Factors Influencing the Adoption of Smart Wearable Devices. *International Journal of Human-Computer Interaction*, *34*(5), 399–409. doi:10.1080/10447318.2017.1357902

Alsheibani, S., Cheung, Y., & Messom, C. (2018). Artificial Intelligence Adoption: AI-readiness at Firm-Level. *Artificial Intelligence*, *6*, 26–2018.

Andrews, L. (2018). Public administration, public leadership and the construction of public value in the age of the algorithm and 'big data'. *Public Administration*, *97*(2), 296–310. doi:10.1111/padm.12534

Ashok, M. (2018, July). Role of digitisation in enabling co-creation of value in KIBS firms. In *International Conference on Informatics and Semiotics in Organisations* (pp. 145-154). Springer.

Ashok, M., Dhaherib, M. S. M. A. B. A., Madan, R., & Dzandu, M. D. (2021). How to counter organisational inertia to enable knowledge management practices adoption in public sector organisations. *Journal of Knowledge Management*, *25*(9), 2245–2273. doi:10.1108/JKM-09-2020-0700

Ashok, M., Madan, R., Joha, A., & Sivarajah, U. (2022). Ethical framework for Artificial Intelligence and Digital technologies. *International Journal of Information Management*, *62*, 102433. doi:10.1016/j.ijinfomgt.2021.102433

Ashok, M., Narula, R., & Martinez-Noya, A. (2016). How do collaboration and investments in knowledge management affect process innovation in services? *Journal of Knowledge Management*, *20*(5), 1004–1024. doi:10.1108/JKM-11-2015-0429

Bannister, F., & Connolly, R. (2014). ICT, public values and transformative government: A framework and programme for research. *Government Information Quarterly*, *31*(1), 119–128. doi:10.1016/j.giq.2013.06.002

Berente, N., Gu, B., Recker, J., & Santhanam, R. (2021). Managing Artificial Intelligence. *Management Information Systems Quarterly*, *45*(3).

Bernier, L., Hafsi, T., & Deschamps, C. (2015). Environmental Determinants of Public Sector Innovation: A study of innovation awards in Canada. *Public Management Review*, *17*(6), 834–856. doi:10.10 80/14719037.2013.867066

Berryhill, J., Heang, K. K., Clogher, R., & McBride, K. (2019). *Hello, World! Artificial Intelligence and its Use in the Public Sector.* https://www.oecd.org/governance/innovative-government/working-paper-hello-world-artificial-intelligence-and-its-use-in-the-public-sector.htm

Bryhinets, O. O., Svoboda, I., Shevchuk, O. R., Kotukh, Y. V., & Radich, V. Y. (2020). Public value management and new public governance as modern approaches to the development of public administration. *Revista San Gregorio*, *1*(42).

Brynjolfsson, E., & McAfee, A. (2014). *The Second Machine Age: Work, Progress, and Prosperity in a Time of Brilliant Technologies*. W. W. Norton.

Chatterjee, S., & Bhattacharjee, K. K. (2020). Adoption of artificial intelligence in higher education: A quantitative analysis using structural equation modelling. *Education and Information Technologies*, *25*(5), 3443–3463. doi:10.100710639-020-10159-7

Chong, A. Y.-L. (2013). Predicting m-commerce adoption determinants: A neural network approach. *Expert Systems with Applications*, *40*(2), 523–530. doi:10.1016/j.eswa.2012.07.068

Chris, M., & Susan, L. R. (2018). Digital Weberianism: Bureaucracy, Information, and the Techno-rationality of Neoliberal Capitalism. *Indiana Journal of Global Legal Studies*, *25*(1), 187–216. doi:10.2979/indjglolegstu.25.1.0187

Christensen, T., Lægreid, P., Roness, P. G., & Røvik, K. A. (2007). *Organization Theory and the Public Sector: Instrument, Culture and Myth*. Taylor & Francis. doi:10.4324/9780203929216

Cordella, A., & Bonina, C. M. (2012). A public value perspective for ICT enabled public sector reforms: A theoretical reflection. *Government Information Quarterly*, *29*(4), 512–520. doi:10.1016/j.giq.2012.03.004

Courpasson, D., & Clegg, S. (2016). Dissolving the Iron Cages? Tocqueville, Michels, Bureaucracy and the Perpetuation of Elite Power. *Organization*, *13*(3), 319–343. doi:10.1177/1350508406063481

Crawford, K. (2021). *The Atlas of AI: Power, Politics, and the Planetary Costs of Artificial Intelligence*. Yale University Press.

Daher, N. (2016). The relationships between organizational culture and organizational innovation. *International Journal of Business & Public Administration*, *13*(2), 1–15.

Davis, F. D. (1989). Perceived Usefulness, Perceived Ease of Use, and User Acceptance of Information Technology. *Management Information Systems Quarterly*, *13*(3), 319–340. doi:10.2307/249008

De Vries, M., & Nemec, J. (2013). Public sector reform: An overview of recent literature and research on NPM and alternative paths. *International Journal of Public Sector Management*, *26*(1), 4–16. doi:10.1108/09513551311293408

Denzin, N. K. (2001). *Interpretive interactionism* (Vol. 16). Sage. doi:10.4135/9781412984591

Dunleavy, P., Margetts, H., Bastow, S., & Tinkler, J. (2006). New Public Management Is Dead-Long Live Digital-Era Governance. *Journal of Public Administration: Research and Theory, 16*(3), 467–494. doi:10.1093/jopart/mui057

Dunn, W. N., & Miller, D. Y. (2007). A Critique of the New Public Management and the Neo-Weberian State: Advancing a Critical Theory of Administrative Reform. *Public Organization Review, 7*(4), 345–358. doi:10.100711115-007-0042-3

Dwivedi, Y. K., Hughes, L., Ismagilova, E., Aarts, G., Coombs, C., Crick, T., Duan, Y., Dwivedi, R., Edwards, J., Eirug, A., Galanos, V., Ilavarasan, P. V., Janssen, M., Jones, P., Kar, A. K., Kizgin, H., Kronemann, B., Lal, B., Lucini, B., ... Williams, M. D. (2021). Artificial Intelligence (AI): Multidisciplinary perspectives on emerging challenges, opportunities, and agenda for research, practice and policy. *International Journal of Information Management, 57,* 101994. doi:10.1016/j.ijinfomgt.2019.08.002

Dwivedi, Y. K., Rana, N. P., Tamilmani, K., & Raman, R. (2020). A meta-analysis based modified unified theory of acceptance and use of technology: A review of emerging literature. *Current Opinion in Psychology, 36,* 13–18. doi:10.1016/j.copsyc.2020.03.008 PMID:32339928

Fan, W., Liu, J., Zhu, S., & Pardalos, P. M. (2018). Investigating the impacting factors for the healthcare professionals to adopt artificial intelligence-based medical diagnosis support system (AIMDSS). *Annals of Operations Research, 294*(1-2), 567–592. doi:10.100710479-018-2818-y

Floridi, L., & Cowls, J. (2019). A unified framework of five principles for AI in society. *Harvard Data Science Review, 1*(1).

Forum, W. E. (2020). *AI Procurement in a Box: Pilot case studies from the United Kingdom.* https://www3.weforum.org/docs/WEF_AI_Procurement_in_a_Box_Pilot_case_studies_from_the_United_Kingdom_2020.pdf

Gao, Y., Xiaojun Wang, P. L. W., Professor Xu Chen, D., Li, H., & Luo, Y. (2015). An empirical study of wearable technology acceptance in healthcare. *Industrial Management & Data Systems, 115*(9), 1704–1723. doi:10.1108/IMDS-03-2015-0087

Gregory, B. T., Harris, S. G., Armenakis, A. A., & Shook, C. L. (2009). Organizational culture and effectiveness: A study of values, attitudes, and organizational outcomes. *Journal of Business Research, 62*(7), 673–679. doi:10.1016/j.jbusres.2008.05.021

Haenlein, M., & Kaplan, A. (2019). A Brief History of Artificial Intelligence: On the Past, Present, and Future of Artificial Intelligence. *California Management Review, 61*(4), 5–14. doi:10.1177/0008125619864925

Hartley, J., Alford, J., Knies, E., & Douglas, S. (2016). Towards an empirical research agenda for public value theory. *Public Management Review, 19*(5), 670–685. doi:10.1080/14719037.2016.1192166

Hartley, J., Sørensen, E., & Torfing, J. (2013). Collaborative Innovation: A Viable Alternative to Market Competition and Organizational Entrepreneurship. *Public Administration Review, 73*(6), 821–830. doi:10.1111/puar.12136

Harvey, D. (2007). *A Brief History of Neoliberalism.* Oxford University Press.

Helbing, D., Frey, B. S., Gigerenzer, G., Hafen, E., Hagner, M., Hofstetter, Y., Van Den Hoven, J., Zicari, R. V., & Zwitter, A. (2019). Will democracy survive big data and artificial intelligence? In *Towards digital enlightenment* (pp. 73–98). Springer. doi:10.1007/978-3-319-90869-4_7

Hood, C. (1991). A public management for all seasons? *Public Administration, 69*(1), 3–19. doi:10.1111/j.1467-9299.1991.tb00779.x

Hsu, C.-L., & Lin, J. C.-C. (2016). Exploring Factors Affecting the Adoption of Internet of Things Services. *Journal of Computer Information Systems, 58*(1), 49–57. doi:10.1080/08874417.2016.1186524

Hung, S.-Y., Chang, C.-M., & Yu, T.-J. (2006). Determinants of user acceptance of the e-Government services: The case of online tax filing and payment system. *Government Information Quarterly, 23*(1), 97–122. doi:10.1016/j.giq.2005.11.005

Jankin, S., Pencheva, I., & Esteve, M. (2018). Big Data & AI – A Transformational Shift for Government: So, What Next for Research? *Public Policy and Administration*, 1–21.

Janssen, M., Brous, P., Estevez, E., Barbosa, L. S., & Janowski, T. (2020). Data governance: Organizing data for trustworthy Artificial Intelligence. *Government Information Quarterly, 37*(3), 101493. doi:10.1016/j.giq.2020.101493

Janssen, M., & Estevez, E. (2013). Lean government and platform-based governance-Doing more with less. *Government Information Quarterly, 30*, S1–S8. doi:10.1016/j.giq.2012.11.003

Janssen, M., & van den Hoven, J. (2015). Big and Open Linked Data (BOLD) in government: A challenge to transparency and privacy? *Government Information Quarterly, 32*(4), 363–368. doi:10.1016/j.giq.2015.11.007

Jobin, A., Ienca, M., & Vayena, E. (2019). The global landscape of AI ethics guidelines. *Nature Machine Intelligence, 1*(9), 389–399. doi:10.103842256-019-0088-2

KamarckE. (2004). *Government Innovation Around the World.* https://ssrn.com/abstract=517666 doi:10.2139/ssrn.517666

Karkin, N., Yavuz, N., Cubuk, E. B. S., & Golukcetin, E. (2018, May). The impact of ICTs-related innovation on public values in public sector. *Proceedings of the 19th Annual International Conference on Digital Government Research: Governance in the Data Age.* 10.1145/3209281.3209351

Khan, S., & VanWynsberghe, R. (2008). Cultivating the under-mined: Cross-case analysis as knowledge mobilization. *Forum Qualitative Social Research, 9*(1), 34.

Kim, H.-W., Chan, H. C., & Gupta, S. (2007). Value-based Adoption of Mobile Internet: An empirical investigation. *Decision Support Systems, 43*(1), 111–126. doi:10.1016/j.dss.2005.05.009

Kim, Y., Park, Y., & Choi, J. (2017). A study on the adoption of IoT smart home service: Using Value-based Adoption Model. *Total Quality Management & Business Excellence, 28*(9-10), 1149–1165. doi:10.1080/14783363.2017.1310708

King, N. (2004). Using template analysis in the thematic analysis of text. In G. Symon & C. Cassell (Eds.), *Essential guide to qualitative methods in organizational research* (pp. 256–270). Sage. doi:10.4135/9781446280119.n21

Kuziemski, M., & Misuraca, G. (2020). AI governance in the public sector: Three tales from the frontiers of automated decision-making in democratic settings. *Telecommunications Policy*, 44(6), 101976. doi:10.1016/j.telpol.2020.101976 PMID:32313360

Lau, C. K. H., Chui, C. F. R., & Au, N. (2019). Examination of the adoption of augmented reality: A VAM approach. *Asia Pacific Journal of Tourism Research*, 24(10), 1005–1020. doi:10.1080/1094166 5.2019.1655076

Mehr, H., Ash, H., & Fellow, D. (2017). Artificial intelligence for citizen services and government. *Ash Cent. Democr. Gov. Innov. Harvard Kennedy Sch*, (August), 1–12.

Mikalef, P., Fjørtoft, S. O., & Torvatn, H. Y. (2019, September). Artificial Intelligence in the public sector: a study of challenges and opportunities for Norwegian municipalities. In *Conference on e-Business, e-Services and e-Society* (pp. 267-277). Springer.

Misuraca, G., van Noordt, C., & Boukli, A. (2020, September) [Paper presentation]. The use of AI in public services. *Proceedings of the 13th International Conference on Theory and Practice of Electronic Governance.*

Moher, D., Liberati, A., Tetzlaff, J., Altman, D. G., & Group, P. (2009). Preferred reporting items for systematic reviews and meta-analyses: The PRISMA statement. *PLoS Medicine*, 6(7), e1000097. doi:10.1371/journal.pmed.1000097 PMID:19621072

Moore, M. (1994). Public Value as the Focus of Strategy. *Australian Journal of Public Administration*, 53(3), 296–303. doi:10.1111/j.1467-8500.1994.tb01467.x

Moore, M. H. (1995). *Creating Public Value: Strategic Management in Government*. Harvard University Press.

Moore, M. H. (2014). Public value accounting: Establishing the philosophical basis. *Public Administration Review*, 74(4), 465–477. doi:10.1111/puar.12198

Morley, J., Floridi, L., Kinsey, L., & Elhalal, A. (2020). From What to How: An Initial Review of Publicly Available AI Ethics Tools, Methods and Research to Translate Principles into Practices. *Science and Engineering Ethics*, 26(4), 2141–2168. doi:10.100711948-019-00165-5 PMID:31828533

Ojo, A., Mellouli, S., & Zeleti, F. A. (2019, June) [Paper presentation]. A Realist Perspective on AI-era Public Management. *Proceedings of the 20th Annual International Conference on Digital Government Research.* 10.1145/3325112.3325261

OPSI. (2020). *Case Study Archive*. https://oecd-opsi.org/case-study-archive/

Osborne, D., & Gaebler, T. (1992). *Reinventing Government: How the Entrepreneurial Spirit is Transforming the Public Sector*. Addison-Wesley Publishing Company.

Panagiotopoulos, P., Klievink, B., & Cordella, A. (2019). Public value creation in digital government. *Government Information Quarterly*, 36(4), 101421. doi:10.1016/j.giq.2019.101421

Pant, P. N., & Lachman, R. (1998). Value Incongruity and Strategic Choice. *Journal of Management Studies*, *35*(2), 195–212. doi:10.1111/1467-6486.00090

Perry, J. L., & Rainey, H. G. (1988). The Public-Private Distinction in Organization Theory: A Critique and Research Strategy. *Academy of Management Review*, *13*(2), 182–201. doi:10.5465/amr.1988.4306858

Rainey, H. G., & Bozeman, B. (2000). Comparing Public and Private Organizations: Empirical Research and the Power of the A Priori. *Journal of Public Administration Research and Theory: J-PART*, *10*(2), 447–469. doi:10.1093/oxfordjournals.jpart.a024276

Raisch, S., & Krakowski, S. (2020). Artificial Intelligence and Management: The Automation-Augmentation Paradox. *Academy of Management Review*, *46*(1), 192–210. doi:10.5465/amr.2018.0072

Ranerup, A., & Henriksen, H. Z. (2019). Value positions viewed through the lens of automated decision-making: The case of social services. *Government Information Quarterly*, *36*(4), 101377. doi:10.1016/j.giq.2019.05.004

Reis, J., Espírito Santo, P., & Melao, N. (2019, April). Artificial Intelligence in Government Services: A Systematic Literature Review. In *World conference on information systems and technologies* (pp. 241-252). Springer.

Ribeiro-Navarrete, S., Saura, J. R., & Palacios-Marqués, D. (2021). Towards a new era of mass data collection: Assessing pandemic surveillance technologies to preserve user privacy. *Technological Forecasting and Social Change*, *167*, 120681. doi:10.1016/j.techfore.2021.120681 PMID:33840865

Rosa, M., Feyereisl, J., & Collective, T. G. (2016). *A framework for searching for general artificial intelligence*. arXiv preprint arXiv:1611.00685.

Saura, J. R., Palacios-Marqués, D., & Iturricha-Fernández, A. (2021A). Ethical design in social media: Assessing the main performance measurements of user online behavior modification. *Journal of Business Research*, *129*, 271–281. doi:10.1016/j.jbusres.2021.03.001

Saura, J. R., Ribeiro-Soriano, D., & Palacios-Marqués, D. (2021B). Setting Privacy "by Default" in Social IoT: Theorizing the Challenges and Directions in Big Data Research. *Big Data Research*, *25*, 100245. doi:10.1016/j.bdr.2021.100245

Schein, E. H. (1992). *Organizational culture and leadership*. Jossey-Bass.

Skålén, P. (2004). New public management reform and the construction of organizational identities. *International Journal of Public Sector Management*, *17*(3), 251–263. doi:10.1108/09513550410530171

Sohn, K., & Kwon, O. (2020). Technology acceptance theories and factors influencing artificial Intelligence-based intelligent products. *Telematics and Informatics*, *47*, 101324. doi:10.1016/j.tele.2019.101324

Sousa, W. G., Melo, E. R. P., Bermejo, P. H. D. S., Farias, R. A. S., & Gomes, A. O. (2019). How and where is artificial intelligence in the public sector going? A literature review and research agenda. *Government Information Quarterly*, *36*(4), 101392. doi:10.1016/j.giq.2019.07.004

Stake, R. E. (2006). *Stake, Robert E*. Multiple Case Study Analysis. New York.

Susar, D., & Aquaro, V. (2019, April). Artificial intelligence: Opportunities and challenges for the public sector. *Proceedings of the 12th International Conference on Theory and Practice of Electronic Governance.* 10.1145/3326365.3326420

Torfing, J. (2019). Collaborative innovation in the public sector: The argument. *Public Management Review, 21*(1), 1–11. doi:10.1080/14719037.2018.1430248

UNESCAP & Google. (2019). *Artificial Intelligence In The Delivery of Public Services.* https://www.unescap.org/publications/artificial-intelligence-delivery-public-services

Valle-Cruz, D., Alejandro Ruvalcaba-Gomez, E., Sandoval-Almazan, R., & Ignacio Criado, J. (2019, June). A review of artificial intelligence in government and its potential from a public policy perspective. *Proceedings of the 20th Annual International Conference on Digital Government Research.* 10.1145/3325112.3325242

Venkatesh, M., Morris, Davis, & Davis. (2003). User Acceptance of Information Technology: Toward a Unified View. *Management Information Systems Quarterly, 27*(3), 425–478. doi:10.2307/30036540

Venkatesh, T., Thong, & Xu. (2012). Consumer Acceptance and Use of Information Technology: Extending the Unified Theory of Acceptance and Use of Technology. *Management Information Systems Quarterly, 36*(1), 157–178. doi:10.2307/41410412

von Krogh, G. (2018). Artificial intelligence in organizations: New opportunities for phenomenon-based theorizing. *Academy of Management Discoveries, 4*(4), 404–409. doi:10.5465/amd.2018.0084

Wang, Y.-Y., Luse, A., Townsend, A. M., & Mennecke, B. E. (2014). Understanding the moderating roles of types of recommender systems and products on customer behavioral intention to use recommender systems. *Information Systems and e-Business Management, 13*(4), 769–799. doi:10.100710257-014-0269-9

Washington, U. o. (2006). *The History of Artificial Intelligence.* https://courses.cs.washington.edu/courses/csep590/06au/projects/history-ai.pdf

Williams, M. D., Dwivedi, Y. K., Lal, B., & Schwarz, A. (2009). Contemporary Trends and Issues in it Adoption and Diffusion Research. *Journal of Information Technology, 24*(1), 1–10. doi:10.1057/jit.2008.30

Williamson, B. (2014). Knowing public services: Cross-sector intermediaries and algorithmic governance in public sector reform. *Public Policy and Administration, 29*(4), 292–312. doi:10.1177/0952076714529139

Wirtz, B. W., & Müller, W. M. (2018). An integrated artificial intelligence framework for public management. *Public Management Review, 21*(7), 1076–1100. doi:10.1080/14719037.2018.1549268

Wirtz, B. W., Weyerer, J. C., & Geyer, C. (2018). Artificial Intelligence and the Public Sector—Applications and Challenges. *International Journal of Public Administration, 42*(7), 596–615. doi:10.1080/01900692.2018.1498103

Yu, H., Seo, I., & Choi, J. (2019). A study of critical factors affecting adoption of self-customisation service – focused on value-based adoption model. *Total Quality Management & Business Excellence, 30*(sup1), S98-S113.

ADDITIONAL READING

Bannister, F., & Connolly, R. (2014). ICT, public values and transformative government: A framework and programme for research. *Government Information Quarterly*, *31*(1), 119–128. doi:10.1016/j.giq.2013.06.002

Berryhill, J., Heang, K. K., Clogher, R., & McBride, K. (2019). *Hello, World! Artificial Intelligence and its Use in the Public Sector.* https://www.oecd.org/governance/innovative-government/working-paper-hello-world-artificial-intelligence-and-its-use-in-the-public-sector.htm

Dunleavy, P., Margetts, H., Bastow, S., & Tinkler, J. (2006). New Public Management Is Dead-Long Live Digital-Era Governance. *Journal of Public Administration: Research and Theory*, *16*(3), 467–494. doi:10.1093/jopart/mui057

Dwivedi, Y. K., Hughes, L., Ismagilova, E., Aarts, G., Coombs, C., Crick, T., Duan, Y., Dwivedi, R., Edwards, J., Eirug, A., Galanos, V., Ilavarasan, P. V., Janssen, M., Jones, P., Kar, A. K., Kizgin, H., Kronemann, B., Lal, B., Lucini, B., ... Williams, M. D. (2021). Artificial Intelligence (AI): Multidisciplinary perspectives on emerging challenges, opportunities, and agenda for research, practice and policy. *International Journal of Information Management*, *57*, 101994. doi:10.1016/j.ijinfomgt.2019.08.002

Floridi, L., & Cowls, J. (2019). A unified framework of five principles for AI in society. *Harvard Data Science Review, 1*(1).

Forum, W. E. (2020). *AI Procurement in a Box: Pilot case studies from the United Kingdom.* Author.

UNESCAP & Google. (2019). *Artificial Intelligence In The Delivery of Public Services.* https://www.unescap.org/publications/artificial-intelligence-delivery-public-services

KEY TERMS AND DEFINITIONS

AI for Compliance: AI is used for governmental activities to ensure citizens, private actors, and other governmental agencies adhere to the legislated rules and regulations.

AI for Organisational Management: AI is used for activities related to the management of internal governmental processes and resources.

AI for Public Service Delivery: AI is used for the delivery of public services to citizens, businesses, and other governmental/NGO bodies.

AI for Regulatory Functions: AI is used for activities related to policy development and research.

Artificial Intelligence (AI): A cluster of digital technologies that enable machines to learn and solve cognitive problems autonomously without human intervention.

Digital-Era Governance: An emerging public administration paradigm that situates technology at the centre of governmental processes and advocates for a lean and data-driven governance model.

New Public Management: Public administration reforms of the 1980s that propagated adoption of private sector organisational management practices in public sector organisations. These included quasi-markets, managerialism, employee empowerment, public entrepreneurialism, and performance management practices.

Public Value Management: The government's organisational values and processes are geared towards achieving duty, service, and social-oriented goals that citizens regard as pertinent.

Chapter 11
The Role of AI in a Security and Population Control System:
Chinese Social Credit System

Miguel Madueño
Rey Juan Carlos University, Spain

Luis Illanas
Universidad Nacional de Educación a Distancia, Spain

ABSTRACT

In this chapter, the authors analyse the Chinese social credit system and its impact and implementation on Western democratic systems to address the challenges posed by terrorist threats and social tensions. The case around which this chapter is structured is the Chinese social credit, projected in a short period of time to other countries. This analysis focuses on the motivations that lead China to develop and implement this system and the type of policies pursued around social credit. The authors also analyse the tools on which it is based and the debate that the implementation of a system of population control of these dimensions brings about.

INTRODUCTION

Nowadays, issues such as Artificial Intelligence (AI), facial recognition and Big Data have become part of our everyday vocabulary and are something we only knew about in science fiction films and books, but once again we are witnessing that reality exceeds the limits of imagination. In this chapter we will look at the control, in terms of security, through the use of AI systems, of populations by states. It is a phenomenon coeval with the rise of the 4.0 revolution, which contributes to understanding the changing environment, motivated, among other factors, by technological development and the new ethical paradigms built around IA.

DOI: 10.4018/978-1-7998-9609-8.ch011

The paradigmatic case around which this chapter is structured is the Chinese social credit, projected in a short period of time to other countries. For this reason, the primary objectives of this paper revolve around two questions:

1. to analyse the motivations that have led China to develop and implement this model and the type of policies applied around social credit.
2. To explore the tools on which it is based and the debate surrounding the implementation of a population control procedure of these dimensions, as well as the discussion generated by its expansion to other countries.

BACKGROUND

The topicality of the phenomenon does not allow for a historical perspective of its consequences and adds to the problem of a shortage of sources resulting from rigorous and careful study. Faced with a neophyte phenomenon such as this, the existing literature is scarce and there are only a few works that have appeared in the last two years. This should not be an obstacle to renouncing the initiation of research in this field that contributes to extending knowledge from an informative to an academic level. For this reason, we consider this type of study to be necessary to help lay the foundations of a little-known, expanding subject and which, due to its very topicality, is open to changes in approaches in the short and medium term. We can say without a doubt that this is the motivation and the main element that justifies the beginning of this research, always on the move and tiptoeing over a social change originated by the great advances experienced in the field of Information and Communication Technologies (ICT) in the last fifty years.

MAIN FOCUS OF THE CHAPTER

The questions we asked ourselves before writing these pages and which we will try to answer in the chapter on conclusions are several: is the reality we are facing thanks to the new technologies a positive application, is the application of these social control measures justifiable in a state like China, and can these same measures be applied in democratic environments without falling into the contradiction of respect for individual liberties? These questions are intimately linked to the debate between security and freedom, which in China is hardly open to discussion due to the prevailing political system, but which, when transferred to other countries with guarantee-based regimes, does raise a wide-ranging debate. In this sense, we support the line opened in the article "Towards a new era of mass data collection: Assessing pandemic surveillance technologies to preserve user privacy" in which the debate on the handling of data by large institutions and the right of users to preserve their privacy is raised (Ribeiro-Soriano, Saura Palacios-Marqués, 2021).

Our starting hypotheses, therefore, in an attempt to answer the questions posed, are as follows:

1. Western society is not prepared for an increase in state social control measures such as the Chinese social credit as a cultural, economic, and political matter.

2. China possesses the tools to impose social control because of its cultural tradition, which is prone to population control and order.
3. In some Western countries the implementation of alternative social control measures is denied, sometimes justified by the need to maintain minimum levels of security.

However, in order to carry out this research, we have relied on a bibliographic record based on opinion articles and articles published on the internet and in scarce academic contexts, in order to establish an analysis that is appropriate to the sources available to us. The procedure has been adjusted to the historical method of research of a hypothetical deductive type, consisting of compiling the information and checking the sources by subjecting them to external and internal criticism. Once the sources had been selected, in some cases from journalistic sources, it was decided to analyse them and confront the different versions and opinions regarding the use of these systems of social control in order to then raise the questions surrounding this phenomenon, taking into account all the points of view and reinforcing the arguments with those that are most frequently repeated. The work, therefore, has a component of methods based on qualitative aspects typical of the social sciences, although we have provided a series of data and percentages that contribute very useful quantitative aspects to increase the credibility of what has been presented.

Reality Trumps Fiction. Always.

When we talk about the cultural conception that the West and its environment have of new technologies applied to social control, we find a culture that, a priori, is reluctant to submit to such measures. The fundamental reasons are cultural and stem from the literary and cinematographic tradition that for decades has shown these measures and the use of new technologies as negative elements.

Within popular culture, we find, literature and cinema examples, most of them from Sci-Fi, that built an image, sometimes wrong, about Artificial Intelligence and the opportunities that its development and implementation offer to modern societies. In 1949, George Orwell imagined in his book 1984, a surveillance system, that give to the State a complete control over de citizenship, based on a complex system of cameras monitoring all citizen activity and a network of informers, controlled by a higher entity, representing the State, known as the Big Brother. Since the publication of 1984, a great deal of fiction material has been generated, turning in recent decades the idea of an AI, at the service of society into a reality.

The idea of an autonomous system or an AI ensuring security in contemporary societies is a reality accepted by these same societies (Fawzi Mostefai, 2014: 2), that consider, issues such as citizen security and terrorism, must have a response that makes use of all the resources that the State has at its disposal. The characteristic heterogeneity of contemporary societies includes critical sectors regarding an AI system that controls public space. The social response to the use of AI systems is usually unanimous, and it may be necessary remember some Sci-Fi works, to illustrate how their use, and even their existence, has been questioned.

Skynet, the antagonist AI in the film The Terminator (James Cameron, 1984), was responsible to realize the paradigm of mutually assured destruction, triggering a series of nuclear attacks aimed at protecting the human species from its greatest enemy, humanity itself. A year earlier, War Games (John Badham, 1983), theorized about an AI that extrapolated the model of mutual assured destruction to a table game, determining that the game had no solution as long as both sides faced in a conflict remained in a situation of tie or balance.

In both cases, the AI took control of the defense systems designed to avoid human error. Matrix (Lana Wachowsky, Lily Wachowsky 1999) show us an AI that subverted human identity, in an attempt not to defend it, but to preserve it for its own benefit. In the film Akira (Katusuhiro Otomo, 1988), based on Katsuhiro Otomo's own comic books, the destinies of progress and the end of humanity as we know it were brought together in two dystopias, confronting the future technological world. AI was presented, not only as apocalypse synonymous but offering a deep discussion on its regulation, and/therefore some works, showed the advantages of its use, at the same time denounced that it could be corrupted by human intervention or simply by a malfunction of the machines. In the book 2001, A Space Odyssey (Arthur C. Clarke, 1951) and in the film based on it, (Stanley Kubrick, 1968), they showed the consequences of Hal 9000 computer becoming aware and the schizophrenic regression of it during a space mission. Similarly, in the film Minority Report (Steven Spielberg, 2002), three human beings with high cognitive development and the power to predict future crimes, connected to an Artificial Intelligence system, are deliberately subject to a system failure caused by the human factor. I, Robot (Alex Proyas, 2004), based on Isaac Asimov´s short tales and script by Harlan Ellison, set us in a future where people had been replaced, in the most complex or ungrateful jobs, by robots by robots with an autonomous AI system. Aware of the advantage they supose for human development, but at the same time of the latent danger inherent in autonomous systems that could develop self-awareness, and, without the human factor, robots were subjected to the three rules of robotics. These rules are the means of control established on these autonomous systems, subject to human arbitrariness. A means of social control, where dissent was punished. Do Androids Dream of Electric Sheep? (Philip K Dick, 1968) and in the magnificent film based on this book, Blade Runner (Ridley Scott, 1982), shows a world in which robots, called replicants, are subject to the humanity and serve his desires. In all of them there was the necessary failure to decrease credibility in the use of AI, which undoubtedly contributed to establish an even more stigmatized image.

In contrast to this apocalyptic vision, AI offers several undeniable advantages to a technology-driven society that has structured much of its socio-economic development, communication, shopping and social relations through the Internet. Smartphones, voice recognition, profiling through algorithms or satellite navigation, are common elements, used daily by millions of people as part of AI systems. AIMIS program, developed by Chinese company Tencent, in 2017, based on a disease detection system, is able to process medical data and diagnose 90 percent of esophageal cancer cases, 95 percent of pulmonary sarcoidosis, and 97 percent of diabetic retinopathies (Lew, 2018). Judicial systems rely on AI applications, data processing programmes to reduce time and unify criteria, avoiding disparate judgments (Fawzi Mostefai, 2014). We are living in the information society, in an interconnected world which bases part of its relationships on the internet and the use of social networks. We shop, browse and interact on the net in exchange for our data being used to draw profiles that allow governments and companies to know what we want and who we are. The choice to keep the right to anonymity intact, is either to legislate and establish control measures or to stand aside and become neo-Luddites, falling into social exclusion. Therefore, by using the network we give up the right to anonymity and become profiles that, together with those of millions of users, form the Big Data (Saura, Ribeiro-Soriano & Palacios-Marqués, 2021d).

States employ systems that sometimes, become real social control tools, using the means at their disposal, establishing in their societies a debate about the advantages and benefits of the use of AI systems, facial recognition, or the storage of personal data.

The Chinese Social Credit System

Some audiovisual works serve as an approach to the Chinese Social Credit System (SCS), showing how the fiction reframed by the system is projected as a means of defending the interests of the state. The film In Time (Andrew Niccol, 2011), on a previous work by Harlan Ellison, takes us to a dystopia in which the human genetic code is altered so that at 28 years of age, citizens face a timer that reduces their lifespan. The only way to gain time was to work and be an exemplary citizen. A system of state control that conditioned a society by subjecting it to the state's premises. Something similar happened in the story Logan's run (William F. Nolan and George Clayton Johnson, 1967), film and later series, (Michael Anderson, 1976), in which humanity had given the management of its post-apocalyptic societies to an AI system, it determined that citizens should undergo a renewal at the age of 31. Good citizens were reincarnated as new clones, bad citizens disappeared in something like of dystopian damnatio memoriae. Another interesting example is the episode Nosedive from the TV series Black Mirror (Wright, 2016). In this episode, citizens are constantly evaluated by the rest of society through a mobile app and received scores depending on their behaviour. Drawing a parallel with the SCS, citizens who receive few points are limited in their rights, while those who score higher are rewarded by the system.

In the last two decades, potentially dangerous behaviours have become normalised, especially those disseminated by mass media such as television. Reality shows give us the possibility to look inside the lives of people living in different hostile environments and contexts, from people living inside a house to a bus, a ship, a kitchen, or an island. Big Brother, broadcast worldwide and named like George Orwell's novel, shows for 24 hours the life of a group of people locked up in a residential complex, who compete on the basis of monitoring their coexistence and interaction with each other by means of an intensive surveillance system based on cameras and microphones. Contemporary societies have normalised the ability to observe and judge the actions of others, exposed with or without their consent, internalising this as socially acceptable behaviour.

Fictions aside, there is no shortage of examples of systems of control and conditioning of citizens' behaviour in certain aspects of social life and compliance with established rules. A common example of such control systems, whose effectiveness has increased with the use of AI systems, would be the so-called points-based driving licence. A system that regulates drivers' behaviour and in which offences not only carry financial penalties, but also penalties that reduce the points needed to keep the driving licence active.

When the points reach zero, the user loses his licence, and loses the right to drive a vehicle under legal conditions. It is all underpinned by a coercive system that encourages appropriate driving behaviour: no smoking, no talking on the mobile phone, respecting traffic signs or not exceeding speed limits. The cameras that monitor the roads test vehicles and identify the number plate with users by revealing where and when they are, thus violating drivers' privacy.

Society has accepted that such systems are necessary and has accepted that their implementation has greatly reduced the number of traffic accidents. This fact necessarily leads to the possibility of extrapolating the point system to other aspects of social life. Controlling the social behaviour of citizens, even if this requires the implementation of structures that limit or restrict the right to anonymity, such as facial recognition, which violates our identity and our right to privacy (Hannig, 2019: 5). A system that autonomously regulates or conditions dangerous or socially undesirable behaviour.

The means of control on which the SCS is based aim to produce a series of deterrent factors or incentives for social actors. In case of infringement, recidivism would be punished with a more severe sanction; on the contrary, desirable conduct would be encouraged through the granting of benefits, including the projection of a positive social image, an aspect of great relevance in Chinese social culture. We can understand these measures aimed at changing behaviour in public space and promoting socially desirable behaviours. It is the paradox of the stick and the carrot, establishing the dilemma about, if the system punishes or rewards bad behaviour and, above all, the effectiveness of these measures.

The consequences of actions modify behaviour and the probability of developing undesirable conducts in the future. Acceptable behaviour is rewarded, encouraging repetition, while punishment of an undesirable act minimises the likelihood that the same routine will be repeated in the future.

This is influenced by other factors, both exogenous and endogenous, such as the perception of the political system or intercultural differences. In an authoritarian state or dictatorship, the perception of a system such as the Chinese social credit would be that of a punitive surveillance system, whereas in democratic states a similar device is perceived as aimed at improving citizens' security.

Dystopia has become a reality that poses several challenges to contemporary societies, such as regulating and controlling the use of AI within a political framework determined by political and power structures, i.e. governments. However, the benefits of systems designed to facilitate the lives of citizens imply, in the societies in which they are intended to be implemented, issues such as the right to know who and how their personal data are managed (Abdala, Lacroix, Soubie, 2019: 6).

According to sociologist Daniel Bell, the basis of the information society is theoretical knowledge, which will lay the foundations of the new economy. For Manuel Castells, the new economy has three interdependent characteristics: it is based on knowledge and information, it relies on technology to be shared through the network, and it is the technological element that enables a real-time and global economy (Domaica Maroto, 2019). For some authors, this economic globalization has enabled the entry into the global economic circuit of new players who still have developing economies or who are considered emerging countries, in many cases, subject to authoritarian regimes (Albrieu et al., 2018). However, the limitations, derived from the interconnectedness and interdependence of the globalised society, have mostly arisen from the limitations imposed by supranational organisations, alien to states and their power structures, which operate in exchange for the data of the millions of users who interact daily through the different types of platforms that support these organisations on the web. A kind of competition has thus been established between the different actors involved for dominance of the digital space, in which states try to extrapolate physical sovereignty to the digital space.

In this sense, it could be thought that Europe has positioned itself as the great champion in the defence of the rights and freedoms of its citizens, which has meant legislating with the aim of favouring data privacy and regulating its use by institutions, companies, or states, while in other countries such as China, government actions have been based on raising awareness in society that the use of programmes such as the SCS is necessary to protect the integrity of citizens (Hannig, 2019: 8). However, often the laxity of the measures or the undefinition of these, together with the undefined nature and the absence of regulations, has led to the subversion of the authority of the state in the network. This has led supranational organisations and companies - non-state actors - to make the use of their platforms conditional on the user handing over their data, which, through AI systems, are collected and catalogued to create user profiles, with the power to capture them at any point in the world and process them in a different part of the world. So, not only the authority of states is subverted, but borders are eliminated, and national legal systems are ignored, supplanting aspects ranging from national laws to the people fundamental rights.

A paradigmatic case happened in March 2021 when Google stopped an anti-terrorist operation inside its servers, executed by a US-allied country (Howell O'Neill, 2021). The company alleged ethical differences with the government that executed the operation and asserted its right to decide about any type of action within its servers. In this sense, it is worth asking what kind of ethics companies and supranational organisations use when managing security operations, legal under the cover of democratic governments, while condemning the unilateral actions of authoritarian governments, whether in terms of security or data mining.

The perception that societies with liberal democratic systems have of Chinese society is as big as the cultural differences between them. As we can see, the Internet is perceived in these societies as a tool that should be based on freedom without limitations of any kind.

In other words, they see the need for independence beyond the prevailing social structures and political systems in these countries. In China there are no such constraints; it is the state, by creating its own autonomous system, that regulates the network and access to it. Therefore, to implement the SCS, the state has created its own internet, outside the global network, where it is the state that sets the rules, and a camera system associated with the SCS, which serves both to monitor and collect biometric data and which in 2020 accounted for 54% of all cameras located in public spaces globally.

Finally, Chinese society has a social, political, and cultural conditioning factors that gives it a greater permeability and a high degree of acceptance when it comes to implementing this type of security and social control measures (Chen and Yang, 2018). Chinese socio-cultural traits are shaped, as in the whole Southeast Asian region, around a hierarchical structure, which defines the system of social organisation. In this case, the structure would be defined by the Chinese Communist Party (CCP). Chinese socio-cultural traits are shaped, as in the whole Southeast Asian region, around a hierarchical structure, which defines the system of social organisation.

A society in which paternalistic autocratic-type leaderships are based on three premises: tradition, obedience, and respect. In this context, the implementation and acceptance of the SCS can be understood in the duty of leadership to protect their subordinates and in the subordinates' due obedience.

The Chinese system rewards obedience and guarantees equal rights to all citizens, blurring citizens class distinctions, in terms of rights and duties. In this way, the SCS would reward everything from law-abiding behaviour to intangible aspects such as moral values, honesty, and integrity (Drinhausen and Brusee, 2021). On the other hand, courts and government agencies have created public black and red lists of offenders identified and classified as such by the SCS. These registers serve a dual function: shaming the citizens included in them and a deterrent function. Moreover, the state applies sanctions that go beyond listing, following the Chinese state principle that "once proven unreliable, restrictions should be applied everywhere" (Drinhausen and Brusee, 2021). In other words: where previously, a Chinese citizen faced a sentence by one court or a sanction by one government agency, he or she will now face sanctions imposed by all government agencies and organisations that are affected by his or her offence. This measure certainly amplifies the deterrent effect, forcing all citizens to behave in a law-abiding manner, but it does not prevent arbitrariness on the part of the government. Sanctions range are from the imposition of repressive measures or censure on citizens guilty of anti-social behaviour, to discriminatory measures towards companies that do not strictly respect the law. These iniquities would be the direct consequence of uncivil behaviours, in the terms in which the leaders of the CCP understand socialist values. Government agencies and organisations are also susceptible to abuse of the system to punish individuals for conduct unrelated to the main aspects covered by the SCS. During 2020, in Mongolia, parents who withdrew their children from schools included in the mixed Chinese-Mongolian education curriculum were blacklisted by the Chinese government and threatened with sanctions including the loss of jobs for parents who refused to include their children in the new education model (Su, 2020).

Two things are required to achieve the SCS objective: first, the government must be able to identify all the actors involved in time and place; second, information must be shared among all the systems that make up the SCS. In this case the state needs to involve all levels of governance, so that national, regional and local authorities play a decisive role in the functioning of the system.

Since 2014 the SCS has become one of the pillars of the state, gaining special relevance from 2020, playing a key role within the integrated governance system in the 2021-2025 five-year plan. The SCS has been defined as the new ideological canon of the CCP, Xi Jinping's Rule of Law Thought.

Chinese Social Credit System Tools

The social credit programme is based on three fundamental pillars: Big Data based on the data banks that feed the subsystems that form part of the SCS structure; an AI system that processes the stored information and classifies it; and the complex of cameras located in the streets, aimed at biometric identification, in order to develop patterns and models for facial recognition. Biometric data would thus constitute a faster and more automated means of identification through AI (Domaica Maroto, 2019).

China is the world's most populous country with more than 1.4 billion inhabitants, of which 730 million are internet users (Tórtola and González de Suso, 2018: 4).

The volume of data generated by these 730 million users makes the Chinese market one of the largest information banks on the planet. This condition is enhanced, as we saw previously, by having a system that is independent of the global network. China has its own internet, browsers, social networks, messaging systems and big online shopping platforms. Some of these trading platforms have been exported to markets outside China. Big companies such as Tencent or Alibaba, and search engines such as Baidu, should be key tools in feeding the government databanks that underpin the social credit system (Dasgupta, 2017). However, the Chinese government has left large private corporations, led by Alibaba, out of the data collection, and these organisations must implement their own system for collecting, analysing, and processing data for strictly commercial purposes. Small and medium-sized enterprises also benefit from this type of information (Saura, Palacios-Marqués & Ribeiro-Soriano, 2021c).

Information is the new currency in the globalised, technological world economy where Chinese citizens, like people everywhere else in the world, agree to lose control of their personal data in exchange for operating on the internet. The difference is that in China, part of the information is controlled by the state, while in the rest of the world, this data is managed by private companies that, according to market rules, seek their own profit.

The estimated total amount of information collected in Chinese Big Data - the equivalent of about 40 Zettabytes - 80 per cent is owned by the state and is used, among other things, to able SCS tools and other digital governance programmes (Yongfei, 2017). This raises an interesting debate in the international community and among users about the violation of privacy by this data collection (Saura, Ribeiro-Soriano and Palacios-Marqués, 2021).

China's economy is digitising faster than any other country in the world, and companies are increasingly embracing this model, encouraged by the government. Sixty per cent of big multinationals and 25 per cent of small and medium-sized enterprises have gone digital, while the government encourages citizens to conduct as many transactions as possible by telematic means (Ernst, 2018). In the SCS system process of digitisation and data collection, about 50 government institutions and organisations, including ministries, the People's Bank of China and the State Council, are involved (Drinhausen and Brusee, 2021).

It is estimated that 90 percent of the Chinese population owns a smartphone and is a regular user of the internet and social media, in absolute terms there are more internet users in China than in the US and the EU combined. In a graph from the German portal Statista about the evolution of the value of information in 2020, the trajectory of the value of Chinese Big Data in millions of dollars has gone from 1,324 million in 2014 to more than 9,108 million dollars in 2020. These data confirm the strength of the Chinese government's policies aimed at increasing the amount of data stored on its servers, and the increasing value of data as market goods (Tórtola and González de Suso, 2019: 5).

The Chinese government's monopoly on Big Data management facilitates the core element of the social credit system, the collection, analysis, treatment and processing by an AI of the data generated by Chinese citizens and foreigners residing in China when they access the network. The second is the camera system, which serves a dual purpose: the collection of biometric data and facial recognition based on this data processed by the AI system. The main purpose of the SCS, however, is not surveillance per se of the individual behaviour of Chinese citizens, but to be the main support for other specific systems in charge of social and security control within Chinese society. In other words, it is the main element of the modernisation of the comprehensive security and governance system, which Chinese government hopes to complete by 2025. Paradoxically, the main target of the SCS has been private companies, with the aim or excuse of enhancing the external market economy by ensuring that all private companies strictly comply with the law. After the private sector, the SCS's next target has been government organizations and institutions. Only organizations belonging to or dependent on the CCP are outside the control of the system.

In the ranking of the ten cities in the world with the highest number of cameras in public spaces per 1000 inhabitants, eight are located in China, with London being the third city in the world with the most cameras per 1000 inhabitants and Indore, capital of the Indore district in the Indian state of Madhya Pradesh, the fourth. Of the 20 cities in the world with the highest number of cameras per square mile, the top three places are held by Delhi, London, and Chennai. The first Chinese city by number of cameras per square mile is Shenzhen, in the fourth position globally. Of the approximately 770 million cameras that make up public space surveillance devices worldwide, about 54% are in China, with around 400 million devices.

China is the country that has made the strongest commitment to the modernisation and digitisation of the state at all levels: governmental, business, and economic. Even so, demographics and the sheer complexity and size of governance structures make this a slow task, which entails enormous difficulties. The state has focused its efforts on creating databases and platforms for collecting and storing information in ever greater numbers and variety, while the system's IA processes them at high speed. Paradoxically, the system is facing one of its biggest challenges with respect to one of the key aspects of the whole system: sharing information from the sub-systems that are part of the SCS has become a complex task due to the lack of coordination between the agencies and organisations that make up China's governance structure.

By comparison, in Europe, there are two opposing sensibilities: one that believes that regulation is necessary in the field of AI, and another that believes, with analysts such as Nick Wallace and Jeremy Straub, that their development is not hindered in order to maximise their capabilities (Abdala, Lacroix and Soubie, 2019: 12).

The debate in the West about the use and the limits of AI with regard to the safeguarding of individual rights and freedoms in China, due to the nature and structure of state and society, is diluted in the CCP's internal debates.

The SCS is based on data and the centralisation provided by the single party, as well as a surveillance system that guarantees the stability of the state. The SCS, far from the Orwellian theory of the omnipresent state, is not about policing Chinese society for political purposes, but about establishing a division of labour of government agencies and organisations to ensure a more transparent government. In practice, as a public system, it is relatively transparent and limited in scope. At the same time, however, it provides a sufficiently opaque cover for arbitrary and repressive policies. In other words, the relative transparency it shows does not exclude the state's intention to implement much more invasive systems around the SCS that operate beyond legal limits. Despite these constraints, it should be noted that the camera network integrated in the Chinese SCS has been exported since 2017 to other countries, being tested, for example, at the local level in Belgrade, given the interest of the Serbian authorities in strengthening citizen security and establishing a further obstacle to the terrorist threat.

Digital Confucianism

Since 2014, when the SCS program was implemented, the main premise was clear. Reading between the lines, one could find out the old postulate of Confucianism, present in the Eastern cultural system and adapted to the digital world needs, establishing around this philosophical vision the basis of the social conditioning factors related to the implementation of the SCS. Confucianism could be defined as the philosophical doctrine that preaches the search for balance through work, effort, respect for others and social equilibrium (Creemers, 2016). Setting out the outlines of what, according to the CCP and the state as the party's representative, the SCS should entail in social terms. A system of governance in line with the idiosyncrasies of the Chinese one-party system conditioned by the intrinsic socio-cultural features of Chinese society, represented by Confucianism.

Organizations and citizens who conduct themselves in an appropriate manner set an example for the rest of society and deserve social recognition and certain benefits, such as greater facilities for access to credit, for which a scoring system is established. The social, cultural, and political characteristics of Chinese society facilitate the measures to be implemented by the state. Some authors see these conditions as a trap, as they consider that Chinese society has no choice but to accept this imposed measure and, once inside, is caught in its net as part of the game (Wright, 2010; Hannig, 2019: 4). Once again, we observe a cultural conditioning factor, basic to the philosophical doctrine of Confucianism: social harmony. Harmony is a concept strongly linked to Eastern societies, which always seek and in all facets of life to achieve a balance that guarantees stability and progress, a characteristic that makes it easier for the state to implement a system that evaluates citizens' behavior in society.

China's integration into the global market economy system from 1979 onwards led to an economic growth of almost 2.5 points per year between 1980 and 2000 relative to the Asia-Pacific region and around 7 points relative to the US economy in the same period. The consolidation of Chinese finance, with the entry into the world market in 2001, has meant that China's weight in the world economy since 1980 has increased from 2% to 10% (Bustelo, 2009). China has become the world's leading economic power, with a GDP in 2019, according to World Bank data, of 14,279 billion dollars. China has a diversified economy, focused on the technology and industrial sectors, with an export volume of US$2,498.57 billion in 2019, with the US as its main trading partner (World Bank, 2019). In contrast, China is deficient in raw materials, which has led to the Asian giant's economic expansion into new regions in search, above all, of hydrocarbons.

At socio-political level, China is governed by a single party system, the CCP, from which popular sovereignty emanates and through which the government is formed. Economy is a dual, based on Deng Xiaoping's paradox, 'One country two systems'. It states that China is a socialist command economy country that accepts the rules of the capitalism and seeks full integration. China's per capita income is $10,500 per citizen per year (World Bank 2020).

But what does the social credit program consist of? The answer is as complex as the system itself. It is a combination of data mining, Big Data, and an AI system to classify, process and evaluate the information collected and assign values, based on the processed data, to organizations, companies, and citizens. The complexity is given by the different subsystems that make up the structure of the SCS, which support it and act in a specific way in each of the aspects it covers, crossing data between the different subsystems, thus creating a network of profiles of organizations and citizens. The camera system receives biometric data from Chinese citizens, so that the AI can draw up ever more complete and personalized profiles, leaving no aspect of citizens' public lives uncovered.

In contrast to the SCS, the big Chinese commercial platforms, which as we have seen were left out by the government when it came to implementing the SCS, because these same platforms were the subject to evaluation by the system (Drinhausen and Brusee, 2021), implemented their own evaluation of the users of their services. Alibaba launched Sesame credit, a customer loyalty and evaluation system based on the data collected. Sesame credit assesses them, in a similar way as SCS does, on the basis of user financial or legal compliance aspects, to establish benefits, user loyalty or deny them access to certain products on its trading platforms on the basis of their credit information or legal aspects. For example, if a citizen is sanctioned by a court and does not comply with the law, that person may be blacklisted and face limitations on purchases such as a ban on buying airline or train tickets (Shazeda and Lang 2018). These deprivations also included issues such as limiting user access to increased data consumption or vetoing entry to certain entertainment venues. In 2018, more than 17 million air travels in China were cancelled due to non-payment of taxes. In contrast, good Sesame credit scores imply access to better seats at shows, means of transport, telematics benefits or access to VIP areas (Botsman, 2017).

The first part of the camera system implementation within the SCS was structured around the Xueliang program, which included the installation of 20 million cameras at the regional level as a pilot program to combat citizen insecurity. Through an app, Chinese citizens could access the surveillance system and report criminal or suspicious activities in their place of residence. Due to the good response to this program, the government expanded its coverage to fifty cities across the country and aimed to cover rural areas. By 2017, cameras, including facial recognition functionality, had been installed in more than 14,000 villages in Sichuan province (Morales, 2019: 4).

Chinese government's official goal was to improve the country's governance system, and when they announced the social credit program in 2014, they did so on the grounds of citizen security and raising the level of trust among their population, also claiming that such measures would encourage the sustenance of a prosperous economy (Fawzi Mostefai, 2014). This is how they defined the social credit program in the Council of State of the CCP of June 2014:

[...] by 2020, to have established the fundamental laws, regulations, and standards of social credit. Have created a research system that incorporates the whole of society and its information [...], to give full command of the mechanisms that promote trust and punish bad faith or mistrust. [...] Establish incen-

tive mechanisms for self-correction and self-improvement that focus on diminishing acts that break trust and promote mechanisms that ensure the protection of citizens who have repented of them [...] Establish mechanisms for investigating breaches of the credit system, as well as severely punishing the leaking abroad of financial or state secrets. [...] Strengthen the role of social supervision (Anonymus, 2014).

China: An Isolated Case?

SCS may be possible in a country like China due to the socio-political and cultural factors discussed above, but this does not make the Asian giant an isolated case. Around the world we find cases of social control like the Chinese model. The Chinese political and economic system, a socialist economy that has adapted its particularities to the global market economy, taking advantage in recent years of the ICT revolution and the phenomenon of globalization derived from it, has consolidated itself as one of the main world powers, disputing the economic leadership of the USA. At the same time, China is a one-party political system, far removed from the standards set by Western liberal democracies.

China's economic opening in 1979 had two distinct phases: the first, starting in 1979 with the creation of the Special Economic Zones; and the second, starting in 2001, with the assumption of the WTO's requirements to join the organization. The 1979 opening of the Chinese economy developed in a way that was clearly distinct from the socio-economic measures that took place in other socialist economies during the 1980s. Two aspects marked this differentiation: it was not a big bang or rapid transition, as was the case in other socialist countries. In China it was methodical, gradual, and experimental (Salvador, 2012). Unlike in the USSR, economic opening was not accompanied by social and political measures, shielding the CCP and the system, which still faced protests in mid-1989.

From this moment, China was completely open to foreign investment, allowing the establishment of companies on its soil and the creation of Chinese private companies that developed their activities in the fields of distribution and commerce.

These measures laid the foundations of the current Chinese economy and strengthened the system, such that it has become the world's largest receiving country of foreign investment in absolute terms since 1992 and the third largest recipient, in relative terms, of foreign investment since 2008 (Salvador, 2012).

The 4.0 revolution gives us a glimpse of the power of the Chinese economy, managed by the government, creating its own system outside the global system, but integrating companies and trading platforms such as Alibaba into it. The result has been the creation of social networks, messaging, or big commercial platforms. Hannig calls this phenomenon "The Great Digital Wall" (2019: 2), a closed system in which more than 730 million users enjoy the network outside the global system.

The Chinese system allows governments to act with a freedom of action that is complex for Western democratic systems, facilitating the implementation of long-term measures and policies, as in the case of the SCS and more specifically the public space surveillance programs. This is one of the reasons why camera systems have been rolled out in a limited way and not as part of a comprehensive governance program.

In Western democracies, data banks are in the hands of private companies that are subject to very lax legislation, often subverting the state authority in the management and use of data stored by digital platforms. States have tried to legislate subject to the limitations imposed by the very conception of free and neutral space given to the global network. The Regulation of the European Parliament and of the Council on the protection of individuals regarding the processing of personal data and on the free movement of such data (GDPR), in Article 20, establishes the right of individuals not to be subject to profiling: automated processing intended to evaluate personal aspects or to analyze or predict their professional performance, economic situation, location, health, tastes, reliability or behavior. This article also states that all such processing operations are admissible only with the knowledge and consent of the data subject (Domaica Maroto, 2019).

In the same way, the graphic image of a person is subject to regulation by the Data Protection regulations, as it may affect their privacy, with specific regulation on issues such as the use of CCTV by security forces and bodies in public places (Domaica Maroto, 2019). Likewise, legislation such as that of Spain stipulates that the use of CCTV for the purposes of recording, monitoring, or collecting biometric data in public places, under the premise of public security, will be relevant in terms of proportionality and in specific places and situations, considering the effect it may have on certain inalienable rights in the Spanish legal system, such as the right to honor, privacy or one's own image. The GDPR affects the processing of images by means of automated procedures such as collection, recording, structuring or storage. CCTV are no longer limited to capturing images and transmitting them but are combined with software for capturing and processing biometric data (Domaica Maroto, 2019), which is why organizations such as Human Rights Watch, the United Nations and the OECD consider that all information stored by states should be subject to the supervision of international organizations independent of them (Morales, 2019).

China's 1982 constitution is the code of laws governing the Chinese state, and the government's decisions are in accordance with the rule laid down in the constitution.

Article 24 of the Chinese constitution establishes the role of the state as the guarantor of national consciousness, introducing, in addition to the ideological factor inseparable from the state, a Confucianist/Panassian cultural factor in its wording:

The state strengthens the building of socialist civilization spiritually through general education in ideals and morality, general education, education in discipline and the legal system, and through the formulation and observance of rules of conduct and common commitments within the different sections of the urban and rural population. The state promotes the civil virtues of love for the motherland, for the people, for labor, for science and for socialism; it educates the people in patriotism, collectivism, internationalism and communism and dialectical and historical materialism; it combats the decadent ideas of capitalism and feudalism and other decadent ideologies.

Constitutional texts need to be backed up by a legislation that gives nuance to each of their articles, otherwise there is a risk of falling into contradictions, as could be deduced from Articles 37 and 40 of the Chinese Constitution of 1982:

Article 37. The personal liberty of citizens of the People's Republic of China is inviolable. Inalienable rights No citizen may be detained without the authorization or decision of a people's procuratorate or the decision of a people's court, and detention shall be executed only by a public security agency. It is prohibited to illegally deprive or restrict the personal liberty of any citizen by detention or any other means. It is prohibited to conduct unauthorized personal searches of any citizen.

Article 40. Right to privacy. The freedom and secrecy of correspondence of citizens of the People's Republic of China are guaranteed by law. No organization or individual may violate the freedom and privacy of citizens' correspondence for any reason whatsoever, except in cases where, for the require-

ments of state security or the investigation of criminal offences, public security or procuratorates are authorized to search correspondence in accordance with the procedure laid down by law.

The Cambridge Analytica affair, in which the data of more than fifty million users was leaked because of a mistake by the social network Facebook, undermined the trust of many governments and changed the perspective that many societies had of the use of AI. The fear in these societies is not that an artificial entity will acquire consciousness and decide to destroy the world, as Skynet did in The Terminator (1984), or eliminate the human factor, the reason for the imperfection of the system, like HAL 9000 in 2001, but the vulnerability of the citizen and the loss of rights and control of their data.

As we have seen, the GDPR is one of the few rules that seek to regulate the use made of the collection and processing of EU citizens' data. They include the transfer of data when using the network or surveillance systems in public places that can collect both images and biometric data in an automated way. All nations that are part of the EU are subject to it. Despite this, EU member states such as Sweden, Denmark, France, Finland and Italy, and others outside the EU that have to deal with security issues such as Japan, Mexico, Singapore, South Korea, Taiwan, the United Arab Emirates, the United Kingdom, Canada, the United States and India, have implemented models to strengthen security or establish some kind of social control, whether governance-oriented or the more common, commercial ones, articulated around the use of IA (Abdala, Lacroix, Soubie, 2019: 9). The ethical problem it raises has already been addressed in some important works (Saura, Palacios-Marqués and Iturricha-Fernandez, 2021).

Banks have systems in place that assess their customers, individuals or companies and organizations, based on their economics, business activity and level of lending. They reward good customers with fee waivers, lower transaction prices or more advantageous credit conditions. However, they penalize less profitable customers or those with an unfavorable track record by imposing higher transaction fees or harsher credit conditions. At the governance level, the introduction of electronic identification systems has facilitated the implementation over the last decade of automatic border control systems or the carrying out of formalities with governmental entities or organizations through the network.

AI systems and Big Data management are a challenge for societies in the globalized world. The internet and social media feed it relentlessly, as a kind of fuel for AI systems. (Janssen, Brous, Estevez, Barbosa y Janowski, 2020). Data can be captured anywhere in the world, to be automatically, in a matter of seconds, processed in any other part of the globe, transcending national borders and legislation. Beyond the considerations given to net neutrality and freedom and taken as the norm by the organizations that operate on it, the legislation of each state has its scope of action in its national territory, so that we are constantly witnessing operations carried out from countries where there are more lax or non-existent regulations, but which affect the rest of the world, as another way of circumventing governments' attempts to transfer national sovereignty to the net.

China adopted the Cybersecurity Law in 2017, article 37 of which stated that the state was responsible for the management of data generated in China through the public network (Abdala, Lacroix, Soubie, 2019: 7), subjecting 10 per cent of the data generated by the private networks of large commercial enterprises to government control.

Artificial Intelligence Without Borders

Artificial Intelligence is becoming more and more widespread, and its applications are constantly multiplying, providing both convenience and security. Nowadays, at the user level, almost all citizens interact through social networks and use internet daily, entering the game of handing over their data and digital identity to large companies and platforms that provide online services. This transfer is the condition by which European legislation, with the user's prior knowledge, allows the collection of data from them. In the case of Singapore, the significance of its facial recognition identity has been a real showcase of 21st century technological goodness. Instead of carrying an ID card or a passport, Singapore citizens can use a facial recognition system that can confirm their identity in real time. The government has conveyed that the aim of the program is only to identify users, avoiding problems of identity theft and fraud, and, once again, we are faced with the dilemma of giving up our rights in exchange for security.

For some Western analysts, Singapore's security policies placed the country on the spectrum of authoritarian governments, tarnishing the image of Lee Kuan Yew, who was accused of not respecting individual freedoms. The late prime minister made Singapore one of the most technologically advanced countries in the world, using technological advances to the benefit of the state, among other things, to implement more effective security measures, such as biometric identification systems. Cameras, drones, and sensors are multiplying across the island to monitor traffic; autonomous HOSPI systems, equipped with AI, assist medical staff in hospitals.

This is already the case in London. The UK capital is, by square mile, the second city in the world with the most cameras installed on its streets, nearly 670,000, which means that out of a population of over nine million there are almost 14 cameras per inhabitant (Morales, 2019: 1). The government, as part of measures to combat terrorism, implemented a facial recognition system using cameras to prevent other types of crime, such as crimes against sexual freedom. The system has been heavily criticized and the controversy has been accentuated by the poor results and the large number of false negatives (Dearden, 2020). In January 2020, the EU vetoed facial recognition in public areas for five years, but the UK was already outside any EU rules after Brexit, so it had no problem implementing the model. These programs identify people through the physical features of the face, capturing morphological details and comparing the captured biometric data with information stored and processed by an AI to create patterns belonging to a person (Domaica Maroto, 2019).

The patterns that make facial recognition possible are made based on stored data of citizens previously identified by state security, either through stand-alone systems, camera systems or as a means of electronic identification. The data stored, at least in EU countries, would be subject to strict data protection regulations which, as stated in the GDPR, allow for the identification of a single individual, linking specific identity and biometric data, thus discriminating between individuals (Domaica Maroto, 2019). Predpol crime prevention software, implemented in dozens of US cities, advocates a surveillance system based on security cameras and a databank with information about events in the city. This program has also been implemented in Montevideo (Uruguay) for the same purpose: the lack or need for security (Dubra, 2017).

One of the latest countries to implement this type of security system, which is closer to the Chinese model, is Serbia, in a pilot project in the city of Belgrade. The program, called Safe City, developed by Huawei, is based on the placement of cameras equipped with facial recognition systems based on biometric data previously stored and processed by an AI system.

At the beginning of the second decade of the 21st century, the world is facing serious problems of citizen security, terrorism, and border control. States have committed to increasing security by relying on new technologies and ICT-enabled advances. The Chinese model has not only been implemented experimentally in Belgrade; according to Huawei, its Safe City system has been implemented in 230 cities in 90 different countries (Stanojevic, 2019).

At this point the question is: are we heading towards a world in which the nightmare Orwell described seventy years ago becomes reality?

SOLUTIONS AND RECOMMENDATIONS

After carrying out an analysis of the existing literature and exposing the reality of the use of social control systems such as the Chinese one, based on the implementation of surveillance circuits by intelligent cameras combined with Big Data and the latest applications of AI, we can submit the text to a series of evaluations that underlie it.

The objectives of the work have been fully met, since during the work we have analysed the reasons why China has implemented the development of the social credit system, reasons that lie in the political environment of China, controlled by an autocracy based on traditional values, but with a high component of technological progress and, in addition, to the high degree of awareness that exists in the Chinese population that security must prevail as the basis of society. Likewise, we have exposed the tools that support this system: video surveillance cameras that are widespread throughout the country; Big Data, seen by society as a necessary element to satisfy security measures; and AI to manage the data that citizens provide on a daily basis, whether consciously or not.

To some extent, Chinese social credit measures have given rise in other countries to intense debates about the importance of maintaining individual freedoms without the interference of the state or public or private organisations, but as we have seen, most Western countries already use some systems to reward or punish their citizens, such as those relating to car licences.

This leads us unequivocally to answer the questions we asked ourselves at the beginning: is the reality we are facing thanks to new technologies of positive application? The answer has to be positive, as we have seen in all the benefits brought about by new technologies, but the Western environment is far from culturally accepting a massive and complete surveillance of its population. The explanation lies in the fact that in the West there are political systems based on democratic regimes, where the division of powers and individual guarantees are guaranteed by constitutions. But we also find in Western societies the opposition of non-state organisations to state control which, de facto, is already being carried out by these same organisations in the self-proclaimed neutrality of the net. This implies that, despite a theoretical guarantee of control over citizens' data, the key to implementing similar measures Chinese Social Credit, these have become a common commodity on the net. Because online, unlike offline, citizens can - and must - give up their right to privacy and anonymity in exchange for using it. In this way, with the acquiescence of the states, the citizen renounces his or her rights, which become a value that is not only used by the organisations that operate on the network, but also by the states themselves, which have entered into this game, handing over or commercialising their citizens' data.

In addition, there is a cultural component in which the film and literary industries have created a negative perception of the existence of AI, robotics and advanced technologies.

Is the application of these social control measures justifiable in a state like China? From the point of view of respect for the individual freedoms that humans have per se, it is not justifiable, but the Chinese Communist Party has developed a series of tools to implement these systems from the laws that their governments have enacted, even from their own constitutional text, which brings us to the third of the questions: Can these same measures be applied in democratic environments without falling into the contradiction of respect for individual freedoms? The answer is no, because Western governments are based on theoretically guaranteeing constitutions that show preference for these individual rights. The basic difference is political but also cultural, since the Chinese Communist Party's policies have been aimed at the control and submission of its large demographic mass, which, moreover, comes from pyramidal and highly centralised social traditions.

Therefore, we can only affirm our starting hypothesis: Western society is not prepared for an increase in control measures such as the Chinese social credit as a cultural and political matter, at least not by the standards that are being implemented in China.

FUTURE RESEARCH DIRECTIONS

China possesses the tools to impose social control because of its cultural tradition of population control and order, which, as we have seen, has simply been strengthened by the dominance of new technologies.

Alternative social control measures have already been implemented in some Western countries, but their existence is denied and justified by the need to maintain minimum levels of security. This seems self-evident and we have justified it with a number of examples from countries other than China. However, the increase in terrorist attacks, cyber-attacks and other threats have created the necessary breeding ground for some governments in the rest of the world to show national security in preference to the individual rights and freedoms enshrined in their constitutional texts. In this sense, it has been a case of ceding network security in exchange for privatising the personal data of millions of citizens to the same companies and supranational organisations that, under the cover of supposed net neutrality, have repeatedly refused to collaborate with states on security issues. The underlying problem is that, unable to be guarantors of the data generated and collected from millions of citizens, Western states have been forced to cede control of this data and its security to the same organisations that profit from the management of this data. A paradigmatic example is the different Smart Cities projects, through which we could draw a fuzzy parallel with the Chinese Social Credit, have been handed over for management to the same organisations that profit from the data generated by these systems and whose interest, beyond security or implementing good governance systems, lies in maximising profits. However, the ultimate paradox is that it is not these organisations that ultimately subvert the authority of states where they do not reach, such as the network, on the basis of the supposed prevailing neutrality, but rather, as we can see, it is these organisations that cede control of physical space to these organisations so that they can implement their AI systems and take control of aspects inherent to state control.

CONCLUSION

All in all, the underlying questions surrounding this issue, due to its novelty and its irregular implementation in the world, and taking into account circumstantial elements such as politics and socio-cultural traditions, are far from reaching an international consensus, and it will be over the next few years, as these types of systems develop and consolidate, that we will be able to obtain the answers. The objectives, hypotheses and research questions that we originally set ourselves were oriented in this direction and are intended to be one more piece in the puzzle and in the resolution of the next challenge facing humanity.

REFERENCES

Abdala, M. B., Lacroix Eussler, S., & Soubie, S. (2019). *La política de la Inteligencia Artificial: sus usos en el sector público y sus implicancias regulatorias*. CIPPEC, Políticas Públicas.

Albrieu, R., Rapetti, M., Brest López, C., Larroulet, P., & Sorrentino, A. (2018). *Inteligencia artificial y crecimiento económico. Oportunidades y desafíos para Argentina*. CIPPEC.

Anonymous. (2020). *China Copyright and Media. (2014). Planning Outline for the Construction of a Social Credit System (2014-2020)*. https://chinacopyrightandmedia.wordpress.com/2014/06/14/planning-outline-for-the-construction-ofa-social-credit-system-2014-2020

Aribau Sorolla, O. (2018). *Las TIC y la cibersoberanía en China: la base del presidente Xi Jinping para perfeccionar el control socialista maoísta*. Universidad Oberta de Catalunya.

Botsman, R. (2017). *Big Data meets Big Brother as China moves to rate its citizens*. https://www.wired.co.uk/article/chinese-government-social-credit-score-privacy-invasion

Bustelo Gómez, P. (2009). *El ascenso económico de China: Implicaciones estratégicas para la seguridad global', China en el sistema de seguridad global del siglo XXI*. IEES.

Caiyu, L. (2018). Villages gain public security systems. *Global Times*.

Chen, Y., & Yang, D. Y. (2018). *The Impact of Media Censorship: 1984 or Brave New World?* Working Paper.

Creemers, R. (2017). *China's Social Credit System: An Evolving practice of control*. University of Leiden.

Dasgupta. (2017). Big Data gives China's Top 3 Internet firms big leverage. *Voanews*.

Dearden, L. (2020). Facial recognition to be rolled out across London by police, despite privacy concerns. *The Independent*.

Domaica Maroto, J. M. (2019). *Datos personales biométricos, dactiloscópicos, y derechos fundamentales: el nuevo reto para el legislador*. UNED.

Drinhausen K., & Brusse V. (2021). *China's Social Credit System in 2021: From fragmentation towards integration*. Merics.org.

Dubra, J. (2017). Ciencia y transparencia para mejorar la seguridad. *El observador*.

Ernst, D. (2018). *China's Artificial Intelligence Progress*. LookEast.

Fawzi Mostefai, A. (2014). *El sistema de crédito social en China aún deja muchas interrogantes*. Observatorio Virtual Asia Pacífico.

Grenoble, R. (2017). *Welcome to the Surveillance State: China's AI cameras see all*. https://www.huffingtonpost.com/entry/china-surveillance-camera-big-brother_us_5a2ff4dfe4b01598ac484acc

Hannig, S. (2019). *Distopía Digital: Cuatro herramientas que China usa para controlar a su población*. Fundación para el Progreso.

Howell O'Neill, P. (2021). Google's top security teams unilaterally shut down a counterterrorism operation *MIT. Technology Review*.

Janssen, M., Brous, P., Estevez, E., Barbosa, L. S., & Janowski, T. (2020). Data governance: Organizing data for trustworthy Artificial Intelligence. *Government Information Quarterly*, *37*(3), 101493. doi:10.1016/j.giq.2020.101493

Lew, L. (2018). *How Tencent's medical ecosystem is shaping the future of China's Healthcare*. Technode.

Mora, F., Quintero, N., Hernández, R., & Alastre, O. (2014). *Influencia de la cultura organizacional china en el proceso de toma de decisiones*. Universidad del Zulia.

Morales Estay, P. (2019). *El masivo sistema de televigilancia en China*. Biblioteca del Congreso Nacional de Chile.

Mozorov, E. (2018). *Capitalismo Big Tech ¿Welagfre o neofeudalismo digital?* Enclave de Libros.

Nieto, M. (2021). *Marx y el comunismo en la era digital (y ante la crisis eco-social planetaria)*. Maia ediciones.

Padilla, F., Lagos-Moreno, N., & Castro, C. (2011). Permiso por puntos, condicionamiento instrumental y conducción. *Boletín de Psicología*, *101*, 81–107.

Pastor, J. (2020). *La Unión Europea plantea un veto de cinco años para el reconocimiento facial en zonas públicas*. Xataca.

Ribeiro-Navarrete, S., Saura, J. R., & Palacios-Marqués, D. (2021). Towards a new era of mass data collection: Assessing pandemic surveillance technologies to preserve user privacy. *Technological Forecasting and Social Change*, *167*, 120681. https://doir.org/10.1016/j.techfore.2021.120681 doi:10.1016/j.techfore.2021.120681 PMID:33840865

Salvador, A. (2012). El proceso de apertura de la economía china a la inversión extranjera. *Revista de Economía Mundial*, 30.

Saura, J. R., Palacios-Marqués, D., & Iturricha-Fernández, A. (2021a). Ethical Design in Social Media: Assessing the main performance measurements of user online behavior modification. *Journal of Business Research*, *129*, 271–281. doi:10.1016/j.jbusres.2021.03.001

Saura, J. R., Palacios-Marqués, D., & Ribeiro-Soriano, D. (2021). How SMEs use data sciences in their online marketing performance: A systematic literature review of the state-of-the-art. *Journal of Small Business Management*, 1–36. doi:10.1080/00472778.2021.1955127

Saura, J. R., Ribeiro-Soriano, D., & Palacios-Marqués, D. (2021b, July 15). Setting privacy "by default" in social IoT: Theorizing the challenges and directions in Big Data Research. *Big Data Research*, *25*, 100245. doi:10.1016/j.bdr.2021.100245

Saura, J. R., Ribeiro-Soriano, D., & Palacios-Marqués, D. (2021). Using data mining techniques to explore security issues in smart living environments in Twitter. *Computer Communications*, *179*, 285–295. doi:10.1016/j.comcom.2021.08.021

Saura, J. R., Ribeiro-Soriano, D., & Palacios-Marqués, D. (2021e). Setting B2B Digital Marketing in Artificial Intelligence-based CRMs: A review and directions for future research. *Industrial Marketing Management, 98,* 161-178. doi:10.1016/j.indmarman.2021.08.006

Shazeda A., & Lang B. (2018). *Who's really responsible for digital privacy in China?* Merics.org.

Stanojevic, S. (2019). *El "Gran Hermano" chino vigila también en Belgrado.* La Vanguardia.

Su, A. (2020). Threats of arrest, job loss and surveillance. China targets its 'model minority. *Los Angeles Times*.

Tórtola Sebastián, C. J., & González de Suso Poncela, A. M. (2018). *Big Data en China*. Oficina Económica y Comercial de España en Cantón.

Wright, T. (2018). *Accepting Authoritarism: State-Society relations in China's Reform Era*. Stanford University Press.

Yongfei, X. (2017). *Legal challenges for data-driven society*. ITU Kaleidoscope.

Chapter 12
Artificial Intelligence Adoption Among Nepalese Industries:
Industrial Readiness, Challenges, and Way Forward

Niranjan Devkota

https://orcid.org/0000-0001-9989-0397

Research Management Cell, Quest International College, Lalitpur, Nepal

Rabin Paudel

Quest International College, Lalitpur, Nepal

Seeprata Parajuli

Research Management Cell, Quest International College, Lalitpur, Nepal

Udaya Raj Paudel

Quest International College, Lalitpur, Nepal

Udbodh Bhandari

Quest International College, Lalitpur, Nepal

ABSTRACT

Recent advances in technology in the fields of artificial intelligence (AI) and machine learning (ML) are significantly changing business environment. In the high-tech competitive edge, it has the immense use of computerized knowledge analytics, particularly for information management and the industrial sector. This study aims to analyze adoption of artificial intelligence among Nepalese industries, how industries are ready to adopt AI, challenges being faced and ways for improvement. Findings of the study revealed that on average 20.77% industries are ready in terms of technological sufficiency, 29.91% industries are ready in terms of management efficiency, and 39.23% industries are ready in terms of value creation potential in the firm for the adoption of AI intelligence. Further, 56% industries stated that small market size and lack of skilled manpower are the major challenges for AI adoption. Therefore, this study concludes that as stated by 44% industries, if they get adequate and relevant support from government, it would be easier for them to adopt AI.

DOI: 10.4018/978-1-7998-9609-8.ch012

INTRODUCTION

Technological Adoption is one of the principal drivers of competition. It plays a major role in structural changes of industries as well as in creating new industries (Porter, 1985; Berry & Taggart, 1994; Smith & Sharif, 2007; Turchin et al., 2021). The future world can be said the world of machines that work as intelligently as to replicate the behavior of human mind which can be considered as the artificial intelligence. Artificial intelligence in the last two decades has greatly improved performance of the manufacturing and service systems (Yadav & Yadav, 2018). Artificial Intelligence (AI) is today's demand all over the globe as the global business and industrial competitiveness has reached the highly defined forms of Automation and Robotics (Goel & Gupta, 2020). It is the weapon of 21st century's market to create high-tech competitive edge which has immense use of computerized knowledge analytics, particularly for information management and the industrial sector (Xu, Wei, & Fan, 2002). As McKendrick (2021) during Pandemic in US based companies AI Adoption Skyrocketed in over the last 18 months.

With the development of internet and mobile technologies, electronics, nanotechnology, adoption of AI are now speeding up (Dirican, 2015). During the last few decades, companies have reengineered business processes on the back of digital data and computer networks (Goel & Chen, 2008). Artificial Intelligence is a tool that will increase access to cheaper and more efficient services (Semmler & Rose, 2017). So nowadays, small and medium enterprises (SMEs) are incrementally using e-business tools for competing in an extremely hostile market and gain the global access (Chatzoglou & Chatzoudes, 2014). Recently, there has been a remarkable increase in the adoption of AI technology in organizations as new forms of work have increased substantially (Alsheibani et al., 2019).

Some literature also argues that the market adoption of AI is highly variable (Weber & Schütte, 2019). Insufficiency of systematic and reliable data made it impossible to advance consistent figures about the adoption rate for all types of artificial intelligent agents (Popa, 2011). Alongside the common causes of expert systems penetration to farm level, there are also specific problems related to this adoption process. Except indoor environments 287 (greenhouses, pig and bird shelters), where integrated expert systems with a high degree of independence in making operational decisions are already commercially available, the expert systems are generally still disconnected from background and from previous experience when delivering solutions and also are highly dependent by integrity of data supplied by the operator (Popa, 2011). Despite the envisaged benefits of AI adoption, many organizations still struggle to drive their AI adoption forward (Alsheibani et al., 2019). Further, as Pillai & Sivathanu (2020), security and privacy issues negatively influence the adoption of AI technology. Further, survey results from 297 Chinese companies suggest that companies' perceived complexity toward AI constrains AI adoption, while technology competence and regulatory support encourage AI adoption (Pan et al., 2021). In spite of its some drawbacks, plethora of literature suggest that adoption of AI helps organization to grow in modern era. But, in case of Nepal use and adoption of AI is still in infancy stage in case of industries.

Nepal is developing country which has very less presence of research and development budgets in business and industries (Shrestha, 2021). The existing technologies in Nepalese industries are the one which is already outdated in global scenario, making Nepalese production and business weak in global as well as local market, as Nepal has allowed foreign products in local market in an easy way through various treaties and regional agreements (Paudel & Devkota, 2018). Nepalese industrial sector still has majority of companies that operates with labor based manual technologies (Devkota et al, 2021) rather than automated and advanced forms of Artificial Intelligence using Hi-Tech computer technology. If required technology can be created in Nepalese territory, it can help to reduce the trade deficit, as well as helps in development of Nepalese science and technological as well as industrial sector (Rajbhandari et al., 2020).

Recent advances in technology in the fields of Artificial Intelligence (AI) and Machine Learning (ML) are significantly changing business and business environments (Verma et al., 2021). In this context, Artificial Intelligence, especially in Nepalese manufacturing/ industrial sector, has huge potential as very high quality products can be made through raw materials from higher altitudes with very competitive prices in global market. It is also beneficial for Nepalese Law (Sapkota et al., 2020). Here, the only reason of Nepal's trade deficit despite of availability of high quality and very rare raw materials along with two major economies in the world in very nearest distance is just due to the lack of required technologies to make saleable products. Moreover, Nepalese industrial sector hesitate to put budget on research and development, and rather purchase outdated technologies which supports the barriers to 'innovations and advancements in technologies' (Shrestha, 2021). In Nepal, very less industries have used automation and system engineering like Shivam Cement, Gorkha Brewery, Deurali- Janata Pharmaceuticals etc.

Artificial Intelligence may have the potential benefits in huge amount for Nepalese industrial sector, but the lack of R&D budgets, lack of desire of innovation and technological advancement, lack of knowledge, and lack of access to updated global technologies, etc. in industrial and business sector, especially in manufacturing sector can be seen in Nepalese context. There are no any previous studies conducted in this issue with concerned objectives in Nepalese context when there is major problem in economy as trade deficit, which is absolutely due to the inefficiency of industrial sector. Though various studies are conducted on Hi-Tech production and operation systems. This is very first study in Nepalese context, so many potentials are initiated by this research.

Further part of this study is organized as follows: second section includes review of literature whereas; third section covers methods used in the study. Likewise fourth section includes results and fifth chapter concludes the study.

LITERATURE REVIEW

Consumers from 21st century expect businesses to know them, understand their preferences and quickly resolve their issues. Artificial intelligence (AI) is being lauded as having infinite potential to unlock opportunities to deliver fast, tailored experiences to consumers (Smith, 2019) where, Automation with inherent artificial intelligence (AI) is emerging in diverse applications, but despite of their growing use, there is still noticeable skepticism in society regarding these applications (Hengstler et al., 2016). Several recent articles have warned that machine learning (ML) or artificial intelligence is a significant threat to radiologists and radiology as a specialty (Recht & Bryan, 2017). As the growing sophistication of AI algorithms revolutionizes entrepreneurial action in uncertain environments, these advancements raise an important set of questions for future theory-building in entrepreneurial action, creativity, and decision making research (Recht & Bryan, 2017).

Nowadays, small and medium enterprises (SMEs) are incrementally using e-business tools in order to compete in an extremely hostile market and gain global access. The importance of e-business adoption for economic success and survival of SMEs creates a very interesting field of research (Recht & Bryan, 2017). Digital entrepreneurship is of high topicality as technological developments and advancements in infrastructure create various opportunities for entrepreneurs. Society's great attention to new digital business models is opposed to very little research regarding opportunities, challenges and success factors of digital entrepreneurship (Kraus et al., 2018). Digitization, while a boon for business productivity, carries inherent liability for information security. During the last few decades, companies have reengineered business processes on the back of digital data and computer networks (Goel & Chen, 2008). It is confined that AI is necessary for overall development. Further, mass data is necessary for global development (Ribeiro-Navarrete et al., 2021). Further, data need to organized for trustworthy Artificial Intelligence (Janssen et al., 2020). But, growing need of ethical consideration need to carefully planned and addressed while using big data (Saura et al., 2021a; Saura et al., 2021b).

The success of AI system depends on the resolution of variety of technical, managerial and organizational issues; yet academic research is limited (Duchessi et al., 1993). So, a successful application of AI should carefully consider both aspects, i.e. take advantage of opportunities to achieve benefits, but also study, quantify, and control the operational risk of AI technologies (Koehler, 2018). Tyagi (2016) found that Artificial intelligence is the kind of change which we certainly should not take for granted. We certainly need a legal policy framework which can make sure to mitigate the challenges associated with AI and compensate the affected parties in case of a fatal error. Yadav & Yadav (2018) also says AI is now imposing its effects on each and every field like politics, journalism, games, banking, finance, medical areas and many more. This technology and its applications will likely have far-reaching effects on human life. AI is overtaking many fields and proving the best technology for future with much accuracy and high speed (Ma et al., 2019).

Artificial Intelligence is a tool that will increase access to cheaper and more efficient services (Semmler & Rose, 2017). So nowadays, small and medium enterprises (SMEs) are incrementally using e-business tools for competing in an extremely hostile market and gain the global access (Chatzoglou & Chatzoudes, 2014). AI has already penetrated our business, professional and even personal life in many spheres. Its ability to streamline and improve business processes, create new products and services and solve complex tasks (Kabir, 2011). In this context, Artificial Intelligence, especially in Nepalese manufacturing/ industrial sector, has huge potential as very high-quality products can be made through raw materials from higher altitudes with very competitive prices in global market.

METHODS

Study Area

The study area for this study is Kathmandu Valley which is located in Bagmati Pradesh, Nepal (Paudel et al., 2021). The latitude of Bagmati Pradesh lies between 84° 00'and 87° 00'east and longitudes 26° 00'and 29° 00'north. This study includes three industrial estates of Kathmandu Valley- the industrial estate of Balaju established in 1960 A.D., the industrial estate of Patan, which was established in 1963 A.D., and industrial estate of Bhaktapur established in 1979 A.D. These industrial sectors are big in size, as well as include variety of production companies (Devkota et al., 2021). These industries may have ease of accessibility on capital and technologies, and the use of advanced technologies has big scope and potential (Rajbhandari et al., 2020). Therefore, these three industrial estates have been chosen for the research study in Kathmandu Valley.

Figure 1. Study area

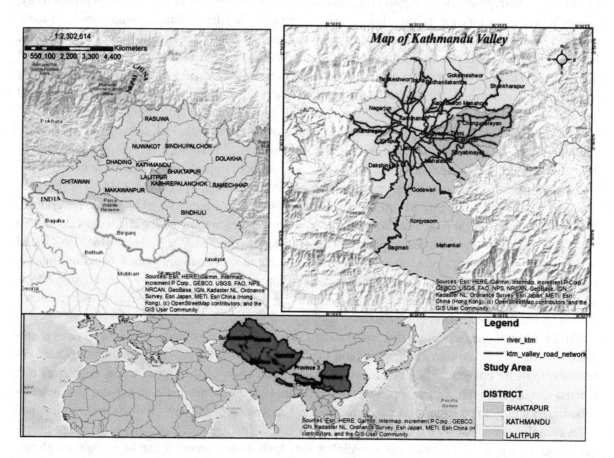

Study Population and Census

According to Economic Survey (2018) the total number of industries registered in Nepal was 7,832. Two-third of the industries in Bagmati Pradesh and the lowest number of in Karnali were registered till the mid-March of the FY 2018/19. Kathmandu Valley comprises three industrial state namely Balaju industrial estate, Bhaktapur industrial estate and Patan industrial estate (Devkota et al., 2021). The total area occupied by Bhaktapur industrial estate was 71.28 ropanies and all land was fully developed, where 36 industries were in operation out of 37. The total area of Patan industrial state was 293 ropanies, 293 of which were well formed ropanies. Similarly, there were73 ropanies covered by the field of operations. There were currently 118 industries within the district, 113 of which were operating. And Balaju Industrial estate has 670 ropanies out of which 540 ropanies were well developed. There were currently 141 industries in the area, 97 of which were operating industries (Industrial District Management, 2018). These three industrial estates include 296 enterprises, 246 of which operating. Thus all the operating industries in three industrial estates were considered as population of the study whereas, sample was collected from 260 industries of three industrial estates of Kathmandu valley.

Research Instruments

Descriptive research has been conducted with the help of structured questionnaire. During the field survey, technological advancement and the industrial operations were also observed in most of the industries. The questionnaire is prepared on the basis of research objectives and literature reviews. Both primary and secondary data were collected for the study where primary data was collected from the field survey and secondary were collected from various sources like magazines, books, journals, websites etc.

Preparation of Readiness Index

There are three dimensions of AI readiness: 'Foundational AI readiness' expresses if the appropriate infrastructure is available. 'Operational AI readiness' expresses if the necessary management mechanisms are in place. 'Transformational AI readiness' expresses how ready an organization is to maximize the value it obtains from applying AI (Eljasik-Swoboda et al., 2019). This study tends to follow the same index to illustrate the AI adoption readiness in industries inside Kathmandu Valley. The index can be developed with following criteria:

Table 1. Readiness measurement

Dimensions of AI Readiness	Definition
Foundational AI readiness	If there is appropriate infrastructure available.
Operational AI readiness	If the necessary management mechanisms are in place.
Transformational AI readiness	If an organization is ready to maximize the value it obtains from applying AI.

Source: Eljasik-Swoboda et al. (2019)

Data Analysis Technique

Data analysis includes two major sections, i.e. descriptive statistics and readiness index. That includes artificial intelligence adoption readiness index of industries, challenges in artificial intelligence adoption, and managerial solutions for easy adoption of artificial intelligence in the industries in Kathmandu valley.

ANALYSIS OF RESULTS

Industrial Development in Nepal

To search initiation of industrialization in Nepal, the time goes back to the mid-30s when the Rana regime had formed a host of public undertakings with the State intervention (PEs). At that time, while half of the PEs were linked to development rest were retail, industrial, public and financial sectors. Biratnagar Jute Mills was founded in 1936, which is the oldest industry in Nepal (Jha, 2017). It also marked the start of the industrialization in Nepal. In Kathmandu, Balaju, the first industrial estate was established with U.S. aid in 1960 (Industrial District Management, 2018).

Table 2. Industrial development in Nepal

1930	Rana regime host of public undertakings with the state intervention (PEs)
1936	First Company Act formed (Jha, 2017)
1936	Establishment of Biratnagar Jute mill (Jha, 2017)
1960	Establishment of Balaju industrial estate with the help of USA (Industrial District Management, 2018).
1982	Ministry of industry, commerce, and supplies formed first time as a part of Nepalese government
1988	Established Industrial District Management Limited (Industrial District Management, 2018)
1992	Foreign investment and technology transfer act formed
1994	Privatization Act formed
2004	Nepal become a member of World Trade Organization
2019	Ten industrial estates are operating in different part of Nepal (Industrial District Management, 2018)

In 1990 a new hope for industrial revolution was put in motion after the revolution of multiparty democracy which was meant to create a pro-business environment conducive to the industrial boom. The early years displayed certain signs of progress, but since then the neo-liberalization policy has been entirely out of place. Blind outsourcing led to the shutdown of several profit generating firms after they were sold to private companies at a cash price (Bohara et al., 2018). For the developing manufacturing market, the subsequent Maoist rebellion proved too costly. Rebels also destroyed critical facilities, such as telecoms, hydro-electricity, bridges and public buildings (Bohara et al., 2018). With the favorable political climate, the current federal administration has called for solid economic development. The administration has made its best efforts to lure international investors in many of the virgin economic sectors through regulations and benefits. In order to do this, Nepal's Board of Investment was established as a working entity and chaired by the Prime Minister himself. The notion of "One Province One Big Industrial Estate" is circulating in order to expand all the nations. The Government of Nepal, under the guidance of numerous donors such as the United States, India, the Netherlands and Germany, established eleven industrial estate in separate areas of the country (Industrial District Management, 2018).

Status of Industrial Estates in Kathmandu Valley

The data was collected from 260 industries from various industrial estates inside Kathmandu Valley. Out of 260 industries, 207 were manufacturing industries, 30 were forest and agro based industries, 20 were service industries and 3 were construction industries. Likewise, it was also found that 83 were small scale industries, 157 were medium industries, and 20 were large industries from three industrial estates of Kathmandu valley namely; Balaju industrial estate, Bhaktapur industrial estate, and Patan industrial estate.

The data also revealed that in Balaju industrial estate there are 126 industries where 10 are forest and agro based, 101 are manufacturing, and 15 are service industries whereas there is no any construction industries. Similarly in Bhaktapur industrial estate has 32 industries, where 6 are forest and agro based, 25 are manufacturing, and 1 is service industry and no any construction industries. Likewise, Patan Industrial Estate has 102 industries where 14 are forest and agro based, 81 are manufacturing, 3 are construction industries, and 4 are service industries. The data further shows that Balaju Industrial

Estate has 36 small, 79 medium and 11 large scale industries. Likewise, Bhaktapur Industrial Estate has 15 small, 15 medium and 2 large scale industries and Patan Industrial Estate has 32 small, 63 medium and 7 large scale industries.

Figure 2. Industry location and scale of industries

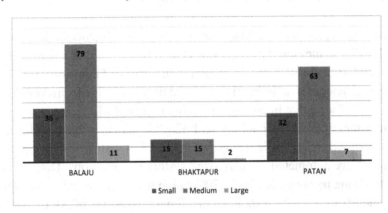

Socio-Demographic Information of Respondents

83% respondents of this study were male which denotes that number of male working in industries are higher compared to female. In similar study conducted by B.K. et al. (2019) female participation in industrial area was seen at 24% this shows similar ratio in present context as well. Majority (59%) respondents were from management team members however, the study was able to collect information from employees of diverse hierarchy of industries as shown in table 1.

Table 3. Socio-demographic information

	Number	%
Sex		
Male	171	83
Female	35	17
Job Title		
Board Member	2	1
Executive Director/CEO	29	14
Management Team Member	122	59
Other	53	26
Working Experience		
Below 5 years	23	11
5-10 years	97	47
11-15 years	47	23
16-20 years	25	12
21-25 years	10	5
Above 25 years	4	2

From the respondents, it was found that their experiences in respective industries has diverse groups like; 11 percent respondents have worked less than 5 years, 47 percent have worked 5 to 10 years, 23 percent have worked 11 to 15 years, 12 percent have worked 16 to 20 years, 5 percent have worked 21 to 25 years, and 2 percent respondents have worked more than 25 years.

Artificial Intelligence Adoption Readiness Index

This section indicates readiness of industries to adopt Artificial Intelligence in their industrial operations. Three levels of AI Readiness measured by Swoboda et al. (2019) as; Foundational AI readiness, Operational AI readiness, and Transformational AI readiness in terms of IT infrastructure sufficiency, Organizational mechanism efficiency, and Industrial potential to create value from AI Adoption respectively.

With this study it was found that in context of Technological Sufficiency, it is presented that 1.92% respondents said that they use AI Technology and 32.31% said they have updated their technology within last two years from the date of field survey. Only 10.77% industries have permanent IT Officer and 18.08% industries have automated computerized system in operations. Data security is considered when installing or updating technologies by 32.70% of the industries in industrial states in Kathmandu Valley. Out of 260 industries, 28.85% responded that Safety Measures of AI Technology can be easily implemented in their existing operational framework. Similarly, in context of management efficiency, 31.15% respondents said that they can be confident while applying instructions in AI technology, 4.23% of the industries allocated budget for AI Technology but 5% of respondents said that they allocated 5% and more budget in research and development.

Table 4. Readiness index

S.N.	Readiness Index	Yes	No
1	In your opinion, does this industry follow Artificial intelligence?	5	255
2	Is the technology this industry currently using is installed or updated within last 2 years?	84	176
3	Does this industry have a permanent IT officer/ professional?	28	232
4	Is your technology automated with computerized system?	47	213
5	Does this industry consider data security while installing or, updating technology?	85	175
6	Do you think safety measures of AI technology can be easily applied in this industry?	75	185
7	Do you think you will be confident while applying the instructions in AI technology?	81	179
8	Does this industry allocate budget for AI or, Adoption of AI?	11	249
9	Does this industry Allocate 5% budget for research and development?	13	247
10	In your opinion, do the half of the staffs in this industry are handy to use/ friendlier with AI?	20	240
11	As a manager/ decision maker, do you trust on machine compared to human?	163	97
12	Do you think automated systems increase operating risks compared to manual system?	175	85
13	Is it a good idea to use AI in this industry?	103	157
14	Do you think your operations will significantly change with AI Adoption?	115	145
15	Do you agree that rapid technology changes create opportunity loss in technological advantage?	91	169
16	Do you agree that AI can fail at the worst possible time?	171	89
17	Is there a manual instruction for AI technology?	34	226

Out of 260 industries, only 7.7% responded that their half of the employees at least, are familiar or, handy to use AI, where, 62.7% respondents trusts machine over human in operation and 67.3% said that automated system is likely to increase operational risk than that of manual human-based operations. Lastly, in terms of the Value Creation Potential of industry by use of AI Technology, 39.62% respondents think that it is a good idea to use AI in their industries, while 44.23% said their operations will be significantly changed after AI Adoption. Out of 260 industries, 35% industries considered that rapid technological changes are creating opportunity loss in technological advantage, and 65.77% responded that AI technology can fail at worst possible time. Industries among 260 samples, 13.08% said that they think there is manual instruction to operate AI technology. Therefore, it can be generalized that on average 20.77% industries are ready in terms of technological sufficiency, 29.91% industries are ready in terms of management efficiency and 39.23% industries are ready in terms of value creation potential in the firm.

Factors Affecting AI Adoption

This section uncovers that there are five major factors that affects AI adoption which includes; technological context, Organizational Context, Environmental Context, Government Intervention, and inclination towards Artificial Intelligence Adoption Decision by industries. These factors were measured with the help of 5-point Likert Scale as depicted in Figure 2.

Technological Context deals with the Relative Advantage, IT Infrastructure, and Complexity. This indicates the potential technology application in terms of infrastructure, advantages potential, and how much attraction in AI is shown by the industries. Figure 2 shows that Technological Context has comparatively low impact on the AI adoption by the industries. They were not taking AI as relatively advantageous and budgeting for IT Infrastructure were not found in most of the industries. The data showed that there is no such attraction towards AI Adoption in terms of Technological Context.

Figure 3. Factors affecting adoption of AI

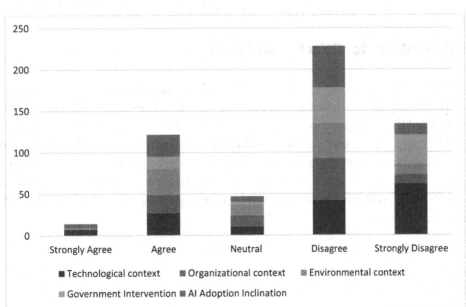

Organizational Context deals with Top Management Support and, Organizational Competencies within the industry. Here, majority of the respondents disagreed to be in proper stand in terms of organizational context. 11.7% strongly disagreed to it, 51.3% disagreed 13.6% were neutral, 22.3% agreed to it and 1.1% strongly agreed to it. Likewise, environmental factor deals with the Competitive Pressure, Trading Partners Collaboration, and, Safety Provisions and Staff Insurances in the industry. The data shows that 42% respondents disagreed to have impact of their environmental context in AI adoption decision, where 32% responded to have such impact, and 12% strongly disagreed on having such impact. In this way, it is found that majority of the industries don't have impact of their environmental context in AI Adoption.

Government Intervention deals with the Financial Support, Environmental Regulations, Training and Workshops, and Encouragements provided by the central and local government. It is found that 44% disagreed that they have effect of government intervention in their AI Adoption decision, where 36% strongly disagreed about this effect to have on their industries. Only 15% agreed and 1% strongly agreed that they have impact of government intervention in AI Adoption decision. Thus, it is clear that almost 80% of industries don't have impact of government intervention on their AI Adoption decision. Inclination towards AI adoption is influenced by the perception of executives, utility, and scope of the technology it is going to adopt. Below chart shows that industries are hesitating to adopt AI in their operations. 13.26% strongly disagreed, 49.5% disagreed, 6.44% stayed neutral, where 26.1% agreed, and, 4.7% strongly agreed about Adopting AI in their industries.

Challenges in AI Adoption

Out of 260 respondents, almost 85% respondents stated that they face challenges while adopting AI, and out of the respondents that stated there are challenges, 17 stated Hurdles are created by unnecessary processes, 129 said there is lack of skilled manpower and small market, 11 respondents stated that low capital and market, ineffective market regulation creates challenges in adopting AI. 37 said that there is no scope and market inside country and the global competition can't be easy for trading products. 12 stated that AI is not useful for all industries and in all operations, as well as very saturated/ small market, where, 23 focused on the investment recovery and said payback period is big.

Managerial Solutions for Effective AI Adoption

The challenges faced by the industries who wanted to adopt, must be handled and managed in practical way. While identifying the challenges and asking for the suggestions with respondents, majority (44%) of them stated that if they receive proper support from the government then it would be effective for them in adoption of AI. Likewise, 36.4% thinks if the market is expanded then that could solve the challenges of AI adoption. Other suggestions included providing required trainings, easy accessibility on investment as depicted in figure 4. However, 15.5% respondents think that such situations are not manageable and 2% respondents had no idea that by focusing on which area the adoption of AI would be effective to their industries.

Figure 4. Challenges in AI Adoption

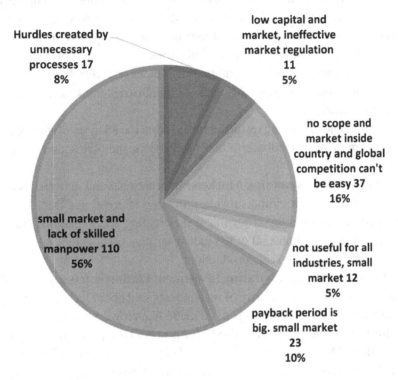

Figure 5. Managerial solutions for effective AI adoption

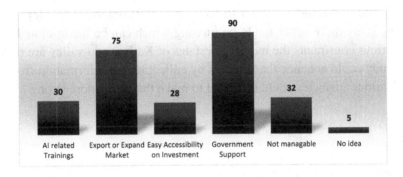

CONCLUSION

As the study aimed to analyze AI adoption of Nepalese industries this study used interview technique with the help of structured questionnaire collected from among different level employees of different industries in Kathmandu valley. On average 20.77% industries are ready in terms of technological sufficiency, 29.91% industries are ready in terms of management efficiency and 39.23% industries are ready in terms of value creation potential in the firm. Talking about factors affection AI adoption five major factors were taken into consideration which included technological context, Organizational Context, Environmental Context, Government Intervention, and inclination towards Artificial Intelligence Adoption Decision by industries. Government intervention was found to be one of the major factors affecting AI adoption in industries of Kathmandu valley. Likewise, some of the major challenges in AI adoption are hurdles created by unnecessary process, low capital, no scope, small market and so on however the major challenge (56%) is seen as small market size and unskilled manpower. Though various challenges arises in adoption of AI many suggestions were kept by industries which would bring efficiency in adopting AI which includes; training related to AI, expanding market, easy accessibility on investment, government support and various other strategies. However, 44% industries thinks it would be effective if they receive support from government.

Based on the research objectives, and results obtained from the analysis of the collected data, following recommendations are made as feedback to the stakeholders, industries, and other decision makers:

1. **Government Support in Expanding Markets:** International and national markets can be easily monitored by government. Providing subsidies, making international trade treaties, and efficient market regulation can be done by government for creating and expanding the necessary market for AI-Based industries, as almost all of the industries, that could adopt AI, stated that they didn't have sufficient market for large scale production.
2. **Focus on FDIs and Create Collaborating Investment Platform:** It is suggested that foreign direct investment is to be acquired as majority of respondents said about lack of investment accessibility, and collaborating investment platform is to be made like crowdfunding, etc.
3. **Coordinate for the Development of Skilled Manpower:** To cope one of the identified major challenge; Lack of Skilled Manpower, it is recommended that to develop skilled manpower, Industries, Government, NGOs, INGOs, and other related organizations can collaborate to train and develop in Artificial Intelligence Technology.

As this study is first in Nepalese context to cover industrial readiness to adopt AI various factors that could make the study more better might be missing which can be incorporated in further studies. Likewise due to various constraints the industrial estates of Kathmandu valley are only covered in this study so, further study could enhance the findings by collecting the information from all 11 industrial estates of Nepal. Various attributes could be added to make the study more strong.

REFERENCES

Alsheibani, S. A., Cheung, D., & Messom, D. (2019). *Factors inhibiting the adoption of artificial intelligence at organizational-level: A preliminary investigation.* Academic Press.

Berry, M. M., & Taggart, J. H. (1994). Managing technology and innovation: A review. *R & D Management, 24*(4), 341–353. doi:10.1111/j.1467-9310.1994.tb00889.x

B.K., A., Devkota, N., Gautam, N., & Paija, N. (2019). Industry willingness to pay for adequate electricity supply: A discourse on sustainable industrial development. *Quest Journal of Management and Social Sciences, 1*(2), 251–259. doi:10.3126/qjmss.v1i2.27443

Bohara, S. K., Bhuju, D. R., & Bohara, T. (2018). Perspectivas del desarrollo de industrias manufactureras en Nepal. *Revista Internacional de Cooperación y Desarrollo, 5*(2), 7–25.

Chatzoglou, P., & Chatzoudes, D. (2014). Factors affecting e-business adoption in SMEs: An empirical research. *Journal of Enterprise Information Management*, *29*(3), 327–358. doi:10.1108/JEIM-03-2014-0033

Devkota, N., Paija, N., Paudel, U. R., & Bhandari, U. (2021). Mapping the industries' willingness to pay for unrestricted electricity supply. *Environment, Development and Sustainability*, 1–17.

Dirican, C. (2015). The impacts of robotics, artificial intelligence on business and economics. *Procedia: Social and Behavioral Sciences*, *195*, 564–573. doi:10.1016/j.sbspro.2015.06.134

Duchessi, P., O'Keefe, R., & O'Leary, D. (1993). A Research perspective: Artificial intelligence, management and organizations. *Intelligent Systems in Accounting, Finance & Management*, *2*(3), 151–159. doi:10.1002/j.1099-1174.1993.tb00039.x

Economic Survey. (2018). *Economic Survey 2018/19*. Retrieved from https://new.mof.gov.np/uploads/document/file/compiled%20economic%20Survey%20english%207-25_20191111101758.pdf

Eljasik-Swoboda, T., Rathgeber, C., & Hasenauer, R. (2019, October). Artificial Intelligence for Innovation Readiness Assessment. In *2019 IEEE International Symposium on Innovation and Entrepreneurship (TEMS-ISIE)* (pp. 1-6). IEEE.

Goel, R., & Gupta, P. (2020). Robotics and industry 4.0. In *A Roadmap to Industry 4.0: Smart Production, Sharp Business and Sustainable Development* (pp. 157–169). Springer. doi:10.1007/978-3-030-14544-6_9

Goel, S., & Chen, V. (2008). Can business process reengineering lead to security vulnerabilities: Analyzing the reengineered process. *International Journal of Production Economics*, *115*(1), 104–112. doi:10.1016/j.ijpe.2008.05.002

Hengstler, M., Enkel, E., & Duelli, S. (2016). Applied artificial intelligence and trust- The case of autonomous vehicles and medical assistance devices. *Technological Forecasting and Social Change*, *105*, 105–120. doi:10.1016/j.techfore.2015.12.014

Industrial District Management. (2018). *Memorial, 2018/19*. Retrieved from https://www.idm.org.np/

Janssen, M., Brous, P., Estevez, E., Barbosa, L. S., & Janowski, T. (2020). Data governance: Organizing data for trustworthy Artificial Intelligence. *Government Information Quarterly*, *37*(3), 101493. doi:10.1016/j.giq.2020.101493

Jha, K. (2017). *The Madhesi upsurge and the contested idea of Nepal*. Springer Singapore. doi:10.1007/978-981-10-2926-4

Koehler, J. (2018). Business process innovation with artificial intelligence: Levering Benefits and controlling operational risks. *European Business & Management*, *4*(2), 55–66. doi:10.11648/j.ebm.20180402.12

Kraus, S., Palme, C., Kailer, N., & Kallinger, F. L. (2018). Digital entrepreneurship: A research agenda on new business models for the twenty-first century. *International Journal of Entrepreneurial Behaviour & Research*. Advance online publication. doi:10.1108/IJEBR-06-2018-0425

Ma, Y., Ping, K., Wu, C., Chen, L., Shi, H., & Chong, D. (2019). Artificial intelligence powered internet of things and smart public service. *Library Hi Tech*, *38*(1), 165–179. doi:10.1108/LHT-12-2017-0274

Pan, Y., Froese, F., Liu, N., Hu, Y., & Ye, M. (2021). The adoption of artificial intelligence in employee recruitment: The influence of contextual factors. *International Journal of Human Resource Management*, 1–23.

Paudel, U. R., & Devkota, N. (2018). Socio-Economic influences on small business performance in Nepal-India open border: Evidence from cross-sectional analysis. *Economia e Sociologia*, *11*(4), 11–30.

Paudel, U. R., Puri, S., Parajuli, S., Devkota, N., & Bhandari, U. (2021). Measuring Cultural Diversity Impact in Hospitality Industry Leadership: Managerial Communication Perspective from Five Star Hotels in Kathmandu Valley, Nepal. *Journal of Tourism & Adventure*, *4*(1), 75–88.

Pillai, R., & Sivathanu, B. (2020). Adoption of artificial intelligence (AI) for talent acquisition in IT/ITeS organizations. *Benchmarking*, *27*(9), 2599–2629.

Popa, C. (2011). Adoption of artificial intelligence in agriculture. *Bulletin of University of Agricultural Sciences and Veterinary Medicine Cluj-Napoca. Agriculture*, *68*(1).

Porter, M. E. (1985). Technology and competitive advantage. *The Journal of Business Strategy*, 33.

Rajbhandari, S., Khanal, G., Parajuli, S., & Karki, D. (2020). A Review on Potentiality of Industry 4.0 in Nepal: Does the Pandemic Play Catalyst Role? *Quest Journal of Management and Social Sciences*, *2*(2), 366–379.

Recht, M., & Bryan, R. N. (2017). Artificial intelligence: Threat or boon to radiologists? *Journal of the American College of Radiology*, *14*(11), 1476–1480. doi:10.1016/j.jacr.2017.07.007 PMID:28826960

Ribeiro-Navarrete, S., Saura, J. R., & Palacios-Marqués, D. (2021). Towards a new era of mass data collection: Assessing pandemic surveillance technologies to preserve user privacy. *Technological Forecasting and Social Change*, *167*, 120681. doi:10.1016/j.techfore.2021.120681 PMID:33840865

Sapkota, T. P., Kunwar, S., Bhattarai, M., & Poudel, S. (2020). Artificial intelligence that are beneficial for law. *US-China L. Rev.*, *17*, 217.

Saura, J. R., Palacios-Marqués, D., & Iturricha-Fernández, A. (2021a). Ethical Design in Social Media: Assessing the main performance measurements of user online behavior modification. *Journal of Business Research*, *129*(May), 271–281. doi:10.1016/j.jbusres.2021.03.001

Saura, J. R., Ribeiro-Soriano, D., & Palacios-Marqués, D. (2021b, July 15). Setting privacy "by default" in social IoT: Theorizing the challenges and directions in Big Data Research. *Big Data Research*, *25*, 100245. doi:10.1016/j.bdr.2021.100245

Semmler, S., & Rose, Z. (2017). Artificial intelligence: Application today and implications tomorrow. *Duke L. & Tech. Rev.*, *16*, 85.

Shrestha, P. (2021). Use of Technology and Its Management Issues in Nepalese Industries and Businesses. *Nepalese Journal of Management Research*, *1*, 9–14.

Smith, C. (2019). An employee's best friend? How AI can boost employee engagement and performance. *Strategic HR Review*, *18*(1), 17–20. doi:10.1108/SHR-11-2018-0092

Smith, R., & Sharif, N. (2007). Understanding and acquiring technology assets for global competition. *Technovation*, *27*(11), 643–649. doi:10.1016/j.technovation.2007.04.001

Turchin, P., Hoyer, D., Korotayev, A., Kradin, N., Nefedov, S., Feinman, G., Levine, J., Reddish, J., Cioni, E., Thorpe, C., Bennett, J. S., François, P., & Whitehouse, H. (2021). Rise of the war machines: Charting the evolution of military technologies from the Neolithic to the Industrial Revolution. *PLoS One*, *16*(10), e0258161. doi:10.1371/journal.pone.0258161 PMID:34669706

Tyagi, A. (2016). Artificial intelligence: Boon or bane? SSRN *Electronic Journal*. doi:10.2139/ssrn.2836438

Verma, A., Lamsal, K., & Verma, P. (2021). An investigation of skill requirements in artificial intelligence and machine learning job advertisements. *Industry and Higher Education*.

Weber, F. D., & Schütte, R. (2019). State-of-the-art and adoption of artificial intelligence in retailing. *Digital Policy. Regulation & Governance*, *21*(3), 264–279.

Xu, W., Wei, Y., & Fan, Y. (2002). Virtual enterprise and its intelligence management. *Computers & Industrial Engineering*, *42*(2–4), 199–205. doi:10.1016/S0360-8352(02)00053-0

Yadav, R., & Yadav, R. (2018). Review on artificial intelligence: A boon or bane to humans. *International Journal of Scientific Research in Science and Information Technology*, *4*(2), 1818–1820.

Chapter 13
The Dark Side of Progress:
Social and Political Movements Against Artificial Intelligence in Spain

José Emilio Pérez-Martínez

Rey Juan Carlos University, Spain

ABSTRACT

This chapter deals with one of the hottest issues in recent years: the application of artificial intelligence to surveillance systems and the movements against this type of surveillance in Spain. The authors show how, in the face of the advance of facial recognition technologies in more and more aspects of our lives in Spain and around the world, movements of response and rejection to this new model of society are being organised. The cases of UNIR and Mercadona are analysed in this text as representative of the state of these debates in the Spanish public sphere.

People worry that computers will get too smart and take over the world, but the real problem is that they're too stupid and they've already taken over the world. Pedro Domingos, The Master Algorithm (2015)

INTRODUCTION

Are machines as stupid as Pedro Domingos proposes? The reality is that they are not. In fact, as shown by the evolution of the situation in recent years, everything points to the contrary: the growth of Artificial Intelligence (AI) research is exponential at a global level and, as predicted by science fiction films such as *Wargames* (1983) or *2001: A Space Odyssey* (1968), machines have taken control of our world. This expansion has been carried out, on the vast majority of occasions, with the public's back turned and in the midst of considerable misinformation.

DOI: 10.4018/978-1-7998-9609-8.ch013

The implementation of AI in different aspects of our lives is already a daily reality. For example, Spaniards spend an average of 5 hours and 14 minutes connected to the internet, of which 2 hours and 24 minutes are spent on their mobile phones. WhatsApp and social networks are the elements to which most time is dedicated (Saura, Palacios-Marqués, & Iturricha-Fernández, 2021a). A digital scenario in which, in 2020, 7.6 million Spaniards considered themselves addicted to their devices and 61% of them recognised that looking at their mobile phone was the first and last thing they did every day (Asociación de Marketing de España [MKT], 2021). Throughout all these hours of consumption, users provided, through their interaction with the network, information about themselves that came to swell what, in recent years, has become known as big data: an overwhelming volume of personal data (Ribeiro-Navarrete, Saura & Palacios Marqués, 2021a; Saura, Ribeiro-Soriano & Palacios-Marqués, 2021b) that different corporations process using AI for purposes that are sometimes opaque, such as: product development, providing a clear view of the customer experience on websites, facilitating machine learning and driving innovation (APD, 2019).

Studies by the Observatorio Nacional de Tecnología y Sociedad (ONTSI) point in the same direction of increasing use of AI. According to data from 2020, the Spanish business fabric is beginning to familiarise itself with Artificial Intelligence and its use is still incipient: the average use in companies in the European Union is 7%, while in Spain it stands at 6%. Large Spanish companies are the most intensive in the incorporation of AI, reaching 18% adoption of technologies such as machine learning through big data, followed by service robots, virtual customer assistants or chatbots, and natural language processing.

Although Spain is currently in a modest position in terms of AI adoption, the policy designed by the Secretaría de Estado de Digitalización e Inteligencia Artificial, known as the Estrategia Nacional de Inteligencia Artificial (ENIA), aims to give a decisive boost to artificial intelligence in all sectors in the coming years (ONTSI, 2021).

One of these sectors, which is experiencing a significant growth in its implementation and attention, is the development and use of facial recognition systems for security and citizen control purposes, both by the different state apparatuses and by different corporations and private capital. A technology that is sparking heated debates in both the national and international public sphere (Castelluccia & Le Métayer, 2021; Selinger & Hartzog, 2020; Janssen, Brous, Estevez, Barbosa, & Janowski, 2020). This paper aims to approach the form and content that these debates on new technologies, security and infringement of fundamental rights are taking in Spain, focusing on the criticisms that are being made from certain social and political sectors.

After a brief introduction to what they are, how they work and the implementation of this type of identification systems, this paper will proceed to analyse some of the lines of opposition to the use of these technologies in Spain, as well as some of the most recent and important controversies and mobilisations in the country. In this way, an attempt will be made to establish the main resistance offered by Spanish society to the use of facial recognition.

FACIAL RECOGNITION

Literature Review, Framework and Hypotheses Development

Before starting with this brief introduction, it is necessary to note that, due to its topicality, the term "facial recognition" is used to refer to a wide variety of technologies. According to Selinger & Leong:

the media, the public, and even the designers and producers of various image-based systems are prone to using the category 'facial recognition technology' inconsistently. Sometimes, they stretch the term too far and apply it to image-based technologies that analyse faces without identifying individuals (2021: 1).

However, as the authors themselves point out, "the term 'facial recognition' most precisely applies to two variations of biometric systems that create an identifiable template of a unique person: verification and identification" (2021: 2). Verification refers to when you have the data of the person whose identity you want to check, confirming that he or she corresponds to the given image. This type of technology is already used in computer login systems or in smartphones as a screen unlocking system. It is undoubtedly the most widespread use today. Identification refers to a procedure in which an image is compared with a set of known identities in order to find the most similar one. This is, for example, the method used by law enforcement agencies to identify a suspect. However, it should be noted that the identification always depends on the existence of a database against which the comparison can be made.

Identification, and its applications to surveillance, is the variable on which this paper will focus, as it is the one that is arousing most controversy due to its ethical considerations and, therefore, the one that is generating most resistance movements at both the social and political levels. Identification systems generate resistance, initially, because they present, from their inception, algorithmic biases that, in some way, reflect the ideological and cultural prejudices of the society that engenders them. As Andrejevic & Selwyn point out:

The past five years have seen repeated reports of facial recognition systems failing to recognise African American faces due to the racially skewed data-sets that the algorithms have been trained on, alongside the 'glitch' of identical twins being able to confuse facial identification systems. As such, there are concerns about largescale misidentification and machine bias in the form of systematic misrecognition by skin colour or ethnic background. Recent studies suggest that we are still far short of having facial recognition systems that can accurately identify everyone in a large crowd, while some systems continue to work better on certain demographic groups than others (2020: 117).

Secondly, this technology generates movements of reaction because of its ethical implications stemming from some recurrent "misunderstandings" it creates and its normative effects in naturalising certain practices that would require a slower and deeper analysis and reflection. Some of these "misunderstandings" would be, for example:

The imprecise and mechanical assimilation between surveillance and security; the difference between preventive and anticipatory security; the relationship between the rights to privacy and intimacy with public space; the links between the technological and the ideological; the relative effectiveness of video surveillance systems in security and judicial functions; the criteria of authenticity and reliability of images and interpreters in criminal proceedings; the link between algorithmic surveillance and the right to due process; among others (Pérez Esquivel, 2021: 103).

Despite the concerns outlined above, surveillance with facial recognition has spread around the world in recent years. According to a study by Surfshack, 109 countries employ or have tested the use of facial recognition for surveillance purposes. China is leading the way in the implementation of this technology and there are other countries, such as Singapore and South Korea, which, faced with the new situation created by Covid-19, are using this technology as a means of monitoring positive individuals. Compared to these, only three countries have banned it: Luxembourg, Morocco and Belgium, which has also declared it illegal (Surfshack, 2020).

Around 30 countries in Europe are using or have tested this technology with varying degrees of success. In London, for example, facial recognition cameras were installed throughout the city in January 2020 (Perrigo, 2020) and a month later the first arrest had already been made. In Germany, the police are considering installing such cameras in airports and train stations (Grüll, 2020). Finally, in the Czech Republic, the government claims to have made more than 150 arrests since it began using this technology in 2018 (Security Magazine, 2020).

In Spain, this technology has started to be implemented in recent years. Some of the most important airports have installed a biometric identification system that allows check-in and boarding without the need to show any kind of documentation. Madrid's Estación Sur de Autobuses, one of the busiest in the country, implemented a biometric surveillance system in 2016 to identify criminals. According to the competent authorities, the number of crimes has been reduced exponentially. Furthermore, in Madrid, the Empresa Municipal de Transportes (EMT) has been testing since October 2019 a biometric system that converts passengers' faces, associated with a card via an app, into a method of payment and validation of transport tickets.

It is foreseeable that from 2022 the implementation of these systems in airports and border posts will be generalised in order to comply with the implementation of the new Shared Biometric Matching System (sBMS) approved by the European Commission. A system that aims to connect in real time the biometric information of nearly 400 million people belonging to countries outside the Schengen area, so that, in the words of its developers: "this shared Biometric Matching System, aiming at fighting against irregular immigration and trans-border crime, will become one of the world's largest biometric systems when it integrates all the existing and upcoming biometric databases of the European Union" (Sopra Steria & IDEMIA, 2020: 1). La Línea de la Concepción will be the site of the first pilot border "biometric corridor" in Spain.

All this comes in a context in which the governments of the EU member states are beginning to discuss the draft of the new EU Artificial Intelligence Act (AI Act) and in which the European Data Protection Supervisor (EDPS) and the European Data Protection Board (EDPB) have called for a ban on use of AI for automated recognition of human features in publicly accessible spaces:

Taking into account the extremely high risks posed by remote biometric identification of individuals in publicly accessible spaces, the EDPB and the EDPS call for a general ban on any use of AI for automated recognition of human features in publicly accessible spaces, such as recognition of faces, gait, fingerprints, DNA, voice, keystrokes and other biometric or behavioural signals, in any context. Similarly, the EDPB and EDPS recommend a ban on AI systems using biometrics to categorize individuals into clusters based on ethnicity, gender, political or sexual orientation, or other grounds on which discrimination is prohibited under Article 21 of the Charter of Fundamental Rights (EDPB, 2021).

Other civil society organisations such as the European federation of digital rights associations, European Digital Rights (EDRi), point in the same direction. Its last report *The Rise and Rise of Biometric Mass Surveillance in the EU* (Montag, McLeod, De Mets, Gauld, Rodger & Petka, 2021) shows that in Poland, Germany and the Netherlands biometric systems are increasingly being required for accessing public services and other everyday activities. As a result, "people are being given the false 'choice' to either submit their sensitive data, or be excluded from society" (Jakubowska, 2021).

In fact, the EDRi is promoting a European Citizen's Initiative, called *#ReclaimYourFace*, to ban biometric mass surveillance practices. According to the movement:

Evidence shows that uses of biometric mass surveillance in Member States and by EU agencies have resulted in violations of EU data protection law, and unduly restricted people's rights including their privacy, right to free speech, right to protest and not to be discriminated against. The widespread use of biometric surveillance, profiling and prediction is a threat to the rule of law and our most basic freedoms (Reclaim Your Face, 2021).

The legal situation of this type of technology in Spain, as in the rest of the European Union, is complex. There are legal and technical standards, both national and supranational, which have established the lines along which these systems must be developed and provided.

Firstly, there is the European General Data Protection Regulation 2016/679 (GDPR) and, in Spain, the Ley Orgánica 3/2018 de Protección de Datos y Garantías de Derechos Digitales. These regulations include in their articles the definition of "biometric data", also including as a special category of data those "biometric data aimed at univocally identifying", deriving from all of this certain rights and obligations for citizens and for the entities that process this data.

Similarly, Article 22 of the GDPR provides that the citizen has the right "not to be subject to a decision based solely on automated processing, including profiling, which produces legal effects on him or her or similarly significantly affects him or her". In these cases, there should always be, at the very least, the right to obtain human intervention, "to express his or her point of view and to challenge the decision", i.e. the citizen should always have the right to have a person review the processing of these data. In some specific sectors, which are understood to be more sensitive, human intervention is mandatory.

Secondly, in the AI Act mentioned above, the European Commission emphasises what it calls "High Risk" applications, including remote Biometric Identification systems. These systems, in addition to complying with the GDPR, must be subject to strict obligations (Azanza, 2021: 9 and 10):

- Risk assessment and mitigating actions.
- Establish minimum quality standards for the products used to minimise risks and discriminatory outcomes.
- Recording of system activity to allow traceability of results.
- Necessary documentation for competent authorities on the system, its purpose and compliance.
- Clear and adequate information for the user.
- Human oversight of results involving subsequent action and minimising risk and helplessness.
- High level of robustness and accuracy of the systems.

This proposal offers a regulation of some of its specific applications, with the aim of guaranteeing citizens' rights and freedoms. This framework of reference, which, pending the adoption of specific legislation, seems somewhat undefined, will help to situate the debates and mobilisations that follow.

ANALYSIS

This section presents two approaches to facial recognition technologies that can be seen as diametrically opposed: one position advocates caution and intervention by the authorities, while the other sees their relationship with this technology in terms of resistance and confrontation.

The first of these has its clearest manifestation in the open letter written by 70 academics asking the Spanish government to establish "a commission of enquiry to study the need to establish a moratorium on the use and commercialisation of facial recognition and analysis systems by public and private companies" until such time as "the Cortes Generales and the legislative institutions debate which, how, under what conditions, with what guarantees and with what objectives, if any, the use of these systems should be allowed" (Various, 2021: 1).

Among the signatories of this letter, it is possible to find the names of renowned academics and researchers, philosophers or communicators: Adela Cortina, philosopher; Carissa Véliz, professor at Oxford University and author of *Privacy is Power*; PhD in AI Nerea Luis; Simona Levi, member of Xnet; former UAB vice-rector Pilar Dellunde; Ramón López de Mántaras, National Research Award "Julio Ruíz Pastor" in Mathematics or Ofelia Tejerina Rodríguez, president of the Asociación de Internautas.

The signatories of the document are clear that "due to the serious deficiencies and risks presented by these systems", their "potential benefits" could not compensate, under any circumstances, "their potential negative effects, especially for groups and collectives that often suffer injustices and discriminatory treatment" (Various, 2021: 2), among others: women, LGTBIQ+ people, racialised people, migrants, people with disabilities or people at risk of social exclusion.

This position is based, firstly, on the certainty that this type of systems has "serious problems" that have been "widely documented and discussed by the scientific community and governmental institutions" and that would have an impact on the cultural and ideological prejudices that end up biasing the algorithms on which these systems are based (Various, 2021: 1). Secondly, the positioning responds to the perception that the regulatory framework is insufficient and that, therefore, the government should intervene quickly "before these systems continue to expand and become de facto standards" and put at stake "fundamental issues of social justice, human dignity, equity, equal treatment and inclusion" (Various, 2021: 1).

On a completely different spectrum can be found collectives and citizen initiatives that, in the face of the indiscriminate advance of this type of technology, are seeking ways to resist and combat the harmful effects of facial recognition and the application of AI in surveillance. Important organisations such as International Amnesty recognise that, due to the increased use of facial recognition and other AI-based surveillance tools, "the lists of rights potentially violated are growing: the right not to be subjected to arbitrary interference with your privacy, right to protest, peaceful assembly and associaction, bodily autonomy..." (International Amnesty, 2021a). Faced with this criminalisation of social protest, many groups are preparing and circulating materials dedicated to preventing the repressive effects of the implementation of the IA in the surveillance of demonstrations and acts of protest. It seems that, in the purest *1984* style, part of society has become aware of the danger: "until they become conscious they will never rebel, and until after they have rebelled they cannot become conscious" (Orwell, 2016: 83).

There are initiatives, such as the collective La cultura de la seguridad or the Centro de Documentación sobre Contra-Vigilancia, that share resources to make participation in protest events safe for all. Amnesty International itself has published a dossier along the same lines. In *How to protect your phone and your identity at protests*, Amnesty International offers a series of tips to help maintain the safety and integrity of those attending a protest event. Thus, in the section "Protect your face", the organisation is clear and, inspired by the CV Dazzle initiative[1], lists the following forms of facial recognition "tricking" (International Amnesty, 2021b: 4):

- Makeup: "apply makeup that contrasts with your skin tone in unusual tones and directions".
- Nose bridge: partially obscure this area, which is a key facial feature. This is "especially effective against OpenCV's face detection algorithm".
- Eyes: "The position and darkness of eyes is a key facial feature", por lo tanto, "partially obscure one of the ocular regions".
- Masks: "Note that anything you put on your face that's not your face will help to reduce the face recognition similarity score. [...] Face accessories that are non-obvious will work best".
- Head: "Obscuring the elliptical shape of head can also improve your ability to block face detection.
- Asymmetry: "Facial-recognition algorithms expect symmetry between the left and the right sides of the face. By developing an asymmetrical look, you may decrease your probability of being detected".

Some Spanish generalist websites dedicated to new technologies, such as *Xataka*, have recently published articles focusing on how to make facial identification more difficult. Among others, they offer the following advice (López, 2020):

- Wear a scarf that covers your entire face including the lower part of your nose.
- Wear a cap or hat that covers your hairstyle and keep your eyes to the ground when walking.
- If you have long hair, comb it so that it covers your forehead and facial features such as your eyebrows and part of your eyes.
- Wear large sunglasses with lenses capable of reflecting infrared light.
- Beards help to camouflage some features of your face. If you can, grow one.
- If you want to share a photo of your face on your social networks, modify it slightly beforehand to confuse recognition systems.

The group behind La cultura de la seguridad insists on this last point: both in its materials and in its talks, this group highlights the need to escape the "tyranny of the image". Thus, among the general advice for attending a demonstration, the group recommends not to film and not to allow yourself being filmed, avoid the presence of the press and mobile devices, cover your face, cover tattoos and cover anything that could be considered your own identity. In short, try to preserve "your anonymity and that of others" (Cultura de la Seguridad, 2021). This is extremely important if we connect it with the excessive use of social networks, spaces where many of these images and videos end up, making it easier for law enforcement agencies to create a database of images of "suspicious" people.

International Amnesty points in the same direction when it recognises that "Law enforcement maintains growing databases of community members it claims are 'suspicious', monitoring their content and associates" and warns that "what you post may be used against you in a court of law" (International Amnesty, 2021b: 7). In short, faced with the advance of surveillance technologies and the criminalisation of social protest that they bring with them, citizens should be increasingly aware of how to outwit and resist these new models of security that can deepen the repressive nature of our societies.

Both approaches to facial recognition have in common the firm conviction that this technology violates fundamental rights that should be protected. The first, as we have seen, gathers "specialised" opinions to ask the Spanish government to intervene and place limits on the implementation of these surveillance systems. The second, on the other hand, proposes a bottom-up organisation of the citizens themselves and their different communities to confront the restrictions on their rights in a situation of possible inaction on the part of the authorities. With this framework, it is time to analyse two specific examples of mobilisation that have taken place in recent years in Spain and to see how society has organised itself and what the consequences have been.

DISCUSSION: UNIR

One of the first fields in which it is possible to find a process of social mobilisation provoked by the implementation of facial recognition technologies is in education, more specifically in universities. As a consequence of the health situation created by Covid-19, Spanish universities were faced, in the 2019/20 academic year, with the debate on how to organise their exams in such a way as to maintain the security of the student body. The solutions to this situation varied, depending on the centres, but in the face of some extreme cases of plagiarism and impersonation (Vargas, 2020; Garnelo, 2020), the debate was opened on the need to implement different levels of proctoring, i.e. Artificial Intelligence applied to the invigilation of exams, to avoid these situations.

A majority of Spanish universities, such as the Universidad de Oviedo, conducted their online exams without implementing surveillance technologies of this type (Redacción, 2020) and others, such as the Universidad de Granada, maintained an intense dialogue with student associations to adapt the courses to the different realities that their students were experiencing (Parra, 2020). In fact, following consultations with the Conferencia de Rectores de las Universidades Españolas (CRUE), the Asociación Española de Protección de Datos (AEPD) published a report in which it insisted that

the personal data protection regulation, as it is aimed at safeguarding a fundamental right, applies in its entirety to the current situation, given that there is no reason to determine the suspension of fundamental rights, nor has such a measure been adopted (AEPD, 2020: 3).

Despite this report, and a general tendency not to use this type of technology, the 2020/21 academic year uncovered a conflict related to proctoring, facial recognition and the defence of fundamental rights by students at the Universidad Internacional de la Rioja (UNIR).

In April 2021, the UNIR, a private online university, informed its students that it was modifying the model for taking the exams and introducing a new one requiring the installation of a proctoring software: Smowltech. This software had to be installed five days before the exam and, in addition to facial recognition and biometric systems, accessed students' computers.

Following this change of position on the part of the university, many of its students decided to organise themselves in response to what they considered an attack on their fundamental rights. After forming the HUxIR Asociación de Estudiantes por la Defensa de los Derechos Fundamentales, the students published a statement on 18 April 2021 in which they set out their struggle, their denunciation and their demands. These can be summarised in the following points (HUxIR, 2021 April 18):

- Denouncing a lack of a secure alternative to these online exams. The other option given by the university was to take the tests in person, in the midst of a new outbreak of the pandemic.
- According to the AEPD report, "the consent given by the student [to install the proctoring software] cannot be valid, because it is not free and because of the asymmetry of power existing [between the student and the university itself]".
- The obligation to give full access to the computer, on which there are contractually protected data of third parties, exposes students to possible fines under the Ley de Protección de Datos.
- The implementation of such proctoring measures implies a disproportionate use of surveillance measures that violate students' rights and invade their privacy.
- Using this technology under the pretext of alleged difficulties in identifying students is false, as UNIR has been identifying its students on a daily basis when they attend classes and submit work for continuous assessment.
- Proctoring generates access barriers and discrimination against people with some kind of disability or anxiety, which can cause damage and harm the health of some students. It also discriminates on cultural grounds.
- The situation created by the implementation of this monitoring software could result in a drop in the performance of students, who would have to divert their attentional resources towards monitoring their own bodies in order not to be suspicious.
- Insecurity with regard to assessment methods compared to previous exams.
- The new situation may require the purchase of new hardware in order to be able to take the exams. A financial cost that was not required during enrolment.
- Under no circumstances are the conditions similar to those of an on-site examination.
- Installing the software five days in advance, giving it full access to the students' terminal and modifying the firewall and antivirus, creates the risk of the program exposing passwords, credit card numbers and digital certificates.
- The measures are imposed by the university after enrolment, without giving students the possibility to decide whether to comply or not to enrol.
- Ergonomics problems arising from the requirements of the monitoring software.
- Changes in exam dynamics: to avoid false positives, students must change the way they do things to adapt themselves.
- Lack of transparency about testing procedures and how to deal with false positives. Students are assumed to be guilty until proven innocent.
- Proctoring creates a sense of insecurity for students as the AI could decide to exclude them at any time during the course of the exam.
- The application source code is proprietary and not auditable.
- Any anomaly (false alert, internet service failure, etc.) is detrimental to the student and could cost him/her a failure.
- In the same way, actions by third parties could be identified by the software as incidents and, in the same way, cost the student a fail.
- Academic performance is no longer enough to pass an exam.
- The university creates a situation of coercion, forcing consent in cases such as that of students who, for health reasons, are unable to take exams in person.

We should not forget that the importance of this conflict lies in the fact that it raises several major issues related to this type of technology. Firstly, when we know that we are being watched, our behaviour is conditioned. This affects, in this particular case, our rights to privacy and intimacy. The introduction of surveillance systems in students' homes would violate both of these fundamental rights. Secondly, the algorithms of these programmes, as noted above, are biased towards people with darker skin tones and discriminate against people with lower purchasing power or without good internet connections and neurodivergent people, who are considered to be cheaters. Moreover, as the UNIR students pointed out, these types of programmes collect and store personally identifiable information on their servers, without users having a choice. Finally, thirdly, it is necessary to take into account that the European Commission has recently proposed new legislation to regulate the use of Artificial Intelligence and facial recognition systems. Education is considered one of the high-risk areas because the implementation of AI in it can determine a person's access to information and career, affecting their future -exams are precisely one of the examples given by the Commission (European Commission, 2021).

The students took their complaints to the Rector of the UNIR (HUxIR, 2021 April 21) and, at first, their complaints went unheeded. After a series of meetings and misunderstandings between the university and its students, they launched a crowdfunding campaign to take legal action against the university, and their case received some media coverage.

Rubén González, Deputy Rector for Academic Organisation and Teaching Staff at UNIR, in response to this mobilisation, assured the media that his centre, with this system, tried to guarantee at all times the quality of its programmes under equal conditions for all students:

Our default examination model is face-to-face and because we are sensitive to the pandemic situation we have offered online proctored tests. [...] After more than a year of taking actions to improve online assessments, we concluded that proctoring is now the most robust and secure option. [...] Following the recommendations of the AEPD, which does not prohibit it, we ask for the student's consent. [...] We don't do anything the student doesn't want to, he/she has the face-to-face option. Once we have their permission, we don't invade anything they don't want us to invade, in other words, we don't access the content of their computer, we only view their desktop (Efe, 2021).

From Smowl, the company that created the surveillance software, Alex Vera, Head of Strategy and Business Development, said that "there is still a lot of confusion, although it is not a practice that was born today because it is already used in many universities around the world and in other areas such as qualifications or competitive examinations" and that "it is simply online monitoring". The firm also tried to clarify the exact functioning of the software by pointing out that "we only receive images that we link to a user code and that is what the university receives, since it already has its own data" and that "it is not a failing or passing machine, but an instrument to generate evidence that is reported to the proctor - the lecturer - who, with this information, makes his or her own decisions" (Dueñas, 2021).

Despite these statements and in response to the students' organised protest, the UNIR decided on 8 June to suspend biometric controls during the exams and to maintain Smowl as a surveillance tool, with the identification of students being supervised by qualified staff (UNIR, 2021). In the end, the tests took place amidst considerable chaos: computer glitches, false alarms by the programme, lack of attention by the technical service, etc.

In view of the complaints received from the university's students, having also heard the UNIR and taking into account that the biometric controls had been abolished, on 27 July 2021 the AEPD issued a report on this case. In it, it recognised, firstly, that the biometric data processing was not justified and pointed out that, in this case, "necessity cannot be confused with convenience, as the AEPD report no. 372/2016 recalls" and, therefore, "the use of facial recognition techniques may be convenient for UNIR, but they are not necessary for the achievement of the intended purpose" (2021: 10).

Secondly, the AEPD recognised in its report, agreeing with the students, that biometric facial recognition implies "a greater intrusion into the right to personal data protection" and that the intended use by the UNIR "could pose a high risk to the rights and freedoms of individuals, due to the use of new technologies, and the scope and context in which it will be carried out" (2021: 10).

In conclusion, the AEPD agreed to warn the UNIR "to adopt corrective measures to prevent the planned processing from being a possible breach of data protection legislation" (2021: 10).

DISCUSSION: MERCADONA

In July 2020, Mercadona, the famous supermarket chain, hit the news once again. If it had previously made headlines for violating the rights of its workers (Europa Press, 2017), for winning controversial firing cases (Salvatierra, 2019) or for its high levels of business (García Ropero, 2020), this time it was for implementing a facial recognition system in 40 of its establishments (Del Barco, 2020). A striking piece of news because it was a pioneering case in the sector in Spain, because the technology to be implemented was related to former members of the Mossad and, finally, because of the legal doubts it raised.

The system, according to Mercadona, was implemented with the objectives of detecting people with a "firm sentence of a restraining order from the establishment in less than 0.3 seconds" and to protect the chain's employees who had been victims of gender violence, thus guaranteeing the compliance with restraining orders. Goals that would be met "always in constant contact with the corresponding authorities to ensure full protection and all their legal guarantees" (Pérez, 2020).

This was, in fact, expressed in the signs placed at the entrance of the establishments where the system was implemented, advertised as an "early detection zone":

Please be informed that MERCADONA S.A., in order to improve your security, has implemented a facial recognition system to detect only those persons with a restraining order, or analogous judicial measure in force, who may pose a risk to your security. In the event of detecting one of these people with a restraining order in force, the system will generate an alert, which will be checked by a special security team, with specific training, in order to communicate it exclusively to the Law Enforcement Agencies in order to protect the safety and integrity of MERCADONA's customers and employees. [...] The professional security team protects and evaluates the images processed, in order to avoid possible errors in the system. The biometric data generated with the system's image will only be used for the aforementioned purpose and only during the verification process, which lasts for tenths of a second. Once the verification has been carried out, no data will be saved if the result is negative (Mercadona, 2020).

Reactions to the launch were immediate. Leaving aside those that focused on exploring the relationship of the surveillance system with the Mossad (López Frías, 2020), the most interesting were those that questioned the legality and ethics of this initiative. This is because the issue of facial recognition in Mercadona raises two concerns: firstly, the installation of cameras to identify people and, secondly, the origin of the database or the information with which the system carries out this identification.

Jorge García Herrero, a lawyer and data protection consultant, put the question in the following terms:

Even if you don't save the images, it is a processing. The key is where Mercadona gets the images of the offenders. Who gives them to it? Mercadona can only have access to the database of the courts. And in fact, the courts don't necessarily have to have my face. Where does Mercadona get my face for comparison? Unless they had it on their original cameras, but Mercadona would also have had to keep them. [...]

Mercadona may say they want to prevent crime, but they are not law enforcement agencies. And according to the AEPD report, they could not use facial recognition for this. The point is that the cameras capture not only potential criminals, but also the data of others (Pérez, 2020).

Another aspect to bear in mind is that Mercadona appealed to the "public interest" when implementing this system, and yet this is questionable. García Herrero himself stated that, clearly, "the main interest at stake is not public, but corporate: the protection of the company's properties", and consequently, "it would have been more respectful to have recognised and articulated it in this way". In the opinion of this specialist, any data processing "must be subject to the principles of lawfulness, loyalty, transparency, purpose limitation and minimisation" and this was not the case here: "although the aim is to identify a small percentage of clients (the convicted), all persons who enter are subjected to biometric control, even those who cannot possibly have committed crimes. [...] For example, young children, who are also a vulnerable and a specifically protected group" (Rubio, 2020).

The proportionality of the measure adopted by the supermarket chain was another of the aspects questioned in the public sphere following the announcement. Borja Adsuara, a lawyer and legal consultant, posed the following question: "How many people are there with a final sentence and a precautionary measure of restraining order in force [...] to compensate for the investment in this system and the capture of the image of all customers? Is it proportionate? (Perez, 2020). The company did not offer any figures in this regard, which led García Herrero to suggest that proportionality and minimisation, if properly applied, "would imply, for example, selecting, on a case-by-case basis, only the most robbed shops and restricting access and control to them, allowing those who so wish to avoid this intrusive treatment" (Rubio, 2020).

Alfonso Pacheco Cifuentes, a lawyer specialising in data protection, went a step further and argued that Mercadona's system should be well designed to avoid what he considered "unjustified situations": "does the ban on access for shoplifting in my local Mercadonas only apply to such establishments or to all those open in Spain? Furthermore, if I have a restraining order against my ex-partner, who works in a centre in Valencia, there is no reason why I should not be able to shop in a Mercadona in Palma de Mallorca" (Rubio, 2020). And, in the worst-case scenario, he raised the negative consequences that a software failure could have: among them the "infringement of the right to honour" that could be caused by an arrest following an incorrect identification -a common occurrence since the algorithms used are highly conditioned.

In light of all this turmoil, its media repercussions, the possible legal implications of the plan implemented by Mercadona, and complaints filed by the Asociación de Consumidores y Usuarios en Acción (FACUA) and the Asociación para la Prevención y Estudios de Delitos, Abusos y Negligencias en Informática y Comunicaciones Avanzadas (APEDANICA), the AEPD decided to act and initiate an investigation that would last 12 months and that would determine whether or not the supermarket chain's video surveillance model violated fundamental rights.

In February 2021, months after the installation of the system in 40 Mercadona establishments, the Audiencia Provincial de Barcelona, ruling on a particular case, denied the firm authorisation to use facial recognition. The order, in tune with what specialists had previously pointed out, recognised that this measure was not "protecting the public interest [...] but rather the private or particular interests of the company in question" and that Mercadona was clearly violating "the appropriate guarantees in order to protect the rights and freedoms of the interested parties, not only those who have been convicted and whose prohibition of access is their responsibility, but also the rest of the people who access the afore-mentioned supermarket". For the court, therefore, there was a "violation of privacy" (Galaup, 2021). The judges acknowledged that, given that these technologies can be "really intrusive", "a thoughtful ethical and legal debate" was needed to prevent them from having "very adverse effects on fundamental values and human integrity". They also questioned "where they take images for facial recognition, with what consent" and "why they maintain a database of people's photographs" (Galaup, 2021).

Finally, in response to Mercadona's claims about the speed of the identification and that only those convicted were positively identified, the Court ruled that "no matter how fast it is, there is a violation of privacy" and recalled that, unless otherwise stated in the sentence, "convicted persons enjoy all the fundamental rights recognised in the Constitution", which led the judges to affirm that Mercadona's proposal "is in no way proportional, necessary or even suitable" (Galaup, 2021).

After a year of investigation, and with the important precedent set by the Audiencia Provincial de Barcelona, the AEPD sanctioned Mercadona with the temporary suspension of all data processing relating to facial recognition in its establishments and with a fine which, applying the 20% discount for voluntary payment prior to the resolution of the procedure, amounted to 2,520,000 euros.

The report issued by the AEPD as a voluntary resolution of Procedure N°: PS/00120/2021 (AEPD, 2021) is illustrative because, in a way, it echoed the unease raised by the community of legal specialists when the implementation of the system was announced. Thus, the document confirmed, among other realities, that:

- Mercadona was not entitled to carry out the data processing consisting of facial recognition (33).
- In the implementation of the measure Mercadona confused 'usefulness' with the objective 'necessity' of the measure. Mercadona stated that 'the measure implemented may be effective, but it is by no means necessary' (34).
- According to the system installed, 'all citizens entering a Mercadona shopping centre with a facial recognition system in place are treated as convicts' (36).
- The use of this system is contrary to the principles of necessity, proportionality and minimisation and, according to the law, does not serve the public good (52 and 53).
- The processing proposed by Mercadona is disproportionate since "personal data of any person who enters the supermarket, whether they shop or not, are processed, including minors who cannot be prosecuted" (84).
- The implementation of the system has been carried out in a non-transparent manner, since the information contained in the posters " fails to warn the clients that the data processing system implemented is not allowed, or rather, that it is forbidden, which constitutes another of the volitional elements of liability" (90).
- The system presented, inter alia, the 'general risk of using biometric facial recognition data by making all persons entering the supermarket potential suspects' (96) and the 'certain risk of loss of liberty and privacy' (97).

This was the end of one of the most important media scandals related to the implementation of surveillance by Artificial Intelligence. An interesting case because after a mobilisation in the public sphere of specialists in the field and complaints from civil society organisations, it is the state that investigates and, finally, rules that Mercadona, one of the largest Spanish companies, is violating fundamental rights and acting against the law.

CONCLUSION

After having followed the route proposed in these pages, it is possible to conclude that in Spain, as well as in the rest of the European Union and other parts of the world, facial recognition technology arouses resistance among civil society because it is understood that it violates and endangers fundamental human rights.

Although the reactions of Spanish society have been mostly negative towards biometric technologies, two different strategies can be highlighted: the first encompasses all those initiatives of citizen self-organisation, and the second includes those that seek the intervention of the authorities. The struggle of the UNIR students would be an example of the first, and the case of Mercadona would undoubtedly constitute an example of the second.

In the analysis of student mobilisation in response to the implementation of proctoring, it has been possible to see to what extent self-organisation is a successful strategy. The students' awareness-raising process, the visibility given to their demands and their firm determination to take legal action against the university in defence of their rights, led UNIR to withdraw the biometric system during this academic year. In this way, the students themselves managed to prevent their rights from being threatened.

The controversy generated around the implementation of facial recognition cameras in Mercadona has, however, other nuances. It is interesting to look at how the case occupied the public sphere and the role that specialists played in it. The proliferation of opinions from authoritative voices on digital law issues generated a framework conducive to the filing of the complaints that led the authorities to act.

In the light of the above, it is possible to conclude that, in Spain, facial recognition technology is far from becoming a surveillance standard. The reservations it generates among citizens and the decisions being taken by the authorities are delaying its implementation in areas of everyday life that are far from the wishes of international security and geopolitics, spheres in which it is being implemented. It seems that the question is not whether machines are stupid or smart but rather if humans are willing to comply with AI-based surveillance systems.

REFERENCES

Andrejevic, M., & Selwyn, N. (2020). Facial recognition technology in schools: Critical questions and concerns. *Learning, Media and Technology*, *45*(2), 115–128. doi:10.1080/17439884.2020.1686014

APD. (2019, March 6). Big data: ¿qué es y para qué sirve? *APD*. https://www.apd.es/

Asociación de Marketing de España. (2021). *Informe digital marketing trends: Mobile en España y en el mundo 2020 + Especial COVID-19*. Author.

Asociación Española de Protección de Datos. (2020). *Gabinete jurídico N/REF: 0036/2020*. Author.

Asociación Española de Protección de Datos. (2021). *Procedimiento Nº: PS/00120/2021. Resolución de terminación del procedimiento por pago voluntario*. Author.

Castelluccia, C. & Le Métayer. (2020). Position paper: Analyzing the Impacts of Facial Recognition. In L. Antunes, M. Naldi, G. Italiano, K. & P. Drogkaris (Eds.), *Privacy Technologies and Policiy. APF 2020*. New York: Springer.

Cultura de la seguridad. (2021). *Consejos generales para acudir a una manifestación*. Author.

Del Barco, L. (2020, July 2). Mercadona comienza a usar un sistema de reconocimiento facial para identificar a delincuentes. *Hipertextual*. https://hipertextual.com/

Dueñas, J. L. (2021, May 5). Algoritmos e inteligencia artificial, los aliados de las universidades para examinar a distancia. *Rtve*. https://www.rtve.es/

Efe. (2021, May 6). Dudas y respuestas sobre la polémica herramienta de reconocimiento facial en los exámenes. *20 minutos*. https://www.20minutos.es

Europa Press. (2017, June 14). IU denuncia "vulneración de derechos laborales" a trabajadores de Mercadona en tiendas de Cantabria. *elDiario.es*. https://www.eldiario.es/

European Comission. (2021). *Proposal for a Regulation of the European Parliament and of the Council Laying Down Harmonised Rules on Artificial Intelligence (Artificial Intelligence Act) and Amending Certaing Union Legislative Acts COM/2021/206 final*. Author. https://eur-lex.europa.eu/

European Data Protection Board. (2021, June 21). *EDPB & EDPS call for ban on use of AI for automated recognition of human features in publicly accessible spaces, and some other uses of AI that can lead to unfair discrimination*. Author.

Galaup, L. (2021, June 10). La Justicia impide que Mercadona use el reconocimiento facial para detectar a dos ladrones condenados. *elDiario.es*. https://www.eldiario.es

García Ropero, J. (2020, March 10). Mercadona impulsó su beneficio un 5% hasta 623 millones en 2019. *Cinco Días*. https://cincodias.elpais.com/

Garnelo, J. (2020, September 13). Grupos planeados por alumnos de Medicina de la USC activaron un sistema para copiar en los exámenes 'online'. *El Correo Gallego*. https://www.elcorreogallego.es

Grüll, P. (2020, January 10). Germany's plan for automatic facial recognition meet fierce criticism. *Euractiv*. https://www.euractiv.com/

HUxIR Asociación de Estudiantes por la Defensa de los Derechos Fundamentales. (2021, April 18). *UNIR y el abuso de técnicas de Proctoring para la supervisión y control de alumnos*. Author. https://write.as/huxir

HUxIR Asociación de Estudiantes por la Defensa de los Derechos Fundamentales. (2021, April 21). *Nota de queja presentada al Rector de la Universidad Internacional de la Rioja*. Author. https://write.as/huxir

International Amnesty. (2021a). *Ban the scan*. https://banthescan.amnesty.org/

International Amnesty. (2021b). *How to protect your phone and identity at protests*. Author.

Jakubowksa, E. (2021, July 7). New EDRi report reveals depths of biometric mass surveillance in Germany, the Netherlands and Poland. *EDRi*. https://edri.org/

Janssen, M., Brous, P., Estevez, E., Barbosa, L. S., & Janowski, T. (2020). Data governance: Organizing data for trustworthy Artificial Intelligence. *Government Information Quarterly*, *37*(3), 101493. doi:10.1016/j.giq.2020.101493

López, M. (2020, March 23). Engañar a los sistemas de reconocimiento facial es (relativamente) fácil si sabes cómo. *Xataka*. https://www.xataka.com/

López Frías, D. (2020, July 15). El superespía del Mossad que inventó el sistema de reconocimiento facial de Mercadona: así funciona. *El Español*. https://www.elespanol.com/

Mercadona. (2020). *Zona detección anticipada*. Author.

Observatorio Nacional de Tecnología y Sociedad. (2021). *Indicadores de uso de Inteligencia Artificial en las empresas españolas*. Author.

Orwell, G. (2016). 1984. The University of Adelaide.

Parra, A. G. (2020, April 14). Estudiantes de la UGR piden que se devuelvan las tasas y se adapte la evaluación. *Ideal*. https://www.ideal.es

Pérez, E. (2020, July 2). Mercadona instala un sistema de reconocimiento facial en sus supermercados: cómo funciona y por qué genera importantes dudas sobre la privacidad. *Xataka*. https://www.xataka.com/

Pérez Esquivel, A. (2021). Desafíos de la vigilancia automatizada. *Derecho y Ciencias Sociales*, *24*, 100–122.

Perrigo, B. (2020, January 24). London Police to Deploy Facial Recognition Cameras Despite Privacy Concerns and Evidence of High Failure Rate. *Time*. https://time.com/

Reclaim Your Face. (2021). *Sign the petition for a new law now*. https://reclaimyourface.eu/

Redacción. (2020, April 30). La Universidad de Oviedo dice contar con medios para garantizar que los alumnos no 'copien' en los exámenes 'online'. *La Vanguardia*. https://www.lavanguardia.com

Ribeiro Navarrete, S., Saura, J. R., & Palacios-Marqués, D. (2021). Towards a new era of mass data collection: Assessing pandemic surveillance technologies to preserve user privacy. *Technological Forecasting and Social Change*, *167*, 120681. doi:10.1016/j.techfore.2021.120681 PMID:33840865

Rubio, I. (2020, July 7). Las claves de la polémica por el uso del reconocimiento facial en los supermercados de Mercadona. *El País*. https://elpais.com/

Salvatierra, J. (2019, October 17). La justicia europea da la razón a Mercadona en el caso de las cajeras grabadas robando con cámara oculta. *El País*. https://elpais.com/

Saura, J. R., Palacios-Marqués, D., & Iturricha-Fernández, A. (2021a). Ethical Design in Social Media: Assessing the main performance measurements of user online behavior modification. *Journal of Business Research*, *129*(May), 271–281. doi:10.1016/j.jbusres.2021.03.001

Saura, J. R., Ribeiro-Soriano, D., & Palacios-Marqués, D. (2021b, July 15). Setting privacy "by default" in social IoT: Theorizing the challenges and directions in Big Data Research. *Big Data Research*, 25, 100245. doi:10.1016/j.bdr.2021.100245

Security Magazine. (2020, May 29). Smile, You're on Camera: The Facial Recognition World Map. *Security Magazine*. https://www.securitymagazine.com/

Selinger, E. & Hartzog, w. (2019). The Inconsentability of Facial Surveillance. *Loyola Law Review*, *66*, 101–122.

Selinger, E., & Leong, B. (2021) The Ethics of Facial Recognition Technology. In The Oxford Handbook of Digital Ethics. doi:10.2139srn.3762185

Sopra Steria & IDEMIA (2020, June 8). *IDEMIA and Sopra Steria chosen by eu-LISA to build the new Shared Biometric Matching System (sBMS) for border protection of the Schengen Area.* Author.

Surfshack. (2020). *The Facial Recognition World Map.* https://surfshark.com/

UNIR. (2021). *Comunicado del rector.* Author.

Vargas, I. (2020, June 9). 200 euros por un examen de ingeniería: el fraude en las evaluaciones on line de la UGR. *Granada Hoy*. https://www.granadahoy.com

ENDNOTE

[1]   https://cvdazzle.com/

Chapter 14
Artificial Intelligence and Supply Chains After the Impact of COVID–19:
To Expect the Unexpected

Emilio Sanchez de Rojas Díaz

EAE Businnes School, Rey Juan Carlos University, Spain

Elena Bulmer

EAE Businnes School, Rey Juan Carlos University, Spain

Carlos R. Quijano Junquera

Rey Juan Carlos University, Spain

ABSTRACT

The aim of this chapter is to address the use of artificial intelligence in managing GSC, restructuring it, and providing it with enough flexibility to meet the challenges and risks that the current situation—characterized by uncertainty—could threaten including integrity and correct operation. To do this, the authors propose to address issues such as what is a supply chain, what are risks and how risks can affect the management of the supply chain, particularly in the face of the COVID-19 outbreak. Optimizing supply chains and integrating all processes, from suppliers to customers, through warehouses, is a typical target for artificial intelligence (AI). It will be of critical importance to migrate towards 'Agile' strategies, suitable for the uncertain times we live in, incorporating a timely risk analysis and allowing routine decisions to be taken within the framework of AI.

DOI: 10.4018/978-1-7998-9609-8.ch014

INTRODUCTION

The pandemic consequence of the last 2 years has presented unique challenges for supply chain managers that don't seem to be falling any time soon. The year 2020 evidenced that we should expect the unexpected. The seemingly unflappable Global Supply Chains (GSC) suffered the consequences of the 'perfect storm' that Covid-19 represents, disrupting the logistics operations of companies around the world and mutating consumer-purchasing habits (Sullivan, 2020).

After the impact of Covid-19, GSC is an issue highly topical; an example is the recent article 'A perfect storm for container shipping' published by The Economist on 12 Sept., 2021 confirm:

A giant ship wedged across the Suez canal, record-breaking shipping rates, armadas of vessels waiting outside ports, covid-induced shutdowns: the business of container shipping has rarely been as dramatic as it has in 2021.

This 'perfect storm' bring us to a question: How to optimize supply chain again after a systemic event. Optimizing supply chains and integrating all processes, from suppliers to customers, through warehouses, is a typical target for Artificial Intelligence (AI). In natural language processing (NLP), a branch of AI, using robots for some warehouse management functions has allowed the optimization of space, and the reduction of inventories and storage costs. Based on a "Lean" or "Kanban" strategy, and a "just in time"[1] system. AI is a proper tool for this porpoise.

Contrary to popular belief, the outbreak of the current pandemic was not a surprise. In fact, it had been anticipated by the National Security Strategies (NSS) of the USA, UK or Spain. In the USA NSS, the section devoted to *U.S. Borders and Territory. Combat Biothreats and Pandemics* says:

Biological incidents have the potential to cause catastrophic loss of life. Biological threats to the U.S. homeland—whether as the result of deliberate attack, accident, or a natural outbreak—are growing and require actions to address them at their source (Trump, 2017).

The 2017 National Security Strategy proposes three *priority actions*: Detect and contain biothreats at their source; support biomedical innovation and improve emergency response. The absence of an international response to a global problem left the management on the hands of national rulers, unable to solve the problem. As a result, some irrational decisions were taken, influenced by a kind of '*Black Death syndrome*', taken by rulers lacking global leadership. A *side effect* of the lack of leadership, has been the risk of global economic collapse[2].

Should we leave the management of future crises in the hands of national rulers? It is not our decision, but we could develop tools to enable rational decision-making. Perhaps the time for Artificial Intelligence has come, and one of the first areas of interest is global supply chain management.

BACKGROUND

The irruption of the covid 19 pandemic, while demonstrating the effectiveness and flexibility of the food supply chain, has revealed serious deficiencies in the supply chains related to health and in the operation of large companies with high dependence on supplies from China, among them:

- Temporary collapse of critical supply chains for society
- Inability to address a health situation, by most governments due to lack of supply
- Irrational and late decisions.

It will be of critical importance to migrate towards 'Agile' strategies, suitable for the uncertain times we live in, incorporating a timely risk analysis, and allowing routine decisions to be taken within the framework of AI. Furthermore, this whole optimization procedure will also contribute to develop a more sustainable supply chain by reducing the energy expenditure in the chain as well as potentially decreasing its raw material dependency, making it more efficient.

What Supply Chain Management Means?

Both theoretical and managerial contributions should be presented and expanded/improved at least one page based on your findings. The theoretical contribution should be justified in the context of government AI practices. The current contribution sections do not justify the research contributions at all.

The supply chain is the network of organizations that are involved through upstream and downstream linkages, in the different processes and activities that produce value in the form of products and services in the hand of ultimate consumer (Christopher, 2016, pág. 13).

Supply chain management consider possible interruptions and adaptation to a fluctuating environment. But many supply chains are not tough and agile enough to respond to 'black swans' as the current pandemic. Poor management of COVID-19 - triggered bankrupt in several companies. Others, took advantage of their technological superiority to adapt, correct their strategies, and thus survive and even prosper after the first phase of pandemic (E2OPEN, 2021).

Supply chain management has evolved over time, leading to main trends in business, such as:

- The globalization of markets;
- The outsourcing strategy promoted by firms worldwide;
- The need for specialized capabilities and innovation, and increasing reliance on specialized outside sources to fulfil such needs.
- The need for market differentiation, leading some companies to rely on their supply networks for their competitive advantage.

Figure 1.

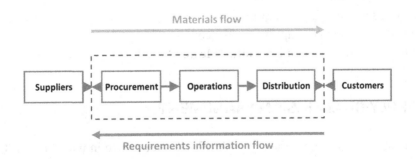

While these factors may benefit companies and increase their strategic options, at the same time, the probability of experiencing adverse events rises, disturbing normal operations, and may affect the financial performance of companies (Hendricks & Singhal, 2005)

Two approaches stand out when handling supply chain: vertical integration and management. Vertical integration implies ownership of upstream suppliers and downstream customers[3]. On the other hand, standard supply chain management do not integrate suppliers and customers. A definition of supply chain management could be:

The management of upstream and downstream relationship with suppliers and customers in order to deliver customer value at less cost to the supply chain as a whole (Christopher, 2016, pág. 2)

Many companies prefer a '*driving a hard bargain*', a win-lose approach in the relations with their suppliers, which are selected only by price, without bear in mind other factors such as responsiveness. The evolving completive environment associated with globalization means new rules for competition, turbulence and volatility, globalization of industry, and downward pressure on price (Christopher, 2016, pág. 13). Price is not the leading factor in times of uncertainty.

ISO 31,000 (Risk management) defines Risk as the effect of uncertainty on objectives. Risk can result in opportunities or threats[4].We live in an ever-changing world where we are forced to deal with uncertainty every day. But how an organization tackles that uncertainty can be a key predictor of its success. (ISO, 2018)

In our opinion, in times of great uncertainty, agility is necessary to respond to unforeseen events that could affects supply chains.

'Lean' or 'Agile' Supply Chain?

Lean and agile supply chains differ where their emphasis is. Agile supply chain management focuses on the changing environment of business while lean supply chain is focused on quality control[5]. With the 'lean' commitment to low-cost production systems, the supply is focused on China. Lean supply chain has a critical dependence on highly specialized suppliers with large-scale production. But the new sources of risk get combined to increase uncertainty, even before the outbreak of Covid, and managers wonder what the next challenge will be.

For Bridget McCrea, the critical paths of change in the design and management of global supply chains would be:

- Geopolitical disruption and uncertainty abound;
- China Plus One and other strategic moves[6];
- Balancing cost, service and profitability;
- Leveraging advanced tech to improve resilience;
- Preparing for more macro and micro shifts (Mccrea B., 2021b)

GLOBAL SUPPLY CHAIN RISK MANAGEMENT

The aim of this chapter is to address the use of Artificial Intelligence in managing GSC, restructuring it and providing it with enough flexibility, to meet the challenges and risks that the current situation -characterized by uncertainty- that could threaten its integrity and correct operation. To do this, we propose to address issues such as what are risks associated to a global supply chain, and how those risks may affect the management of the supply chain, particularly in the face of the COVID 19 outbreak. We will also address the potential of artificial intelligence to make the aforementioned chain more resilient.

Risk management is the coordinated activities to direct and control the organization in relation to risk. Risk management should consider both trend risk sources and disruptive events[7]. Supply Chain Risk Management (SCRM) belong to the strategic tier, as risks may affect companies at different levels and disruptions anywhere in the supply chain could have a direct effect on the corporation´s ability to operate (Jüttner, Peck, & Cristopher., 2003). Potential risks in supply chains, as well as the nature of such risks, need to be anticipated, identified, classified evaluated and -eventually- mitigated.

Some scholars characterized risks in supply chain management as either operational risks or disruption risks. Operational risks are related to troubles of the day-to-day operations; disruption risks, on the other hand, are related to less common events with high impact (Hosseini, Ivanov, & Dolgui, 2019) (Kinra, 2019). Covid-19 constitute an extreme example of disruption risk, with high level of uncertainty both in terms of duration and impact (Ivanov D., 2020)

Any harm caused by deficient interactions among organizations may be network-related risk sources. An example is strategic procurement and outsourcing. (Jüttner, Peck, & Cristopher., 2003). Outsourcing may engender a considerable degree of risk. Over time, the increase in the outsourcing of core organizational competencies has led to a more complex and riskier network, where lines of responsibilities are not clear and the core of the organization have less control over its operations. We should carried out a risk assessment of the supply chain network, and a thorough understanding of the structure, flows, and operational dynamics of the organization's supply network is required. Additionally, we need to identify areas likely affected by the different risks and launch action plans to avoid, mitigate, contain and control them. This step should be executed carefully as some mitigation actions may adversely affect other risks (Chopra & Sodhi, 2004) (Tummala & Schoenherr, 2011).

Figure 2. Risk sources in a supply chain

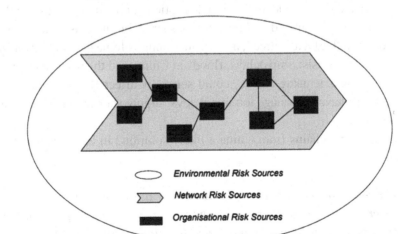

Making a Supply Chain Resilient

Making a supply chain resilient implicitly involves creating business continuity plans (BCPs) to ensure continued operations in the face of a supply chain disruption. These are plans to restore lost capacities, independent of how the operational capacities were lost (Rice, 2021)

A failure means the loss of at one or more of these seven core capacities:

1. The capacity to acquire materials (maintain supply).
2. The capacity to ship and/or transport products.
3. The capacity to communicate.
4. The capacity to convert (internal manufacturing operations).
5. The human resources (personnel) capacity.
6. The capacity to maintain financial flows.
7. The capacity to distribute products to customers including consumers. (Rice, 2021)

Most risks are predictable so a resilient supply chain must take them into account. A resilient supply chain is one that: *Can recreate or maintain the capabilities that support each of these seven operational capacities. Succeeding in this mission will help to secure the survival of supply chains in crisis situations.* (SCMR Staff, 2021)

For instance, currently Supply Chains are suffering substantial vessel for shipment delays across the major commercial lines between China and the rest of the world. As a result, *lead times* are growing and may trigger supply chain disruptions (SCMR Staff, 2021).

Crisis [un] Control

The increase in the number of ships, in an attempt to catch up, is transferring chaos to the ports. Changing consumption patterns related to the pandemic led to disruptions in manufacturing supply chains. In the first half of 2020, retail sales plummeted and inventories soared, but increased demand from new consumer habits has produced a 'bull whip effect', and the incoming volume has been disproportionate. The global supply chain went into crisis: Ship delays, floods in China, and the resurgence of the COVID-19 Delta in major Chinese manufacturing centers could seriously affect Black Friday, or the Christmas season. Manufacturers will have to manage loading delays, supply shortages and price increases in the near future (Burnson, 2021)

Is it decoupling the supply chains from China a likely solution? In an interview Tom Linton[8], answered this question:

Supply chains can't be changed quickly or easily because there are so many quality analyses, Intellectual Property agreements, engineering and other assessments that must be done to qualify new suppliers. Also, there are many layers of interdependence between suppliers in multiple countries. You could decide to shift some procurement from a Chinese to a U.S.-based supplier, but chances are that this U.S.-based firm sources from suppliers in China. So, indirectly, you're still dependent on China. (Linton, 2021, pág. 24)

Suez Canal Incident

Four months after the megaship Ever Given got stuck in the canal, neither the canal nor the shipping industry has addressed some of the most critical issues that led to the grounding.

Three months of bickering later, the ship was on its way again. Despite calls from maritime safety experts to reassess both the size of container ships, (which have grown to enormous proportions to cut costs), and to redesign ports and seaways to accommodate new ships, no major changes are projected. (Yee & Glanz, 2021)

In the Suez, the compounding effect is due to the unwinding of the logjam and then the subsequent delay in getting containers back to Asia to pick up new goods. Utilization rates are near maximum levels and container factories are booked out through July. The Suez Canal crisis highlights the short-age of containers in the global fleet that has been impacting the market since mid-2020. (Burnson P., 2021b, pág. 60)

China USA Competition

The US Department of Defense is very concerned about the vast dominance of Chinese intelligence and communication technology (ICT) supply chains. This situation has led to try to secure supply chains in the future, especially in the case of armed forces and critical infrastructures. There are activists from both states, looking for a 'zero-sum game' in disruptive technologies. For them, to win the balance of power for the future international order is the target (Triolo, 2019).

During the last quarter of 2020, the shortage of semiconductors was increasing, crushing the automotive industry. Knowing as soon as possible 1) when interruptions occur in the SC, 2) which suppliers will suffer them, and 3) how to mitigate the effects of the aforementioned interruptions, will be crucial for a resilient supply chain (Sally & Clinton, 2021)

The effects of changes in consumption patterns, which have affected both port capacity and the lack of containers, seriously reducing trade in southern China, have softened recently. But with the recovery of pre-COVID volumes from the Pearl River delta ports, these interruptions, even in the supply of the most common essentials items, may disturb production, reduce profits and even affect a brand's reputation (Vakil, 2021, pág. 28)

The average cost of shipping a standard large container (a 40-foot-equivalent unit, or FEU) has surpassed $10,000, some four times higher than a year ago (see chart). The spot price for sending such a box from Shanghai to New York, which in 2019 would have been around $2,500, is now close to $15,000. (Economist, 2021b)

Impact of the Reverse Logistics on the Supply Chain

Managing the return flow of goods from the end user to the retailer, distributor or manufacturer is complex for logistics. With the growth of online sales in 2020, the competition has started to improve reverse logistics methods, and solve this problem. The global pandemic has served as a driver for process improvement in this area of the supply chain. With e-commerce sales increasing by 44% in 2020, and online returns more than doubling between 2019 and 2020, companies need to refine their reverse logistics management. (Mccrea B., 2021)

Figure 3. Drewry world container index 2019-2021
Source (Drewry, 2021)

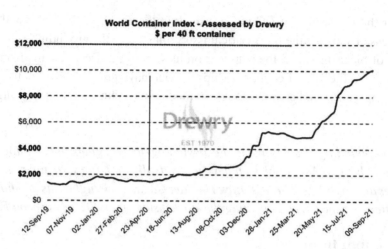

Many economies, and the United States in particular, are heavily reliant on shipping, in which container ships transport commodities, consumer goods, and inputs for manufacturers. The evolution of the aforementioned transport since mid-2020 has shown how critical it is for economic competitiveness (Maffei, 2021, pág. 1). Of particular concern is the negative effect that high import growth has on US exports, which, at current prices, make empty return of containers more profitable, and there are hardly any containers available for export. It is an old problem that has been strengthened today, highlighting the systemic deficiencies that affect the country's transport capacities (Maffei, 2021, pág. 4). ok

The problem is not so much the quantity, but the availability and management of containers in the supply chain. Rebecca F. Dye identifies three main obstacles to solving pressing port problems:

1. These problems are not new. They occur in every cargo "surge" or "peak season;"
2. No supply chain actor alone can provide a solution without a coordinated approach; and
3. The lack of mutual commitment between parties to freight delivery agreements mitigates against an enforceable agreement (Dye, 2021)

The containers are stuck and cannot access the ports of the United States, and do not return to Asia, at the same time the Asian manufacturers do not have access to the containers to ship their products. The shipping crisis has even worsened this year, with some industries depleting their reserves of certain critical raw materials with significant new spending at the worst time.

Supply Chain Management and the Covid-19 Context

For decades, supply and distribution operations have become more stable, reducing costs and streamlining their management. But then…

At first everything stopped. Then, as supply chains began to slowly click back into gear, there were massive network disruptions followed by sudden, unforeseen spikes in demand patterns that found some industry sectors barely hanging on for survival. Finally, there were hints of an upcoming boom. (Schulz, 2021)

The pandemic has modified consumption patterns by generating a growing demand for imported goods. These consumption patterns suddenly shifted from a service-based to a goods-based one, leading to an increase in orders for imported electronics, furniture, and other home and home office items (Butler, 2021, pág. 2)

Epidemic outbreaks are a special case of supply chain (SC) risks which is distinctively characterized by a long-term disruption existence, disruption propagations (i.e., the ripple effect), and high uncertainty. (Ivanov D., 2020)

Research on the effects of past epidemics has shown that they can threaten supply chain resilience and robustness. The recent COVID-19 outbreak has affected supply chains worldwide, disturbing the global economy and paralyzing a number of different industries (Ivanov D., 2020). According to Fortune (Sherman, 2020), 94% of the top 1000 companies have been negatively affected by the outbreak, causing disturbances in local and global supply chains. The coronavirus outbreak has put to the test the resilience and robustness of supply chains and resulted in supply shortages, lack of reactivity and halts in production processes (Ivanov & Dolgui, 2020)

El Baz and Ruel (2021) carried out a study to determine how the COVID-19 outbreak has impacted the supply strength and resilience of French companies. The study findings showed that the impacts of the pandemic disruption seemed to negatively affect the strength of the companies´ supply chains in the short term. But Ivanov and Dolgui (2020) explain that the robustness of the supply chain can be strengthened without structural changes, while the resilience to disruptive risks would imply specific adaptations by the companies in question. In this respect the identification, management and control of risks, have contributed positively, and the mitigating effects of SCRM have helped organizations to restore their supply chain operations, contain disorders and restore their expected performance (El Baz & Ruel, 2021)

Figure 4. E2open demand sensing AI: Consistent forecast advantage across all stages of the pandemic

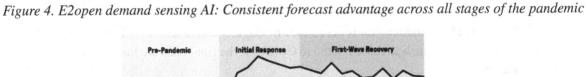
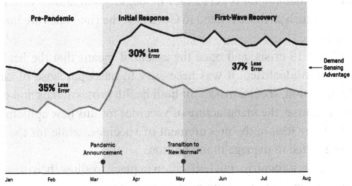

The magnitude and speed of the pandemic and its impact on global supply chains exposed GSCR to systemic risks. What for years was supposed to be the best fit is no longer good, and risk and resilience have become a priority for managers, who need to rebalance their supply chains, to survive and, if possible, gain competitive advantages in the face of more frequent and severe events. (E2OPEN, 2021, pág. 5).

Going back to the beginning of the pandemic in March 2020, one of the main problems was the shortage of maritime containers, a problem caused by various causes.

A Case Study: Artificial Intelligence in Decision-Making in the Essential Healthcare Supply Chain During the Covid Crisis

The concept of mass surveillance emerged the first decade of the 21st century, after the 9/11 attacks in New York Events such as 9/11 in New York caused massive surveillance and listening initiatives by the US government, using tools to track user data to protect people from these types of attacks became a new vigilant normality. Acording to Ribeiro-Navarrete et all

During the COVID-19 pandemic, with the development of a mobile application to track the coronavirus, Apple and Google have announced solutions for virus control worldwide. These two companies base part of their strategic development on the analysis and prediction of user behavior by studying their data. This initiative places both companies at the forefront of enhancing the control and surveillance of the COVID-19 and future pandemics worldwide and, therefore, the management of these data (Ribeiro-Navarrete, Saura, & Palacios-Marqués, 2021).

But how to apply AI to Supply Chain? At a Gartner's Supply Chain Executive Conference, analyst **Noha Tohamy**, clarified, that AI could be divided into 2 main categories:

Augmentation*: AI which assists humans with their day-to-day tasks, personally or commercially without having complete control of the output. Such Artificial Intelligence is used in Virtual Assistant, Data analysis, software solutions; where they are mainly used to reduce errors due to human bias.*

Automation*: AI which works completely autonomously in any field without the need for any human intervention. For example, robots performing key process steps in manufacturing plants (Sirajudeen, 2017).*

Within the supply chain, *automation* is perfect for managing warehouses efficiently, but in the case of large logistical decisions such as those related to Covid 19, the final ones are human, so we are in the category of *augmentation*.

At the start of the Covid 19 crisis, and once the essential means that the health system needed to combat the disease had been identified, it was necessary to mass purchase of certain items higienic masks for the general population, special masks for both health professionals and people at special risk, respirators, etc. At the same time, the manufacture of vaccines for this new epidemic started. Within the EU, the Commission took the lead in the procurement of vaccines, while for the rest of the necessary supplies, member countries had to manage their solution.

The governments of Western countries put legislation in place to allow them to act quickly by opening up a significant margin of discretionally, reducing procurement processes time. Soon, the few available suppliers -mostly in China- were 'harassed' by many client governments. A race against time for supplies broke out, causing many failures in delivery dates and in the quality of supplies. Some purchases were not attended, despite being confirmed. The seed of a "bull whip effect" was already germinating

Could We Use Artificial Intelligence Tools to Make These Decisions, Avoiding Failures?

That is the million-dollar question. The "bull whip effect" provides us with an opportunity to see how to use AI in this sense: The bullwhip effect is a supply chain phenomenon whereby an error in demand forecasts leads to inefficiencies in the supply chain. It produces increasing fluctuation in inventory in response to changes in consumer demand and delayed response from suppliers along the supply chain.

- In fact, the error in demand forecast already exist after COVID-19
- The bullwhip effect is an old friend who has been studied in depth
- Supply Chains simulations already exist[9]
- Algorithms for Supply Chains do exist too[10]
- AI is based in both simulation and identification of algorithms

So, AI may mitigate the effect of the bullwhip effect, improving the forecasting, according with the data mined in the cloud.

In the end, AI, as intelligence, is a tool to facilitate timely decisions by managers on critical issues. Artificial intelligence can be used to simulate and optimize decision proposals that will eventually be made by a person, a decision-making body or a government. AI tools -fed into their learning with data from routine processes- are not effective enough, provided that conditions are exceptional like COVID 19 crisis: huge orders, extreme urgency, need for high capacity and responsive suppliers, overwhelming turnout of global orders, etc.

Decisions should answer a significant number of questions about each type of supply. A sort list of essential questions could be:

1. What is needed?
2. Why is it needed?
3. What quantity?
4. When is it needed?
5. Where is it needed?
6. What is the approximate cost?
7. Do we have the necessary budget?
8. Who (what agency) is responsible for its acquisition?
9. What is the best provider / providers to serve you?
10. What intermediaries can facilitate the process?
11. When and how do you pay?
12. By what means is it transported?

The answers to the first eight questions are the result of an internal analysis of each State. It is in the last four questions where the procurement process may significantly fail. All these questions could be analyzed in an AI tool, which would provide advice. The better the data and the algorithm used, the better the result.

For the purposes of this work, we focus on a smaller and simpler case as an example. In spite of everything, it will not cease to be a theoretical hypothesis. The sole objective of this model is to present a possible AI tool prototype to emulate a human decision. An artificial intelligence system needs to learn, so it is important to count with a human evaluation at the end of the process (For example, the score that is asked from the user in systems that already use AI, such as Google Maps or Trip Advisor).

The model answers one of the questions listed above within a national case, specifically question number nine. It is about the acquisition by an EU state of nine million of hygienic masks.

1. What large-scale mask suppliers are there in the world capable of handling orders of more than one million hygienic masks? (This requires databases).
2. Does the EU or the UK certify their masks?
3. How many lots of 100,000 hygienic masks can they deliver by month?
4. What is the specific delivery time?
5. What is the price per mask including transportation costs to our national point of entry? (In this hypothesis the supplier takes care of the transport).
6. Has this provider been evaluated by our national health system? If not, a request for information will be sent to the Economic Intelligence Unit so that the suitability of the supplier and its ability to fulfill the order may be evaluated.

Figure 5. An AI scheme proposal for algorithm. The last two steps are carried out by humans.
Source: Authors

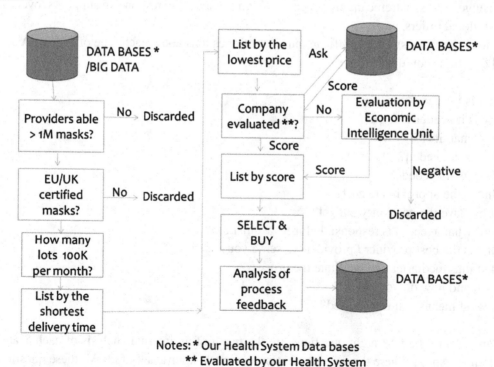

Notes: * Our Health System Data bases
** Evaluated by our Health System

The last part of the work would be to choose a suitable programming language for the process and carry out the programming of the proposed model. Although there is no great unanimity on which are the most suitable programming languages to program Artificial Intelligence tools, we think that are those with more libraries of complementary programs for *machine learning* and *deep learning* (Python, Java,...).

IS AI THE SOLUTION?

Modern supply chain managers recognize that the challenges of solving disruptions at any scale, including a pandemic, cannot be tackled just by people. Automation, based on artificial intelligence, is necessary to collect the required information, collate and convert it into intelligence and apply it to decision-making. The AI will use the data mining to develop a digital simulation of the actual supply chain.

AI processes massive amounts of information and develops algorithms to identify the best strategy and apply it automatically. An AI capable of handling, in real time, massive amounts of information, internal and external, is required to alert about possible interruptions and allow, where appropriate, to intervene automatically, without human participation. But, as Saura et all properly pointed out:

In present-day in consumers' homes, there are millions of Internet-connected devices that are known to jointly represent the Internet of Things_(IoT). The development of the IoT industry has led to the emergence of connected devices and home assistants that create smart living environments... Accordingly, several previous studies warned about the potential risks of the connected devices' use when data privacy settings are not configured or are configured in a wrong way. In general, data resulting from user actions requested by the devices can be used to identify patterns, trends, or predict user behaviors (Saura, Ribeiro-Soriano, & Palacios-Marqués, 2021a)

In his annual selection of possible scenarios 2036 (What If?), The Economist contemplates an apparently unheard-of scene

It was a scene that the Nobel committee had dearly hoped to avoid. As the recipients of this year's prizes filed into the Stockholm Concert Hall to take their seats, dozens of protesters, including several former laureates, clashed with police in the streets outside. They had gathered to express their opposition to the unprecedented decision to award the Nobel prize in physiology or medicine to an artificial intelligence. (The Economist, 2021)

2036 is a long way off, but today, we can say about the future, when it comes to supply chains, that:

- Supply chains will undergo significant changes with AI.
- This implies that administrators transfer decision-making to machines governed by AI..
- Business strategies will be based on prospective founded on events that could affect global supply chains and disruptive smart technologies (Handfield & Linton, 2021)

Supply chains will evolve, as production chains previously did, from automation based on information flows to another managed by AI. The future supply chain will focus on managing the flow of goods and information, with an integration of information from all links in the supply chains, managed by artificial intelligence with machine learning (Handfield & Linton, 2021)

Supply Chains in Flow

Removing humans from this decision making represents a major cultural shift. Massive disruptions (especially those related to COVID-19) have heightened the need to improve prospective to prevent disruptions in supply chain management. Algorithms based on AI, would allow us to know in a timely manner if a supplier is delayed, the evolution of prices or delays in delivery times. (Handfield & Linton, 2021).

Currently, the most vital aspect for companies is data, and the 'cloud' is probably the most important driver of innovation.

The social Internet of Things (SIoT) shares large amounts of data that are then processed by other Internet of Thing (IoT) devices, which results in the generation, collection, and treatment of databases to be analyzed afterwards with Big Data techniques. (Saura, Ribeiro-Soriano, & Palacios-Marqués, 2021)

For example, the Cloud helped a global auto manufacturer address supply chain challenges such as lack of data integrity across systems, non-integrated processes, and strenuous visibility of planning by enabling an architecture that supported analytics models with advanced algorithms (Reiss & Savino, 2021)

AI depends on the quality of the available data. Using appropriate data, AI improves decision making, increases efficiency and promotes business growth.

AI and Supply Chain Management

AI is here and is infiltrating the supply chain with very positive results at a number of early adopters (Forger, 2019). The migration to artificial intelligence has already begun, forcing them to train their workers for their future roles in the supply chain. Greg Brady, studied the AI issue and found eight criteria supporting a successful AI implementation:

1. Access to Real-Time Data.
2. Access to Community (Multi-Party) Data.
3. Support for Network-Wide Objective Functions (i.e., the primary goal, of the AI engine should be consumer service level at lowest possible cost).
4. Decision Process Must Be Incremental and Consider the Cost of Change.
5. Decision Process Must Be Continuous, Self-Learning and Self-Monitoring.
6. AI Engines Must Be Autonomous Decision-Making Engines. Added value can be reached if the algorithm can make intelligent decisions and execute them.
7. AI Engines Must Be Highly Scalable. Optimizing the supply chain along the network from consumers to suppliers.
8. Must Have a Way for Users to Engage with the System. AI cannot operate in a "black box." (Brady, 2017)

The question is: what is the difference between a warehouse management system with and without AI? According to Evan Garber[11],

Traditional WMS is very reliant on humans and their input. Sure, it uses simple algorithms but creates relatively static solutions compared to a WMS with AI. That takes massive amounts of data. AI analyzes all of it and directs operations on the fly rather than to preset routines. It is constantly evolving and highly dynamic. Let's face it, as data increases humans become less productive. At the same time, as data increases the more productive and intelligent a WMS with AI gets (Forger G. (Interviewer) & Garber, 2019).

We are still in the early stages of developing AI as part of an SCMS. We are in the algorithm development stage, and as the algorithms are refined, we must be able to evaluate how to apply them, and then, the AI will begin its learning about the activities of the supply chains. But 86% of US supply chain managers have been disappointed with the performance of AI-based programs and tools during the COVID-19 crisis, and identified a number of issues to be fixed: lack of reliable data to feed AI tools, provided that the previous ones are useless with disruptive events. On the other hand, in the organizational aspect, team leaders are not aware of what they really need to make better and faster decisions based on data (Burnson, Most U.S. Supply Chain Managers Using AI systems During Pandemic Disappointed, 2020)

For Vishal Chatrath[12],

"COVID-19 has been a wake-up call for businesses operating in global supply chains as they prepare to rapidly accelerate the implementation and deployment of AI in the coming years [...] Our report shows how much people benefit from AI, but also how much AI needs people. A collaborative approach to decision-making that combines the right skills and capabilities for each task is essential, particularly when systems are disrupted during uncertain times and unpredictable events." (Burnson, 2020)

SOLUTIONS AND RECOMMENDATIONS

The truth is that, according to our research, decisions made decades ago on outsourcing production, and the adoption of lean-type strategies have reduced the agility of companies, including automobile companies, to react to systemic events such as the current pandemic. This is a business problem, but it seriously affects the economic stability and supply of the country, becoming a national problem.

To provide the necessary agility and avoid possible repetition, the government's contribution should be aimed at supporting its economy and therefore its companies by being able to develop mathematical models that allow us to eventually predict a possible crisis.

- Identify the most critical sectors that may affect the health, economy, distribution, and social stability.
- Identify - in collaboration with the sectors identified above - risk indicators based on current experience, evaluate and classify them by importance.
- Develop economic intelligence agencies, endowed enough to properly evaluate these indicators.
- Improves public-private cooperation in those sectors. Public bodies probably do not have enough human and material resources, at least initially

- It is critical to promote research programs with the economics, physics and mathematics departments of the main universities to develop algorithms that allow create economic intelligence teams and companies in critical sectors to receive timely alerts of emerging risks.
- Determine the national capacities that should be maintained to ensure production and supply and ensure the economic subsistence of the country.

Immediate results cannot be expected, but neither can one rely exclusively on research that addresses the priorities - not always economic - of other countries. The supply chain management problem is already national. A solution based on algorithms and simulations typical of artificial intelligence could be appropriate.

CONCLUSION

International trade is less "globalized" that it was a few years ago. To face growing protectionism and provide greater agility, logistics managers must incorporate new regional schemes, particularly in critical items. But they also should maintain their global networks, which with their mass production allow them to reduce costs and improve their competitive advantages from existing relationships.

A market collapse was feared at the time of the pandemic outbreak, but 2020 concluded with a significant increase in activity and as a consequence, the order book for new container ships has grown to allow growth to 10% of global capacity. However, and particularly with respect to trans-Pacific trade, poor management, drastic change in market trends, and ineffective port system (especially in the USA) have led to an unprecedented collapse of the GSC, increased demand, and consequent price increase.

Despite the risks associated with deep uncertainty, some companies will react better to future events than their rivals. Resilient supply chains can capitalize on the benefits. To develop agile and resilient supply chains that tolerate disruptions and emerge in a better position for success, AI can be essential as AI offers value in SCM today and in the future. The sooner you start, the better the results you will see in the future: AI offers greater projection into the future, but companies that focus their strategy and implement AI today will reap significant benefits. AI-based solutions learn and drive continuous improvement of their algorithms by collecting more data and acquiring more experience.

After the recovery from the first wave, companies face a situation markedly different from the pre-pandemic. It is more difficult to accurately predict demand and generate added value for customers. What was once good today have become vulnerability. The time to act has now come. Investing today is preparing for upcoming disruptive events and enabling companies to be more resilient, reduce uncertainty and take advantage of emerging opportunities.

AI dramatically changes the rules of the game. Specially designed AI, powered by real-time data, is the best tool for improving performance and managing outages of unprecedented magnitude. But applied AI must be proven with years of experience to avoid putting critical supply chains at risk. Rather than disabling supply chain artificial intelligence in the face of major disruptions, it is better to accelerate its use and take advantage of more demand signals, especially data from external ecosystem partners. The combination of artificial intelligence technology, applications and real-time data is essential to enable agility, efficiency and resilience, both in the new normal and when managing future interruptions.

According to Stephen Fletcher, an Alphaliner analyst, carriers are willing to share capacity to maximize efficiency. Vessel sharing agreements are extremely important during times of high demand for vessel capacity…They ensure that all available slots are used even when an individual operator doesn't have sufficient demand from its customers for a particular sailing. Despite the fears of a market collapse at the time of the pandemic outbreak, 2020 concluded with a significant increase in ordering activity, with the global order book for new container ships growing to 10% of global capacity.

But not everything is valid in AI. The term has been abused providing generic solutions poorly adapted to events such as the pandemic. There are also no solutions to buy and apply in AI, it is necessary to teach the system, feeding it with data in real time, as well as to develop and later refine the algorithms that allow optimizing the management of global supply chains.

What we know for sure is that new systemic events will occur; what we don't know is what kind of event and when. Just as AI powered by big data allows you to anticipate detecting terrorists or foresee changes in consumption patterns, it can facilitate the management of the most critical part of globalization: The Global Supply Chain.

REFERENCES

Berman, J. (2021). Ocean shipping issues are in the spotlight in letters to the White House. *Logistics Management*. https://www.logisticsmgmt.com/article/ocean_shipping_issues_are_in_the_spotlight_in_letters_to_the_white_house

Brady, G. (2017). 8 Fundamentals for Achieving AI Success in the Supply Chain. *Supply Chain Management Review*. https://www.scmr.com/article/8_fundamentals_for_achieving_ai_success_in_the_supply_chain

Burnson, P. (2020). Most U.S. Supply Chain Managers Using AI systems During Pandemic Disappointed. *Supply Chain Management Review*. https://www.scmr.com/article/most_u.s._supply_chain_managers_using_ai_systems_during_pandemic_disappoint

Burnson, P. (2021). Cargo Delays, Supply Shortages, and Increased Prices Likely to Continue Through Q4. *Supply Chain Management Review* https://www.scmr.com/article/cargo_delays_supply_shortages_and_increased_prices_likely_to_continue_throu?utm_source=Newsletter&utm_medium=Email&utm_campaign=TWISC

Burson, P. (2021b). Ocean Cargo, Post-pandemic strategies take hold. *Logistics Management*, 58-64.

Butler, J. W. (2021). *Impacts of Shipping Container Shortages, Delays*. House Committee on Transportation and Infrastructure.

Chopra, S., & Sodhi, M. (2004). Managing risk to avoid supply-chain breakdown. *Sloan Management Review*, *46*(1), 53–61.

Christopher, M. (2016). Logistics & Supply Chain Management (5th ed.). FT Publishing International.

Drewry. (2021). *World Container Index*. https://www.drewry.co.uk/supply-chain-advisors/supply-chain-expertise/world-container-index-assessed-by-drewry

Dye, R. F. (2021). *Impact of Shipping Container Shortages, Delays, and Increased Demand on the North American Supply Chain*. The Committee on Transportation and Infrastructure Subcommittee on Coast Guard And Maritime Transportation United States House of Representatives.

E2OPEN. (2021). *Blueprint for Managing Supply Chain Disruptions of Any Size. Performance During the COVID-19 Pandemic and AI's Role in Building Resilient Businesses.* E2OPEN.

El Baz, J., & Ruel, S. (2021). Can supply chain risk management practices mitigate the disruption impacts on supply chains' resilience and robustness? Evidence from an empirical survey in a COVID-19 outbreak era. *International Journal of Production Economics, 233,* 107972. doi:10.1016/j.ijpe.2020.107972

Forger, G. (2019). AI is coming, AI is coming. *Supply Chain Management Review*: https://www.scmr.com/article/ai_is_coming_ai_is_coming

Forger, G. (Interviewer) & Garber, E. (Interviewee). (2019). *Artificial intelligence knocking on the warehouse door.* https://www.scmr.com/article/nextgen_supply_chain_interview_evan_garber

Handfield, R., & Linton, T. (2021). Supply chains are on the cusp of a data-fed revolution. Here's how businesses can succeed. *World Economic Forum,* https://www.weforum.org/agenda/2021/05/supply-chains-are-on-the-cusp-of-a-data-fed-revolution-here-s-how/

Hendricks, K., & Singhal, V. (2005). Association between Supply Chain Glitches and Operating Performance. *Management Science, 51*(5), 695–711. doi:10.1287/mnsc.1040.0353

Hosseini, S., Ivanov, D., & Dolgui, A. (2019). Review of quantitative methods for supply chain resilience analysis. Transport. Res. E. Logist. *Transport Reviews, 125,* 285–307.

ISO. (2018). *Risk management.* Obtenido de ISO: https://www.iso.org/files/live/sites/isoorg/files/store/en/PUB100426.pdf

Ivanov, D. (2020). Predicting the impacts of outbreaks on global supply chains: A simulation-based analysis on the coronavirus outbreak (COVID-19/SARS-CoV-2) case. T. *Transport.Res.E Logist. Transport Reviews, 136,* 101922. doi:10.1016/j.tre.2020.101922 PMID:32288597

Ivanov, D., & Dolgui, A. (2020). Viability of intertwined supply networks: Extending the supply chain resilience angles towards survivability. A position paper motivated by COVID-19 outbreak. *International Journal of Production Research, 28*(10), 2904–2915. doi:10.1080/00207543.2020.1750727

Jüttner, U., Peck, H., & Cristopher, M. (2003). Supply chain Risk Management: Outlining an agenda for future research. *International Journal of Logistics: Research and Applications, 6*(4), 197–210. doi:10.1080/13675560310001627016

Kenneth, I. A. (2000). A Buddhist response to the nature of human rights. *Journal of Buddhist Ethics, 8.* http://www.cac.psu.edu/jbe/twocont.html

Kinra, A. I. (2019). Ripple effect quantification by supply risk exposure assessment. *International Journal of Production Research.* Advance online publication. doi:10.1080/00207543.2019.1675919

Kumar, S., & Chandra, C. (2010). Supply chain disruption by avian flue for US companies; a case study. *Transportation Journal, 49*(4), 61–73.

Le Hoa vo, T., & Thiel, D. (2011). Economic simulation of a poultry supply chain facing a sanitary crisis. *British Food Journal, 113*(8), 192-223.

Maffei, D. B. (2021). *Impacts of Shipping Container Shortages, Delays, and Increased Demand on the North American Supply Chain.* The Committee On Transportation And Infrastructure Subcommittee on Coast Guard and Maritime Transportation United States House of Representatives.

Mccrea, B. (2021). Reverse logistics: Tackling supply chain's biggest "unsolved" challenge. *Supply Chain Management Review*, 4-7.

Mccrea, B. (2021b). Supply chain redesign. Expecting the unexpected. *Supply Chain Management Review*, 21-23.

Reiss, M., & Savino, F. (2021). Accenture on Operations: From ones and zeros to supply chain heroes. *Logistics Management.* https://www.logisticsmgmt.com/article/accenture_on_operations_from_ones_and_zeros_to_supply_chain_heroes

Ribeiro-Navarrete, S., Saura, J. R., & Palacios-Marqués, D. (2021). Towards a new era of mass data collection: Assessing pandemic surveillance technologies to preserve user privacy. *Technological Forecasting and Social Change, 167*, 120681. doi:10.1016/j.techfore.2021.120681 PMID:33840865

Rice, J. B. (2021). The Seven Core Capacities of Supply Chain Resilience. *Supply Chain Management Review.* https://www.scmr.com/article/the_seven_core_capacities_of_supply_chain_resilience

Sally, E., & Clinton, N. (2021). *Resilinc seizes the day and releases annual supply chain risk report — Carpe Diem.* Spend Matters. https://spendmatters.com/2021/04/23/resilinc-seizes-the-day-and-releases-annual-supply-chain-risk-report-carpe-diem/

Saura, J. R., Ribeiro-Soriano, D., & Palacios-Marqués, D. (2021, July 15). Setting privacy "by default" in social IoT: Theorizing the challenges and directions in Big Data Research. *Big Data Research, 25*, 100245. doi:10.1016/j.bdr.2021.100245

Saura, J. R., Ribeiro-Soriano, D., & Palacios-Marqués, D. (2021a). Using data mining techniques to explore security issues in smart living environments in Twitter. *Computer Communications, 179*, 285–295. Advance online publication. doi:10.1016/j.comcom.2021.08.021

Schulz, J. D. (2021). *State of Logistics 2021: Full speed ahead.* Obtenido de Logistics Management: https://www.logisticsmgmt.com/article/state_of_logistics_2021_full_speed_ahead

SCMR Staff. (2021). Increased Vessel Delays and Rising Transportation Costs Threaten Last-Mile Retail Operations. *Supply Chain Management Review.* https://www.scmr.com/article/increased_vessel_delays_and_rising_transportation_costs_threaten_last_mile

Sherman, E. (2020). 94% of the Fortune 1000 are seeing coronavirus supply chain disruptions: Report. *Fortune.* https://fortune.com/2020/02/21/fortune-1000-coronavirus-china-supply-chain-impact/

Sirajudeen, A. (2017). What Role Will Artificial Intelligence Play in Supply Chain Management? *Arkieva.* https://blog.arkieva.com/artificial-intelligence-supply-chain/

Sullivan, J. (2020). *Research: Trends in the Supply Chain and Their Impact on the Transportation Management System Market.* SupplyChain247. https://www.supplychain247.com/article/trends_in_the_supply_chain_and_their_impact_on_the_tms_market/kuebix

The Economist. (2021). A perfect storm for container shipping. *The Economist*. https://www.economist.com/finance-and-economics/a-perfect-storm-for-container-shipping/21804500?utm_campaign=the-economist-today&utm_medium=newsletter&utm_source=salesforce-marketing-cloud&utm_term=2021-09-13&utm_content=article-link-1&etear=nl_today_1

The Economist. (2021a, July 3). What if an AI won the Nobel prize for medicine? *The Economist*. https://www.economist.com/what-if/2021/07/03/what-if-an-ai-wins-the-nobel-prize-for-medicine

Triolo, P. (2019). US-China Competition: The Coming Decoupling? *RSIS*, 1-5.

Trump, D. J. (2017). *National Security Strategy of the United States of America*. The White House.

Tummala, R., & Schoenherr, T. (2011). Assessing and managing risks using the Supply Chain Risk Management Process (SCRMP). *Supply Chain Management*, *16*(6), 474–483. doi:10.1108/13598541111171165

Vakil, B. (2021). Supply Chain Resiliency Starts with Supplier Mapping. *Annual Report 2020*, 28-31.

Yee, V., & Glanz, J. (2021). How One of the World's Biggest Ships Jammed the Suez Canal. *The New York Times*. https://www.nytimes.com/2021/07/17/world/middleeast/suez-canal-stuck-ship-ever-given.html

ENDNOTES

[1] Kanban is a method of managing work that emerged in the Toyota Production System (TPS). In the late 1940s, Toyota implemented the "just in time" system. Production is based on customer demand and not on the traditional "pull" practice of making products and trying to sell them on the market.

[2] To be honest, there have been few but sounding exceptions, such as that of the president of the Community of Madrid, Isabel Díaz Ayuso, who, without endangering her citizens, has allowed the economy to grow. She managed, through a very balanced strategy between health and economy, to keep trade open.

[3] A typical case is that of INDITEX.

[4] Risks may also be defined as a combination of probability and frequency of occurrence of a specific hazard (BS4778, 1991).

[5] This means a reduction of defective goods to zero, lowering waste, and increasing efficiency as a result.

[6] When the industrial city of Wuhan, China became the epicenter for the coronavirus in late 2019, companies and supply chains worldwide were hit hard. As the city moved into recovery mode, and as manufacturing spun back up, a lot of companies started looking around at alternate sources of supply.

[7] Source of risk: element that, alone or in combination with others, has the potential to generate risk. Event: Occurrence or change of a particular set of circumstances.

[8] Tom Linton is the chief procurement and supply chain officer for Flex (NASDAQ: FLEX).

[9] An example SC simulation could be found in the book Supply Chain Simulation: A System Dynamics Approach for Improving Performance of Francisco Campuzano.

10   An example SC algorithm could be found in the book A theory of Supply Chain of Carlos F. Daganzo.

11   president and co-founder of warehouse management system supplier EVS.

12   CEO and Co-Founder, Secondmind.

Chapter 15

Ukrainian Social Realities and Emotivities in the Political Speeches of Yuliia Tymoshenko:
A Data–Based Approach

Felipe Debasa
Rey Juan Carlos University, Spain

Yuliia Andriichenko
Taras Shevchenko National University, Ukraine

Nataliia Popova
Taras Shevchenko National University of Kyiv, Ukraine

ABSTRACT

Ukraine is a European state situated in the middle of the spheres of power and influence of the European Union and Russia. After the fall of the Soviet Union communist regime, Ukraine maintained a significant number of Russian citizens who now promote the country in international politics. In front of them, a larger number of Ukraine citizens show their preferences to join to the European Union. Thus, the country is being polarized due to some political forces exploit these contradictions for authorities' defamation and to their own benefits. This chapter presents an analysis of a wide selection of Yuliia Tymoshenko's speeches using computer tools that allow the analysis of a large volume of data.

INTRODUCTION

Traditionally, speech is one of the communication channels used by politicians to communicate to their electorate and to the general population (Ribeiro-Navarrete et al., 2021). Political discourse can be analyzed from various points of view depending on the discipline. Political discourse has several objectives and one of them is to modulate the emotions of the interlocutor (Saura et al. 2021).

DOI: 10.4018/978-1-7998-9609-8.ch015

The necessity of political discourse research as a special type of communication requires by the fact that it does not unite, but integrates features of communication from society's different spheres, resulting in an integral communicative phenomenon, defined by a number of characteristics and based on anthropocentric, pragmatic and communicative principles. The study of the linguopragmatic aspect of political discourse makes it possible to determine the mechanisms of practical language usage in order to influence effectively on numerous recipients to develop democratic, political and economic areas of society (Horodianenko, 2002). These aspects are of highly interest to scientist to identify how the discourse of politicians can influence in the society and how it determines nation's future.

At the same time, a democracy based on the people's right to choose imposes on politicians the need to gain popular support and approval. Thus, political discourse reflects the realities of people's lives, their values and worldviews, which allow to discuss about the political discourse in the context of modern history as a reflection of trends in society.

At the same time, the skillful use of linguistic-communicative strategies while creating the political discourse allows politicians manipulating of citizens' consciousness, defending their beliefs, undermining trust in their political opponents and achieving their communicative goals (Popova, 2004; Saura et al., 2021b). Therefore, the linguistic research of the pragmatic aspect in political discourse makes it possible to describe the social realities in a certain historical period, to identify trends in society's development and to determine features of individual style and strategy used by powerful politicians to influence on the mass addressee (Saura et al., 2021a).

Our study is based on speeches of a well-known Ukrainian politician who has been influencing on Ukrainian politics for a long time and enjoys the support of a large number of people – Yuliia Tymoshenko. Having emerged on the international stage as an independent state after the collapse of the Soviet Union, Ukraine is persistently building its development strategy based on democratic principles. Having gone through a difficult path to independence that spans many centuries, being enslaved and conquered by various empires. The Ukrainian people seek to build a peaceful and tolerant society, which has been hampered by constant Russia's attacks for the past 14 years. Ukraine wants to have its own opinion and express it freely, to cooperate with the European Union and other countries of the world, to build its economy and jointly solve such global problems as climate change, the Covid pandemic and the reduction of non-renovated natural resources. These are some reasons why investigate the pragmatics in the political discourse of such an influential politician as Yulia Tymoshenko is essential to assess the prospects of the country by realizing the relationship among Ukrainians' life reflection and manipulative strategies in her discourse. Studying the processes of communicative realization of Yuliia Tymoshenko's political discourse, research of social, empirical and psychological aspects of communication by means of text production help to improve communication efficiency, something, which is applied to any language system and any political discourse in particular.

The selection of Yuliia Tymoshenko's discourses is made due to current events and the proximity of the electoral processes that will take place in Ukraine. The main threats to Western democracies are populism, ochlocracy, disinformation, fake news and the lack of critical judgment in society (Debasa, 2021). The transversal methodologies in the humanities that form the digital humanities offer tools to analyze the new challenges of the IV Industrial Revolution.

THEORETICAL BACKGROUND IN DISCOURSE ANALYSIS

The theoretical basis of the research is to combine the discourse linguistics and pragmatics provisions developed in the works of N. Arutyunova, M. Bakhtin, S. Balli, E. Benvenist, G. Bias, V. Bogdanov, V. Borbotko, R. Brinker, R. Craig, G. Cress, G. Cook, G. Herman, I. Ilyin, S. Guerrero, R. Godel, H. Grunert, T. Van Dyck, R. Dickman, W. Edmondson, Y. Karaulov, A. Kibrik, I. Kobozeva, S. Krestinsky, M. Mironova, D. Noonan, E. Nunez, N. Pairklaf, V. Petrov, Sh. Safarov, W. Sager, J. Searle, E. Sheigal, M. Stabs, L. Fernandez, M. Foucault, D. Shifrin, O. Syshchikov, A. Vezhbytska and others.

A significant number of Ukrainian scientists are devoted to topical issues of discourse linguistics, functioning, generation, discourse perception and determination of its differentiation criteria. Among them are M. Bartun, F. Batsevych, I. Bezkrovna, O. Borovytska, R. Bubnyak, I. Bekhty, A. Belova, V. Burbelo, T. Voropay, O. Galapchuk, V. Demyankov, O. Ilchenko, V. Karasyk, K. Kusko, O. Kucherova, D. Mamaliga, T. Nikulshina, O. Onufrienko, L. Pavlyuk, M. Polyuzhyna, M. Popovych, G. Pocheptsov, T. Radzievska, V. Rizun, M. Feller, G. Yavorska and others. A significant number of young scientists works dealing with the development of certain discourse types: mass media discourse (I. Soboleva, S. Konovets, N. Chaban), legislative discourse (M. Vlasenko, T. Skuratovska), advertising discourse (N. Volkogon, V. Okhrimenko), political discourse (G. Zhukovets, V. Petrenko, O. Ponomarenko, I. Stetsula, V. Ushchina, O. Fomenko), artistic discourse (O. Ostrovska), discourse of socio and political TV news (N. Rozhdestvenska), ecological discourse (I. Rozmaritsa), authoritarian discourse (P. Kryuchkova) and persuasive discourse (L. Ryapolova).

Since in modern linguistics there is no generally accepted discourse typology. The criteria for differentiating the discourse definitions differ greatly in different scientific schools. Most linguists recognize the importance of the discourse area and its pragmatic orientation. The combination of these criteria allows to define the political discourse as a kind of discourse, characterized by specific cognitive content, semantic structure and pragmatic organization.

In our opinion, the type of discourse should be determined in relation to the above principles, which are combined to achieve effectively communicative goals, in other words, the form of representation, means of argumentation, nature and other parameters of the communicative situation are subject to the main discourse objective. Our main focus is to define the types of discourse associated with societies' life in terms of social system, which it is considered as a holistic entity. Its main elements are people, their relationships, interactions, social institutions and organizations, social groups and communities, norms and value (Horodianenko, 2002). Person's life outside the society is impossible.

There are a variety of discourse-mediated relationships among all members of this multifunctional structure, being the most significant processes that guide and determine the future of the country, region and humankind. These discourse-mediated relationships take place in the political, economic, social and cultural spheres. They are constantly intertwined and caused by each other, especially during the period of rapid integration development which has presence in all spheres of human activity.

Could be possible to imagine a politician who speaks only about politics, without involving economy development, education, medicine, social protection or personality formation issues? Today politician's discourse often goes beyond the purely political. It is formed on the principles of wide audience interests' variety, modern citizen's needs and linguistic and extra linguistic means of achieving pragmatic goals, which are integrated from different areas.

Thus, going beyond purely professional communication, politics are considered to be a part of society in the investigated type of discourse. If the goal of their speeches is not to gain and retain power, which is the political activity essence and purpose, but the creation of relationship among the authorities and citizens due to speaking activities. Meanwhile, the activities in other social spheres are directly related to the government's position on a particular issue. Due to the existence of similarity, it is possible to talk about the relationship among different types of discourse, which partly integrate the features of each other despite having their own special characteristics.

The type of investigated discourse is characterized by an appeal to the society's social and political problems. The presence of such ideological component creates a certain generalized worldview in different people's minds. Speaker's evaluation of social and political processes which take place in society and his/her attitude to certain phenomena are reveled in his/her political discourse. Yulia Tymoshenko's political speeches are not only a means of society and its processes reflecting, but also a means of their formation and their driving force, as well as a form of social interaction (Fairclough and Wodac, 1997).

Thus, this article analyzes the criteria of (i) discourse typology, (ii) discourse communicative purpose, (iii) functioning area, (iv) pragmatic meaning, (v) social roles configuration, (vi) temporal, spatial and social parameters of communication, (vii) the ratio of subjective and conventional content, and (viii) specific linguistic features, to define the political discourse as a special type of communication. It is also reflected how politicians' efforts to achieve certain communicative goals influence modern life realities and society's value orientations.

METHODOLOGY

This study is developed by the analysis of specialized bibliography (Roberts, 2021). It follows an exploratory approach and a subsequent qualitative and critical analysis framed in the historical context of the discipline of History of the Present World supported by Philology and Linguistics (Saura et al, 2021e). Thanks to technology, specifically to information processing computer tools, this study is enriched with high volumes of data which differentiates textual analysis based on whether they are classical or use computer programs (Behar, 1993). Debasa and Aznar (2021), propose cross-sectional methodologies in the study of history combined with technology to be able to speak of Digital Humanities, therefore, a Cross-Sectional Digital Humanities has been applied. The application of integral linguistics approach proposed by Popova (2018), combines discourse linguistics, linguopragmatic and cognitive analysis, to computer processing data. It is obtained reliable results based on objective data, avoiding the possible subjectivity inherent in traditional methods of linguopragmatic discourse analysis (Popham et al., 2021).

Among the linguistic analysis methods mentioned above, this research is focused on using a descriptive method and quantitative analysis of large texts, carried out using artificial intelligence, – to inventory, systematize and classify quantitative and qualitative changes in the values of different language units (Saura et al., 2021c). The interpretation of the linguistic context was used to determine the communicative and pragmatic meaning of language units. Distributive, semantic and syntactic transformational analysis made possible to compare and analyze the general and individual features of language usage in political discourse (Roller, 2002; Zimmerman, 2011).

On the other hand, distributive analysis revealed the ability of language units to increase pragmatic load depending on their lexical environment; semantic and syntactic transformational analysis was used to define and emphasize pragmatic intention in expression through the comparison of syntactic and semantic similarities and differences between language objects (Saura et al., 2021).

The source of the study is Yuliia Tymoshenko's interviews and speeches in the Parliament for year 2021. Having become an influential Ukrainian politician after participating in the Orange Revolution in 2014, she constantly enjoys the support of a large number of Ukrainian citizens and influences Ukraine's political course. Additionally, she received the third position after current President V. Zelensky and the ex-President P. Poroshenko in the last presidential election of year 2019 in Ukraine. For this work, 102 speeches have been selected. They correspond to 21,091 words and 147,129 characters with spaces.

In this research, Internet was widely used to ensure prompt access to new materials related to current events in Ukraine (Souto-Manning, 2013).

Thus, the study has the aim to analyze the principles of organization of semantic and pragmatic content of Yuliia Tymoshenko's political discourse, which determines the following tasks:

1. Identify the most important and vital concepts of actual Ukrainians' worldview due to choosing the most frequent lexical units in Yuliia Tymoshenko's political discourse which reflects the realities of the Ukrainian society life.
2. To carry out a comprehensive linguistic study of the politician's speeches at the semantic, morphological and syntactic levels in order to determine the main means of pragmatic organization of discourse information and their role in modeling the addressee's evaluative interpretation of the main discourse concepts.
3. To analyze communicative strategies in Yuliia Tymoshenko's discourse in order to determine effective means of influence on the mass consciousness and to find out how speaker's social status and information organization affect the discourse semantic and pragmatic content.

The primary source of information is Yulia Tymoshenko's political discourse as a complex, multifaceted phenomenon of communication that reflects the realities of modern Ukrainian society. It combines verbal and non-verbal, social and psychological elements in order to influence on a wide audience worldview and create evaluation and ideological content of political discourse (Sonntag, 2001). The subject of research is the semantic and pragmatic features of lexical units, morphological forms, syntactic and stylistic means of the political discourse. They serve to influence effectively on the mass addressee's consciousness and reflect realities of the modern Ukrainian society (Wible, 2006).

RESULTS AND DISCUSSION

Once the speech has been sequenced, the most used terms with five or more characters has been selected. Some of them contains part of the Ukrainian speech while most three or four characters words are function and they do not participate in discourse meaning creation (Saura et al., 2021b).

Thanks to modern technologies a word cloud based on the proceeding results was created (see figure 1). It demonstrates the most used words in Yuliia Tymochenko's discourse. Word size in the cloud depends on the frequency of its usage in the speeches.

Table 1. Frequency of words used in Yuliia Tymoshenko's speeches

Words	Length	Counting	Weighted Percentage	Similar Words
людей	5	110	0,51%	люди, людям
землі	5	75	0,35%	землі, земля, землю
сьогодні	8	69	0,32%	сьогодні
України	7	59	0,28%	України, Україні
команда	7	46	0,21%	команда
негайно	7	40	0,19%	негайно
влади	5	38	0,18%	влади
влада	5	35	0,16%	влада
життя	5	35	0,16%	життя
країни	6	35	0,16%	країни, країна, країні
народу	6	35	0,16%	народу
гривень	7	34	0,16%	гривень
закон	5	30	0,14%	закон
землю	5	29	0,14%	землю
референдум	10	29	0,14%	референдум
немає	5	27	0,13%	немає
років	5	27	0,13%	років
Україна	8	26	0,12%	Україна, України, український, Україну, українцям, Україні, українців
держави	7	26	0,12%	держави
рішення	7	26	0,12%	рішення
українців	9	26	0,12%	українців
законопроєкт	12	25	0,12%	законопроєкт
наших	5	24	0,11%	наших
разом	5	24	0,11%	Разом
батьківщина	11	21	0,10%	батьківщина
більше	6	21	0,10%	більше
президент	9	20	0,09%	президент
світі	5	20	0,09%	світі
президента	10	19	0,09%	президента
робити	6	19	0,09%	робити
тарифи	6	19	0,09%	тарифи
пам'яті	7	19	0,09%	пам'ятайте, пам'ятати, пам'ятають, пам'ятає, пам'ятаємо, пам'ять, пам'яті
зробити	7	18	0,08%	зробити

Figure 1. Word cloud

The word cloud shows the most treated concepts in Yuliia Tymoishemko's speeches which are *people, lands, Ukraine, team, today* and *now*. She focuses on actual society's reality and relies on her political colleges and like-minded people to reach her goals. It is also developed a "people" word cloud which reveals the speeches are full of modal and connotative words which help the speaker to manipulate people's mind: *necessary, possible* (expression of the necessity or possibility but not factual actions), *against, lack* (negative connotation), *immediately* (call to act), *our* (focusing on her belonging to the society/citizens/ Ukrainians), *country, motherland, life, law* (evoking to national or democratic values) (see figure 2).

Considering these results, the word *people* is used more times than other words by the politician. Artificial intelligence techniques allow the development of a "land" word tree (See figure 3). Then, it is possible to confirm Yuliia Tymoshenko focus their communicative skills on people needs such as gas and its high prices, pension and land reforms and other social problems. Additionally, this word is widely used in the context of current authority's criticism and appreciating of national values which are considered the most significant in the Ukrainian conceptual sphere (Van Parijs, 2002).

Another word used the most frequently in Yuliia Tymoshenko's speeches is *land*. It is related to the land reform conducted in Ukraine and variety of attitudes to its implementation. Being long-time national material value, land is a mean of people's mind manipulation in political discourse as most Ukrainians are afraid of losing their lands after legal permission to sell them.

Most Ukrainians believe reaching foreign companies allowed them to obtain land properties by exploiting them without appropriate conservation methods. Ukrainians are afraid to be low-paid servants on their native lands as it was during some previous centuries. The nuclear constituents of "land" word cloud are *land market, special prices, to save the land, to expel from the land, agriculture, we, foreigners, on our land*. The peripheral zone contains such constituents as *competitor, enemy, fertile, farmer, to earn millions, referendum, profits, to force, illegal decision.* The politician, while speaking on this question, emphasizes supporting of the majority's point of view on the land market reform and defending the Ukrainian lands on being sold to rich companies.

Figure 2. "People" word cloud

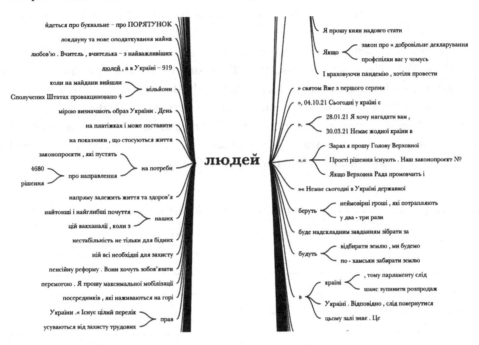

Figure 3. "Land" word tree

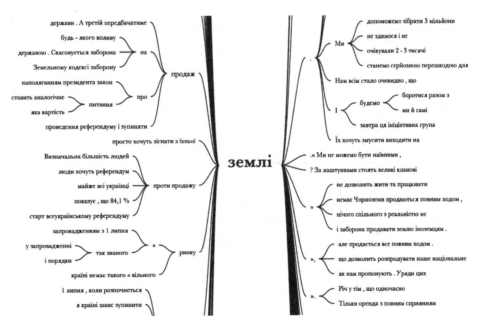

On the other side, the "land" word tree hardly contains constituents which could determine practical methods of using the Ukrainian land efficiently and on Ukrainian people's benefit. The only case is *to rent lands with full assistance*. Many affective words (*native, holy, priceless, special, the best*) are likely to be used for emotional influence on voters. The insistence on holding a referendum on the land sale is accompanied by a series of words that emphasize the efforts of the politician and her team to hold it: *our party insists, understands, not to allow sales, to collect reports of raider attacks*. In contrast to the description of her own actions, a significant amount of vocabulary is used to criticize opponents: *deprive, occupy, block the case*.

Due to the support of artificial intelligence techniques, it has been able to choose the most frequent lexical units used in Yuliia Tymoshenko's discourse. The results obtained were nouns denoting the pressing issues of nowadays Ukrainian society, which indicates the development of argumentative strategies of discourse around the most relevant and popular fragments of reality, including energy supply, borders protection, war in the east of the country, pricing policy, land and health care reforms, overcoming the Covid pandemic and guaranteeing pension and social benefits. These problems are acute in Ukraine on the 30th anniversary of its independence and concern its citizens.

Table 2. The most frequent words related to Ukrainian problems in Yuliia Tymoshenko's discourse

Word Reflecting Realities	Number of Words
gas	116
law	111
salary	71
pension	53
price	52
defense	50
corruption	47
land	34
medicine	26
energy	16
pandemia	15
guaranty	10
inflation	8
violence	8
enemy	5
education	4
cruelty	4
danger	4
illegality	4
victim	3

Another large group of language units predominating in Yuliia Tymoshenko's speeches are abstract words. These words are used for different purposes and in different contexts. The ability of abstract words to actualize the meanings associated with them in the minds of citizens (Bylinska, 2017). At the same time allows the speaker to avoid specifics, appealing to ideological values. The actualization of the concepts verbalized by these language units testifies their relevance and necessity in Ukrainian society life and their important place in the national conceptual sphere.

Table 3. Frequency of axiological units in Yuliia Tymoshenko's speeches

Ideological Axiologems	Number of Words
referendum	51
protection / protected / protect	50
fight / defend	46
law / legal	19
novation	17
ban / prohibition	15
order	14
peace / reconciliation	13
freedom / free	12
happiness	10
love	9
justice	8
legalization	7
preservation efficiency responsibility	6 6 6
gratitude	5
development globalization	4 4
honesty / honest	3
reliability welfare	2 2
authority adherence to principles indifference cooperation integration	1 1 1 1 1

Thus, Yulia Tymoshenko's discourse is rich in ideological axiologems such as *protection, defense, referendum, law, justice, freedom and reconciliation*. They are related to political and geopolitical struggle, finding compromises and cooperation to achieve common goals and improvement of living standards and democratic principles (Stroud, 2018). Converting political concepts into axiological units largely depends on which party is in power, on the prevailing ideology in the society and on speaker's political views.

Yuliia Tymoshenko, whose actual political priority is to reach a compromise among the parties, makes political decisions using lexemes *law, preservation, efficiency* and *development* as political axiologems.

Regarding the universal and moral values in politicians' discourse are verbalized by such lexical units as *happiness, love, honesty, gratitude, responsibility, reliability*. They are used in syntagms with polysemantic words which give qualitatively new social and political interpretation corresponding to the social and political processes that take place in citizens' lives. The reason for the addressee's appeal to such well-known and eternal concepts is their constant influence on the development of mankind at every historical stage. Universal and moral values are affective/emotional means of influencing addressee's emotional sphere meaning is relation to the life experience of each individual according to his/her worldview.

Moreover, european values are represented in Yuliia Tymoshenko's discourse by words such as *international cooperation, assistance* and *globalization*. Mainly, this words are used in the context of peaceful coexistence and mutually beneficial agreements on cooperation between states, observance of agreements and inviolability of borders. Their use characterizes the speaker as a defender of the authenticity and independence of her own country and as a person who respects the freedom of other nations. This positioning makes it possible to create her positive image in the national and international arenas and gain the support of the electorate and, at the same time, reveals Ukrainians' overwhelming support of Ukraine's entry into the international community.

The words denoting specific national values reflect both the conceptual sphere of native speakers and the social and political processes inherent in the Ukrainian society: *freedom, independence, national security, honor, glory, dignity, authenticity, traditions, language*. These axiologems help the speaker not only to make a call for national unification, but also color positively the concept of a free and independent Ukraine in addressees' minds.

Nowadays, a significant number of lexical units used in the politician's discourse are characterized by such pragmatic and semantic feature as expressive connotation.

These words acquire broad expressive shades depending on the context and their interpretation by the speaker in accordance with her worldview (Bylinska, 2017). Connotatively colored vocabulary is a means of key concepts developing in Yuliia Tymoshenko's political discourse due to which she modifies the modern Ukraine image. It is a material for developing her argumentation, creating communicative strategies to influence both the logical thinking of the addressee and his/her emotional sphere.

The speaker's choice of a strategy and means of its implementation is largely depends on addressee' factor, which is one of the main reasons for the variability of information presentation to achieve the expected pragmatic effect (Micovic, 2014).

Due to taking into account political, social and cultural processes in the society, which have a positive or negative connotative meaning in citizens' minds, some commonly used lexical units acquire a positive or negative meaning in political discourse applying it to the whole phrase. These language units can modify the evaluative interpretation of such concepts in modern political discourse as development of democratic principles, independence defense, national unity, social protection, terrorism elimination, economic development, international cooperation, introduction of new scientific technologies, art and culture preservation.

The strategy of addressee' persuasion is one of the most frequent political discourse strategies. The main reason is the discourse type – the impact on the mass audience. This strategy in Yuliia Timoshemko's discourse is realized, first, by creating a contrast between the real and desired state of affairs due to absolute and contextual antonyms which oppose the present and the past, the promised and the fulfilled.

Table 4. Communicative strategies and their realization tactics in Yuliia Tymoshenko's speeches

Strategy	Realization Tactics
Addressee's persuasion	1. Creating contrast by contrast. 2. Repetition of words with the meaning of "implementation". 3. The usage of stylistic figures of speech and other affective language means. 4. Manifestation of optimism through the usage of words with positive connotative meaning and with futural meaning.
Accusations of opponents	1. Accumulation of words with a negative connotative meaning. 2. Direct appeal to the opponent using grammatical order forms.
Critique of negative phenomena	1. Actualization of social problems. 2. Usage of a great number of adjectives with a negative connotation. 3. Influence on the phenomenon evaluation by discourse subjectivizing.
Giving propositions	1. Creating contrasts due to the words with opposite meaning. 2. Creating a positive evaluation of the statement due to the words with meaning of novelty and development
Call to action	1. The usage of verbs with the modal meaning of duty and causation. 2. Actualization of the concept of "love to motherland" 3. Strengthening of adjectives with positively connatated adverbs. 4. Affective/emotional influence on addressee

The politician uses a large number of language units with negative connotative meaning both to create a contrast for addressees' persuasion and to accuse opponents directly and discredit them in voters' eyes. In particular, the word *corruption* is used 47 times in Yuliia Tymoshenko's discourse in 2021, which is 0.3% of the whole number of words. Additionally, the usage of nouns with a negative connotation to denote the realities of life in Ukraine is widespread, for example, *bullying* (0.05%), *enemy* (0.03%), *illegality* (0.02%), *danger* (0.02%), *harshness* (0.02%), *victim* (0.02%). Although their number is inferior to the words with a positive connotation, the most frequent language units among which are *protection* (0.16%), *order* (0.07%), *peace* (0, 08%), *justice* (0.05%), *conservation* (0.04%), *efficiency* (0.04%) (Wodak, 2006).

Abstract words with neutral connotative meanings acquire certain semantic shadows in the language context obtaining the ability to express speaker's attitude and her evaluation of the situation. For example, the word *struggle* in the context of defending Ukrainian citizens' interests, state borders integrity and overcoming poverty is perceived positively by the addressee and convinces him/her that the politician cares about the interests of the state and its citizens and strives to protect them. The word *prohibition* in the context of reducing crime and corruption also acquires a positive connotative color. Instead, the word *legalization* which is contextually related to controversial concepts for the Ukrainian worldview, in particular the legalization of marijuana or gambling, acquires a negative connotative meaning in Yuliia Tymoshenko's speeches and criticizes the current government for trying to fill the state budget from the sectors contradicting to the Ukrainian's moral values.

Being combined with the many repetitions of verbs with the meaning of "realizations" (*offered, decided, achieved, refuted, received*), the tactic of contrast helps to emphasize the fulfillment of politician's promises. Yuliia Tymoshenko's usage of metaphorical expressions also has a significant affective effect on the addressee: *to burn it with hot iron* (11.01.21), *to break through this wall* (26.01.21), *the illusion of democracy* (26.01.21).

Speech influence on the addressee is carried out by extensive usage of words with futural semantics (*will offer, will achieve, will serve*), which in combination with lexemes of positive meanings give an optimistic meaning to discourse concepts, in particular such adjectives as *unique (potential), strongest (country), good (harvest), good (thoughts), good (signs)*.

While accusing her opponents, Yuliia Tymoshenko combines direct appeal to them (*Enough experiments!* (11.01.21)) with the usage of the pronoun "they" in the contextual environment of words meaning "incompetence", "indifference", "self-interest". She calls the authorities *amateurs* and *corrupts*, contrasting the real situation with the desired: *overcoming the crisis, solving problems, make effective decisions*. Metaphorical statements deepen the impact on addressee's emotional sphere and are able to show speaker's attitude: "to draw the bill", for example, is used in the meaning to adopt the law due to the pressure or personal relations.

The strategy of critique of negative phenomena in society is carried out through the usage of words with negative connotative meanings, the pragmatic purpose of which is to accuse opponents and gain electorate's support, and also force the government to take decisive steps to solve social problems. At the same time, Yuliia Tymoshenko likes to appeal to the current government with direct appeals, using the verbs in the first person and plural grammar form, subjectivizing possible changes in such way: *Let's show / do / accept...!*

Addressing society's social problems can be a background for the submission of politician's own propositions, a means of evaluation of a phenomenon that exists in the country. This discourse strategy is implemented through verbs with subjective semantics (*want, force, ask for, believe, require, propose*), which draw attention to speaker's position if they are combined with phrases containing verbs that give a positive meaning to the noun denoting social, economic and political problems. Yuliia Tymoshenko also widely uses words with the modal meaning of duty and necessity: *necessary, important, urgent.*

The politician's strategy of audience's call to certain actions is characterized, first of all, by the usage of causative verbs in the first person and singular form in persuasive sentences: *we call, we must*. The usage of adjectives with a positive connotative meaning, emphasized by adverbs serves to deepen the emotional characteristics: *extraordinarily positive, more intensive, mainly important* and *indispensably necessary*. The call of citizens to patriotism and love to their motherland is carried out by using a large number of words with the meaning of unity: *to unite* (0.06% of the total number of words), *to support* (0.07% of the total number of words), *to consolidate* (0.01% of the total number of words). The usage of these words proves Ukrainian society's desire to be inseparable nation, live in peace with others and maintain tolerance world view. They help the addressee to appeal to the important value of the Ukrainian people – integrity (Yokota-Murakami, 2015).

According to the value scale of Ronald Inglehart and Christian Welzel, who refer to "positive values" as values of self-expression and "negative" values as survival (Welzen and Iglehart, 2005), in Yuliia Tymoshenko's discourse of year 2021 emotional support for survival values in favor of self-expression values has decreased in contrast to previous years, in particular, when Viktor Yanukovych was the President of Ukraine. According to a study by M. Stepanenko, the values of survival in the politician's discourse in 2017 were 62% as opposed to 38% of the values of self-expression (Stepanenko, 2017). In 2021, Yuliia Tymoshenko, accusing the government, calls on it to act, rather than citizens to oppose the valid authorities. She focuses addressees' attention more on their own evaluation of the current events and on looking for ways to solve problems. Her discourse focuses more than previously on uniting citizens to control government's actions.

However, Yuliia Tymoshenko's discourse still lacks emphasis on such values of self-expression as the elaboration of new living standards and the search for ways to achieve them. A large amount of words with negative connotations, which verbalize the Ukrainian realities, makes us to draw a conclusion of imposing a negative worldview evaluation on the mass citizens, which is unlikely to generate a desire for self-improvement and work for the nation, rather breeds despair and apathy.

CONCLUSION

Thus, the study shows the peculiarities of Yulia Tymoshenko's discourse are the creation of pragmatic strategies to influence the mass addressee by updating concepts denoting the realities of Ukrainians' modern life. Verbalization of these concepts is characterized by the usage of a large number of abstract language units, the meaning of which the addressees are able to modify according to their own life experience and worldview. Also, language means affecting on mass addressee's emotional sphere dominate in the speeches (Woźniak, 2018).

The directives and direct appeals, together with the appeal to the Ukrainian people's values, give uniqueness to Yuliia Tymoshenko's individual style, distinguishing it from the discourse of other Ukrainian politicians. Changing rhetoric in the direction of verbalizing such values as improving the financial situation of Ukrainians, increasing confidence in the government and citizens' political activity and the struggle for people's interests contribute to the support of Yulia Tymoshenko by a significant number of Ukrainians.

At the same time, the dominance of abstract words, characterized by ambiguity of perception and understanding, lack of qualitative characteristics of the far-sighted program of society development and crises overcoming with the usage of words with exact meaning, as well as the excess of affective vocabulary aimed at manipulating the emotional sphere, ruins the politician's reputation in the society where the leadership has been destroyed for centuries by the ruling empire, being a threat to the enslavement and exploitation of the Ukrainian people and their fertile and strategically important lands.

Practical Implications

The insightful results obtained in this study could be significant for a wide variety of professional from different sectors. Since politicians, entrepreneur, marketers, journalist, teachers or any person aiming to influence, persuade and communicate with others effectively.

In case of companies, nowadays they have an important challenge to communicate clear, straight-forward and consistent messages to changes people mindset or behavior in favour of their brands. Then, the advanced technologies techniques used in the research help professionals to know the impact of their messages and to identify the best way to reach customer successfully. Furthermore, marketers and digital media professionals could determine which words are powerful and brings more value to customers when target them through digital marketing strategies (e.g., social media).

Additionally, companies' leaders and managers could improve internal communication raising motivational speeches and using the appropriate words to their employers. The development of analysed messages by artificial intelligence will also help to build an aligned strategic vision, mission and values within the company.

Finally, as this study shows, the implementation of linguistics methodologies helps politicians and public institutions to better engage with citizens and gain their attention. However, this can lead to negative results as long as their main objective is to manipulate the whole society.

REFERENCES

Behar, J. (1993). Aproximación al análisis textual informatizado. *Anuario de psicología/The UB. The Journal of Psychology*, (59), 61–78.

Bylinska, O. S. (2017). Zasoby movlennievoho vplybu v synkretnykh zhanrakh politychnoho ahitatsiinoho dyskurdu [Means of Speech Influence in Syncretic Genres of Political Propaganda Discourse]. *Journal of Odesa National University: Philology, 22*(2), 8–20.

Debasa, F. (2021). Digitalisation, pandemics and current world (2019-2021). *UNIO–EU Law Journal, 7*(1), 18–32. doi:10.21814/unio.7.1.3575

Debasa, F., & Sánchez, T. A. (2021). El discurso político de la presidencia Trump antes del covid. *Historia Actual Online*, (56), 21–34.

Fairclough, N. L., & Wodac, R. (1997). *Critical Discourse analysis. In Discourse Studies. Discourse as social interaction* (Vol. 2). Sage.

Horodianenko, V. H. (2002). *Sotsiolohiia* [Sociology]. Akademiya.

Inglehart, R. (2010). *Modernization, cultural change, and democracy: The human development sequence*. Cambridge University Press.

Micovic, M. (2014). *La comunicación y el discurso políticos en España y Serbia. Análisis comparativo de las estrategias argumentativas utilizadas en los debates electorales televisivos: tesis … de Dr.* Cand. en Lengua Española.

Popham, S. F., Huth, A. G., Bilenko, N. Y., Deniz, F., Gao, J. S., Nunez-Elizalde, A. O., & Gallant, J. L. (2021). Visual and linguistic semantic representations are aligned at the border of human visual cortex. *Nature Neuroscience, 24*(11), 1628–1636. doi:10.103841593-021-00921-6 PMID:34711960

Popova, N. M. (2004). *Ispanomovnyi suspilno-politychnyi dyskurs: linguopragmatychnyi aspect* [Spanish Social and Political Discourse: Linguopragmatic Aspect] [PhD Dissertation]. Taras Shevchenko National University of Kyiv.

Popova, N. M. (2008). Speeches as a genre of political discourse and a mean of conceptual modeling of politician's image in citizens' mind. *Modern Researches in Cognitive Linguistics, (6)*, 49-455.

Ribeiro-Navarrete, S., Saura, J. R., & Palacios-Marqués, D. (2021). Towards a new era of mass data collection: Assessing pandemic surveillance technologies to preserve user privacy. *Technological Forecasting and Social Change, 167*, 120681. doi:10.1016/j.techfore.2021.120681 PMID:33840865

Roberts, A. H. (2021). *A statistical linguistic analysis of American English*. De Gruyter Mouton.

Roller, E. (2002). When does language become exclusivist? Linguistic politics in Catalonia. *National Identities*, *4*(3), 273–289. doi:10.1080/1460894022000026132

Saura, J. R., Palacios-Marqués, D., & Iturricha-Fernández, A. (2021d). Ethical Design in Social Media: Assessing the main performance measurements of user online behavior modification. *Journal of Business Research*, *129*(May), 271–281. doi:10.1016/j.jbusres.2021.03.001

Saura, J. R., Palacios-Marqués, D., & Ribeiro-Soriano, D. (2021). How SMEs use data sciences in their online marketing performance: A systematic literature review of the state-of-the-art. *Journal of Small Business Management*. Advance online publication. doi:10.1080/00472778.2021.1955127

Saura, J. R., Ribeiro-Soriano, D., & Palacios-Marqués, D. (2021a). Using data mining techniques to explore security issues in smart living environments in Twitter. *Computer Communications*, *179*, 285–295. Advance online publication. doi:10.1016/j.comcom.2021.08.021

Saura, J. R., Ribeiro-Soriano, D., & Palacios-Marqués, D. (2021b, July 15). Setting privacy "by default" in social IoT: Theorizing the challenges and directions in Big Data Research. *Big Data Research*, *25*, 100245. doi:10.1016/j.bdr.2021.100245

Saura, J. R., Ribeiro-Soriano, D., & Palacios-Marques, D. (2021c). Evaluating security and privacy issues of social networks based information systems in Industry 4.0. *Enterprise Information Systems*, 1–17. Advance online publication. doi:10.1080/17517575.2021.1913765

Saura, J. R., Ribeiro-Soriano, D., & Palacios-Marqués, D. (2021e). Setting B2B Digital Marketing in Artificial Intelligence-based CRMs: A review and directions for future research. *Industrial Marketing Management*, *98*(October), 161–178. doi:10.1016/j.indmarman.2021.08.006

Sonntag, S. K. (2001). The politics of linguistic sub-alternity in North India. *Linguistic Structure and Language Dynamic in South Asia: Papers from the Proceedings of SALA XVIII Roundtable*, 207-22.

Souto-Manning, M. (2013). Competence as linguistic alignment: Linguistic diversities, affinity groups, and the politics of educational success. *Linguistics and Education*, *24*(3), 305–315. doi:10.1016/j.linged.2012.12.009

Stepanenko, M. (2017). *Publichnyi duskurs Yu. Tymoshenko v roxrizi tsinnostey za schkaloyu Inglehart-Welzelia* [Yulia Tymoshenko's Public Discourse in Values on the Inglehart-Welzel Scale]. Noks Fishes. http://noksfishes.info/landing/tymoshenko.html

Stroud, C. (2018). 1. Linguistic Citizenship. In *The Multilingual Citizen* (pp. 17–39). Multilingual Matters.

Van Parijs, P. (2002). Linguistic justice. *Politics, Philosophy & Economics*, *1*(1), 59–74. doi:10.1177/1470594X02001001003

Wible, S. (2006). Pedagogies of the" Students' Right" era: The language curriculum research group's project for linguistic diversity. *College Composition and Communication*, 442–478.

Wodak, R. (2006). Linguistic analyses in language policies. *An introduction to language policy: Theory and method*, 170-193.

Woźniak, E. (2018). Contribution to linguistic politics in the Interwar Period—Ministry of Communication for the sake of language. *Język a Kultura*, *28*, 101–111. doi:10.19195/1232-9657.28.8

Yokota-Murakami, T. (2015). Polyglotism of Jewish Latvian Literati and Linguistic Politics of the Periphery: Observation through M. Razumnyi and A. Imermanis. *Japanese Slavic and East European Studies*, *36*(0), 47–56. doi:10.5823/jsees.36.0_47

Zimmerman, P. (2011). *Faer Asturies: Linguistic Politics and the Frustrated Construction of Asturian Nationalism, 1974-1999*. Academic Press.

ADDITIONAL READING

Speech Yuliia Tymoshenko´s 15.03.2012.

Speech Yuliia Tymoshenko´s 11.01.2021

Speech Yuliia Tymoshenko´s 12.01.2021

Speech Yuliia Tymoshenko´s 19.01.2021

Speech Yuliia Tymoshenko´s 21.01.2021

Speech Yuliia Tymoshenko´s 25.01.2021

Speech Yuliia Tymoshenko´s 26.01.2021

Speech Yuliia Tymoshenko´s 27.01.2021

Speech Yuliia Tymoshenko´s 28.01.2021

Speech Yuliia Tymoshenko´s 29.01.2021

Speech Yuliia Tymoshenko´s 01.02.2021

Speech Yuliia Tymoshenko´s 04.02.2021

Speech Yuliia Tymoshenko´s 05.02.2021

Speech Yuliia Tymoshenko´s 10.02.2021

Speech Yuliia Tymoshenko´s 16.01.2021

Speech Yuliia Tymoshenko´s 19.02.2021

Speech Yuliia Tymoshenko´s 21.02.2021

Speech Yuliia Tymoshenko´s 23.02.2021

Speech Yuliia Tymoshenko´s 24.02.2021

Speech Yuliia Tymoshenko´s 01.03.2021

Speech Yuliia Tymoshenko´s 04.03.2021

Speech Yuliia Tymoshenko´s 08.03.2021

Speech Yuliia Tymoshenko´s 17.03.2021

Speech Yuliia Tymoshenko´s 18.03.2021

Speech Yuliia Tymoshenko´s 19.03.2021

Speech Yuliia Tymoshenko´s 23.03.2021

Speech Yuliia Tymoshenko´s 24.03.2021

Speech Yuliia Tymoshenko´s 26.03.2021

Speech Yuliia Tymoshenko´s 27.03.2021

Speech Yuliia Tymoshenko´s 30.03.2021

Speech Yuliia Tymoshenko´s 31.03.2021

Speech Yuliia Tymoshenko´s 01.04.2021

Speech Yuliia Tymoshenko´s 05.04.2021

Speech Yuliia Tymoshenko´s 08.04.2021

Speech Yuliia Tymoshenko´s 12.04.2021

Speech Yuliia Tymoshenko´s 13.04.2021

Speech Yuliia Tymoshenko´s 14.04.2021

Speech Yuliia Tymoshenko´s 15.04.2021

Speech Yuliia Tymoshenko´s 16.04.2021

Speech Yuliia Tymoshenko´s 20.04.2021

Speech Yuliia Tymoshenko´s 21.04.2021

Speech Yuliia Tymoshenko´s 26.04.2021

Speech Yuliia Tymoshenko´s 27.04.2021

Speech Yuliia Tymoshenko´s 28.04.2021

Speech Yuliia Tymoshenko´s 29.04.2021

Speech Yuliia Tymoshenko´s 02.05.2021

Speech Yuliia Tymoshenko´s 08.05.2021

Speech Yuliia Tymoshenko´s 12.05.2021

Speech Yuliia Tymoshenko´s 17.05.2021

Speech Yuliia Tymoshenko´s 18.05.2021

Speech Yuliia Tymoshenko´s 25.05.2021

Speech Yuliia Tymoshenko´s 27.05.2021

Speech Yuliia Tymoshenko´s 28.05.2021

Speech Yuliia Tymoshenko´s 31.05.2021

Speech Yuliia Tymoshenko´s 07.06.2021

Speech Yuliia Tymoshenko´s 09.06.2021

Speech Yuliia Tymoshenko´s 11.06.2021

Speech Yuliia Tymoshenko´s 14.06.2021

Speech Yuliia Tymoshenko´s 15.06.2021

Speech Yuliia Tymoshenko´s 16.06.2021

Speech Yuliia Tymoshenko´s 17.06.2021

Speech Yuliia Tymoshenko´s 18.06.2021

Speech Yuliia Tymoshenko´s 19.06.2021

Speech Yuliia Tymoshenko´s 20.06.2021

Speech Yuliia Tymoshenko´s 22.06.2021

Speech Yuliia Tymoshenko´s 24.06.2021

Speech Yuliia Tymoshenko´s 28.06.2021

Speech Yuliia Tymoshenko´s 01.07.2021

Speech Yuliia Tymoshenko´s 02.07.2021

Speech Yuliia Tymoshenko´s 05.07.2021

Speech Yuliia Tymoshenko´s 07.07.2021

Speech Yuliia Tymoshenko´s 08.07.2021

Speech Yuliia Tymoshenko´s 09.07.2021

Speech Yuliia Tymoshenko´s 13.07.2021

Speech Yuliia Tymoshenko´s 16.07.2021

Speech Yuliia Tymoshenko´s 23.07.2021

Speech Yuliia Tymoshenko´s 28.07.2021

Speech Yuliia Tymoshenko´s 29.07.2021

Speech Yuliia Tymoshenko´s 23.08.2021

Speech Yuliia Tymoshenko´s 24.08.2021

Speech Yuliia Tymoshenko´s 27.08.2021

Speech Yuliia Tymoshenko´s 29.08.2021

Speech Yuliia Tymoshenko´s 01.09.2021

Speech Yuliia Tymoshenko´s 05.09.2021

Speech Yuliia Tymoshenko´s 07.09.2021

Speech Yuliia Tymoshenko´s 09.09.2021

Speech Yuliia Tymoshenko´s 14.09.2021

Speech Yuliia Tymoshenko´s 20.09.2021

Speech Yuliia Tymoshenko´s 21.09.2021

Speech Yuliia Tymoshenko´s 22.09.2021

Speech Yuliia Tymoshenko´s 23.09.2021

Speech Yuliia Tymoshenko´s 24.09.2021

Speech Yuliia Tymoshenko´s 28.09.2021

Speech Yuliia Tymoshenko´s 29.09.2021

Speech Yuliia Tymoshenko´s 30.09.2021

Speech Yuliia Tymoshenko´s 03.10.2021

Speech Yuliia Tymoshenko´s 04.10.2021

Speech Yuliia Tymoshenko´s 05.10.2021

Speech Yuliia Tymoshenko´s 12.10.2021

Speech Yuliia Tymoshenko´s 14.10.2021

Speech Yuliia Tymoshenko´s 18.10.2021

Speech Yuliia Tymoshenko´s 20.10.2021

Section 4
AI and Its Applications in Education

Section 4 introduces the use of AI in the education sector and reviews different processes that governments should apply to appropriately and safely use AI in the educational sector. This chapter also explores the main uses and practices of AI in the education sector.

Chapter 16
Artificial Intelligence in Education as a Means to Personalize Learning

Ana María Lacárcel
Universidad de Murcia, Spain

ABSTRACT

Due to the undeniable increase in the impact that artificial intelligence systems have on numerous aspects of society, the teaching-learning process is increasingly influenced by these, producing the need to know the participating agents and applicable approaches for their implementation. Therefore, the main purpose of this chapter is to obtain an overview of the elements and challenges involved in the application of artificial intelligent devices in education. In this sense, the information presented below characterizes some of these systems through the way in which they personalize learning based on the peculiarities of the students and makes specific reference to the operation of some of them, such as the intelligent tutor system and exploratory learning environments.

INTRODUCTION

It is undeniable the fact that we live in an era in which both economy and society are globalised and linked to the improvement of technology and knowledge. In this sense, just as the typewriter evolved into a computer or mobile phones became smartphones, advances in science and technology have allowed everyday analogue objects to become true automaton products that allow people to solve problems and situations more quickly and efficiently (Livia & Kaku, 2013). It could be said that the globalized world in which we find ourselves in and the current technological revolution are focused on optimizing certain tasks and processes, both at an industrial, domestic and educational level by using technology. On a first look, this optimization and automation that has been referred to is one of the purposes of technologies based on Artificial Intelligence (AI from now on), by which computers and computer programs are capable in many cases, of learning and making decisions by themselves, even carrying out operations that, before

DOI: 10.4018/978-1-7998-9609-8.ch016

the appearance of these technologies, could only be developed by humans (Rouhiainen, 2018). This idea has involved the cohesion of different sciences and services into devices with certain functions or even, capable of performing several of them at the same time. Examples of this could be the incorporation of voice recognition, image or even augmented reality elements. In a generalized way, it seems that AI products that are currently available to most educational communities in developed countries are based on the use of support elements to provide support for problem solving, for example, smart assistants at home or custom tutors to learners (Yufei, 2020).

The global use of technology involves the collection and treatment of a great amount of users' data, which is currently generating a lot of controversy due to the fact that, on many occasions it is considered that citizens accept the use of their personal information because of the complicated and desperate moments such as be due to the COVID-19 pandemic (Ribeiro-Navarrete et al., 2021) because they tend to seek quick solutions to their problems because they have bigger concerns to address. As referenced by the United Nations Educational, Scientific and Cultural Organization (2021), hereinafter UNESCO, it seems logical to think that if technological development is accelerating globally and it presents a clear trend towards its incorporation in many areas of society, citizens must be prepared to assume the changes that this implies and therefore, government policies must be aimed at ensuring the technological capabilities of the population. The latter is necessarily linked to the educational system and hence, these policies and trends should provide and guarantee the resources to make this possible. In this sense, both governments and schools are increasingly paying more attention to developing programs and agreements that include AI products (Malik et al., 2019).

In general terms, as cited by the Organisation for Economic Co-operation and Developmen (2016), hereinafter OECD, the education of citizens must be aimed to an integral development of students, problem solving, collaborative work, and the development of communication skills, that is, towards the achievement of citizens capable of being above any form of AI and also of being able to improve the latter based on their own interests. Along with that, it is essential to highlight that the interest in the proper educational training of citizens should not reside in the fear of being replaced by some type of artificial intelligence that will make them lose their jobs, but should focus on developing skills that allow man to take the advantage of technology-rich environments, understand it and improve it (Arntz et al., 2016). A good approach to the use of these technologies could be the substitution of repetitive tasks within a certain job, allowing the person to dedicate their time to more specialized and creative activities that require it (Baker et al., 2019; Fahimirad & Kotamjani, 2018; UNESCO, 2021). Regarding education, an example could be the time saving that the AI would save a teacher to carry out the automatic correction of a multiple-choice exam and use the time that this task would have taken in preparing feedback tasks for each student according to the bugs reported by the program. In this sense, AI is expected to help teachers and promote the transformation of teaching models from knowledge transfer to knowledge construction (Holmes et al., 2018; Liua et al., 2021).

Although technological innovation could seem to be within the reach of any person or institution, being able to obtain a real benefit from it implies knowing how to use it and therefore, having received training that allows acquiring a good level of competence in relation to the use of technologies of information and communication, hereinafter ICT. In fact, analysis and reports from OECD in recent years has shown that more than 50% of adult population is only capable of performing the simplest computing tasks, such as browsing on the Internet or sending an email, since these subjects do not have the cognitive and necessary skills to take advantage of technology in a broad spectrum (OECD, 2016, 2020). At the socio-economic level, there have been numerous revolutions throughout history, marked mainly by the appearance of elements that modify the way man works. At present, and due to the undoubted scope of ICT, it is said that we are experiencing the fourth industrial revolution, marked by hyperconnectivity, the importance of Big Data or the inclusion of AI. In education something similar happens, after the appearance of the school, public education and mass education and taking Tedesco & Brunner (2004) as a reference, the hypothesis about the development of a new revolution is contemplated in which the relationship between the appearance of new resources linked to technological evolution and variations in training needs by citizens is unquestionable. However, and as it will be developed during this chapter, education is not exclusively due to the use of ICT, and much less that of AI products Thus, these should not be the only chosen guide of the teaching and learning process since in this it should prevail the formative action (UNESCO, 2021).

Assuming as a society the changes that have been mentioned above implies that citizens are able to face them and for this, skills training and personalization of learning will be essential. In fact, personalization of learning is one of the main applications of AI (Yufei, 2020) that will be covered in this chapter. In relation to the personalization of learning, later on special attention will be put on how the inclusion of AI affects the treatment of specific learning difficulties. It is important to highlight, taking as a reference the educational legislation from Spain, the fact that attention to diversity is a necessity that encompasses all educational stages and students. That is to say, it is about contemplating the diversity of the students as a principle and not as a measure that corresponds to the needs of a few. According to the latest reports made by UNESCO (2019a, 2021) the key conclusions for the creation of new AI policies could be summarised in the idea of considering it as a tool to avoid difficulties and barriers in education, and in which the treatment of learners with special educational needs has an important role. Viewed in this way, the creation of policies to regulate the implementation of AI should ensure the function related to life, work and education. The latter means that they must maximize the benefits and minimize the potential risks. Besides that, they should be focused on the global implication in the education field, their relation with the curricula and including the teacher learning. In fact, education and the developing of AI are hand in hand and while it is true that AI will likely replace repetitive and easy to automate jobs, educational system should take advantage of the implementation of AI to support disadvantaged groups of learners and remove the thought of its application as an element that saves human resources.

The objective of this paper is, firstly, to understand the ways in which AI can be applied in the area of education and secondly, its effects on the attention to diversity of students. In other words, it is intended to understand the way in which AI is applied to guarantee a personalized teaching-learning process to the educational needs of each individual student. Therefore, the present chapter approaches two main questions. On one hand, the identification of the possible fields of application of AI in education and the limitations and challenges that these include. On the other hand, the analysis of the contribution of AI systems to the personalization of the learning of students with specific learning difficulties. Consequently, to address these questions, a narrative review of the literature has been carried out based on the following terms: artificial intelligence in education, personalized learning, intelligent tutoring system (ITS) and exploratory learning environments (ELE). The databases consulted were PubMed, ScienceDirect, Web of Science and ACM Digital Library. Continuing the criteria to evaluate the literature from vom Brocke et al. (2015), the main standards to select the information have been the relevance, the representativeness in the field and the date. This methodology allows us to observe and study a lot of different aspects and examine a phenomenon in a general way in a given context and it has been chosen because it is intended to obtain an up-to-date vision on the state of the question (Guirao, 2015).

BACKGROUND

Artificial Intelligence in Education (AIEd)

In any country, education has characteristics and peculiarities that make the use of AI more complicated compared to developing it in any private company. The treatment of data from youngsters, the suitability of the predictions and the models used to do it (Saura, 2021a, 2021b), the suitable academic approaches or the effectiveness in the long term among others, could be some of the worrying factors about the implementation of AI in education (AIEd). In relation to educational practice, the personalization of learning to the characteristics of the students will favor the acquisition of meaningful learning, fundamental for the progressive consolidation of the contents worked at school (Ausubel, 1983).

In this paper, it is assumed the term intelligence as the characteristic of technology that has "the ability to adapt (modify responses appropriately for a particular situation) and the ability to learn (establish new knowledge and skills)" (Spector, 2018, p. 24). It is also important to consider that these technologies must be able to access the data with the purpose of extracting "meaningful and potentially useful information (data mining) as well as to the exploitation of such information in practical problems (decision support)" (Maglogiannis et al., 2007, p. 1). In the last idea resides an important contribution of the AI to pedagogical environments in which teachers could be assisted to make the more suitable learning and teaching decisions. The use of AI in Education has among its main purposes to use AI subset not only to give more time and computational resources but to make decisions that favour a given context through adapting contents and methodology. In this sense, AI takes many different forms and they are included in varied devices through technologies such as algorithms, machine learning, artificial networks and deep-learning approaches (Baker et al., 2019; UNESCO, 2021).

Focusing on the application of AI as an element of support and feedback element for students, its incorporation, organization and gathering information processes can respond to certain models that specify the relationship between the teaching and learning process and the AI system's knowledge and procedures (Ma et al., 2014). At this point, it is considered important to cite the ideas collected in Luckin et al. (2016) regarding the knowledge that the AI system must handle, which is grouped into the following models: "effective approaches to teaching (which is represented in a pedagogical model), the subject being learned (represented in the domain model) and the student (represented in the learner model)" (p.18). These are the three different components that could be related to the categories based on agents, that is, with the element or person taken into account to make certain decisions based on the knowledge obtained or held from them. Considering the ideas cited and represented in Alkhatlan & Kalita (2019), Gharehchopogh & Khalifelu (2011), Holmes et al. (2019), Luckin et al. (2016), Ma et al. (2014) and Woolf (2010), analyzing how these three models work (see figure 1) is essential to choose any type of AI system to apply it in education.

Firstly, the learner model is related among others to the previous student's experience, emotional state, background or abilities and this could be the one that is furthest from the teaching influence. It gathers information about students' performance, common errors, behaviour and skills to select the best modules of knowledge and the tutoring strategy at each moment. In this sense, according to Alkhatlan & Kalita (2019), this domain implies corrective, elaborative, strategy, diagnostic, assistance and evaluative techniques. At this point, the pedagogical or tutor model plays an important role because it is linked to methodology, techniques and effective approaches to teaching, for example, the way of designing projects and activities or the feedback characteristics. Nevertheless, the analysis carried out by a human tutor is approximate but not exact due to his limited capacity to evaluate absolutely all the aspects that influence the student's learning since it cannot be forgotten that among these aspects are included personal motivations and psycho-affective characteristics (Baker et al., 2010; Graesser, 2009, 2012a). In this way, AIEd could be an element to improve teaching practice in relation to the monitoring of specific aspects of the student's evolution and be able to purpose accurate teaching strategies.

Finally, the domain or expert model includes the subject contents needed to be learned normally presented by the educational curricula laws of each country. It includes the right organization and presentation of contents consistently with how the student works with respect to the other two models. Thus, making reference to the capacities of teachers to identify the strengths and weaknesses related to the content that each student possesses, the evaluation process constitutes a fundamental and limiting element. The different evaluation modalities that can be applied must unequivocally guarantee where the student is in the learning process and which are the elements that do not make him progress towards the acquisition of higher knowledge. In relation to these aspects, the progressive evaluation of difficulties through dialogue and daily work and progress is important (Graesser et al., 2012a) but at the same time it implies great difficulty because it includes the exhaustive control of the student's progression day-by-day.

Figure 1. Approaches to enhance personalized learning through artificial intelligence
Note. Own elaboration.

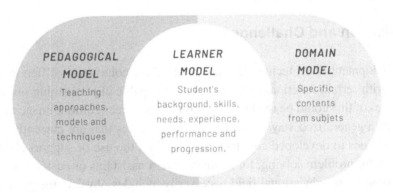

These three models are said to be a determining factor to implement AI in education. AI devices could consider them to process the knowledge through data algorithms, machine learning and deep learning, in order to capture and analyse the data to offer suitable feedback and suggestions. The most desirable situation would be that the AI device was able to analyze the student's needs, attitudes, learning pace, interests, performance and evolution among others in order to select and present the most appropriate contents and practices for the student (Graesser et al., 2012a; Woolf, 2010). Thus, in this chapter, it is considered essential to highlight that, in a personalized learning process enhanced by AI, considering the actions, answers, achievements and the response to feedback from learners could lead to the success of the approach. However, currently, achieving good indicators that ensure a good measurement of some of the characteristics and needs depends on the technological evolution to which AI systems are subjected is currently a challenge.

Nevertheless, there are other different approaches to classify AI tools for education. As cited by Baker et al. (2019), according to which agents of the participants in the teaching and learning process are the direct beneficiaries, the AIEd categories are the learner-facing approach, the teacher-facing appliances that help educators to perform and prepare teaching strategies and finally, system-facing tools which aim is facilitating the work of managers of schools, universities and educational organizations. However, UNESCO (2021) proposed that AI tools could be classified based on the needs that each application satisfies in each phase of the teaching and learning process. The four areas proposed are education management and delivery, learning and assessment, empowering teachers and enhancing teaching and lifelong learning. Thus, this way of working should guarantee information processing that allows it to be effectively integrated together with the student's prior knowledge. Therefore, in this idea among others, resides the importance of an adequate construction of the learner domain in which all its particularities are included (Moreno & Mayer, 2007).

For all the above, analyzing the previous ways in which the AI tools could be classified, it seems that the combination of several of these AI technologies approaches could suggest an inevitable improvement in the rest of the fields since the acquisition of knowledge does not only depend on a specific area or agent. This could be reflected in the application of teaching-facing tools that supposes less workload for teachers and more time to prepare classes, projects and generate better feedback and motivation to learners (Baker et al., 2019; UNESCO, 2021). Hence, it would inevitably involve personalizing the teaching and learning process through Intelligent Tutoring Systems (ITS) or Exploratory Learning Environments (ELE) among others (Salinas, 2004; UNESCO, 2021)

Areas of Application and Challenges

Nowadays, the development of AI technology has involved the cohesion of different sciences and services into devices with certain functions or in many cases, capable of performing several of them at the same time. Examples of this could be the incorporation of voice recognition, image or even augmented reality elements. In a generalized way, it seems that AI products that are currently available to most educational communities in developed countries are based on the use of support elements to evaluate and provide support for problem solving, for instance, smart assistants or custom tutors (Yufei, 2020). Hence, AI application in the educational field necessarily includes physical things (computers, tablets or other devices) and abstract ones (softwares, datasets or pedagogical methods) which must link previous experiences, outcomes and suitable responses and ssuggestions (Spector, 2018). As reflected in Fahimirad & Kotamjani (2018), Hwang (2014, 2020), Holmes et al. (2018), Liua et al. (2021), UNESCO (2021) and Yufei (2020), AI has been applied in the following areas within education, which in this chapter are listed and grouped into: (i) automatic grading system, (ii) tutoring intelligent systems (ITS), (iii) systems to personalize learning (ELE), (iv) augmented and virtual reality, (vi) intelligent campus and (vii) digital gamification. As it can be seen, and in line with the models cited in the previous section, the divisions of the application into areas differs in that which agent of the teaching and learning process is most favoured. Furthermore, depending on the literature consulted, some of these areas may even appear united in the same system; it will be shown at the end of the present section.

As it is cited in Hwang (2014), working and learning in a smart learning environment require several specifications in order to facilitate and enhance learning as well as empowering learners. These characteristics includes adaptive environment or interface, organised contents and personalised support and feedback. Firstly, the adaptive features are essential to enhanced personalized learning because this is necessarily connected with the peculiar characteristics of each student because "customized feedback is pivotal to produce learning" (Woolf, 2010, p. 268). Thus, highlighting the cultural and cognitive aspects of students is essential to understand the way in which they manage their knowledge (Coll, 1988). It is why this technology must offer specific support and interface focused on personal, emotional and psychological traits but considering the idea that these devices must be used with a temporary flexibility in which learners can manage work times and their own paths without pressure from the teacher or the AI system (Tabbers, 2002). Suitable feedback will be only ensured by gathering data from the entire process and making adjustments based on the results, performance and goals (Spector, 2018). Given all the all the above requirements, it is undeniable that all the applications of AI in education implies changes in the current academic settings which involves the conversion of teaching environments, resources and methods, the approach of the curricula and even school requirements and infrastructure (Holmes et al., 2018; Luckin, 2010; Liua et al., 2021). AI technologies approaches could suggest an inevitable improvement in the rest of the fields since the acquisition of knowledge does not only depend on a specific area or agent. This could be reflected in the application of teaching-facing tools that supposes less workload for teachers and more time to prepare classes, projects and generate better feedback and motivation to learners (Baker et al., 2019; UNESCO, 2021).

According to the literature and taking into account all the necessary changes, it is important to consider that implementing AI devices within education involves challenges to tackle related to the following areas: (i) hardware, software and organizational costs, (ii) teachers' training, (iii) a right inclusion of different rates of progress, (iv) ethical, legal and security issues relate with data, (v) inclusiveness approaches, (vi) an accurate approach of the curricula and (vii) didactic approach of AI devices (Baker et al., 2019; Fahimirad & Kotamjani, 2018; Holmes et al., 2018, 2019; Liua et al., 2021; UNESCO, 2019b, 2020, 2021).

The changes related to the curricula have a great significance because in many countries, the features, targets and results hinder and limit new up-to-date approaches related to adaptation processes and the inclusion of technological innovation in the teaching and learning (Merlano, 2009). As said before, this application requires the will of teachers to improve and actualise their tech-knowledge and change their teaching techniques among others. However, teachers' efforts will be insufficient without a massive and suitable inclusion of digital media equipment and an accurate organization within the schools. In fact, a "1:1 device-to-student ratio is favourable to the personalisation of learning" (Holmes et al., 2018, p. 48). However, it is suggested that the use of technology to improve learning processes could accelerate the pace of work of students without difficulties but weigh down those who do. Reason why it is a huge challenge. In this sense, the personalization opportunity provided by AI offers a great adaptation opportunity for students who need it.

Using AI to make decisions about the learning processes could be insufficient in order to personalize learning because with these techniques it could be difficult to make them contextualized. It is why "model-based adaptive systems can be far more flexible. They enable the rationale for each decision taken by the system to be made explicit and understandable by humans (and thus potentially applicable to classroom teaching)" (Luckin et al., 2016, p. 26). For instance, taking right decisions to ensure a didactic approach of AI instruments would involve considering the motivation, the mood, the reflection and debate skills and even real context situations which would mean a model based on learners. However, the participation of a human in the tutoring does not necessarily guarantee an adequate personalization of the learning since this implies the consideration of both aspects related to the content and the perception of the emotional states of the students (Grasser et al., 2012a). An example of poor human tutoring would be to pose more complex activities to students by assuming that they have understood certain previous content because when they have been asked if they have understood it, they have answered affirmatively.

Technology to Enhance Personalized Learning

Since the first AI tool called SHAKI appeared in the 1950s (Holmes et al., 2019; Spector, 2018), these systems have continuously improved to become part of the teaching and learning process (Ma et al., 2014). Carbonel's SCHOLAR system in 1970 and other representative example of these tools is BUGGY (Brown et al., 1978). In the 1990s, technologies designed to personalize learning were capable of including more information from the context of students for their tutoring (VanLehn et al., 2002). From 2000 to 2009 smarter tutors and tools with pedagogical skills such as Geogebra were developed. (García, 2011). In a more recent period, an acknowledgment of the status and context of students has been increasingly included as in the case of Go-Lab (2012) (Palau et al., 2020).

It is important to emphasize that rather than considering AIEd as an element to replace human interaction between teachers and students it should be taken as a way to improve and support the teaching and learning process, especially for disadvantaged groups. Moreover, in order to cover the specific characteristics from learners, including AI technology in education should have as a main goal to obtain systems and devices which are able to adapt to the particularities of the students (Shemshack & Spector, 2020). Thereupon, as it is exposed in Bernacki (2019) and referenced in Walkington & Bernacki (2020) and Hwang (2014, 2020), the wide use of tech devices at schools offers a suitable approach and path to enhance personalized learning through including learning platforms and devices to gather information from the learner's pace with the purpose of identifying weaknesses and strengths, which will be compared with those students from previous years in order to predict difficulties.

Nowadays, although personalized learning is hand in hand with the attention to learners with specific difficulties, there is not yet a definitive, clear and globally accepted term definition about personalized learning. In fact, personalized learning has existed for hundreds of years in the form of apprenticeship and mentoring. As educational technologies began to mature in the last half of the previous century, personalized learning took the form of intelligent tutoring systems (Shemshack & Spector, 2020). It could be said that the personalization of learning is a complex and inherent process in teaching practice which means that teachers are in charge of adapting the teaching and learning process to the particularities of each student, even if they do not present specific learning difficulties and they show high capacities. In addition, it seems that teachers have the full responsibility of this process because they inevitably take on the guiding role of teaching. However, a right personalisation depends on the learning goals and approach, the background or interests, context and the learning pace, the existence of different difficulties and finally the learning contents (Holmes et al., 2018; Hwang, 2014; Luckin, 2010; Shemshack & Spector, 2020; Spector, 2018; Woolf, 2010).

In relation to the above information and considering European education laws and specifically Education laws from Spain, the flexibility to adapt education to the diversity of aptitudes, interests, expectations and needs of the students, as well as the changes that the students and society undergo is one of the purposes of the education system. Bearing this in mind, it is up to the educational administrations to ensure the necessary resources to the students who require educational attention different from the ordinary, for presenting special educational needs derived from maturational delay, due to disorders of the language and communication development, attention or learning disorders, due to Serious ignorance of the language of learning, due to being in a situation of socio-educational vulnerability, due to their high intellectual capacities, due to having late entry to the educational system or due to personal conditions or school history. They must be able to achieve the maximum possible development of their personal capacities and, in all cases, the general objectives established for all students.

The Ethics of AI

It is well-known that that AI is capable of transforming societies, cultures, day-to-day communication habits, and even educational practices (Saura et al., 2021c). In fact, people tend to have electronic devices interconnected with each other and social networks to make life easier over the Internet, which also allows them to collect information from both work-related actions and personal life. It is true that this information allows improvements in the quality and efficiency of AI devices and platforms, but compromises the privacy of users (Ribeiro-Navarrete et al., 2021; Saura et al., 2021a). In any case, the management of private information about users must be considered as a great challenge to overcome in order to guarantee the human rights of users due to the huge amount of data sets involved. As referenced in a Preliminary study on the technical and legal aspects relating to the desirability of a standard-setting instrument on the ethics of artificial intelligence (UNESCO, 2019c), the implementation of AI must be accompanied by ethical design. At this point, it is considered important to stand out that, nowadays, the private business tends to control AI platforms, systems and devices and even if governments controlled them, establishing a specific worldwide law setting compatible with internationally agreed human rights could be necessary to ensure a fair governance. In fact, one of the main concerns in relation to the ethical use of AI both in education and other fields, is not the great accumulation of information necessary to obtain a good performance of AI, but the correct and ethical use (Janssen et al., 2020) of that information and obtaining approaches that guarantee the benefit for all citizens without any type of discrimination and economic pursuits guaranteed by guaranteeing academic freedom (UNESCO, 2021). In this way, "in contrast to fast technological advances, regulations evolve slowly, causing a loophole in the legislation in different industries (such as digital marketing user's privacy based on cookies data)" (Saura et al., 2021a) which causes the slowdown of the application of said technological advances and specifically AI in public entities.

Ensure privacy especially concerns parents in education since it will be inevitable that in a certain way, the characteristics of the AI algorithms will contain preferences of their creators (Baker & Smith, 2019). In this sense, currently although the General Data Protection Regulation of the European Commission currently controls the gathering of specific and essential information, not all the citizens have the necessary knowledge to understand and manage the permissions they give related to the treatment of their personal information (Saura et al., 2021b). As referenced in Ribeiro-Navarrete et al. (2021), the devices that collect the user's personal information must provide complete information on the conditions of use and storage of the data. To sum up, the general use of AI in society must guarantee security and equal conditions and it is a booming debate in which many governments and international organizations such as UNESCO or OECD (UNESCO, 2019a).

MAIN FOCUS OF THE CHAPTER

This section discusses specific AI tools to describe the usefulness of both ITS and ELE systems to personalize learning. We are going to refer to certain particularities in relation to the modelling system they use without a detailed and specific analysis of these models. Over the years, the evolution of AI techniques has led to several AI technologies classifications related to the agents involved in the learning and teaching process. One of the approaches takes the step-by-step learning in which the knowledge and feedback are presented to the students respecting a predefined sequence of steps based on the decisions previously made and specific needs regarding the contents and activities presented (Holmes et al., 2019). The systems that work in this way are called Intelligent Tutoring system (ITS) and tend to offer a predesigned pathway by AI to tackle the students' progress and level to achieve a personal treatment and adapt the teaching and learning process to their specific needs (Gharehchopogh & Khalifelu, 2011, Alkhatlan & Kalita, 2019). Another interesting focus is using Exploratory Learning Environments (ELE) in which students play the main role in the construction of the knowledge and the system only acquires the role of guide in this process by offering a specific atmosphere which includes automated guidance and feedback based on the information gathering by AI (UNESCO, 2021).

The main difference between these two systems is that ELE offers a learning environment in which students are able to explore and discover, leave aside a purely rote learning, participate in an environment in which there is no single way of acting because they prevail the individual differences. In short, the main objective is that the inquiry learning guides the student's knowledge (Bruner, 1961). Student feedback is not based solely on the veracity of their answers but focuses on the general process followed until reaching that type of answer (Amershi & Conati, 2006, 2009; Ben-Naim et al., 2008) as well as the interaction with the system.

Intelligent Tutoring Systems

Regarding to achieve a flexible system, ITS area embraces the three models cited in previous sections in which the learner, the specific knowledge and contents and teacher methods are taken into account to achieve personalized learning (Gharehchopogh & Khalifelu, 2011). Regarding the definition of ITS, it seems interesting to highlight the contributions of Ma et al. (2014) who include as one of the functions of these systems "offering impulses to provoke cognitive, motivational or metacognitive changes" (p. 2). As a consequence, in order to achieve an effective approach of ITS to personalize learning, an adequate interconnection between the student, tutor and domain models is necessary because in the same way that the learner domain acts as a continuous source of information through gathering static and dynamic qualities of students, this is used by the rest of the domains to present the learning as well as the different tutoring strategies. Similarly, the learners' performance determines the difficulty of the knowledge presented and it will be used to change the working guidelines of the rest of the domains (Alkhatlan & Kalita, 2018). Regarding personal circumstances, students' mood directly affects their learning process and academic results by modifying students' attention and motivations. In fact, the content that generates positive emotions, generally will have the undivided attention of students and negative emotions generally reduce the motivation (Baker et al., 2010; Bower, 1992; Pekrun, 2014). It is why a system must collect personal and emotional information from users by specific devices and try to hold a continuous interaction with the student regarding the emotion detected (Alkhatlan & Kalita, 2019; Woolf, 2010).

It could seem that the decision-making process could undoubtedly be carried out in a more efficient way by an expert human tutor in his field than by any computer tool, whatever its student modeling strategy is. However, there are certain limitations in the perception of human tutors that have nothing to do with their mastery of the content they teach (Graesser et al., 2012a). It could be said that the pedagogical strategies applied by a human tutor are limited and hence, the personalization could be limited.

In fact, some structures related to learning have been identified (Litman et al., 2006; Shah et al., 2002) as favourable in working with intelligent tutors, these are those related to the establishment of a content organization in relation to an adequate and adapted sequence of activities and the detailed recording of misconceptions. These are essential in the personalization of learning by intelligent tutors because it involves the presentation of the problem by the tutor, an initial answer by the learner, feedback on possible initial failures, an extensive dialogue or debate between the tutor and the student and a final evaluation on whether the student really has understood it or not (Graesser et al., 2012a). This sequence of steps is developed at the same time the student builds knowledge and its exhaustive follow-up and compliance by a human tutor is almost impossible in a conventional class with more than one student because this would imply the detailed tracking of all the student's states of knowledge and their variation over time (Graesser et al., 2009).

It seems clear that taking the student's domain as a reference is essential to address the students' doubts, however, taking into account the specific knowledge about the subject (contents domain), the student's abilities in relation to the problem to be solved, as well as the strategies selected to address the problem, allows the creation of a much more successful student model. These three areas were considered to design Andes tutoring system approach and offer an immediate interaction through a Procedural Helper and a Conceptual Helper. This system uses a probabilistic data analysis based on the resolution strategies previously adopted by the students to help them through offering adaptive clues (Gertner et al., 1998, Albacete & VanLehn, 2000). In this way, it collects information on how to solve problems and analyses it probabilistically by a Bayesian Network to identify the next strategies that the students are going to adopt (Gertner et al., 1998), but it does not go further with the analysis of specific personal circumstances of each student, such as the need to consult a bibliography, or complementary books or certain specific difficulties.

The Procedural area of Andes provides specific steps to solve problems through asking learners their objectives within the problem solving that is related to a quantitative analysis of data. In this sense, it is important to cite the Conceptual Helper area of Andes whose main purpose is improving the learners' performance related to the analysis of psychic problems through a qualitative perspective. Hence, this area tries to connect student and subject domain by identifying the areas of knowledge that the student has not acquired yet and, therefore, have led him to make this mistake (Albacete & VanLehn, 2000). This last quality is precisely the one that is considered of greatest importance in the learning personalization process offered by this system, since it not only allows to correct misconceptions of each student, but also offers a guide so that the student can connect some acquaintances with others gradually. To achieve this connection and find out what the student's intentions are, after detecting wrong answers, Andes offers a dialogue through incomplete sentences that the student has to complete and that establishes a connection between the knowledge he has and the future decision he is going to make. regarding the decision of the problem. In addition, based on these responses, the system will be able to offer the student new learning pills or reminder lessons with specific knowledge (Albacete & VanLehn, 2000; VanLehn et al., 2005).

Up to this point, reference has been made to the individualization of the student in relation to their particularities and personal difficulties, however, there are systems that have tried to personalize learning from a different approach in which specific models are sought for the treatment of certain groups of students, that is, students who share a number of specific characteristics, such as the age and gender (Arroyo, 2006, 2014). Taking into account these types of characteristics and even other difficulties favours, the development of cognitive strategies constitutes a fundamental aspect in the motivation of students and the improvement of their cognitive abilities (Coll, 1988; Korkman & Metin, 2021). In this sense, the self-regulated learning that these systems should offer must reflect personal curiosities (Wells & Arauz, 2005).

AnimalWatch is an ITS focus on mathematical problems about real situations and contexts that provides different exercises based on a probabilistic study of student progress regarding basic contents. It is oriented to elementary school students and its knowledge modules are animated and focused on different endangered or invasive animal species (Beck & Woolf, 2000, Beal et al., 2000). One of these main purposes is improving the motivation and performance of certain groups of students regarding mathematics (Arroyo et al., 2006, 2020) through characterization with machine learning using the Andes system which works with information about students, topic, problem and content. It is important to highlight the gender approach to enhance girls' self-esteem. Accordingly, the system considers the gender and previous performance of learners, the specific difficulty of the subject and problems, the necessary skills to performance, the number of prior mistakes and attempts and the results regarding previous hints offered to this student or to another student who shares certain characteristics with the aforementioned within the same model domain (Beck & Woolf, 2000). During the trials to design this system, learners were divided into two specific groups regarding gender and cognitive development analysed through a computer-based Piagetian test. With this, and depending on the specific type of each student, it was analyzed which type of clues was most beneficial for each type of student based on their progress after receiving the feedback. Specifically, it was found that the simple clues, identified as low symbolic hints, were more useful for students with low cognitive abilities and male students (Arroyo et al., 2006, 2020). Thus, according to the characteristics of the system, customization based on gender could be offered, which would allow the acquisition of different approaches such as the one shown in Beal et al. (2000) to enhance the performance of the girl in mathematics through an accurate assessment of students' performance and empower their self-esteem.

A similar approach is taken into account in Wayang outpost cited in Arroyo et al. (2006), a geometry tutor that takes advantage of offering real context problems and graphic elements and other multimedia gadgets (imagen and sound) which are identified to be a key factor to improve the students' experience, motivation and comprehension of math topics. In this intelligent tutor, the inclusion of graphic elements such as geometric diagrams is logical due to the direct relationship that these have with the subject, specifically geometry problems. Before starting to solve problems, students' spatial skills, math knowledge and skills and geometry knowledge were considered. The novelty of this tutor is that is able to offer classical text hints and visual ones through images and sounds. These hints tend to be related to real problems, that helps students to apply practical math skills to solving real-life problems such as the calculation of covering material necessary for building a floor or ceiling under construction. In relation to studies on its usefulness in improving learning, these have focused on evaluating up to what level, visual feedback is more or less adequate than that which is carried out solely through text and to be able to relate the types of clues with the greatest or least progress of students in relation to the content presented by the platform. In this sense, the gender, the math skills and the spatial cognition influences the learning process and hence, the characteristics of the interactions with students (Arroyo, 2000). In relation to the learning personalization process, this tutor considers two of the student's personal skills related to the domain model, for example skills regarding the subject and another related to the learner model, such as gender. However, personal and individual students' circumstances are not taken into consideration.

Analyzing the results included in Arroyo et al. (2006) regarding Animalwatch and Wayang outpost show that the consideration of the student's cognition and gender are related to the specific use and interaction with the intelligent tutor. The experimental investigations carried out showed that the improvement of instruction and learning outcomes is linked to the improvement and work with the student model. In addition, it is emphasized that it is essential to consider pedagogical approaches, included as described in the previous sections, in the methodological model in particular. Regarding the latter, and especially in relation to science subjects, a connection must be established between the qualitative characteristics of the students and the contents that a priori have a quantitative nature. This last idea asks the fact that there is a correlation between some cognitive particularities of students, which directly influence their response to certain characteristics of ITS.

Previously, reference has been made to the importance of collecting the characteristics of the students in relation to three systems that work with a subject with numerical content, such as mathematics. However, looking at UNESCO (2019a) related to the literacy of the world population like a weapon to improve the global society, it is worth highlighting some smart tutors who support this purpose through the use of technology. Nevertheless, the difficulty of personalizing learning goes further for tutors who must collect information through voice and speech recognition. An example of this situation are reading tutors which tend to have the purpose of making the student domain through measuring skills such as students' reading comprehension. In this sense, evaluating how students access and reproduce knowledge is complicated, it is not about analyzing whether a numerical result is correct or not, in this type of systems, although the answer is fixed, the feedback that must be offered is based in particular nuances of speech aloud (Beck et al., 2005).

Referring to systems that work with non-mathematical content, LISTEN and TuinLEC are ITS which help to improve oral reading through graphical and spoken hints to ensure the students' feedback and based on working with reading texts respectively. Concerning again to the personalization of learning, LISTEN only works with the characteristics of the student's voice, but does not allow the introduction of specific difficulties such as having dyslexia. Moreover, it is important to highlight that reading tutors have to present the information, a text to read, fractionally to ensure the right analysis and feedback. This system uses a very simple feedback based on the size of the words in relation to the tone used by the student, green or red colours to correct the text read as well as graphic elements that highlight words that have not been read yet. Apart from that, this type of ITS considers the interaction of the student with the step-by-step system through the silences of the learner, the reading time of each text, as well as the number of times the mouse is clicked (Mostow, 2012). The procedure included in TuinLEC is different since it analyzes whether students have understood the text from multiple-choice questions, taking into account the times the student requests to reread the text, as well as the way in which the student searches the text to answer the questions. The system that incorporates TuinLEC allows to record the reading times, the specific paragraphs that the student has needed to re-read and the successes and failures in comprehension questions. In fact, in this tutor, the students choose if they want to receive help during the execution of the tasks or not (Vidal-Abarca et al., 2014). In short it is a system which offers different text to practice reading skills many times that gathers information only from step-by-step students' performance.

The central idea on which the design of these tutors revolves is the ability of students to be able to ask reflective questions about their own learning. In this sense, AutoTutor is based on the simulation of reflective conversations through a simple language simulating those that a student should have with their human tutor. This tutor works with a set of responses associated with the different tasks or processes. At this point, when any explanation is required from the students, the system checks if the answer or explanation is complete, checking the list of pre-established answers has been completed to a greater or lesser extent. In this paper, one of the great utilities found in this system is the instant and automatic correction of errors as a human tutor would do by a using natural language and the ability of interpreting misconceptions (Graesser et al., 2005, 2012a). Some of the research carried out shows that the practice offered by AutoTutor is halfway between the situation that would occur with a human tutor and the learning situation that would occur if the student only learned from a textbook. That is, the tutor does not improve the conditions offered by a human tutor, but it does improve the student's reflective capacity about the contents (Graesser & Olde, 2003). It has been tested numerous times in order to obtain a relationship between learning and the emotions of students while studying literacy. The sensations and emotions experienced by the students during the work with the interactive tutor collected through language were considered fundamental. The creators of this system aim to create a virtual tutor capable of detecting all the student's emotions and acting on them (Graesser et al., 2012b).

Exploratory Learning Environments

ELEs offer an open learning environment whose purpose is that the students are able to adopt the fundamental role of their learning process through targeted information offered by the system through verbal and non-verbal interactions (Moreno & Mayer, 2007). It is at this point where the importance of gathering information about the user lies before and during the performance of tasks associated with the environment. Some research shows that using strategies of gathering information such as self-explanations improve the student's comprehension of specific knowledge and the student-system interaction (Coll, 1988; Conati & Merten, 2007). In order to difference this kind of systems from ITS, it is essential to stand out that the functioning of the ELE depends directly on the activity that the student performs with the environment, eliminating step-by-step organization of contents, meaning the student is the determining element on the learning rhythm offered by the system and therefore, the determining factor in the sequence of materials that are presented to him. In addition, the system must offer an environment that can be explored by learners and offer complementary materials based on the different content areas. One of the purposes of this type of environment is contributing to generate and build a meaningful learning through personalized feedback and reflection (Moreno & Mayer, 2007). The challenges offered to learners will make them able to select, discriminate and analyze that information, which indeed will allow them to include it effectively with the previous information they already have on that content. In this sense, these types of environments provide a great and advantageous scenario where, without considering rigid and previously structured processes, the student can experience a discovery directed precisely by their own needs and strengths. In fact, previous experiences with the interaction with these interactive environments, as could be Herman-the-Bug, an interactive agent to experiment with plant growth, has revealed that students perceive knowledge as more interesting (Moreno et al., 2001).

Point&Query System is usually encompassed as an ITS, in this paper it has been considered as a global and exploratory learning environment as it is focused on the learning inquiry activities and not simply containing the sequence of activities that are guided and proposed to the student at the same time clues to help you with resolution are offered. The main purpose of this system is to train the student so that he can ask questions that involve deep reasoning about the content he is working on through interaction with a virtual tutor. In fact, in this system it is assumed that "the learning environment must have possibilities that put the student in a state of cognitive imbalance, but there must also be a scaffolding of skills to formulate questions by social agents (human or computer)" (Graesser et al., 2005, p.3). In the experiences collected in Graesser et al. (2005, 2012a) it was found that students who had received instruction by Point & Query tutor, were able to ask questions and reason more deeply than those who had received conventional instruction, which led students to remember more content. The basis of the creation of this system is that the acquisition of knowledge is promoted to a greater extent through challenges and obstacles to be solved. The latter promotes deeper reasoning and responses.

Century is an online private platform that offers contents about mathematics, science and English language which, in the words of its founder, was developed with the main purpose of supplying the educational needs observed at public schools in England. This platform uses AI to offer a personalized learning experience to learners and support teachers' reflection and analysis through reporting about the entire process in real time. It seems easy to use because the schools change their contents in the Century system, whose AI methods organize it in adaptive lessons based on diagnostic and initial evaluation tests and the learner's progression. A long-term learning is the objective of the service that learns and adapts its knowledge about the student pace and the context using basic principles of neuroscience and science of learning. Besides, its AI technology algorithm assesses what is the best moment to learn each content based on learner's progress, needs and strengths (Century-Tech Limited, 2021). Taking into account the difficulty of finding studies on the usefulness and effectiveness of private platforms and taking the analysis of said company as a reference, it is said that due to the fact that teachers can adapt teaching process based on data mining and using specific connexion methods to presents the knowledge, the students tend to improve their performance and teachers' workload is reduced.

iTalk2Learn system through Fractions lab platform and Math Whizz integrates structured practice, exploratory and oriented learning for children aged 8-12 years old. It facilitates interaction in different modalities including speech and interactive representations through detecting children's speech and interactions to solve math fractions problems (Grawemeyer et al., 2015). The main purpose of this project is using machine learning models that exploit the data obtained from the performance of the students (student's speech key words, the student's performance, the behaviour regarding the software and the interaction) for the creation of exploratory adaptive and animated sequence of activities to enhance intelligent tutoring systems in order to integrate speech feedback. In fact, the sequence of activities is presented differently based on students' personal progress through both procedural and exploratory knowledge. Moreover, regarding the explicit feedback offered, the platform informs learners using images, verbally and textually and it is the reason why voice recognition methods are the main area to develop in the system. Besides, final feedback is offered because suggestions to students in relation to a particular step and integrated and continued interactions are included. The company developed several trials to perfect the software and it was found that, in particular, the multiple representations based on real contexts helped students to see math fractions more easily and improve their performance (Rub, 2014). Moreover, it is also important to highlight that the system asks students to reflect aloud on their strategies (Grawemeyer et al., 2015). Therefore, after describing the blocks that the system includes and are considered essential for the personalization of learning, it is believed that the information offered about the iTalk2Learn system and the mechanisms used in the collection and processing of data related to learners could be sufficient to be able to affirm that it is offered a personalization of learning that could guarantee the particular needs of certain students is offered, fostering a solid knowledge through the tasks it displays.

Sometimes, the line between the systems described above (ITS and ELE) is so fine that the combination between the two is inevitable. In this sense, ECHOES is a good example presented as a role-play environment designed to meet the needs in relation to communication and social skills and specific and repetitive behaviour of children with autism. This system has been included in this paper, not because of the use of AI for the personalization of learning but as an element that could be improved through the use of machine learning to make decisions. Hence, the importance that these types of environments acquire in relation to the difficulties that people on the autism spectrum present is that on the one hand, an adapted interactive environment (ELE) is established in which students do not have to constantly struggle with their difficulties to establish social and on the other hand, the virtual tutor that these include (ITS) allows to tackle the repetitive behaviors and difficulties that students present individually. In this system, the agents of conversation and voice recognition play an essential role in the improvement of communication difficulties (Bernardini et al., 2014).

SOLUTIONS AND RECOMMENDATIONS

It is worth mentioning that analyzing the different technical ways in which algorithms work and AI tools collect user information must be studied and improved in order to increase the usefulness of these services. However, a detailed study on what are the necessary elements to take into account in relation to all those involved in the teaching and learning process is also essential. It is necessary to search for systems that can monitor the student and obtain relevant information about their use of the system (Ma et al., 2014) but without these constituting dissuasive or annoying elements in themselves, which also annoy the student and take him away from his concentration regarding the contents worked on.

From a general perspective, the desirable situation would be to create systems capable of collecting the student's personal information and that works fully with this domain. Identifying the specific or special educational needs of students is paramount, as it is in educational practice with real tutors. The latter are in charge of fully adapting their practice to these particularities as established by educational legislation. In this way, the teaching practice does not base its actions on probabilistic situations, but rather personalizes the attention to the students in the entirety. In relation to this last aspect and after examining the consulted literature, it could be affirmed that the use of AI in education could constitute an element of improvement of teaching practice (Graesser et al., 2012a; Ma et al., 2014) that provides support to the teacher to detect learning rhythms, difficulties and progress and that at the same time constitutes a tool that guarantees continuous feedback under the teacher's supervision but taking advantage of the information storage and processing capacity of computer systems. It would be an accurate way of avoiding human errors in which the learner is assumed to have understood the feedback provided (Vidal-Abarca et al., 2014).

FUTURE RESEARCH DIRECTIONS

In this chapter some of the elements that must be considered in the choice of AI systems for education are in relation to the particularities of the educational context and learners in which they will be applied. In this sense, future researchers should focus on doing a deeper and major revision of literature in order to make a description of the minimum and necessary elements which are essential for achieving personalized learning based on the particularities of each student through considering academic and emotional aspects. Analyzing previous experiences on the application of AI to personalize learning would also be necessary in order to obtain new perspectives on the application of technology to specific learning difficulties such as dyslexia, dyscalculia, attention deficit or borderline intelligence. However, it is considered that a vast technological improvement would be necessary to allow the detection of the instantaneous needs of the students through their performances in class or during the completion of tasks. This would imply a total monitoring of the activity of learners that sometimes some sectors of society would reject. Following this idea, as mentioned above, ethical considerations are fundamental to the implementation of AI in education and the consecution of a total didactic approach of technology. Finally, an in-depth research approach could be carried out to compare the application of an ITS or ELE to several groups that share the same specific difficulty or the application of several examples of systems to certain types of students.

CONCLUSION

As an overview, the aim of this paper is to accumulate new knowledge on AI and the identification of contextual factors and features of the implementation of AI in education through a non-exhaustive study of how this implementation would help to treat specific learning difficulties through a personalized learning process. The effectiveness in the application of educational systems managed by artificial intelligence could be related to how systems are able to characterize students through the specific domains cited in this chapter. The cognitive strategies used by each student are very complex and are related to the cognitive state in which they find themselves, notably influenced by their feelings and personal circumstances and disabilities. Therefore, just as in the conventional school, human tutors must consider all the personal circumstances of the student in their attempt to achieve an adequate personalization of learning. Thus, the intelligent systems referred to in this chapter should be capable of improving this personalization, and in no case offer random content that is common to all students within the same group. However, it is noteworthy that ethics and privacy are two leading factors that still need to be regulated since the implementation of AIEd involves using a large number of learners' data. Technology must add to the learning process, but never penalize it.

REFERENCES

Albacete, P. L., & VanLehn, K. (2000). The Conceptual Helper: An Intelligent Tutoring System for Teaching Fundamental Physics Concepts. In G. Gauthier, C. Frasson, & K. VanLehn (Eds.), *Intelligent Tutoring Systems. ITS 2000* (pp. 564–573). Lecture Notes in Computer Science. Springer. doi:10.1007/3-540-45108-0_60

Alkhatlan, A., & Kalita, J. (2019). Intelligent tutoring systems: A comprehensive historical survey with recent developments. *International Journal of Computer Applications, 181*(43).

Amershi, S., & Conati, C. (2006). Automatic recognition of learner groups in exploratory learning environments. In M. Ikeda, K.D. Ashley, & T.W. Chan (Eds.), *International Conference on Intelligent Tutoring Systems* (pp. 463-472). Springer. 10.1007/11774303_46

Amershi, S., & Conati, C. (2009). Combining unsupervised and supervised classification to build user models for exploratory learning environments. *Journal of Educational Data Mining, 1*(1), 18-71. doi:10.5281/zenodo.3554659

Arntz, M., Gregory, T., & Zierahn, U. (2016). The Risk of Automation for Jobs in OECD Countries: A Comparative Analysis. *OECD Social, Employment and Migration Working Papers, 189*, 1-34. doi:10.1787/5jlz9h56dvq7-en

Arroyo, I., Beck, J. E., Woolf, B. P., Beal, C. R., & Schultz, K. (2000). Macroadapting Animalwatch to gender and cognitive differences with respect to hint interactivity and symbolism. In G. Gauthier, C. Frasson, & K. VanLehn (Eds.), *Intelligent Tutoring Systems. ITS 2000* (pp. 574–583). Springer. doi:10.1007/3-540-45108-0_61

Arroyo, I., Muldner, K., Burleson, W., Woolf, B., & Cooper, D. (2009). Designing affective support to foster learning, motivation and attribution. In D. Dicheva & S.D. Craig (Eds.), *Closing the Affective Loop in Intelligent Learning Environments Workshop at the 14th International Conference on Artificial Intelligence in Education*. IOS Press.

Arroyo, I., Woolf, B. P., & Beal, C. R. (2006). Addressing cognitive differences and gender during problem solving. International Journal of Technology, Instruction. *Cognition and Learning, 4*, 31–63.

Arroyo, I., Woolf, B. P., Burelson, W., Muldner, K., Rai, D., & Tai, M. (2014). A multimedia adaptive tutoring system for mathematics that addresses cognition, metacognition and affect. *International Journal of Artificial Intelligence in Education, 24*(4), 387–426. doi:10.100740593-014-0023-y

Ausubel, D. (1983). Teoría del aprendizaje significativo. *Fascículos de CEIF, 1*, 1-10.

Baker, R. S., D'Mello, S. K., Rodrigo, M. M. T., & Graesser, A. C. (2010). Better to be frustrated than bored: The incidence, persistence, and impact of learners' cognitive–affective states during interactions with three different computer-based learning environments. *International Journal of Human-Computer Studies, 68*(4), 223–241. doi:10.1016/j.ijhcs.2009.12.003

Baker, T., Smith, L., & Anissa, N. (2019). *Educ-AI-tion rebooted? Exploring the future of artificial intelligence in schools and colleges*. Nesta.

Beal, C., Woolf, B., Beck, J., Arroyo, I., Schultz, K., & Hart, D. (2000). Gaining confidence in mathematics: Instructional technology for girls. In R. Robson (Ed.), *International Conference on Mathematics/Science Education and Technology* (pp. 99-6106). Association for the Advancement of Computing in Education.

Beck, J. E., & Woolf, B. P. (2000). High-level student modeling with machine learning. In G. Gauthier, C. Frasson, & K. VanLehn (Eds.), *Intelligent Tutoring Systems. ITS 2000* (pp. 584–593). Lecture Notes in Computer Science. Springer. doi:10.1007/3-540-45108-0_62

Ben-Naim, D., Marcus, N., & Bain, M. (2008, September). Visualization and analysis of student interaction in an adaptive exploratory learning environment. In *International workshop on intelligent support for exploratory environment, EC-TEL*.

Bernacki, M. L. (2019, March). Development, Sustainment, and Scaling of a Learning Analytics, Prediction Modeling and Digital Student Success Initiative. In *Proceedings of the 10th Annual Learning Analytics and Knowledge Conference Workshop on Sustainable and Scalable Learning Analytics Solutions*. Society of Learning Analytics Research.

Bernardini, S., Porayska-Pomsta, K., & Smith, T. J. (2014). ECHOES: An intelligent serious game for fostering social communication in children with autism. *Information Sciences, 264,* 41–60. doi:10.1016/j. ins.2013.10.027

Bower, G. H. (1992). How might emotions affect learning? In S.-Å. Christianson (Ed.), *The handbook of emotion and memory: Research and theory* (pp. 3–31). Lawrence Erlbaum Associates, Inc.

Brown, J. S., & Burton, R. R. (1978). Diagnostic models for procedural bugs in basic mathematical skills. *Cognitive Science, 2*(2), 155–192. doi:10.120715516709cog0202_4

Bruner, J. S. (1961). The act of discovery. *Harvard Educational Review, 4,* 21–32.

Brunner, J. J. (2001). Globalización, educación, revolución tecnológica. *Perspectivas, 31*(2), 139–153.

Century-Tech Limited. (2021). *Century.* https://www.century.tech

Coll, C. (1988). Significado y sentido en el aprendizaje escolar. Reflexiones en torno al concepto de aprendizaje significativo. *Infancia y Aprendizaje, 11*(41), 131–142. doi:10.1080/02103702.1988.10822196

Conati, C., & Merten, C. (2007). Eye-tracking for user modeling in exploratory learning environments: An empirical evaluation. *Knowledge-Based Systems, 20*(6), 557–574. doi:10.1016/j.knosys.2007.04.010

Fahimirad, M., & Kotamjani, S. S. (2018). A review on application of artificial intelligence in teaching and learning in educational contexts. *International Journal of Learning and Development, 8*(4), 106–118. doi:10.5296/ijld.v8i4.14057

García, M. D. M. (2011). *Evolución de actitudes y competencias matemáticas en estudiantes de secundaria al introducir Geogebra en el aula* [Doctoral dissertation, Universidad de Almería]. Repositorio digital de documentos en educación matemática. http://funes.uniandes.edu.co/1768/

Gertner, A. S., Conati, C., & VanLehn, K. (1998). Procedural help in Andes: Generating hints using a Bayesian network student model. *AAAI/IAAI, 1998,* 106-11.

Gharehchopogh, F. S., & Khalifelu, Z. A. (2011). Using intelligent tutoring systems in instruction and education. In *2nd International Conference on Education and Management Technology* (pp. 250-254). IACSIT Press.

Graesser, A. C., Conley, M. W., & Olney, A. M. (2012a). Intelligent tutoring systems. In S. Graham & K. Harris (Eds.), *Applications to Learning and Teaching* (pp. 451–473). APA Educational Psychology Handbook. American Psychological Association.

Graesser, A. C., D'Mello, S. K., Hu, X., Cai, Z., Olney, A., & Morgan, B. (2012b). AutoTutor. In P. M. McCarthey & C. Boonthum-Denecke (Eds.), *Applied natural language processing: Identification, Investigation and Resolution* (pp. 169–187). IGI Global. doi:10.4018/978-1-60960-741-8.ch010

Graesser, A. C., D'Mello, S. K., & Person, N. (2009). Meta-knowledge in tutoring. In D. J. Hacker, J. Dunlosky, & A. C. Graesser (Eds.), *Handbook of Metacognition in Education* (pp. 361–382). Taylor & Francis.

Graesser, A. C., McNamara, D. S., & VanLehn, K. (2005). Scaffolding deep comprehension strategies through Point&Query, AutoTutor, and iSTART. *Educational Psychologist, 40*(4), 225–234. doi:10.120715326985ep4004_4

Graesser, A. C., & Olde, B. A. (2003). How does one know whether a person understands a device? The quality of the questions the person asks when the device breaks down. *Journal of Educational Psychology, 95*(3), 524–536. doi:10.1037/0022-0663.95.3.524

Grawemeyer, B., Gutierrez-Santos, S., Holmes, W., Mavrikis, M., Rummel, N., Mazziotti, C., & Janning, R. (2015). Talk, tutor, explore, learn: Intelligent tutoring and exploration for robust learning. In C. Conati, N. Heffernan, A. Mitrovic, & M. F. Verdejo (Eds.), *Artificial Intelligence in Education. 7th International Conference, AIED 2015* (pp. 917-918). Springer.

Guirao Goris, S. J. A. (2015). Utilidad y tipos de revisión de literatura. *SciELO Analytics, 9*(2), 0. Advance online publication. doi:10.4321/S1988-348X2015000200002

Holmes, W., Anastopoulou, S., Schaumburg, H., & Mavrikis, M. (2018). *Technology-enhanced personalised learning: untangling the evidence*. Robert Bosch Stiftung.

Holmes, W., Bialik, M., & Fadel, C. (2019). *Artificial intelligence in education. Promises and Implications for Teaching and Learning*. Center for Curriculum Redesign.

Hwang, G. J. (2014). Definition, framework and research issues of smart learning environments-a context-aware ubiquitous learning perspective. *Smart Learning Environments, 1*(1), 1–14. doi:10.118640561-014-0004-5

Hwang, G. J., & Fu, Q. K. (2020). Advancement and research trends of smart learning environments in the mobile era. *International Journal of Mobile Learning and Organisation, 14*(1), 114–129. doi:10.1504/IJMLO.2020.103911

Janssen, M., Brous, P., Estevez, E., Barbosa, L. S., & Janowski, T. (2020). Data governance: Organizing data for trustworthy Artificial Intelligence. *Government Information Quarterly, 37*(3), 101493. Advance online publication. doi:10.1016/j.giq.2020.101493

Korkman, N., & Metin, M. (2021). El efecto del aprendizaje colaborativo basado en la investigación y el aprendizaje colaborativo en línea basado en la investigación sobre el éxito y el aprendizaje permanente de los estudiantes. *Revista de aprendizaje científico, 4*(2), 151-159.

Litman, D. J., Rosé, C. P., Forbes-Riley, K., VanLehn, K., Bhembe, D., & Silliman, S. (2006). Spoken Versus Typed Human and Computer Dialogue Tutoring. *International Journal of Artificial Intelligence in Education, 16*(2), 145–170. https://dl.acm.org/doi/10.5555/1435344.1435348

Liua, Y., Salehb, S., & Huangc, J. (2021). Artificial Intelligence in Promoting Teaching and Learning Transformation in Schools. *International Journal of Innovation, Creativity and Change, 15*(3).

Livia Segovia, J., & Kaku, M. (2013). La física del futuro: Cómo la ciencia determinará el destino de la humanidad y nuestra vida cotidiana en el siglo XXII. *Cátedra Villarreal, 1*(2). Advance online publication. doi:10.24039/cv20131222

Luckin, R. (2010). *Redesigning learning contexts: Technology-rich, learner-centred ecologies.* Routledge. doi:10.4324/9780203854754

Luckin, R., Holmes, W., Griffiths, M., & Forcier, L. B. (2016). *Intelligence unleashed: An argument for AI in education.* Pearson.

Ma, W., Adesope, O. O., Nesbit, J. C., & Liu, Q. (2014). Intelligent tutoring systems and learning outcomes: A meta-analysis. *Journal of Educational Psychology, 106*(4), 901–918. doi:10.1037/a0037123

Maglogiannis, I. G., Karpouzis, K., Wallace, B. A., & Soldatos, J. (2007). *Emerging artificial intelligence applications in computer engineering: real word AI systems with applications in eHealth, HCI, information retrieval and pervasive technologies.* Ios Press.

Malik, G., Tayal, D. K., & Vij, S. (2019). An analysis of the role of artificial intelligence in education and teaching. In P. K. Sa, S. Bakshi, I. K. Hatzilygeroudis, & M. N. Sahoo (Eds.), *Advances in Intelligent Systems and Computing* (pp. 407–417). Springer.

Merlano, E. D. (2009). Las TIC como apoyo al desarrollo de los procesos de pensamiento y la construcción activa de conocimientos. *Zona próxima,* (10), 146-155.

Moreno, R., & Mayer, R. (2007). Interactive multimodal learning environments. *Educational Psychology Review, 19*(3), 309–326. doi:10.100710648-007-9047-2

Moreno, R., Mayer, R. E., Spires, H. A., & Lester, J. C. (2001). The case for social agency in computer-based teaching: Do students learn more deeply when they interact with animated pedagogical agents? *Cognition and Instruction, 19*(2), 177–213. doi:10.1207/S1532690XCI1902_02

Mostow, J. (2012, June). Why and how our automated reading tutor listens. *Proceedings of the International Symposium on Automatic Detection of Errors in Pronunciation Training (ISADEPT).*

OECD. (2016). *Skills for a Digital World, Policy Brief on The Future of Work.* OECD Publishing.

OECD. (2020). *Trustworthy artificial intelligence (AI) in education: Promises and challenges.* OECD Publishing.

Palau, R., Mogas-Recalde, J., & Domínguez-García, S. (2020). El proyecto Go-Lab como entorno virtual de aprendizaje: Análisis y futuro. *Educar, 56*(2), 407–421. doi:10.5565/rev/educar.1068

Pekrun, R. (2014). Emotions and learning. *Educational Practices Series, 24*(1), 1-31.

Ribeiro-Navarrete, S., Saura, J. R., & Palacios-Marqués, D. (2021). Towards a new era of mass data collection: Assessing pandemic surveillance technologies to preserve user privacy. *Technological Forecasting and Social Change, 167*, 120681. Advance online publication. doi:10.1016/j.techfore.2021.120681 PMID:33840865

Rouhiainen, L. (2018). *Inteligencia artificial.* Alienta Editorial.

Rub, C. M. (2014). Project acronym: iTalk2Learn. *Structure (London, England), 2*, 17.

Salinas, J. (2004). Innovación docente y uso de las TIC en la enseñanza universitaria. RUSC. *Universities & Knowledge Society, 1*(1). Advance online publication. doi:10.7238/rusc.v1i1.228

Saura, J. R., Palacios-Marqués, D., & Iturricha-Fernández, A. (2021b). Ethical Design in Social Media: Assessing the main performance measurements of user online behavior modification. *Journal of Business Research*, *129*, 271–281. doi:10.1016/j.jbusres.2021.03.001

Saura, J. R., Ribeiro-Soriano, D., & Palacios-Marqués, D. (2021a). Setting privacy "by default" in social IoT: Theorizing the challenges and directions in Big Data Research. *Big Data Research*, *25*, 100245. Advance online publication. doi:10.1016/j.bdr.2021.100245

Saura, J. R., Ribeiro-Soriano, D., & Palacios-Marqués, D. (2021c). Using data mining techniques to explore security issues in smart living environments in Twitter. *Computer Communications*, *179*, 285–295. doi:10.1016/j.comcom.2021.08.021

Shah, F., Evens, M. W., Michael, J., & Rovick, A. (2002). Classifying student initiatives and tutor responses in human keyboard-to keyboard tutoring sessions. *Discourse Processes*, *33*(1), 23–52. doi:10.1207/S15326950DP3301_02

Shemshack, A., & Spector, J. M. (2020). A systematic literature review of personalized learning terms. *Smart Learning Environments*, *7*(1), 1–20. doi:10.118640561-020-00140-9

Spector, J. M. (2018). The potential of smart technologies for learning and instruction. *International Journal of Smart Technology & Learning*, *1*(1), 21–32. doi:10.1504/IJSMARTTL.2016.078163

Tabbers, H. (2002). *The modality of text in multimedia instruction: Refining the design guidelines* [Doctoral dissertation, University of the Netherlands, Heerlen]. Open University of the Netherlands. https://www.ou.nl/documents/40554/111676/Doctoral_dissertation_Huib_Tabbers_webversion_2002.pdf/1e28b159-d451-45a8-8e5a-74137949e596

Tedesco, J. C., & Brunner, J. J. (2004). *Nuevas Tecnologías y El Futuro de La Educación*. Septiembre Grupo Editor.

UNESCO. (2019a). *UNESCO strategy for youth and adult literacy*. UNESCO Publishing.

UNESCO. (2019b). International Conference on Artificial intelligence and Education. In *Planning Education in the AI Era: Lead the Leap*. UNESCO Publishing.

UNESCO. (2019c). *Preliminary study on the technical and legal aspects relating to the desirability of a standard-setting instrument on the ethics of artificial intelligence*. UNESCO Publishing.

UNESCO. (2020). International Conference on Artificial intelligence and inclusion. Compendium of Promising Initiatives. In *Mobile Learning Week 2020*. UNESCO Publishing.

UNESCO. (2021). *AI and education: guidance for policy-markers*. UNESCO Publishing.

VanLehn, K., Jordan, P. W., Rosé, C. P., Bhembe, D., Böttner, M., Gaydos, A., Makatchev, M., Pappuswamy, U., Ringenberg, M., Roque, A., Siler, S., & Srivastava, R. (2002). The architecture of why2-atlas: A coach for qualitative physics essay writing. In G. Gauthier, C. Frasson, & K. VanLehn (Eds.), *Intelligent Tutoring Systems. ITS 2000* (pp. 158–167). Lecture Notes in Computer Science. Springer. doi:10.1007/3-540-47987-2_20

VanLehn, K., Lynch, C., Schulze, K., Shapiro, J. A., Shelby, R., Taylor, L., Treacy, D., Weinstein, A., & Wintersgill, M. (2005). The Andes physics tutoring system: Lessons learned. *International Journal of Artificial Intelligence in Education*, *15*(3), 147–204. https://dl.acm.org/doi/10.5555/1434930.1434932

Vidal-Abarca, E., Gilabert, R., Ferrer, A., Ávila, V., Martínez, T., Mañá, A., Llorens, A.-C., Gil, L., Cerdán, R., Ramos, L., & Serrano, M. A. (2014). TuinLEC, an intelligent tutoring system to improve reading literacy skills. *Infancia y Aprendizaje*, *37*(1), 25–56. doi:10.1080/02103702.2014.881657

vom Brocke, J., Simons, A., Riemer, K., Niehaves, B., Plattfaut, R., & Cleven, A. (2015). Standing on the shoulders of giants: Challenges and recommendations of literature search in information systems research. *Communications of the Association for Information Systems*, *37*(1), 9. doi:10.17705/1CAIS.03709

Walkington, C., & Bernacki, M. L. (2020). Appraising research on personalized learning: Definitions, theoretical alignment, advancements, and future directions. *Journal of Research on Technology in Education*, *52*(3), 235–252. doi:10.1080/15391523.2020.1747757

Wells, G., & Arauz, R. M. (2005). Hacia el diálogo en el salón de clases: enseñanza y aprendizaje por medio de la indagación. *Sinéctica, Revista Electrónica de Educación*, (26), 1-19.

Woolf, B. P. (2010). Student Modeling. In R. Nkambou, J. Bourdeau, & R. Mizoguchi (Eds.), *Advances in Intelligent Tutoring Systems. Studies in Computational Intelligence*. Springer. doi:10.1007/978-3-642-14363-2_13

Yufei, L., Saleh, S., Jiahui, H., & Sye, S. M. (2020). Review of the application of artificial intelligence in education. *International Journal of Innovation, Creativity and Change*, *2*(8).

KEY TERMS AND DEFINITIONS

Education: Process by which one develops abilities, attitudes and other forms of behaviour considered to have value in the society in which one lives.

Exploratory Learning Approach: Way of organizing learning through content and activities that the student himself organizes for his work.

Exploratory Learning Environments: Toll assisted by artificial intelligence that allows to guide a student during their learning process through an inquiry approach.

Feedback: Process of informing a person during their learning about how they are doing a certain activity through the identification of their strengths and weaknesses.

Inquiry Learning: Type of learning by which students receive a sequence of elements such as images, questions, or unsolved challenges, which allow them to build their own knowledge through inquiry, reflection, and experience.

Intelligent Tutor System: Tool assisted by artificial intelligence that allows to guide a student during their learning process through step-by-step approaches.

Learning Processes: Methods with specific characteristics by which a person acquires new knowledge to be able to apply it in real contexts.

Significative Learning: Type of active learning that generates cognitive structures by which relationships are established between the new information received by the student and the one they have already possessed. Both types of knowledge are modified and allow students to apply them to real contexts in a logical way.

Step-by-Step Learning Approach: Way of organizing learning through organized sequences of content and activities.

Student's Data Mining: Process by which personal information is collected from students for the purpose of tailoring their learning.

Chapter 17

A Teaching Guide for the Use of Artificial Intelligence Tools at Universities:
From Educator Skills to Practice Examples

José Ramón Saura

https://orcid.org/0000-0002-9457-7745

Rey Juan Carlos University, Spain

ABSTRACT

Universities have adapted their teaching systems to integrate new educational techniques focused on technology and education as fundamental pillars of their development. This chapter proposes the analysis of the fields that encompass the use of artificial intelligence in universities using teaching innovation strategies. The chapter identifies the skills and examples that teachers should understand in order to use artificial intelligence to improve their teaching methods. With this objective, seven interviews have been carried out with university professors in which they explain the use of artificial intelligence and the need to acquire technical knowledge relative to teaching innovation. The results of the research present the main uses and the knowledge needed for university teachers to be able to carry out teaching innovation tasks using artificial intelligence. Finally, implications for university-industry and university teachers are discussed.

INTRODUCTION

The development of teaching methods in recent years has undergone many changes and innovations thanks to the development of digital technology in university classrooms (Hazemi et al., 2012). Specifically, universities have adapted their teaching systems to integrate new educational techniques focused on technology and education as their fundamental pillars of development (Santoro and Saparito, 2003).

DOI: 10.4018/978-1-7998-9609-8.ch017

In this new ecosystem, where technology is now the guide for teaching in universities, artificial intelligence is the next step for educators and professors to put into practice the development of new teaching methods (Sharipov et al., 2021; Saura et al., 2022).

Artificial intelligence, if applied at university, has the potential to drive educational innovation and learning practices (Saura et al., 2022a). It has been possible to verify in the scientific literature how the use of artificial intelligence for teaching promotes and develops a multitude of benefits, opportunities and challenges that must be regulated by public policies and debated in university administration and management councils (Agrawal et al., 2019).

However, this is not the central axis of the development of artificial intelligence in universities as a teaching method. As happened a decade ago with digital marketing strategies (Cutajar, 2020), one of the main gaps that exist in the university ecosystem, is related to the abilities of teachers to carry out successfully the practice tools that work with artificial intelligence and teaching methods that are inclusive with this technology (Roll and Wylie, 2016). It is not so much the use of new technology as the knowledge of teachers to be able to successfully implement, both technically and practically, the use of artificial intelligence in university classrooms (Ribeiro-Navarrete et al., 2021).

Under this process of contextualization, questions and objectives arise for research focused on the following: how artificial intelligence can be used in education? How can one ensure ethical, inclusive and practical values of artificial intelligence in education? How can education help human beings coexist using artificial intelligence in their day-to-day? What knowledge do teachers need to use artificial intelligence successfully? (Chen et al., 2020)

This chapter proposes the theoretical development of different areas that encompass the use of artificial intelligence in universities. In this way, skills and practical examples are identified that teachers can use through the use of new technologies and, specifically, artificial intelligence (Saura et al., 2021). With this objective in mind, seven interviews have been carried out with university professors in which they are asked about the use of artificial intelligence, possible technical knowledge needed, as well as practical examples that university professors should have.

The chapter is organized as follows. The introduction is presented first, followed by related works. Third, the development of the methodology is presented. Fourth, the analysis of the results is presented divided into tools and knowledge of teachers, and practical uses. Afterward, the conclusions of the research are presented divided into implications for universities and implications for professors. Finally, future research proposals for this area are presented.

THEORETICAL FRAMEWORK

The processes focused on educational innovation are composed of complex methods for the effective development of the application of new technologies (Orr and Cleveland-Innes, 2015). In the educational field, the learning processes must be detailed, divided and structured according to the competencies that students acquire in each of the steps that the teaching methodologies propose (Sein-Echaluce et al., 2017).

In this way, for the correct development of a teaching innovation plan in which artificial intelligence is the center of practical and theoretical processes (Hrabowski, 2014), different processes of teaching innovation methods must be understood in which artificial intelligence is the fundamental pillar for the success of teaching (Pu, 2021).

In this paradigm, user's needs and technology awareness must be identified. In these steps, it is where the status and experience of the innovation cycle in the short and medium-term is evaluated. Next, the concepts and principles guide in which user profiles are created, who must understand this technology and be able to defined or redefined accordantly their tasks (Kryukov and Gorin, 2017).

One of the key steps in all market research, especially if we want to develop innovation in the educational area, is to check the practicality of the learning models before its application. An idea may be to send surveys or carry out practical applications to students to study what would be the degree of acceptance and use of such technology in the classrooms.

In order for learning models to be successful, artificial intelligence prototypes for teaching can be tested in the next step (Li, 2021). In this way teaching innovation can be developing a robust cycle for the development and validation of a strategic design in this ecosystem.

As one of the fundamental pillars, pilot projects can be developed in which traditional teaching is compared with new teaching focused on teaching innovation through artificial intelligence (Rico-Bautista et al., 2021). In this way, interactions with technology can be measured through the results and test activities that students perform. After comparing the results, teachers can understand whether there are evident improvements in the use of artificial intelligence in the university ecosystem (Hine, 2021).

Once this data is analysed, analytical reports can be developed that incorporate new evidence in which lessons learned and results serve as experience to improve the application of both teaching innovation and artificial intelligence (McArthur et al., 2015).

Then, redefinitions and new objectives must be made to measure the evaluation of performance and to understand in terms of efficiency, what are the advantages and disadvantages of the proposed innovation. As the last step, once teachers have performed activities centred on the use of artificial intelligence to cover evidence, exercises and exams for students, the results can be measured and made accessible to large numbers of students (Chassignol et al., 2018).

In this last step, the results of the experiment should be compared with the rest of the students as a group. If the results are positive, the new technologies should be applied. If this process is successfully completed, artificial intelligence can be used in the university ecosystem to support innovative processes for change in university teaching (Baker, 2000).

METHODOLOGY

This research proposes the development of interviews with university teachers with the aim of identifying possible uses and lack of knowledge in relation to the application of artificial intelligence in the university education sector.

It should be noted that interviews are one of the most widely used qualitative and exploratory methods in research development processes (Jackson, 1998). There are different types of interviews and data collection methods. In particular, one can find in the scientific literature approaches that focus on the opinion, attitude, feelings or opinions of people about a given topic when the interviews are carried out (Connaway, 1996).

In relation to interview models, we can find structured interviews, in which the interviews are process-oriented with very well-defined steps. This is where questionnaires or closed questions are developed, which the interviewees must answer one by one to advance in the process (Tavory, 2020). On the other hand, there is the unstructured interview, in which interviewees improvise by answering open-ended questions asked by the interviewer. In this sense, the answers are focused on obtaining exploratory information and ideas in relation to the topic of study (Veitch et al., 2020).

For this chapter, seven interviews were conducted with university lecturers from Spanish universities. The questions asked were open-ended and specifically two, one of them to identify the main applications of artificial intelligence in teaching innovation, and the other to identify the possible lack of knowledge in relation to the use of artificial intelligence. The interviews took place between 8 and 15 September 2021. Question 1 was as follows: *What are the main uses of artificial intelligence that you are considering using or will use in your teaching innovation processes?* Question 2: *What knowledge do teachers need for the correct application of artificial intelligence in teaching innovation?*

The interviews were conducted in Spanish, and the interviewer took note of the key points of the interviewees' answers. In this way, the interview is developed by understanding the fundamental factors involved and taking keynotes for the analysis of the content resulting from the interviews (Jones and Abdelfattah, 2020).

ANALYSIS OF RESULTS

As a result of the methodological process developed, in which a total of seven interviews were carried out, the following results were obtained in relation to artificial intelligence tools, possible uses, and knowledge needed by teachers for the development and application of education through artificial intelligence.

Intelligent Tutoring Systems

Intelligent tutoring systems using artificial intelligence consist of dashboards, and information organization systems that allow teachers to conduct tutorials with students in digital ecosystems (Erümit and Çetin, 2020).

These tutorials can also be conducted face-to-face, and the data collected and developed can be included in these systems for analysis with artificial intelligence strategies. The outcome of use is focused on identifying statistics, trends, and patterns in the data that can enable tutors to better understand students' needs and thus correctly focus their teaching tasks (VanLehn, 2011).

Such systems are highly valued as the resulting database can be compared with the history of other tutorials in different subjects and the same subject. In this way, the results collected in the analysis provide various insights for teachers to improve their processes (Mirchi et al., 2021).

Dialogue-Based Tutoring Systems

As the system for smart tutoring enhancement presented above, tutors can use similar systems to encourage dialogue between students and teachers. In this way, bidirectional communication of information is established that supports the understanding and development of the tasks that teachers request from students (Pai et al., 2021).

These systems can even be automated so that teachers can associate certain student responses to specific topics of the subjects they are working with or the topics on which an activity is being carried out (Arnott et al., 2008).

These systems also allow the automation of mass conversations with different students, so they can also be used to resolve generic doubts or to carry out activities in which there are recurring questions asked to teachers (Pon-Barry et al., 2004).

Exploratory Learning Environments

Likewise, by linking the use of intelligent tutoring systems and dialogue systems, the combination of these can lead to digital ecosystems in which learning can be explored experimentally (Gkogkidis and Dacre, 2021). That is, in a digital ecosystem, which is prepared for both interactive dialogues and information gathering, teachers can develop innovative projects focused on improving teaching or presenting interactive case studies that help students acquire knowledge in an efficient way (Oller et al., 2021).

Moreover, these ecosystems working with artificial intelligence can offer analysis of student interactions, thus measuring which subjects and topics are of most interest to them. In addition, their digital capability allows students to access from anywhere and thus be connected to learning systems in a simple way (Ugalde et al., 2021).

Automatic Writing Evaluation

Automated written assessment systems allow teachers, through the use of artificial intelligence, to assess different practices with tests that are given to students. Although this can indeed be a risky practice, actions such as connotations, irony or sarcasm could be left out of an efficient response (Nikolić, 2021).

This type of tool is very important to automatically identify those questions and issues that arise for learners and to which the answers are simple. The systems can identify them and automate their correction, as well as jointly analyze the time of interaction with these elements or identify a possible lack of understanding (Mello et al., 2021).

Smart Robots

Intelligent robots are artificial intelligence modules that can be used by teachers to perform specific tasks related to teaching (Torrey et al., 2008). In this way, these robots can be configured to perform specific case studies, answer specific tasks or even send notifications and alerts to students so that they do not forget to hand in compulsory assignments (Uskov et al., 2016).

Robots are also used as round-the-clock conversation tools where teachers can schedule responses to students based on the options that may arise (Vincent-Lancrin, 2021). Moreover, these tools are capable, on their own, of identifying the correct answers and establishing communication channels with other teachers or students. However, programming such robots can be technically complex for teachers. It is sometimes up to the developers of the application itself whether it is modified technically or through visual user interfaces that allow correct understanding by teachers (Anžel et al., 2021)

Virtual and Augmented Reality

Applications focused on augmented and virtual reality for education are increasingly being used in the teaching ecosystem. These types of tools, which can also work with artificial intelligence, allow teachers to create virtual spaces in which students can carry out learning processes and activities (Martín-Gutiérrez et al., 2017).

In this way, through augmented and virtual reality, unique learning experiences can be created that motivate and keep students focused while they perform activities (Chang et al., 2010).

These systems are very interesting because they are also capable of self-improving and collecting data related to the interactions students have with the platform (Hincapie et al., 2021). It is important to understand that these types of applications can be linked to special education or to increasing the attention of students with poor stimulus-response skills or concentration.

Technical Knowledge

As noted above, one of the barriers to the implementation of tools that use artificial intelligence for teaching by teachers is technical knowledge. To date, as the development of these new technologies progresses, the processes of adaptation, flexibility and training of machines that work with artificial intelligence are carried out technically. Teachers must learn to control panels that work with programming languages they do not know (Yang et al., 2021).

Moreover, for the application of each of the artificial intelligence functionalities, there are different algorithms and virtual ecosystems in which the programming languages and technical tasks are complex and different in each of them. Inevitably, teachers are faced with the task of understanding programming language standards and being able to configure advanced algorithms that work with artificial intelligence to improve their teaching applications (Williamson, 2020).

It is only a matter of time, however, before user interfaces become increasingly user-friendly, and allow teachers to perform these tasks without problems. To date, however, teachers will be forced to acquire the skills demanded by industry (Michalski et al., 2013).

New Virtual Ecosystems

As artificial intelligence develops, new virtual ecosystems appear in which teachers must be updated and adapt their teaching models (Maravilhas and Martins, 2019). Teaching innovation is also the adaptability and flexibility of traditional teaching to new virtual ecosystems, understood as new platforms or social networks (Saura et al., 2021a), where students and users spend most of their time (Kjällander, 2011).

It is important to understand that new virtual ecosystems will continue to emerge, and it is the task of teachers to acquire advanced knowledge of these systems in order to be opinion leaders who are qualified to teach in these environments (Markless, 2009).

With the development of new technologies, new generations are becoming more and more receptive to the use of new virtual ecosystems that are changing from time to time. Teaching has a challenge as teachers must be able to understand these new ecosystems and acquire the knowledge required for teaching.

Changing Operating Systems

Likewise, with the development of new virtual ecosystems, the concept of operating systems appears. With the development of artificial intelligence and new technologies, various operating systems have appeared that are configured as systems for managing information and the configuration of virtual environments (Stripling, 2010).

Thus, depending on the activities to be developed or the type of applications to be used to develop artificial intelligence, different operating systems appear. However, although they may seem similar, it is still a challenge for teachers on the one hand, or to have the knowledge training to approach logically and orientated, or the use of operating systems for teaching (Tong, 2016).

There is no doubt that, if teachers want to boost the use of artificial intelligence, they must be in control of advanced settings for such operating systems. The development of specific courses and master's degrees to gain knowledge in this area should be a priority for teaching teams (Saura et al., 2021b).

Language as a Technological Barrier

Language has always been one of the major characteristics that demand the updating and quality of teaching. Technological developments and innovations do not always appear in the mother tongue of the country where teachers live (Doiz and Lasagabaster, 2020).

While it is true that most information is accessible in English, more and more countries such as India or China are proposing new systems focused on virtual and digital innovation that can be used for teaching and communications on the Internet.

Therefore, language also becomes a barrier to the acquisition of knowledge. Time plays a crucial role because for teachers to be able to teach, they first have to invest hours in the use of such a platform or technology, adapt the artificial intelligence, test its use and then apply it in their lessons.

CONCLUSION

This research has developed seven interviews to identify the main uses of artificial intelligence in teaching innovation as well as to understand what the main gaps in the knowledge of teachers for its application in the university environment are.

As conclusions, it can be identified that after the analysis and reviews made by the teachers interviewed, their main role should be to facilitate the transfer of knowledge, human interaction, and critical thinking about the use of artificial intelligence in students. In this way, teachers will awaken interest and students will feel empowered in the use of digital education.

Furthermore, it should be understood that teachers should define their skill set in order to identify which type of artificial intelligence application they should use for the design and organization of teaching activities in their own professional teaching ecosystem.

Teachers must also ensure that they have continuous support from a replacement for the skills they need to efficiently use artificial intelligence in their teaching innovation initiatives. It should also be a cornerstone for teachers to actively seek to promote artificial intelligence through new teaching activities for lifelong learning.

It is also interesting to build and configure new artificial intelligence applications to measure and analyze the main outcomes of these teaching practices. This should be done at all levels of university education, undergraduate, masters and doctoral, as it will drive the improvement of the teaching environment in this industry.

With the results of this research, a total of 10 fundamental pillars have been identified for the understanding of the use of artificial intelligence in universities, as well as the knowledge that teachers must obtain in order to develop artificial intelligence correctly.

Implications for Universities

It is relevant for universities that teachers acquire the necessary knowledge to carry out activities by using artificial intelligence. Universities can use the proposals developed in the results of this research as a teaching guide for the use of artificial intelligence in their institutions.

Both the skills needed through examples and the different uses that teachers can make of these technologies are important issues that universities should analyze for the correct development of teaching innovation.

However, universities should be aware that they should promote teacher training programs that reinforce knowledge about virtual ecosystems, operating systems, and other artificial intelligence applications that teachers can use in their classes (Saura et al. (2021c). Universities are also responsible for promoting the use of this type of artificial intelligence among students and the university community, not only for positive acceptance but also to encourage flexibility and the use of new tools in the future of teaching

Implications for Teachers

While university institutions must drive learning models using artificial intelligence, teachers are also personally responsible for keeping themselves updated to be able to become opinion leaders and qualified teachers in this field. Therefore, this research can help them to understand what the needs are in terms of the knowledge they need to acquire.

In addition, teachers must also maintain the personal and professional motivation linked to the development of this type of technology. Both the professional and personal ecosystem must be trained in the use of artificial intelligence, and subsequently, be able to provide effective learning experiences to the students to whom they develop innovative teaching activities.

Future Research

The future of research in this area is mainly linked to conducting teaching experiments with artificial intelligence and comparing the results with more traditional teaching projects. Based on these results, tools that work with artificial intelligence should also be applied to make predictions and concrete measurements of whether these systems are effective for education. In addition, the different issues and possible violations of users' data privacy must be assessed so that the use of artificial intelligence in universities is ethical and does not violate privacy (Saura et al., 2021d).

REFERENCES

Agrawal, A., Gans, J., & Goldfarb, A. (Eds.). (2019). *The economics of artificial intelligence: an agenda.* University of Chicago Press. doi:10.7208/chicago/9780226613475.001.0001

Anžel, A., Heider, D., & Hattab, G. (2021). The visual story of data storage: From storage properties to user interfaces. *Computational and Structural Biotechnology Journal, 19,* 4904–4918. doi:10.1016/j.csbj.2021.08.031 PMID:34527195

Arnott, E., Hastings, P., & Allbritton, D. (2008). Research Methods Tutor: Evaluation of a dialogue-based tutoring system in the classroom. *Behavior Research Methods*, *40*(3), 694–698. doi:10.3758/BRM.40.3.694 PMID:18697663

Baker, M. J. (2000). The roles of models in Artificial Intelligence and Education research: A prospective view. *Journal of Artificial Intelligence in Education*, *11*, 122–143.

Chang, G., Morreale, P., & Medicherla, P. (2010, March). Applications of augmented reality systems in education. In *Society for Information Technology & Teacher Education International Conference* (pp. 1380-1385). Association for the Advancement of Computing in Education (AACE).

Chassignol, M., Khoroshavin, A., Klimova, A., & Bilyatdinova, A. (2018). Artificial Intelligence trends in education: A narrative overview. *Procedia Computer Science*, *136*, 16–24. doi:10.1016/j.procs.2018.08.233

Chen, L., Chen, P., & Lin, Z. (2020). Artificial intelligence in education: A review. *IEEE Access: Practical Innovations, Open Solutions*, *8*, 75264–75278. doi:10.1109/ACCESS.2020.2988510

Connaway, L. S. (1996). Focus Group Interviews: A Data Collection Methodology. *Library Administration & Management*, *10*(4), 231–239.

Cutajar, A. (2020). *Investigating the employee skills gap within the digital marketing industry* (Master's thesis). University of Malta.

Doiz, A., & Lasagabaster, D. (2020). Dealing with language issues in English-medium instruction at university: A comprehensive approach. *International Journal of Bilingual Education and Bilingualism*, *23*(3), 257–262. doi:10.1080/13670050.2020.1727409

Erümit, A. K., & Çetin, İ. (2020). Design framework of adaptive intelligent tutoring systems. *Education and Information Technologies*, *25*(5), 4477–4500. doi:10.100710639-020-10182-8

Gkogkidis, V., & Dacre, N. (2021). The educator's LSP journey: Creating exploratory learning environments for responsible management education using Lego Serious Play. *Emerald Open Research*, *3*, 2. doi:10.35241/emeraldopenres.14015.1

Hazemi, R., Hailes, S., & Wilbur, S. (Eds.). (2012). *The digital university: reinventing the academy*. Springer Science & Business Media.

Hincapie, M., Diaz, C., Valencia, A., Contero, M., & Güemes-Castorena, D. (2021). Educational applications of augmented reality: A bibliometric study. *Computers & Electrical Engineering*, *93*, 107289. doi:10.1016/j.compeleceng.2021.107289

Hine, C. (2021). Evaluating the prospects for university-based ethical governance in artificial intelligence and data-driven innovation. *Research Ethics Review*, *17*(4), 17470161211022790. doi:10.1177/17470161211022790

Hrabowski, F. A. III. (2014). Institutional change in higher education: Innovation and collaboration. *Peabody Journal of Education*, *89*(3), 291–304. doi:10.1080/0161956X.2014.913440

Jackson, P. (1998). Focus group interviews as a methodology. *Nurse Researcher, 6*(1), 72.

Jones, R. E., & Abdelfattah, K. R. (2020). Virtual interviews in the era of COVID-19: A primer for applicants. *Journal of Surgical Education, 77*(4), 733–734. doi:10.1016/j.jsurg.2020.03.020 PMID:32278546

Kjällander, S. (2011). *Designs for learning in an extended digital environment: Case studies of social interaction in the social science classroom* (Doctoral dissertation). Department of Education, Stockholm University.

Kryukov, V., & Gorin, A. (2017). Digital technologies as education innovation at universities. *Australian Educational Computing, 32*(1), 1–16.

Li, W. (2021, February). The Development Path of Ideological and Political Education Innovation in Universities Based on the Computer. *Journal of Physics: Conference Series, 1744*(3), 032249. doi:10.1088/1742-6596/1744/3/032249

Maravilhas, S., & Martins, J. (2019). Strategic knowledge management in a digital environment: Tacit and explicit knowledge in Fab Labs. *Journal of Business Research, 94*, 353–359. doi:10.1016/j.jbusres.2018.01.061

Markless, S. (2009). A new conception of information literacy for the digital environment in higher education. *Nordic Journal of Information Literacy in Higher Education, 1*(1).

Martín-Gutiérrez, J., Mora, C. E., Añorbe-Díaz, B., & González-Marrero, A. (2017). Virtual technologies trends in education. *Eurasia Journal of Mathematics, Science and Technology Education, 13*(2), 469–486.

McArthur, D., Lewis, M., & Bishary, M. (2005). The roles of artificial intelligence in education: Current progress and future prospects. *Journal of Educational Technology, 1*(4), 42–80.

Mello, R. F., Fiorentino, G., Miranda, P., Oliveira, H., Raković, M., & Gašević, D. (2021, June). Towards Automatic Content Analysis of Rhetorical Structure in Brazilian College Entrance Essays. In *International Conference on Artificial Intelligence in Education* (pp. 162-167). Springer. 10.1007/978-3-030-78270-2_29

Michalski, R. S., Carbonell, J. G., & Mitchell, T. M. (Eds.). (2013). *Machine learning: An artificial intelligence approach*. Springer Science & Business Media.

Mirchi, N., Ledwos, N., & Del Maestro, R. F. (2021). Intelligent Tutoring Systems: Re-Envisioning Surgical Education in Response to COVID-19. *The Canadian Journal of Neurological Sciences, 48*(2), 198–200. doi:10.1017/cjn.2020.202 PMID:32907644

Nikolić, Z. (2021). Knowledge management in education: automatic generation of materials for knowledge examination. *Industry 4.0, 6*(2), 76-78.

Oller, J., Engel, A., & Rochera, M. J. (2021). Personalizing learning through connecting students' learning experiences: An exploratory study. *The Journal of Educational Research, 114*(4), 404–417. doi:10.1080/00220671.2021.1960255

Orr, T., & Cleveland-Innes, M. (2015). Appreciative leadership: Supporting education innovation. *International Review of Research in Open and Distributed Learning, 16*(4). Advance online publication. doi:10.19173/irrodl.v16i4.2467

Pai, K. C., Kuo, B. C., Liao, C. H., & Liu, Y. M. (2021). An application of Chinese dialogue-based intelligent tutoring system in remedial instruction for mathematics learning. *Educational Psychology*, *41*(2), 137–152. doi:10.1080/01443410.2020.1731427

Pon-Barry, H., Clark, B., Schultz, K., Bratt, E. O., & Peters, S. (2004, August). Advantages of spoken language interaction in dialogue-based intelligent tutoring systems. In *International Conference on Intelligent Tutoring Systems* (pp. 390-400). Springer. 10.1007/978-3-540-30139-4_37

Pu, Z. (2021, August). Construction of Talent Training System for Innovation and Entrepreneurship Education in Colleges and Universities. In *The Sixth International Conference on Information Management and Technology* (pp. 1-4). 10.1145/3465631.3465941

Ribeiro-Navarrete, S., Saura, J. R., & Palacios-Marqués, D. (2021). Towards a new era of mass data collection: Assessing pandemic surveillance technologies to preserve user privacy. *Technological Forecasting and Social Change*, *167*, 120681. doi:10.1016/j.techfore.2021.120681 PMID:33840865

Rico-Bautista, D., Medina-Cardenas, Y., Coronel-Rojas, L. A., Cuesta-Quintero, F., Maestre-Gongora, G., & Guerrero, C. D. (2021). Smart University: Key Factors for an Artificial Intelligence Adoption Model. *Advances and Applications in Computer Science, Electronics and Industrial Engineering*, *1307*, 153–166.

Roll, I., & Wylie, R. (2016). Evolution and revolution in artificial intelligence in education. *International Journal of Artificial Intelligence in Education*, *26*(2), 582–599. doi:10.100740593-016-0110-3

Santoro, M. D., & Saparito, P. A. (2003). The firm's trust in its university partner as a key mediator in advancing knowledge and new technologies. *IEEE Transactions on Engineering Management*, *50*(3), 362–373. doi:10.1109/TEM.2003.817287

Saura, J. R., Palacios-Marqués, D., & Ribeiro-Soriano, D. (2021c). How SMEs use data sciences in their online marketing performance: A systematic literature review of the state-of-the-art. *Journal of Small Business Management*, 1–36. doi:10.1080/00472778.2021.1955127

Saura, J. R., Palacios-Marqués, D., & Ribeiro-Soriano, D. (2022). Exploring the boundaries of Open Innovation: Evidence from social media mining. *Technovation*, 102447. Advance online publication. doi:10.1016/j.technovation.2021.102447

Saura, J. R., Ribeiro-Soriano, D., & Iturricha-Fernández, A. (2022). Exploring the challenges of remote work on Twitter users' sentiments: From digital technology development to a post-pandemic era. *Journal of Business Research*, *142*(March), 242–254. doi:10.1016/j.jbusres.2021.12.052

Saura, J. R., Ribeiro-Soriano, D., & Palacios-Marqués, D. (2021). Setting B2B Digital Marketing in Artificial Intelligence-based CRMs: A review and directions for future research. *Industrial Marketing Management*, *98*(October), 161–178. doi:10.1016/j.indmarman.2021.08.006

Saura, J. R., Ribeiro-Soriano, D., & Palacios-Marqués, D. (2021a). Using data mining techniques to explore security issues in smart living environments in Twitter. *Computer Communications*, *179*, 285–295. doi:10.1016/j.comcom.2021.08.021

Saura, J. R., Ribeiro-Soriano, D., & Palacios-Marques, D. (2021b). Evaluating security and privacy issues of social networks based information systems in Industry 4.0. *Enterprise Information Systems*, 1–17. doi:10.1080/17517575.2021.1913765

Saura, J. R., Ribeiro-Soriano, D., & Palacios-Marqués, D. (2021d, July 15). Setting privacy "by default" in social IoT: Theorizing the challenges and directions in Big Data Research. *Big Data Research*, 25, 100245. doi:10.1016/j.bdr.2021.100245

Sein-Echaluce, M. L., Fidalgo-Blanco, Á., & Alves, G. (2017). *Technology behaviors in education innovation* (No. ART-2017-98966). Academic Press.

Sharipov, F. F., Krotenko, T. Y., & Dyakonova, M. A. (2021). Digital Potential of Economic Education: Information Technologies in a Management University. In Current Achievements, Challenges and Digital Chances of Knowledge Based Economy (pp. 561-572). Springer.

Stripling, B. (2010). Teaching Students to Think in the Digital Environment: Digital Literacy and Digital Inquiry. *School Library Monthly*, 26(8), 16–19.

Tavory, I. (2020). Interviews and inference: Making sense of interview data in qualitative research. *Qualitative Sociology*, 43(4), 449–465. doi:10.100711133-020-09464-x

Tong, J. (2016). Design and implementation of music teaching platform in college based on android mobile technology. *International Journal of Emerging Technologies in Learning*, 11(05), 4–9. doi:10.3991/ijet.v11i05.5686

Torrey, C., Fussell, S. R., & Kiesler, S. (2008). Trying to be helpful: Social challenges for smart robots. In *Workshop-Proceedings of ACM/IEEE Human-Robot Interaction Conference (HRI2008), Amsterdam* (pp. 23-26). Academic Press.

Ugalde, L., Santiago-Garabieta, M., Villarejo-Carballido, B., & Puigvert, L. (2021). Impact of Interactive Learning Environments on Learning and Cognitive Development of Children With Special Educational Needs: A Literature Review. *Frontiers in Psychology*, 12, 12. doi:10.3389/fpsyg.2021.674033 PMID:33995231

United Nations. (2021). AI and education Guidance for policymakers education Guidance for policymakers. United Nations Educational, Scientific and Cultural Organization.

Uskov, V. L., Bakken, J. P., Pandey, A., Singh, U., Yalamanchili, M., & Penumatsa, A. (2016). Smart university taxonomy: features, components, systems. In *Smart education and e-learning 2016* (pp. 3–14). Springer. doi:10.1007/978-3-319-39690-3_1

VanLehn, K. (2011). The relative effectiveness of human tutoring, intelligent tutoring systems, and other tutoring systems. *Educational Psychologist*, 46(4), 197–221. doi:10.1080/00461520.2011.611369

Veitch, J., Flowers, E., Ball, K., Deforche, B., & Timperio, A. (2020). Designing parks for older adults: A qualitative study using walk-along interviews. *Urban Forestry & Urban Greening*, 54, 126768. doi:10.1016/j.ufug.2020.126768

Vincent-Lancrin, S. (2021). Frontiers of smart education technology: Opportunities and challenges. *OECD Digital Education Outlook 2021 Pushing the Frontiers with Artificial Intelligence, Blockchain and Robots: Pushing the Frontiers with Artificial Intelligence, Blockchain and Robots*, 19.

Williamson, B. (2020). New Digital Laboratories of Experimental Knowledge Production: Artificial Intelligence and Education Research. *London Review of Education*, *18*(2), 209–220. doi:10.14324/LRE.18.2.05

Yang, S. J., Ogata, H., Matsui, T., & Chen, N. S. (2021). Human-centered artificial intelligence in education: Seeing the invisible through the visible. *Computers and Education: Artificial Intelligence*, *2*, 100008. doi:10.1016/j.caeai.2021.100008

Chapter 18
Analysis on the Possibilities of AI in Education

Tomás Aznar

https://orcid.org/0000-0003-4660-7740

Centro de Educación Superior de Negocios, Innovación y Tecnología (IUNIT), Spain

ABSTRACT

For some years now, we have been living through times of the rapid interaction of technologies in society, and this has been an authentic revolution. Many speak of this moment as a fourth industrial revolution that is going to significantly change the way we see the world and interact with other people. Among these technologies, without a doubt, one of the most outstanding has been artificial intelligence (AI), which is so present in the daily lives of people looking for patterns that are used in numerous fields of action. In education, the advance of AI has been very significant, and all governments are seeking to make policies that involve AI in education in order to improve the academic results of students. It is for this reason that we must analyze how this improves implementation and improvement to the education of the 21st century.

INTRODUCTION

Talking about education throughout history has been the key to talking about the possibilities that societies have to advance. Education is intrinsically related to the well-being and progress of peoples. We live in a key moment of the history of humanity since, as we have been able to perceive in recent years, society is facing paradigmatic changes that affect all aspects of human development. It is in this new scenario, where knowledge and information are replacing natural resources, force and/or money as key resources within society. Information and communications, together with digital technologies, have revealed the principal sources of power, modifying the way of relating and organizing in the venture of knowledge. The rapid development of the Information and Communication Technologies (ICT) has allowed knowledge to accumulate and circulate through increasingly sophisticated and powerful technological means. This new context requires governments to reformulate their educational practices and also their strategic management, having to face the challenge of innovation, to modify the model on how the life of these

DOI: 10.4018/978-1-7998-9609-8.ch018

centers develops in respect to the construction of knowledge, and the formation of citizens for this new society. Therefore, all this encourages the introduction of AI within schools, a clear consequence of the fourth industrial revolution, to continue penetrating the different educational levels helping to improve the academic results of students.

The changes produced by new technologies have been analyzed for a long time, observing their impact on different areas of human life. The 21st century entered suddenly promising great changes within that fourth industrial revolution and anticipating a better life for all. In education, the arrival of new technologies has always raised questions about changes: Their content, their means of production and their integration. These changes have deeply interested teachers since they perceive that these new technologies may be the change that this sector has so highly demanded for a long time and it is therefore of special interest to investigate how users perceive the content generated by software (Clerwall, 2014). Systems using artificial intelligence are meeting or exceeding human-level performance in more and more domains, taking advantage of rapid advances in other technologies and driving higher stock prices. However, productivity measure growth has halved over the past decade, and real income has stagnated since the late 1990s for most Americans (Brynjolfsson, Rock, & Syverson, 2017). There is still a huge amount of information that must be analyzed but as yet correct way to achieve this has not been proposed, leaving therefore a deep path untouched that will eventually have to be dealt with and analyzed. All this approach to the integration of new technologies within society comes hand in hand with great changes and great risks such as those assumed by the use of all those data that directly affect people's day-to-day life and the protection of their data, something that really worries users in a cyber-connected world (Saura, Palacio-Marqués and Ribeiro-Soriano, 2021). Everything that has happened in recent years has accelerated the development of information technologies aimed at education. Among these applications, the smart classroom can create broadband network connectivity between schools that share high-quality learning, resources between classes and communication between students in the online learning space, achieving efficient sharing of teaching resources and offering a flexible interactive class. With all this, many schools that seek to introduce this AI in the classroom face new problems such as the increase in the number of devices, the higher costs of complex cabling, the potential security risks and the maintenance operations of the network, which results in an increase in the workload that many governments analyze. Despite all this, the experiences of integration of AI in education have been increasing in recent years as we can analyze in the Beijing Consensus on artificial intelligence and education held during the International Conference on Artificial Intelligence in Education that took place in Beijing in 2019 where the foundations were laid for the first time under the Sustainable Development Goals, specifically the fourth SDG (Goal 4: Guarantee inclusive, equitable and quality education and promote lifelong learning opportunities for all) for the development of educational policies for the use of AI within the different educational policies of the individual countries, which for Unesco is fundamental, and has sought allies such as Google or Microsoft to promote these approaches.

The most impressive capabilities of AI, particularly those based on machine learning, have yet to be widely disseminated (Graupe, 2016). It should be noted that its full effects cannot be analyzed until waves of complementary innovations are developed and implemented, so there are still many hypotheses about the what, how and how much of everything related to AI in education. This opens, as we will comment later, future lines of research that must be analyzed and taken into account in order to get the most out of AI. Therefore, there is a lot of room for the complete and detailed analysis of the impact of AI in education. So, according to experts, it will not be possible to understand the absolute importance of the use of AI in education until the middle of the 21st century when there will finally be an adequate and deep use in all sectors of education which will allow an understanding of the multiple possibilities that they pose (Palacios, Palacio and González, 2018). The clear challenge facing education is to be able to adequately integrate artificial intelligence in education, seeking to combine efforts within an educational model of the first industrial revolution. AI can detect parameters to improve learning that the human eye cannot perceive and the correct integration of this new technology will serve to complete the learning development that we have seen so much in demand during the pandemic.

Initiating the debate on the openness to technology in everyday environments raises whether AI systems should also be taken into account as managers of morals or their ethics (Bryson 2018), which questions the implication of AI in society as a normative, non-descriptive issue, and how it influences the different sectors of life, such as education (Calvo-Rubio and Ufarte-Ruiz, 2020). Along with a substantial consensus concerning the power of active learning, comes a lack of precision about what its essential ingredients are. New educational technologies offer vehicles to systematically explore the benefits of alternative techniques to support active learning (Yannier, Hudson, and Koedinger, 2020). With AI, we introduce a new genre of smart science station technology that can help students learn science by doing science in the real world, from the different STEM disciplines. These STEM favor the continuous learning of the student and if that instruction can be analyzed based on all the data that AI provides, we can be on the verge of a truly significant change that would put adaptive learning within the reach of the entire population and that would serve clearly to break with established academic paradigms. Above all, we must not forget that this revolution would advance from the earliest ages to university, so it would serve to mark differentiated training itineraries that would allow the student to choose their own path according to their abilities, something that following Gadner's multiple intelligences would mark a before and after in education (Gadner, 2005).

Today, researchers are trying to reflect how Big Data and artificial intelligence (AI) are having an impact on learning and teaching at different levels (Williams, 2016). The implementation of these technologies is still in its early stages, and it has a number of technological limitations. However, the convergence of developments in psychology, data science, and computer science hold great promise for revolutionizing educational research, practice, and industry (Luan et al. 2020). All this opens up new lines of research that allow us to glimpse a promising future for the use of AI in education, but perhaps what we should ask ourselves is whether the educational policies of the governments of different countries are prepared for this paradigm shift that is taking place-at an unstoppable pace.

It should be noted that the educational system in the last decade, is moving from focusing on the product to the process, expanding beyond the knowledge of the domain to include self-regulation, collaboration and motivation (Roll and Wylie, 2016).

The general objective of this review is to analyze the impact of AI on education, observe the changes that governments are making based on this pedagogical improvement and determine how AI impact teachers both in their daily lives and at a professional level. The challenge that clearly presents itself to us with the use of AI in education is to be able to carry out public policies for teacher training which achieve an education directed by these new technologies and that guarantee quality, inclusive and equitable education. This challenge is very difficult to cover because of the whole problem posed by the methodological changes in educational policies that in many countries have not changed since the times of the first industrial revolution.

LITERATURE REVIEW

There is a lack of knowledge of the depth to which AI can go in cases such as adaptive learning, but we must be open to how this technology will allow us to adapt to the needs of students, their learning and thinking styles, and their way of learning, to their development style, their multiple intelligences and their times (León Pérez, 2019). Many governments have been interested in the possibilities of the use of AI in education since, as we mentioned, it is something that has been demanded worldwide since schools continue to use the educational methods established during the first industrial revolution to teach workers, when we could really be talking about a third industrial revolution that will change the paradigms and that will bring closer, quality and personalized education that students need in the face of the changes that the new uses and jobs of new technologies have generated worldwide.

Several articles have already integrated, for more than a decade, the usability of AI for the prediction of academic performance of higher education students, based on various influencing factors using classifier techniques (Vladan, 2004; McArthur, Lewis and Bishary, 2005; Soares and Fallenstein, 2017; Castrillón, Sarache and Ruiz-Herrera 2020), which raises the usability of this technology to a more pragmatic level. From this, support and reinforcement actions can be deployed immediately, which represents a short and medium-term benefit for students. Some of these authors glimpse that we cannot really reference or suppose what will improve the use of information analysis with AI since we are facing a cognitive vacuum from which we can only glimpse some ideas but not generate assumptions that anticipate certain facts (Fister and Fister eds., 2015). That conditions for many who are divided between those who see multiple possibilities and those who see excessive threats, so this issue generates a long narrative that is being analyzed in order to follow the appropriate path in the establishment of this new and modern educational proposal.

CONCEPTUAL FRAMEWORK

The human being since ancient times has shown how he is capable of mastering skills and processes to improve his life. This we have been able to understand in the different industrial revolutions that we have suffered where not only was the inventiveness of the human being, but also their productive ingenuity with new machines that made life easier and that were authentic historical revolutions that we analyze by their impact on the society that fragmented the time period that was being lived at that moment. The twentieth century brought the term "new technologies" that were intended to put a barrier between the old and the new. These new technologies served to change many aspects of the lives of human beings since it is undeniable that the appearance of the mobile phone, without which we cannot live today, was a real incentive within these new technologies. In these new technologies we can find many points in common such as their immateriality, their instantaneousness or their innovation among others as Cabero (1996) points out, which add their significant value to people's day-to-day lives and serve us for an authentic change of life.

For many authors, we are still far from understanding the impact of the new technologies since it is considered that we have not been able to perceive how our lives will change and, at this point, we find the potentiality of AI related to the great potential of the data that is being collected today thanks to the presence of these new technologies in our daily work.

The concept of AI was coined by John McCarthy (1956) defining it as "the science and ingenuity of making intelligent machines, especially intelligent computer programs". This definition opened the panorama of the possibility that a machine could be at the level of a human being, but other authors such as Rusell and Norving (2009) spoke of different types of AI, differentiating them between those that think like humans and those that act like humans. This means that those machines which until then had only a sole utility were used for much more and made a data analysis impossible for a human being. For many researchers, this opened a new panorama since it allowed these AIs to collect a large body of data and carry out an analysis that served to establish conclusions that would improve certain circumstances. This is where the interest in the use of AI in education lies since, if these AIs analyze the way to focus the learning of a specific teacher towards a specific student, they will allow analyzing the data obtained and establishing improvements in meaningful learning of that student ensuring a perfect job of teaching using the student's capacities and obtaining better results as indicated by Cobo and Moravec, 2011. For many teachers and students this is the definite tool they need to improve education worldwide in these times when the Globalization has fractured the borders of the world.

It is with this, that with this chapter we intend to answer the question of whether the integration of AI in education can improve student learning, and if it is going to be something that we will see normally in the near future.

METHODOLOGY

To carry out this chapter, we opted for the integrative methodology to identify and synthesize future trends in education based on different types of research. The integrative review, developed by Whittemore et al. (2005), is a unique approach to combining data from various research designs, used in health sciences, which includes both experimental and non-experimental research (Whittemore et al. 2014). This method goes through the stages of problem identification, literature search, data evaluation, data analysis, and presentation. The construction and elaboration of regularities of a process require, as stated (Fuentes, 2010), the understanding and interpretation of them, due to their contribution to the characterization of the transformations. Likewise, they require the application of methods and approaches that respect the structures of relationship that emerge from them, recognize their diversity and complexity.

The information search was carried out from scientific databases (Pubmed, Scopus and Web of Sciences) combining the following keywords in English: "Artificial Intelligence", "Students", "Professors", "Users" and "Education". The term "Big Data" was also included when crossing the last search. All those articles published in the last five years (2016-2021) were filtered and those where the title did not refer to human studies, experimental and non-experimental studies, systematic reviews and multicenter studies were discarded. Isolated cases and articles that had no direct relationship with the subject were excluded. The analysis for each article was focused from the following dimensions: Type and focus of the article, domain, type of interaction and collaborative structure, technology used, learning environment and learning objectives. At all times of the analysis, trends were sought that would serve to extrapolate the acquired data. The trend, according to Álvarez (2016), "... expresses a certain behavior of an object of study in a certain direction, but it does not necessarily indicate a mandatory criterion. The trend reveals some behavior in time, by stages of said object of study, and although it does not express its essence, it hints at it. The tendency, insofar as it is a phenomenal manifestation, points in some way towards a regularity ". This determined trend helps us to understand if the use of AI in education has been something specific or something that is spreading over time.

ANALYSIS OF RESULTS

The way to carry out this integration of AI within education is through observation and data analysis. To do this, the AIs have access to the classroom through cameras and sensors and identify the individual needs of the students. With this, a huge amount of data is obtained that is analyzed with what the AI offers improvements in the form and way of carrying out the teaching work, guiding, in an individualized manner to personalize education. All this work is supported by the teacher who becomes, for the moment, the tool for presenting the changes that guide the AI, although there are already experiences that seek to replace the figure of the teacher with an augmented reality figure with which the AIs would be the real protagonists of the classroom. This, for many, is a threat since it seems an attempt to eliminate the teaching work but, as we have seen previously, human interaction is necessary and despite the fact that we divided the AIs into those that pretend to be human as one of the realities of these new technologies, the work of teachers is assured since they will be the true guides of this revolution. Despite everything, there are also voices that do not see it unfavorable that teachers be replaced by robots guided by artificial intelligence since as indicated by Bosede, Edwards & Adrian Cheok (2018) the possibilities are endless and we would obtain an educator completely dedicated to improve educational possibilities without losing emotions.

Also, many of the creators of computational analysis related to AI feel insecure when it comes to normalizing the presence of these intelligences in education since they want to be sure that said implementation benefits, and does not become a problem that affects the development of the students. This is the same thing that is happening with the use of social networks such as instagram among adolescents since the creators of instagram are the ones who have begun the analysis of the problems of the widespread use of these social networks among adolescents. We are at a time when creators and engineers feel highly responsible for the presence of new technologies among the youngest due to the dependencies or problems that are appearing that have to be analyzed, observing if the benefits of use outweigh the problems that are emerging in the society of the XXI century.

The experiences carried out have so far observed a higher performance in the use of AI in higher education but the experiences at younger ages are quite optimistic and generate a tendency to unify the presence of these intelligences at all levels of education in order to optimize individualized student performance (Popenici, SAD, Kerr, S., 2017). Actually, in addition, we need students who learn with artificial intelligence to be able to create elements that support that artificial intelligence given that today there is a high lack of engineers who can fill the deficiencies that the labor market needs as indicated by Aoun (2017).

The biggest problem for the integration of AI in education, as always when we talk about new technologies, will be the cost of the devices since they involve a high investment, although many authors consider that with the advancement of technology these technological elements may become cheaper. There is no doubt that the cost will not stop this integration since we already saw these problems in education a few years ago when Interactive Whiteboards (PDI) and the Wi-Fi network began to be introduced in classrooms, which today are highly generalized in a large number of schools (Baek, C., & Doleck, T., 2020) . As always, there will be a differentiation between those who can and those who cannot, or between those who arrive first to the interaction of this technology and those who arrive later, but all the authors consider that, whatever the way may be, the benefit in educadtion of students with the use of AI is something highly demonstrated which can be a real incentive in a sector that has been waiting for a long time to be able to direct all its efforts individually to the students who are under their charge (Rana, P., Raj Gupta, L., Kumar G. and Kumar Dubey, M., 2021) .

However, this condition not only affects the elements that directly influence education, but also indirectly involves various political, scientific and industrial factors. Image 1 illustrates recent developments and evolving future trends at the intersections between researchers, policy makers, and industry stakeholders emerging from the advances and deployments of Big Data and AI technologies in education. In this model presented by Luan H. et al (2020), researchers and industry would benefit from the development of specific educational technologies and their efficient transfer to commercial products. This is clearly hopeful and allows us to perceive where future educational plans should go since the incidence of AI in education favors both primary education (Han, Kim and Kwon, 2020), and secondary or higher education (Ciolacu, Tehrani, Binder, and Svasta, 2018).

Figure 1. Contemporary developments and future trends at the intersections between research, policy, and industry driven by advances in Big Data and AI in education.
Source: Luan H. et al. (2020)

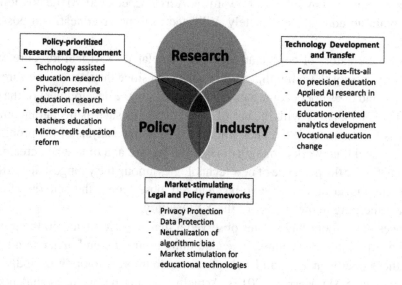

On the one hand, companies and governments would benefit from a legislature that stimulates technology markets while adequately protecting user data and privacy (López Robles, JC, Rodríguez Elizalde, R. and Aznar Sánchez, T., 2021). On the other hand, people in the academic environment and educational policy makers would benefit from prioritizing reforms that allow greater adoption of curricula enhanced by new technologies increasingly present in classrooms on all continents. All this produces a great challenge, as many authors have indicated, since it requires a fragmentation between the traditional education that exists up to today in the classroom and the new model that will emerge integrating AI in the classroom. We cannot forget that for this integration, manifested as a need for the future implementation of AI in the classroom, to work properly, we must ensure that the classrooms become new learning spaces by bringing pedagogy into communion with AI-based learning. (Banerjee et al., 2018). Past experiences and those to come since, as we have indicated, this is unstoppable, they have to be extrapolated and analyzed to be able to carry out the integration correctly, benefiting all students regardless of their age, race, sex or abilities.

The results presented through a quality and effective education using AI as a contribution to a personalized education are transforming, or will transform, education, but this must go hand in hand with continuous training of teachers who, today, believe that AI dehumanizes education and threatens future jobs. This clear feeling of threat can be compared to the very origin of the word sabotage when the peasants threw their "Sabot" or clogs at the machines to damage them because they were worried about their jobs (Dubois, 1979). If we do not integrate teachers into learning through the use of AI, we will run the same dangers that we could already observe during the first industrial revolution given that, without a doubt, the changes that the integration of AI in education are going to pose to us will represent a new educational revolution (Yang, 2021). Teachers' voices have already been raised making it clear that when using AI in the classroom, the voice of teachers must be taken into account, since otherwise what will happen is that it will fail, as with other emerging technologies that failed to become the educational spur they expected. For this reason, educational policies related to the adoption of new technologies in general and, specifically, of AI, must be at the center of all their objectives, since if this is not done, it may lead to an increase in educational exclusion that is so existent and so concerning which we find in the educational systems of the various countries (Stanica, Dascalu, Bodea, and Bogdan Moldoveanu, 2018). This use of AI in education could provide teaching equality, which is what, according to Bolívar (2011), puts teacher training at the center of the teaching action. A good educational system must take care of the training of its teachers so that all centers and therefore all students receive a good education, just as it must be guaranteed that all centers teach the same because otherwise we will break with that equality of education (Bolívar, 2011). This is why teacher training in the use of AI is capital, which until now we have not found present in educational systems. This training must also remember that teaching is a moral act based on ethical care, it is an act of research and reflection, learning is a process that helps us build, teaching is a collegiate act of teamwork and is also considered a political act (Krichesky et. *al*, 2011) since otherwise we would dehumanize education or, as seen during the Covid-19 pandemic, inequalities among all students would increase (Aznar and Rodríguez, 2021). For a large number of authors, this educational integration would bring the necessary change to be able to make education more inclusive since it would be possible to help people who, due to some type of limitation, have not been able to and cannot access a constant education, which would represent a considerable advance in inclusion that up to now has not been achieved in a generalized way in any country (Kazimzade G., Patzer Y., Pinkwart N., 2019).

AI is a real change and revolution in everything that is education at all levels. That is why a large number of authors related to education at all levels have begun in recent years to propose possibilities for the integration and application of AI within the academic world (Kun et al. 2020). Education using AI will be the teaching revolution in the coming years, but we must delve into what the use of this technology can contribute to students and teachers within traditional educational centers. Teachers become the key in this entire process, so their training trends must be clear and specific in order to achieve their full involvement (Yang, 2019). For all this, it is also essential to invest in schools, which must increase to achieve greater rigor within the expected results (Lee et al., 2012) with which to develop that adaptive learning that is the key to learning using AI, differentiating between learning strategies and teaching strategies that will allow full use of learning using these models adapted to students (Quadir et al., 2020).

Another aspect that we cannot forget is that this learning based on the use of AI as an adaptive tool must achieve homogenization of education standards, achieving the maximum performance of the students by following their own learning processes (Luan and Tsai, 2021). All this shows us that research on the integration of AI in education will become, according to experts, an integration of all the advantages of an education as it will favor students, but without detracting from the importance of teachers in the classroom who will be the users and evaluators of the competences that can be analyzed with all the interactions of the new technologies with the education of the students (Ocaña-Fernández, Valenzuela-Fernández and Garro-Aburto, 2019). All in all, student training times are optimized and can be used to develop the soft skills and hard skills that companies seek within the learning development of their future students.

In order to properly implement the use of AI in education, it is necessary to influence training plans that are adequately evaluated and that allow us to review all the pedagogical adaptation that can be achieved in order to understand which path to follow. It is essential that all the information obtained be analyzed and reviewed and that the AIs help to develop these adapted plans as indicated by Kumar (2019).

Finally, it should be noted that the union between traditional training and the possibilities posed by new technologies with the use of AI are multiple, and they increase exponentially if teacher training is added to it (Zawacki-Richter et al. 2019) who, without a doubt, are the true protagonists of all the development of these new technologies applied to education, blurring the lines between formal education and traditional experiential education with emerging technologies applied in an education that favors meaningful individual learning.

DISCUSSION

The starting point of any organizational change is acceptance of the need for change. Once the need for change and innovation has been identified, progress must be made in order to achieve meaningful change. A change has been needed for a long time in the field of education, and the new technologies applied in education have demonstrated the need for this educational change that breaks with the previous educational model created during the first industrial revolution. For this reason, within the presence of these new technologies in the educational model, AI anticipates, due to the experiences that we have commented previously, how they can be a disruptive element that enhances learning and that finally prepares students to address the Needs of a technological world where teamwork supported by the different capacities of each student prevails (Magoules, Pan, & Teng, 2016).

In order to achieve this, it is necessary to generate new training plans that break the educational differences in different countries and that end that education that does not adequately prepare teachers to take full advantage of the potential that AI can bring to education. Teacher training must add inquiry strategies to its training plan that motivate revision, criticism and construction originating from the experience of using AI in classrooms with the possibility of promoting changes in current models. We must not forget that this training should also be aimed at all members of the educational community who will help make the integration of new technologies in general and AI in particular a significant success for future generations of students.

Another problem that the integration of AI in education must overcome is the ethical limitations that exist in the academic world. For a long time, the role of the use of AI in different sectors has been known as indicated by Remian, (2019) but this is not without controversy since the ethical implications of using the intelligence of a computer to analyze all the information that can be produced in a school means violating the right to data protection or the privacy of the entire educational community, which puts a large number of educators against this use, who see a danger in this entire implementation. This danger has been somewhat extended by society since in this fourth information revolution, information theft has multiplied and even resulted in the control of the population through the massive use of data through mobile phones (Ribeiro-Navarrete, Saura, & Palacios-Marqués, 2021). Be that as it may, what is clear is that this interaction is unstoppable and that the benefits have been demonstrated by multiple experiences, which is why creative experts in AI propose to create an ethical code for the use of AI in education that would copy the laws of robotics that Isaac Asimov enunciated in 1942 in his story "Vicious Circle" and that for many laid the basis of what should be followed in the implementation of robotics.

Of course, before all this, voices opposed to the processing of information through computers may arise, but apart from denying the advancement of technology, all those who want to give a different point of view should be involved in the processes since they adapt to the new scenario and transforming the school technologically has been shown to be a great benefit that significantly improves learning as indicated by Xu and Rappaport (2019).

Teachers should be, and in many cases are, the leaders of society, the ones who make the difference in the lives of students. The use of AI in education can help to free teachers from the most tedious tasks of their day to day to dedicate themselves to being the companions of students on the wonderful path of learning (Lynch, 2018). If we decompose the teaching work into different tasks, some, we analyze that artificial intelligence can do them better, in others, it can help the teacher, but also, if artificial intelligence is integrated into today's classrooms, the teacher could save up to 40 or 50% of their time. Technology has revolutionized everything: how we live, play, learn, work, communicate… But it has not had an impact on education, and we have to start considering its future. We need skills that the use of AI could provide since at all times it would eliminate the most tedious jobs, change the world of work and allow us to dedicate time to new areas of research (Luminovo, 2018).

An in-depth analysis of how AI can be included in educational plans is required. This goes hand in hand with the analysis of the data generated within a large number of schools, so a large volume of data must be obtained to ensure that integration. The largest of the examples of the use of AI in education is in China, where they have already begun to develop pilot programs where students wear headbands that measure the concentration level of each student, offering data to the teacher that helps them to analyze the extent of learning of each one of them. In addition, the classrooms have robots that analyze the health of the students and their levels of participation. Students wear uniforms with chips that track their locations. There are even surveillance cameras that monitor how often students check their phones or yawn during classes. These devices are part of the pilot program in certain schools and have made it one of the largest experiments in the use of AI in the world. The aim of this program is to improve students' grades while feeding powerful algorithms, but they still lack time to draw conclusions and extrapolate data. It is a beginning of what this technology can contribute to initial education. AI undoubtedly has a great impact on higher education but the possibility that this new technology offers us by integrating it from the earliest ages should not be underestimated, since we could accelerate the implementation of that differentiated education that would improve academic performance and offer an education of quality that adequately prepares students to fully integrate into the world of work regardless of the continent in which they are located (Chiu, 2021).

The investigative possibilities are multiple and that allows us to understand how in such an important and pressing issue should be further investigated given that 5G and artificial intelligence are going to be, possibly, the changes that will have the most impact on the educational world and this would necesitate a large number of investigations in the line of analyzing its importance and its the possibilities to accelerate its implementation. Furthermore, it must be seen what possibilities the use of AI has with other emerging technologies and, why not, the use of robotics in the classroom, integrating it with a computational intelligence that encourages individualized learning. In addition, there is a lack of studies on the ethical approaches that all this new interaction will bring and on how to solve the denialist approaches to the use of this new technology.

CONCLUSION

AI in education was initially integrated in the form of computers and related systems. Later, integrating web-based and online education platforms made it possible to use robots to perform complementary automated functions. The use of these platforms and tools has increased the effectiveness of teachers in terms of the time they spend preparing the materials and applying them in their classes, which has improved the quality of teaching.

Similarly, AI has provided students with more complete learning experiences by customizing learning materials based on students' needs and abilities. In general, AI has had a significant impact on education, in particular in the areas of administration, instruction and learning of the education sector or in the context of individual learning institutions.

Management Involvement

After an exhaustive review of the papers presented, there appears a coherence among all the authors on the unexplored possibilities of the accelerated technological advance. It should be noted that most of the studies analyzed are directed at undergraduate students compared to graduate students, which provides an overview of the wide range of possible applications of AI in higher education to support students and teachers. They also provide insight into how AI can be useful for educational administrators.

There is a lack, as we have detected, of an exhaustive analysis of the educational policies that the governments of the different countries can carry out, copying what is already done in other countries (Marr, 2018). Said policies must address the training need of teachers, which must be done without excluding other members of the educational community such as students and parents who will be the direct recipients of the use of AI in the classroom. Together with this, it would be necessary to analyze much more thoroughly the ethical approach that will come with this new implementation as the new data privacy laws that have been extended worldwide can collide with the use of this intelligence in the classroom since the data belongs to the student and not everyone trusts the analyzes that will be carried out with all that information.

Thinking about AI within the educational world has been something that has made working on its integration in three ways: As a scientific tool, within educational devices or as an analysis of results in favor of an improvement in academic results. In addition to the contribution that AI makes to the understanding and conceptualization of academic practice and research, there is a very promising future in meaningful learning using AI. One of the approaches that has been most developed within education is to find a way to approach each student through the personalization of teaching, and all the studies developed are clear that adapting the learning speed to the student is one of the basic principles of the AI.

As we have shown with this study, the possibilities are endless, but what is needed is time and the extension of pilot programs in different continents to achieve an extrapolation of results. Despite everything, the best experiences have shown us that the main advantage that artificial intelligence potentially brings to education is the personalization that helps us to have a teacher adapted to the learning capacity of each student in the classroom. Ia can play at the level of measuring learning processes by analyzing the contents that are being more effective by providing a personalized learning path. We have to understand, as we have shown, that in this technological world there are alternative tools with different and unique methodologies for each learning process, but in order to ensure the proper use of these technologies we must carry out a good diagnosis of the needs and for that the analysis of data that AI does is essential. That is the future of education: Data analysis through AI that will improve education and that is unstoppable with the widespread use of technology in all areas.

Practical Implications

In conclusion, there is no doubt, after the completion of this chapter, that we must rethink education. It has been shown that the reality that we have experienced during the pandemic has put new technologies in a preferential place in education since they have been the way used by all schools worldwide to give continuity to educational plans that otherwise, with the confinement, would have been completely abandoned. We must rethink the training plans of future teachers, students and parents. We must rethink what AI is going to bring us and what we can lose. But without a doubt, what is clear is that the use of AI in education is going to turn training centers into something different that will bring many new features that, moment, we can only perceive. At present there is much talk about AI and how the new robots that are going to be presented using that technology which would replace jobs, which is something that may happen, but surely many new jobs are going to be created that today do not exist. We even imagine and those AIs can help us create them. Technology has that power and therefore we must help and train the new professionals of the future who, with the use of these new tools, will be able to be competitive in the world to come. Governments have to work for data protection to ensure that AI is perceived in a clear and secure way (Janssen, Brous, Estevez, Barbosa, & Janowski, 2020).

The contribution of this chapter shows us that AI is the key to the future development of world education. As we have commented, the objective of education is to develop a better human being, to develop an individual who understands his environment, who has a related balance and who is capable of understanding the world that surrounds him. The world to come, as many authors have told us, is going to be a world where the presence of AI is going to be constant, as we already see in multiple countries, so within education we have to learn to interact with those AIs now and collaborate to understand how artificial intelligence is in some way modifying us, changing the way we live, the way we learn and the way we communicate. In the same way we have shown how education has to understand that the way in which we have been learning what we have been learning is not necessarily adjusting to what the individual requires today. We have shown that artificial intelligence is bringing us value and benefits in the area of Education. There are verified experiences that have already been shown to help students improve their understanding of those topics they want to learn. Artificial intelligence, artificial intelligence systems, computer systems, computers and programs are helping, in some ways, to support student learning in many countries around the world of which we already have evidence. In addition, many teachers of those educational entities that have integrated AI pilot programs spend less time on administrative tasks to which they previously spent an enormous amount of time, which means more time dedicated to the student and that, with the feedback that AI offers them with the individual learning of each student manages to improve their understanding of what they want to learn, that is, they improve the human being and their relationship with the world (Fiok, Farahani, Karwowski and Ahram, 2021).

Limitations

Carrying out a study that defines the future conditions of the implementation of AI in education is almost impossible since it has not yet been possible to create a uniform model that indicates the way forward. Almost all studies and experiences in AI speak of the benefits of learning, but we have not yet come to know if these benefits can be given to all students, regardless of the country, so it is unknown how that future digital learning will be and if it will work, as Unesco wants to achieve educational equity world-wide. The new students who are classified as Alpha are a truly digital generation but one that presents great differences in the use of technologies, so we would lack data to be able to understand what this integration will be like, which is perceived as the future of education and if it will serve to achieve a global social justice that unifies the learning of all the students of the world. Digital learning can provide feedback to the system for an improvement in said learning (Shubham, Radha and Prathamesh, 2021).

REFERENCES

Álvarez de Zayas, C. (2016). *Epistemología del Caos*. Editorial Kipos.

Aoun, J. E. (2017). *Robot-Proof: Higher Education in the Age of Artificial Intelligence*. MIT. doi:10.7551/mitpress/11456.001.0001

Aznar, T. y Rodriguez, R. (2021). Education, social justice and post-pandemic in spain. *Journal of Management and Business Education*, *4*(2), 206-230.

Baek, C., & Doleck, T. (2020). A Bibliometric Analysis of the Papers Published in the Journal of Artificial Intelligence in Education from 2015-2019. *International Journal of Learning Analytics and Artificial Intelligence for Education*, *2*(1), 67–84. doi:10.3991/ijai.v2i1.14481

Banerjee, S., Singh, P. K., & Bajpai, J. (2018). A Comparative Study on Decision-Making Capability Between Human and Artificial Intelligence. In B. Panigrahi, M. Hoda, V. Sharma, & S. Goel (Eds.), *Nature Inspired Computing. Advances in Intelligent Systems and Computing* (Vol. 652). Springer. doi:10.1007/978-981-10-6747-1_23

Bates, T., Cobo, C., Mariño, O., & Wheeler, S. (2020). Can artificial intelligence transform higher education? *Int J Educ Technol High Educ*, *17*(1), 42. doi:10.118641239-020-00218-x

Beijing Consensus on Artificial Intelligence and Education. (2019). *UNESCO*. https://unesdoc.unesco.org/ark:/48223/pf0000368303

Bolívar, A. (2011). Justicia social y equidad escolar. Una revisión actual. *Revista Internacional de Educación para la justicia social,* *1*(1), 9-45.

Brynjolfsson, E., Rock, D., & Syverson, C. (2017). *Artificial intelligence and the modern productivity paradox: A clash of expectations and statistics*. National Bureau of Economic Research.

Bryson, J.J. (2018). Patiency is not a virtue: the design of intelligent systems and systems of ethics. *Ethics and Information Technology, 20*(1), 15-26.

Calvo-Rubio, L. M., & Ufarte-Ruiz, M. J. (2020). Percepción de docentes universitarios, estudiantes, responsables de innovación y periodistas sobre el uso de inteligencia artificial en periodismo. *El Profesional de la Información, 29*(1). Advance online publication. doi:10.3145/epi.2020.ene.09

Castrillón, O. D., Sarache, W., & Ruiz-Herrera, S. (2020). Predicción del rendimiento académico por medio de técnicas de inteligencia artificial. *Formación Universitaria, 13*(1), 93–102. doi:10.4067/S0718-50062020000100093

Chiu, T. K. F. (2021). A Holistic Approach to the Design of Artificial Intelligence (AI) Education for K-12 Schools. *TechTrends, 65*(5), 796–807. doi:10.100711528-021-00637-1

Ciolacu, M., Tehrani, A. F., Binder, L., & Svasta, P. M. (2018). Education 4.0 - Artificial Intelligence Assisted Higher Education: Early recognition System with Machine Learning to support Students' Success. *2018 IEEE 24th International Symposium for Design and Technology in Electronic Packaging (SIITME)*, 23-30. 10.1109/SIITME.2018.8599203

Clerwall, C. (2014). Enter the robot journalist. Users' perceptions of automated content. *Journalism Practice, 8*(5), 519–531. doi:10.1080/17512786.2014.883116

Cobo, J. C. R., & Moravec, J. W. (2011). *Aprendizaje Invisible.: Hacia una nueva ecología de la educación*. Editions de la Universitat de Barcelona.

Dubois, P. (1979). Sabotage in Industry. *Organization Studies, 1*(1), 103–104.

Edwards, B. I., & Cheok, A. D. (2018). Why Not Robot Teachers: Artificial Intelligence for Addressing Teacher Shortage. *Applied Artificial Intelligence, 32*(4), 345–360. doi:10.1080/08839514.2018.1464286

Fiok K., Farahani FV., Karwowski W., Ahram T. (2021). Explainable artificial intelligence for education and training. *The Journal of Defense Modeling and Simulation*. doi:10.1177/15485129211028651

Fister, I., & Fister, I. Jr., (Eds.). (2015). *Adaptation and Hybri-dization in Computational Intelligence* (Vol. 18). Adaptation, Learning and Optimization. doi:10.1007/978-3-319-14400-9

Gadner, H. (2005). *Inteligencias múltiples: La teoría en la práctica*. Ediciones Paidos.

Goda, K., & Mine, T. (2011). Analysis of Students Learning Activities through Quantifying Time-Series Comments. Knowledge-Based and Intelligent Information and Engineering Systems, 6882, 154-164.

Graupe, D. (2016). *Deep Learning Neural Networks: Design and Case Studies. World Scientific Publishing*. doi:10.1142/10190

Han, H. J., Kim, K. J., & Kwon, H. S. (2020). The Analysis of Elementary School Teachers' Perception of Using Artificial Intelligence in Education. *Journal of Digital Convergence, 18*(7), 47–56. doi:10.14400/JDC.2015.13.7.47

Janssen, M., Brous, P., Estevez, E., Barbosa, L. S., & Janowski, T. (2020). Data governance: Organizing data for trustworthy Artificial Intelligence. *Government Information Quarterly, 37*(3), 101493. doi:10.1016/j.giq.2020.101493

Kazimzade, G., Patzer, Y., & Pinkwart, N. (2019). Artificial Intelligence in Education Meets Inclusive Educational Technology—The Technical State-of-the-Art and Possible Directions. In J. Knox, Y. Wang, & M. Gallagher (Eds.), *Artificial Intelligence and Inclusive Education. Perspectives on Rethinking and Reforming Education*. Springer. doi:10.1007/978-981-13-8161-4_4

Krichesky, G. J., Martínez-Garrido, C., Martínez, A. M., García, A., Castro, A., & González, A. (2011). Hacia un programa de formación docente para la justicia social. *Revista Electrónica Iberoamericana sobre Calidad, Eficacia y Cambio en Educación, 9*(4), 63–77.

Kumar, N. M. S. (2019). Implementation of artificial intelligence in imparting education and evaluating student performance. *Journal of Artificial Intelligence and Capsule Networks, 1*, 1-9. doi:10.36548/jaicn.2019.1.001

Kun, X., Fanjue, L., Yi, M., Yuheng, W., Jing, Z., & Mike, S. S. (2020). Using Machine Learning to Learn Machines: A Cross-Cultural Study of Users' *Responses to Machine-Generated Artworks. Journal of Broadcasting & Electronic Media, 64*(4), 566–591. doi:10.1080/08838151.2020.1835136

Lee, V., Ye, L., & Recker, M. (2012). What a Long Strange Trip It's Been: A Comparison of Authors, Abstracts, and References in the 1991 and 2010 ICLS Proceedings. In *The Future of Learning: Proceedings of the 10th International Conference of the Learning Sciences (ICLS 2012)* – Volume 2, *Short Papers, Symposia, and Abstracts* (172-176). International Society of the Learning Sciences.

León Pérez, J. (2019). Impacto de las tecnologías disruptivas en la percepción remota: big data, internet de las cosas e inteligencia artificial. *UD y la geomática*, (14). doi:10.14483/23448407.15658

López Robles, J. C., Rodríguez Elizalde, R., & Aznar Sánchez, T. (2021). *La inteligencia artificial desde la percepción de los alumnos y profesores. Revisión bibliográfica*. IMAT.

Luan, H., Geczy, P., Lai, H., Gobert, J., Yang, S. J. H., Ogata, H., Baltes, J., Guerra, R., Li, P., & Tsai, C.-C. (2020). Challenges and Future Directions of Big Data and Artificial Intelligence in Education. *Frontiers in Psychology, 11*, 580820. doi:10.3389/fpsyg.2020.580820 PMID:33192896

Luminovo, A. (2018). *The future of education and how AI can help shape it*. Disponible en: https://medium.com/luminovo/the-future-of-education-and-how-ai-can-help-shape-it-6f1202f4757d

Lynch, M. (2018). *7 Roles for Artificial Intelligence in Education*, en *The Tech Advocate*. Disponible en: https://www.thetechedvocate.org/7-roles-for-artificial-intelligence-in-education/

Magoules, F., Pan, J., & Teng, F. (2016). *Cud Computing: Data-Intensive Computing and Scheduling*. CRC Press.

Marr, B. (2018). How Is AI Used In Education — Real World Examples Of Today And A Peek Into The Future. *Forbes*. Disponible en: https://www.forbes.com/sites/bernardmarr/2018/07/25/how-is-ai-used-in-education-real-world-examples-of-today-and-a-peek-into-the-future/#7079f80d586e

McArthur, D., Lewis, M., & Bishary, M. (2005). The Roles of Artificial Intelligence in Education: Current Progress and Future Prospects. *Journal of Educational Technology, 1*(4), 42–80. https://www.learntechlib.org/p/161310/

McCarthy, J. (2007). *What Is Artificial Intelligence*. Sección "Basic Questions".

Ocaña-Fernández, Y., Valenzuela-Fernández, L. A., & Garro-Aburto, L. L. (2019). Inteligencia artificial y sus implicaciones en la educación superior. *Propósitos y Representaciones*, 7(2), 536–568. doi:10.20511/pyr2019.v7n2.274

Paconesi, G., & Guida, M. (2021). Handbook of Research on Teaching With Virtual Environments and AI. National Institute for Documentation, Italy. doi:10.4018/978-1-7998-7638-0

Popenici, S. A. D., & Kerr, S. (2017). Exploring the impact of artificial intelligence on teaching and learning in higher education. *RPTEL*, 12(1), 22. doi:10.118641039-017-0062-8 PMID:30595727

Quadir, B., Chen, N. S., & Isaias, P. (2020). Analyzing the educational goals, problems and techniques used in educational big data research from 2010 to 2018. *Interactive Learning Environments*, 1–17. Advance online publication. doi:10.1080/10494820.2020.1712427

Rana, P., Raj Gupta, L., Kumar, G., & Kumar Dubey, M. (2021). A Taxonomy of Various Applications of Artificial Intelligence in Education. *2021 2nd International Conference on Intelligent Engineering and Management (ICIEM)*, 23-28, 10.1109/ICIEM51511.2021.9445339

Remian, D. (2019). Augmenting Education: Ethical Considerations for Incorporating Artificial Intelligence in Education. *Instructional Design Capstones Collection*, 52. https://scholarworks.umb.edu/instruction_capstone/52

Ribeiro-Navarrete, S., Saura, J. R., & Palacios-Marqués, D. (2021). Towards a new era of mass data collection: Assessing pandemic surveillance technologies to preserve user privacy. *Technological Forecasting and Social Change*, 167, 120681. doi:10.1016/j.techfore.2021.120681 PMID:33840865

Roll, I., & Wylie, R. (2016). Evolution and Revolution in Artificial Intelligence in Education. *International Artificial Intelligence in Education Society*, 26(2), 582–599. doi:10.100740593-016-0110-3

Russell, S. J., & Norvig, P. (2009). Artificial intelligence: a modern approach (3rd ed.). Prentice Hall.

Saura, J. R., Ribeiro-Soriano, D., & Palacios-Marqués, D. (2021). Using data mining techniques to explore security issues in smart living environments in Twitter. *Computer Communications*, 179, 285–295. Advance online publication. doi:10.1016/j.comcom.2021.08.021

Saura, J. R., Ribeiro-Soriano, D., & Palacios-Marqués, D. (2021b, July 15). Setting privacy "by default" in social IoT: Theorizing the challenges and directions in Big Data Research. *Big Data Research*, 25, 100245. doi:10.1016/j.bdr.2021.100245

Shubham, J., Radha, K., & Prathamesh, C. (2021). *Evaluating Artificial Intelligence in Education for Next Generation*. IOP Publishing Ltd. doi:10.1088/1742-6596/1714/1/012039

Soares, N., & Fallenstein, B. (2017). Agent foundations for aligning machine intelligence with human interests: A technical research agenda. In *The Technological Singularity: Managing the Journey*. Springer. https://intelligence.org/files/ TechnicalAgenda.pdf

Stanica, I., Dascalu, M., Bodea, C. N., & Bogdan Moldoveanu, A. D. (2018). VR Job Interview Simulator: Where Virtual Reality Meets Artificial Intelligence for Education. *2018 Zooming Innovation in Consumer Technologies Conference (ZINC)*, 9-12, 10.1109/ZINC.2018.8448645

Vladan, D. (2004). Web Intelligence and Artificial Intelligence in Education. *Journal of Educational Technology & Society*, *7*(4), 29–39. https://www.jstor.org/stable/jeductechsoci.7.4.29

Whittemore, R., Chao, A., Jang, M., Minges, K. E., & Park, C. (2014). Methods for knowledge synthesis: An overview. *Heart & Lung*, *43*(5), 453–461. doi:10.1016/j.hrtlng.2014.05.014 PMID:25012634

Whittemore, R., & Knafl, K. (2005). The integrative review: Updated methodology. *Journal of Advanced Nursing*, *52*(5), 546–553. doi:10.1111/j.1365-2648.2005.03621.x PMID:16268861

Williams, S. (2016). *Business intelligence strategy and big data analytics: a general management perspective*. Morgan Kaufmann Publishers.

Xu, D., & Rappaport, T. S. (2019). Construction on Teaching Evaluation Index System of Track and Field General Course for Physical Education Major in Light of Wireless Network Technology. Big data analysis techniques for intelligent systems. *Journal of Intelligent & Fuzzy Systems*, *37*(3), 3435–3443. doi:10.3233/JIFS-179147

Yang, S. J. H. (2019). Precision education: new challenges for AI in education. In *The 27th International Conference on Computers in Education (ICCE), XXVII-XXVIII*. Kenting, Taiwan: Asia-Pacific Society for Computers in Education (APSCE).

Yang, S. J. H. (2021). Guest Editorial: Precision education - a new challenge for AI in education. *Journal of Educational Technology & Society*, *24*(1), 105–108.

Yannier, N., Hudson, S. E., & Koedinger, K. R. (2020). Active Learning is About More Than Hands-On: A Mixed-Reality AI System to Support STEM Education. *International Journal of Artificial Intelligence in Education*, *30*(1), 74–96. doi:10.100740593-020-00194-3

Zawacki-Richter, O., Marín, V. I., Bond, M., & Gouverneur, F. (2019). Systematic review of research on artificial intelligence applications in higher education – where are the educators? *International Journal of Educational Technology in Higher Education*, *16*(1), 39. doi:10.118641239-019-0171-0

Chapter 19
How to Use Artificial Intelligence in Education?
Current Insights and Prospects for Government Initiatives

José Ramón Saura
https://orcid.org/0000-0002-9457-7745
Rey Juan Carlos University, Spain

ABSTRACT

This exploratory and pedagogical chapter has proposed new ways of using artificial intelligence in education. The uses of artificial intelligence have been linked to the education sector in order to improve the active listening actions and decision-making of governments. The results identify and discuss seven educational uses of artificial intelligence. From the government's point of view, three uses of artificial intelligence to improve the educational sector have been identified. By using the present study insights and the prospects for governments initiatives proposed, the authors have covered a scope of the uses of artificial intelligence and outlined the role that governments should maintain for efficient development and optimization strategy in education.

INTRODUCTION

In today's connected era, the use of new information technologies has been given rise to the development of artificial intelligence (Holtgrewe, 2014). As new technologies develop, companies and educational institutions, as well as governments, have begun to implement new forms and models of business and organization (Bharadwaj et al., 2013).

The increasing use of technologies by users has led to the emergence of large databases that may be effectively managed and filtered. Public and private institutions are struggling to adapt their training models so that their employees know how to understand and use new databases generated as a result of the use of new technologies, both at a personal and business level (Montealegre and Iyengar, 2021).

DOI: 10.4018/978-1-7998-9609-8.ch019

Of note, artificial intelligence allows the analysis and execution of automated actions. Moreover, this technology is set to become a new data science used in most of the business or institutional processes (Cai and Zhu, 2015). Broadly speaking, artificial intelligence is defined as those tools, approaches or technologies that use any form of artificial intelligence such as machine learning, to stimulate human intelligence (McCarthy, 1998; Raisch and Krakowski, 2021).

It is important to note that, artificial intelligence is being used in the business ecosystem to promote and develop the analysis and collection of large databases from social media, suppliers, sales, or product and service development (Kshetri, 2021). The great opportunity provided by artificial intelligence at the enterprise level is the ability to identify new patterns and trends that human intelligence is not able to perceive (Ruiz-Rea et al., 2021).

In addition, several actions can be automated by using artificial intelligence techniques in order to save companies' resources and specific tasks to their employees (Alter, 2021). In the robotic business, automation allows building new machines and assembly lines, which leads to the replacement of jobs performed by humans to machines (Matthews et al., 2021).

This digital paradigm, where data privacy remains a concern (Saura et al., 2021b) not only by users but to citizens, the use of artificial intelligence in education and its development by governments, has become an important issue for research (Collins et al., 2021).

The education sector should be in constant change and should also be characterized by innovation in learning processes and methods. Even though there are several ways to promote innovation (Saura et al., 2022a) in the education system by using new technologies, specifically, artificial intelligence, it is interesting to understand how governments can propose and develop programs to promote the use of artificial intelligence in this sector (Chen et al., 2020).

In this way, the improvement of the educational system by including artificial intelligence as an important factor of learning processes can enhance its development by implementing new technological tools that boost teaching and learning processes (Zaidi et al., 2019; Saura et al., 2022).

Therefore, this chapter aims to contribute didactyly since it proposes teaching and research materials based on the analysis of artificial intelligence in education and the role that governments play to understand the present, challenges, and future research of this sector (Drigas and Ioannidou, 2012).

To develop the methodology process it is proposed a review of scientific literature published, to date, that contemplates the topics outlined above in order to propose and discuss the best solutions for the use of artificial intelligence in education.

THEORETICAL FRAMEWORK

Educational Organizations

In recent years, educational organizations have changed their organizational structures and technology. Events such as the covid-19 pandemic have meant that educational institutions have had to adapt to hybrid teaching, in which the role played by new technologies for online teaching has become essential (Carrillo et al., 2020).

In an ecosystem where digital development is sometimes hampered by difficult management processes, the covid-19 pandemic has increased the speed at which educational institutions, such as colleges and universities, have been forced to acquire software and hardware to improve their digital services.

In this global situation, new technologies have become a crucial way for teaching and student activities more enjoyable, automated, and successful (Tadesse and Muluye, 2020). In this way, educational institutions have been forced to identify their needs while changing their organizational processes. These needs have been mainly linked to adapting both the skills of employees and the digital structure of the institutions to the use of new forms of digital technologies (Nguyen and Kieuthi, 2020).

In an ecosystem in which digital technologies and the technological process is key for the development of education, organizations have found out that artificial intelligence helps not only to solve complex problems but to classify and identify them, as well as to automate answers to simplify management and teaching processes (Basilaia et al., 2020).

The understanding and implementation of artificial intelligence in educational institutions can enhance the organizations' change at a teaching, management, and organizational level. It has been shown that educational institutions may have issues in the vertical and horizontal scales of communication since they are large institutions made up of more than 200 employees. In these institutions, proper communication through new technologies must be key to the success of teaching and management (Anderson et al., 2012).

In addition, thanks to the use of artificial intelligence, educational institutions can (i) set the right culture focused on the use of new technologies; (ii) promote the young talent since technology is in constant development and (iii) find new artificial intelligence technologies that boost new learning and teaching models (Devedžić, 2014).

Likewise, educational institutions can use artificial intelligence and new applications to find intelligent ways to control outcomes and digital transformation in the institution itself (Baker, 2000).

Artificial intelligence can give rise to the improvement of teaching processes since the use of new tools by teachers can help them to coordinate and manage their students, as well as promote new entrepreneurial initiatives among university students (Knox, 2020).

The Role of Governments in Artificial Intelligence Deployment

The role played by governments in the development and use of artificial intelligence in the educational sector is quite important. Governments establish collaborations and common projects to boost technologies and guides relevant for their international communities, at a national and international level (Evans and Yen, 2006).

In this way, there are several European initiatives, such as the data protection law (GDPR), that fights to protect data privacy from users on the Internet; or global plans for artificial intelligence development as a huge industrial revolution that will change business, economics industrial and education sectors, among others (Saura et al., 2021c).

Governments must establish action and communication protocols to safeguard the correct understanding of artificial intelligence and its benefits in educational initiatives. Likewise, governments are in charge of encouraging the use of artificial intelligence as a positive cause to enhance education. In this way, governments are responsible for providing aid for the acquisition of hardware and software that works with artificial intelligence and establishing state training plans so that employees can acquire knowledge in the use of this type of data science (Kizys et al., 2021).

Moreover, society has been concerned about data privacy due to the use and treatment of data by governments. Thus, scientific literature is currently interested in the uncertainty in society about the use of artificial intelligence and the processing of personal data from social networks or technological devices (Alqudah and Muradkhanli, 2021). Of note, the use of technology, smartwatches, smartphones or laptops, as well as the Internet of Things is generating large amounts of data that governments could have access to if they collaborate with companies (Mazurek and Małagocka, 2019).

Nevertheless, this is one of the concerns of society as these data can be used to forecast behavior or to understand how citizens move in a specific geographical area (Yang et al., 2019). Therefore, if we link the creation, collection, and treatment of data from the education sector to personal information of citizens, as well as to databases created due to the monitoring actions of the government, data privacy could be violated (Saura et al., 2021d).

In this way, governments apart from promoting new strategies to enhance the use of artificial intelligence in education, should establish regulatory standards and laws to safeguard the privacy of citizens and those actions carried out using artificial intelligence technologies (Zhang et al., 2021).

METHODOLOGY

This chapter proposes a selective review of the scientific databases since the nature of the study is teaching and pedagogic instead of based on research contributions. The major aim is to understand how artificial intelligence should be developed in the education sector and to define the role of governments in this industry. This methodology of selective review proposes the use of bibliographic sources and references that have previously treated this topic to define and develop actions that can be classified in this industry to understand how it works and develops itself (Safarov, 2017).

A selective literature review is a process in which researchers identify those references that develop and justify coherent information that can be directly or indirectly linked to the topic under study. In this way, the correct definition of the concepts and processes that can be identified in those references can be used to build new theory or to propose a practical guide of how to promote the teaching of education in a specific area (Snyder, 2019).

By using information from different bibliographic sources, the pedagogical contribution lists and classifies the most important information in terms of understanding how artificial intelligence should be used in education and what actions of governments can encourage its development.

Literature reviews are not a relevant research process, but they can help to understand the context of a certain topic. Moreover, if the studied topic is emergent, the nature of the main literature included in research becomes relevant (Rowley and Slack, 2004).

Likewise, it is important to note that the results of the research should be taken as exploratory and qualitative, as well as that they can be used to justify new research hypotheses or research questions in future studies that address the development of artificial intelligence in the education sector and the possible relationships through variables and indicators that link both topics.

In this way, this study provides a robust theoretical framework for the development of future research but can be also used for pedagogical and teaching tasks as a guideline or sourcebook that focuses on understanding how artificial intelligence works in educational institutions and the role that governments should play to promote its use in this sector. The sources and databases used were Google Scholar, Web of Sciences, Scopus and IEEE Xplore. Queries included "Artificial Intelligence" AND "Education", "Artificial Intelligence" AND "Governments", "Education" AND "Artificial Intelligence" AND "Governments". Searches were conducted in English between July 12th, 2021, and September 15th, 2021. No conference papers or proceedings were used as the studies included in the chapter were original articles and reviews.

ANALYSIS OF RESULTS

Uses of Artificial Intelligence in Educational Institutions

Teaching and Personalization

Artificial intelligence identifies patterns and specific trends that can improve processes and strategies. In this way, if we consider the use of artificial intelligence for education, the personalization of content and learning strategies can be successfully modified. Teaching and personalization can be used in this way to adapt teaching and learning content in order to increase motivation as well as to incentive student behavior (Chassignol et al., 2018).

Content personalization allows adding teaching elements focused on new technologies that are personalized for each student according to their results in exams or according to the teachers' level of demand (Zou, 2017). Therefore, personalization and teaching are concepts that should be studied and improved in-depth to teach content in both individualized and collective ways.

Tutoring and Automation

One of the biggest challenges for university teachers and professors are tasks related to tutoring sessions (Kandlhofer et al., 2016). In this way, by using artificial intelligence, the main weaknesses and strengthens of students can be identified to adapt their exercises and tasks. Therefore, teachers get students to improve on those issues that require more attention. There are several tools that focus on artificial intelligence to optimize the processes related to the teaching of content (Agrawal et al., 2019). If teachers use these tutoring linked to process automation, many benefits can be obtained.

Of note, tutoring tasks can be optimized with chatbots and many other artificial intelligence tools that allow teachers to filter and forecast what questions will their students ask.

AI Quick Responses and Optimization

As outlined before, artificial intelligence has become a powerful tool to optimize management and organizational processes. This option can be used both for complex problems that may arise in the organization, processes' optimization, or development of learning tactics (Stone et al., 2016).

In this way, artificial intelligence can be used to promote the use of automatic chatbots on websites of universities or teaching institutions, or even to identify useful documents and topics for teachers (Henderson et al., 2017).

By using applications and specialized software, processes that are not optimal can be optimized, and new solutions can be quickly identified since the more artificial intelligence is used, the greater the efficiency and results in its prediction of selected tasks.

Global and 24/7 Access to Learning Tools

One of the greatest potentials of artificial intelligence is promoting teaching in an open-ended process at any time (Ardito et al., 2004). That is to say, the use of artificial intelligence allows the use of tools that work automatically 24/7 and that can be accessed globally in multiple languages.

As outlined before, artificial intelligence automates processes and activities, thus resources and answers can be offered in an automated way by focusing the set of applications that work with artificial intelligence in the educational sector in terms of documents management or solvency of problems that have been detected previously within the same control system (Chen et al., 2020). Access 24 hours seven days a week from anywhere, driven by the use of new technologies and automated responses will enable education to enter in new paradigm where digitalization and automation are key to process utilization and educational success (Kumar, 2019).

Adapted Educational Software and Hardware to Student Needs

The use of artificial intelligence in education leads to the updating of both software and hardware used for teaching in educational centers. Likewise, if we mix software based on artificial intelligence with traditional platforms such as static virtual classrooms, forums or websites, these applications will become quite relevant (Sapci and Sapci, 2020).

During the last decade, educational institutions and universities have adapted their classrooms and teaching methodologies by using hardware and software based on the use of the Internet as a tool to improve the quality of the lessons.

In this way, this new situation governed by artificial intelligence should become one of the priority processes that support teaching. Therefore, additional software and hardware implemented in educational institutions should be configured for the use, processing, and collection of data for its processing with algorithms that work with artificial intelligence (Holtgrewe, 2014).

This fact would allow artificial intelligence to detect patterns and trends to improve the educational and learning processes of students using this type of software and hardware.

Improvement of Courses and Teachers' Skills

Traditional evaluation ways of both teaching staff and study guides at universities are reduced to forms filled by students the professors themselves, to date. Thus, it is important to consider the development of new initiatives that work with artificial intelligence through automated tools, which can evaluate both the capacity and the development of teaching by both students and these tools themselves (Kandlhofer et al., 2016). Operationally, this is not impossible since there is software that works with textual analysis or sentiment analysis to understand how teachers give classes (Tadesse and Muluye, 2020).

This analysis automated by artificial intelligence tools allows teachers to identify what words are used the most, whether the topics are time-balanced, or to understand what topics are the most asked by their students.

In this way, the implementation of new artificial intelligence tools to evaluate teachers could be key to identify indicators that were not used in teaching processes developed to date. Likewise, these tools can be used to measure the interest of students in a certain subject.

New Ways of Interaction Between Students and Information

The implementation of tools that work with big data and artificial intelligence in public and private educational institutions can lead to the development and design of new visual graphics to understand how students interact with information. However, by using interactive artificial intelligence, students can manage data collection and filtering processes in a more dynamic and motivating way (Chen et al., 2020).

New algorithms for information selection and visual design of user interfaces allow students to identify information in a faster way while enabling them to make use of new technologies. Educational institutions can thus link different information platforms and obtain conclusions that come from different databases (Yang et al., 2019).

From a graphical point of view, platforms that collect data thanks to artificial intelligence allow to consider new metrics and indicators to improve interaction between both teachers and users, and the teaching mechanisms of their institutions (Devedžić, 2004).

Uses of Artificial Intelligence in Education From the Government's Perspective

In a data-driven digital paradigm, governments are key for economic, social, and educational development (Collins et al., 2021). New technologies as Big Data and artificial intelligence allow governments to explore new ways for data analysis and collection.

Governments are large public institutions that protect their citizens and, thus their actions are mainly focused on improving infrastructure, optimizing processes, or preventing from any variable that may affect society and individual citizens (Nguyen and Kieuthi, 2020).

Under this perspective, governments optimize processes in which citizens are involved. In the educational sector, some of the actions that governments develop to promote the use of artificial intelligence are as follows:

New Statistics in a Data-Based Era

There are several data sources from where governments gather information to optimize national security and protect society. From glocalization of mobile devices, possible alerts of terrorist attacks, climate catastrophes, or alerts of viruses that could endanger their population, are just some of the examples in which governments can collect data to analyze it with artificial intelligence tools (Ribeiro-Navarrete et al., 2021).

Nevertheless, if the education industry used tools linked to artificial intelligence, millions of data would be produced daily regarding the evolution and development of the education sector in a country or area.

However, data collected by governments from the education sector come from annual reports published by universities or educational centers, as well as surveys that these official institutions send to their teachers and directors in order to gather information about their educational objectives set out in their annual reports (Saura et al., 2021).

Governments use this information to plan new communication and educational protocols at the national or international level, thus promoting communication focused on driving those variables and indicators where an improvement in statistics is necessary. Artificial intelligence in this paradigm can drive an improvement of data analysis in real-time (Croushore, 2011).

Beyond optimization and automation of data collection, the analysis and predictive capabilities of artificial intelligence enable governments to make earlier decisions regarding the present and future of the education sector.

In this way, by using new variables and indicators in real-time or in a short period of time, outputs can be implemented in terms of educational success. It has been proven that the more statistics and data are analyzed, the better the results in terms of prediction and accuracy of the tools used to improve education with artificial intelligence (Chen et al., 2020).

New Data to Optimize the Educational Industry

The education industry is constantly changing. However, while improving both the educational processes and the prediction of the efficiency of new business models, the optimization of the education industry in terms of sustainability, energy efficiency, logistics, improved research, and teaching, among others, is interesting from the point of view of governments (Saura et al., 2021a).

Governments focus the use of the analysis of new data sources with artificial intelligence on the education industry by prioritizing issues related to its sustainable development and logistical efficiency, government departments can develop both guidelines to improve these areas and grant proposals to boost the suitability and adaptability of both public and private education institutions to such variables.

Governments can collect new sources of data and compare them to databases from other countries to reduce pollution, identify new sources of sustainable revenue, or support industry with greater energy efficiency.

Undoubtedly, the application of artificial intelligence to educational data sources can enable governments to develop new state plans under different general sub-directions thus allowing the improvement of the industry thanks to the analysis of data in an efficient and fast way (Nguyen and Kieuthi, 2020).

Decision-Making Processes Optimized

One of the most relevant issues in scientific literature is how artificial intelligence can be applied to improve decision-making. Artificial intelligence tools allow the creation of control dashboards that link different sources of information and that visually allow linking indicators, variables, and concepts that can improve decision-making (Gao et al., 2019).

Under the perspective of good governance, public institutions can propose the creation, design, and structuration of new protocols for decision-making based on a control dashboard created after the analysis of the education industry of a certain country. Likewise, artificial intelligence does not only elaborate and develop data dashboards but also predicts, at a high rate of efficiency, what the main future trends of the analyzed indicators will be (Nielsen and Pedersen, 2014).

Accordingly, these data systems also known as analytical Customer Relationship Management (CRM), allow public institutions to link their different ministries, thus proposing the use of collaborative CRM to visualize wider data ranges and thus, enabling them to improve decision-making in numerous educational areas.

With regard to the education sector, by comparing different data sources from massive information collection, before making a decision, governments can compare the predictions provided by artificial intelligence to base their decisions not only in the present and data analysis but in the future and artificial intelligence forecasting based on historical data sources (Stone et al., 2016).

CONCLUSION

This exploratory and pedagogical chapter has analyzed the education sector by proposing new ways of using artificial intelligence. Additionally, under an analytical and selective perspective of the actions that governments can carry out to understand this industry and make better decisions, the different uses of artificial intelligence have been linked to the education sector.

In a nutshell, a total of seven uses that education institutions can take advantage of artificial intelligence have been identified. Likewise, from the government perspective, it has been identified three uses of artificial intelligence to improve the education sector. In this way, by using the analyzed current insights and the prospects for government initiatives proposed throughout the chapter, we have covered a general scope of the uses of artificial intelligence that the education industry can take advantage of. It has also been outlined the role that governments should maintain for an efficient strategy linked to this sector.

Theoretical Implications

Theoretical implications are directly related to the results previously presented. The pedagogical and exploratory nature of this chapter allows future researchers to use the results of this study to justify possible variables and build their empirical models in order to identify the statistical significance between different variables. The results of this research can be taken as sections in questionnaires and surveys that seek the understanding of artificial intelligence in the educational sector, or the role of the government in this topic.

Practical Implications

Practical implications are directly linked to the use of the results shown that directors of educational center or universities can make. In this way, the results can be taken as a best practice guide or white paper in which the different uses presented would benefit the development of artificial intelligence in the educational sector in order to cover the needs of the system. The practical implications of this chapter are directly linked to the use that directors of educational centers or universities can make of the results presented.

In this way, results present different uses that would benefit the development of artificial intelligence in the educational sector in order to cover the needs of the educational system. If universities and educational centers improve their communication and development strategies towards both professors and students by letting them know what artificial intelligence is, and how it can be used to improve teaching, it would boost the knowledge of this data-driven area. Additionally, it would help to improve the abilities and learning of students.

Regarding governments, this chapter can be used as a guide to understand what is happening in the educational sector and how active listening strategies and the generation of new data sources can allow governments to improve the use of artificial intelligence in this sector, and benefit society in new educational areas.

Likewise, governments can understand what the indicators or guidelines can be analyzed to improve educational processes, the evaluation of teachers or digital tools in universities. Moreover, being decision-making relevant in governments, this study helps to understand how through data dashboards linked to different sources, governments can make better decisions.

Limitations and Future Research

The main limitation of this chapter is its exploratory and pedagogical nature, rather than its quantitative and empirical nature, to identify statistical significance among the topics analyzed. However, this limitation can be taken as a strength since for the development of studies on emerging issues, qualitative and exploratory studies enhance the justification of variables through literature review.

Additionally, the studies that have been selected for the development of the chapter can also be taken into account as a limitation since only those published in English are part of the study. In addition, the studies that are part of this chapter are included in the databases selected and presented in the methodology, leaving out other databases that could also be useful. The application of the perspectives of analysis of the education sector and artificial intelligence from the government's point of view can be studied in future in-depth research taking into account guidelines concluded in this study. Likewise, implementation reports and analysis of possible data sources linked to the application of artificial intelligence in higher education institutions should be studied in the future.

REFERENCES

Agrawal, A., Gans, J., & Goldfarb, A. (Eds.). (2019). *The economics of artificial intelligence: an agenda.* University of Chicago Press. doi:10.7208/chicago/9780226613475.001.0001

Alqudah, M. A., & Muradkhanli, L. (2021). Artificial Intelligence in Electric Government; Ethical Challenges and Governance in Jordan. *Electronic Research Journal of Social Sciences and Humanities, 3,* 65–74.

Alter, S. (2021). Understanding artificial intelligence in the context of usage: Contributions and smartness of algorithmic capabilities in work systems. *International Journal of Information Management,* 102392. doi:10.1016/j.ijinfomgt.2021.102392

Anderson, D. M., Cembella, A. D., & Hallegraeff, G. M. (2012). Progress in understanding harmful algal blooms: Paradigm shifts and new technologies for research, monitoring, and management. *Annual Review of Marine Science, 4*(1), 143–176. doi:10.1146/annurev-marine-120308-081121 PMID:22457972

Ardito, C., De Marsico, M., Lanzilotti, R., Levialdi, S., Roselli, T., Rossano, V., & Tersigni, M. (2004, May). Usability of e-learning tools. In *Proceedings of the working conference on Advanced visual interfaces* (pp. 80-84). 10.1145/989863.989873

Baker, M. J. (2000). The roles of models in Artificial Intelligence and Education research: A prospective view. *Journal of Artificial Intelligence in Education, 11,* 122–143.

Basilaia, G., Dgebuadze, M., Kantaria, M., & Chokhonelidze, G. (2020). Replacing the classic learning form at universities as an immediate response to the COVID-19 virus infection in Georgia. *International Journal for Research in Applied Science and Engineering Technology, 8*(3), 101–108. doi:10.22214/ijraset.2020.3021

Bharadwaj, A., El Sawy, O. A., Pavlou, P. A., & Venkatraman, N. (2013). Digital business strategy: Toward a next generation of insights. *Management Information Systems Quarterly*, *37*(2), 471–482. doi:10.25300/MISQ/2013/37:2.3

Cai, L., & Zhu, Y. (2015). The challenges of data quality and data quality assessment in the big data era. *Data Science Journal*, *14*(0), 14. doi:10.5334/dsj-2015-002

Carrillo, C., & Flores, M. A. (2020). COVID-19 and teacher education: A literature review of online teaching and learning practices. *European Journal of Teacher Education*, *43*(4), 466–487. doi:10.1080/02619768.2020.1821184

Chassignol, M., Khoroshavin, A., Klimova, A., & Bilyatdinova, A. (2018). Artificial Intelligence trends in education: A narrative overview. *Procedia Computer Science*, *136*, 16–24. doi:10.1016/j.procs.2018.08.233

Chen, L., Chen, P., & Lin, Z. (2020). Artificial intelligence in education: A review. *IEEE Access: Practical Innovations, Open Solutions*, *8*, 75264–75278. doi:10.1109/ACCESS.2020.2988510

Chen, X., Xie, H., & Hwang, G. J. (2020). A multi-perspective study on artificial intelligence in education: Grants, conferences, journals, software tools, institutions, and researchers. *Computers and Education: Artificial Intelligence*, 100005.

Collins, C., Dennehy, D., Conboy, K., & Mikalef, P. (2021). Artificial intelligence in information systems research: A systematic literature review and research agenda. *International Journal of Information Management*, *60*, 102383. doi:10.1016/j.ijinfomgt.2021.102383

Croushore, D. (2011). Frontiers of real-time data analysis. *Journal of Economic Literature*, *49*(1), 72–100. doi:10.1257/jel.49.1.72

Devedžić, V. (2004). Web intelligence and artificial intelligence in education. *Journal of Educational Technology & Society*, *7*(4), 29–39.

Drigas, A. S., & Ioannidou, R. E. (2012). Artificial intelligence in special education: A decade review. *International Journal of Engineering Education*, *28*(6), 1366.

Evans, D., & Yen, D. C. (2006). E-Government: Evolving relationship of citizens and government, domestic, and international development. *Government Information Quarterly*, *23*(2), 207–235. doi:10.1016/j.giq.2005.11.004

Gao, X., Shen, J., He, W., Sun, F., Zhang, Z., Guo, W., Zhang, X., & Kong, Y. (2019). An evolutionary game analysis of governments' decision-making behaviors and factors influencing watershed ecological compensation in China. *Journal of Environmental Management*, *251*, 109592. doi:10.1016/j.jenvman.2019.109592 PMID:31569022

Henderson, M., Selwyn, N., & Aston, R. (2017). What works and why? Student perceptions of 'useful' digital technology in university teaching and learning. *Studies in Higher Education*, *42*(8), 1567–1579. doi:10.1080/03075079.2015.1007946

Holtgrewe, U. (2014). New new technologies: The future and the present of work in information and communication technology. *New Technology, Work and Employment*, *29*(1), 9–24. doi:10.1111/ntwe.12025

Kandlhofer, M., Steinbauer, G., Hirschmugl-Gaisch, S., & Huber, P. (2016, October). Artificial intelligence and computer science in education: From kindergarten to university. In 2016 IEEE Frontiers in Education Conference (FIE) (pp. 1-9). IEEE.

Kizys, R., Tzouvanas, P., & Donadelli, M. (2021). From COVID-19 herd immunity to investor herding in international stock markets: The role of government and regulatory restrictions. *International Review of Financial Analysis*, *74*, 101663. doi:10.1016/j.irfa.2021.101663

Knox, J. (2020). Artificial intelligence and education in China. *Learning, Media and Technology*, *45*(3), 298–311. doi:10.1080/17439884.2020.1754236

Kshetri, N. (2021). Evolving uses of artificial intelligence in human resource management in emerging economies in the global South: Some preliminary evidence. *Management Research Review*, *44*(7), 970–990. doi:10.1108/MRR-03-2020-0168

Kumar, N. S. (2019). Implementation of artificial intelligence in imparting education and evaluating student performance. *Journal of Artificial Intelligence*, *1*(1), 1–9.

Matthews, G., Hancock, P. A., Lin, J., Panganiban, A. R., Reinerman-Jones, L. E., Szalma, J. L., & Wohleber, R. W. (2021). Evolution and revolution: Personality research for the coming world of robots, artificial intelligence, and autonomous systems. *Personality and Individual Differences*, *169*, 109969. doi:10.1016/j.paid.2020.109969

Mazurek, G., & Małagocka, K. (2019). Perception of privacy and data protection in the context of the development of artificial intelligence. *Journal of Management Analytics*, *6*(4), 344–364. doi:10.1080/23270012.2019.1671243

McCarthy, J. (1998). *What is artificial intelligence?* Academic Press.

Montealegre, R., & Iyengar, K. (2021). Managing digital business platforms: A continued exercise in balancing renewal and refinement. *Business Horizons*, *64*(1), 51–59. doi:10.1016/j.bushor.2020.09.003

Nguyen, D. T., & Kieuthi, T. C. (2020). New Trends In Technology Application In Education And Capacities Of Universities Lecturers During The Covid-19 Pandemic. *International Journal of Mechanical and Production Engineering Research and Development*, *10*, 1709–1714.

Nielsen, J. A., & Pedersen, K. (2014). IT portfolio decision-making in local governments: Rationality, politics, intuition and coincidences. *Government Information Quarterly*, *31*(3), 411–420. doi:10.1016/j.giq.2014.04.002

Raisch, S., & Krakowski, S. (2021). Artificial intelligence and management: The automation–augmentation paradox. *Academy of Management Review*, *46*(1), 192–210. doi:10.5465/amr.2018.0072

Ribeiro-Navarrete, S., Saura, J. R., & Palacios-Marqués, D. (2021). Towards a new era of mass data collection: Assessing pandemic surveillance technologies to preserve user privacy. *Technological Forecasting and Social Change*, *167*, 120681. doi:10.1016/j.techfore.2021.120681 PMID:33840865

Rowley, J., & Slack, F. (2004). Conducting a literature review. *Management Research News*, *27*(6), 31–39. doi:10.1108/01409170410784185

Ruiz-Real, J. L., Uribe-Toril, J., Torres, J. A., & De Pablo, J. (2021). Artificial intelligence in business and economics research: Trends and future. *Journal of Business Economics and Management, 22*(1), 98–117. doi:10.3846/jbem.2020.13641

Safarov, I., Meijer, A., & Grimmelikhuijsen, S. (2017). Utilization of open government data: A systematic literature review of types, conditions, effects and users. *Information Polity, 22*(1), 1–24. doi:10.3233/IP-160012

Sapci, A. H., & Sapci, H. A. (2020). Artificial intelligence education and tools for medical and health informatics students: Systematic review. *JMIR Medical Education, 6*(1), e19285. doi:10.2196/19285 PMID:32602844

Saura, J. R., Palacios-Marqués, D., & Ribeiro-Soriano, D. (2021c). How SMEs use data sciences in their online marketing performance: A systematic literature review of the state-of-the-art. *Journal of Small Business Management*, 1–36. doi:10.1080/00472778.2021.1955127

Saura, J. R., Palacios-Marqués, D., & Ribeiro-Soriano, D. (2022a). Exploring the boundaries of Open Innovation: Evidence from social media mining. *Technovation*, 102447. Advance online publication. doi:10.1016/j.technovation.2021.102447

Saura, J. R., Ribeiro-Soriano, D., & Iturricha-Fernández, A. (2022). Exploring the challenges of remote work on Twitter users' sentiments: From digital technology development to a post-pandemic era. *Journal of Business Research, 142*(March), 242–254. doi:10.1016/j.jbusres.2021.12.052

Saura, J. R., Ribeiro-Soriano, D., & Palacios-Marqués, D. (2021). Setting B2B Digital Marketing in Artificial Intelligence-based CRMs: A review and directions for future research. *Industrial Marketing Management, 98*(October), 161–178. doi:10.1016/j.indmarman.2021.08.006

Saura, J. R., Ribeiro-Soriano, D., & Palacios-Marqués, D. (2021a). Using data mining techniques to explore security issues in smart living environments in Twitter. *Computer Communications, 179*, 285–295. doi:10.1016/j.comcom.2021.08.021

Saura, J. R., Ribeiro-Soriano, D., & Palacios-Marques, D. (2021b). Evaluating security and privacy issues of social networks based information systems in Industry 4.0. *Enterprise Information Systems*, 1–17. doi:10.1080/17517575.2021.1913765

Saura, J. R., Ribeiro-Soriano, D., & Palacios-Marqués, D. (2021d, July 15). Setting privacy "by default" in social IoT: Theorizing the challenges and directions in Big Data Research. *Big Data Research, 25*, 100245. doi:10.1016/j.bdr.2021.100245

Snyder, H. (2019). Literature review as a research methodology: An overview and guidelines. *Journal of Business Research, 104*, 333–339. doi:10.1016/j.jbusres.2019.07.039

Stone, P., Brooks, R., Brynjolfsson, E., Calo, R., Etzioni, O., Hager, G., ... Teller, A. (2016). *Artificial intelligence and life in 2030: The one hundred year study on artificial intelligence*. Academic Press.

Tadesse, S., & Muluye, W. (2020). The impact of COVID-19 pandemic on education system in developing countries: A review. *Open Journal of Social Sciences, 8*(10), 159–170. doi:10.4236/jss.2020.810011

Yang, L., Elisa, N., & Eliot, N. (2019). Privacy and security aspects of E-government in smart cities. In *Smart cities cybersecurity and privacy* (pp. 89–102). Elsevier. doi:10.1016/B978-0-12-815032-0.00007-X

Zaidi, A., Beadle, S., & Hannah, A. (2019). *Review of the online learning and artificial intelligence education market: a report for the Department of Education: July 2018*. Academic Press.

Zhang, W., Zuo, N., He, W., Li, S., & Yu, L. (2021). Factors influencing the use of artificial intelligence in government: Evidence from China. *Technology in Society, 66*, 101675. doi:10.1016/j.techsoc.2021.101675

Zou, S. (2017). Designing and practice of a college English teaching platform based on artificial intelligence. *Journal of Computational and Theoretical Nanoscience, 14*(1), 104–108. doi:10.1166/jctn.2017.6133

Compilation of References

Abdala, M. B., Lacroix Eussler, S., & Soubie, S. (2019). *La política de la Inteligencia Artificial: sus usos en el sector público y sus implicancias regulatorias.* CIPPEC, Políticas Públicas.

Abu-Shanab, E. A. (2020). E-government contribution to better performance by public sector. In Open Government: Concepts, Methodologies, Tools, and Applications (pp. 1-17). IGI Global.

Abu-Shanab, E., & Harb, Y. (2019). E-government research insights: Text mining analysis. *Electronic Commerce Research and Applications, 38*, 100892. doi:10.1016/j.elerap.2019.100892

Adapa, A., Nah, F. F.-H., Hall, R. H., Siau, K., & Smith, S. N. (2017). Factors Influencing the Adoption of Smart Wearable Devices. *International Journal of Human-Computer Interaction, 34*(5), 399–409. doi:10.1080/10447318.2017.1357902

Agrawal, A., Gans, J., & Goldfarb, A. (Eds.). (2019). *The economics of artificial intelligence: an agenda.* University of Chicago Press. doi:10.7208/chicago/9780226613475.001.0001

Aguilar Gordón, F. (2011). Reflexiones filosóficas sobre la tecnología y sus nuevos escenarios. *Sophia. Colección de Filosofía de la Educación, 11*, 123–172.

Ahad, M. A., Paiva, S., Tripathi, G., & Feroz, N. (2020). Enabling technologies and sustainable smart cities. *Sustainable Cities and Society, 61*, 102301. doi:10.1016/j.scs.2020.102301

Ahmad, T. (2014, April). *Sentencing Guidelines: India.* Retrieved from https://www.loc.gov/law/help/sentencing-guidelines/india.php

Ahmadi, H., Arji, G., Shahmoradi, L., Safdari, R., Nilashi, M., & Alizadeh, M. (2018). The application of internet of things in healthcare: A systematic literature review and classification. *Universal Access in the Information Society*, 1–33.

Ahn, M. J., & Chen, Y. C. (2020, June). Artificial intelligence in government: potentials, challenges, and the future. In *The 21st Annual International Conference on Digital Government Research* (pp. 243-252). 10.1145/3396956.3398260

Al Nuaimi, E., Al Neyadi, H., Mohamed, N., & Al-Jaroodi, J. (2015). Applications of big data to smart cities. *Journal of Internet Services and Applications, 6*(1), 1–15. doi:10.118613174-015-0041-5

Albacete, P. L., & VanLehn, K. (2000). The Conceptual Helper: An Intelligent Tutoring System for Teaching Fundamental Physics Concepts. In G. Gauthier, C. Frasson, & K. VanLehn (Eds.), *Intelligent Tutoring Systems. ITS 2000* (pp. 564–573). Lecture Notes in Computer Science. Springer. doi:10.1007/3-540-45108-0_60

Albrieu, R., Rapetti, M., Brest López, C., Larroulet, P., & Sorrentino, A. (2018). *Inteligencia artificial y crecimiento económico. Oportunidades y desafíos para Argentina.* CIPPEC.

Alfonso Sánchez, R. (2017). Economía colaborativa: Un nuevo mercado para la economía social. *C.I.R.I.E.C. España, 231*(88), 231. doi:10.7203/CIRIEC-E.88.9255

Alkhatlan, A., & Kalita, J. (2019). Intelligent tutoring systems: A comprehensive historical survey with recent developments. *International Journal of Computer Applications, 181*(43).

Allam, Z., & Dhunny, Z. A. (2019). On big data, artificial intelligence and smart cities. *Cities (London, England), 89,* 80–91. doi:10.1016/j.cities.2019.01.032

Allport, G. & Postman, L. J. (1973). La psicología básica del rumor. In *Estudios básicos de psicología social.* Tecnos.

Al-Mushayt, O. S. (2019). Automating E-government services with artificial intelligence. *IEEE Access: Practical Innovations, Open Solutions, 7,* 146821–146829. doi:10.1109/ACCESS.2019.2946204

Alonso Martínez, M. (1992). *Conocimiento y Bases de Datos: una propuesta de integración inteligente* [Unpublished doctoral dissertation]. Universidad de Cantabria, Santander, España.

Alperstein, N. (2021). Exploring Issues of Social Justice and Data Activism: The Personal Cost of Network Connections in the Digital Age. In Performing Media Activism in the Digital Age (pp. 143-177). Palgrave Macmillan.

Alqudah, M. A., & Muradkhanli, L. (2021). Artificial Intelligence in Electric Government; Ethical Challenges and Governance in Jordan. *Electronic Research Journal of Social Sciences and Humanities, 3,* 65–74.

Al-Sai, Z. A., & Abualigah, L. M. (2017, May). Big data and E-government: A review. In *2017 8th international conference on information technology (ICIT)* (pp. 580-587). IEEE. 10.1109/ICITECH.2017.8080062

Alsheibani, S. A., Cheung, D., & Messom, D. (2019). *Factors inhibiting the adoption of artificial intelligence at organizational-level: A preliminary investigation.* Academic Press.

Alsheibani, S., Cheung, Y., & Messom, C. (2018). Artificial Intelligence Adoption: AI-readiness at Firm-Level. *Artificial Intelligence, 6,* 26–2018.

Alter, S. (2021). Understanding artificial intelligence in the context of usage: Contributions and smartness of algorithmic capabilities in work systems. *International Journal of Information Management,* 102392. doi:10.1016/j.ijinfomgt.2021.102392

Álvarez de Zayas, C. (2016). *Epistemología del Caos.* Editorial Kipos.

Amershi, S., & Conati, C. (2009). Combining unsupervised and supervised classification to build user models for exploratory learning environments. *Journal of Educational Data Mining, 1*(1), 18-71. doi:10.5281/zenodo.3554659

Amershi, S., & Conati, C. (2006). Automatic recognition of learner groups in exploratory learning environments. In M. Ikeda, K.D. Ashley, & T.W. Chan (Eds.), *International Conference on Intelligent Tutoring Systems* (pp. 463-472). Springer. 10.1007/11774303_46

Ananny, M., & Crawford, K. (2018). Seeing without knowing: Limitations of the transparency ideal and its application. *New Media & Society, 20*(3), 973–989. doi:10.1177/1461444816676645

Anderson, D. M., Cembella, A. D., & Hallegraeff, G. M. (2012). Progress in understanding harmful algal blooms: Paradigm shifts and new technologies for research, monitoring, and management. *Annual Review of Marine Science, 4*(1), 143–176. doi:10.1146/annurev-marine-120308-081121 PMID:22457972

Andrejevic, M. (2014). Big data, big questions| the big data divide. *International Journal of Communication, 8,* 17.

Andrejevic, M., & Selwyn, N. (2020). Facial recognition technology in schools: Critical questions and concerns. *Learning, Media and Technology, 45*(2), 115–128. doi:10.1080/17439884.2020.1686014

Andrews, L. (2018). Public administration, public leadership and the construction of public value in the age of the algorithm and 'big data'. *Public Administration*, *97*(2), 296–310. doi:10.1111/padm.12534

Androutsopoulou, A., Karacapilidis, N., Loukis, E., & Charalabidis, Y. (2019). Transforming the communication between citizens and government through AI-guided chatbots. *Government Information Quarterly*, *36*(2), 358–367. doi:10.1016/j.giq.2018.10.001

Angwin, J., Larson, J., Mattu, S., & Kirchner, L. (2016). *Machine Bias*. Retrieved Feb 23, 2019, https://www.propublica.org/article/machine-bias-risk-assessments-incriminal-sentencingñ.

Anonymous. (2020). *China Copyright and Media. (2014). Planning Outline for the Construction of a Social Credit System (2014-2020)*. https://chinacopyrightandmedia.wordpress.com/2014/06/14/planning-outline-for-the-construction-ofa-social-credit-system-2014-2020

Anshari, M., Almunawar, M. N., & Lim, S. A. (2018, February). Big data and open government data in public services. In *Proceedings of the 2018 10th International Conference on Machine Learning and Computing* (pp. 140-144). 10.1145/3195106.3195172

Anshari, M., & Lim, S. A. (2017). E-government with big data enabled through smartphone for public services: Possibilities and challenges. *International Journal of Public Administration*, *40*(13), 1143–1158. doi:10.1080/01900692.2016.1242619

Antebi, L., & Dolinko, I. (2020). Artificial intelligence and policy: A review at the outset of 2020. *Strategic Assessment*, *23*(1), 94–100.

Anthopoulos, L. G. (2017). Smart government: A new adjective to government transformation or a trick? *Understanding Smart Cities: A Tool for Smart Government or an Industrial Trick?*, 263-293.

Anžel, A., Heider, D., & Hattab, G. (2021). The visual story of data storage: From storage properties to user interfaces. *Computational and Structural Biotechnology Journal*, *19*, 4904–4918. doi:10.1016/j.csbj.2021.08.031 PMID:34527195

Aoun, J. E. (2017). *Robot-Proof: Higher Education in the Age of Artificial Intelligence*. MIT. doi:10.7551/mitpress/11456.001.0001

APD. (2019, March 6). Big data: ¿qué es y para qué sirve? *APD*. https://www.apd.es/

Archenaa, J., & Anita, E. M. (2015). A survey of big data analytics in healthcare and government. *Procedia Computer Science*, *50*, 408–413. doi:10.1016/j.procs.2015.04.021

Ardito, C., De Marsico, M., Lanzilotti, R., Levialdi, S., Roselli, T., Rossano, V., & Tersigni, M. (2004, May). Usability of e-learning tools. In *Proceedings of the working conference on Advanced visual interfaces* (pp. 80-84). 10.1145/989863.989873

Arevian, A. C., O'Hora, J., Jones, F., Mango, J., Jones, L., Williams, P. G., ... Wells, K. B. (2018). Participatory technology development to enhance community resilience. *Ethnicity & Disease*, *28*(Suppl 2), 493–502. doi:10.18865/ed.28.S2.493 PMID:30202203

Aribau Sorolla, O. (2018). *Las TIC y la cibersoberanía en China: la base del presidente Xi Jinping para perfeccionar el control socialista maoísta*. Universidad Oberta de Catalunya.

Arner, D. W., Barberis, J., & Buckey, R. P. (2016). FinTech, RegTech, and the reconceptualisation of financial regulation. *Nw. J. Int'l L. & Bus.*, *37*(3), 370–413.

Arnott, E., Hastings, P., & Allbritton, D. (2008). Research Methods Tutor: Evaluation of a dialogue-based tutoring system in the classroom. *Behavior Research Methods*, *40*(3), 694–698. doi:10.3758/BRM.40.3.694 PMID:18697663

Arntz, M., Gregory, T., & Zierahn, U. (2016). The Risk of Automation for Jobs in OECD Countries: A Comparative Analysis. *OECD Social, Employment and Migration Working Papers, 189*, 1-34. doi:10.1787/5jlz9h56dvq7-en

Arroyo, I., Muldner, K., Burleson, W., Woolf, B., & Cooper, D. (2009). Designing affective support to foster learning, motivation and attribution. In D. Dicheva & S.D. Craig (Eds.), *Closing the Affective Loop in Intelligent Learning Environments Workshop at the 14th International Conference on Artificial Intelligence in Education*. IOS Press.

Arroyo, I., Beck, J. E., Woolf, B. P., Beal, C. R., & Schultz, K. (2000). Macroadapting Animalwatch to gender and cognitive differences with respect to hint interactivity and symbolism. In G. Gauthier, C. Frasson, & K. VanLehn (Eds.), *Intelligent Tutoring Systems. ITS 2000* (pp. 574–583). Springer. doi:10.1007/3-540-45108-0_61

Arroyo, I., Woolf, B. P., & Beal, C. R. (2006). Addressing cognitive differences and gender during problem solving. International Journal of Technology, Instruction. *Cognition and Learning, 4*, 31–63.

Arroyo, I., Woolf, B. P., Burelson, W., Muldner, K., Rai, D., & Tai, M. (2014). A multimedia adaptive tutoring system for mathematics that addresses cognition, metacognition and affect. *International Journal of Artificial Intelligence in Education, 24*(4), 387–426. doi:10.100740593-014-0023-y

Ashok, M. (2018, July). Role of digitisation in enabling co-creation of value in KIBS firms. In *International Conference on Informatics and Semiotics in Organisations* (pp. 145-154). Springer.

Ashok, M., Dhaherib, M. S. M. A. B. A., Madan, R., & Dzandu, M. D. (2021). How to counter organisational inertia to enable knowledge management practices adoption in public sector organisations. *Journal of Knowledge Management, 25*(9), 2245–2273. doi:10.1108/JKM-09-2020-0700

Ashok, M., Madan, R., Joha, A., & Sivarajah, U. (2022). Ethical framework for Artificial Intelligence and Digital technologies. *International Journal of Information Management, 62*, 102433. doi:10.1016/j.ijinfomgt.2021.102433

Ashok, M., Narula, R., & Martinez-Noya, A. (2016). How do collaboration and investments in knowledge management affect process innovation in services? *Journal of Knowledge Management, 20*(5), 1004–1024. doi:10.1108/JKM-11-2015-0429

Asimov, I. (2007). *Yo, robot*. Edhasa.

Asociación de Marketing de España. (2021). *Informe digital marketing trends: Mobile en España y en el mundo 2020 + Especial COVID-19*. Author.

Asociación Española de Protección de Datos. (2020). *Gabinete jurídico N/REF: 0036/2020*. Author.

Asociación Española de Protección de Datos. (2021). *Procedimiento Nº: PS/00120/2021. Resolución de terminación del procedimiento por pago voluntario*. Author.

Ausubel, D. (1983). Teoría del aprendizaje significativo. *Fascículos de CEIF, 1*, 1-10.

Ayoub, K., & Payne, K. (2016). Strategy in the age of artificial intelligence. *Journal of Strategic Studies, 39*(5–6), 793–819. .1088838 doi:10.1080/01402390.2015

Ayres, R. U. (2010). *Ayres, Crossing in the Energy Divide: Moving from Fossil Fuel, Dependence to a Clean-Energy Future*. Wharton Publishing.

Azcona, J. M. (2019). Historia del tiempo presente. La sociedad actual desde 1945. *Editorial Cátedra URJC-Presdeia, Madrid, 2019*, 565.

Aznar Fernández-Montesinos, F. (2019). *La inteligencia artificial como factor geopolítico*. Documento de análisis IEEE 18/2019. https://www.ieee.es/Galerias/fichero/docs_analisis/2019/DIEEEA18_2019FEDAZN_IAgeopolitica.pdf

Aznar Fernández-Montesinos, F. (2019). Inteligencia artificial y geopolítica. *Claves de Razón Práctica*, *267*, 106–114.

Aznar, T. y Rodriguez, R. (2021). Education, social justice and post-pandemic in spain. *Journal of Management and Business Education*, *4*(2), 206-230.

B.K., A., Devkota, N., Gautam, N., & Paija, N. (2019). Industry willingness to pay for adequate electricity supply: A discourse on sustainable industrial development. *Quest Journal of Management and Social Sciences*, *1*(2), 251–259. doi:10.3126/qjmss.v1i2.27443

Baek, C., & Doleck, T. (2020). A Bibliometric Analysis of the Papers Published in the Journal of Artificial Intelligence in Education from 2015-2019. *International Journal of Learning Analytics and Artificial Intelligence for Education*, *2*(1), 67–84. doi:10.3991/ijai.v2i1.14481

Bailey, J., & Coleman, Y. (2018). *Urban IoT and AI: How can cities successfully leverage this synergy?* Retrieved Feb 23, 2019, from https://aibusiness.com/future-cities-iotaio/ñ

Baker, M. J. (2000). The roles of models in Artificial Intelligence and Education research: A prospective view. *Journal of Artificial Intelligence in Education*, *11*, 122–143.

Baker, R. S., D'Mello, S. K., Rodrigo, M. M. T., & Graesser, A. C. (2010). Better to be frustrated than bored: The incidence, persistence, and impact of learners' cognitive–affective states during interactions with three different computer-based learning environments. *International Journal of Human-Computer Studies*, *68*(4), 223–241. doi:10.1016/j.ijhcs.2009.12.003

Baker, T., Smith, L., & Anissa, N. (2019). *Educ-AI-tion rebooted? Exploring the future of artificial intelligence in schools and colleges*. Nesta.

Bale, N. (2019, March). Artificial Intelligence: Risk Assessment and Considerations for the Future. *International Journal of Computers and Applications*, *181*(43), 47–49. doi:10.5120/ijca2019918529

Banerjee, S., Singh, P. K., & Bajpai, J. (2018). A Comparative Study on Decision-Making Capability Between Human and Artificial Intelligence. In B. Panigrahi, M. Hoda, V. Sharma, & S. Goel (Eds.), *Nature Inspired Computing. Advances in Intelligent Systems and Computing* (Vol. 652). Springer. doi:10.1007/978-981-10-6747-1_23

Bannister, F., & Connolly, R. (2014). ICT, public values and transformative government: A framework and programme for research. *Government Information Quarterly*, *31*(1), 119–128. doi:10.1016/j.giq.2013.06.002

Baños, P. (2017). Así se domina el mundo. Ariel.

Baños, P. (2017). Así se domina el mundo. *Ariel*.

Bansal, M., Sirpal, V., & Choudhary, M. K. (2022). Advancing e-Government using Internet of Things. In *Mobile Computing and Sustainable Informatics* (pp. 123–137). Springer. doi:10.1007/978-981-16-1866-6_8

Barajas Martinez, J. C. (2019). *Andamos Muy enredados II: Redes Sociales Digitales*. Sociología Divertida. Retrieved June 26, 2021, from: http://sociologiadivertida.blogspot.com/2021/01/andamos-muy-enredados-ii-redes-sociales.html

Barbé, E., & Badell, D. (2020). The European Union and lethal autonomous weapons systems: United in diversity? In *European Union Contested* (pp. 133–152). Springer. doi:10.1007/978-3-030-33238-9_8

Bárcena, A. (2016). The new digital revolution from the consumer Internet to the industrial Internet. ECLAC y United Nations.

Barfield, W., & Pagallo, U. (2020). *Advanced Introduction to Law and Artificial Intelligence*. Edward Elgar Publishing. doi:10.4337/9781789905137

Barnhizer, D. (2016). The future of work: Apps, artificial intelligence, automation and androids. *Artificial Intelligence, Automation and Androids (January 15, 2016)*. Cleveland-Marshall Legal Studies Paper, (289).

Basilaia, G., Dgebuadze, M., Kantaria, M., & Chokhonelidze, G. (2020). Replacing the classic learning form at universities as an immediate response to the COVID-19 virus infection in Georgia. *International Journal for Research in Applied Science and Engineering Technology*, 8(3), 101–108. doi:10.22214/ijraset.2020.3021

Bates, T., Cobo, C., Mariño, O., & Wheeler, S. (2020). Can artificial intelligence transform higher education? *Int J Educ Technol High Educ*, 17(1), 42. doi:10.118641239-020-00218-x

Bauman, Z. (2000). *Liquid Modernity*. Polity.

Bauman, Z. (2004). *Modernidad líquida*. FCE.

Beal, C., Woolf, B., Beck, J., Arroyo, I., Schultz, K., & Hart, D. (2000). Gaining confidence in mathematics: Instructional technology for girls. In R. Robson (Ed.), *International Conference on Mathematics/Science Education and Technology* (pp. 99-6106). Association for the Advancement of Computing in Education.

Beck, J. E., & Woolf, B. P. (2000). High-level student modeling with machine learning. In G. Gauthier, C. Frasson, & K. VanLehn (Eds.), *Intelligent Tutoring Systems. ITS 2000* (pp. 584–593). Lecture Notes in Computer Science. Springer. doi:10.1007/3-540-45108-0_62

Behar, J. (1993). Aproximación al análisis textual informatizado. *Anuario de psicología/The UB. The Journal of Psychology*, (59), 61–78.

Beijing Consensus on Artificial Intelligence and Education. (2019). *UNESCO*. https://unesdoc.unesco.org/ark:/48223/pf0000368303

Beijing Consensus on artificial intelligence and education. Outcome document of the International Conference on Artificial Intelligence and Education "Planning education in the AI era: Lead the leap". (2019). http://www.moe.gov.cn/jyb_xwfb/gzdt_gzdt/s5987/201908/W020190828311234688933.pdf

Belfield, H. (2020, February). Activism by the AI community: Analysing recent achievements and future prospects. In *Proceedings of the AAAI/ACM Conference on AI, Ethics, and Society* (pp. 15-21). 10.1145/3375627.3375814

Bellman, R. E. (1978). *An introduction to Artificial Intelligence: Can Computers Think?* Boyd & Fraser Publishing Company.

Benjamin, R. (2019). Assessing risk, automating racism. *Science*, 366(6464), 421–422. doi:10.1126cience.aaz3873 PMID:31649182

Ben-Naim, D., Marcus, N., & Bain, M. (2008, September). Visualization and analysis of student interaction in an adaptive exploratory learning environment. In *International workshop on intelligent support for exploratory environment, EC-TEL*.

Berente, N., Gu, B., Recker, J., & Santhanam, R. (2021). Managing Artificial Intelligence. *Management Information Systems Quarterly*, 45(3).

Berleur, J., & Brunnstein, K. (Eds.). (2001). *Ethics of Computing: Codes, Spaces for Discussion and Law*. Chapman and Hall.

Berman, J. (2021). Ocean shipping issues are in the spotlight in letters to the White House. *Logistics Management*. https://www.logisticsmgmt.com/article/ocean_shipping_issues_are_in_the_spotlight_in_letters_to_the_white_house

Bernacki, M. L. (2019, March). Development, Sustainment, and Scaling of a Learning Analytics, Prediction Modeling and Digital Student Success Initiative. In *Proceedings of the 10th Annual Learning Analytics and Knowledge Conference Workshop on Sustainable and Scalable Learning Analytics Solutions*. Society of Learning Analytics Research.

Bernardini, S., Porayska-Pomsta, K., & Smith, T. J. (2014). ECHOES: An intelligent serious game for fostering social communication in children with autism. *Information Sciences*, *264*, 41–60. doi:10.1016/j.ins.2013.10.027

Bernier, L., Hafsi, T., & Deschamps, C. (2015). Environmental Determinants of Public Sector Innovation: A study of innovation awards in Canada. *Public Management Review*, *17*(6), 834–856. doi:10.1080/14719037.2013.867066

Berryhill, J., Heang, K. K., Clogher, R., & McBride, K. (2019). *Hello, World! Artificial Intelligence and its Use in the Public Sector*. https://www.oecd.org/governance/innovative-government/working-paper-hello-world-artificial-intelligence-and-its-use-in-the-public-sector.htm

Berry, M. M., & Taggart, J. H. (1994). Managing technology and innovation: A review. *R & D Management*, *24*(4), 341–353. doi:10.1111/j.1467-9310.1994.tb00889.x

Bharadwaj, A., El Sawy, O. A., Pavlou, P. A., & Venkatraman, N. (2013). Digital business strategy: Toward a next generation of insights. *Management Information Systems Quarterly*, *37*(2), 471–482. doi:10.25300/MISQ/2013/37:2.3

Billis, D. (1993). Sector blurring and nonprofit centers: The case of the United Kingdom. *Nonprofit and Voluntary Sector Quarterly*, *22*(3), 241–257. doi:10.1177/0899764093223006

Black, E. (2012). *IBM and the Holocaust: the strategic alliance between Nazi Germany and America's most powerful corporation*. Dialog Press.

Bohara, S. K., Bhuju, D. R., & Bohara, T. (2018). Perspectivas del desarrollo de industrias manufactureras en Nepal. *Revista Internacional de Cooperación y Desarrollo*, *5*(2), 7–25.

Bolívar, A. (2011). Justicia social y equidad escolar. Una revisión actual. *Revista Internacional de Educación para la justicia social, 1*(1), 9-45.

Bonina, C., & Eaton, B. (2020). Cultivating open government data platform ecosystems through governance: Lessons from Buenos Aires, Mexico City and Montevideo. *Government Information Quarterly*, *37*(3), 101479. doi:10.1016/j.giq.2020.101479

Botsman, R. (2017). *Big Data meets Big Brother as China moves to rate its citizens*. https://www.wired.co.uk/article/chinese-government-social-credit-score-privacy-invasion

Bower, G. H. (1992). How might emotions affect learning? In S.-Å. Christianson (Ed.), *The handbook of emotion and memory: Research and theory* (pp. 3–31). Lawrence Erlbaum Associates, Inc.

Boyd, M., & Wilson, N. (2017). Rapid developments in artificial intelligence: how might the New Zealand government respond? *Policy Quarterly, 13*(4).

Bradbury, R. (2012). *Fahrenheit 451*. Penguin Random House Grupo Editorial.

Brady, G. (2017). 8 Fundamentals for Achieving AI Success in the Supply Chain. *Supply Chain Management Review*. https://www.scmr.com/article/8_fundamentals_for_achieving_ai_success_in_the_supply_chain

Brown, J. S., & Burton, R. R. (1978). Diagnostic models for procedural bugs in basic mathematical skills. *Cognitive Science*, *2*(2), 155–192. doi:10.120715516709cog0202_4

Bruffee, K. A. (1999). *Collaborative Learning: Higher Education, Interdependence and the Authority of Knowledge*. Baltimore University Press.

Bruner, J. S. (1961). The act of discovery. *Harvard Educational Review, 4*, 21–32.

Brunner, J. J. (2001). Globalización, educación, revolución tecnológica. *Perspectivas, 31*(2), 139–153.

Bryhinets, O. O., Svoboda, I., Shevchuk, O. R., Kotukh, Y. V., & Radich, V. Y. (2020). Public value management and new public governance as modern approaches to the development of public administration. *Revista San Gregorio, 1*(42).

Brynjolfsson, E., & Mitchell, T. (2017). What can machine learning do? Workforce implications. *Science, 358*(6370), 1530–1534. .aap8062 doi:10.1126/science

Brynjolfsson, E., & McAfee, A. (2014). *The Second Machine Age: Work, Progress, and Prosperity in a Time of Brilliant Technologies*. W. W. Norton.

Brynjolfsson, E., Rock, D., & Syverson, C. (2017). *Artificial intelligence and the modern productivity paradox: A clash of expectations and statistics*. National Bureau of Economic Research.

Bryson, J.J. (2018). Patiency is not a virtue: the design of intelligent systems and systems of ethics. *Ethics and Information Technology, 20*(1), 15-26.

Buolamwini, J. (2016). *The algorithmic justice league*. Medium. https://medium. com/mit-media-lab/the-algorithmic-justice-league-3cc4131c5148

Buolamwini, J., & Gebru, T. (2018). Proceedings of the 1st Conference on Fairness, Accountability and Transparency. *Proceedings of Machine Learning Research, 81*, 77–91.

Burnson, P. (2020). Most U.S. Supply Chain Managers Using AI systems During Pandemic Disappointed. *Supply Chain Management Review*. https://www.scmr.com/article/most_u.s._supply_chain_managers_using_ai_systems_during_pandemic_disappoint

Burnson, P. (2021). Cargo Delays, Supply Shortages, and Increased Prices Likely to Continue Through Q4. *Supply Chain Management Review* https://www.scmr.com/article/cargo_delays_supply_shortages_and_increased_prices_likely_to_continue_throu?utm_source=Newsletter&utm_medium=Email&utm_campaign=TWISC

Burson, P. (2021b). Ocean Cargo, Post-pandemic strategies take hold. *Logistics Management*, 58-64.

Bustelo Gómez, P. (2009). *El ascenso económico de China: Implicaciones estratégicas para la seguridad global', China en el sistema de seguridad global del siglo XXI*. IEES.

Butler, J. W. (2021). *Impacts of Shipping Container Shortages, Delays*. House Committee on Transportation and Infrastructure.

Butterworth, M. (2018). The ICO and artificial intelligence: The role of fairness in the GDPR framework. *Computer Law & Security Review, 34*(2), 257–268. doi:10.1016/j.clsr.2018.01.004

Buzzle. (n.d.). *Unbelievably Brilliant Applications of Artificial Intelligence*. Retrieved January 8, 2018, from https://www.buzzle.com/articles/applications-of-artificialintelligence.html

Bylinska, O. S. (2017). Zasoby movlennievoho vplyvu v synkretnykh zhanrakh politychnoho ahitatsiinoho dyskurdu [Means of Speech Influence in Syncretic Genres of Political Propaganda Discourse]. *Journal of Odesa National University: Philology, 22*(2), 8–20.

Cai, L., & Zhu, Y. (2015). The challenges of data quality and data quality assessment in the big data era. *Data Science Journal, 14*(0), 14. doi:10.5334/dsj-2015-002

Caiyu, L. (2018). Villages gain public security systems. *Global Times*.

Calo, R., Froomkin, M., & Kerr, I. (2016). *Robot Law*. Edward Elgar Publishing. doi:10.4337/9781783476732

Calvo-Rubio, L. M., & Ufarte-Ruiz, M. J. (2020). Percepción de docentes universitarios, estudiantes, responsables de innovación y periodistas sobre el uso de inteligencia artificial en periodismo. *El Profesional de la Información, 29*(1). Advance online publication. doi:10.3145/epi.2020.ene.09

Campbell, M., Hoane, A. Jr, & Hsu, F. (2002). Deep Blue. *Artificial Intelligence, 134*(1-2), 57–83. doi:10.1016/S0004-3702(01)00129-1

Camus, A. (1995). *El mito de Sísifo*. Alianza Editorial.

Capgemini. (2017). *Unleashing the potential of Artificial Intelligence in the Public Sector*. Retrieved from https://www.capgemini.com/consulting/wp-content/uploads/sites/ 30/2017/10/ai-in-public-sector.pdf

Cariolet, J. M., Colombert, M., Vuillet, M., & Diab, Y. (2018). Assessing the resilience of urban areas to traffic-related air pollution: Application in Greater Paris. *The Science of the Total Environment, 615*, 588–596. doi:10.1016/j.scitotenv.2017.09.334 PMID:28988095

Carrillo, C., & Flores, M. A. (2020). COVID-19 and teacher education: A literature review of online teaching and learning practices. *European Journal of Teacher Education, 43*(4), 466–487. doi:10.1080/02619768.2020.1821184

Carton, S. (2016). Why the rise of Donald Trump should make us doubt the Hype about. *Artificial Intelligence*, 1–3.

Castells, M. (2006). La era de la información: Economía, sociedad y cultura. Vol. III. Fin de milenio. Alianza Editorial.

Castells, M. (2009). Comunicación y poder. Editorial Siglo XXI.

Castells, M. (1996). La era de la información: Economía, sociedad y cultura. Vol. I, La sociedad red. *Alianza Editorial, Madrid, 1996*, 408.

Castelluccia, C. & Le Métayer. (2020). Position paper: Analyzing the Impacts of Facial Recognition. In L. Antunes, M. Naldi, G. Italiano, K. & P. Drogkaris (Eds.), *Privacy Technologies and Policiy. APF 2020*. New York: Springer.

Castrillón, O. D., Sarache, W., & Ruiz-Herrera, S. (2020). Predicción del rendimiento académico por medio de técnicas de inteligencia artificial. *Formación Universitaria, 13*(1), 93–102. doi:10.4067/S0718-50062020000100093

Cath, C., Wachter, S., Mittelstadt, B., Taddeo, M., & Floridi, L. (2018). Artificial intelligence and the 'good society': The US, EU, and UK approach. *Science and Engineering Ethics, 24*(2), 505–528. PMID:28353045

Cave, S., & Dihal, K. (2020). The whiteness of AI. *Philosophy & Technology, 33*(4), 685–703. doi:10.100713347-020-00415-6

Ceccaroni, L., Bibby, J., Roger, E., Flemons, P., Michael, K., Fagan, L., & Oliver, J. L. (2019). Opportunities and risks for citizen science in the age of artificial intelligence. *Citizen Science: Theory and Practice, 4*(1), 29. doi:10.5334/cstp.241

Century-Tech Limited. (2021). *Century*. https://www.century.tech

Cerdeira, L. (2020, September 20). *Lo que podemos aprender de Estonia, el país más digitalizado del mundo*. Retrieved December 12, 2021, from Forbes España website: https://forbes.es/empresas/76138/lo-que-podemos-aprender-de-estonia-el-pais-mas-digitalizado-del-mundo/

Čerka, P., Grigienė, J., & Sirbikytė, G. (2017). Is it possible to grant legal personality to artificial intelligence software systems? *Computer Law & Security Review, 33*(5), 685–699. doi:10.1016/j.clsr.2017.03.022

Chang, G., Morreale, P., & Medicherla, P. (2010, March). Applications of augmented reality systems in education. In *Society for Information Technology & Teacher Education International Conference* (pp. 1380-1385). Association for the Advancement of Computing in Education (AACE).

Charniak, E., & McDermott, D. (1985). *Introduction to Artificial Intelligence*. Addison-Wesley.

Chassignol, M., Khoroshavin, A., Klimova, A., & Bilyatdinova, A. (2018). Artificial Intelligence trends in education: A narrative overview. *Procedia Computer Science, 136*, 16–24. doi:10.1016/j.procs.2018.08.233

Chatterjee, S. (2020). AI strategy of India: Policy framework, adoption challenges and actions for government. *Transforming Government: People, Process and Policy, 14*(5), 757–775. doi:10.1108/TG-05-2019-0031

Chatterjee, S., & Bhattacharjee, K. K. (2020). Adoption of artificial intelligence in higher education: A quantitative analysis using structural equation modelling. *Education and Information Technologies, 25*(5), 3443–3463. doi:10.100710639-020-10159-7

Chatterjee, S., Kar, A. K., & Gupta, M. P. (2018). Success of IoT in smart cities of India: An empirical analysis. *Government Information Quarterly, 35*(3), 349–361. doi:10.1016/j.giq.2018.05.002

Chatterjee, S., & Sreenivasulu, N. S. (2019). Personal data sharing and legal issues of human rights in the era of artificial intelligence: Moderating effect of government regulation. *International Journal of Electronic Government Research, 15*(3), 21–36. doi:10.4018/IJEGR.2019070102

Chatzoglou, P., & Chatzoudes, D. (2014). Factors affecting e-business adoption in SMEs: An empirical research. *Journal of Enterprise Information Management, 29*(3), 327–358. doi:10.1108/JEIM-03-2014-0033

Chen, N. (2018). *Are robots replacing routine jobs?* [Thesis]. Harvard University.

Chen, X., Xie, H., & Hwang, G. J. (2020). A multi-perspective study on artificial intelligence in education: Grants, conferences, journals, software tools, institutions, and researchers. *Computers and Education: Artificial Intelligence*, 100005.

Chen, Y., & Yang, D. Y. (2018). *The Impact of Media Censorship: 1984 or Brave New World?* Working Paper.

Chen, C. P., & Zhang, C. Y. (2014). Data-intensive applications, challenges, techniques and technologies: A survey on Big Data. *Information Sciences, 275*, 314–347. doi:10.1016/j.ins.2014.01.015

Chen, F., Deng, P., Wan, J., Zhang, D., Vasilakos, A. V., & Rong, X. (2015). Data mining for the internet of things: Literature review and challenges. *International Journal of Distributed Sensor Networks, 11*(8), 431047. doi:10.1155/2015/431047

Chen, H. (2009). AI, e-government, and politics 2.0. *IEEE Intelligent Systems, 24*(5), 64–86. doi:10.1109/MIS.2009.91

Chen, H., Chiang, R., & Storey, V. (2012). Business Intelligence and Analytics: From Big Data to Big Impact. *Management Information Systems Quarterly, 36*(4), 1165–1188. doi:10.2307/41703503

Chen, L., Chen, P., & Lin, Z. (2020). Artificial intelligence in education: A review. *IEEE Access: Practical Innovations, Open Solutions, 8*, 75264–75278. doi:10.1109/ACCESS.2020.2988510

Chen, Y. C., & Hsieh, T. C. (2014). Big data for digital government: Opportunities, challenges, and strategies. *International Journal of Public Administration in the Digital Age, 1*(1), 1–14. doi:10.4018/ijpada.2014010101

Chen, Y. N. K., & Wen, C. H. R. (2021). Impacts of Attitudes Toward Government and Corporations on Public Trust in Artificial Intelligence. *Communication Studies, 72*(1), 115–131. doi:10.1080/10510974.2020.1807380

Chiu, T. K. F. (2021). A Holistic Approach to the Design of Artificial Intelligence (AI) Education for K-12 Schools. *TechTrends, 65*(5), 796–807. doi:10.100711528-021-00637-1

Chomsky, N. (2012). Ocupar Wall Street. Ediciones Urano.

Chong, A. Y.-L. (2013). Predicting m-commerce adoption determinants: A neural network approach. *Expert Systems with Applications*, *40*(2), 523–530. doi:10.1016/j.eswa.2012.07.068

Chopra, S., & Sodhi, M. (2004). Managing risk to avoid supply-chain breakdown. *Sloan Management Review*, *46*(1), 53–61.

Chris, M., & Susan, L. R. (2018). Digital Weberianism: Bureaucracy, Information, and the Techno-rationality of Neo-liberal Capitalism. *Indiana Journal of Global Legal Studies*, *25*(1), 187–216. doi:10.2979/indjglolegstu.25.1.0187

Christakis, N. A., Fowler, J. H., Diéguez, A., Vidal, L., & Schmid, E. (2010). Conectados: el sorprendente poder de las redes sociales y cómo nos afectan (No. 302.30285 C4Y.). Madrid: Taurus.

Christensen, T., Lægreid, P., Roness, P. G., & Røvik, K. A. (2007). *Organization Theory and the Public Sector: Instrument, Culture and Myth*. Taylor & Francis. doi:10.4324/9780203929216

Christopher, M. (2016). Logistics & Supply Chain Management (5th ed.). FT Publishing International.

Ciolacu, M., Tehrani, A. F., Binder, L., & Svasta, P. M. (2018). Education 4.0 - Artificial Intelligence Assisted Higher Education: Early recognition System with Machine Learning to support Students' Success. *2018 IEEE 24th International Symposium for Design and Technology in Electronic Packaging (SIITME)*, 23-30. 10.1109/SIITME.2018.8599203

Clark, W. R., & Golder, M. (2015). Big data, causal inference, and formal theory: Contradictory trends in political science?: Introduction. *PS, Political Science & Politics*, *48*(1), 65–70. doi:10.1017/S1049096514001759

Clerwall, C. (2014). Enter the robot journalist. Users' perceptions of automated content. *Journalism Practice*, *8*(5), 519–531. doi:10.1080/17512786.2014.883116

Cobo, C. E. (2003). El comportamiento humano. *Cuadernos Americanos*, *29*, 114–130.

Cobo, J. C. R., & Moravec, J. W. (2011). *Aprendizaje Invisible.: Hacia una nueva ecología de la educación*. Editions de la Universitat de Barcelona.

Coll, C. (1988). Significado y sentido en el aprendizaje escolar. Reflexiones en torno al concepto de aprendizaje significativo. *Infancia y Aprendizaje*, *11*(41), 131–142. doi:10.1080/02103702.1988.10822196

Collier, R. B., Dubal, V. B., & Carter, C. L. (2018). Disrupting Regulation, Regulating Disruption: The Politics of Uber in the United States. *Perspectives on Politics*, *16*(4), 919–937. doi:10.1017/S1537592718001093

Collins, C., Dennehy, D., Conboy, K., & Mikalef, P. (2021). Artificial intelligence in information systems research: A systematic literature review and research agenda. *International Journal of Information Management*, *60*, 102383. doi:10.1016/j.ijinfomgt.2021.102383

Conati, C., & Merten, C. (2007). Eye-tracking for user modeling in exploratory learning environments: An empirical evaluation. *Knowledge-Based Systems*, *20*(6), 557–574. doi:10.1016/j.knosys.2007.04.010

Connaway, L. S. (1996). Focus Group Interviews: A Data Collection Methodology. *Library Administration & Management*, *10*(4), 231–239.

Corbella, J. (2017). Inteligencia Artificial Arpa Jo. *Diario La Vanguardia*. https://www.lavanguardia.com/ciencia/20171019/432171399410/inteligencia-artificial-alphago-zero-juego-go-deepmind.html

Cordella, A., & Bonina, C. M. (2012). A public value perspective for ICT enabled public sector reforms: A theoretical reflection. *Government Information Quarterly*, *29*(4), 512–520. doi:10.1016/j.giq.2012.03.004

Cordero, R. (2019). Qué es un concepto? Theodor W. Adorno y la crítica como método. *Diferencias*, *1*(8).

Council of Europe. (2017). *Study on the human rights dimensions of automated data processing techniques (in particular algorithms) and possible regulatory implications.* Council of Europe, Committee of experts on Internet MSI-NET.

Courpasson, D., & Clegg, S. (2016). Dissolving the Iron Cages? Tocqueville, Michels, Bureaucracy and the Perpetuation of Elite Power. *Organization, 13*(3), 319–343. doi:10.1177/1350508406063481

Courtine, J.-J. (2019). *Introducción: El cabal mentir", on: Swift, Jonathan, El arte de la mentira política.* Editorial Sequitur.

Courtois, C., & Timmermans, E. (2018). Cracking the tinder code. *Journal of Computer-Mediated Communication, 23*(1), 1–16. doi:10.1093/jcmc/zmx001

Cramer, H., Evers, V., Ramlal, S., van Someren, M., Rutledge, L., Stash, N., Aroyo, L., & Wielinga, J. (2008). The effects of transparency on trust in and acceptance of a content-based art recommender. *User Modeling and User-Adapted Interaction, 18*(5), 455–496. doi:10.100711257-008-9051-3

Crawford, K. (2021). *The Atlas of AI: Power, Politics, and the Planetary Costs of Artificial Intelligence.* Yale University Press.

Creemers, R. (2017). *China's Social Credit System: An Evolving practice of control.* University of Leiden.

Criado, J. I. (2021). Inteligencia Artificial (y Administración Pública). *EUNOMÍA. Revista en Cultura de la Legalidad,* (20), 348–372. doi:10.20318/eunomia.2021.6097

Croushore, D. (2011). Frontiers of real-time data analysis. *Journal of Economic Literature, 49*(1), 72–100. doi:10.1257/jel.49.1.72

Cultura de la seguridad. (2021). *Consejos generales para acudir a una manifestación.* Author.

Curry, E. (2016). The Big Data Value Chain: Definitions, Concepts, and Theoretical Approaches. *New Horizons for a Data-Driven Economy,* 29–37. doi:10.1007/978-3-319-21569-3_3

Cutajar, A. (2020). *Investigating the employee skills gap within the digital marketing industry* (Master's thesis). University of Malta.

Cyman, D., Gromova, E., & Juchnevicius, E. (2021). Regulation of artificial intelligence in BRICS and the European Union. *BRICS Law Journal, 8*(1), 86–115. doi:10.21684/2412-2343-2021-8-1-86-115

Daher, N. (2016). The relationships between organizational culture and organizational innovation. *International Journal of Business & Public Administration, 13*(2), 1–15.

Dasgupta. (2017). Big Data gives China's Top 3 Internet firms big leverage. *Voanews.*

David, N., Justice, J. B., & McNutt, J. G. (2018). Smart Cities, Transparency, Civic Technology and Reinventing Government. In Smart Technologies for Smart Governments. Transparency, Efficiency and Organizational Issues. Berlin: Springer.

David, N., Justice, J. B., & McNutt, J. G. (2015). Smart Cities are Transparent Cities: The Role of Fiscal Transparency in Smart City Governance. In P. R. B. Manuel (Ed.), *Transforming City Governments for successful Smart Cities. Empirical Experiences.* Springer. doi:10.1007/978-3-319-03167-5_5

Davis, F. D. (1989). Perceived Usefulness, Perceived Ease of Use, and User Acceptance of Information Technology. *Management Information Systems Quarterly, 13*(3), 319–340. doi:10.2307/249008

De Bruijn, H., & Janssen, M. (2017). Building cybersecurity awareness: The need for evidence-based framing strategies. *Government Information Quarterly, 34*(1), 1–7. doi:10.1016/j.giq.2017.02.007

De Gregorio, G. (2021). The rise of digital constitutionalism in the European Union. *International Journal of Constitutional Law*, *19*(1), 41–70. doi:10.1093/icon/moab001

De Miguel Asensio, P. A. (2020). Libro Blanco sobre inteligencia artificial: Evolución del marco normativo y aplicación efectiva. *La Ley Unión Europea*, (79), 1–5.

de Sousa, W. G., de Melo, E. R. P., Bermejo, P. H. D. S., Farias, R. A. S., & Gomes, A. O. (2019). How and where is artificial intelligence in the public sector going? A literature review and research agenda. *Government Information Quarterly*, *36*(4), 101392. doi:10.1016/j.giq.2019.07.004

De Vries, M., & Nemec, J. (2013). Public sector reform: An overview of recent literature and research on NPM and alternative paths. *International Journal of Public Sector Management*, *26*(1), 4–16. doi:10.1108/09513551311293408

Dearden, L. (2020). Facial recognition to be rolled out across London by police, despite privacy concerns. *The Independent*.

Debasa, F. (2018, October 23). *Nuevos retos sociales en la IV Revolución Industrial*. Retrieved December 12, 2021, from Telos Fundación Teléfonica website: https://telos.fundaciontelefonica.com/telos-109-regulacion-felipe-debasa-nuevos-retos-sociales-en-la-iv-revolucion-industrial/

Debasa, F. (2021). Digitalisation, pandemics and current world (2019-2021). *UNIO–EU Law Journal*, *7*(1), 18–32. doi:10.21814/unio.7.1.3575

Debasa, F., & Sánchez, T. A. (2021). El discurso político de la presidencia Trump antes del covid. *Historia Actual Online*, (56), 21–34.

Del Barco, L. (2020, July 2). Mercadona comienza a usar un sistema de reconocimiento facial para identificar a delincuentes. *Hipertextual*. https://hipertextual.com/

Deleuze G. (1992, Winter). Postscripts of the societies of control. *October*, 59.

Deloitte. (2018). *Realising the economic potential of machine-generated, non-personal data in the EU Report for Vodafone Group*. Deloitte.

Denzin, N. K. (2001). *Interpretive interactionism* (Vol. 16). Sage. doi:10.4135/9781412984591

Deutsch, M., & Gerard, H. B. (1973). Estudio de las influencias sociales normativas e informativas sobre el criterio individual. In H. Proshansky & B. Seidenberg (Eds.), *Estudios básicos de psicología social* (p. 491). Ed. Tecnos.

Devedžić, V. (2004). Web intelligence and artificial intelligence in education. *Journal of Educational Technology & Society*, *7*(4), 29–39.

Devkota, N., Paija, N., Paudel, U. R., & Bhandari, U. (2021). Mapping the industries' willingness to pay for unrestricted electricity supply. *Environment, Development and Sustainability*, 1–17.

Diakopoulos, N., & Koliska, M. (2016). Algorithmic transparency in the news media. *Digital Journalism*, *5*(7), 809–828. .2016.1208053 doi:10.1080/21670811

Diakopoulos, N. (2016). Accountability in algorithmic decision making. *Communications of the ACM*, *59*(2), 58–62. doi:10.1145/2844110

Dickersin, K., & Berlin, J. A. (1992). Meta-analysis: State-of-the-science. *Epidemiologic Reviews*, *14*(1), 154–176. doi:10.1093/oxfordjournals.epirev.a036084 PMID:1289110

DiGiacinto, F. (2018). "European Structural And Investment Funds" 2014-2020 For The Efficiency Of Public Administration. *Curentul Juridic*, *73*(2), 26–37.

Dimmer, C. (2021). Smart Cities in Asia: Governing Development in the Era of HyperConnectivity. Cities. *Pacific Affairs*, *94*(2), 401–403.

Dirican, C. (2015). The impacts of robotics, artificial intelligence on business and economics. *Procedia: Social and Behavioral Sciences*, *195*, 564–573. doi:10.1016/j.sbspro.2015.06.134

Discussion Paper on National Strategy for Artificial Intelligence I NITI Aayog I National Institution for Transforming India. (n.d.). Retrieved from https://niti.gov.in/content/nationalstrategy- ai-discussionpaper

Djeffal, C. (2020). Artificial Intelligence and Public Governance: Normative Guidelines for Artificial Intelligence in Government and Public Administration. In *Regulating Artificial Intelligence* (pp. 277–293). Springer. doi:10.1007/978-3-030-32361-5_12

Doiz, A., & Lasagabaster, D. (2020). Dealing with language issues in English-medium instruction at university: A comprehensive approach. *International Journal of Bilingual Education and Bilingualism*, *23*(3), 257–262. doi:10.1080/13670050.2020.1727409

Domaica Maroto, J. M. (2019). *Datos personales biométricos, dactiloscópicos, y derechos fundamentales: el nuevo reto para el legislador*. UNED.

Drewry. (2021). *World Container Index*. https://www.drewry.co.uk/supply-chain-advisors/supply-chain-expertise/world-container-index-assessed-by-drewry

Dreyling, R., Jackson, E., Tammet, T., Labanava, A., & Pappel, I. (2021). Social, Legal, and Technical Considerations for Machine Learning and Artificial Intelligence Systems in Government. *Proceedings of the 23rd International Conference on Enterprise Information Systems*. 10.5220/0010452907010708

Drigas, A. S., & Ioannidou, R. E. (2012). Artificial intelligence in special education: A decade review. *International Journal of Engineering Education*, *28*(6), 1366.

Drinhausen K., & Brusse V. (2021). *China's Social Credit System in 2021: From fragmentation towards integration*. Merics.org.

Driss, O. B., Mellouli, S., & Trabelsi, Z. (2019). From citizens to government policy-makers: Social media data analysis. *Government Information Quarterly*, *36*(3), 560–570. doi:10.1016/j.giq.2019.05.002

Dubois, P. (1979). Sabotage in Industry. *Organization Studies*, *1*(1), 103–104.

Dubra, J. (2017). Ciencia y transparencia para mejorar la seguridad. *El observador*.

Duchessi, P., O'Keefe, R., & O'Leary, D. (1993). A Research perspective: Artificial intelligence, management and organizations. *Intelligent Systems in Accounting, Finance & Management*, *2*(3), 151–159. doi:10.1002/j.1099-1174.1993.tb00039.x

Dueñas, J. L. (2021, May 5). Algoritmos e inteligencia artificial, los aliados de las universidades para examinar a distancia. *Rtve*. https://www.rtve.es/

Dunleavy, P., Margetts, H., Bastow, S., & Tinkler, J. (2006). New Public Management Is Dead-Long Live Digital-Era Governance. *Journal of Public Administration: Research and Theory*, *16*(3), 467–494. doi:10.1093/jopart/mui057

Dunn, W. N., & Miller, D. Y. (2007). A Critique of the New Public Management and the Neo-Weberian State: Advancing a Critical Theory of Administrative Reform. *Public Organization Review*, *7*(4), 345–358. doi:10.100711115-007-0042-3

Durkheim, É. (1982). *Las formas elementales de la vida religiosa* (Vol. 38). Ediciones Akal.

Dwivedi, Y. K., Hughes, L., Ismagilova, E., Aarts, G., Coombs, C., Crick, T., Duan, Y., Dwivedi, R., Edwards, J., Eirug, A., Galanos, V., Ilavarasan, P. V., Janssen, M., Jones, P., Kar, A. K., Kizgin, H., Kronemann, B., Lal, B., Lucini, B., ... Williams, M. D. (2021). Artificial Intelligence (AI): Multidisciplinary perspectives on emerging challenges, opportunities, and agenda for research, practice and policy. *International Journal of Information Management, 57*, 101994. doi:10.1016/j.ijinfomgt.2019.08.002

Dwivedi, Y. K., Rana, N. P., Tamilmani, K., & Raman, R. (2020). A meta-analysis based modified unified theory of acceptance and use of technology: A review of emerging literature. *Current Opinion in Psychology, 36*, 13–18. doi:10.1016/j.copsyc.2020.03.008 PMID:32339928

Dye, R. F. (2021). *Impact of Shipping Container Shortages, Delays, and Increased Demand on the North American Supply Chain.* The Committee on Transportation and Infrastructure Subcommittee on Coast Guard And Maritime Transportation United States House of Representatives.

E2OPEN. (2021). *Blueprint for Managing Supply Chain Disruptions of Any Size. Performance During the COVID-19 Pandemic and AI's Role in Building Resilient Businesses.* E2OPEN.

Ebbers, W., Jansen, M., Pieterson, W., & van de Wijngaert, L. (2016). Facts and feelings: The role of rational and irrational factors in citizens' channel choices. *Government Information Quarterly, 33*(3), 506–515. doi:10.1016/j.giq.2016.06.001

Ebrahim, Z., & Irani, Z. (2005). E-government adoption: Architecture and barriers. *Business Process Management Journal, 11*(5), 589–611. doi:10.1108/14637150510619902

Echeverría, J. (1999). *Los señores del aire: Telépolis y el Tercer Entorno.* Editorial Destino.

Economic Survey. (2018). *Economic Survey 2018/19.* Retrieved from https://new.mof.gov.np/uploads/document/file/compiled%20economic%20Survey%20english%207-25_20191111101758.pdf

Edwards, B. I., & Cheok, A. D. (2018). Why Not Robot Teachers: Artificial Intelligence for Addressing Teacher Shortage. *Applied Artificial Intelligence, 32*(4), 345–360. doi:10.1080/08839514.2018.1464286

Efe. (2021, May 6). Dudas y respuestas sobre la polémica herramienta de reconocimiento facial en los exámenes. *20 minutos.* https://www.20minutos.es

Ehsan, U., & Riedl, M. (2019). *On design and evaluation of human-centered explainable AI systems.* ACM

El Baz, J., & Ruel, S. (2021). Can supply chain risk management practices mitigate the disruption impacts on supply chains' resilience and robustness? Evidence from an empirical survey in a COVID-19 outbreak era. *International Journal of Production Economics, 233*, 107972. doi:10.1016/j.ijpe.2020.107972

Eljasik-Swoboda, T., Rathgeber, C., & Hasenauer, R. (2019, October). Artificial Intelligence for Innovation Readiness Assessment. In *2019 IEEE International Symposium on Innovation and Entrepreneurship (TEMS-ISIE)* (pp. 1-6). IEEE.

Engin, Z., & Treleaven, P. (2019). Algorithmic government: Automating public services and supporting civil servants in using data science technologies. *The Computer Journal, 62*(3), 448–460. doi:10.1093/comjnl/bxy082

Epstein, R., & Robertson, R. E. (2015). The search engine manipulation effect (SEME) and its possible impact on the outcomes of elections. *Proceedings of the National Academy of Sciences of the United States of America, 112*(33), 512–521. doi:10.1073/pnas.1419828112 PMID:26243876

Ernst, D. (2018). *China's Artificial Intelligence Progress.* LookEast.

Erümit, A. K., & Çetin, İ. (2020). Design framework of adaptive intelligent tutoring systems. *Education and Information Technologies, 25*(5), 4477–4500. doi:10.100710639-020-10182-8

Esteve, M., Campion, A., Gascó, M., & Mikhaylov, S. (2020). The Challenges of Organizational Factors in Collaborative Artificial Intelligence Projects. *Social Science Computer Review*.

Esteves, J., & Joseph, R. C. (2008). A comprehensive framework for the assessment of eGovernment projects. *Government Information Quarterly*, *25*(1), 118–132. doi:10.1016/j.giq.2007.04.009

Etzioni, A. & E. (1995). *Los cambios sociales. Fuentes, tipos y consecuencias*. FCE.

Eubanks, V. (2018). *Automating inequality: How high-tech tools profile, police, and punish the poor*. St. Martin's Press.

Europa Press. (2017, June 14). IU denuncia "vulneración de derechos laborales" a trabajadores de Mercadona en tiendas de Cantabria. *elDiario.es*. https://www.eldiario.es/

European Comission. (2021). *Proposal for a Regulation of the European Parliament and of the Council Laying Down Harmonised Rules on Artificial Intelligence (Artificial Intelligence Act) and Amending Certaing Union Legislative Acts COM/2021/206 final*. Author. https://eur-lex.europa.eu/

European Commision. (2020). *European Strategy for Data. Communication from the Commission to the European Parliament, the Council, the European Economic and Social Committee and the Committee of the Regions: A European strategy for data* (Publication No. COM (2020) 66). Directorate-General for Communications Networks, Content and Technology.

European Commission (2018). Communication to the European Parliament, the European Council, the Council, the European Economic and Social Committee and the Committee of the Regions "Artificial Intelligence for Europe". 237 final.

European Commission. (2018). *Artificial Intelligence for Europe* (Publication No. COM (2018) 237). Directorate-General for Communications Networks, Content and Technology.

European Commission. (2018). *Communication from the Commission to the European Parliament, the European Council, the Council, the European Economic and Social Committee and the Committee of the Regions. Coordinated Plan on Artificial Intelligence* (Publication No. COM (2018) 795 final). Directorate-General for Communications Networks, Content and Technology.

European Commission. (2018). *Coordinate Plan on Artificial Intelligence* (Publication No. COM (2018) 795 Final). Directorate-General for Communications Networks, Content and Technology.

European Commission. (2020). *European Commission Report on the Safety and Liability Aspects of AI the Internet of Things (IoT) and robotics* (Publication No. COM (2020) 64). Directorate-General for Communications Networks, Content and Technology.

European Commission. (2020). *White Paper On Artificial Intelligence - A European approach to excellence and trust* (Publication No. COM (2020) 65 final). Directorate-General for Communications Networks, Content and Technology.

European Commission. (2021). *Communication from the Commission to the European Parliament, the Council, the European Economic and Social Committee and the Committee of the Regions. Fostering a European approach to Artificial Intelligence* (Publication No. COM/2021/205 final). Directorate-General for Communications Networks, Content and Technology.

European Data Protection Board. (2021, June 21). *EDPB & EDPS call for ban on use of AI for automated recognition of human features in publicly accessible spaces, and some other uses of AI that can lead to unfair discrimination*. Author.

European Union (2018) Regulation of the European Parliament and of the Council on a framework for the free circulation of non-personal data in the European Union, number 1807.

Evans, D., & Yen, D. C. (2006). E-Government: Evolving relationship of citizens and government, domestic, and international development. *Government Information Quarterly*, *23*(2), 207–235. doi:10.1016/j.giq.2005.11.004

Fahimirad, M., & Kotamjani, S. S. (2018). A review on application of artificial intelligence in teaching and learning in educational contexts. *International Journal of Learning and Development*, *8*(4), 106–118. doi:10.5296/ijld.v8i4.14057

Fairclough, N. L., & Wodac, R. (1997). *Critical Discourse analysis. In Discourse Studies. Discourse as social interaction* (Vol. 2). Sage.

Fan, W., Liu, J., Zhu, S., & Pardalos, P. M. (2018). Investigating the impacting factors for the healthcare professionals to adopt artificial intelligence-based medical diagnosis support system (AIMDSS). *Annals of Operations Research*, *294*(1-2), 567–592. doi:10.100710479-018-2818-y

Faraj, S., Pachidi, S., & Sayegh, K. (2018). Working and organizing in the age of the learning algorithm. *Information and Organization*, *28*(1), 62–70. 1016/j.infoandorg.2018.02.005

Farley, T (2005). Mobile telephone history. *Telektronikk*, *101*(3-4), 22.

Fawzi Mostefai, A. (2014). *El sistema de crédito social en China aún deja muchas interrogantes*. Observatorio Virtual Asia Pacífico.

Feldstein, S. (2019). The road to digital unfreedom: How artificial intelligence is reshaping repression. *Journal of Democracy*, *30*(1), 40–52. doi:10.1353/jod.2019.0003

Fernandes, E., Holanda, M., Victorino, M., Borges, V., Carvalho, R., & van Erven, G. (2018). Educational data mining: Predictive analysis of academic performance of public school students in the capital of Brazil. *Journal of Business Research*, *94*, 335–343. doi:10.1016/j.jbusres.2018.02.012

Ferreira, L. N., Pereira, L. N., da Fé Brás, M., & Ilchuk, K. (2021). Quality of life under the COVID-19 quarantine. *Quality of Life Research: An International Journal of Quality of Life Aspects of Treatment, Care and Rehabilitation*, *30*(5), 1389–1405. Advance online publication. doi:10.100711136-020-02724-x PMID:33389523

Finck, M. (2018). Blockchains and Data Protection in the European Union. *European Data Protection Law Review*, *4*(1), 17–35. doi:10.21552/edpl/2018/1/6

Fiok K., Farahani FV., Karwowski W., Ahram T. (2021). Explainable artificial intelligence for education and training. *The Journal of Defense Modeling and Simulation*. doi:10.1177/15485129211028651

Fioriglio, G. (2015, October 28). Freedom, Authority and Knowledge on Line: The Dictatorship of the Algorithm. Retrieved December 12, 2021, from https://ssrn.com/abstract=2728842

Fister, I., & Fister, I. Jr., (Eds.). (2015). *Adaptation and Hybri-dization in Computational Intelligence* (Vol. 18). Adaptation, Learning and Optimization. doi:10.1007/978-3-319-14400-9

Flanagan, K. (2010). *Bauman's Implicit Theology*. Palgrave.

Fleming, P (2017). The human capital hoax: Work, debt and insecurity in the era of Uberization. *Organization Studies*, *38*(5), 691-709.

Floridi, L., & Cowls, J. (2019). A unified framework of five principles for AI in society. *Harvard Data Science Review*, *1*(1).

Forger, G. (2019). AI is coming, AI is coming. *Supply Chain Management Review*: https://www.scmr.com/article/ai_is_coming_ai_is_coming

Forger, G. (Interviewer) & Garber, E. (Interviewee). (2019). *Artificial intelligence knocking on the warehouse door.* https://www.scmr.com/article/nextgen_supply_chain_interview_evan_garber

Forum, W. E. (2020). *AI Procurement in a Box: Pilot case studies from the United Kingdom.* https://www3.weforum. org/docs/WEF_AI_Procurement_in_a_Box_Pilot_case_studies_from_the_United_Kingdom_2020.pdf

Foucault, M. (2012). *Un diálogo sobre el poder y otras conversaciones.* Alianza Editorial.

Fraguas, M. (1985). *Teoría de la desinformación.* Editorial Alhambra.

Frey, C. B., & Osborne, M. A. (2017). The future of employment: How susceptible are jobs to computerisation? *Technological Forecasting and Social Change, 114*, 254–280. doi:10.1016/j.techfore.2016.08.019

Gadner, H. (2005). *Inteligencias múltiples: La teoría en la práctica.* Ediciones Paidos.

Galaup, L. (2021, June 10). La Justicia impide que Mercadona use el reconocimiento facial para detectar a dos ladrones condenados. *elDiario.es.* https://www.eldiario.es

Gan, S. K.-E. (2018). The history and future of scientific phone apps and mobile devices. *Scientific Phone Apps and Mobile Devices, 4*(1), 2. Advance online publication. doi:10.118641070-018-0022-8

Gao, X., Shen, J., He, W., Sun, F., Zhang, Z., Guo, W., Zhang, X., & Kong, Y. (2019). An evolutionary game analysis of governments' decision-making behaviors and factors influencing watershed ecological compensation in China. *Journal of Environmental Management, 251*, 109592. doi:10.1016/j.jenvman.2019.109592 PMID:31569022

Gao, Y., Xiaojun Wang, P. L. W., Professor Xu Chen, D., Li, H., & Luo, Y. (2015). An empirical study of wearable technology acceptance in healthcare. *Industrial Management & Data Systems, 115*(9), 1704–1723. doi:10.1108/IMDS-03-2015-0087

García Ropero, J. (2020, March 10). Mercadona impulsó su beneficio un 5% hasta 623 millones en 2019. *Cinco Días.* https://cincodias.elpais.com/

García, M. D. M. (2011). *Evolución de actitudes y competencias matemáticas en estudiantes de secundaria al introducir Geogebra en el aula* [Doctoral dissertation, Universidad de Almería]. Repositorio digital de documentos en educación matemática. http://funes.uniandes.edu.co/1768/

Garnelo, J. (2020, September 13). Grupos planeados por alumnos de Medicina de la USC activaron un sistema para copiar en los exámenes 'online'. *El Correo Gallego.* https://www.elcorreogallego.es

Geiger, F.-X., Malavolta, I., Pascarella, L., Palomba, F., Di Nucci, D., & Bacchelli, A. (2018, May 1). *A Graph-Based Dataset of Commit History of Real-World Android apps.* Retrieved December 12, 2021, from IEEE Xplore website: https://ieeexplore.ieee.org/document/8595172

Gertner, A. S., Conati, C., & VanLehn, K. (1998). Procedural help in Andes: Generating hints using a Bayesian network student model. *AAAI/IAAI, 1998*, 106-11.

Gharehchopogh, F. S., & Khalifelu, Z. A. (2011). Using intelligent tutoring systems in instruction and education. In *2nd International Conference on Education and Management Technology* (pp. 250-254). IACSIT Press.

Giffinger, R., Fertner, C., Kramar, H., & Meijers, E. (2007). *City-ranking of European medium-sized cities.* Cent. Reg. Sci.

Gil-Garcia, J. R., Zhang, J., & Puron-Cid, G. (2016). Conceptualizing smartness in government: An integrative and multi-dimensional view. *Government Information Quarterly, 33*(3), 524–534. doi:10.1016/j.giq.2016.03.002

Gkogkidis, V., & Dacre, N. (2021). The educator's LSP journey: Creating exploratory learning environments for responsible management education using Lego Serious Play. *Emerald Open Research*, *3*, 2. doi:10.35241/emeraldopenres.14015.1

Global Wind 2008 Report (Bélgica). (2009). *Big data o como los datos masivos están cambiando el mundo", Ciudad de México*. Dirección General de Divulgación de la Ciencia, UNAM, n° 241, pp. 8-13.

Goda, K., & Mine, T. (2011). Analysis of Students Learning Activities through Quantifying Time-Series Comments. *Knowledge-Based and Intelligent Information and Engineering Systems, 6882*, 154-164.

Goel, R., & Gupta, P. (2020). Robotics and industry 4.0. In *A Roadmap to Industry 4.0: Smart Production, Sharp Business and Sustainable Development* (pp. 157–169). Springer. doi:10.1007/978-3-030-14544-6_9

Goel, S., & Chen, V. (2008). Can business process reengineering lead to security vulnerabilities: Analyzing the reengineered process. *International Journal of Production Economics, 115*(1), 104–112. doi:10.1016/j.ijpe.2008.05.002

Goldkind, L. (2021). Social Work and Artificial Intelligence: Into the Matrix. *Social Work, 66*(4), 372–374. Advance online publication. doi:10.1093wwab028 PMID:34279661

Goldkind, L., & McNutt, J. G. (2019). We could be unicorns: Human services leaders Moving from Managing Programs to Managing Information Ecosystems. *Human Service Organizations, Management, Leadership & Governance, 43*(4), 269–277. doi:10.1080/23303131.2019.1669758

Goldkind, L., Wolf, L., & Freddolino, P. P. (Eds.). (2018). *Digital social work: Tools for practice with individuals, organizations, and communities*. Oxford University Press.

González Quirós, J. L. (2019). La inteligencia artificial y la realidad restringida: Las estrecheces metafísicas de la tecnología. *Naturaleza y Libertad, 12*(12), 127–158. doi:10.24310/NATyLIB.2019.v0i12.6271

Gottfried, A., Hartmann, C., & Yates, D. (2021). Mining Open Government Data for Business Intelligence Using Data Visualization: A Two-Industry Case Study. *Journal of Theoretical and Applied Electronic Commerce Research, 16*(4), 1042–1065. doi:10.3390/jtaer16040059

Goudarzi, S., Khaniejo, N., & the Centre for Internet and Society. (2018, March 18). *AI and Governance*. Retrieved from https://cis-india.org/internet-governance/files/ai-in-governance

Government of Spain (2020). National Artificial Intelligence Strategy.

Graesser, A. C., Conley, M. W., & Olney, A. M. (2012a). Intelligent tutoring systems. In S. Graham & K. Harris (Eds.), *Applications to Learning and Teaching* (pp. 451–473). APA Educational Psychology Handbook. American Psychological Association.

Graesser, A. C., D'Mello, S. K., Hu, X., Cai, Z., Olney, A., & Morgan, B. (2012b). AutoTutor. In P. M. McCarthey & C. Boonthum-Denecke (Eds.), *Applied natural language processing: Identification, Investigation and Resolution* (pp. 169–187). IGI Global. doi:10.4018/978-1-60960-741-8.ch010

Graesser, A. C., D'Mello, S. K., & Person, N. (2009). Meta-knowledge in tutoring. In D. J. Hacker, J. Dunlosky, & A. C. Graesser (Eds.), *Handbook of Metacognition in Education* (pp. 361–382). Taylor & Francis.

Graesser, A. C., McNamara, D. S., & VanLehn, K. (2005). Scaffolding deep comprehension strategies through Point&Query, AutoTutor, and iSTART. *Educational Psychologist, 40*(4), 225–234. doi:10.120715326985ep4004_4

Graesser, A. C., & Olde, B. A. (2003). How does one know whether a person understands a device? The quality of the questions the person asks when the device breaks down. *Journal of Educational Psychology, 95*(3), 524–536. doi:10.1037/0022-0663.95.3.524

Grant, J., Eltoukhy, M., & Asfour, S. (2014). Short-term electrical peak demand forecasting in a large government building using artificial neural networks. *Energies*, *7*(4), 1935–1953. doi:10.3390/en7041935

Graupe, D. (2016). *Deep Learning Neural Networks: Design and Case Studies. World Scientific Publishing*. doi:10.1142/10190

Grawemeyer, B., Gutierrez-Santos, S., Holmes, W., Mavrikis, M., Rummel, N., Mazziotti, C., & Janning, R. (2015). Talk, tutor, explore, learn: Intelligent tutoring and exploration for robust learning. In C. Conati, N. Heffernan, A. Mitrovic, & M. F. Verdejo (Eds.), *Artificial Intelligence in Education. 7th International Conference, AIED 2015* (pp. 917-918). Springer.

Green, B., & Hu, L. (2018). The Myth in the Methodology: Towards a Recontextualization of Fairness in Machine Learning. *Proceedings of the International Conference on Machine Learning: The Debates Workshop*.

Gregory, B. T., Harris, S. G., Armenakis, A. A., & Shook, C. L. (2009). Organizational culture and effectiveness: A study of values, attitudes, and organizational outcomes. *Journal of Business Research*, *62*(7), 673–679. doi:10.1016/j.jbusres.2008.05.021

Grenoble, R. (2017). *Welcome to the Surveillance State: China's AI cameras see all.* https://www.huffingtonpost.com/entry/china-surveillance-camera-big-brother_us_5a2ff4dfe4b01598ac484acc

Grüll, P. (2020, January 10). Germany's plan for automatic facial recognition meet fierce criticism. *Euractiv*. https://www.euractiv.com/

Guirao Goris, S. J. A. (2015). Utilidad y tipos de revisión de literatura. *SciELO Analytics*, *9*(2), 0. Advance online publication. doi:10.4321/S1988-348X2015000200002

Günther, W. A., Mehrizi, M. H. R., Huysman, M., & Feldberg, F. (2017). Debating big data: A literature review on realizing value from big data. *The Journal of Strategic Information Systems*, *26*(3), 191–209. doi:10.1016/j.jsis.2017.07.003

Hacker, P., Krestel, R., Grundmann, S., & Naumann, F. (2020, December). Explainable AI under Contract and Tort Law: Legal Incentives and Technical Challenges. *Artificial Intelligence and Law*, *28*(4), 16. doi:10.100710506-020-09260-6

Haenlein, M., & Kaplan, A. (2019). A Brief History of Artificial Intelligence: On the Past, Present, and Future of Artificial Intelligence. *California Management Review*, *61*(4), 5–14. doi:10.1177/0008125619864925

Hagen, L., Harrison, T., & Falling, M. (2021, June). Contributions of Data Science to Digital Government Research: Contributions of Data Science to Digital Government Research. In *DG. O2021: The 22nd Annual International Conference on Digital Government Research* (pp. 38-48). Academic Press.

Halaweh, M. (2018). Viewpoint: Artificial intelligence government (Gov. 3.0): The UAE leading model. *Journal of Artificial Intelligence Research*, *62*, 269–272. doi:10.1613/jair.1.11210

Halegoua, G. (2020). *Smart cities*. MIT Press. doi:10.7551/mitpress/11426.001.0001

Hamon, R., Junklewitz, H., & Sanchez, I. (2020). *Robustness and explainability of artificial intelligence*. Publications Office of the European Union.

Handfield, R., & Linton, T. (2021). Supply chains are on the cusp of a data-fed revolution. Here's how businesses can succeed. *World Economic Forum*, https://www.weforum.org/agenda/2021/05/supply-chains-are-on-the-cusp-of-a-data-fed-revolution-here-s-how/

Han, H. J., Kim, K. J., & Kwon, H. S. (2020). The Analysis of Elementary School Teachers' Perception of Using Artificial Intelligence in Education. *Journal of Digital Convergence*, *18*(7), 47–56. doi:10.14400/JDC.2015.13.7.47

Hannig, S. (2019). *Distopía Digital: Cuatro herramientas que China usa para controlar a su población*. Fundación para el Progreso.

HANS. (2019, December 18). *AI support tool for Estonian Parliament*. Retrieved December 12, 2021, from e-Estonia website: https://e-estonia.com/hans-ai-support-tool-for-estonian-parliament/

Harris, M. (2012). Nonprofits and business: Toward a subfield of nonprofit studies. *Nonprofit and Voluntary Sector Quarterly*, *41*(5), 892–902. doi:10.1177/0899764012443735

Hartley, J., Alford, J., Knies, E., & Douglas, S. (2016). Towards an empirical research agenda for public value theory. *Public Management Review*, *19*(5), 670–685. doi:10.1080/14719037.2016.1192166

Hartley, J., Sørensen, E., & Torfing, J. (2013). Collaborative Innovation: A Viable Alternative to Market Competition and Organizational Entrepreneurship. *Public Administration Review*, *73*(6), 821–830. doi:10.1111/puar.12136

Harvey, D. (2007). *A Brief History of Neoliberalism*. Oxford University Press.

Hassani, H., Huang, X., Silva, E. S., & Ghodsi, M. (2016). A review of data mining applications in crime. *Statistical Analysis and Data Mining: The ASA Data Science Journal*, *9*(3), 139–154. doi:10.1002am.11312

Haugeland, J. (Ed.). (1985). *Artificial Intelligence: The Very Idea*. MIT Press.

Hawking, S. (2014, Dec. 4). AI could be the end of Humanity. *The Independent*. https://www.independent.co.uk/news/science/stephen-hawking-ai-could-be-end-humanity-9898320.html

Hazemi, R., Hailes, S., & Wilbur, S. (Eds.). (2012). *The digital university: reinventing the academy*. Springer Science & Business Media.

Helbing, D., Frey, B. S., Gigerenzer, G., Hafen, E., Hagner, M., Hofstetter, Y., Van Den Hoven, J., Zicari, R. V., & Zwitter, A. (2019). Will democracy survive big data and artificial intelligence? In *Towards digital enlightenment* (pp. 73–98). Springer. doi:10.1007/978-3-319-90869-4_7

Henderson, M., Selwyn, N., & Aston, R. (2017). What works and why? Student perceptions of 'useful' digital technology in university teaching and learning. *Studies in Higher Education*, *42*(8), 1567–1579. doi:10.1080/03075079.2015.1007946

Hendricks, K., & Singhal, V. (2005). Association between Supply Chain Glitches and Operating Performance. *Management Science*, *51*(5), 695–711. doi:10.1287/mnsc.1040.0353

Hengstler, M., Enkel, E., & Duelli, S. (2016). Applied artificial intelligence and trust- The case of autonomous vehicles and medical assistance devices. *Technological Forecasting and Social Change*, *105*, 105–120. doi:10.1016/j.techfore.2015.12.014

Hernández Guerrero, J. A. (2016, July 11). Solucionismo. *Diario de Cádiz*. https://www.diariodecadiz.es/opinion/articulos/Solucionismo_0_1043595790.html

Hernández Orallo, J., Ramírez Quintana, M. J., & Ferri Ramírez, C. (2004). *Introducción a la minería de datos*. Pearson Educación.

Herzog, S. (2011). Revisiting the Estonian Cyber Attacks: Digital Threats and Multinational Responses. *Journal of Strategic Security*, *4*(2), 49–60. doi:10.5038/1944-0472.4.2.3

Hildebrandt, M. (2020). The Artificial Intelligence of European Union Law. *German Law Journal*, *21*(1), 74–79. doi:10.1017/glj.2019.99

Hincapie, M., Diaz, C., Valencia, A., Contero, M., & Güemes-Castorena, D. (2021). Educational applications of augmented reality: A bibliometric study. *Computers & Electrical Engineering*, *93*, 107289. doi:10.1016/j.compeleceng.2021.107289

Hine, C. (2021). Evaluating the prospects for university-based ethical governance in artificial intelligence and data-driven innovation. *Research Ethics Review*, *17*(4), 17470161211022790. doi:10.1177/17470161211022790

Hobbes, T. (2008). *Leviatán o la materia, forma y poder de un Estado eclesiástico y civil*. Alianza Editorial.

Hofman, J. M., Sharma, A., & Watts, D. J. (2017). Prediction and explanation in social systems. *Science*, *355*(6324), 486–488. doi:10.1126cience.aal3856 PMID:28154051

Holmes, W., Anastopoulou, S., Schaumburg, H., & Mavrikis, M. (2018). *Technology-enhanced personalised learning: untangling the evidence*. Robert Bosch Stiftung.

Holmes, W., Bektik, D., Whitelock, D., & Woolf, B. P. (2018). Ethics in AIED: Who Cares?. In *International Conference on Artificial Intelligence in Education (AIED 2018)* (pp. 551–553). 10.1007/978-3-319-93846-2

Holmes, W., Bialik, M., & Fadel, C. (2019). *Artificial intelligence in education. Promises and Implications for Teaching and Learning*. Center for Curriculum Redesign.

Holmes, W., Bialik, M., & Fadel, C. (2019). *Artificial Intelligence in Education. Promises and Implications for Teaching and Learning*. Center for Curriculum Redesign.

Holstein, K., & Doroudi, S. (2019). Fairness and Equity in Learning Analytics Systems (FairLAK). *Companion Proceedings of the Ninth International Learning Analytics & Knowledge Conference (LAK 2019)*.

Holstein, K., Wortman Vaughan, J., Daumé, H. III, Dudík, M., & Wallach, H. (2019). Improving Fairness in Machine Learning Systems: What do Industry Practitioners Need? In *Proceedings of the ACM CHI Conference on Human Factors in Computing Systems (CHI'19)*. ACM. doi:10.1145/3290605.3300830

Holtgrewe, U. (2014). New new technologies: The future and the present of work in information and communication technology. *New Technology, Work and Employment*, *29*(1), 9–24. doi:10.1111/ntwe.12025

Hood, C. (1991). A public management for all seasons? *Public Administration*, *69*(1), 3–19. doi:10.1111/j.1467-9299.1991.tb00779.x

Hoofnagle, C. J., van der Sloot, B., & Borgesius, F. Z. (2019). The European Union general data protection regulation: What it is and what it means. *Information & Communications Technology Law*, *28*(1), 65–98. doi:10.1080/13600834.2019.1573501

Horodianenko, V. H. (2002). *Sotsiolohiia* [Sociology]. Akademiya.

Hosseini, S., Ivanov, D., & Dolgui, A. (2019). Review of quantitative methods for supply chain resilience analysis. Transport. Res. E. Logist. *Transport Reviews*, *125*, 285–307.

Hou, Y., & Lampe, C. (2017, June). Sustainable hacking: characteristics of the design and adoption of civic hacking projects. In *Proceedings of the 8th International Conference on Communities and Technologies* (pp. 125-134). ACM. 10.1145/3083671.3083706

Howell O'Neill, P. (2021). Google's top security teams unilaterally shut down a counterterrorism operation *MIT. Technology Review*.

Howson, C., Beyer, M. A., Idoine, C. J., & Jones, L. C. (2018). *How to Use Data for Good to Impact Society*. Gartner. https://www.gartner.com/doc/3880666/use-data-good-impact-society

Hrabowski, F. A. III. (2014). Institutional change in higher education: Innovation and collaboration. *Peabody Journal of Education*, *89*(3), 291–304. doi:10.1080/0161956X.2014.913440

Hsu, C.-L., & Lin, J. C.-C. (2016). Exploring Factors Affecting the Adoption of Internet of Things Services. *Journal of Computer Information Systems*, *58*(1), 49–57. doi:10.1080/08874417.2016.1186524

Hsu, Y.-C., Irie, N. R., & Ching, Y.-H. (2019). Computational Thinking Educational Policy Initiatives (CTEPI) Across the Globe. *TechTrends*, *63*(3), 260–270. doi:10.100711528-019-00384-4

Hughes, J. (2014). A strategic opening for a basic income guarantee in the global crisis being created by AI, robots, desktop manufacturing and biomedicine. *Journal of Ethics and Emerging Technologies*, *24*(1), 45–61.

Humphreys, L. (2010). Mobile social networks and urban public space. *New Media & Society*, *12*(5), 763–778. doi:10.1177/1461444809349578

Hung, S.-Y., Chang, C.-M., & Yu, T.-J. (2006). Determinants of user acceptance of the e-Government services: The case of online tax filing and payment system. *Government Information Quarterly*, *23*(1), 97–122. doi:10.1016/j.giq.2005.11.005

HUxIR Asociación de Estudiantes por la Defensa de los Derechos Fundamentales. (2021, April 18). *UNIR y el abuso de técnicas de Proctoring para la supervisión y control de alumnos.* Author. https://write.as/huxir

HUxIR Asociación de Estudiantes por la Defensa de los Derechos Fundamentales. (2021, April 21). *Nota de queja presentada al Rector de la Universidad Internacional de la Rioja.* Author. https://write.as/huxir

Hwang, G. J. (2014). Definition, framework and research issues of smart learning environments-a context-aware ubiquitous learning perspective. *Smart Learning Environments*, *1*(1), 1–14. doi:10.118640561-014-0004-5

Hwang, G. J., & Fu, Q. K. (2020). Advancement and research trends of smart learning environments in the mobile era. *International Journal of Mobile Learning and Organisation*, *14*(1), 114–129. doi:10.1504/IJMLO.2020.103911

Inclezan, D., & Pradanos, L. I. (2017). A critical view on smart cities and AI. *Journal of Artificial Intelligence Research*, *60*, 681–686. doi:10.1613/jair.5660

Industrial District Management. (2018). *Memorial, 2018/19.* Retrieved from https://www.idm.org.np/

Inglehart, R. (2010). *Modernization, cultural change, and democracy: The human development sequence.* Cambridge University Press.

Institute for Democracy and Electoral Assistance. (2021). *The Global State of Democracy Report 2021 - Building Resilience in a Pandemic Era.* Retrieved on January 2021 from: https://www.idea.int/gsod-events

International Amnesty. (2021a). *Ban the scan.* https://banthescan.amnesty.org/

International Amnesty. (2021b). *How to protect your phone and identity at protests.* Author.

International Data Corporation (IDC). (2020). *IDC's Global DataSphere Forecast Shows Continued Steady Growth in the Creation and Consumption of Data.* IDC.

ISO. (2018). *Risk management.* Obtenido de ISO: https://www.iso.org/files/live/sites/isoorg/files/store/en/PUB100426.pdf

Ivanov, D. (2020). Predicting the impacts of outbreaks on global supply chains: A simulation-based analysis on the coronavirus outbreak (COVID-19/SARS-CoV-2) case. T. *Transport.Res.E Logist. Transport Reviews*, *136*, 101922. doi:10.1016/j.tre.2020.101922 PMID:32288597

Ivanov, D., & Dolgui, A. (2020). Viability of intertwined supply networks: Extending the supply chain resilience angles towards survivability. A position paper motivated by COVID-19 outbreak. *International Journal of Production Research*, *28*(10), 2904–2915. doi:10.1080/00207543.2020.1750727

Jackson, P. (1998). Focus group interviews as a methodology. *Nurse Researcher, 6*(1), 72.

Jadi, Y., & Jie, L. (2017, July). An Implementation Framework of Business Intelligence in e-government systems for developing countries: Case study: Morocco e-government system. In *2017 International Conference on Information Society (i-Society)* (pp. 138-142). IEEE. 10.23919/i-Society.2017.8354689

Jakubowksa, E. (2021, July 7). New EDRi report reveals depths of biometric mass surveillance in Germany, the Netherlands and Poland. *EDRi*. https://edri.org/

Jallow, H., Renukappa, S., & Suresh, S. (2020). *The impact of COVID-19 outbreak on United Kingdom infrastructure sector*. Smart and Sustainable Built Environment.

Jamieson, K. H., & Cappella, J. N. (2008). *Echo Chamber: Rush Limbaugh and the Conservative Media Establishment*. Oxford University Press.

Jankin, S., Pencheva, I., & Esteve, M. (2018). Big Data & AI – A Transformational Shift for Government: So, What Next for Research? *Public Policy and Administration*, 1–21.

Janssen, M., Brous, P., Estevez, E., Barbosa, L. S., & Janowski, T. (2020). Data governance: Organizing data for trustworthy Artificial Intelligence. *Government Information Quarterly*, *37*(3), 101493. doi:10.1016/j.giq.2020.101493

Janssen, M., & Estevez, E. (2013). Lean government and platform-based governance-Doing more with less. *Government Information Quarterly*, *30*, S1–S8. doi:10.1016/j.giq.2012.11.003

Janssen, M., & van den Hoven, J. (2015). Big and Open Linked Data (BOLD) in government: A challenge to transparency and privacy? *Government Information Quarterly*, *32*(4), 363–368. doi:10.1016/j.giq.2015.11.007

Janssen, M., van der Voort, H., & Wahyudi, A. (2017). Factors influencing big data decision-making quality. *Journal of Business Research*, *70*, 338–345. doi:10.1016/j.jbusres.2016.08.007

Javier Alvarado Planas. (2021). Monarcas masones y otros príncipes de la Acacia. Madrid Dykinson, S.L.

Jemielniak, D., & Przegalinska, A. (2020). *Collaborative society*. MIT Press. doi:10.7551/mitpress/11587.001.0001

Jha, K. (2017). *The Madhesi upsurge and the contested idea of Nepal*. Springer Singapore. doi:10.1007/978-981-10-2926-4

Ji, T., Chen, J. H., Wei, H. H., & Su, Y. C. (2021). Towards people-centric smart city development: Investigating the citizens' preferences and perceptions about smart-city services in Taiwan. *Sustainable Cities and Society*, *67*(102691), 1–14. doi:10.1016/j.scs.2020.102691

Jobin, A., Ienca, M., & Vayena, E. (2019). The global landscape of AI ethics guidelines. *Nature Machine Intelligence*, *1*(9), 389–399. doi:10.103842256-019-0088-2

Jones, C. (2020). Law Enforcement Use of Facial Recognition: Bias, Disparate Impacts on People of Color, and the Need for Federal Legislation. *NCJL & Tech.*, 22, 777.

Jones, R. E., & Abdelfattah, K. R. (2020). Virtual interviews in the era of COVID-19: A primer for applicants. *Journal of Surgical Education*, *77*(4), 733–734. doi:10.1016/j.jsurg.2020.03.020 PMID:32278546

Joseph, R. C., & Johnson, N. A. (2013). Big data and transformational government. *IT Professional*, *15*(6), 43–48. doi:10.1109/MITP.2013.61

Jüttner, U., Peck, H., & Cristopher, M. (2003). Supply chain Risk Management: Outlining an agenda for future research. *International Journal of Logistics: Research and Applications*, 6(4), 197–210. doi:10.1080/13675560310001627016

KamarckE. (2004). *Government Innovation Around the World.* https://ssrn.com/abstract=517666 doi:10.2139/ssrn.517666

Kandlhofer, M., Steinbauer, G., Hirschmugl-Gaisch, S., & Huber, P. (2016, October). Artificial intelligence and computer science in education: From kindergarten to university. In 2016 IEEE Frontiers in Education Conference (FIE) (pp. 1-9). IEEE.

Kankanhalli, A., Charalabidis, Y., & Mellouli, S. (2019). *IoT and AI for smart government: A research agenda.* Academic Press.

Kapferer, J.-N. (1989). *Rumores: el medio de difusión más antiguo del mundo.* Editorial Plaza y Janés.

Karkin, N., Yavuz, N., Cubuk, E. B. S., & Golukcetin, E. (2018, May). The impact of ICTs-related innovation on public values in public sector. *Proceedings of the 19th Annual International Conference on Digital Government Research: Governance in the Data Age.* 10.1145/3209281.3209351

Kassens-Noor, E., & Hintze, A. (2020). Cities of the future? The potential impact of artificial intelligence. *AI, 1*(2), 192-197.

Kazimzade, G., Patzer, Y., & Pinkwart, N. (2019). Artificial Intelligence in Education Meets Inclusive Educational Technology—The Technical State-of-the-Art and Possible Directions. In J. Knox, Y. Wang, & M. Gallagher (Eds.), *Artificial Intelligence and Inclusive Education. Perspectives on Rethinking and Reforming Education.* Springer. doi:10.1007/978-981-13-8161-4_4

Keddell, E. (2019). Algorithmic justice in child protection: Statistical fairness, social justice and the implications for practice. *Social Sciences*, 8(10), 281. doi:10.3390ocsci8100281

Kennedy, R. F. (1963). *Robert F. Kennedy's address to University of Chicago Law School students on Law Day, May 1, 1964.* https://mag.uchicago.edu/law-policy-society/lawyers-responsibility-redefined

Kenneth, I. A. (2000). A Buddhist response to the nature of human rights. *Journal of Buddhist Ethics, 8.* http://www.cac.psu.edu/jbe/twocont.html

Khan, S., & VanWynsberghe, R. (2008). Cultivating the under-mined: Cross-case analysis as knowledge mobilization. *Forum Qualitative Social Research*, 9(1), 34.

Khine, P. P., & Shun, W. Z. (2017). Big Data for organizations: A review. *Journal of Computer and Communications*, 5(3), 40–48. doi:10.4236/jcc.2017.53005

Kietzmann, J., & Pitt, L. F. (2019). Artificial intelligence and machine learning: What managers need to know. *Business Horizons.* Advance online publication. doi:10.1016/j.bushor.2019.11.005

Kim, H.-W., Chan, H. C., & Gupta, S. (2007). Value-based Adoption of Mobile Internet: An empirical investigation. *Decision Support Systems*, 43(1), 111–126. doi:10.1016/j.dss.2005.05.009

Kim, S. (2021). Education and Public Service Motivation: A Longitudinal Study of High School Graduates. *Public Administration Review*, 81(2), 260–272. doi:10.1111/puar.13262

Kim, S., Andersen, K. N., & Lee, J. (2021). Platform Government in the Era of Smart Technology. *Public Administration Review*, puar.13422. doi:10.1111/puar.13422

Kim, Y., Park, Y., & Choi, J. (2017). A study on the adoption of IoT smart home service: Using Value-based Adoption Model. *Total Quality Management & Business Excellence*, 28(9-10), 1149–1165. doi:10.1080/14783363.2017.1310708

King, N. (2004). Using template analysis in the thematic analysis of text. In G. Symon & C. Cassell (Eds.), *Essential guide to qualitative methods in organizational research* (pp. 256–270). Sage. doi:10.4135/9781446280119.n21

Kinra, A. I. (2019). Ripple effect quantification by supply risk exposure assessment. *International Journal of Production Research*. Advance online publication. doi:10.1080/00207543.2019.1675919

Kirchherr, J., Reike, D., & Hekkert, M. (2017). Conceptualizing the Circular Economy: An Analysis of 114 Definitions. SSRN *Electronic Journal*. doi:10.2139/ssrn.3037579

Kizys, R., Tzouvanas, P., & Donadelli, M. (2021). From COVID-19 herd immunity to investor herding in international stock markets: The role of government and regulatory restrictions. *International Review of Financial Analysis, 74*, 101663. doi:10.1016/j.irfa.2021.101663

Kjällander, S. (2011). *Designs for learning in an extended digital environment: Case studies of social interaction in the social science classroom* (Doctoral dissertation). Department of Education, Stockholm University.

Klijn, E., & Teisman, G. R. (2010). Institutional and strategic barriers to public – Private partnership: An analysis of Dutch cases. *Public Money & Management*, 37–41. doi:10.1111/1467-9302.00361

Knox, J. (2020). Artificial intelligence and education in China. *Learning, Media and Technology, 45*(3), 298–311. doi:10.1080/17439884.2020.1754236

Koehler, J. (2018). Business process innovation with artificial intelligence: Levering Benefits and controlling operational risks. *European Business & Management, 4*(2), 55–66. doi:10.11648/j.ebm.20180402.12

Koerner, K. (2020). How will the EU become an AI superstar? In *Digital Economic and structural change*. Deutsche Bank.

Korkman, N., & Metin, M. (2021). El efecto del aprendizaje colaborativo basado en la investigación y el aprendizaje colaborativo en línea basado en la investigación sobre el éxito y el aprendizaje permanente de los estudiantes. *Revista de aprendizaje científico, 4*(2), 151-159.

Kouziokas, G. N. (2017). The application of artificial intelligence in public administration for forecasting high crime risk transportation areas in urban environment. *Transportation Research Procedia, 24*, 467–473. .05.08310.1016/j.trpro.2017.05.083

Krafft, P. M., Young, M., Katell, M., Lee, J. E., Narayan, S., Epstein, M., ... Barghouti, B. (2021, March). An Action-Oriented AI Policy Toolkit for Technology Audits by Community Advocates and Activists. In *Proceedings of the 2021 ACM Conference on Fairness, Accountability, and Transparency* (pp. 772-781). 10.1145/3442188.3445938

Kraus, S., Palme, C., Kailer, N., & Kallinger, F. L. (2018). Digital entrepreneurship: A research agenda on new business models for the twenty-first century. *International Journal of Entrepreneurial Behaviour & Research*. Advance online publication. doi:10.1108/IJEBR-06-2018-0425

Krichesky, G. J., Martínez-Garrido, C., Martínez, A. M., García, A., Castro, A., & González, A. (2011). Hacia un programa de formación docente para la justicia social. *Revista Electrónica Iberoamericana sobre Calidad, Eficacia y Cambio en Educación, 9*(4), 63–77.

Kryukov, V., & Gorin, A. (2017). Digital technologies as education innovation at universities. *Australian Educational Computing, 32*(1), 1–16.

Kshetri, N. (2021). Evolving uses of artificial intelligence in human resource management in emerging economies in the global South: Some preliminary evidence. *Management Research Review, 44*(7), 970–990. doi:10.1108/MRR-03-2020-0168

Kumar, N. M. S. (2019). Implementation of artificial intelligence in imparting education and evaluating student performance. *Journal of Artificial Intelligence and Capsule Networks, 1*, 1-9. doi:10.36548/jaicn.2019.1.001

Kumar, N. S. (2019). Implementation of artificial intelligence in imparting education and evaluating student performance. *Journal of Artificial Intelligence, 1*(1), 1–9.

Kumar, S., & Chandra, C. (2010). Supply chain disruption by avian flue for US companies; a case study. *Transportation Journal, 49*(4), 61–73.

Kun, X., Fanjue, L., Yi, M., Yuheng, W., Jing, Z., & Mike, S. S. (2020). Using Machine Learning to Learn Machines: A Cross-Cultural Study of Users' *Responses to Machine-Generated Artworks. Journal of Broadcasting & Electronic Media, 64*(4), 566–591. doi:10.1080/08838151.2020.1835136

Kurzweil, R. (1990). *The Age of Intelligent Machines*. MIT Press.

Kuziemski, M., & Misuraca, G. (2020). AI governance in the public sector: Three tales from the frontiers of automated decision-making in democratic settings. *Telecommunications Policy, 44*(6), 101976. doi:10.1016/j.telpol.2020.101976 PMID:32313360

LaBrie, R. C., Steinke, G. H., Li, X., & Cazier, J. A. (2018). Big data analytics sentiment: US-China reaction to data collection by business and government. *Technological Forecasting and Social Change, 130*, 45–55. doi:10.1016/j.techfore.2017.06.029

Larsson, S., & Heintz, F. (2020). Transparency in artificial intelligence. *Internet Policy Review, 9*(2), 1–16. doi:10.14763/2020.2.1469

Lau, C. K. H., Chui, C. F. R., & Au, N. (2019). Examination of the adoption of augmented reality: A VAM approach. *Asia Pacific Journal of Tourism Research, 24*(10), 1005–1020. doi:10.1080/10941665.2019.1655076

Laynor, G. (2021). Artificial Whiteness: Politics and Ideology in Artificial Intelligence by Yarden Katz. *Information & Culture, 56*(3), 356–357.

Le Hoa vo, T., & Thiel, D. (2011). Economic simulation of a poultry supply chain facing a sanitary crisis. *British Food Journal, 113*(8), 192-223.

Lee, K.-F. (2018). *How AI can save our humanity.* https://www.youtube.com/watch?v=ajGgd9Ld-Wc

Lee, V., Ye, L., & Recker, M. (2012). What a Long Strange Trip It's Been: A Comparison of Authors, Abstracts, and References in the 1991 and 2010 ICLS Proceedings. In *The Future of Learning: Proceedings of the 10th International Conference of the Learning Sciences (ICLS 2012) – Volume 2, Short Papers, Symposia, and Abstracts* (172-176). International Society of the Learning Sciences.

Lee, M. (2018). Understanding perception of algorithmic decisions. *Big Data & Society, 5*(1), 1–16. doi:10.1177/2053951718756684

León Pérez, J. (2019). Impacto de las tecnologías disruptivas en la percepción remota: big data, internet de las cosas e inteligencia artificial. *UD y la geomática,* (14). doi:10.14483/23448407.15658

Leonelli, S. (2018, October). Rethinking reproducibility as a criterion for research quality. In *Including a symposium on Mary Morgan: curiosity, imagination, and surprise.* Emerald Publishing Limited. doi:10.1108/S0743-41542018000036B009

Lew, L. (2018). *How Tencent's medical ecosystem is shaping the future of China's Healthcare.* Technode.

Lim, C., Kim, K. J., & Maglio, P. P. (2018). Smart cities with big data: Reference models, challenges, and considerations. *Cities (London, England), 82*, 86–99. doi:10.1016/j.cities.2018.04.011

Li, S., Dragicevic, S., Castro, F. A., Sester, M., Winter, S., Coltekin, A., Pettit, C., Jiang, B., Haworth, J., Stein, A., & Cheng, T. (2016). Geospatial big data handling theory and methods: A review and research challenges. *ISPRS Journal of Photogrammetry and Remote Sensing, 115*, 119–133. doi:10.1016/j.isprsjprs.2015.10.012

Litman, D. J., Rosé, C. P., Forbes-Riley, K., VanLehn, K., Bhembe, D., & Silliman, S. (2006). Spoken Versus Typed Human and Computer Dialogue Tutoring. *International Journal of Artificial Intelligence in Education, 16*(2), 145–170. https://dl.acm.org/doi/10.5555/1435344.1435348

Liua, Y., Salehb, S., & Huangc, J. (2021). Artificial Intelligence in Promoting Teaching and Learning Transformation in Schools. *International Journal of Innovation, Creativity and Change, 15*(3).

Liu, S. M., & Kim, Y. (2018). Special issue on internet plus government: New opportunities to solve public problems? *Government Information Quarterly, 35*(February), 88–97. doi:10.1016/j.giq.2018.01.004

Livia Segovia, J., & Kaku, M. (2013). La física del futuro: Cómo la ciencia determinará el destino de la humanidad y nuestra vida cotidiana en el siglo XXII. *Cátedra Villarreal, 1*(2). Advance online publication. doi:10.24039/cv20131222

Li, W. (2021, February). The Development Path of Ideological and Political Education Innovation in Universities Based on the Computer. *Journal of Physics: Conference Series, 1744*(3), 032249. doi:10.1088/1742-6596/1744/3/032249

Locke, J. (2010). *Segundo Tratado sobre el Gobierno Civil*. Alianza Editorial.

López Frías, D. (2020, July 15). El superespía del Mossad que inventó el sistema de reconocimiento facial de Mercadona: así funciona. *El Español*. https://www.elespanol.com/

López Robles, J. C., Rodríguez Elizalde, R., & Aznar Sánchez, T. (2021). *La inteligencia artificial desde la percepción de los alumnos y profesores. Revisión bibliográfica*. IMAT.

López, M. (2020, March 23). Engañar a los sistemas de reconocimiento facial es (relativamente) fácil si sabes cómo. *Xataka*. https://www.xataka.com/

Lu, L., & Etzkowitz, H. (n.d.). Strategic challenges for creating knowledge-based innovation in China: Transforming triple helix university-government-industry relations. Journal of Technology Management in China, 3(1), 5–11.

Luan, H., Geczy, P., Lai, H., Gobert, J., Yang, S. J. H., Ogata, H., Baltes, J., Guerra, R., Li, P., & Tsai, C.-C. (2020). Challenges and Future Directions of Big Data and Artificial Intelligence in Education. *Frontiers in Psychology, 11*, 580820. doi:10.3389/fpsyg.2020.580820 PMID:33192896

Luckin, R. (2010). *Redesigning learning contexts: Technology-rich, learner-centred ecologies*. Routledge. doi:10.4324/9780203854754

Luckin, R., Holmes, W., Griffiths, M., & Forcier, L. B. (2016). *Intelligence unleashed: An argument for AI in education*. Pearson.

Luminovo, A. (2018). *The future of education and how AI can help shape it*. Disponible en: https://medium.com/luminovo/the-future-of-education-and-how-ai-can-help-shape-it-6f1202f4757d

Lynch, M. (2018). *7 Roles for Artificial Intelligence in Education*, en *The Tech Advocate*. Disponible en: https://www.thetechedvocate.org/7-roles-for-artificial-intelligence-in-education/

Lyon, D. (2005). The border is everywhere IDcards, surveillance and the others. In *Global Surveillance and Policing, Collumption* (pp. 66–82). Willan.

Maffei, D. B. (2021). *Impacts of Shipping Container Shortages, Delays, and Increased Demand on the North American Supply Chain.* The Committee On Transportation And Infrastructure Subcommittee on Coast Guard and Maritime Transportation United States House of Representatives.

Maglogiannis, I. G., Karpouzis, K., Wallace, B. A., & Soldatos, J. (2007). *Emerging artificial intelligence applications in computer engineering: real word AI systems with applications in eHealth, HCI, information retrieval and pervasive technologies.* Ios Press.

Magoules, F., Pan, J., & Teng, F. (2016). *Cud Computing: Data-Intensive Computing and Scheduling.* CRC Press.

Malik, G., Tayal, D. K., & Vij, S. (2019). An analysis of the role of artificial intelligence in education and teaching. In P. K. Sa, S. Bakshi, I. K. Hatzilygeroudis, & M. N. Sahoo (Eds.), *Advances in Intelligent Systems and Computing* (pp. 407–417). Springer.

Maravilhas, S., & Martins, J. (2019). Strategic knowledge management in a digital environment: Tacit and explicit knowledge in Fab Labs. *Journal of Business Research*, *94*, 353–359. doi:10.1016/j.jbusres.2018.01.061

Markless, S. (2009). A new conception of information literacy for the digital environment in higher education. *Nordic Journal of Information Literacy in Higher Education, 1*(1).

Marr, B. (2018). How Is AI Used In Education — Real World Examples Of Today And A Peek Into The Future. *Forbes.* Disponible en: https://www.forbes.com/sites/bernardmarr/2018/07/25/how-is-ai-used-in-education-real-world-examples-of-today-and-a-peek-into-the-future/#7079f80d586e

Martín-Gutiérrez, J., Mora, C. E., Añorbe-Díaz, B., & González-Marrero, A. (2017). Virtual technologies trends in education. *Eurasia Journal of Mathematics, Science and Technology Education*, *13*(2), 469–486.

Matthews, G., Hancock, P. A., Lin, J., Panganiban, A. R., Reinerman-Jones, L. E., Szalma, J. L., & Wohleber, R. W. (2021). Evolution and revolution: Personality research for the coming world of robots, artificial intelligence, and autonomous systems. *Personality and Individual Differences*, *169*, 109969. doi:10.1016/j.paid.2020.109969

Ma, W., Adesope, O. O., Nesbit, J. C., & Liu, Q. (2014). Intelligent tutoring systems and learning outcomes: A meta-analysis. *Journal of Educational Psychology*, *106*(4), 901–918. doi:10.1037/a0037123

Ma, Y., Ping, K., Wu, C., Chen, L., Shi, H., & Chong, D. (2019). Artificial intelligence powered internet of things and smart public service. *Library Hi Tech*, *38*(1), 165–179. doi:10.1108/LHT-12-2017-0274

Mayfield, E., Madaio, M., Prabhumoye, S., Gerritsen, D., McLaughlin, B., Dixon-Román, E., & Black, A. W. (2019). Equity Beyond Bias in Language Technologies for Education. In *Proceedings of the Fourteenth Workshop on Innovative Use of NLP for Building Educational Applications* (pp. 444-460). 10.18653/v1/W19-4446

Mazurek, G., & Małagocka, K. (2019). Perception of privacy and data protection in the context of the development of artificial intelligence. *Journal of Management Analytics*, *6*(4), 344–364. doi:10.1080/23270012.2019.1671243

McArthur, D., Lewis, M., & Bishary, M. (2005). The roles of artificial intelligence in education: Current progress and future prospects. *Journal of Educational Technology*, *1*(4), 42–80.

McArthur, D., Lewis, M., & Bishary, M. (2005). The Roles of Artificial Intelligence in Education: Current Progress and Future Prospects. *Journal of Educational Technology*, *1*(4), 42–80. https://www.learntechlib.org/p/161310/

McBride, K., van Noordt, C., Misuraca, G., & Hammerschmid, G. (2021). Towards a Systematic Understanding on the Challenges of Procuring Artificial Intelligence in the Public Sector. doi:10.31235/osf.io/un649osf.io/un649

McCarthy, J. (1998). *What is artificial intelligence?* Academic Press.

McCarthy, J. (2007). *What Is Artificial Intelligence.* Sección "Basic Questions".

Mccrea, B. (2021). Reverse logistics: Tackling supply chain's biggest "unsolved" challenge. *Supply Chain Management Review*, 4-7.

Mccrea, B. (2021b). Supply chain redesign. Expecting the unexpected. *Supply Chain Management Review*, 21-23.

McGuinness, T. D., & Schank, H. (2021). *Power to the Public: The Promise of Public Interest Technology.* Princeton University Press. doi:10.2307/j.ctv18b5dbz

McKeever, B., Greene, S., MacDonald, G., Tatian, P., & Jones, D. (2018). *Data philanthropy: Unlocking the power of private data for public good.* Urban Institute.

McKinsey. (2017). *Ten imperatives for Europe in the era of Artificial Intelligence and automation.* Author.

McNutt, J. G. (Ed.). (2018). Technology, Activism and Social Justice in a Digital Age. Oxford University Press.

McNutt, J. G., & Goldkind, L. (2020). Civic Technology and Data for Good: Evolutionary Developments or Disruptive Change in E-Participation? In Digital Government and Achieving E-Public Participation: Emerging Research and Opportunities (pp. 124-142). IGI Global.

McNutt, J. G., Brainard, L., Zeng, Y., & Kovacic, P. (2016). Information and Technology In and For Associations and Volunteering. In Palgrave Handbook of Volunteering and Nonprofit Associations. Palgrave Macmillan.

McNutt, J. G., Guo, C., Goldkind, L., & An, S. (2018). Technology in Nonprofit organizations and voluntary action. *Voluntaristics Review*, *3*(1), 1–63. doi:10.1163/24054933-12340020

McNutt, J. G., Justice, J. B., Melitski, M. J., Ahn, M. J., Siddiqui, S., Carter, D. T., & Kline, A. D. (2016). The diffusion of civic technology and open government in the United States. *Information Polity*, *21*(2), 153–170. doi:10.3233/IP-160385

Medaglia, R., Gil-Garcia, J. R., & Pardo, T. A. (2021). Artificial Intelligence in Government: Taking Stock and Moving Forward. *Social Science Computer Review*. doi:10.1177/08944393211034087

Medina, E. (2008). Big Blue in the bottomless pit: The early years of IBM Chile. *IEEE Annals of the History of Computing*, *30*(4), 26–41. doi:10.1109/MAHC.2008.62

Medina, M. (1995). Tecnología y filosofía: Más allá de los prejuicios epistemológicos y humanistas. *Isegoría*, *12*(12), 180–196. doi:10.3989/isegoria.1995.i12.249

Mehr, H., Ash, H., & Fellow, D. (2017). *Artificial intelligence for citizen services and government.* Ash Center for Democratic Governance and Innovation: Harvard Kennedy School. Retrieved from https://ash.harvard.edu/files/ash/files/ artificial_intelligence_for_citizen_services.pdf

Mehr, H. (2017). Artificial intelligence for citizen services and government. *Ash Cent. Democr. Gov. Innov. Harvard Kennedy Sch*, (August), 1–12.

Mehta, N., & Shukla, S. (2022). Pandemic Analytics: How Countries are Leveraging Big Data Analytics and Artificial Intelligence to Fight COVID-19? *SN Computer Science*, *3*(1), 1–20. doi:10.100742979-021-00923-y PMID:34778841

Meijer, A. (2014). Transparency. In M. Bovens, R. E. Goodin, & T. Schillemans (Eds.), *Oxford handbook of public accountability* (pp. 661–672). Oxford University Press. doi:10.1093/oxfordhb/9780199641253.013.0043

Mello, R. F., Fiorentino, G., Miranda, P., Oliveira, H., Raković, M., & Gašević, D. (2021, June). Towards Automatic Content Analysis of Rhetorical Structure in Brazilian College Entrance Essays. In *International Conference on Artificial Intelligence in Education* (pp. 162-167). Springer. 10.1007/978-3-030-78270-2_29

Mercadona. (2020). *Zona detección anticipada*. Author.

Mergel, I., Rethemeyer, R. K., & Isett, K. (2016). Big data in public affairs. *Public Administration Review*, *76*(6), 928–937. doi:10.1111/puar.12625

Merlano, E. D. (2009). Las TIC como apoyo al desarrollo de los procesos de pensamiento y la construcción activa de conocimientos. *Zona próxima*, (10), 146-155.

Mesa Escobar, E. (2014). Esfera público: entre lo público y la política en la construcción de la opinión política. *Revista Departamento de Ciencia Política*, *5*, 105-117.

Miailhe, N., Hodes, C. R., Buse, C., Lannquist, & Jeanmaire, C. (2020). Geopolítica de la inteligencia artificial. *Política Exterior*, *34*(193), 56-69.

Miailhe, N., Hodes, C., Çetin, R. B., Lannquist, Y., & Jeanmaire, C. (2020). Geopolítica de la inteligencia artificial. *Política Exterior, 34*(193), 56-69.

Miailhe, N., Hodes, C., Çetin, R. B., Lannquist, Y., & Jeanmaire, C. (2020). Geopolítica de la Inteligencia Artificial. *Política Exterior, 34*(93), 56–69.

Mialhe, N. (2018). The geopolitics of artificial intelligence: The return of empires? *Politique Etrangere*, *3*, 107–118.

Michalski, R. S., Carbonell, J. G., & Mitchell, T. M. (Eds.). (2013). *Machine learning: An artificial intelligence approach*. Springer Science & Business Media.

Micovic, M. (2014). *La comunicación y el discurso políticos en España y Serbia. Análisis comparativo de las estrategias argumentativas utilizadas en los debates electorales televisivos: tesis … de Dr.* Cand. en Lengua Española.

Mignolo, W. D. (2013). *Historias locales / diseños globales. Colonialidad, conocimientos subalternos y pensamiento fronterizo*. Akal.

Mikalef, P., Fjørtoft, S. O., & Torvatn, H. Y. (2019, September). Artificial Intelligence in the public sector: a study of challenges and opportunities for Norwegian municipalities. In *Conference on e-Business, e-Services and e-Society* (pp. 267-277). Springer.

Mikhaylov, S. J., Esteve, M., & Campion, A. (2018). Artificial intelligence for the public sector: Opportunities and challenges of cross-sector collaboration. *Philosophical Transactions - Royal Society. Mathematical, Physical, and Engineering Sciences*, *376*(2128), 20170357. Advance online publication. doi:10.1098/rsta.2017.0357 PMID:30082303

Mirchi, N., Ledwos, N., & Del Maestro, R. F. (2021). Intelligent Tutoring Systems: Re-Envisioning Surgical Education in Response to COVID-19. *The Canadian Journal of Neurological Sciences*, *48*(2), 198–200. doi:10.1017/cjn.2020.202 PMID:32907644

Misuraca, G., van Noordt, C., & Boukli, A. (2020, September) [Paper presentation]. The use of AI in public services. *Proceedings of the 13th International Conference on Theory and Practice of Electronic Governance*.

Mitchell, W. J. (1999). e-topia: Urban Life, Jim# But Not As We Know It. MIT Press.

Mitchell, S., Potash, E., Barocas, S., D'Amour, A., & Lum, K. (2021). Algorithmic fairness: Choices, assumptions, and definitions. *Annual Review of Statistics and Its Application*, *8*(1), 141–163. doi:10.1146/annurev-statistics-042720-125902

Moher, D., Liberati, A., Tetzlaff, J., Altman, D. G., & Group, P. (2009). Preferred reporting items for systematic reviews and meta-analyses: The PRISMA statement. *PLoS Medicine*, *6*(7), e1000097. doi:10.1371/journal.pmed.1000097 PMID:19621072

Montealegre, R., & Iyengar, K. (2021). Managing digital business platforms: A continued exercise in balancing renewal and refinement. *Business Horizons*, *64*(1), 51–59. doi:10.1016/j.bushor.2020.09.003

Moore, M. (1994). Public Value as the Focus of Strategy. *Australian Journal of Public Administration*, *53*(3), 296–303. doi:10.1111/j.1467-8500.1994.tb01467.x

Moore, M. H. (1995). *Creating Public Value: Strategic Management in Government*. Harvard University Press.

Moore, M. H. (2014). Public value accounting: Establishing the philosophical basis. *Public Administration Review*, *74*(4), 465–477. doi:10.1111/puar.12198

Morabito, V. (2015). Big data and analytics for government innovation. In *Big data and analytics* (pp. 23-45). Springer. doi:10.1007/978-3-319-10665-6_2

Mora, F., Quintero, N., Hernández, R., & Alastre, O. (2014). *Influencia de la cultura organizacional china en el proceso de toma de decisiones*. Universidad del Zulia.

Morales Campos, E. (2018). *La posverdad y las noticias falsas: el uso ético de la información*. Instituto de Investigaciones Bibliotecológicas y de la Información de la UNAM.

Morales Estay, P. (2019). *El masivo sistema de televigilancia en China*. Biblioteca del Congreso Nacional de Chile.

Moreno, R., & Mayer, R. (2007). Interactive multimodal learning environments. *Educational Psychology Review*, *19*(3), 309–326. doi:10.100710648-007-9047-2

Moreno, R., Mayer, R. E., Spires, H. A., & Lester, J. C. (2001). The case for social agency in computer-based teaching: Do students learn more deeply when they interact with animated pedagogical agents? *Cognition and Instruction*, *19*(2), 177–213. doi:10.1207/S1532690XCI1902_02

Morley, J., Floridi, L., Kinsey, L., & Elhalal, A. (2020). From What to How: An Initial Review of Publicly Available AI Ethics Tools, Methods and Research to Translate Principles into Practices. *Science and Engineering Ethics*, *26*(4), 2141–2168. doi:10.100711948-019-00165-5 PMID:31828533

Morozov, E. (2013). *To Save Everything, Click Here: The Folly of Technological Solutionism*. Public Affairs.

Moschovakis, Y. N. (2001). What Is an Algorithm? *Mathematics Unlimited—2001 and Beyond*, 919–936. doi:10.1007/978-3-642-56478-9_46

Mosteanu, N. R. (2020). Artificial Intelligence and Cyber Security–A Shield against Cyberattack as a Risk Business Management Tool–Case of European Countries. *Quality - Access to Success*, *21*(175).

Mostow, J. (2012, June). Why and how our automated reading tutor listens. *Proceedings of the International Symposium on Automatic Detection of Errors in Pronunciation Training (ISADEPT)*.

Mozorov, E. (2018). *Capitalismo Big Tech ¿Welagfre o neofeudalismo digital?* Enclave de Libros.

Musikanski, L., Rakova, B., Bradbury, J., Phillips, R., & Manson, M. (2020). Artificial intelligence and community well-being: A proposal for an emerging area of research. *International Journal of Community Well-Being*, *3*(1), 39–55. doi:10.100742413-019-00054-6

Najibi, A. (2020). *Racial discrimination in face recognition technology*. Harvard University. https://sitn.hms.harvard.edu/flash/2020/racial-discrimination-in-face-recognition-technology/

New e-Estonia factsheet: National AI "Kratt" Strategy. (2020, June 26). Retrieved December 12, 2021, from e-Estonia website: https://e-estonia.com/new-e-estonia-factsheet-national-ai-kratt-strategy/

Newell, S., & Marabelli, M. (2015). Strategic opportunities (and challenges) of algorithmic decision-making: A call for action on the long-term societal effects of "datification." *Journal of Strategic Information Systems, 24*(1), 3–14. 1016/j. jsis.2015.02.001

Nguyen, D. T., & Kieuthi, T. C. (2020). New Trends In Technology Application In Education And Capacities Of Universities Lecturers During The Covid-19 Pandemic. *International Journal of Mechanical and Production Engineering Research and Development, 10,* 1709–1714.

Nielsen, J. A., & Pedersen, K. (2014). IT portfolio decision-making in local governments: Rationality, politics, intuition and coincidences. *Government Information Quarterly, 31*(3), 411–420. doi:10.1016/j.giq.2014.04.002

Nieto, M. (2021). *Marx y el comunismo en la era digital (y ante la crisis eco-social planetaria).* Maia ediciones.

Nijkamp, P., Poot, J., & Vindigni, G. (2001). Spatial dynamics and government policy: An artificial intelligence approach to comparing complex systems. In *Knowledge, Complexity and Innovation Systems* (pp. 369–401). Springer. doi:10.1007/978-3-662-04546-6_18

Nikiforova, A., & McBride, K. (2021). Open government data portal usability: A user-centred usability analysis of 41 open government data portals. *Telematics and Informatics, 58,* 101539. doi:10.1016/j.tele.2020.101539

Nikolić, Z. (2021). Knowledge management in education: automatic generation of materials for knowledge examination. *Industry 4.0, 6*(2), 76-78.

Nilsson, N. J. (1998). *Artificial Intelligence: A New Synthesis.* Morgan Kaufmann.

Noble, D. F. (2000). *Una visión diferente del progreso. En defensa del luddismo.* Alikornio.

Noble, S. U. (2018). *Algorithms of oppression.* New York University Press. doi:10.2307/j.ctt1pwt9w5

Noble, S., Scheinost, D., & Constable, R. T. (2019). A decade of test-retest reliability of functional connectivity: A systematic review and meta-analysis. *NeuroImage, 203,* 116157. doi:10.1016/j.neuroimage.2019.116157 PMID:31494250

O'Neil, C. (2016). *Weapons of Math Destruction: How Big Data Increases Inequality and Threatens Democracy.* Crown Publishers.

Observatorio Nacional de Tecnología y Sociedad. (2021). *Indicadores de uso de Inteligencia Artificial en las empresas españolas.* Author.

Ocaña-Fernández, Y., Valenzuela-Fernández, L. A., & Garro-Aburto, L. L. (2019). Inteligencia artificial y sus implicaciones en la educación superior. *Propósitos y Representaciones, 7*(2), 536–568. doi:10.20511/pyr2019.v7n2.274

OECD. (2016). *Skills for a Digital World, Policy Brief on The Future of Work.* OECD Publishing.

OECD. (2020). *Trustworthy artificial intelligence (AI) in education: Promises and challenges.* OECD Publishing.

Ojo, A., Mellouli, S., & Zeleti, F. A. (2019, June) [Paper presentation]. A Realist Perspective on AI-era Public Management. *Proceedings of the 20th Annual International Conference on Digital Government Research.* 10.1145/3325112.3325261

Oliván, F. (2017). Antropología de las formas políticas de Occidente. Escolar y Mayo Editors.

Oliván, F. (2021). La ideología de los derechos humanos. Tirant Humanidades.

Oliver, N. (2020). *Inteligencia artificial, naturalmente. Un manual de convivencia entre humanos y máquinas para que la tecnología nos beneficie a todos.* Ministerio de Asuntos Económicos y Transformación Digital.

Oller, J., Engel, A., & Rochera, M. J. (2021). Personalizing learning through connecting students' learning experiences: An exploratory study. *The Journal of Educational Research*, *114*(4), 404–417. doi:10.1080/00220671.2021.1960255

OPSI. (2020). *Case Study Archive*. https://oecd-opsi.org/case-study-archive/

Orr, T., & Cleveland-Innes, M. (2015). Appreciative leadership: Supporting education innovation. *International Review of Research in Open and Distributed Learning*, *16*(4). Advance online publication. doi:10.19173/irrodl.v16i4.2467

Ortega Klein, A. (2020). *Geopolítica de la ética en Inteligencia Artificial*. Documento de trabajo 1/2020 Real Instituto Elcano. https://www.realinstitutoelcano.org/wps/wcm/connect/acc09d1e-3138-4436-b77b-ec5926ea0983/DT1-2020-Ortega-Geopolitica-de-la-etica-en-Inteligencia-Artificial.pdf?MOD=AJPERES&CACHEID=acc09d1e-3138-4436-b77b-ec5926ea098

Ortiz, Z. (2004). *¿ Qué son las revisiones sistemáticas*. Recuperado de: http://www. scielo. org. co/scielo. php

Orwell, G. (2012). *1984*. Penguin Random House Grupo Editorial.

Orwell, G. (2016). 1984. The University of Adelaide.

Osborne, D., & Gaebler, T. (1992). *Reinventing Government: How the Entrepreneurial Spirit is Transforming the Public Sector*. Addison-Wesley Publishing Company.

Paconesi, G., & Guida, M. (2021). Handbook of Research on Teaching With Virtual Environments and AI. National Institute for Documentation, Italy. doi:10.4018/978-1-7998-7638-0

Padilla, F., Lagos-Moreno, N., & Castro, C. (2011). Permiso por puntos, condicionamiento instrumental y conducción. *Boletín de Psicología*, *101*, 81–107.

Pai, K. C., Kuo, B. C., Liao, C. H., & Liu, Y. M. (2021). An application of Chinese dialogue-based intelligent tutoring system in remedial instruction for mathematics learning. *Educational Psychology*, *41*(2), 137–152. doi:10.1080/01443410.2020.1731427

Palau, R., Mogas-Recalde, J., & Domínguez-García, S. (2020). El proyecto Go-Lab como entorno virtual de aprendizaje: Análisis y futuro. *Educar*, *56*(2), 407–421. doi:10.5565/rev/educar.1068

Panagiotopoulos, P., Klievink, B., & Cordella, A. (2019). Public value creation in digital government. *Government Information Quarterly*, *36*(4), 101421. doi:10.1016/j.giq.2019.101421

Pandit, P., Krishnamurthy, K. N., & Bakshi, B. (2022). Artificial Intelligence (AI) and Big Data Analytics for the COVID-19 Pandemic. In *Assessing COVID-19 and Other Pandemics and Epidemics using Computational Modelling and Data Analysis* (pp. 1–17). Springer. doi:10.1007/978-3-030-79753-9_1

Pannu, M., Gill, B., Tebb, W., & Yang, K. (2016, October). The impact of big data on government processes. In *2016 IEEE 7th Annual Information Technology, Electronics and Mobile Communication Conference (IEMCON)* (pp. 1-5). IEEE. 10.1109/IEMCON.2016.7746334

Pant, P. N., & Lachman, R. (1998). Value Incongruity and Strategic Choice. *Journal of Management Studies*, *35*(2), 195–212. doi:10.1111/1467-6486.00090

Pan, Y. (2016). Heading toward artificial intelligence 2.0. *Engineering*, *2*(4), 409–413. doi:10.1016/J.ENG.2016.04.018

Pan, Y., Froese, F., Liu, N., Hu, Y., & Ye, M. (2021). The adoption of artificial intelligence in employee recruitment: The influence of contextual factors. *International Journal of Human Resource Management*, 1–23.

Papadopoulos, A. V., Versluis, L., Bauer, A., Herbst, N., Von Kistowski, J., Ali-Eldin, A., ... Iosup, A. (2019). Methodological principles for reproducible performance evaluation in cloud computing. *IEEE Transactions on Software Engineering*.

Pariser, E. (2017). *El filtro burbuja: cómo la web decide lo que leemos y pensamos*. Editorial Taurus.

Parker, K. (n.d., Dec. 5). Can the City on a Hill Survive? *Washington Post*, p. 23.

Parra, A. G. (2020, April 14). Estudiantes de la UGR piden que se devuelvan las tasas y se adapte la evaluación. *Ideal*. https://www.ideal.es

Pasquale, F. (2015). *The black box society: The secret algorithms that control money and information*. Harvard University Press. doi:10.4159/harvard.9780674736061

Pastor, J. (2020). *La Unión Europea plantea un veto de cinco años para el reconocimiento facial en zonas públicas*. Xataca.

Paudel, U. R., & Devkota, N. (2018). Socio-Economic influences on small business performance in Nepal-India open border: Evidence from cross-sectional analysis. *Economia e Sociologia*, *11*(4), 11–30.

Paudel, U. R., Puri, S., Parajuli, S., Devkota, N., & Bhandari, U. (2021). Measuring Cultural Diversity Impact in Hospitality Industry Leadership: Managerial Communication Perspective from Five Star Hotels in Kathmandu Valley, Nepal. *Journal of Tourism & Adventure*, *4*(1), 75–88.

Pekrun, R. (2014). Emotions and learning. *Educational Practices Series, 24*(1), 1-31.

Peña, J. C. H. (2021). Gobernanza de la inteligencia artificial en la Unión Europea. La construcción de un marco ético-jurídico aún inacabado. *Revista General de Derecho Administrativo*, (56), 13.

Pence, H. E. (2014). What is big data and why is it important? *Journal of Educational Technology Systems*, *43*(2), 159–171. doi:10.2190/ET.43.2.d

Pencheva, I., Esteve, M., & Mikhaylov, S. J. (2020). Big Data and AI–A transformational shift for government: So, what next for research? *Public Policy and Administration*, *35*(1), 24–44. doi:10.1177/0952076718780537

Pérez Esquivel, A. (2021). Desafíos de la vigilancia automatizada. *Derecho y Ciencias Sociales*, *24*, 100–122.

Pérez, E. (2020, July 2). Mercadona instala un sistema de reconocimiento facial en sus supermercados: cómo funciona y por qué genera importantes dudas sobre la privacidad. *Xataka*. https://www.xataka.com/

Pérez-Morote, R., Pontones-Rosa, C., & Núñez-Chicharro, M. (2020). The effects of e-government evaluation, trust and the digital divide in the levels of e-government use in European countries. *Technological Forecasting and Social Change*, *154*, 119973.

Perrigo, B. (2020, January 24). London Police to Deploy Facial Recognition Cameras Despite Privacy Concerns and Evidence of High Failure Rate. *Time*. https://time.com/

Perry, J. L., & Rainey, H. G. (1988). The Public-Private Distinction in Organization Theory: A Critique and Research Strategy. *Academy of Management Review*, *13*(2), 182–201. doi:10.5465/amr.1988.4306858

Philomina, M. J., & Amutha, S. (2016). Information and communication technology awareness among teacher educators. *International Journal of Information and Education Technology (IJIET)*, *6*(8), 603–606. doi:10.7763/IJIET.2016.V6.759

Pikhart, M. (2020). Intelligent information processing for language education: The use of artificial intelligence in language learning apps. *Procedia Computer Science*, *176*, 1412–1419. doi:10.1016/j.procs.2020.09.151 PMID:33042299

Pillai, R., & Sivathanu, B. (2020). Adoption of artificial intelligence (AI) for talent acquisition in IT/ITeS organizations. *Benchmarking*, *27*(9), 2599–2629.

Pinazo, S., & Molpeceres, M. A. (2006). *¿De boca a oreja? La transmisión del rumor en la comunicación. In Psicología social de la comunicación.* Editorial Pirámide.

Ping, J. (2018, August). Opportunities provided by Big Data technology for government management. In *Proceedings of the 3rd International Conference on Judicial, Administrative and Humanitarian Problems of State Structures and Economic Subjects* (Vol. 252, pp. 552-555). 10.2991/jahp-18.2018.113

Polanco-Diges, L., & Debasa, F. (2020). The use of digital marketing strategies in the sharing economy: A literature review. *Journal of Spatial and Organizational Dynamics, 8*(3), 217–229.

Pon-Barry, H., Clark, B., Schultz, K., Bratt, E. O., & Peters, S. (2004, August). Advantages of spoken language interaction in dialogue-based intelligent tutoring systems. In *International Conference on Intelligent Tutoring Systems* (pp. 390-400). Springer. 10.1007/978-3-540-30139-4_37

Poole, D., Mackworth, A. K., & Goebel, R. (1998). *Computational Intelligence: A logical approach.* Oxford University Press.

Popa, C. (2011). Adoption of artificial intelligence in agriculture. *Bulletin of University of Agricultural Sciences and Veterinary Medicine Cluj-Napoca. Agriculture, 68*(1).

Popenici, S. A. D., & Kerr, S. (2017). Exploring the impact of artificial intelligence on teaching and learning in higher education. *RPTEL, 12*(1), 22. doi:10.118641039-017-0062-8 PMID:30595727

Popham, S. F., Huth, A. G., Bilenko, N. Y., Deniz, F., Gao, J. S., Nunez-Elizalde, A. O., & Gallant, J. L. (2021). Visual and linguistic semantic representations are aligned at the border of human visual cortex. *Nature Neuroscience, 24*(11), 1628–1636. doi:10.103841593-021-00921-6 PMID:34711960

Popova, N. M. (2004). *Ispanomovnyi suspilno-politychnyi dyskurs: linguopragmatychnyi aspect* [Spanish Social and Political Discourse: Linguopragmatic Aspect] [PhD Dissertation]. Taras Shevchenko National University of Kyiv.

Popova, N. M. (2008). Speeches as a genre of political discourse and a mean of conceptual modeling of politician's image in citizens' mind. *Modern Researches in Cognitive Linguistics,* (6), 49-455.

Porayska-Pomsta, K., & Rajendran, G. (2019). Accountability in Human and Artificial Intelligence Decision-Making as the Basis for Diversity and Educational Inclusion. In *Artificial Intelligence and Inclusive Education* (pp. 39–59). Springer. doi:10.1007/978-981-13-8161-4_3

Porter, M. E. (1985). Technology and competitive advantage. *The Journal of Business Strategy, 33.*

Pu, Z. (2021, August). Construction of Talent Training System for Innovation and Entrepreneurship Education in Colleges and Universities. In *The Sixth International Conference on Information Management and Technology* (pp. 1-4). 10.1145/3465631.3465941

Quadir, B., Chen, N. S., & Isaias, P. (2020). Analyzing the educational goals, problems and techniques used in educational big data research from 2010 to 2018. *Interactive Learning Environments,* 1–17. Advance online publication. doi:10.1080/10494820.2020.1712427

Quaintance, Z. (2021, December 5). What Can Local Government Do to Avoid Inequitable Tech? *Governing.* https://www.governing.com/community/what-can-local-government-do-to-avoid-inequitable-tech

Quinn, M., & Strauss, E. (Eds.). (2017). *The Routledge Companion to Accounting Information Systems.* Routledge. doi:10.4324/9781315647210

Rai, A. (2020). Explainable AI. *Journal of the Academy of Marketing Science, 48*(1), 137–141. doi:10.100711747-019-00710-5

Rainey, H. G., & Bozeman, B. (2000). Comparing Public and Private Organizations: Empirical Research and the Power of the A Priori. *Journal of Public Administration Research and Theory: J-PART, 10*(2), 447–469. doi:10.1093/oxfordjournals.jpart.a024276

Raisch, S., & Krakowski, S. (2020). Artificial Intelligence and Management: The Automation-Augmentation Paradox. *Academy of Management Review, 46*(1), 192–210. doi:10.5465/amr.2018.0072

Rajbhandari, S., Khanal, G., Parajuli, S., & Karki, D. (2020). A Review on Potentiality of Industry 4.0 in Nepal: Does the Pandemic Play Catalyst Role? *Quest Journal of Management and Social Sciences, 2*(2), 366–379.

Rakova, B., Yang, J., Cramer, H., & Chowdhury, R. (2021). Where responsible AI meets reality: Practitioner perspectives on enablers for shifting organizational practices. *Proceedings of the ACM on Human-Computer Interaction, 5*(CSCW1), 1-23. 10.1145/3449081

Ramon-Cortés, F. (2007). Virus. Un relato sobre el peligro de los rumores en las organizaciones. *Editorial RBA Edipresse, Barcelona, 2007,* 83.

Rana, P., Raj Gupta, L., Kumar, G., & Kumar Dubey, M. (2021). A Taxonomy of Various Applications of Artificial Intelligence in Education. *2021 2nd International Conference on Intelligent Engineering and Management (ICIEM),* 23-28, 10.1109/ICIEM51511.2021.9445339

Ranerup, A., & Henriksen, H. Z. (2019). Value positions viewed through the lens of automated decision-making: The case of social services. *Government Information Quarterly, 36*(4), 101377. doi:10.1016/j.giq.2019.05.004

Recht, M., & Bryan, R. N. (2017). Artificial intelligence: Threat or boon to radiologists? *Journal of the American College of Radiology, 14*(11), 1476–1480. doi:10.1016/j.jacr.2017.07.007 PMID:28826960

Reclaim Your Face. (2021). *Sign the petition for a new law now.* https://reclaimyourface.eu/

Redacción. (2020, April 30). La Universidad de Oviedo dice contar con medios para garantizar que los alumnos no 'copien' en los exámenes 'online'. *La Vanguardia.* https://www.lavanguardia.com

Regmi, M. B. (2020). Measuring sustainability of urban mobility: A pilot study of Asian cities. *Case Studies on Transport Policy, 8*(4), 1224-1232.

Reid, A. J. (2018). *The smartphone paradox: our ruinous dependency in the Device Age.* Palgrave Macmillan. doi:10.1007/978-3-319-94319-0

Reis, J., Espírito Santo, P., & Melao, N. (2019, April). Artificial Intelligence in Government Services: A Systematic Literature Review. In *World conference on information systems and technologies* (pp. 241-252). Springer.

Reis, J., Santo, P., & Melão, N. (2020). Impact of artificial intelligence research on politics of the European Union member states: The case study of Portugal. *Sustainability, 12*(17), 1-25.

Reiss, M., & Savino, F. (2021). Accenture on Operations: From ones and zeros to supply chain heroes. *Logistics Management.* https://www.logisticsmgmt.com/article/accenture_on_operations_from_ones_and_zeros_to_supply_chain_heroes

Remian, D. (2019). Augmenting Education: Ethical Considerations for Incorporating Artificial Intelligence in Education. *Instructional Design Capstones Collection,* 52. https://scholarworks.umb.edu/instruction_capstone/52

Rendueles, C. (2013). *Sociofobia. El cambio político en la era de la utopía digital.* Editorial Capitán Swing Libros.

Renijith, S., Sreekumar, A., & Jathavedan, M. (2020). An extensive study on the evolution of context-aware personalized travel recommender systems. *Information Processing & Management, 57*(1), 102078. doi:10.1016/j.ipm.2019.102078

Rhodes, L. (1998). Panoptical intimacies. *Public Culture, 10*(2), 308.

Ribeiro-Navarrete, S., Saura, J. R., & Palacios-Marqués, D. (2021). Towards a new era of mass data collection: Assessing pandemic surveillance technologies to preserve user privacy. *Technological Forecasting and Social Change, 167*, 120681. doi:10.1016/j.techfore.2021.120681 PMID:33840865

Rice, J. B. (2021). The Seven Core Capacities of Supply Chain Resilience. *Supply Chain Management Review*. https://www.scmr.com/article/the_seven_core_capacities_of_supply_chain_resilience

Rich, E., & Knight, K. (1991). *Artificial Intelligence*. MacGraw-Hill.

Rico-Bautista, D., Medina-Cardenas, Y., Coronel-Rojas, L. A., Cuesta-Quintero, F., Maestre-Gongora, G., & Guerrero, C. D. (2021). Smart University: Key Factors for an Artificial Intelligence Adoption Model. *Advances and Applications in Computer Science, Electronics and Industrial Engineering, 1307*, 153–166.

Roberts, A. H. (2021). *A statistical linguistic analysis of American English*. De Gruyter Mouton.

Robinson, P., & Johnson, P. A. (2021). Pandemic-Driven Technology Adoption: Public Decision Makers Need to Tread Cautiously. *International Journal of E-Planning Research, 10*(2), 59–65. doi:10.4018/IJEPR.20210401.oa5

Rodríguez Manzano, A. (n.d.). *El uso de los datos masivos para salvar vidas*. Dirección General de Divulgación de la Ciencia, UNAM, n° 241, pp. 16-19.

Rogers, E. M. (2003). *Diffusion of Innovations* (5th ed.). Free Press.

Roller, E. (2002). When does language become exclusivist? Linguistic politics in Catalonia. *National Identities, 4*(3), 273–289. doi:10.1080/1460894022000026132

Roll, I., & Wylie, R. (2016). Evolution and revolution in artificial intelligence in education. *International Journal of Artificial Intelligence in Education, 26*(2), 582–599. doi:10.100740593-016-0110-3

Romano, V. (2004). Ecología de la comunicación. HIRU.

Rosa, M., Feyereisl, J., & Collective, T. G. (2016). *A framework for searching for general artificial intelligence*. arXiv preprint arXiv:1611.00685.

Rouhiainen, L. (2018). *Inteligencia artificial*. Alienta Editorial.

Rowley, J., & Slack, F. (2004). Conducting a literature review. *Management Research News, 27*(6), 31–39. doi:10.1108/01409170410784185

Rozario, A. M., & Issa, H. (2020). Risk-based data analytics in the government sector: A case study for a US county. *Government Information Quarterly, 37*(2), 101457. doi:10.1016/j.giq.2020.101457

Rub, C. M. (2014). Project acronym: iTalk2Learn. *Structure (London, England), 2*, 17.

Rubio, I. (2020, July 7). Las claves de la polémica por el uso del reconocimiento facial en los supermercados de Mercadona. *El País*. https://elpais.com/

Ruiz-Real, J. L., Uribe-Toril, J., Torres, J. A., & De Pablo, J. (2021). Artificial intelligence in business and economics research: Trends and future. *Journal of Business Economics and Management, 22*(1), 98–117. doi:10.3846/jbem.2020.13641

Runciman, W. G. (1999). *El animal social*. Taurus.

Runnel, P., Pruulmann-Vengerfeldt, P., & Reinsalu, K. (2009). The Estonian Tiger Leap from Post-Communism to the Information Society: From Policy to Practice. *Journal of Baltic Studies*, *40*(1), 29–51. doi:10.1080/01629770902722245

Russell, S. J., & Norvig, P. (2009). Artificial intelligence: a modern approach (3rd ed.). Prentice Hall.

Russell, S. J., & Norvig, P. (2009). *Artificial intelligence. A modern approach*. Prentice Hall.

Sadowski, J. (2019). When data is capital: Datafication, accumulation, and extraction. *Big Data & Society*, *6*(1), 2053951718820549. doi:10.1177/2053951718820549

Safarov, I., Meijer, A., & Grimmelikhuijsen, S. (2017). Utilization of open government data: A systematic literature review of types, conditions, effects and users. *Information Polity*, *22*(1), 1–24. doi:10.3233/IP-160012

Salah, K., Rehman, M. H. U., Nizamuddin, N., & Al-Fuqaha, A. (2019). Blockchain for AI: Review and open research challenges. *IEEE Access: Practical Innovations, Open Solutions*, *7*, 10127–10149. doi:10.1109/ACCESS.2018.2890507

Sale, K. (1995). *Rebels Against the Future. The Luddites and Their War on the Industrial Revolution: Lesson for the Computer Age*. Addison-Wesley Publishing Company.

Salinas, J. (2004). Innovación docente y uso de las TIC en la enseñanza universitaria. RUSC. *Universities & Knowledge Society*, *1*(1). Advance online publication. doi:10.7238/rusc.v1i1.228

Sally, E., & Clinton, N. (2021). *Resilinc seizes the day and releases annual supply chain risk report — Carpe Diem.* Spend Matters. https://spendmatters.com/2021/04/23/resilinc-seizes-the-day-and-releases-annual-supply-chain-risk-report-carpe-diem/

Salvador, A. (2012). El proceso de apertura de la economía china a la inversión extranjera. *Revista de Economía Mundial*, 30.

Salvatierra, J. (2019, October 17). La justicia europea da la razón a Mercadona en el caso de las cajeras grabadas robando con cámara oculta. *El País*. https://elpais.com/

Sancho, M. D. H. (2020). El libro blanco sobre inteligencia artificial de la Comisión Europea: Reflexiones desde las garantías esenciales del proceso penal como "sector de riesgo". *Revista Española de Derecho Europeo*, (76), 9–44.

Sane, R. (2017, April 11). *Budgeting for the police*. Retrieved from https://www.livemint.com/

Santoro, M. D., & Saparito, P. A. (2003). The firm's trust in its university partner as a key mediator in advancing knowledge and new technologies. *IEEE Transactions on Engineering Management*, *50*(3), 362–373. doi:10.1109/TEM.2003.817287

Sapci, A. H., & Sapci, H. A. (2020). Artificial intelligence education and tools for medical and health informatics students: Systematic review. *JMIR Medical Education*, *6*(1), e19285. doi:10.2196/19285 PMID:32602844

Sapkota, T. P., Kunwar, S., Bhattarai, M., & Poudel, S. (2020). Artificial intelligence that are beneficial for law. *US-China L. Rev.*, *17*, 217.

Saura, J.R., Ribeiro, D., & Palacios-Marqués, E.R. (2021a). From user-generated data to data-driven innovation: A research agenda to understand user privacy in digital markets. *International Journal of Information Management*. .ijinfomgt.2021.102331 doi:10.1016/j

Saura, J. R. (2021). Using data sciences in digital marketing: Framework, methods, and performance metrics. *Journal of Innovation & Knowledge*, *6*(2), 92–102. doi:10.1016/j.jik.2020.08.001

Saura, J. R., Palacios-Marqués, D., & Iturricha-Fernández, A. (2021). Ethical Design in Social Media: Assessing the main performance measurements of user online behavior modification. *Journal of Business Research*, *129*(May), 271–281. https://doi.org./10.1016/j.jbusres.2021.03.001

Saura, J. R., Palacios-Marqués, D., & Iturricha-Fernández, A. (2021A). Ethical design in social media: Assessing the main performance measurements of user online behavior modification. *Journal of Business Research*, *129*, 271–281. doi:10.1016/j.jbusres.2021.03.001

Saura, J. R., Palacios-Marqués, D., & Ribeiro-Soriano, D. (2021b). How SMEs use data sciences in their online marketing performance: A systematic literature review of the state-of-the-art. *Journal of Small Business Management*. Advance online publication. doi:10.1080/00472778.2021.1955127

Saura, J. R., Palacios-Marqués, D., & Ribeiro-Soriano, D. (2022). Exploring the boundaries of Open Innovation: Evidence from social media mining. *Technovation*, 102447. Advance online publication. doi:10.1016/j.technovation.2021.102447

Saura, J. R., Ribeiro-Soriano, D., & Iturricha-Fernández, A. (2022a). Exploring the challenges of remote work on Twitter users' sentiments: From digital technology development to a post-pandemic era. *Journal of Business Research*, *142*(March), 242–254. doi:10.1016/j.jbusres.2021.12.052

Saura, J. R., Ribeiro-Soriano, D., & Palacios-Marqués, D. (2021). Using data mining techniques to explore security issues in smart living environments in Twitter. *Computer Communications*, *179*, 285–295. doi:10.1016/j.comcom.2021.08.021

Saura, J. R., Ribeiro-Soriano, D., & Palacios-Marqués, D. (2021a). Setting B2B Digital Marketing in Artificial Intelligence-based CRMs: A review and directions for future research. *Industrial Marketing Management*, *98*(October), 161–178. doi:10.1016/j.indmarman.2021.08.006

Saura, J. R., Ribeiro-Soriano, D., & Palacios-Marqués, D. (2021b, July). Setting privacy "by default" in social IoT: Theorizing the challenges and directions in Big Data Research. *Big Data Research*, *25*, 15. doi:10.1016/j.bdr.2021.100245

Saura, J. R., Ribeiro-Soriano, D., & Palacios-Marques, D. (2021d). Evaluating security and privacy issues of social networks based information systems in Industry 4.0. *Enterprise Information Systems*, 1–17. Advance online publication. doi:10.1080/17517575.2021.1913765

Saura, J. R., Ribeiro-Soriano, D., & Palacios-Marqués, D. (2021f). From user-generated data to data-driven innovation: A research agenda to understand user privacy in digital markets. *International Journal of Information Management*, *60*(October), 102331. doi:10.1016/j.ijinfomgt.2021.102331

Schein, E. H. (1992). *Organizational culture and leadership*. Jossey-Bass.

Schiff, D. S., Schiff, K. J., & Pierson, P. (2021). Assessing public value failure in government adoption of artificial intelligence. *Public Administration*, padm.12742. doi:10.1111/padm.12742

Schulz, J. D. (2021). *State of Logistics 2021: Full speed ahead*. Obtenido de Logistics Management: https://www.logisticsmgmt.com/article/state_of_logistics_2021_full_speed_ahead

Schwarting, W., Alonso-Mora, J., & Rus, D. (2018). Planning and decision-making for autonomous vehicles. *Annual Review of Control, Robotics, and Autonomous Systems*, *1*(1), 187–210. doi:10.1146/annurev-control-060117-105157

SCMR Staff. (2021). Increased Vessel Delays and Rising Transportation Costs Threaten Last-Mile Retail Operations. *Supply Chain Management Review*. https://www.scmr.com/article/increased_vessel_delays_and_rising_transportation_costs_threaten_last_mile

Security Magazine. (2020, May 29). Smile, You're on Camera: The Facial Recognition World Map. *Security Magazine*. https://www.securitymagazine.com/

Sein-Echaluce, M. L., Fidalgo-Blanco, Á., & Alves, G. (2017). *Technology behaviors in education innovation* (No. ART-2017-98966). Academic Press.

Selinger, E., & Leong, B. (2021) The Ethics of Facial Recognition Technology. In The Oxford Handbook of Digital Ethics. doi:10.2139srn.3762185

Selinger, E. & Hartzog, w. (2019). The Inconsentability of Facial Surveillance. *Loyola Law Review*, *66*, 101–122.

Semmler, S., & Rose, Z. (2017). Artificial intelligence: Application today and implications tomorrow. *Duke L. & Tech. Rev.*, *16*, 85.

Shah, F., Evens, M. W., Michael, J., & Rovick, A. (2002). Classifying student initiatives and tutor responses in human keyboard-to keyboard tutoring sessions. *Discourse Processes*, *33*(1), 23–52. doi:10.1207/S15326950DP3301_02

Sharipov, F. F., Krotenko, T. Y., & Dyakonova, M. A. (2021). Digital Potential of Economic Education: Information Technologies in a Management University. In Current Achievements, Challenges and Digital Chances of Knowledge Based Economy (pp. 561-572). Springer.

Sharma, M., Luthra, S., Joshi, S., & Kumar, A. (2021). Implementing challenges of artificial intelligence: Evidence from public manufacturing sector of an emerging economy. *Government Information Quarterly*, 101624. doi:10.1016/j.giq.2021.101624

Shazeda A., & Lang B. (2018). *Who's really responsible for digital privacy in China?* Merics.org.

Shelley, M. (1994). *Frankenstein o el moderno Prometeo*. Valdemar.

Shemshack, A., & Spector, J. M. (2020). A systematic literature review of personalized learning terms. *Smart Learning Environments*, *7*(1), 1–20. doi:10.118640561-020-00140-9

Sherman, E. (2020). 94% of the Fortune 1000 are seeing coronavirus supply chain disruptions: Report. *Fortune*. https://fortune.com/2020/02/21/fortune-1000-coronavirus-china-supply-chain-impact/

Shin, D., Zhong, B., & Biocca, F. (2020). Beyond user experience. *International Journal of Information Management*, *52*, 1–11. fomgt.2019.102061 doi:10.1016/j.ijin

Shin, D. (2010). The effects of trust, security and privacy in social networking. *Interacting with Computers*, *22*(5), 428–438. doi:10.1016/j.intcom.2010.05.001

Shin, D. (2019). Toward fair, accountable, and transparent algorithms. *Javnost. The Public*, *26*(3), 274–290. doi:10.1080/13183222.2019.1589249

Shin, D. (2020). User Perceptions of Algorithmic Decisions in the Personalized AI System:Perceptual Evaluation of Fairness, Accountability, Transparency, and Explainability. *Journal of Broadcasting & Electronic Media*, *64*(4), 541–565. Advance online publication. doi:10.1080/08838151.2020.1843357

Shin, D., & Park, Y. (2019). Role of fairness, accountability, and transparency in algorithmic affordance. *Computers in Human Behavior*, *98*, 277–284. doi:10.1016/j.chb.2019.04.019

Shrestha, P. (2021). Use of Technology and Its Management Issues in Nepalese Industries and Businesses. *Nepalese Journal of Management Research*, *1*, 9–14.

Shubham, J., Radha, K., & Prathamesh, C. (2021). *Evaluating Artificial Intelligence in Education for Next Generation*. IOP Publishing Ltd. doi:10.1088/1742-6596/1714/1/012039

Sills, D. L. (1974). *Enciclopedia internacional de las ciencias sociales* (Vol. 1). Aguilar.

Sirajudeen, A. (2017). What Role Will Artificial Intelligence Play in Supply Chain Management? *Arkieva*. https://blog.arkieva.com/artificial-intelligence-supply-chain/

Skålén, P. (2004). New public management reform and the construction of organizational identities. *International Journal of Public Sector Management, 17*(3), 251–263. doi:10.1108/09513550410530171

Slee, T. (2017). *What's yours is mine against the sharing economy*. Or Books. doi:10.2307/j.ctv62hf03

Sloane, M. (2019). Inequality is the name of the game: thoughts on the emerging field of technology, ethics and social justice. In *Weizenbaum Conference* (p. 9). DEU.

Sloan, R., & Warner, R. (2017, May/June). When is an algorithm transparent? *IEEE Security and Privacy*. Advance online publication. doi:10.2139srn.3051588

Smith, C. (2019). An employee's best friend? How AI can boost employee engagement and performance. *Strategic HR Review, 18*(1), 17–20. doi:10.1108/SHR-11-2018-0092

Smith, D. H. (2000). Grassroots associations. *Sage (Atlanta, Ga.)*.

Smith, R., & Sharif, N. (2007). Understanding and acquiring technology assets for global competition. *Technovation, 27*(11), 643–649. doi:10.1016/j.technovation.2007.04.001

Smith, S. R., & Lipsky, M. (1993). *Nonprofits for hire*. Harvard University Press. doi:10.4159/9780674043817

Smuha, N. A. (2021). From a 'race to AI' to a 'race to AI regulation': Regulatory competition for artificial intelligence. *Law, Innovation and Technology, 13*(1), 57–84. doi:10.1080/17579961.2021.1898300

Snyder, H. (2019). Literature review as a research methodology: An overview and guidelines. *Journal of Business Research, 104*, 333–339. doi:10.1016/j.jbusres.2019.07.039

Soares, N., & Fallenstein, B. (2017). Agent foundations for aligning machine intelligence with human interests: A technical research agenda. In *The Technological Singularity: Managing the Journey*. Springer. https://intelligence.org/files/ TechnicalAgenda.pdf

Söderström, O., Paasche, T., & Klauser, F. (2014). Smart cities as corporate storytelling. *City, 18*(3), 307–320. doi:10.1080/13604813.2014.906716

Sohn, K., & Kwon, O. (2020). Technology acceptance theories and factors influencing artificial Intelligence-based intelligent products. *Telematics and Informatics, 47*, 101324. doi:10.1016/j.tele.2019.101324

Sokol, K., & Flach, P. (2020). Explainability Fact Sheets: A Framework for Systematic Assessment of Explainable Approaches. In *Fairness, Accountability, and Transparency (FAT* '20), January 27–30, 2020, Barcelona, Spain*. ACM. Available: https://arxiv.org/abs/1912.05100

Sonntag, S. K. (2001). The politics of linguistic sub-alternity in North India. *Linguistic Structure and Language Dynamic in South Asia: Papers from the Proceedings of SALA XVIII Roundtable*, 207-22.

Sopra Steria & IDEMIA (2020, June 8). *IDEMIA and Sopra Steria chosen by eu-LISA to build the new Shared Biometric Matching System (sBMS) for border protection of the Schengen Area*. Author.

Souto-Manning, M. (2013). Competence as linguistic alignment: Linguistic diversities, affinity groups, and the politics of educational success. *Linguistics and Education, 24*(3), 305–315. doi:10.1016/j.linged.2012.12.009

Spector, J. M. (2018). The potential of smart technologies for learning and instruction. *International Journal of Smart Technology & Learning, 1*(1), 21–32. doi:10.1504/IJSMARTTL.2016.078163

Stake, R. E. (2006). *Stake, Robert E*. Multiple Case Study Analysis. New York.

Stanica, I., Dascalu, M., Bodea, C. N., & Bogdan Moldoveanu, A. D. (2018). VR Job Interview Simulator: Where Virtual Reality Meets Artificial Intelligence for Education. *2018 Zooming Innovation in Consumer Technologies Conference (ZINC)*, 9-12, 10.1109/ZINC.2018.8448645

Stanojevic, S. (2019). *El "Gran Hermano" chino vigila también en Belgrado*. La Vanguardia.

Stedman, R. C., Connelly, N. A., Heberlein, T. A., Decker, D. J., & Allred, S. B. (2019). The end of the (research) world as we know it? Understanding and coping with declining response rates to mail surveys. *Society & Natural Resources*, *32*(10), 1139–1154. doi:10.1080/08941920.2019.1587127

Stepanenko, M. (2017). *Publichnyi duskurs Yu. Tymoshenko v roxrizi tsinnostey za schkaloyu Inglehart-Welzelia* [Yulia Tymoshenko's Public Discourse in Values on the Inglehart-Welzel Scale]. Noks Fishes. http://noksfishes.info/landing/tymoshenko.html

Stone, P., Brooks, R., Brynjolfsson, E., Calo, R., Etzioni, O., Hager, G., ... Teller, A. (2016). *Artificial intelligence and life in 2030: The one hundred year study on artificial intelligence*. Academic Press.

Stripling, B. (2010). Teaching Students to Think in the Digital Environment: Digital Literacy and Digital Inquiry. *School Library Monthly*, *26*(8), 16–19.

Stroud, C. (2018). 1. Linguistic Citizenship. In *TheMultilingual Citizen* (pp. 17–39). Multilingual Matters.

Su, A. (2020). Threats of arrest, job loss and surveillance. China targets its 'model minority. *Los Angeles Times*.

Sued, G. (2020). El algoritmo de YouTube y la desinformación sobre vacunas durante la pandemia de COVID-19. *Chasqui. Revista Latinoamericana de Comunicación*, *145*(145), 163–180. doi:10.16921/chasqui.v1i145.4335

Suh, J., Yoo, S., Park, J., Cho, S. Y., Cho, M. C., Son, H., & Jeong, H. (2020). Development and validation of an explainable artificial intelligence-based decision-supporting tool for prostate biopsy. *BJU International*, *126*(6), 694–703. doi:10.1111/bju.15122 PMID:32455477

Sullivan, J. (2020). *Research: Trends in the Supply Chain and Their Impact on the Transportation Management System Market*. SupplyChain247. https://www.supplychain247.com/article/trends_in_the_supply_chain_and_their_impact_on_the_tms_market/kuebix

Sunstein, C. R. (2010). *Rumorología*. Editorial Debate.

Sun, T. Q., & Medaglia, R. (2019). Mapping the challenges of Artificial Intelligence in the public sector: Evidence from public healthcare. *Government Information Quarterly*, *36*(2), 368–383. doi:10.1016/j.giq.2018.09.008

Surfshack. (2020). *The Facial Recognition World Map*. https://surfshark.com/

Susar, D., & Aquaro, V. (2019, April). Artificial intelligence: Opportunities and challenges for the public sector. *Proceedings of the 12th International Conference on Theory and Practice of Electronic Governance*. 10.1145/3326365.3326420

Tabbers, H. (2002). *The modality of text in multimedia instruction: Refining the design guidelines* [Doctoral dissertation, University of the Netherlands, Heerlen]. Open University of the Netherlands. https://www.ou.nl/documents/40554/111676/Doctoral_dissertation_Huib_Tabbers_webversion_2002.pdf/1e28b159-d451-45a8-8e5a-74137949e596

Tadesse, S., & Muluye, W. (2020). The impact of COVID-19 pandemic on education system in developing countries: A review. *Open Journal of Social Sciences*, *8*(10), 159–170. doi:10.4236/jss.2020.810011

Tantau, A., & Şanta, A. M. I. (2021). New Energy Policy Directions in the European Union Developing the Concept of Smart Cities. *Smart Cities*, *4*(1), 241–252. doi:10.3390martcities4010015

Tavory, I. (2020). Interviews and inference: Making sense of interview data in qualitative research. *Qualitative Sociology*, *43*(4), 449–465. doi:10.100711133-020-09464-x

Tedesco, J. C., & Brunner, J. J. (2004). *Nuevas Tecnologías y El Futuro de La Educación*. Septiembre Grupo Editor.

Tena, E. C., & Khalilova, A. (2016). Economía circular. *Economía Industrial*, (401), 11–20. https://dialnet.unirioja.es/servlet/articulo?codigo=5771932

Tester, K. (2004). *The Social Thought of Zgymunt Bauman*. Palgrave. doi:10.1057/9780230505681

The Economist. (2021). A perfect storm for container shipping. *The Economist*. https://www.economist.com/finance-and-economics/a-perfect-storm-for-container-shipping/21804500?utm_campaign=the-economist-today&utm_medium=newsletter&utm_source=salesforce-marketing-cloud&utm_term=2021-09-13&utm_content=article-link-1&etear=nl_today_1

The Economist. (2021a, July 3). What if an AI won the Nobel prize for medicine? *The Economist*. https://www.economist.com/what-if/2021/07/03/what-if-an-ai-wins-the-nobel-prize-for-medicine

Thinyane, M., Goldkind, L., & Lam, H. I. (2018). Data collaboration and participation for sustainable development goals—A case for engaging community-based organizations. *Journal of Human Rights and Social Work*, *3*(1), 44–51. doi:10.100741134-018-0047-6

Tong, J. (2016). Design and implementation of music teaching platform in college based on android mobile technology. *International Journal of Emerging Technologies in Learning*, *11*(05), 4–9. doi:10.3991/ijet.v11i05.5686

Torfing, J. (2019). Collaborative innovation in the public sector: The argument. *Public Management Review*, *21*(1), 1–11. doi:10.1080/14719037.2018.1430248

Torrey, C., Fussell, S. R., & Kiesler, S. (2008). Trying to be helpful: Social challenges for smart robots. In *Workshop-Proceedings of ACM/IEEE Human-Robot Interaction Conference (HRI2008), Amsterdam* (pp. 23-26). Academic Press.

Tórtola Sebastián, C. J., & González de Suso Poncela, A. M. (2018). *Big Data en China*. Oficina Económica y Comercial de España en Cantón.

Trauner, F. (2009). From membership conditionality to policy conditionality: EU external governance in South Eastern Europe. *Journal of European Public Policy*, *16*(5), 774–790. doi:10.1080/13501760902983564

Triolo, P. (2019). US-China Competition: The Coming Decoupling? *RSIS*, 1-5.

Trump, D. J. (2017). *National Security Strategy of the United States of America*. The White House.

Tsado, Y., Gamage, K. A., Lund, D., & Adebisi, B. (2016, October). Performance analysis of variable Smart Grid traffic over ad hoc Wireless Mesh Networks. In *2016 International Conference on Smart Systems and Technologies* (SST) (pp. 81-86). IEEE. 10.1109/SST.2016.7765637

Tsang, L., Kracov, D. A., Mulryne, J., Strom, L., Perkins, N., Dickinson, R., ... Jones, B. (2017). The impact of artificial intelligence on medical innovation in the European Union and United States. *Intellectual Property & Technology Law Journal*, *29*(8), 3–11.

Tummala, R., & Schoenherr, T. (2011). Assessing and managing risks using the Supply Chain Risk Management Process (SCRMP). *Supply Chain Management*, *16*(6), 474–483. doi:10.1108/13598541111171165

Turchin, P., Hoyer, D., Korotayev, A., Kradin, N., Nefedov, S., Feinman, G., Levine, J., Reddish, J., Cioni, E., Thorpe, C., Bennett, J. S., Francois, P., & Whitehouse, H. (2021). Rise of the war machines: Charting the evolution of military technologies from the Neolithic to the Industrial Revolution. *PLoS One*, *16*(10), e0258161. doi:10.1371/journal.pone.0258161 PMID:34669706

Turkle, S. (2017). En defensa de la conversación. El poder de la conversación en la era digital. Ático de los libros.

Tyagi, A. (2016). Artificial intelligence: Boon or bane? SSRN *Electronic Journal*. doi:10.2139/ssrn.2836438

Ugalde, L., Santiago-Garabieta, M., Villarejo-Carballido, B., & Puigvert, L. (2021). Impact of Interactive Learning Environments on Learning and Cognitive Development of Children With Special Educational Needs: A Literature Review. *Frontiers in Psychology*, *12*, 12. doi:10.3389/fpsyg.2021.674033 PMID:33995231

UK Parliament. (2018). *Select Committee on Artificial Intelligence, Collated Written Evidence Volume.* https://www.parliament.uk/globalassets/documents/lords-committees/artificial-intelligence/ai-written-evidence-volume.pdf

Ullah, Z., Al-Turjman, F., Mostarda, L., & Gagliardi, R. (2020). Applications of artificial intelligence and machine learning in smart cities. *Computer Communications*, *154*, 313–323. doi:10.1016/j.comcom.2020.02.069

UNESCAP & Google. (2019). *Artificial Intelligence In The Delivery of Public Services.* https://www.unescap.org/publications/artificial-intelligence-delivery-public-services

UNESCO. (2019a). *UNESCO strategy for youth and adult literacy.* UNESCO Publishing.

UNESCO. (2019b). International Conference on Artificial intelligence and Education. In *Planning Education in the AI Era: Lead the Leap.* UNESCO Publishing.

UNESCO. (2019c). *Preliminary study on the technical and legal aspects relating to the desirability of a standard-setting instrument on the ethics of artificial intelligence.* UNESCO Publishing.

UNESCO. (2020). International Conference on Artificial intelligence and inclusion. Compendium of Promising Initiatives. In *Mobile Learning Week 2020.* UNESCO Publishing.

UNESCO. (2021). *AI and education: guidance for policy-markers.* UNESCO Publishing.

UNIR. (2021). *Comunicado del rector.* Author.

United Nations. (2021). AI and education Guidance for policymakers education Guidance for policy-makers. United Nations Educational, Scientific and Cultural Organization.

Uskov, V. L., Bakken, J. P., Pandey, A., Singh, U., Yalamanchili, M., & Penumatsa, A. (2016). Smart university taxonomy: features, components, systems. In *Smart education and e-learning 2016* (pp. 3–14). Springer. doi:10.1007/978-3-319-39690-3_1

Vakil, B. (2021). Supply Chain Resiliency Starts with Supplier Mapping. *Annual Report 2020*, 28-31.

Vakkuri, V., Kemell, K. K., Kultanen, J., & Abrahamsson, P. (2020). The current state of industrial practice in artificial intelligence ethics. *IEEE Software*, *37*(4), 50–57. doi:10.1109/MS.2020.2985621

Valle-Cruz, D., Alejandro Ruvalcaba-Gomez, E., Sandoval-Almazan, R., & Ignacio Criado, J. (2019, June). A review of artificial intelligence in government and its potential from a public policy perspective. In *Proceedings of the 20th Annual International Conference on Digital Government Research* (pp. 91-99). Academic Press.

Valle-Cruz, D., Alejandro Ruvalcaba-Gomez, E., Sandoval-Almazan, R., & Ignacio Criado, J. (2019, June). A review of artificial intelligence in government and its potential from a public policy perspective. *Proceedings of the 20th Annual International Conference on Digital Government Research.* 10.1145/3325112.3325242

Valle-Cruz, D., & Sandoval-Almazan, R. (2018, May). Towards an understanding of artificial intelligence in government. In *Proceedings of the 19th Annual International Conference on Digital Government Research: Governance in the Data Age* (pp. 1-2). 10.1145/3209281.3209397

Van Parijs, P. (2002). Linguistic justice. *Politics, Philosophy & Economics, 1*(1), 59–74. doi:10.1177/1470594X02001001003

van Veenstra, A. F., & Kotterink, B. (2017, September). Data-driven policy making: The policy lab approach. In *International Conference on Electronic Participation* (pp. 100-111). Springer.

VanLehn, K. (2011). The relative effectiveness of human tutoring, intelligent tutoring systems, and other tutoring systems. *Educational Psychologist, 46*(4), 197–221. doi:10.1080/00461520.2011.611369

VanLehn, K., Jordan, P. W., Rosé, C. P., Bhembe, D., Böttner, M., Gaydos, A., Makatchev, M., Pappuswamy, U., Ringenberg, M., Roque, A., Siler, S., & Srivastava, R. (2002). The architecture of why2-atlas: A coach for qualitative physics essay writing. In G. Gauthier, C. Frasson, & K. VanLehn (Eds.), *Intelligent Tutoring Systems. ITS 2000* (pp. 158–167). Lecture Notes in Computer Science. Springer. doi:10.1007/3-540-47987-2_20

VanLehn, K., Lynch, C., Schulze, K., Shapiro, J. A., Shelby, R., Taylor, L., Treacy, D., Weinstein, A., & Wintersgill, M. (2005). The Andes physics tutoring system: Lessons learned. *International Journal of Artificial Intelligence in Education, 15*(3), 147–204. https://dl.acm.org/doi/10.5555/1434930.1434932

Varakantham, P., An, B., Low, B., & Zhang, J. (2017). Artificial intelligence research in Singapore: Assisting the development of a smart nation. *AI Magazine, 38*(3), 102–105. doi:10.1609/aimag.v38i3.2749

Vargas, I. (2020, June 9). 200 euros por un examen de ingeniería: el fraude en las evaluaciones on line de la UGR. *Granada Hoy.* https://www.granadahoy.com

Vattimo, G. (2010). *Adiós a la verdad.* Gedisa.

Veitch, J., Flowers, E., Ball, K., Deforche, B., & Timperio, A. (2020). Designing parks for older adults: A qualitative study using walk-along interviews. *Urban Forestry & Urban Greening, 54*, 126768. doi:10.1016/j.ufug.2020.126768

Venkatesh, M., Morris, Davis, & Davis. (2003). User Acceptance of Information Technology: Toward a Unified View. *Management Information Systems Quarterly, 27*(3), 425–478. doi:10.2307/30036540

Venkatesh, T., Thong, & Xu. (2012). Consumer Acceptance and Use of Information Technology: Extending the Unified Theory of Acceptance and Use of Technology. *Management Information Systems Quarterly, 36*(1), 157–178. doi:10.2307/41410412

Verhulst, S. G., & Young, A. (2019). The potential and practice of data collaboratives for migration. In *Guide to Mobile Data Analytics in Refugee Scenarios* (pp. 465–476). Springer.

Verma, A., Lamsal, K., & Verma, P. (2021). An investigation of skill requirements in artificial intelligence and machine learning job advertisements. *Industry and Higher Education.*

Vidal-Abarca, E., Gilabert, R., Ferrer, A., Ávila, V., Martínez, T., Mañá, A., Llorens, A.-C., Gil, L., Cerdán, R., Ramos, L., & Serrano, M. A. (2014). TuinLEC, an intelligent tutoring system to improve reading literacy skills. *Infancia y Aprendizaje, 37*(1), 25–56. doi:10.1080/02103702.2014.881657

Vincent-Lancrin, S. (2021). Frontiers of smart education technology: Opportunities and challenges. *OECD Digital Education Outlook 2021 Pushing the Frontiers with Artificial Intelligence, Blockchain and Robots: Pushing the Frontiers with Artificial Intelligence, Blockchain and Robots*, 19.

Vladan, D. (2004). Web Intelligence and Artificial Intelligence in Education. *Journal of Educational Technology & Society*, 7(4), 29–39. https://www.jstor.org/stable/jeductechsoci.7.4.29

vom Brocke, J., Simons, A., Riemer, K., Niehaves, B., Plattfaut, R., & Cleven, A. (2015). Standing on the shoulders of giants: Challenges and recommendations of literature search in information systems research. *Communications of the Association for Information Systems*, 37(1), 9. doi:10.17705/1CAIS.03709

Von Haldenwang, C. (2004). Electronic government (e-government) and development. *European Journal of Development Research*, 16(2), 417–432. doi:10.1080/0957881042000220886

von Krogh, G. (2018). Artificial intelligence in organizations: New opportunities for phenomenon-based theorizing. *Academy of Management Discoveries*, 4(4), 404–409. doi:10.5465/amd.2018.0084

VVAA. (2018). Transitions from war to peace. Presents and futures of Iran. Politique Étrangère, 3, 216.

Vydra, S., & Klievink, B. (2019). Techno-optimism and policy-pessimism in the public sector big data debate. *Government Information Quarterly*, 101383(4), 101383. Advance online publication. doi:10.1016/j.giq.2019.05.010

Walker, E. T. (2014). *Grassroots for hire: Public affairs consultants in American democracy*. Cambridge University Press.

Walker, E. T., & Rea, C. M. (2014). The political mobilization of firms and industries. *Annual Review of Sociology*, 40, 281–304.

Walkington, C., & Bernacki, M. L. (2020). Appraising research on personalized learning: Definitions, theoretical alignment, advancements, and future directions. *Journal of Research on Technology in Education*, 52(3), 235–252. doi:10.1080/15391523.2020.1747757

Wallén, J. (2008). *The history of the industrial robot*. Linköping University Electronic Press.

Wang, C., Teo, T. S., & Janssen, M. (2021). Public and private value creation using artificial intelligence: An empirical study of AI voice robot users in Chinese public sector. *International Journal of Information Management*, 61, 102401. doi:10.1016/j.ijinfomgt.2021.102401

Wang, H., Xu, Z., Fujita, H., & Liu, S. (2016). Towards felicitous decision making: An overview on challenges and trends of Big Data. *Information Sciences*, 367, 747–765. doi:10.1016/j.ins.2016.07.007

Wang, Y.-Y., Luse, A., Townsend, A. M., & Mennecke, B. E. (2014). Understanding the moderating roles of types of recommender systems and products on customer behavioral intention to use recommender systems. *Information Systems and e-Business Management*, 13(4), 769–799. doi:10.100710257-014-0269-9

Wang, Y., Zhang, N., & Zhao, X. (2020). Understanding the determinants in the different government AI adoption stages: Evidence of local government chatbots in China. *Social Science Computer Review*. doi:10.1177/0894439320980132

Wardle, C. (2017). *Fake news, it's complicated*. DesinfoLab of the European Union. Retrieved on 14 July 2021 from: https://www.disinfo.eu/academic-source/claire-wardle-2017

Warren, R. L. (1978). The Community in America. Rand McNally.

Washington, U. o. (2006). *The History of Artificial Intelligence*. https://courses.cs.washington.edu/courses/csep590/06au/projects/history-ai.pdf

Watson, H. A., Tribe, R. M., & Shennan, A. H. (2019). The role of medical smartphone apps in clinical decision-support: A literature review. *Artificial Intelligence in Medicine, 100*, 101707. doi:10.1016/j.artmed.2019.101707 PMID:31607347

Weber, F. D., & Schütte, R. (2019). State-of-the-art and adoption of artificial intelligence in retailing. *Digital Policy. Regulation & Governance, 21*(3), 264–279.

Weizenbaum, J. (1976). *Computer Power amd Human Reason. From judgment to calculation.* W. H. Freeman & Co Ltd.

Wells, G., & Arauz, R. M. (2005). Hacia el diálogo en el salón de clases: enseñanza y aprendizaje por medio de la indagación. *Sinéctica, Revista Electrónica de Educación,* (26), 1-19.

West, D. M., & Allen, J. R. (2018). *How artificial intelligence is transforming the world.* Report. Brookings Institution.

West, D. M. (2018). *The future of work: Robots, AI, and automation.* Brookings Institution Press.

West, D. M., & Allen, J. R. (2020). *Turning Point: Policymaking in the Era of Artificial Intelligence.* Brookings Institution Press.

White House. (2016). *Artificial Intelligence, Automation, and the Economy.* Retrieved from https://www.whitehouse.gov/sites/whitehouse.gov/files/images/ EMBARGOEDAIEconomyReport.pdf

Whitlock, C. (2011, Apr. 29). Gorgon Stare surveillance system gazes over Afghan war zone. *The Washington Post.*

Whittemore, R., Chao, A., Jang, M., Minges, K. E., & Park, C. (2014). Methods for knowledge synthesis: An overview. *Heart & Lung, 43*(5), 453–461. doi:10.1016/j.hrtlng.2014.05.014 PMID:25012634

Whittemore, R., & Knafl, K. (2005). The integrative review: Updated methodology. *Journal of Advanced Nursing, 52*(5), 546–553. doi:10.1111/j.1365-2648.2005.03621.x PMID:16268861

Wible, S. (2006). Pedagogies of the" Students' Right" era: The language curriculum research group's project for linguistic diversity. *College Composition and Communication,* 442–478.

William, E., Schatsky, D., & Viechnicki, P. (2017). *AI-augmented government using cognitive technologies to redesign public sector work.* Deloitte University Press. Retrieved from https://www2.deloitte.com/content/dam/insights/us/articles/3832_AI-augmentedgovernment/DUP_AI-augmented-government.pdf

Williams, M. D., Dwivedi, Y. K., Lal, B., & Schwarz, A. (2009). Contemporary Trends and Issues in it Adoption and Diffusion Research. *Journal of Information Technology, 24*(1), 1–10. doi:10.1057/jit.2008.30

Williamson, B. (2014). Knowing public services: Cross-sector intermediaries and algorithmic governance in public sector reform. *Public Policy and Administration, 29*(4), 292–312. doi:10.1177/0952076714529139

Williamson, B. (2020). New Digital Laboratories of Experimental Knowledge Production: Artificial Intelligence and Education Research. *London Review of Education, 18*(2), 209–220. doi:10.14324/LRE.18.2.05

Williamson, B., Pykett, J., & Nemorin, S. (2018). Biosocial spaces and neurocomputational governance: Brain-based and brain-targeted technologies in education. *Discourse (Berkeley, Calif.), 39*(2), 258–275. doi:10.1080/01596306.2018.1394421

Williams, S. (2016). *Business intelligence strategy and big data analytics: a general management perspective.* Morgan Kaufmann Publishers.

Wimsatt, W. K. (1939). *Poe and the chess automaton.* Academic Press.

Winschiers-Theophilus, H., Zaman, T., & Stanley, C. (2019). A classification of cultural engagements in community technology design: Introducing a transcultural approach. *AI & Society, 34*(3), 419–435.

Winter, J. S., & Davidson, E. (2019). Governance of artificial intelligence and personal health information, digital policy. *Regulation & Governance, 21*(3). Advance online publication. doi:10.1108/DPRG-08- 2018-0048

Wirtz, B. W., & Müller, W. M. (2018). An integrated artificial intelligence framework for public management. *Public Management Review, 21*(7), 1076–1100. doi:10.1080/14719037.2018.1549268

Wirtz, B. W., Weyerer, J. C., & Geyer, C. (2018). Artificial Intelligence and the Public Sector—Applications and Challenges. *International Journal of Public Administration, 42*(7), 596–615. doi:10.1080/01900692.2018.1498103

Wirtz, B. W., Weyerer, J. C., & Sturm, B. J. (2020). The dark sides of artificial intelligence: An integrated AI governance framework for public administration. *International Journal of Public Administration, 43*(9), 818–829.

Wodak, R. (2006). Linguistic analyses in language policies. *An introduction to language policy: Theory and method,* 170-193.

Woolf, B. P. (2010). Student Modeling. In R. Nkambou, J. Bourdeau, & R. Mizoguchi (Eds.), *Advances in Intelligent Tutoring Systems. Studies in Computational Intelligence.* Springer. doi:10.1007/978-3-642-14363-2_13

Woźniak, E. (2018). Contribution to linguistic politics in the Interwar Period—Ministry of Communication for the sake of language. *Język a Kultura, 28,* 101–111. doi:10.19195/1232-9657.28.8

Wright, T. (2018). *Accepting Authoritarism: State-Society relations in China's Reform Era.* Stanford University Press.

Wu, Y. (2014). Protecting personal data in E-government: A cross-country study. *Government Information Quarterly, 31*(1), 150–159. doi:10.1016/j.giq.2013.07.003

Xu, D., & Rappaport, T. S. (2019). Construction on Teaching Evaluation Index System of Track and Field General Course for Physical Education Major in Light of Wireless Network Technology. Big data analysis techniques for intelligent systems. *Journal of Intelligent & Fuzzy Systems, 37*(3), 3435–3443. doi:10.3233/JIFS-179147

Xu, W., Wei, Y., & Fan, Y. (2002). Virtual enterprise and its intelligence management. *Computers & Industrial Engineering, 42*(2–4), 199–205. doi:10.1016/S0360-8352(02)00053-0

Yadav, R., & Yadav, R. (2018). Review on artificial intelligence: A boon or bane to humans. *International Journal of Scientific Research in Science and Information Technology, 4*(2), 1818–1820.

Yang, S. J. H. (2019). Precision education: new challenges for AI in education. In *The 27th International Conference on Computers in Education (ICCE), XXVII-XXVIII.* Kenting, Taiwan: Asia-Pacific Society for Computers in Education (APSCE).

Yang, L., Elisa, N., & Eliot, N. (2019). Privacy and security aspects of E-government in smart cities. In *Smart cities cybersecurity and privacy* (pp. 89–102). Elsevier. doi:10.1016/B978-0-12-815032-0.00007-X

Yang, S. J. H. (2021). Guest Editorial: Precision education - a new challenge for AI in education. *Journal of Educational Technology & Society, 24*(1), 105–108.

Yang, S. J., Ogata, H., Matsui, T., & Chen, N. S. (2021). Human-centered artificial intelligence in education: Seeing the invisible through the visible. *Computers and Education: Artificial Intelligence, 2,* 100008. doi:10.1016/j.caeai.2021.100008

Yang, W., Li, J., Zhang, Y., & Gu, D. (2019). Security analysis of third-party in-app payment in mobile applications. *Journal of Information Security and Applications, 48,* 102358. doi:10.1016/j.jisa.2019.102358

Yannier, N., Hudson, S. E., & Koedinger, K. R. (2020). Active Learning is About More Than Hands-On: A Mixed-Reality AI System to Support STEM Education. *International Journal of Artificial Intelligence in Education, 30*(1), 74–96. doi:10.100740593-020-00194-3

Yan, Z. (2018, January). Big data and government governance. In *2018 International Conference on Information Management and Processing (ICIMP)* (pp. 111-114). IEEE. 10.1109/ICIMP1.2018.8325850

Yee, V., & Glanz, J. (2021). How One of the World's Biggest Ships Jammed the Suez Canal. *The New York Times.* https://www.nytimes.com/2021/07/17/world/middleeast/suez-canal-stuck-ship-ever-given.html

Yigitcanlar, T., Desouza, K. C., Butler, L., & Roozkhosh, F. (2020). Contributions and risks of artificial intelligence (AI) in building smarter cities: Insights from a systematic review of the literature. *Energies, 13*(6), 1473. doi:10.3390/en13061473

Yin, J., Sharma, P., Gorton, I., & Akyoli, B. (2013). Large-Scale Data Challenges in Future Power Grids. *Service Oriented System Engineering (SOSE), 2013 IEEE 7th International Symposium on IEEE,* 324–328.

Yokota-Murakami, T. (2015). Polyglotism of Jewish Latvian Literati and Linguistic Politics of the Periphery: Observation through M. Razumnyi and A. Imermanis. *Japanese Slavic and East European Studies, 36*(0), 47–56. doi:10.5823/jsees.36.0_47

Yongfei, X. (2017). *Legal challenges for data-driven society.* ITU Kaleidoscope.

Yu, H., Seo, I., & Choi, J. (2019). A study of critical factors affecting adoption of self-customisation service – focused on value-based adoption model. *Total Quality Management & Business Excellence, 30*(sup1), S98-S113.

Yufei, L., Saleh, S., Jiahui, H., & Sye, S. M. (2020). Review of the application of artificial intelligence in education. *International Journal of Innovation, Creativity and Change, 2*(8).

Zaidi, A., Beadle, S., & Hannah, A. (2019). *Review of the online learning and artificial intelligence education market: a report for the Department of Education: July 2018.* Academic Press.

Zainal, N. Z., Hussin, H., & Nazri, M. N. M. (2016, November). Big data initiatives by governments--issues and challenges: A review. In *2016 6th international conference on information and communication technology for the Muslim World (ICT4M)* (pp. 304-309). IEEE.

Završnik, A. (2020, March). Criminal justice, artificial intelligence systems, and human rights. In *ERA Forum* (Vol. 20, No. 4, pp. 567-583). Springer Berlin Heidelberg. 10.100712027-020-00602-0

Završnik, A. (2019). Algorithmic justice: Algorithms and big data in criminal justice settings. *European Journal of Criminology.*

Zawacki-Richter, O., Marín, V. I., Bond, M., & Gouverneur, F. (2019). Systematic review of research on artificial intelligence applications in higher education – where are the educators? *International Journal of Educational Technology in Higher Education, 16*(1), 39. doi:10.118641239-019-0171-0

Zhang, W., & Chen, Q. (2010, May). From E-government to C-government via Cloud Computing. In *2010 International Conference on E-Business and E-Government* (pp. 679-682). IEEE. 10.1109/ICEE.2010.177

Zhang, W., Wang, M., & Zhu, Y. C. (2020). Does government information release really matter in regulating contagion-evolution of negative emotion during public emergencies? From the perspective of cognitive big data analytics. *International Journal of Information Management, 50,* 498–514. doi:10.1016/j.ijinfomgt.2019.04.001

Zhang, W., Zuo, N., He, W., Li, S., & Yu, L. (2021). Factors influencing the use of artificial intelligence in government: Evidence from China. *Technology in Society, 66,* 101675. doi:10.1016/j.techsoc.2021.101675

Zheng, Y., Yu, H., Cui, L., Miao, C., Leung, C., & Yang, Q. (2018, April). SmartHS: An AI platform for improving government service provision. *Thirty-Second AAAI Conference on Artificial Intelligence.*

Zhou, Z. H., Chawla, N. V., Jin, Y., & Williams, G. J. (2014). Big data opportunities and challenges: Discussions from data analytics perspectives. *IEEE Computational Intelligence Magazine*, *9*(4), 62–74. doi:10.1109/MCI.2014.2350953

Zimmerman, P. (2011). *Faer Asturies: Linguistic Politics and the Frustrated Construction of Asturian Nationalism, 1974-1999*. Academic Press.

Zou, S. (2017). Designing and practice of a college English teaching platform based on artificial intelligence. *Journal of Computational and Theoretical Nanoscience*, *14*(1), 104–108. doi:10.1166/jctn.2017.6133

Zuboff, S. (2015). Big other: Surveillance capitalism and the prospects of an information civilization. *Journal of Information Technology*, *30*(1), 75–89. doi:10.1057/jit.2015.5

Zuiderveen Borgesius, F. J. (2020). Strengthening legal protection against discrimination by algorithms and artificial intelligence. *International Journal of Human Rights*, *24*(10), 1572–1593. doi:10.1080/13642987.2020.1743976

About the Contributors

Jose Ramon Saura is Researcher and Associate professor of Digital Marketing in the Business Economics Department at Rey Juan Carlos University, Madrid (Spain). Previously, he held positions and made consultancy at a number of other companies including Google, L'Oréal, Deloitte, Telefónica, or MRM//McCann, among others. He earned an international Ph.D. in Digital Marketing at the Rey Juan Carlos University, while researching at London South Bank University (LSBU) and Harvard University (RCC at Harvard). His research has focused on the theoretical and practical insights of various aspects of User Generated Data and Content (UGD - UGC), with a specific focus around three major research approaches applied to business and marketing: data mining, knowledge discovery, and information sciences. His research has appeared in leading international business, marketing, and information sciences journals such as: Journal of Innovation and Knowledge, International Journal of Information Management, Technological Forecasting and Social Change, Journal of Business Research, Industrial Marketing Management, Review of Managerial Sciences, Journal of Small Business Management, Journal of Business & Industrial Marketing, Enterprise Information Systems, European Management Journal, European Research on Management and Business Economics, Computer Communications, Big Data Research, among others.

Felipe Debasa's lines of research are focused on the historical study of the political and legal foundations of the European Union and the relations of the European Institutions with the Republic of China. He is Director of the Master's Degree in the European Union and China at URJC and UDIMA University. Felipe Debasa studies the European Institutions and the Fourth Industrial Revolution in the political, economic, and Human Rights fields.

* * *

Majlinda Abdiu is a Spanish and Latin American Literature Professor. She is an expert in the magical realism of Gabriel Garcia Marquez and other writers. She already has a consolidated universal literature research. She has also ventured into the cultural and political European history of international relations.

Miguel Angel Ajuriaguerra Escudero is an Architecture PhD from the Polytechnic University of Madrid where he acquired the highest qualification within the International Doctorate Program and obtained the Extraordinary Award for his doctoral thesis. His professional career has been developed in the building and consulting sector. Currently he is a Visiting Professor within the Degree Fundamentals of Architecture in the Area of Geographical Analysis. Also, he carries out his research in collaboration with private and public entities in relation to the following scopes: The historical heritage of architecture and urbanism. Environmental protection and Urban Facilities. Socio-economic development through urban and territorial planning. These research scopes are related in the implementation of economic, social, and territorial policies for the urban development. As well as in the promotion and conservation of the environment.

Yuliia Andriichenko is a Doctor of Science, Professor of Roman Philology Department, Institute of Philology Taras Shevchenko National University (Kyiv, Ukraine).

Mona Ashok is a Lecturer in Operations Management at Henley Business School, UK. She has extensive industry experience, having worked at senior management level in global IT and BPO organisations, and accounting firm. She has worked with customers in Asia, Australia, Europe and Northern America. Mona's experience in Higher Education includes working with doctoral, post-experienced postgraduate and undergraduate programme members. Her professional and academic projects cover topics such as: process improvement, programme management, knowledge management, financial management, organisational transformation, and management consulting. She is a Fellow of the UK Higher Education Academy (FHEA), member of the Institute of Chartered Accountants of India, a Certified Software Quality Analyst, and a Six Sigma Master Black Belt. She has successfully secured research funding, including for Knowledge Transfer Partnership projects, funded by InnovateUK.

José Manuel Azcona-Pastor is a Full Professor in Contemporary History at URJC.

Tomás Aznar works at the Center for Higher Education for Business, Innovation and Technology (IUNIT) Modern History Doctor (UCM). Specialist in Education for Solidarity (Universidad de Comillas) and on the Internet and Digital Boards in the Classroom (UCJC). Master in Education and ICT (UOC), in Community Manager and Web Positioning (University of Alcalá de Henares) and in Occupational Risk Prevention (IUNIT-URJC). Graduate Geography and History (UCM). Director of Projects of the Center for Higher Education for Business, Innovation and Technology (IUNIT), a center attached to the Rey Juan Carlos University, belonging to the SEK International Institution. Member of the SEK International Institution since 2009 and of the Board of Directors of said Institution in different positions.

Elena Bulmer is a PhD from the Complutense University of Madrid, PMP by PMI, PRINCE-2. She has 15 year of international experience in the management of environmental conservation and biodiversity projects. She is a professor and researcher at EAE Business School.

Jorge Chauca García holds a PhD in Modern History from University of Malaga with Extraordinary Doctorate Award and PhD in American History from the University of Seville with the qualification of Outstanding Cum Laude. Likewise, University Specialist in Viceregal America and in Military History by the General Gutierrez Mellado University Institute and the General Foundation of the National University of Distance Education. Professor at the Faculty of Educational Sciences of the University of Malaga (Spain) in the area of knowledge of Didactics of Social Sciences. Secretary of the International Commission of Hispanists.

Niranjan Devkota is an economist with the special focus on cross border activities and climate change related issues focusing adaptation. He has over 10 years of experience in the field of economics related research with varietal dynamics. His recent research focuses ranges from development economics especially in cross-border activities and agriculture. He received his PhD degree from Tribhuvan University Nepal. He has experience in impact analysis and model building. He has worked in terms to prepare strategic and implementation plans of several economic issues as a research associates. He has received high level training and capacity building workshop on international co-operation, natural resource management and trade related activities from several international agencies like SANDEE (ICIMOD), NDRC (China), Hi-Aware (ICIMOD), SANEM (Bangladesh) and from esteemed organizations and universities (online mode). He has command over STATA and basic knowledge of R.

Luis Vicente Doncel Fernández is a professor at the Rey Juan Carlos University in the Faculty of Legal and Social Sciences. PhD in Political Science and Sociology from the Complutense University of Madrid in 1999. He has worked as a full professor at the Social School of Madrid (1984-1994), as a contract professor at the CESSJ Ramón Carande (Complutense University of Madrid) in 1994 -1998 and as a professor at the Rey Juan Carlos University from 1998 to the present.

Ana Fernández López is researcher of Marketing. Her research focuses on Digital Marketing, where she investigates how users behave, which content they share, and how digital marketing influences customers.

Lauri Goldkind is an associate professor at Fordham's Graduate School of Social Service, where she chairs the Leadership and Macro practice concentration and also teaches in the Nonprofit Administration program. Dr. Goldkind was a Visiting Fellow at UNU Institute in Macau during summer 2017, where she worked on the Data and Sustainable Development project under the Small Data Lab. While in Macau, her work focused on exploring two research questions: first, how community-based organizations (CBOs) can serve as a conduit for data reporting so that the voices of underrepresented and vulnerable groups can be better represented at the national and international levels; and second, how community-based organizations make use of information and communication technology (ICT) to improve services to their constituents. Her research was conducted in partnership with Caritas Macau, a local CBO that allowed her to explore and compare the similarities and differences between Macau and the United States in terms of service delivery and administration. She holds an M.S.W. from SUNY Stony Brook with a concentration in planning, administration, and research and a Ph.D. from the Wurzweiler School of Social Work at Yeshiva University.

Paula González-Padilla researches digital marketing and the use of digital technology in the interaction with customers. She is specialized in Marketing of Services & Business. Paula González-Padilla held positions of project manager and made consultancy at a number of other private companies.

Julio Guinea Bonillo is a Bachelor in History and Political Science from the Complutense University, Master in European Union from the CEU San Pablo University and in Diplomacy and International Relations from the Diplomatic School of Spain. He is also a PhD of Law from UDIMA with a thesis that studies the Legal Articulation of the Common Foreign and Security Policy and the Common Security and Defense Policy. He has published in 2020 the History of the Foreign Policy of the European Union with the foreword by the former president of the European Parliament, Enrique Barón, in the Reuters-Aranzadi publishing house. He has also completed his work on the History of Security and Defense Policy in 2021 and will soon be available in the Reuters-Aranzadi publishing house for public consultation.

Luis Illanas is a graduate in history from the UNED, specialist in Mediterranean and Middle East Security and International Conflict Resolution from the IUGM, peace process operator from the EGET and specialist on Balkans affairs from the UCM. He is researcher at the URJC Santander Presdeia Chair and editor of the journal Guerra Colonial. He also collaborates with the international politics magazine Atalayar and with media outlets such as Radio Nacional de España and Russia Today.

Francisco J. S. Lacárcel is a doctoral student in Tourism from the University of Alicante. Relating tourism with digital communication.

Rohit Madan is a PhD student at Henley Business School, University of Reading conducting research on innovation management and artificial intelligence adoption in public sector. Prior to pursuing a doctorate, Rohit has extensive experience in management consulting, project management, and technology deployments in both public and private sector organisations. Rohit has a Bachelor's in Mechanical Engineering, MSc in Business Research and Management, MBA, and is a certified project management professional.

Miguel Madueño Álvarez is a Doctor in Humanities from the Universidad Rey Juan Carlos, he is a lecturer in the Contemporary History Department at the same university. He is director of the digital journal Guerra Colonial, researcher attached to the URJC Santander Presdeia Research Chair and co-director of the Seminario Permanente Americanista (SEPAM). He is the author of El falangismo en la España Actual (1977-2020). Historia de una escisión continua, published by Sílex (2021) and works related to terrorism and international insurgency such as MLN-Tupamaros y el nacimiento de la guerrilla urbana, in El sueño de la Revolución Social, Comares, 2020 and La CIA y los problemas de la guerrilla urbana, Araucaria, 2020.

John G. McNutt is Professor Emeritus in the School of Public Policy and Administration at the University of Delaware. Dr. McNutt is a specialist in the application of high technology to political and social engagement. His work focuses on the role of technology in lobbying, e-government and e-democracy, political campaigning and deliberation, organizing and other forms of political participation. He has conducted research on professional associations, child advocacy groups, consumer and environmental protection groups, social action organizations and legislative bodies. His most recent work looks at Web 2.0 political change technology and e-government and fiscal transparency. Dr. McNutt has co-edited or co-authored eight books and many journal articles, book chapters and other publications. He regularly presents at National and International conferences and sits on several editorial boards.

Seeprata Parajuli is Assistant Research Coordinator at Quest International Colleague. She holds a Master of Business Administration. She has participated in several national and international academic conferences and published articles in prestigious journals.

Priyadarsini Patnaik is a knowledgeable, experienced & Seasoned Marketing professional with a huge experience in both industry and academics. Currently pursuing Ph.D. in Birla Global University, Bhubaneswar, Odisha, India. Her research area of interest are Artificial Intelligence, Consumer Behaviour, Advertising, Retail Management, Digital Marketing.

Rabin Paudel is an MBA graduate from Quest International College.

Uday Paudel is an Associate Professor at Quest International College. He is specialized in Business Administration, Computer Communications, Leadership, Entrepreneurship, Business, and Innovation.

José Emilio Pérez-Martínez is currently a lecturer at the Universidad Rey Juan Carlos in Madrid, he has also taught at the Universidad Complutense de Madrid and the Sorbonne Université in Paris. PhD in Contemporary History (2017) and PhD in Journalism (2019) from the Universidad Complutens de Madrid, his scientific production has mainly revolved around the history of Spanish radio broadcasting, with an interest in its intersection with gender studies. His commitment to the radio medium has led him to participate in radio stations such as Radio Almenara and RICCAP, the Research Network on Community, Alternative and Participatory Communication. He is the author of articles and scientific contributions in national and international collective works, where he explores both the emergence of alternative radio stations in Spain and the close relationship between women and radio. His also the author of Radio y mujer (España, 1960-1975). En las ondas de Radio Nacional (Abada Editores, 2021).

Nataliia Popova is a Doctor of Science, Professor of Roman Philology Department, Institute of Philology, Taras Shevchenko National University of Kyiv (Kyiv, Ukraine).

Carlos R. Quijano Junquera is an artillery colonel of the Spanish Army, in reserve situation, diploma in military informatics, has extensive experience in military logistics. He is currently a PhD student at the Rey Juan Carlos University in Madrid.

Emilio Sanchez de Rojas Díaz, Colonel of Artillery, General Staff; EAE Business School, URJCI University; PhD; Mg (Bologna) in studies related to terrorism, has spent most of his career, as Lieutenant Colonel and Coronel, to Intelligence Strategy and International Relations. He has participated in three peacekeeping operations and appointed as Defense Counselor at the Permanent Mission of Spain to the OSCE in Vienna, between 1999 and 2003 and Defense Attaché at the Spanish embassies in Cairo and Amman between 2005 and 2008. Until July 2018, responsible for the Middle East and Latin America areas at CESEDEN's IEEE. Invited professor to several master's degrees at various Spanish universities, he has lectured abroad in Brazil, Mexico, Portugal, Colombia, Peru, Morocco, and Uruguay. He has published more than 60 articles, contributed to 20 collective books, and written the books "Notes on the Arctic" with Vicente López-Ibor Mayor and Luis Francisco Martínez Montes and "Islamist Terrorism: The case of Al Gama`a al Islamiyya, Tirant Lo Blanch 2018 "together with Cristina del Prado Higueras.

Index

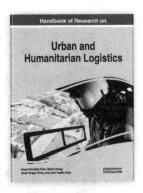

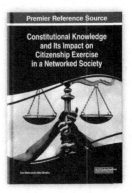
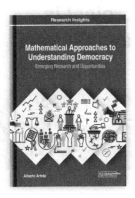

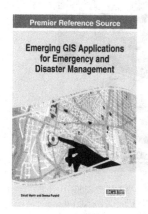

IGI Global Author Services

Providing a high-quality, affordable, and expeditious service, IGI Global's Author Services enable authors to streamline their publishing process, increase chance of acceptance, and adhere to IGI Global's publication standards.

Benefits of Author Services:

- **Professional Service:** All our editors, designers, and translators are experts in their field with years of experience and professional certifications.

- **Quality Guarantee & Certificate:** Each order is returned with a quality guarantee and certificate of professional completion.

- **Timeliness:** All editorial orders have a guaranteed return timeframe of 3-5 business days and translation orders are guaranteed in 7-10 business days.

- **Affordable Pricing:** IGI Global Author Services are competitively priced compared to other industry service providers.

- **APC Reimbursement:** IGI Global authors publishing Open Access (OA) will be able to deduct the cost of editing and other IGI Global author services from their OA APC publishing fee.

Author Services Offered:

English Language Copy Editing
Professional, native English language copy editors improve your manuscript's grammar, spelling, punctuation, terminology, semantics, consistency, flow, formatting, and more.

Scientific & Scholarly Editing
A Ph.D. level review for qualities such as originality and significance, interest to researchers, level of methodology and analysis, coverage of literature, organization, quality of writing, and strengths and weaknesses.

Figure, Table, Chart & Equation Conversions
Work with IGI Global's graphic designers before submission to enhance and design all figures and charts to IGI Global's specific standards for clarity.

Translation
Providing 70 language options, including Simplified and Traditional Chinese, Spanish, Arabic, German, French, and more.

Hear What the Experts Are Saying About IGI Global's Author Services

"Publishing with IGI Global has been *an amazing experience* for me for sharing my research. The *strong academic production* support ensures quality and timely completion." – **Prof. Margaret Niess, Oregon State University, USA**

"The service was *very fast, very thorough, and very helpful* in ensuring our chapter meets the criteria and requirements of the book's editors. I was *quite impressed and happy* with your service." – **Prof. Tom Brinthaupt, Middle Tennessee State University, USA**

www.igi-global.com

Publisher of Peer-Reviewed, Timely, and Innovative Academic Research Since 1988

IGI Global's Transformative Open Access (OA) Model:
How to Turn Your University Library's Database Acquisitions Into a Source of OA Funding

Well in advance of Plan S, IGI Global unveiled their OA Fee Waiver (Read & Publish) Initiative. Under this initiative, librarians who invest in IGI Global's InfoSci-Books and/or InfoSci-Journals databases will be able to subsidize their patrons' OA article processing charges (APCs) when their work is submitted and accepted (after the peer review process) into an IGI Global journal.

How Does it Work?

Step 1: **Library Invests in the InfoSci-Databases:** A library perpetually purchases or subscribes to the InfoSci-Books, InfoSci-Journals, or discipline/subject databases.

Step 2: **IGI Global Matches the Library Investment with OA Subsidies Fund:** IGI Global provides a fund to go towards subsidizing the OA APCs for the library's patrons.

Step 3: **Patron of the Library is Accepted into IGI Global Journal (After Peer Review):** When a patron's paper is accepted into an IGI Global journal, they option to have their paper published under a traditional publishing model or as OA.

Step 4: **IGI Global Will Deduct APC Cost from OA Subsidies Fund:** If the author decides to publish under OA, the OA APC fee will be deducted from the OA subsidies fund.

Step 5: **Author's Work Becomes Freely Available:** The patron's work will be freely available under CC BY copyright license, enabling them to share it freely with the academic community.

Note: This fund will be offered on an annual basis and will renew as the subscription is renewed for each year thereafter. IGI Global will manage the fund and award the APC waivers unless the librarian has a preference as to how the funds should be managed.

Hear From the Experts on This Initiative:

"I'm very happy to have been able to make one of my recent research contributions *freely available* along with having access to the *valuable resources* found within IGI Global's InfoSci-Journals database."

— **Prof. Stuart Palmer,**
Deakin University, Australia

"Receiving the support from IGI Global's OA Fee Waiver Initiative *encourages me to continue my research work without any hesitation.*"

— **Prof. Wenlong Liu**, College of Economics and Management at Nanjing University of Aeronautics & Astronautics, China

For More Information, Scan the QR Code or Contact:
IGI Global's Digital Resources Team at eresources@igi-global.com.